lonely planet

Morocco

Frances Linzee Gordon
Dorinda Talbot
Damien Simonis

Morocco

4th edition

Published by
Lonely Planet Publications
Head Office: PO Box 617, Hawthorn, Vic 3122, Australia
Branches: 155 Filbert St, Suite 251, Oakland, CA 94607, USA
10a Spring Place, London NW5 3BH, UK
71 bis rue du Cardinal Lemoine, 75005 Paris, France

Printed by
SNP Printing Pte Ltd, Singapore

Photographs by

Glenn Beanland	Adrienne Costanzo	Geoff Crowther
Karyn Duggan	Hugh Finlay	Richard I'Anson
Frances Linzee Gordon	Maria Rainone	Damien Simonis
Dorinda Talbot	Chris Wyness	Photo Younis

Front cover: 'Patriotism in Chefchaouen' by Frances Linzee Gordon

First Published
July 1989

This Edition
January 1998

National Library of Australia Cataloguing in Publication Data

Morocco

4th ed.
Includes index
ISBN 0 86442 501 5

1. Morocco – Guidebooks. I. Linzee Gordon, Frances, 1966-

916.4045

Frances Linzee Gordon

Frances grew up in the Highlands of Scotland, but later went to London University, where she read Latin. Overwhelmed by feelings of usefulness and employability, she decided modern languages might be the thing, and worked in Spain, Germany and Belgium for a couple of years.

Frances has travelled in nearly 40 different countries and has qualifications in nine languages. She is a Fellow of the Royal Geographical Society in London and holds a licentiateship of the Royal Photographical Society. Frances has contributed to LP's *Mediterranean Europe, Western Europe* and *Africa* guides. Other passions include dangerous and silly sport, being rude about the Brits, and electric blankets. She lives in London, but no longer with her zebra finch, George.

Dorinda Talbot

Born in Melbourne, Australia, Dorinda began travelling when 18 months old and has since seen a fair slice of the world, including South East Asia, the USA and Europe.

After studying journalism at Deakin University in Victoria, Dorinda worked as a reporter in Alice Springs (where she covered the famous Azaria Chamberlain inquest and learned to jump out of aeroplanes), before embarking on the traditional Aussie sojourn to London. She has worked for numerous magazine titles in London, as a kitchen-hand in a Pall Mall club and as a banana vendor in Brixton.

Dorinda has contributed to LP's *Mediterranean Europe* and *Canada* guides. When not sweating her eyebrows off in far-flung corners of the world, she lives as a bag lady in London.

Damien Simonis

Damien Simonis is an Australian freelance journalist based in London.

After completing a degree in modern languages, he worked as a reporter and subeditor on the *Australian* in Sydney and the *Age* in Melbourne, before putting several years' hard labour on newspapers including the *Guardian*, the *Independent* and the *Sunday Times* in London.

Damien has worked, studied and travelled extensively in Europe and the Arab world.

In addition to revising the third edition of this guide, Damien has updated Lonely Planet's guides to *Jordan & Syria, Egypt & the Sudan, Spain* and *Italy*, as well as contributing to shoestring guides including *Middle East, Africa* and *Mediterranean Europe*.

From the Authors

Many people contributed to this book, providing information, guidance, hospitality, good humour, or simply a shared enthusiasm for the country of Morocco. Full credit and appreciation is given to them at the back of this book on page 534.

This Book

This book started life as one third of the *Morocco, Tunisia & Algeria* guide, which was written and updated by Geoff Crowther and Hugh Finlay. The third edition was expanded and revised by Damien Simonis. This fourth edition was further expanded and revised by Frances Linzee Gordon and Dorinda Talbot.

From the Publisher

This edition of *Morocco* was edited at Lonely Planet's Melbourne office by Peter Cruttenden, with help from Carolyn Papworth and Martin Hughes.

Verity Campbell was responsible for the mapping and design, with mapping assistance from Rachael Scott, Geoff Stringer, Anthony Phelan and Trudi Canavan. Verity, Trudi, Greg Herriman.

Thanks to Peter d'Onghia for his expertise in the Berber language, Simon Bracken for the cover, Michelle Glynn for indexing, Jane Rawson and Carolyn for help with the captions, and Russell Kerr for his 11th hour assistance.

Special thanks to Andrew Tudor and Dan Levin for their Quark XPress expertise, David Andrew for writing and illustrating the bird-watching section and to co-ordinating author Frances Linzee Gordon for her enthusiasm and professionalism.

Thanks also to Michael Sklovsky, who provided extra information for the Arts & Crafts colour section and generously allowed Lonely Planet staff to photograph items from his Ishka Handcrafts stores in Melbourne.

Finally thanks to all those travellers who took the time and effort to write to us with suggestions and comments; they are listed at the back of the book on page 535.

Contents

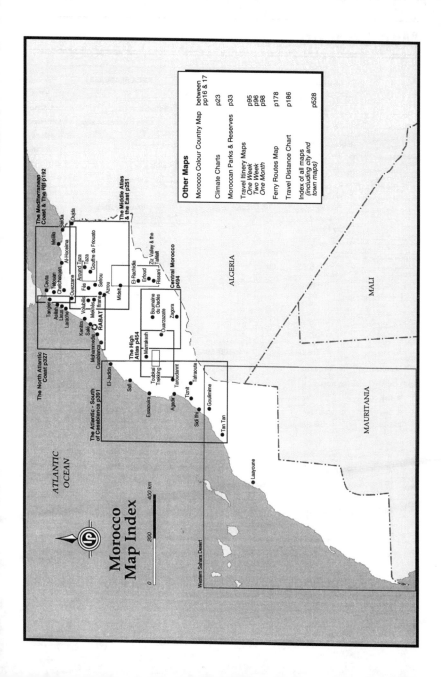

Morocco Map Index

ATLANTIC OCEAN

0   200   400 km

The North Atlantic Coast p327

The Mediterranean Coast & The Rif p192

The Middle Atlas & the East p251

Oujda
Saïdia
Melilla
Al-Hoceima
Ceuta
Tetouan
Chefchaouen
Tangier
Asilah
Larache
Lixus
Ouazzane
Goulfre du Friouato
Around Taza
Taza
Fès
Volubilis
Meknès
Ifrane
Azrou
Sefrou
El-Rachidia
Erfoud
Rissani
Ziz Valley & the Tafilalt

RABAT
Kenitra
Salé
Midelt

Central Morocco p404

The Atlantic – South of Casablanca p391

Mohammedia
Casablanca
El-Jadida
Safi
Essaouira

The High Atlas p454

Marrakesh
Boumalne du Dadès
Ouarzazate
Zagora

Toubkal Trekking
Taroudannt
Taliouine
Agadir
Tiznit
Sidi Ifni
Goulimine
Tan Tan

Western Sahara

Laayoune

ALGERIA

MALI

MAURITANIA

Other Maps

Morocco Colour Country Map   between pp16 & 17

Climate Charts   p23

Moroccan Parks & Reserves   p33

Travel Itinerary Maps
One Week   p95
Two Week   p96
One Month   p98

Ferry Routes Map   p178

Travel Distance Chart   p186

Index of all maps
(including city and
town maps)   p528

Map Legend

ROUTES

┼┼┼┼┼┼┼┼─O─┼─ .... Train Route, with Station
‑‑‑‑‑‑‑‑‑‑‑‑‑‑‑ .... Ferry
‑‑‑‑‑‑‑‑‑‑‑‑‑‑‑ .... Walking Track

Regional Maps

.... Freeway
.... Highway
.... Primary Road
============ .... Unsealed Road
.... Minor Road

City Maps

.... Highway
‑‑‑‑‑‑‑‑‑‑ .... Unsealed Highway
.... Primary Road
‑‑‑‑‑‑‑‑‑‑ .... Unsealed Road
.... Street
============ .... Unsealed Street
.... Lane

AREA FEATURES

.... City Park, National Park
.... Building
.... Pedestrian Mall, Plaza
.... Market
+ + + + + ... Cemetery
.... Built-Up Area
.... Ancient or City Wall

BOUNDARIES

.... International Boundary
‑ ‑ ‑ ‑ ‑ .... Disputed Boundary

HYDROGRAPHIC FEATURES

.... River, Creek
.... Intermittent River or Creek
─»»─ ─))─ .... Rapids, Waterfalls
.... Lake, Intermittent Lake

SYMBOLS

✪	CAPITAL	National Capital	✈	Airport	▲	Mountain
◉	Capital	Regional Capital	∴	Archaeological Site	🏛	Museum
●	City	City	❸	Bank	♉	Palmerie
●	Town	Town	🏖	Beach	)(	Pass
●	Village	Village	⚲	Bird Sanctuary	⛽	Petrol Station
			▭ ⛪	Cathedral, Church	★	Police Station
■		Place to Stay	⌒	Cave, Grotto	▭	Pool
⛺		Camping Ground	○	Embassy	✉	Post Office
☍		Caravan Park	⊕	Hammam	×	Spot Height
⌂		Youth Hostel	✚	Hospital	◎	Spring
⌂		Hut or Chalet	❶	Information		Surf Beach
▼		Place to Eat	🗼	Lighthouse	☎	Telephone
▼		Pub or Bar	〰	Lookout		Trail Head
☕		Café	▮	Monument	⊖	Transport
			☪	Mosque		Windsurfing

Note: not all symbols displayed above appear in this book

Introduction

The country of Morocco stands at the western extremity of the Arab and Muslim world. From here was launched Islam's most successful penetration of Western Europe – the occupation of Spain. Separated from Europe by only the 15km of the Strait of Gibraltar, Morocco is at once a crossroads and a frontier state – a gateway for Europeans into Africa and for Africans and Arabs into Europe. For many travellers, it is their first taste of Africa.

Known to the Arabs as *al-Maghreb al-Aqsa*, the 'farthest land of the setting sun', Morocco has long held a romantic allure for the westerner. Since the 18th century, some of Europe's greatest writers and painters have sought inspiration here. In 19th century France, paintings depicting scenes from Morocco were exhibited in the salons of Paris and set off a craze for all things 'Eastern'. Many artists chose to remain in Morocco; all claim to have been altered in some way by it.

For many, its greatest charm lies in the labyrinths of the imperial cities – Marrakesh, Fès, Meknès and Rabat. Morocco is certainly home to an astonishingly rich architectural tradition, and its medieval cities, Roman ruins, Berber fortresses and beautiful Islamic monuments are among the best examples of their kind in the world.

The countryside holds no lesser attractions. From Marrakesh the snowcapped High Atlas Mountains are clearly visible and lure a growing number of trekkers. Also recognised for their hiking potential are the Middle Atlas and Anti-Atlas ranges. Huge sections of these isolated regions still remain the sole preserve of the Berber tribespeople and their animals. Many of these areas are also rich in wildlife.

Morocco boasts great diversity of flora and fauna and is well known among bird enthusiasts for the vast numbers of migrants it attracts.

For others, the main draw-card is sand.

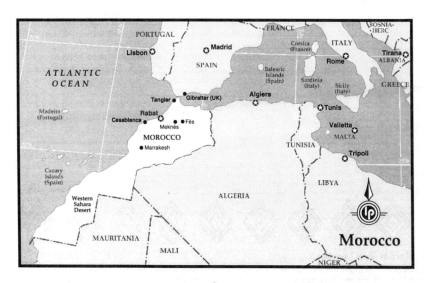

The wide beaches along the Atlantic and Mediterranean coasts attract many, as do the dunes found in the eerie solitude of the desert.

This inhospitable, but strangely beautiful, region extends over a large area of the country, dropping off the back of the Atlas and sweeping into the vast Saharan emptiness of Algeria. Some of the more accessible areas are geared up to tourism in a way rarely found in other parts of the country and those keen to explore the desert should find ample opportunity to do so.

The country's greatest resource is perhaps its people. Moroccans lay claim to an incredibly diverse ancestry. Phoenicians and Romans once held sway here, warrior Arabs from the east dominated much of the country's history, Andalusian refugees sought refuge from southern Spain and thousand of slaves from sub-Saharan Africa were introduced to the country as warriors or concubines.

All have mixed with the indigenous Berber tribes and left their mark on Moroccan culture. Although the hard mercantile tradition of the people initially can be a little hard to adjust to, the overall impression of visitors is of an open, uninhibited and extraordinarily hospitable people. For many, the encounters with the locals form the most enduring memories of their travels.

Such diverse ancestry and influences also can be seen in the country's rich culinary tradition. According to some, Moroccan cuisine ranks among the greatest in the world. Traditionally labour-intensive, many dishes are prepared over a number of days from recipes that have been jealously guarded within families for generations. Moroccan food, particularly in the touristy zones, can be very variable, but for those prepared to seek out the best, it is astounding.

A land of incredible colour, frenetic activity and endless variety, Morocco can feel like an assault on the senses. For those still in search of the exotic and the unfamiliar, Morocco won't disappoint. The sights and smells of the souq, the mesmerising geometric designs of the carpets or just the taste of freshly brewed mint tea, all make for a visit not quickly forgotten.

Berber eye symbol
Believed to avert the evil eye which is deflected in four directions by the central cross.

Facts about the Country

HISTORY

The early history of the area now known as Morocco remains largely shrouded in mystery. Perched on the very edge of the known world in ancient times, only scant shreds of evidence throw any light on the society or societies that inhabited this territory. Even after the arrival of the Phoenicians in North Africa, hotly followed by the Romans, Vandals, Byzantines and Arabs, much of what we know of the original inhabitants remains obscure. Modern historians, relying on the limited and often very unreliable accounts of contemporary writers, have offered us little more than broad assumptions.

This applies not only to Morocco, but also to the rest of North Africa, known to the Arabs as the *Maghreb*, meaning 'sunset' or 'west'. The invaders of the region rarely made great inroads, whether from the coast or from the cities, and in Morocco this was particularly the case.

Notoriously difficult to subdue were the Berbers, as the local peoples came to be known. When threatened by invasion, they simply recoiled into the rugged fastnesses of the Sahara desert and Atlas mountains, well out of reach of the outsiders. This split between Berber native and urban invader has basically remained a constant throughout Morocco's history. Central rulers, even of Berber tribes themselves, have very rarely managed to exercise real power over the entire reach of the country.

Prehistory

Morocco's early history tends to be lumped together with that of the rest of the Maghreb. Archaeological evidence indicating the presence of *Homo erectus* dates back at least 200,000 years, although some scholars believe it may date back still further. At this time, much of the Sahara was covered in forest, scrub and savannah grasses, and teeming animal life inhabited the area. From around 6000 BC, rainfall in this area began to fall off dramatically and the grasslands began to give way to arid, inhospitable desert.

Evidence suggests the appearance of two different races in North Africa between about 15,000 and 10,000 BC. The first, the Oranian branch, is named after the city and important archaeological area of Oran in Algeria; the second, the Capsian line, is named after Qafsah (ancient Capsa) in Tunisia.

The origins of both remain very obscure and the cause of much speculation. It would appear that a kind of fusion took place with the indigenous peoples, the long-term result of which was a spread of Neolithic (New Stone Age) culture. Rock paintings, particularly in the Hoggar in modern Algeria, are the best source of knowledge about this period, although there have been several finds in Morocco too. Many of the results of these discoveries are on view in the Archaeological Museum in Rabat.

It is from these peoples that the Berbers are thought to owe their descent. Although little is known about them for certain, they are thought to have been mainly pastoralists, although some hunting and land cultivation continued to be practised too. By the time the Phoenicians appeared on the scene (the first of the invaders from the east), the local inhabitants were well established, although with what kind of social organisations and divisions remains uncertain.

Carthage

First on the scene in a long series of foreign invaders were the powerful and wealthy Phoenician traders. Sailing from their capital in Tyre (in modern-day Lebanon), they patrolled the North African coast in search of suitable staging posts for the lucrative trade in raw metals from Spain. The foundation of the first of these places has been positively dated to the 8th century BC. Carthage, in modern Tunisia, became their principal and most powerful base, but the Phoenicians also had posts in Sicily, the Balearic Islands and all the way along the North African coast to the Atlantic.

In Morocco, they were ensconced in Tamuda (near present-day Tetouan), Tingis (Tangier), Lixus and Mogador (Essaouira). The latter marked their farthest advance along the Atlantic coast. However, these possessions remained in Phoenician hands only until the end of the 3rd century BC.

By the 4th century BC, Carthage had become one of the richest cities in the Mediterranean world. It attracted the avaricious eye of the Greeks and later the Romans. Mighty clashes between these rival powers soon followed.

In the 5th century BC, as Carthage approached the apogee of its power, some of its more illustrious sons set out on voyages of discovery. One of the most famous, Hanno the navigator, headed off down the Atlantic coast of Morocco. Many historians now believe that his purpose was merely to locate new and valuable sources of fish. Nevertheless, he returned with tales of a fabulous and legendary gold route. Much later, his stories were confirmed as the area became a well known and lucrative source of both gold and slaves.

By the 3rd century, after repeated clashes with the Greek settlements in Sicily, Carthage came into direct conflict with the expanding power of Rome. Several long and bitter wars ensued and, at one stage, Hannibal, the most famous Carthaginian leader, came quite close to destroying Rome.

The Romans gradually recovered, however, and the third Punic War culminated in the massive defeat of Carthage in 146 BC. The Romans, determined that its old rival should never again rise from the ashes, completely flattened the entire city.

One factor that may have contributed indirectly to the eventual downfall of Carthage was the notorious conscription system and financing of its large mercenary armies. In Africa, the indigenous people were treated particularly harshly. A huge wartime tribute of 50% was exacted on local produce, while natives were drafted into the army, often without pay.

Forming the majority of their subjects were the Libyans, a collective term for the people inhabiting the areas to the south and east of Carthage. Fed up with Carthaginian control over large tracts of the land of modern Tunisia, the Libyans, together with the formidable Numidian forces to the west (led by the powerful king, Massinissa), carried on a steady campaign of harassment against their Carthaginian overlords.

It is difficult to gauge with certainty the impact of the Carthiginian legacy on its subjects. By the time the Arabs appeared on the scene some eight centuries later, the Libyans, Numidians and, in the far west, the Mauri (Mauretanians or Moors), had all come to be known by outside observers as the 'Berbers'.

Those who remained in Carthaginian-controlled territory were heavily exploited. Some claim that these farmers profited from the more advanced agricultural methods they learnt from their oppressors. Many modern historians now dispute this, calling into question any single benefit that was felt by the subjects of this empire.

There is no doubt, however, of one effect of the Carthaginian regime: the marginalisation of certain groups of the indigenous population. Some took refuge in the hinterland of the Sahara desert and Atlas Mountains, where they reverted to seminomadic lifestyles. From these wild and inaccessible regions, they were to launch the first of a continual wave of attacks upon whatever unsuspecting foreign power was foolhardy enough to breach the coast.

Rome

The sack of Carthage in 146 BC meant that Rome was here to stay. During the hundred or so years of its occupation of Africa, however, it remained content just to maintain the garrisons it had posted there. These guards ensured the protection of the ports along the trade routes and kept a watchful and suspicious eye on the course of events unrolling in the interior of the country.

The Berbers

Morocco is still populated by the descendants of an ancient race that has inhabited Morocco since Neolithic times. The Berbers, famous throughout history as warriors, were notoriously resistant to being controlled by any system beyond the tribe.

Phoenicians, Romans, Arabs, even the French and Spanish felt the full fury of their wrath, and the Moroccan sultans also failed to gain full allegiance from all the clans of the mountain tribes.

In the Rif, until comparatively recently, a deadly insult was, 'your father died in his bed'.

Many Berbers have quite distinctive racial features, such as light skin, blue eyes, and in some case blond or red hair. Their ethnic origin remains obscure and the subject of hot debate, though many claim they are Caucasian people.

Though the country has long been dominated by the Arabs, the Berbers have managed to hang onto their culture with amazing tenacity.

Berber dialects are still spoken by many, the tradition of Berber crafts remain alive and the strong tribal structure still predominates. Some tribes will marry only within the clan. ■

Towards the end of the pre-Christian era, however, Rome's interest in North Africa grew keener. Colonists were settled here, local agricultural production was cranked up, and increasingly direct control was sought.

Beyond the cluster of small trading enclaves on the coast, the Mauretanian kingdom (including what is now Morocco and much of northern Algeria) had remained largely untainted by either Carthaginian or Roman influence. In 33 BC, however, Bocchus II of Mauretania died, bequeathing his entire kingdom to Rome. The Romans, not wishing to expend unnecessary energy and resources, preferred to foster local rule.

In about 40 AD, the kingdom was split into two provinces – Mauretania Caesariensis, with its capital in Caesarea (in modern Algeria), and Mauretania Tingitana, with its capital at Tingis (Tangier). Several Roman colonies were also established at this time including Lixus, succeeding the Phoenicians, and Volubilis. The latter became a minor centre of Graeco-Roman culture.

On the whole, however, Morocco remained virtually cut off from the rest of Roman North Africa. This was in a large measure due to the extensive and imposing presence of the Rif and Atlas mountain ranges; access was always easier by sea to ports like Tingis. The proud tribes of the Rif Mountains, in particular, retained their independence and occasionally launched small but wearing campaigns against imperial power.

During the first three centuries AD, Roman North Africa was comparatively stable and wealthy. Providing 60% of the empire's grain needs and other commodities such as olive oil, it had become an important breadbasket for the empire, supplying food to lands flung far across the kingdom. Rich, Romanised North Africans gradually began to enter the Roman administration and eventually provided an emperor, the Libyan Septimius Severus, who took power in 193 AD.

The latter half of the 3rd century brought strife to the empire, and Rome's African possessions did not remain untouched. As Rome strove to rationalise its position, parts of Tunisia, northern Algeria, Libya and Egypt were all maintained, while Mauretania Tingitana was abandoned to local tribes. The exception was the city of Tingis which remained a Romanised enclave protecting the strategic crossing between Spain and North Africa.

The 4th century, in what was left of Romanised Africa, was marked above all by the increasingly rapid spread of Christianity. Constantine's conversion in 313 AD had been the catalyst for this, as had the resulting schism launched by Donatus. His followers, the Donatists, promoted a version of Christianity firmly rooted in North

African traditions. Some historians view the movement more as a rejection of Roman society. Whatever its intents and purposes, the crumbling Roman empire, weakened by attack on all sides, was already beyond repair.

Vandals & Byzantium

In 429 AD, King Gaeseric (or Genseric), who had been busy marauding in southern Spain, decided to take the entire Vandal people (about 80,000 men, women and children) across to Africa. Bypassing Tingis, he managed within a few years to scupper the Roman forces and wring hefty concessions from them. By the middle of the 5th century, his ships were in control of almost the entire western Mediterranean. Rome was all but a spent force.

Vandal control over the former Roman provinces was never cast-iron, and their unbridled exploitation of the local economy only served to accelerate its decline. In addition, tribes from the surrounding areas, including the Atlas mountains, kept up a campaign of continual harassment.

Eventually, the former masters of North Africa put an end to Vandal rule. Emperor Justinian, ruler of the eastern half of what had been the Roman empire, was keen to restore it to its former glory, and sent an army to retake the core of North Africa in 533.

The dream of a Roman renaissance did not come off and the empire split in two. The eastern half had its capital in Constantinople (modern Istanbul) and came to be known as Byzantium. Little is known about subsequent Byzantine rule in North Africa, which appears to have been both ineffectual and uneventful. What is certain is that it had very little impact on the unfettered tribes of the Maghreb. Instead, a new and much more powerful force was about to unleash itself upon the world.

The Coming of Islam

In the distant peninsula of Arabia in the early 7th century, a new and obscure religion was emerging. Within a hundred years, the destiny of North Africa was to be forever altered. By 640, Islam's green banner was flying over the towns of Egypt, but it was some time before the Arab armies ventured further westwards.

When they did, it was initially tentatively. The first campaign west of Egypt took them along the coast through several Libyan towns to modern-day Tunisia. By 649, the Byzantines had been defeated. With depleted forces, however, the Arabs were unable to capitalise properly on their successes. Another attempt was made again in the 660s, but divided by internal conflicts over who should be caliph (successor of the Prophet and effectively secular and spiritual leader of the Muslim world), they were weakened and defeated by opposing forces.

It was not until Uqba bin Nafi al-Fihri began his campaign of conquest that the full military force of Islam was brought to bear on North Africa. From 669, in a highly successful three year campaign, he swept across the top of the continent.

Islam's first great city in the Maghreb, Kairouan (Qayrawan) in modern Tunisia, was founded. With an army of Arab cavalry and Islamised Berber infantry from Libya, he marched into the Atlas and is said to have conquered land as far afield as the Atlantic coast.

A lull ensued, but in 681 Uqba went on the rampage again, mostly in Morocco. Things began well, but finished disastrously, and in 683 he was defeated by the Berber chieftain, Qusayla. This led to the eviction of the Arabs from the entire region of the Maghreb as far east as Libya. Qusayla occupied Kairouan, and the Byzantine cities sat tight, careful not to provoke trouble on either side.

Their days were numbered, however, and by 698 the Arabs had succeeded in evicting the Byzantines from North Africa. Various Berber tribes continued to resist, including those led by the legendary princess Al-Kahina.

It was then Musa bin Nusayr's turn to take command of the conquering armies. Succeeding eventually in gaining a foothold in Morocco, he went about befriending, rather than alienating, the local Berber population. This wise policy and the new religion was well received by the tribespeoples. Islam, with its roots in a tough desert and tribal environment, probably appealed to Berber sensibilities.

By 710, Musa considered his work in Morocco done. His wandering eye now fell on Europe and, with his lieutenant Tariq (the name 'Gibraltar' is a bastardisation of Jebel Tariq – 'Tariq's Mountain') he set about conquering Spain. By 732 they had made their deepest advance, reaching Poitiers in France.

Moroccan Dynasties

Islam had arrived in Morocco, but not so warmly received were the Arab invaders who had introduced it. Treating Berbers, including Islamic converts, as second class citizens, the Arab overlords began to be deeply resented. A wave of religious fervour, issuing from the East and inspired by the Kharijite heresy, suddenly swept across the Islamic world. Taken up zealously by the Berbers and moulded to their cause, it resulted in the Arab governors being completely evicted.

Although a substantial population of Arab citizens remained, by 740 all effective Arab rulers had been expelled from the Maghreb. Tunisia and Algeria would again succumb to Arab control and, in the 15th century, fall into the hands of the Ottomans, but Morocco was never to come under the direct sway of the eastern Arab dynasties again.

Idriss, an Arab noble fleeing persecution from the ruling Abbassid dynasty in Baghdad, arrived in Morocco in the 780s. Winning the respect of enough Berber tribes, he soon established a dominant dynasty in northern Morocco. This is generally considered to be the first Moroccan state.

Idriss is also credited with the founding of Fès, and his rapid rise to power was sufficiently alarming for the Caliph in Baghdad, Harun ar-Rashid, to send a mission to kill him. Idriss was finally dispatched in 791 with a draught of poison. His son, just a baby on his father's death, assumed power in 803 at the tender age of 11. By the time he died in 829, a stable Idrissid state that dominated all of northern Morocco had been established.

This state of affairs did not last long. By the middle of the following century, the Idrissids had been reduced to one of a number of bit players on a wider stage. Among them, the Fatimid dynasty had managed to install itself in Tunisia, in Cairo and even in Fès for a short period. This rival dynasty was responsible for encouraging the so-called invasion of the Maghreb by the Beni Hillal Arab tribesmen from the East.

Long at odds with the Fatimids were the Umayyad Muslims of Al-Andalus who, in their turn, had become increasingly meddlesome in the affairs of northern Morocco.

Into this general chaos came a new force from a new direction. Inspired by the Qur'anic teacher, Abdallah bin Yasin, the Sanhaja confederation of Berber Saharan tribes began to wage war throughout southern and central Morocco. Because of their dress, they were known as 'the veiled ones' (al-mulathamin) and later as the 'people of the monastery' (al-murabitin) – the Almoravids.

In 1062 their leader, Youssef ben Tachfin, founded Marrakesh as his capital and led troops on a march of conquest that, at its height, saw a unified empire stretching from Senegal in Africa to Saragossa in northern Spain.

This brilliant flash was just that, for as quickly as they had risen, the Almoravids crumbled in the face of another Moroccan dynasty. These new Muslim overlords were strictly conservative and came to be known as 'those who proclaim the unity of God' (al-muwahhidin) – the Almohads.

Inspired by the teachings of Mohammed ibn Tumart against the growing religious laxness of the Almoravids, Abd al-Mu'min, his successor, began a successful campaign against them. In the 30 years to 1160, the Almohads conquered all of Almoravid Morocco, as well as what are now Algeria, Tunisia and parts of Libya. In the following years, Muslim Spain also fell.

The greatest of his successors, Yacoub al-Mansour ('the Victorious'), continued the fight against dissidents in the Maghreb and the Reconquista in Spain. By his death in 1199, Morocco's greatest dynasty was at the height of its power. Many of the empire's cities flourished in this golden age of Moroccan cultural development. Trouble was never far away, however.

The Almohads tended to treat most of their subjects as conquered enemies and drained them of their wealth for the enrichment of their cities. Marrakesh was the principal beneficiary. The empire was expanding too quickly, however, and suddenly it began to crumble under its own weight.

As it caved in, the Maghreb divided into three parts: Ifriqiyya (Tunisia) came under the Hafsids; Algeria under the Banu Abd al-Wad; and Morocco under the Merenids. Although borders have changed and imperial rulers have come and gone, this division has remained more or less intact until today.

The Merenids ruled until 1465 (although a rival family, the Wattasids, held effective power from as early as 1420). The mid-14th century marked the pinnacle of Merenid rule. Many of the monuments that survive to this day (especially religious schools *(medersas)* were built by the Merenids. They also built Fès el-Jdid (New Fès) as their capital.

As the dynasty declined, Morocco slid into chaos. Spotting an opportunity, the adventurous maritime power of Portugal took Ceuta (Sebta) in 1415. Only a few years earlier, a Spanish force had debarked in northern Morocco to sack Tetouan in reprisal for piracy.

The Wattasids then took over as the next ruling dynasty. By the early 16th century, however, Morocco was effectively divided into two shaky kingdoms: that of the Wattasids in Fès and the Saadians in Marrakesh.

Growing European interference caused Morocco to turn in on itself. Portugal's seizure of Sebta had symbolised the beginning; by 1515 Lisbon possessed a string of bases along the Moroccan coast. Spain took Melilla in 1497.

The rise of the Saadian dynasty, originally from Arabia, was largely due to the popularity that they won by their determination to turf out the Portuguese. After winning back some of the coastal bases from Lisbon, they began expanding northwards. Marrakesh became their capital from 1524 and they wrested Fès from the Wattasids in 1554.

Ottoman & European Threats

The next threat to Moroccan independence was the rapidly expanding Ottoman Empire. It eventually came to control all of the Maghreb up to Tlemcen in modern Algeria. War and empire-building create strange bedfellows and Mohammed ash-Sheikh, the Saadian sultan, entered into an alliance with Spain to check the Turkish advance. It proved an uneasy arrangement, but probably helped to keep Morocco out of Turkish hands.

No sooner did the Turkish threat recede than a Portuguese army, headed by King Dom Sebastian, arrived in northern Morocco. They had come to help Mohammed al-Mutawwakil regain his throne, after he had been deposed by his Saadian uncle with Turkish intervention.

The ensuing Battle of the Three Kings in 1578 finally put an end to Portuguese pretensions in Morocco, although by this stage many of their coastal footholds had been lost anyway. Not long after the Battle of the Three Kings, the Saadian sultan Ahmed al-Mansour undertook a foreign campaign of his own, looting Timbuktu and taking home a rich booty in gold and slaves.

With the Christian reconquest of the peninsula at the turn of the century, the Catholic monarchy in Spain began to pursue a violent policy of national and religious unity. This led to waves of Muslim refugees seeking asylum in Morocco. A whole community of these exiles set up shop in Salé and Rabat, and soon acquired de facto autonomy as a base for the highly successful corsairs.

These famous pirates roamed not only the Mediterranean and Atlantic coasts, but

DAMIEN SIMONIS   FRANCES LINZEE GORDON   FRANCES LINZEE GORDON

DAMIEN SIMONIS   FRANCES LINZEE GORDON

DAMIEN SIMONIS   FRANCES LINZEE GORDON

Top Left, Middle & Right: Water seller, Meknès; Carding wool, Meknès; Potion seller, Spice Souq, Marrakesh Medina

Middle Left & Right: Busker, Taroudannt; Coal seller, Marrakesh souq

Bottom Left & Right: Wedding procession, Taroudannt; Collecting wood, Moulay Bousselham

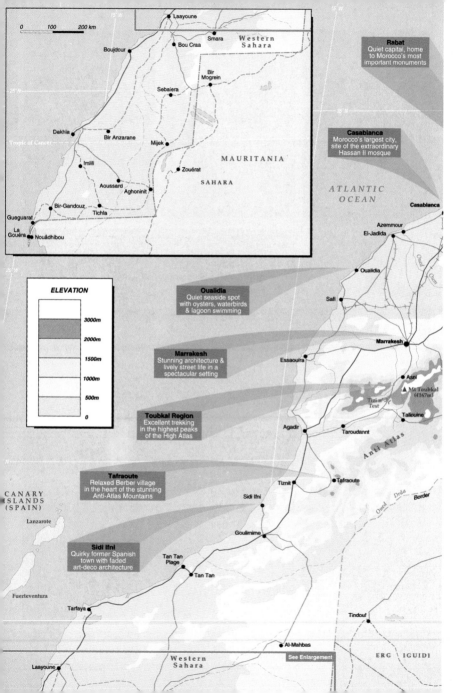

ELEVATION

3000m
2000m
1500m
1000m
500m
0

0   100   200 km

Western Sahara

Laayoune
Smara
Bou Craa
Boujdour
Bir Mogrein
Sebaiera
Dakhla
Bir Anzarane
Mijek
Imlili
Zouérat
Aoussard
Aghoninit
Bir-Gandouz
Tichla
Gueguarat
La Gouéra
Nouâdhibou

MAURITANIA

SAHARA

Tropic of Cancer

Rabat
Quiet capital, home to Morocco's most important monuments

Casablanca
Morocco's largest city, site of the extraordinary Hassan II mosque

ATLANTIC OCEAN

Casablanca
Azemmour
El-Jadida
Oualidia
Safi
Marrakesh
Essaouira
Asni
Mt Toubkal (4167m)
Tizi n' Test
Taliouine
Agadir
Taroudannt

Anti Atlas

Oualidia
Quiet seaside spot with oysters, waterbirds & lagoon swimming

Marrakesh
Stunning architecture & lively street life in a spectacular setting

Toubkal Region
Excellent trekking in the highest peaks of the High Atlas

Tafraoute
Relaxed Berber village in the heart of the stunning Anti-Atlas Mountains

Sidi Ifni
Quirky former Spanish town with faded art-deco architecture

Tiznit
Tafraoute
Sidi Ifni
Goulimime
Oued Drâa
Border

CANARY ISLANDS (SPAIN)

Lanzarote
Fuerteventura

Tan Tan Plage
Tan Tan
Tarfaya
Tindouf

Laayoune
Al-Mahbas

Western Sahara

See Enlargement

ERG   IGUIDI

he French Protectorate (1912-56)

he treaty of Fès, by which Morocco be-
me a French protectorate, was signed on
March 1912. The sultan was to maintain
ly the semblance of power, with effective
ntrol resting firmly with the governor, or
sident-general, General Lyautey and his
ccessors. Spain controlled the northern
anche of the country and Tangier was
ade an international zone in 1923.

The Moroccan people were not im-
essed. As usual, it was the Berber tribes
the mountains who reacted most strongly
d who remained beyond colonial control.
fter WWI, the Berber leader Abd el-Krim
arshalled a revolt in the Rif and Middle
tlas Mountains, and for five years had the
paniards and French on the run. Spain
me close to a massive and embarrassing
efeat, and France only managed to end all
ffective Berber resistance in 1934.

The process of colonisation in the French
ne was rapid. From a few thousand before
912, the number of foreigners living in
orocco rose to more than 100,000 by
929. Thereafter, the Great Depression put
dampener on significant growth.

The French contribution was threefold: it
ilt roads and railways, developed the port
f Casablanca virtually from scratch, and
oved the political capital to Rabat. In the
ench zone, *villes nouvelles* (new towns)
ere built next to the old medinas. This was
rgely a result of an enlightened policy on
yautey's part – in Algeria he had wit-
essed the wholesale destruction of many
d cities by his countrymen. The Spaniards
llowed suit in their zone, but on a much
ore modest scale.

WWII brought a new wave of Europeans
to Morocco, virtually doubling their num-
ers. It also brought hardship to many as
rices rose and industry came to a standstill.
fter Franco came to power in Spain in
939 and Hitler overran France in 1940,
panish Morocco became a seat of Nazi
ropaganda, which tended, curiously, to fo-
ent Moroccan nationalist aspirations in
e rest of the country.

Various local opposition groups began to
form, but the French administration ignored
pleas for reform. The Allied landings in
North Africa in 1943 further muddied the
waters. However the Free French Forces, in
spite of US President Roosevelt's sympathy
for the nationalists' cause, were adamant
that nothing in Morocco should change. In
January 1944 the Istiqlal (Independence)
party led by Allal al-Fasi, one of Morocco's
most intractable nationalists, demanded full
independence.

When the war ended, nationalist feeling
grew and the French became increasingly
inflexible. Moroccans boycotted French
goods and terrorist acts against the administration multiplied. The sultan, Mohammed
V, sympathised with the nationalists – so
much so that the French authorities in Rabat
had him deposed in 1953. This act served
only to make him a hero in the people's
eyes. In 1955, Paris allowed his return and
talks finally began on handing power to the
Moroccans.

Madrid's administration of the Spanish
zone after the war was considerably less
heavy-handed than that of the French. In
fact the area even became something of a
haven for Moroccan nationalists. Spain had
not been consulted on the expulsion of the
sultan and continued to recognise him. By
this time there was virtually no cooperation
at all between the French and Spanish
zones.

Independence

Mohammed V returned to Morocco in November 1955 to a tumultuous welcome.
Within five months he was able to appoint
Morocco's first independent government as
the French protectorate formally came to an
end. Shortly afterwards, Spain pulled out of
its zone in the north, but hung on to the enclaves of Ceuta, Melilla and Ifni. It abandoned the latter in 1970, but Madrid has
shown no desire to give up the other two
since.

The sultan resumed virtually autocratic
rule and, when the Istiqlal Party divided
into two groups in 1959 (Istiqlal and the
more left-wing Union Nationale des Forces

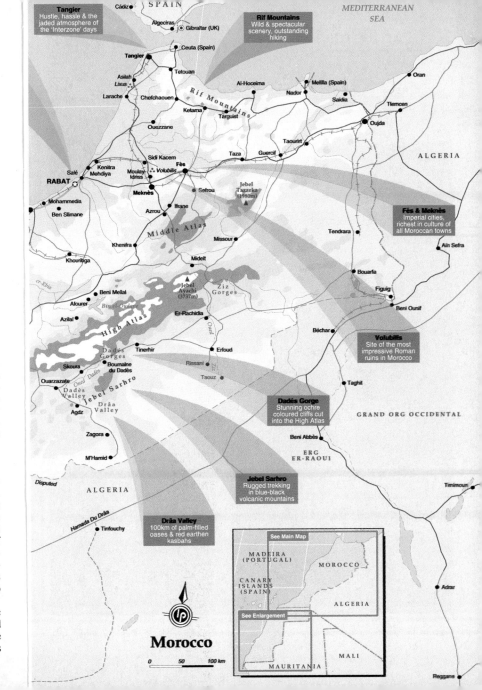

Morocco

DAMIEN SIMONIS

Morocco's only genuine Saharan dune, Erg Chebbi, near Merzouga.

also dared to operate as far afield as the Irish Sea and off the coast of the Americas. The corsairs were subject to no law and were beyond the control of even the sultan himself.

Like those before it, the Saadian dynasty eventually collapsed and was succeeded by one that has been in charge, sometimes only nominally, right up until today – the Alawites (or Alaouites). Like the Saadians before them, they are of Arab origin and claim descent from the Prophet and therefore the right to be considered sherifs.

Alawite Rule

From early in the 17th century, the notion of central rule in Morocco had hardly existed. The Saadians had found themselves continually preoccupied with putting down local rebellions, and into this growing vacuum stepped the Alawites.

It took Moulay ar-Rashid some 30 years before he finally managed to secure the sultanate in the early 1660s. His successor, Moulay Ismail, made Meknès his capital, which he set about turning into a kind of Moroccan Versailles.

His reign, which lasted from 1672 to 1727, was largely spent pacifying tribes inside Morocco which he accomplished, it is said, with boundless and legendary cruelty. As a result of his military efforts, Portugal was left with just one base in Morocco, Mazagan (modern El-Jadida), and Spain had only four small bases on the north coast.

At the time of Ismail's death, Morocco was relatively stable and independent, but his demise saw a degeneration into the usual chaos. Over the following century, the country was characterised by a period of stagnation, periodically rocked by internal strife.

European Interference (to 1912)

Moulay Abd ar-Rahman and Mohammed bin Abd ar-Rahman continued to grapple with internal problems. Also to be faced was the unpleasant fact that powerful European powers were increasingly taking a keen interest in all of the countries o Africa. These concerns materialised with France's occupation of neighb Algeria. The most alarming elemen was the sultan's total inability to d thing about it.

As Europe's big players moved to advantages over each other, the co tion for influence in Morocco grew.

In 1856 Great Britain extracted a guaranteeing free trade. French and S influence also grew, but it waned agai porarily after 1870.

Moulay al-Hassan (1873-94) began economic, administrative and milita forms and managed to keep Europe at length, but could not prevent attemp Spain and Britain to get a foothold the coast (Río de Oro, Ifni and Cap J Europeans stepped up trade and set u dustries in Morocco, but the benefit t Moroccan people was minimal.

Al-Hassan's successor, Moulay Ab Aziz, came to the throne ill-prepare cope with the problems in store for him attempt at tax reform and repeated Fr military intervention caused uproar. Fr bought off Italy (by offering it a free in Libya), Spain (with the promise northern sphere of interest in Morocco), Great Britain (allowing it free reig Egypt and the Sudan), and in 1905 hope pull off the establishment of a protecto with a so-called 'plan of reforms'.

Germany, which had been left out of international wheeling and dealing, trie put pay to all this and called for an inte tional conference, achieving little excep delay the inevitable. Moulay Abd al-H became sultan in 1909, but the situation already slipped beyond the Morocca control.

Germany was pacified by the other Eu pean powers in 1911 with concessions the Congo (after sending a gunboat to A dir and so pushing Germany and France the brink of war), leaving the way free France to move in. Spain had already s troops to the northern zone allocated to it agreement in 1904.

Populaires), Mohammed V posed as mediator, above the mucky business of party politics. He did not have to fulfil this role for long, as he died in 1961. He was succeeded by his son, Hassan II.

The new king finally managed to introduce a constitution in 1972, after a coup attempt in 1971 had delayed its promulgation. Another attempted takeover that same year led him to suspend much of it. When elections were finally held in 1977, supporters of the king won a big majority. Both halves of the Istiqlal had by now gone into the opposition.

Western Sahara

Hassan II owes some of his popularity to his apparent *baraka* (good grace) in surviving two attempts to get rid of him. Above all, it was the famous Green March in November 1975, in which 350,000 Moroccans walked unarmed into the former Spanish Sahara, that really established him as leader.

After various about-faces, Madrid had decided to abandon the phosphate-rich ter-

King of Morocco since 1961, Hassan II enjoys enormous popularity among his people.

ritory in 1974 and pulled the last of its troops out shortly after the Moroccans walked in. Mauritania dropped its claims to any of the territory in 1979 in exchange for Rabat's renouncing any plans to absorb Mauritania, to which it had claimed historical rights.

In the late 1960s it had become clear that the 100,000 or so inhabitants of the territory wanted independence. The Popular Front for the Liberation of Saguia al-Hamra and Río de Oro (Polisario), initially set up to harass the Spaniards, did not take kindly to Moroccan intervention and embarked on a long guerrilla war against the new overlords in Rabat.

Backed by Libya and Algeria, Polisario scored occasional successes against the far superior Moroccan forces. However, with the construction of a ragged defensive wall inside the territory's Mauritanian and Algerian frontiers, Polisario's room to move became extremely limited. In 1984, Morocco and Libya proclaimed a 'union' in Oujda that resulted in the latter withdrawing its support for Polisario. As Algeria's internal problems grew in the late 1980s and early 90s, it too abandoned its Saharan protégés.

In 1991, the United Nations brokered a ceasefire on the understanding that a referendum on the territory's future would be held in 1992. Although the ceasefire has more or less held, the referendum has yet to happen because of a disagreement over who are eligible to vote. Polisario wants only those registered as citizens prior to the Green March to participate, while Rabat naturally wants to include many of the region's new inhabitants.

Polisario claims that Morocco is systematically moving Moroccans into the area in order to bolster future votes in its favour.

In late 1996, the USA, frustrated and fed up with the stagnation of affairs (and the on-going cost, calculated at some US$250 million to date), threatened to block an extension of UN operations if there was no further progress towards a political settlement. In November of the same year, UN operations were renewed for a further six months. By March 1997, however, still no advance had been made.

Disappointed by the state of affairs, the Security Council, led by secretary-general Kofi Annan, appointed a former US secretary of state, James Baker, as special envoy to deal with the issue. Baker's immediate mandate is to find a compromise between the two sides which will allow a referendum to proceed.

In May 1997, the first meeting took place with representatives from Morocco, Algeria, Mauritania and Polisario. More talks are scheduled throughout 1997 and 1998.

Although both sides seem ready to co-operate, and relations seem to be improving, (culminating in 1996 with the exchange of prisoners, and the first direct talks between palace officials and Polisario) the task will be a tough one for Baker.

Morocco will not give up its claim to the region, and Polisario has threatened to resume guerrilla warfare if no agreement is reached.

Should the UN abandon the cause altogether, this would lead most probably to a de facto victory to Rabat. Polisario's resources are limited and its former backer, Algeria, is preoccupied with its own serious problems.

Relations with Israel

Morocco has maintained a unique position in the Arab-Israeli conflict. Although the two nations still do not have diplomatic relations (and according to the king, this must await the conclusion of a formal Middle East peace agreement), Morocco has hosted Israeli guests, often in secret, and long before Egypt's President Anwar Sadat went to Israel in 1977.

Various Israeli senior politicians have travelled to Rabat incognito, and Shimon Peres, the former foreign minister, made several open visits, including one to Ifrane in 1987. After signing a peace accord with the PLO in Washington in September 1993, Yitzak Rabin, the then Israeli prime minister, stopped at Rabat on his way home to thank Hassan II for his behind-the-scenes work as intermediary.

The two countries have traditionally had strong ties, with 700,000 Jews of Moroccan origin living in Israel, and around 30,000 Jews living in Morocco. Israeli Jews have long been allowed to holiday in Morocco and, officially at least, there is little bad blood between the resident Jews and the rest of the Moroccan population. Joint business ventures between the two countries have dramatically increased in recent years.

More recently however, political relations with Israel have become more strained. In late March 1997, amid widespread concern about the faltering Middle East peace process, King Hassan called for the Jerusalem committee to meet in Rabat. Israel was urged to halt the provocative development of a Jewish settlement in Arab East Jerusalem and was threatened with the reassessment of relations with 14 Arab countries.

In February 1997, King Hassan made it clear that a state visit from either the Israeli prime minister, Binyamin Netanyahu or his foreign minister, David Levy, would not be appropriate in the present circumstances.

Relations with Algeria

In the early 1990s, Morocco's traditionally stormy relations with Algeria seemed to be on the mend. The Algerian president, Mohammed Boudiaf, lent a sympathetic ear to the Moroccan campaign for the Western Sahara and indicated his desire to see a prompt settlement. His assassination, however, in 1992, signalled the start of a relapse in relations, which culminated in August 1994, when Morocco publicly accused the Algerian security forces of involvement in the hotel shooting of two western tourists. This led to the closure of the border once again.

In 1996, Algeria was next accused of meddling in Western Saharan affairs and, in protest, King Hassan called for the total suspension of the Arab Maghreb Union (AMU). In December 1996, however, with the visit to Morocco of Algeria's interior minister, relations between the two countries appeared to be thawing.

The Moroccan government has shown itself willing to consider the reopening of the border in the future, and adopting a neutral stance towards the Algerian conflict; in return, it will ask for lasting neutrality by Algeria towards the Western Sahara issue.

A genuine settlement of these issues and the reopening of the border appears to lie in the distant future of the next century. In the meantime, Algeria's sad and brutal civil war rages on.

The Present

The 1980s in Morocco were marked above all by economic stagnation and hardship. The situation deteriorated, and in 1984 there were scenes of open rioting over bread price rises in Fès in which at least 100 people died.

Hassan II has friends in useful places, however, and the rulers of Saudi Arabia and the Gulf States are among them. Accorded most favoured trading nation status, these countries sometimes reciprocate when things are particularly bad: in 1985, US$250 million turned up in the central bank at a time when Morocco was practically bereft of foreign exchange reserves. Hassan's pro-allied position during the Gulf War in 1990-91 has done him no harm either.

Although popular sentiment tended to side with Iraq's Saddam Hussein, Hassan managed to keep in with the west and the Gulf States in a low-profile fashion that aroused little rancour among his subjects.

Although things have improved in some sectors recently, unrest has bubbled below the surface and occasionally bursts through. Strikes and riots over low wages and poor social conditions saw unions clashing with the authorities in the early 1990s. In one such event, at least 33 people died and hundreds were jailed. In early 1994, the trade unions were heading for renewed clashes with the authorities over pay and social policy, calling for mass protests and strikes.

The years 1996 and 1997 were characterised above all by an upsurge in violent confrontation between Islamist students and government security forces. The trouble ignited at Casablanca University and rapidly spread to other universities, particularly Marrakesh and Mohammedia. In January 1997, UNEM, the national student union (now controlled by the radical Islamist Al-Adel wal-Ihssan party) called a 24 hour strike in protest at government repression. Some 60 students received sentences ranging from three months to three years and the rectors of eight universities lost their jobs.

Unemployment continues to be the other major headache for the country and a vote-winning electoral issue for politicians. 1996 and 1997 also saw high-profile demonstrations by unemployed graduates. A petition was even presented to King Hassan himself. This caused the government major embarrassment and led to some over-reaction. In January 1997, three protesters, part of a group of 30 students staging peaceful demonstrations in Marrakesh, were sentenced to six months in prison.

In spite of constitutional reforms and the announcement of the forthcoming elections to a new, bicameral parliament due to meet for the first time in October 1997 (see the Government entry later in this chapter), Hassan II remains an absolute ruler.

On the economic front, the pressures of a soaring population, top-heavy public sector and disappointing progress in most industries remain considerable obstacles, but the news is not all black, particularly if Morocco secures a free trade deal with the European Union (see the Economy entry later in this chapter).

Despite the wave of fundamentalist trouble crashing over from neighbouring Algeria and the very real problems confronting Hassan II and his people, it appears his baraka will hold for a while yet.

GEOGRAPHY

Morocco presents by far the most variegated geological smorgasbord in all North Africa and boasts some of the most beautiful countryside in the continent. With its long Atlantic and Mediterranean coasts it has remained to some degree shielded from the rest of the continent by the Atlas Mountain ranges to the east and the Sahara desert to the south.

Including the Western Sahara, occupied by Morocco since the Green March of 1975, the kingdom covers 710,850 sq km, more than a third of it in the disputed territory.

There are four distinct mountain ranges or massifs in Morocco which are considered geologically unstable and leave Morocco subject to earthquakes, such as the one that devastated Agadir in 1960. In the north, the Rif (sometimes confusingly known as the Rif Atlas) forms an arc of largely impenetrable limestone and sandstone mountain territory, shooting steeply back from the Mediterranean to heights of about 2200m and populated largely by Berbers, many of whom are engaged in the cultivation of kif (the local name for marijuana).

Running north-east to south-west from the Rif is the Middle Atlas range (Moyen Atlas), which rises to an altitude of 3290m. It is separated from the Rif by the only real access route linking Atlantic Morocco with the rest of North Africa, the Taza Gap.

The low hills east of Agadir rise to form the highest of the mountain ranges, the High Atlas, which more or less runs parallel to the south of the Middle Atlas. Its tallest peak, Jebel (Mt) Toubkal, is 4165m high and, like much of the surrounding heights, covered in a mantle of snow through the winter and into spring. Farther south again, the lower slopes of the Anti-Atlas drop down into the arid wastes of the Sahara.

The rivers (known as *oued*, from the Arabic *wadi*) are mostly torrential and, depending on seasonal rainfall and melting snows, can flow quite strongly at certain times of the year. The Drâa, Ziz and the Dadès rivers, among others, drain off into the Sahara, although occasionally the Drâa completes its course all the way to the Atlantic coast north of Tan Tan.

Among other rivers that drain into the Atlantic are the Sebou, which rises south of Fès and empties into the ocean at Mehdiya about 40km north of Rabat, and the Oum er-Rbia, which has its source in the Middle Atlas, north-east of Khenifra, and reaches the Atlantic at Azemmour just north of El-Jadida.

Between each of the mountain ranges and the Atlantic lie the plains and plateaux, which are generally well watered and, in places, quite fertile.

South of the Anti-Atlas, the dry slopes, riven by gorges, trail off into the often stony desert of the Western Sahara, which is also the name the rebels of the former Spanish Sahara have given to the territory they want to see independent of Morocco. This is a sparsely populated and unforgiving region bounded to the east and south by Algeria and Mauritania.

CLIMATE

The geological variety of Morocco also gives it a wide range of climatic conditions.

Weather in the coastal regions is generally mild, but it can become a little cool and wet, particularly in the north. Average temperatures in Tangier and Casablanca range from about 12°C (54°F) in winter to 25°C (77°F) in summer, although the daytime temperatures can easily go higher. Rainfall is highest in the Rif and northern Middle Atlas, where only the summer months are almost dry.

While the interior of the country can become stiflingly hot in summer, particularly when the desert winds from the Sahara (known as the *sirocco* or *chergui*, from the Arabic *ash-sharqi*, meaning 'the easterly') are blowing, the Atlantic coast is kept comparatively agreeable by sea breezes. The southern Atlantic coast, however, is more arid. Rainfall here drops off and renders crop-growing less tenable.

The rainy season is from November to January, but can go on as late as April. From 1991 to late 1993, however, drought dried the country out and cut cereal production by around 60%. There was a sigh of relief when heavy rains struck in November 1993, replenishing reservoirs for drinking water, power stations and irrigation.

The lowlands can be quite hot during the

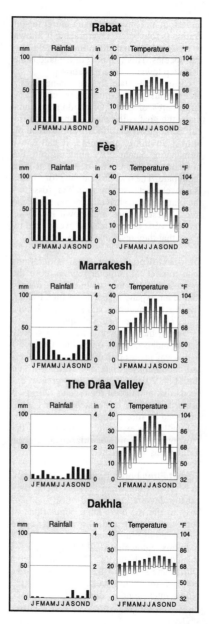

Rabat

Fès

Marrakesh

The Drâa Valley

Dakhla

day, even in winter, with the mercury hitting as high as 30°C, but temperatures drop quickly in the evening. In the mountains, it can get as cold as -20°C (without taking the wind-chill factor into account). As snow can often block mountain passes, it is important to remember to have enough warm clothing to cope with an unwelcome night stuck in an unheated bus. In summer, the opposite is true during the day, particularly when the chergui is up, with temperatures easily exceeding 40°C. This goes for Marrakesh too.

In the desert, temperatures can swing wildly from day to night. This is due to the dryness of the atmosphere, which has almost no humidity.

The chergui, which is sometimes laden with dust, can occur at any time of the year, but is most common in spring.

ECOLOGY & ENVIRONMENT

The first-time visitor to Morocco may be struck by the amount of green encountered in a country more popularly associated with vast stretches of desert. Travellers arriving in northern Morocco after crossing the arid *meseta* (high plateau) of central and southern Spain are surprised by the comparative lushness they find across the Strait of Gibraltar.

Until the first century or so of the Christian era, sweeping savannah and good pasture land covered much of the Maghreb. But the process of desertification that had already been underway for thousands of years gradually forced the mainly Berber population to seek refuge in the mountains of the Atlas.

Desertification and, on a larger scale, deforestation continue apace. Like most other countries in North Africa, demographic pressures have caused increasing environmental havoc. Twenty species of birds and animals found in Morocco at the turn of the century have disappeared. A recent victim, and a great loss for bird enthusiasts, was the slender-billed curlew, which was last recorded in March 1995. Other now defunct species include the famous Barbary lion (hunted to extinction), as well as various species of gazelle and oryx, and the red-necked ostrich. Among the further 34 bird and animal species said to be in acute danger are the leopard, monk seal and bald ibis.

The conservation movement in Morocco is relatively well developed, particularly in comparison with other North African countries. This has more to do with pragmatic, economic reasons than equitable ones. Like many African countries, humanity and the environment in Morocco are much more mutually dependent than in more developed, industrialised countries. Morocco is particularly dependent on its forests for its wellbeing.

These woodland areas are crucial to the country's manufacturing industries, and supply the paper, construction, sawing, mining and crafts industries. They also provide raw materials such as cork, tannin, rubber, medicinal products and fuel. On a local level, the forests are an important source of food, particularly in rural areas where poorer populations depend on them for providing game, mushrooms, edible acorns and berries.

Apart from their well-cited functions of regulating the climate and purifying the air, trees are essential in Morocco for the prevention of soil erosion – a problem which continues to plague the country. As mentioned above, they also provide a key habitat for Morocco's rich wildlife, including species which are already extinct in other parts of the world.

Principal Environmental Problems
Overgrazing In many regions of Morocco, animal husbandry forms the basis of the local economy. Often, when cultivation is restricted by climate or space restrictions (in arid or mountainous zones for example), this is the only possible means of living.

Livestock, when not controlled, can have a devastating impact on the environment.

During very dry periods, the situation is aggravated by hungry herds of animals congregating on a single area of land and exhausting it. The new seedlings are trampled underfoot and any chance of natural regeneration is scuppered. Overgrazing is known to cause a large reduction in plant and animal species. This stripping of the land is the first step towards desertification.

Close to this state are the argane forests on the Souss plain which are threatened by large herds of goats. Of all domestic animals, the goat is the most adapted to difficult ecological conditions. Able to feed on almost anything, anywhere, it can cause tremendous damage. By climbing into the branches of the argane trees, it can strip them bare. The once lush argane forest area is now characterised by so-called 'fossils' – the scattered and shrivelled remains of dead trees. These stumps are known locally as *rochers verts* (argan trees so overgrazed by goats that they resemble green rocks).

Deforestation Poorer tribal populations who inhabit the remoter regions pose the greatest threat to forests. In order to satisfy their ever-expanding needs for fuel, fodder, construction materials and arable land, huge tracts of forest are being cleared.

During the two world wars and shortly before independence, much forest was lost in this way in the north of the country. In certain mountain regions, such as the Rif and the High Atlas, illegal felling greatly exceeds that authorised for regular felling. It often takes place in isolated regions, little surveyed by forest rangers.

Finally, the expansion of towns and the movement of people on pilgrimage and on holiday has also threatened ecosystems.

Forest Fires Forest fires are relatively rare in Morocco, but when they do occur, they can be devastating. In the north, particularly in the Rif area, huge populations of cork, thuya, cedar and, above all, pine tree have been lost in this way.

In this region almost all felling of trees is carried out with the aid of 'controlled' fires. During the season of the chergui (the very hot and dry south-westerly wind which blows intermittently during the summer), these can quickly spread out of control.

Land is also cleared in this way for the extension of roads or the cultivation of crops.

Land Mismanagement Ironically, it is the Moroccan forestry department which has often been guilty of misguided practises. Methods intended for forests of temperate climes have been applied to forests in Morocco, often with disastrous results.

The widespread practice of the thinning of trees is the best example of this. Thinning is carried out with the aim of accelerating the tree's growth by removing the competition supplied by surrounding tree species. In the forests of Mamora, for example, broom has been thinned from under cork oaks. This has led to serious soil erosion, and the oaks have later died from dehydration.

Official mismanagement of the land has also occurred. Hoping to bring aid to local farmers, agricultural organisations have cleared much argane forest on the Souss plain for the purpose of large-scale market gardening. Ill-adapted to this form of cultivation, the top soil of the land has suffered greatly. After three successive years of this type of cultivation, and without the necessary replenishment of the soil by fertiliser, the land becomes sterile.

This practise of thinning Moroccan holm oaks, cork oaks and argane trees has been one of the principal causes of deforestation.

The replanting of foreign species such as the canary pine, again ill-adapted to the soil, has had a similar effect.

Hunting Whether legal or illegal, hunting continues to be the single most important cause of animal extinction. The last Atlas lion, for example, was shot in 1936 in the region of Taza. Fewer than a dozen specimens of panther remain in the central High Atlas, and the hyena, jackal and desert fox have all become extremely rare.

The disappearance or scarcity of these carnivores has caused an imbalance of other species. In the Middle Atlas, for example, populations of macaque monkey and wild boar have grown disproportionately.

Animals most under threat are those hunted for their meat or skin. Common in Morocco until quite recently were the partridge, bustard, rabbit, hare, gazelle, and moufflon. Some are now endangered. The Barbary deer has recently disappeared from Morocco (although a reintroduction programme is currently underway in certain forests of the north).

Outlook Despite various measures and steps taken by the government and backed by international organisations, the situation remains grave. A third of all ecosystems have been seriously damaged and are in danger of disappearing, 10% of vertebrates are considered endangered, and each year 25,000 hectares of forest are lost for ever.

Forests which have already disappeared include the Atlantic pistachio and the wild olive. Those in real danger of disappearing, even by the end of the 20th century, include the forests of Moroccan pine, thuya and Atlas cedar. Considered seriously degraded are the forests of argane, red juniper, holm-oak canary oak (*quercus canariensis*) and tauzin oak (*quercus pyrenaica*).

With the disappearance of so much forest, soil erosion begins to present a serious problem. Every year thousands of topsoil is swept away with the rains falling in the north of the country. The yields of the peasant farms in these areas have begun to fall dramatically because of the impoverishment of the land, and with the silting up of the dams, flooding has been widespread.

In August 1994, villages in southern and eastern Morocco sustained huge damages because of floods, including the loss of hundred of lives.

Morocco's programme of large-scale agriculture has also been criticised. In order to divert water to these vast, cultivated areas, dams have been constructed and water pumps installed. This has led to the lowering of the water table, and many ecosystems (such as the valleys in the pre-Sahara) are no longer able to sustain the animal life that depended upon them.

Protective Measures Genuinely worried

about the loss of habitat and the resulting disappearance of plant and animal species, Morocco has begun to demark certain areas for protection. Toubkal national park in the Atlas Mountains, was the first to be created in 1942 and covers an area of 36,000 hectares. Tazekka followed in 1950, and more recently the park of Souss Massa in 1991. The establishment of further parks in the Atlas Mountains is expected in the next few years and, in 1997, plans were underway to establish a huge, one million hectare protected area in the Moroccan Sahara.

As in many African countries, the greatest obstacle to overcome is the opposition of the local people. Antagonised by the loss of their grazing land, lack of compensation and unsympathetic and harsh policing, the communities have shown themselves unwilling to cooperate.

In an effort to appease the local people and win their si pport, a new government initiative is underway. Park guides are beginning to be recruited from the local communities, and limited access to grazing and felling has been permitted. New industry has also been encouraged, such as craft production for the lucrative tourist industry.

There are hopes also that some of the revenue gained from tourism in the parks may eventually be returned to the community for the development of local projects such as clinics, schools and skill training centres.

Extensive plantation programmes are also underway, some with international backing. The area of the Rif mountains, in particular, has been the centre of much activity, and fire prevention measures have been widely introduced. In the south, particularly in the area around Agadir and Essaouira, and in the Saharan desert near Erfoud, Zagora and Laayoune, work has been carried out to fight the desertification which is threatening the palm groves and some of the inhabited areas. Every year, two million fruit trees are distributed throughout these regions.

Other protective measures include the plantation of wind breaks, natural screens and green belts around built-up areas.

A programme of reintroduction of wild animal species, including the Barbary deer, partridge, several types of gazelle and pheasants, is also underway. In November 1995, around 40 gazelles and oryx were introduced into the Souss Massa National park in a joint international effort involving 16 zoos in France, Germany, Denmark and the Czech Republic.

In 1996, 24 Addax antelopes and Mediterranean monk seals were reintroduced following a French-Moroccan initiative.

Perhaps the most ambitious and publicised effort was the PNR plan (national plan of replanting) which promised to meet the demand for timber of all national industries by the year 2000. However, the project has been widely criticised for its policy of planting rapid-growth trees, most often of foreign varieties such as pines, eucalyptus and acacia, without taking into account the suitability of the species for their environment.

Although these foreign varieties have initially shown high yields, in recent times there have been several major disasters around the country. Entirely because of the unsuitability of the tree species, huge losses caused by the cold, drought and by insect plagues have occurred. In the Gharb, yields from the 100,000 eucalyptus plantations have fallen dramatically.

Responsible Tourism Morocco is a trekker's heaven. Across the country, and particularly around the High Atlas area, there are large mountainous areas which see almost no visitors and which remain almost totally unexplored. While this provides wonderful opportunities for the hiker, travellers should also bear in mind that these regions are extremely susceptible to the impact of tourism. In order to protect both the fragile environment of these places and the hill tribes who inhabit them, it would show both consideration and foresight to bear in mind a few guidelines.

Dress code is important all over Morocco (see Avoiding Offence in the Society & Conduct section in this chapter), but especially in the deeply conservative societies of the hill tribes. Many of the inhabitants have had little or no exposure either to modernisation from inside their country or foreign customs from without.

Inside the villages, travellers will feel most comfortable in buttoned shirts (rather than tee shirts which are seen by villagers as underwear) and, above all, trousers (rather than shorts) for both men and women. The importance of dress in the villages cannot be overemphasised (as many a frustrated and embarrassed trekking tour leader will affirm). An effort to respect this tradition will bring greater rewards for the traveller, too. You are much more likely to attract a friendly reception, generous hospitality, reasonable prices in the souqs and help or assistance should you ever be in need of it.

Again, as in other parts of Morocco, photographers should be aware that cameras can cause offence and, in some cases, extreme upset, particularly when pointed at women. Always ask in advance and, if you do find a cooperative model, it's polite to leave a very small consideration for them.

Contrary to what the majority of guidebooks tell you, it's not a good idea to distribute sweets and pens among village children, however great the temptation. It engenders a grossly distorted image of the westerner (as a do-gooder of limitless resources) which will affect the image of all tourists who come after you. It can also lead to truancy at school as families send out their children to solicit whatever seemingly innocent gift you care to bestow on them.

If you really want to help, an infinitely more appropriate and useful gift is medical supplies, although only in consultation with a local doctor or medical advisor.

On the mountains themselves, the usual trekking etiquette should be followed, particularly the disposal of rubbish. Degradable refuse can be burnt on the spot and the remains buried. The rest – particularly glass, aluminium and tins – should be kept with you for the return journey or until you find a suitable rubbish collection point.

When trekking through cultivated areas, respect the crops and plants of the villagers,

and when collecting firewood, use only dead matter. In order to avoid aggravating the persistent and serious problem of overgrazing in many of the regions, sufficient fodder for all baggage mules and donkeys should be brought with you in the form of barley from the valley. It is a good idea to inquire carefully about this before setting off.

FLORA & FAUNA

God begot living things from water,
Some of them creep, others crawl,
and there are some who crouch.
God creates what he wants.
God is almighty in all things.

(Koran. Sourate XXIV, verse 45)

The biodiversity found in Morocco is among the highest in the Mediterranean basin, the rich landscape providing a diverse habitat for vegetation, animals and birds.

The country can be divided roughly into three ecological zones: the coastal region, consisting of both the Atlantic and Mediterranean littorals; the mountainous region, encompassing the three ranges of the High, Middle and Anti-Atlas; and the desert region which includes the Moroccan steppe area.

Within these zones, over forty different ecosystems have been identified, home to some 4000 species of plants and 400 species of bird. The remarkable forests of Morocco provide perhaps the richest habitat. This ecosystem shelters two thirds of the country's plants and at least a third of its animal species, including many of the country's endemics (those found only in Morocco).

Stretching for more than 3500km from the Algerian border to the Mauritanian frontier, Morocco's vast coastal region teems with life.

The Mediterranean littoral, extending from Algeria to the Spanish enclave of Ceuta, is made up of wild and jagged rocky scree. Among the plants you might find here are various types of algae, sea holly and sea stock. Fish include tuna, swordfish and mullet, although over-fishing continues to deplete this area. Porpoises and dolphins are commonly spotted around the Straits of Gibraltar.

The Atlantic coast is made up of low sandstone cliffs with intermittent, but extensive, beaches of fine sand. Fish include sea bream, tarpon and conger eel, and dolphins are frequently spotted off the coast. The shoreline is home to abundant marine life including various types of sea urchin, mudskipper, limpet and small octopus. These, along with the shellfish marooned in the pools at low tide, attract an excellent variety of seabirds, including the Moroccan cormorant, white-eyed gull, turnstone and sandwich tern. The area is also known for the diversity of anemone and, particularly, mussel species. Just inland, and planted along the humid coastal belts, are eucalyptus and olive groves, plus some cereal crops.

Further south lying on a fertile strip of land between Agadir and Tiznit, is the inland lagoon of Oued Massa, home of the famous Souss Massa National Park generally considered the country's premier habitat for birds (see the special section on Morocco's birdlife in this chapter).

The region is a diverse one, made up of cliffs, sand dunes, farmland and forests. Fauna includes the vast reed beds which line the banks of the Oued Massa, various species of indigenous euphorbia, and tamarisk with its unmistakable pink flowers.

Among the species of mammals present are the shy Egyptian mongoose, the increasingly rare common otter and the Eurasian wild boar. The park is also home to one of the world's last remaining populations of the northern bald ibis.

Small groups of osprey are commonly seen during March and September, as are colonies of pochard and greater flamingo which spend the winter here. In the bay of Agadir, the warming influence of the Gulf Stream can be felt.

Just inland from the coast, and stretching between the towns of Kenitra, Rabat and Meknès, is the Mamora Forest. The woodland is made up principally of cork oaks, but is also home to pine, acacia and eucalyptus plantations, and the rarer Mamora wild pear. The thick undergrowth of the forests provides a rich habitat for many species of resident and migratory birds, including the white stork, colourful roller, spotted flycatcher, and black-shouldered kite. Fauna includes the asphodel, and among the mammals is the exotic African chameleon.

Of the four mountainous regions dividing the country, the Rif is the lowest, but also the wettest, with up to 1000mm of rainfall every year. It's home to the wild olive, holm oak, cedar and various species of pine. Foxes, monkeys and wild boar abound.

The Middle Atlas has been called (somewhat generously) the Switzerland of Morocco, with its villages of wooden chalets with steep-pitched roofs set amid vast forests of cedar, juniper, oak, conifer and ash. Flowers typically found include pitch trefoil and broom. Various lizards (such as the blue and green-eyed variety) are also found here.

The High Atlas boasts the most diverse habitats of the mountain chains, with rocky peaks and enormous plateaux, as well as deep gorges and steep-sided valleys accessible only on foot. The northern slopes are characterised by forests of cedar trees, holm oaks, thuyas and Aleppo pines. At higher altitudes, thuriferous juniper is found. This increasingly rare shrub also features on the southern slopes of the High Atlas, along with red cedar forests.

Flowers in the High Atlas region include thyme, convolvulus and pit trefoil. If you're very lucky, you might come across the high-altitude-loving painted frog which inhabits the riverbeds of this region. Also preferring higher habitats is the mountain gazelle, most commonly seen at altitudes above 2000m. Birdlife includes horned lark and the garrulous red-billed chough.

The higher mountain ranges are the undisputed domain of some of the most impressive raptors in Morocco, including the lammergeier vulture, the beautiful golden eagle (distinguished by its large wingspan) and the acrobatic booted eagle.

Among the mammals inhabiting the region are populations of Barbary sheep and the last and very rarely seen leopards of

Morocco. To the south, on the same latitude as the Canary Islands, are the Anti-Atlas, which protect the Souss plain from the dry wind of the desert.

The large and ancient cedar forests that characterise these ranges provide a rich habitat for a significant number of species including the famous and sociable Barbary ape which is usually easily spotted. Other mammals, but rarely sighted, include the leopard, now close to extinction; the nocturnal common genet; polecat; pine and beach martens; and the red fox. The lynx has also been sighted here.

Birds inhabiting the area include the red crossbill, fire crest, various species of wood-pecker and treecreeper, and the short-toed eagle. Of the plantlife, the Atlas species of cedar grows at altitudes of between four to 9000 feet, and in the cedar glades, orchids, geranium, campanula and scarlet dianthus are commonly found. The area is also home to Morocco's only species of peony.

Many people choose to visit Morocco in spring, when many flowers are in bloom. On the slopes of the Atlas mountains, common flowers include the Barbary nut iris and the germander. In the cedar forests, species include virburnum, campanula and, later in spring, yellow broom.

Spring (particularly from April to May) is also an excellent period for butterflies. Species common to the area include the scarlet cardinal and bright yellow Cleopatra; less frequently seen are the Spanish marbled white, hermit and Larquin's blue. Later in the summer, the cedar forests of the Middle Atlas are known for their several species of fritillary butterfly.

Other kinds of forests found in the Anti-Atlas, and in the eastern foothills of the High Atlas (as well as in the region between Agadir and Essaouira), are the smaller, less dense plantations of the indigenous argane tree. The species favours dry regions and is cultivated for its oil (extracted from the nut), which is used for cooking.

Wildlife common to this habitat includes the Barbary squirrel, which feeds on argane nuts; Moussier's redstart; and the very rare visitor, the dark chanting goshawk.

Continuing south of the Atlas into the hot, arid region of the Moroccan steppe, the landscape changes dramatically. Forests give way to plains of Alfa-grass dotted with the occasional juniper, acacia and sage bushes.

Harsh and inhospitable as the region appears, it is in fact home to a large number of animal species, including the golden jackal, desert fox, Dorcas gazelle and numerous small rodents.

Thousands of species of insects also inhabit the area, as well as the galeode spider and several species of lizard, including the mastigure and the gecko. Hunted almost to extinction in some parts of the world (including eastern Morocco), but still seen in this area, is the Houbara bustard.

Finally there is the inhospitable, desert region of the south, made up of a wide variety of habitats including the famous ergs (sand dunes), the *hammada* (vast pebbly plateau) which stretches to the Mauritanian border, and the extensive plains of tussock grass.

In the oases, lush and productive orchards and gardens are cultivated. The heat is intense during the day, but during the night in winter, it can drop below zero.

This diverse area is home to a large number of species. In the erg, animals include the Berber skink, Fennec fox (frequently illegally trapped) and the sand cat. Rodents here include the jerboa and sand rat.

In the hammada, several species of snake are found, including the horned viper, horseshoe and Montpelier snake, as well as several species of scorpion. A vast number of insects also make their home here, including various kinds of beetles.

A fairly common sight is the spiny-tailed lizard. Mammals include the striped hyena and two species of deer – the Edmi gazelle and the much rarer Addax antelope. On the plain a fairly commonly spotted predator is the Egyptian vulture. Flowers include daisies and the pink asphodels, a member of the lily family.

Apart from the date palms (which have become virtually a monoculture), the oases are home to the Mauritanian toad and the common bulbul.

Finally, while travelling in any region of Morocco, it's worth keeping a look out for the holy shrines *marabouts* dotted throughout the country and recognisable by their domed roofs and whitewashed walls.

They are often surrounded by little islands of vegetation which have been protected over the years, sometimes centuries, because of their sacred situation.

Although tiny, they are undoubtedly the real nature reserves of Morocco, often illustrating the most primitive vegetation of the country.

Cruelty to Animals

Pets are a luxury not often seen in Morocco. Animals are kept for their utilitarian benefits, as draught animals or as sources of food, and have few rights.

The exception are the cats which you will see everywhere in Morocco, commonly snoozing on the roof tops of the medinas. Generally they are left in peace and sometimes plates of food are put out for them, since this is the animal that Mohammed, the Prophet, singled out for kind treatment.

It is the donkey that gets the roughest deal. The archetypal beast of burden, you will seen it being hurried through the medina laden with vast loads of merchandise.

The Arabic word *hmar*, meaning donkey, is often used as a term of abuse, usually implying stupidity or mental slowness. Appropriately, the donkey is the logo that one of Morocco's very few animal welfare organisations has chosen to adopt.

The Societé Protectrice des Animaux et de la Nature (SPANA) was founded in 1959 by a British mother and daughter distressed by the plight of mules, donkeys and horses after a trip around North Africa. The original aim of the women was to educate the owners of the animals in the training care and general wellbeing of their charges.

Although now Moroccan-run, the organisation is still partly funded by its mother charity in Britain, the Society for the Protection of Animals Abroad.

The main objectives of the organisation include the setting up and running of animal hospitals where abandoned or mistreated animals (the large majority of which are donkeys, mules or horses) can be brought. In the souqs, mobile hospitals are set up which the merchants treat just like garages.

Other functions include providing shelter and new homes for abandoned animals; conducting surveillance and health checks on other working animals such as the carriage horses of Marrakesh; the distribution of modern, more humane harnessing equipment; and a campaign to limit the unwanted populations of cats and dogs through sterilisation and, sometimes, destruction.

SPANA has hospitals in Rabat, Marrakesh, Meknès, Tangier and Midelt among other places. If you want more information or want to visit them, you can contact them at 41 Résidence Zohra, Harhoura, Temara 12 000 (☎ 747209; fax 747493; email spana @mtds.net.ma).

continued on page 40

Not just a beast of burden: the camel is the most esteemed animal in Morocco.

Bird-watching in Morocco

Because of its relatively mild climate, rich habitat diversity and importance as a stopover for migratory birds, Morocco has much to offer the bird-watcher. Well over 300 species have been recorded and, with habitats ranging from estuaries and salt marshes to high mountains and true desert, many spectacular, unusual and colourful birds can be seen. These include huge concentrations of migrating storks, hawks and eagles in spring and autumn; colourful bee-eaters and rollers; and the majestic bustards and graceful cranes.

Morocco is a popular destination for keen bird-watchers who look for rarities such as the bald ibis, Audouin's gull, Eleanora's falcon, Levaillant's woodpecker and Moussier's redstart. A few years ago small numbers of the extremely rare slender-billed curlew were discovered wintering at Moulay Bousselham and really put Morocco on the bird-watchers' map. Sadly, there have been no recent sightings and this species is well on the way to extinction. Morocco also remains the last stronghold of another endangered bird, the bald ibis.

Where to See Birds in Morocco

The traveller will notice some birds almost everywhere, but greatest concentrations occur in reserves and at certain times of year. By taking in a variety of habitats and visiting a few reserves, a visitor can be sure of seeing a pleasing variety and number of birds. Many will be encountered close to habitation and popular tourist sights, but with just a bit of effort some of the country's specialities also may be seen.

Most national parks and reserves feature a good variety; those particularly recommended for bird-watching include **Oued Loukkos**, an area of marshes with good numbers of ducks and waders; **Merja Zerga**, a coastal lagoon holding thousands of wintering waterfowl, waders and flamingos; **Lac de Sidi Bourhaba**, an area of marsh land and open water that is good for crested coot, marbled duck and other water birds; **Dayet Aoua**, a mountain lake in the Middle Atlas where there are many water birds and, in the surrounding woods, buntings, short-toed treecreeper, firecrest and Levaillant's woodpecker.

South of **Sidi Yahya** an extensive area of cork-oak forest and scrub holds double-spurred francolin, black-headed bush-shrikes and black-shouldered kite. The plains south of **Zaida** are a good place to look for larks, especially Dupont's; other species noted have included Thekla, shore and thick-billed larks, and trumpeter finch.

The **Essaouira Islands** (including Ile de Mogador), are famed for their breeding population of Eleanora's falcon; **Tamri** is the most reliable site in Morocco to see bald ibis; and Oued Sous is an estuarine area that attracts gulls, waders and flamingos.

Title page: Egrets take wing over Lake Dayet Srji, Merzouga (photograph by Frances Linzee Gordon).

Below: The greater flamingo can be found across the whole region in the shallows of freshwater lakes, estuaries, dams and saltpans.

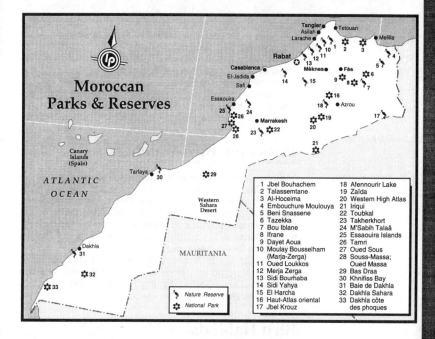

Moroccan
Parks & Reserves

1 Jbel Bouhachem	18 Afennourir Lake
2 Talassemtane	19 Zaïda
3 Al-Hoceima	20 Western High Atlas
4 Embouchure Moulouya	21 Iriqui
5 Beni Snassene	22 Toubkal
6 Tazekka	23 Takherkhort
7 Bou Iblane	24 M'Sabih Talaâ
8 Ifrane	25 Essaouira Islands
9 Dayet Aoua	26 Tamri
10 Moulay Bousselham	27 Oued Sous
(Marja-Zerga)	28 Souss-Massa;
11 Oued Loukkos	Oued Massa
12 Merja Zerga	29 Bas Draa
13 Sidi Bourhaba	30 Khnifiss Bay
14 Sidi Yahya	31 Baie de Dakhla
15 El Harcha	32 Dakhla Sahara
16 Haut-Atlas oriental	33 Dakhla côte
17 Jbel Krouz	des phoques

Nature Reserve

National Park

Some Tips for Watching Birds

A pair of binoculars will be a great aid to observation and will considerably aid identification. Subtleties of plumage and form will be far more apparent through a pair of field glasses. If you get serious about birding you may want to invest in better quality optics. Although expensive, brands such as Leica and Zeiss will last a lifetime and offer unrivalled quality. Both brands come in handy, pocket-sized models. To get the most out of bird-watching, bear the following in mind:

- Try to get an early start because most birds are generally active during the cooler hours of the day.
- Do not disturb birds unnecessarily and never handle eggs or young birds in a nest. Adults will readily desert a nest that has been visited, leaving their young to perish.
- You may be offered the services of a guide at good birding sights. While a guide can often help you find rare or shy birds, some have been known to throw rocks to flush roosting birds. This should be strongly discouraged as birds are easily stressed and will not return to areas that have been persistently disturbed.

- Approach birds slowly and avoid sudden movements or loud talk. Try to dress in drab clothing so as not to stand out. Many species are quite approachable and will allow opportunities for observation and photography. Birds are not usually too concerned about people in a vehicle and stunning views can often be obtained from the roadside.
- Be careful not to alarm guards when birding near Royal residences or government buildings. If you are moved on be courteous. Always ask permission before birding on private property.

Books for Bird-watchers

The popularity of bird-watching has inspired a number of excellent illustrated titles to suit all budgets and levels of interest. *Birds of the Middle East and North Africa*, by Hollom, Porter, Christensen & Willis, is the definitive guide to the region. *Birds of Europe with North Africa and the Middle East*, by Lars Jonsson, is superbly illustrated and covers all species likely to be found in Morocco.

Useful guides to finding birds include *A Bird-watchers' Guide to Morocco* by Patrick and Fedora Bergier, and two booklets by David Gosney, *Finding Birds in Northern Morocco* and *Finding Birds in Southern Morocco*.

Bird Habitats

Many birds are wide-ranging, but most have feeding, breeding or other biological requirements which restrict them to a habitat, or group of habitats. A brief rundown of Moroccan bird habitats follows.

Ocean & Seashore The narrow strip where land meets sea is one of the most dynamic habitats on earth; its inhabitants must be adapted to being inundated twice daily and battered by the elements in between. Many of the creatures found here, such as crustaceans and shellfish, make tasty morsels for humans and birds alike. Some birds adapted to these habitats include waders such as oystercatchers and plovers, and cliff-nesting seabirds such as gulls, gannets and cormorants.

Estuaries occur where rivers meet the sea and many are now important conservation reserves. At low tides the mud floor is exposed and makes a rich feeding ground for migratory waders like sandpipers, stints, curlew, godwits and plovers.

The coasts attract a rich variety of seabirds, including graceful petrels and shearwaters, which live a great part of their lives on the open sea. Look out for marauding skuas that harass seabirds and force them to drop their catch.

Forest Forests and woodlands now cover only a small proportion of Morocco's total land area, and in many parts have been replaced by a mosaic of pastoral and agricultural lands.

Nonetheless, orchards, plantations and gardens can support a surprising number of small birds, such as warblers and pipits. Surviving lowland forests include mixed cork/oak woodlands, which feature warblers, woodpeckers, birds of prey and the beautiful hoopoe.

Grassland Depending on whether it is on a plain or a mountain top, grassland can be short or tall, dense or sparse. Large areas the world over have been modified by grazing and agriculture, but seed-eating birds in particular have adapted well to agriculture and even modified grasslands can contain an interesting range of species. Grassland specialists include various species of larks, pipits and finches; spectacular 'game' birds such as bustards; and birds of prey such as harriers.

Desert Much of Morocco is desert or subdesert – a stark and dramatic landscape shaped by low rainfall. Largely consisting largely of rocky plains and outcrops, sand dunes and sparsely vegetated steppe. The number and variety of life forms are diminished in this harsh environment, but this habitat supports a few interesting birds, such as finches which may be seen feeding around the droppings of tethered camels. Oases are a haven for wildlife of all types and bird-watching can be a treat around wadis, gardens and plantations. Migrating flocks of birds can literally drop out of the sky into an oasis for a few hours' rest and feeding.

Waterways Lakes, swamps, marshes and rivers, can support an astonishing variety of birds. During hot months, waterholes and even large rivers can dry up, so many waterbirds are migratory or nomadic, and leave an area when its resources vanish to seek more productive habitat.

Different groups of birds utilise waterways in different ways: some hunt along the shoreline or probe the mud at the water's edge; others stride on long legs into deeper water to seek prey. The kingfisher perches on overhanging vegetation and dives into the water, and warblers, finches and rails skulk in dense vegetation.

Cities & Towns Since these will be the first stop for nearly all visitors, it's worth mentioning a few birds that will be seen around human settlement. Perhaps most visible are the storks, which are famous for nesting on rooftops and chimney stacks. Swifts, swallows and martins nest under the eaves of buildings, and sparrows, starlings and pigeons are familiar denizens of human settlements the world over.

Huge numbers of white storks pass through Morocco on migration. Many also remain to nest, and their huge untidy nests are a common sight on roofs and other structures.

The Birds

The following is a group-by-group description of some of the birds a visitor could see while in Morocco. Bear in mind that weather and wind can adversely affect viewing conditions and you shouldn't expect to see everything at first attempt. This is not a comprehensive list; we have paid attention to common, unusual or spectacular species and readers should refer to one of the guides mentioned earlier for full information.

Flamingos The greater flamingo is a large, graceful – if bizarre – bird that often concentrates in large flocks at coastal reserves. These flocks are one of the highlights of Morocco, a mass of pink birds sifting through the water for food makes a startling contrast against the stark landscape. Flamingos are best seen at reserves such as Merja Zerga and Oued Sous.

Bustards Stately, long-legged birds of the grasslands, bustards are among the heaviest of flying birds. Of the three species found in Morocco, the great bustard is the largest, while the little bustard stands only 40cm high and can seem to disappear into long grass. The best time to look for bustards is in winter, when great bustards concentrate in fields near Asilah and little bustards can be seen near Oued Loukkos.

Cranes These graceful, long-legged birds superficially resembles the storks and herons, but are typically grassland-dwelling birds. Large flocks of cranes gather near Asilah in winter, where they associate with flocks of bustards.

Swifts & Swallows Although unrelated, these two groups are superficially similar and are commonly seen flying after insects. Both groups have long wings and streamlined bodies adapted to lives in the air; both fly with grace and agility; and both are usually dark in coloration. However, swallows differ in one major respect: they can perch on twigs, fences or even the ground while swifts have weak legs and rarely land except at the nest. In fact, swifts are so adapted to life in the air that some are even known to roost (sleep) on the wing.

Seabirds Into this broad category can be lumped a number of bird families which hunt over the open sea or which are generally coastal species that feed at sea. The former category includes various petrels and shearwaters; among the latter are the beautiful gannet, which feeds by plunging from a great height, and the fish-eating cormorants (shags), which also make use of brackish and freshwater habitats. The Moroccan race of the great cormorant differs from its all-black relatives of Europe in having a white throat and breast.

The great cormorant is a fish-eating bird found along coasts and large waterways. The sub-species found in Morocco has a white face and throat.

Waterfowl This large group includes the familiar ducks and geese. As their name suggests they are found almost exclusively around waterways, though most are equally at home in fresh and salt water habitats. A dozen or so species are commonly seen in Morocco's coastal lagoons, where they may concentrate in tens of thousands during winter. Most of the species, such as mallard, widgeon, garganey and shelduck, are common European visitors. Several sites, such as Lac de Sidi Bourhaba, are particularly good for the rare marbled duck.

Birds of Prey Under this broad heading fall the hawks, eagles, vultures and falcons. Together they number nearly 30 species in Morocco and some outstanding examples are readily found. All birds of prey have sharply hooked bills and talons for tearing flesh. Some have specialised prey or habitat requirements: the osprey is seen around waterways and feeds almost exclusively on fish; harriers hunt by gliding low over fields and dropping onto prey; and kites and vultures are well known for their scavenging habits.

Examples that are sought by keen bird-watchers include Barbary, Eleanora's and Lanner falcons, lamergeier and dark chanting goshawk. The largest of the Old World vultures, the lamergeier or bearded vulture, has a wingspan of nearly 3m; look for in the Dadès Gorge and High Atlas mountains.

The migration spectacle is the best time to see birds of prey. Flocks numbering tens of thousands assemble at points close to Europe (such as the Tangiers peninsula) awaiting suitable conditions to make the crossing.

Spring and autumn migrations feature huge numbers of birds of prey and other species as they cross the Straits of Gibraltar to and from Morocco.

Sandgrouse Swift-flying birds adapted to life on the semiarid steppes and grasslands, the five species of sandgrouse in Morocco are all nomadic and feed on seeds. Sandgrouse can carry water in their breast feathers and can often be seen flying in from miles around to waterholes in the evening.

Crows & Ravens Members of this family should be familiar to all. The common black and white magpie of Europe and North America is represented in Morocco by a race peculiar to north-western Africa which has a patch of naked blue skin behind the eye. In mountainous areas look for the two species of choughs – alpine and common – which are recognisable by their slender, down-curved bills.

Long-legged Wading Birds Many waterways will have a complement of herons, egrets, storks, spoonbills, and/or ibis, though the variety and number never reach the peaks they do in sub-Saharan Africa.

All have long legs and necks, and bills adapted to specific feeding strategies – herons and egrets have dagger-like bills for spearing fish and frogs; spoonbills have peculiar, flattened bills which they swish from side to side and gather small water creatures; and storks have large powerful beaks to snap up small animals and fish.

Two species of storks, white and black, are readily seen by visitors and are a familiar part of the countryside. Storks are migratory and are far more common in spring and summer, when they arrive in vast numbers from south of the Sahara.

The endangered bald ibis was once widespread through Europe, but today is restricted to parts of Morocco and Turkey. Its population seems to be in decline and as few as 200 pairs are thought to remain. The lagoons and cliffs near Tamri are probably the most reliable spots to look for this species.

The bald ibis was once found across Europe, where it was also known as the waldrapp. Its numbers are now dwindling and it is under threat of extinction.

Kingfisher, Bee-eaters, Rollers & Hoopoe The brightly coloured kingfisher is a living jewel that feeds on small fish and other aquatic animals. Two species of bee-eaters – European and blue-cheeked – sally forth from perches in serach of flying insects, particularly (as their name suggests) bees and wasps. The roller is another colourful member of this family, and the bizarre, crested hoopoe is distinct in salmon-pink plumage boldly marked in black and white.

Waders, Gulls & Terns Every year hundreds of thousands of shorebirds pass via Morocco on their way to sub-Saharan Africa, after flying for thousands of kilometres from their breeding grounds in Scandinavia, Greenland and northern Russia. 'Waders' moult from striking summer plumage to rather nondescript winter plumage. Many keen birders relish the challenge of identifying these drab winter plumages.

With few exceptions waders are found near fresh and saline waterways, feeding along the shores or probing intertidal mud for worms. They include the long-distance champions, the sandpipers and plovers, the lapwing and the odd stone curlew – a lanky, cryptic, nocturnal species with weird wailing cries.

The gulls and terns are close relatives of the waders, although they look very different. Many species inhabit the coasts and breed on offshore islands or isolated sandbanks. Audouin's gull is a handsome species that can be seen fairly regularly at Lac de Sidi Bourhaba and Tamri.

The hoopoe, which rejoices under the latin name of Upupa epops, *is related to the kingfisher. It is an uncommon migrant to Morocco and best looked for in spring.*

Owls These nocturnal birds of prey have soft feathers for silent flight, exceptional hearing and can turn their heads in a 180 degree arc to locate prey. The marsh owl roosts in reed beds and dense vegetation during the day and feeds over marshlands at night. Marsh owls are often seen at dusk near the campsite at Merja Zerga.

Woodpeckers Levaillant's woodpeacker is eagerly sought by visiting bird-watchers because it is found only in the mountains of Morocco and Algeria.The wryneck, a superbly camouflaged member of this family, is so named because it can turn its head in an astonioshing arc.

Larks & Pipits Not the most spectacular group of birds, the larks and pipits nonetheless reach a great diversity of species in Morocco and biologically are significant to the grasslands they inhabit. Their identification can pose some challenges, but a few species readily seen in Morocco are unusual and relatively spectacular. Among these are the hoopoe lark, which bears some resemblance to the hoopoe (although it is unrelated), the shore lark and the thick-billed lark.

David Andrew

GOVERNMENT

The kingdom of Morocco is ruled by King Hassan II who came to the throne in 1961. During his reign, the country's constitution has been considerably modernised with the establishment of a Chamber of Representatives (*majlis an-nuwab*) and Morocco has moved closer to becoming a parliamentary democracy – in a superficial sense at least. In practice, the chamber's power is still severely limited and remains little more than a forum for debate. Morocco remains essentially an absolute monarchy.

Hassan II is the latest in a long dynastic line, the Alawites, who have been at the helm, at least in name, since the 17th century. Hassan claims a double role as temporal leader (king) and spiritual and moral guide (*amir al-mu'mineen*, or Commander of the Faithful), from his family's claim of descent from the Prophet Mohammed, through his grandson Al-Hassan bin Ali. As such, these monarchs have been considered sherifs of Morocco, much in the way that Mecca was traditionally ruled by a sherif.

The religious significance of Hassan II's claim to legitimacy should not be underestimated, and goes part of the way to explaining how he has managed to stay in power for so long, when other traditional rulers in the Arab and wider Muslim world have tended to be toppled. The heir apparent is Hassan's eldest son, Crown Prince Sidi Mohammed.

Constitution

Hassan II is playing a delicate game. On the one hand he is trying to present an image of slow, but definite, democratisation to the west – particularly to his European neighbours, with whom he wants closer economic links. On the other, he wishes to maintain his power over the political life of the country. Reforms that he has carried out include the introduction of an elected chamber and a system of multi-party politics.

Under a constitution established in 1972, multi-political parties, trade unions and professional bodies were to take an active part in the country's administration. However, the king reserved for himself the right to name his prime minister and ministers, control of the armed forces, the right to dissolve the Chamber of Representatives and a raft of other powers.

Moreover, despite increasing electoral gains by the opposition parties since this amendment, parliament continues to be dominated by loyalist, centre-right parties; this is because of the way the chamber is organised. In September 1992, the king, keen to sustain his reputation for reform, declared that the constitution should be altered again in order to form a 'gouvernement d'alternance'.

Although this would mean handing over some power to the opposition parties, the major ministries of Finance, Foreign and Internal Affairs would remain firmly in the hands of the loyalists. Similarly, the king would renounce his right to appoint ministers, but not the right to appoint the prime minister. In this way, the government would be more representative of public opinion superficially, but in reality all policy-making would remain the preserve of the monarch.

The opposition turned the offer down since it failed to rectify the gross imbalance of power. In a large demonstration, it used the 50th anniversary of the Istiqlal Party's demand for independence in 1944, to call for greater democracy in modern Morocco.

Frustrated by unsuccessful attempts to entice the opposition parties into government, King Hassan abandoned his proposals and, in February 1995, a centre-right alliance of five pro-monarchy parties was put into power.

In September 1996, a ground-breaking plan was finally announced for the formation of a bicameral legislature. Deputies to the lower chamber would be elected directly; deputies to the upper chamber indirectly from local and regional government, professional bodies and trade unions.

Local elections took place in June 1997 and the Koutla (the alliance of opposition parties including the Istiqlal and USFP parties) nearly doubled their number of seats. However, they did not manage to gain the sweeping majority that was predicted, largely due to an inability to agree on a single candidate.

A better performance is expected in the legislative elections scheduled for the end of September 1997. With the enticement of some of the numerous smaller parties to their side, the opposition alliance is tipped to form the majority. However, these gains will be counterbalanced by the right-dominated and indirectly elected upper house which have dominated Moroccan politics for the last 30 years.

The creation of a bicameral legislature is part of King Hassan II's attempts to improve Morocco's democratic credentials, while still retaining considerable power.

Nevertheless, the wind of change seems to be blowing at long last through Moroccan politics. In February 1997, all the main political parties signed a joint declaration pledging cooperation on reform of the political process. With eyes on Europe and the changes occurring there, particularly the election of the British Labour government 18 years in opposition, the mood is a positive one and from October 1997, a new parliament, government and prime minister is eagerly awaited.

Political Parties

The opposition parties forming the Bloc Démocratique are a ragbag of groups, including Parti Istiqlal, the Union Socialiste des Forces Populaires, the former Communist Parti du Progrès du Socialisme and the smaller Organisation de l'Action Démocratique et Populaire.

Ranged against them are the five main pro-monarchy parties appointed in February 1995.

The Mouvement Populaire, the biggest of them, attracts most of its support from the rural Berber population. The others are: the liberal Union Constitutionelle, the Rassemblement National des Indépendants, the Mouvement Nationale Populaire and the Parti National Démocratique.

The king appoints the prime minister who then selects a Council of Ministers which must be approved by the king. The current prime minister is Abdellatif Filali.

Tiers of Government

For administrative purposes, the country is divided into 39 provinces (wilayat), four of them making up the territory of the Western Sahara. The provinces are subdivided into eight préfectures (Casablanca is made up of five), which are further subdivided into qaidates, under the direction of qaids.

Qaids (or caids) are appointed by the Ministry of the Interior and have similar powers to those of pashas, who are responsible for administering urban municipalities. Other local government officials go by the name of moqadams.

Outlook

In spite of several assassination attempts during the uncertain years of the 1970s, the king's position as head of the government seems secure. Although Morocco is disturbed by the troubles plaguing Algeria next door, few believe the country will experience the same difficulties.

However, because of the widespread frustration among opposition parties anxious to win representation in government, a number of illegal opposition parties has sprung up – especially among the so-called Islamic dissidents. There have also been increasingly violent confrontations between Islamist students and the police.

The government remains very nervous of these groups and has adopted an ambivalent policy towards them. While maintaining a steady and strict surveillance of all dissident political activity, it has dealt harshly with the university-based groups, but has allowed limited expression to the more established and respected radical elements.

In January 1997, Abdelillah Benkirane's Al-Islah wal-Tajdid (Unification and Reform) party was given formal recognition when it merged with the Mouvement Populaire Démocratique et Constitutionel. In 1995, the death sentence on Mohammed Basri, the leader of the USFP, was overturned and he was allowed to return from a

30 year exile. Several radical Islamists remain in jail, however, and Abdessalam Yassine, the leader of Al-Adl wal-Ihsan (Justice & Charity), the most important of such groups in Morocco, has been under house arrest in Salé since 1989. His party will not be allowed to participate in the forthcoming elections; other more moderate Islamic groups will be allowed only token representation.

Amnesty International claims that, despite several releases of prisoners in recent years, more than 600 people remain incarcerated because of their political activities. Dissident Moroccans outside the country hope economic difficulties and Hassan's desire for greater integration into the western economies will lead him to make concessions along the path to a more open government.

The Morocco of today has often been compared to Franco's Spain of the 1950s and 60s. According to some, if Hassan II has a full innings, he might even be succeeded by a full parliamentary democracy.

ECONOMY

After years of mishaps and harsh austerity measures, there are signs that Morocco has turned a difficult corner. A sophisticated privatisation scheme is bearing fruit, grossing US$820 million at the end of 1995, and Morocco has returned to international finance markets after 10 years of tough slimming measures imposed by the International Monetary Fund (IMF).

Along the way, maximum tariffs have come down from 400% to 35%, the dirham has moved close to full convertibility (although this has now been delayed to 1998 at the earliest because of the effects of the exceptional drought of 1995).

Morocco has also become a member of the General Agreement on Tariffs & Trade (GATT) – in fact Marrakesh was chosen as the site for signing the final accord ending the long-contested Uruguay Round in April 1994.

Inflation has been brought down to just 3% in 1996 from highs above 12% in the mid-1980s. Unemployment has fallen officially from 23% (of the working population) in 1996 to 18.7%. According to some forecasts, however, the figure could rise to 25% by 2005 unless reforms are dramatically accelerated. Official estimates say the number of people living below the poverty line has dropped by a third to 12% of the populace since 1985. In that same period, it is claimed that per capita income has nearly doubled to US$1200 per annum.

Analysts expect the IMF-recommended policies to continue to be pursued into the beginning of the next century, although the pace of adjustment has certainly slowed.

The softened approach, although defusing social tensions in the short term, runs the risk of slowing economic growth overall and handicapping the transition from an economy dependent on (unpredictable) rain-fed agriculture to an emerging industrial nation ready for free trade with Europe.

This growth rate (6% to 7%) will also be required if jobs are to be created for the country's underemployed young.

In 1994, the government, anxious about the frustration of this group, set up a special US$100,000 fund to promote job creation. Overall, the economy is expected to grow further over 1997 and 1998, particularly with the continuing economic expansion in Europe.

Among the hopeful signals, however, are plenty of worrying indicators of an uneven economy. Foreign debt, at US$21.9 billion, remains a heavy burden, although Saudi Arabia's decision to forgive US$3 billion in loans in the wake of the Gulf War has eased the load. Morocco is still borrowing heavily. The World Bank says Morocco is the biggest recipient of its aid throughout North Africa and the Middle East.

Government figures put the number of poor by World Bank definitions at around four million, but the opposition claims the real figures are worse and that the gap between wealthy and poor is widening. The average farm or factory worker's wage, for instance, does not rise above Dr1000 a month and is often less.

European Connection

King Hassan II pins great hopes upon anchoring Morocco as firmly as possible to the EU's orbit. Conversely, Morocco is seen by Europe as a useful ally among Arab states and a bulwark against the diffusion of Islamic fundamentalism. To this end, the free trade zone agreement was signed between the EU and the kingdom in 1996, which should consolidate ties on both sides on a long-term basis.

In 1995, during a presidential visit to Morocco of the French President, Jacques Chirac, Hassan II again stated Morocco's ambition to join the EU, which it first applied to do (unsuccessfully) in 1987. Many Mediterranean EU members still fear a flood of cheap agricultural produce that would provide unwelcome competition. As it is, the trade balance between the EU and Morocco only moderately favours Europe. However, there are some quid pro quos to be made, and the EU is well aware of it.

The government has moved to halt illegal immigration to Europe and tackle the flourishing smuggling business in all sorts of consumer items via the Spanish enclaves in the north of the country. In return, western countries have promised US\$1 billion to help persuade farmers in the Rif mountains to grow crops other than kif. The ill-reputed hashish trade is estimated to be worth US\$2 billion (Morocco is said to supply at least 30% of Europe's dope).

European police chiefs fear Morocco could become a major route for South American hard drugs into Europe. The stakes are high and the drugs issue gives Rabat some leverage when bargaining with the EU.

A new link between Europe and the Maghreb was created in November 1996, when the 1,430km gas pipeline came on stream, carrying Algerian gas to Spain via Morocco. Relations with Spain, one of Morocco's most important trading partners, remain mercurial despite this and the friendship treaty signed between Rabat and Madrid in June 1991.

In 1995-6, there were continuing quarrels over Spanish fishing rights in Morocco, Moroccan immigration in Spain and the enclaves of Melilla and Ceuta. Despite this, there are still plans afoot to build a fixed link between Morocco and the Straits of Gibraltar.

Such strong ties to Europe also have a downside. Morocco still exports too much to too few countries (France takes 30% of the total), making it vulnerable to recession in Europe.

Resources

Agriculture still employs about 40% of the population and although Morocco doesn't produce enough grain and cereal to meet its own needs, food exports (mainly fruits and vegetables) make up about 30% of the total exports. Occasional drought, such as in 1995, makes it impossible to predict what contribution the farm sector will make to the economy in any one year.

Marble for Sugar

In the 16th century, a thriving sugar industry existed in Morocco. Located to the south of the High Atlas, the plantations were watered by a complex and sophisticated system of irrigation. Owned by the state, managed by entrepreneurial Europeans and worked by slaves, the 14 or so factories produced large amounts of sugar that were exported all over the world.

The highest quality sugar was reserved for European countries, particularly Italy and France. Britain was considered to be the greatest connoisseur. So valued was the product, and so in demand, that the Saadian sultans, with a taste for luxury and keen to embellish their palaces, would exchange it gram for gram for the best Carraran marble from Italy.

The decline of the factories eventually came with competition from the Americas, though many may have been damaged by rival dynasties trying to undermine the economy. According to historian El-Oufrani, some may have been destroyed by locals protesting against slavery. ■

At the top of its mineral assets are phosphates, of which Morocco is said to have between two-thirds and three-quarters (if you include those in the Western Sahara) of the planet's reserves. It is the world's third biggest exporter of phosphates after the USA and the CIS.

World prices have recovered from their depression in 1991-3 and are set to continue to rise in 1998 and 1999, and now form a major foreign exchange earner. Phosphate mining is controlled by the Office Cherifien des Phosphates, a state monopoly.

Other mineral exports include fluorite, barytes, manganese, iron ore, lead, zinc, cobalt, copper and antimony, but with phosphates accounting for 90% of mineral exports, these are relatively insignificant.

Although Morocco's search for oil has turned up nothing, there are two refineries for processing imported oil at Mohammedia and Sidi Kacem.

Remittances from the 1.7 million Moroccans living abroad (most of whom live in Europe and half in France) are the biggest source of foreign income. In 1992, they brought in Dr19 million.

Tourism, hard hit by the effects of the Gulf War in 1990-1, picked up in 1992, then recovered strongly again in 1996 after a three year recession. It remains the second largest hard-currency earner.

Visitors to Morocco in 1996 numbered 1.65 million (up 8% from 1995), a little over a third of them Europeans, and a large and growing proportion of them French. Likewise, the number of German tourists has increased, the number of Spaniards has levelled, but the number of visitors from Italy and the UK have fallen.

Tourism is thought to provide jobs, both formal and 'informal', for half the working population of cities like Marrakesh. The informal (ie black) 'sector' of the economy is reckoned conservatively to make up 30% of GDP.

POPULATION

The population of Morocco was estimated in 1996 at 27.5 million. About half this total is under 20 years of age and, with a growth rate of 2.2%, the population threatens to become a destabilising factor in a country where a great rift separates the well-off minority and the growing legions of unemployed youth.

As the rural flight to the cities continues, the urban population continues to expand; more than two-thirds of the populace is estimated to live in the cities. By far the most populous city is the Atlantic port and commercial centre of Casablanca, with 3.07 million people. The capital, Rabat, numbers 1.23 million people if Salé is included. Fès is pushing close to three quarters of a million and Marrakesh has over half a million, and Meknès, Oujda and Agadir are not far behind.

PEOPLE
Arabs, Berbers & Moors

The bulk of the population is made up of Berbers or Arabs, although the distinction is not always easily made. The numbers of ethnic Arabs who came to Morocco with the first Islamic invasion of the 7th century, or 400 years later with the Beni Hillal, were comparatively small. Bigger contributions came from Spain as the Catholics evicted the Muslims in the course of the Reconquista. They have to a large degree mixed with Berbers, who in turn have in great measure been Arabised.

When it is said that most of the inhabitants of the northern coastal areas and big cities are Arabic, what is usually meant is Arabic-speaking. Probably less than a quarter of the population is now monolingual in Berber and bilingualism has increased thanks to modern communications and transport.

Little is known of the racial origins of the Berbers. The word 'Berber' comes from an Arabic word possibly borrowed from the Latin (and ultimately ancient Greek) *barbari*, signifying the non-Latin speaking peoples of the Maghreb. The antiquated name for this area of North Africa, Barbary, has the same origins.

The Berbers inhabit the mountain regions

and parts of the desert, and are generally divided into three rough groups identified by dialect. Those speaking Riffian are, not surprisingly, found mainly in the Rif. The dominant group in the Middle Atlas speaks Amazigh (also known as Tamazight or Braber), while in the High Atlas the predominant dialect is known as Chleuh. In truth, the tribal structure is much more fractured.

Europeans have long used the term 'Moors' as a generic description for the whole populace of the Maghreb and even for the whole Muslim world. The name probably more justly refers to a group of people living in the south of Morocco, but who also spread out across Mauritania, Algeria and Mali. 'Moor' was probably derived from the Greek word 'Mauros', which was used to describe these people. Only a small proportion of them, also known as the 'blue people' because of the colour of their attire and the fact that the dye lends a bluish hue to their skin, live on Moroccan soil.

FRANCES LINZEE GORDON

Enjoying a national pastime – people-watching at the old town fountain, Marrakesh.

For simplicity's sake they can be roughly lumped together with the Tuaregs of southern Algeria. In spite of tourist hype, few if any actual Tuaregs live in Morocco. The population of Europeans living in Morocco numbers around 60,000, down from around half a million at independence. Most expats are French, Spanish and Italian. Conversely, there are an estimated 1.7 million Moroccans living abroad, mostly in Europe and particularly France and Spain.

Jews

Morocco once hosted a large population of Jews, roughly divided into those of obscure Berber origin and Arabic speakers who found themselves compelled to leave Andalusian Spain in the face of the Reconquista. By the end of the 1960s this number had dropped significantly, as most Jews opted to migrate to the state of Israel after 1948. The ancient *mellah*, or Jewish quarter, of many Moroccan towns can still often be identified. Nevertheless, there is still a sizeable Jewish population of around 30,000 in Morocco.

Other Ethnic Groups

Growing commercial links with the interior of Africa over the centuries has attracted a population of black Africans from various parts of sub-Saharan Africa into the south of Morocco, particularly into the southern oases and desert settlements. Many originally came as slaves.

Morocco once played host to half a million foreigners, but since the end of the French protectorate in 1956, the number has dropped considerably. Among those who have been absorbed into the general populace are Iberians who came to Morocco when the Muslims were forced out of Spain. They were joined in later times by Spanish traders and workers, many of whom have also assimilated into the Moroccan populace.

EDUCATION

Morocco spends a lot on educating its young – as much as 27% of the state budget according to some claims – but still has a long way to go. In spite of enrolments of nearly four million children in schools and some 230,000 students in the country's 11 universities, UNESCO estimates that around half the adult male population is still illiterate.

The figure among women is higher still – possibly as much as 70%. In January 1997, the World Bank addressed a memorandum to the Moroccan government in which it highlighted education as an area in need of urgent reform, not just for social reasons, but also for economic growth and competitiveness. The need for basic education of women and girls in rural areas was picked out for special attention.

The gulf between the urban and rural populations is also highlighted by literacy figures. As few as 23% of people living in the country can read, as opposed to 64% in the cities.

National service, which applies to males, lasts up to 18 months.

ARTS
Music
Invasion and cultural cross-fertilisation have bequeathed several musical traditions to Morocco. If you are seriously interested in buying recordings of various types of Moroccan music, try Le Comptoir Marocain de Distribution de Disques (☎ 269538) at 26 Ave Lalla Yacout, in Casablanca. It has a wide range of material on LP, cassette and CD. Popular cassettes can be had for a dollar or two at music stands throughout the country.

Arab-Andalusian Music In addition to the more 'standard' musical patrimony from Arab lands further to the east, Morocco knows another classical tradition that developed in Muslim Spain under the guidance of a man called Ziryeb, a musician who settled in Granada in the 9th century.

He developed a suite system known as the *nawba*, which played on alternate use of rhythm and non-rhythm, and vocals and instrumental. In all, there are 24 *nawbat*; they are tightly structured and correspond to the 24 harmonic modes of Andalusian music. Each is purportedly in tune with an hour of the day.

Another musical system that emerged under the guidance of the same man aligned music with the Ptolemaic system of viewing medicine and human health as determined by humours, the four chief fluids of the body (blood, phlegm, choler, melancholy).

As the Muslims were forced out of Spain by the end of the 15th century, the music moved and took root in Morocco. The palaces of Rabat and Oujda, among others, became havens for the preservation of the Andalusian tradition.

Of modern exponents of the art, Sheikh Salah was one of the best, and it is possible to pick up cassettes of his orchestra with little difficulty in Morocco, and even the odd CD in Europe.

Berber Music Long before the Arabs even knew of the existence of Morocco, the Berber tribes had been developing their own music and it was later enhanced by the arrival of various Arab instruments and styles.

Music is not just entertainment – it is also the medium for storytelling and the passing on of oral culture from generation to generation. It can still be heard at *moussems* (pilgrimages), wedding ceremonies, public town or tribal gatherings and festivals, as well as at private celebrations.

The music of any tribe is often a reflection of the musicality of the local dialect too. Instrumental pieces can be heard, but often the music is accompanied by songs and dancing. The latter can involve men *and* women, something that occasionally raises the hackles of some city (generally orthodox Arab) Muslims.

Storytelling is a big part of the musical repertoire of the Berbers. The *heddaoua* (wandering minstrels) move from one small town to another and recite poetry and the like, often in a hazy allusive style usually attributable to the effects of kif. They usually provide musical accompaniment, but dance is not necessarily part of the performance.

Musical Instruments

Some of the instruments you may come across include the following:

amzhad: a single-chord violin, made of wood and a goatskin cover, and played with a horse-hair bow; it is a specifically Berber instrument

andir: a long, narrow trumpet, most often used for celebrations during Ramadan

bendir: other Berber names for this single-headed oriental drum are *tagnza* and *allun*

darbuka: a generic term for a form of drum typical throughout the Arab world; it is usually made of terracotta in the form of a jug, with a goatskin cover on one side

ghaita: a reed oboe, in wide use throughout Morocco

guedra: another kind of drum most commonly used by the so-called 'blue people' to accompany a dance performed solely by women; the dance is one you're less and less likely to see, except perhaps in a hotel's watered-down floor show version

guimbri: a long lute with two or three strings

kanza: very loosely like a guitar, a three stringed instrument with a rectangular base

kemenja: a typical Arab instrument, not un-like the western viola

nira or **lira**: a generic Arabic term for various types of reed flute

qarqba (plural **qaraqib**): large, metal castanets

tbel or **tabala**: a cylindrical wooden drum hung around the neck, or held under the arm

tebilat: two different sized and shaped drums fastened together with leather lacing and covered in skin

zmar: an odd-looking double clarinet ■

PHOTO YOUNIS

Berber women musicians celebrating the feast of Moulay Idriss – singing, and playing the *darbuka* (left), the *tebilat* (middle) and the *bendir* (right).

Contemporary Music Various Moroccan musicians have experimented with moves to combine aspects of their heritage and western influences. Hassan Erraji, a blind *oud* (Arab lute) player who moved to Belgium and studied European as well as Arab classical music, has put out several CDs, including ones entitled *Marhaba*, *La Dounia* and *Nikriz*. Although the Arab roots of his music prevail, he introduces other elements into some of his pieces that are well removed from the Oriental tradition, such as saxophone.

Aisha Kandisha goes several steps further, taking traditional sound and infusing what might seem to some an overwhelming stratum of modern western music, hence perhaps the title of one CD, *Jarring Effects*.

Raï Although identified more with Algeria, *raï* ('opinion') is fast gaining popularity in Morocco and the voices of its leading exponents, such as Cheb Khaled, can be heard in music stores as far east as Egypt and Jordan.

In spite of its distinctly Arabo-African rhythms, which are derivative of Bedouin music, it is probably the most thoroughly westernised music, using a variety of modern electrical instruments to create an often hypnotic effect.

Morocco itself has given rise to several less well known raï performers.

Dance

Talk of dance in the Orient and the first thing to pop into most western minds is the belly dance, something you can see (for a price) at plenty of the more expensive tourist hotels (and occasionally in quite sleazy 'nightclubs' in the bigger cities, especially Casablanca), although it is not essentially a Moroccan art.

You may also get a chance to see so-called folk dancing, which is usually a poor hotel imitation of the real thing out in the Berber backblocks.

Some of the kinds of dance you may be lucky enough to encounter outside the hotels include the following:

ahidous
This is a complex circle dance seen in the Middle Atlas. Usually associated with harvest rites, it is an occasion for the whole community to join in. Alternating circles of men and women dance and sing antiphonally around musicians, usually playing bendirs only, but sometimes other instruments.

ahouach
This is linked to the ahidous of the Atlas Mountains, but is performed in the kasbahs of the south. The dancing is done by women alone, again in a circle around musicians.

guedra
The term takes its name from a kind of drum commonly used to accompany a dance performed solely by women.

gnaoua
This term refers mainly to blacks (often descendants of slaves brought to Morocco from central and west Africa) who perform as musicians and acrobats in southern Morocco. They were once a not uncommon sight in the Djemaa el-Fna in Marrakesh, but have now become a rarity.

PHOTO YOUNIS
Raw percussion in a street parade.

Art & Architecture

Prehistoric Art Most evidence for prehistoric art exists in the form of multiple (and still largely unstudied) Neolithic rock engravings. The best sites are found in southern Morocco, notably in the area between the Anti-Atlas and The Drâa Valley.

Difficult to date accurately, the majority seem to come from a period between 4000 and 2000 BC, and resemble similar finds south of Oran in Algeria. Geometric or symbolic signs are the most commonly-occurring motif and are difficult to interpret. People and animals feature in later engravings which has allowed the classification of three stylistic periods: the hunters, the animal carriers and the daggers of the Atlas.

This rock carving, dating from 3-5000BC, was found in Central Morocco.

Classical Period Situated at one of the furthest boundaries of the Roman empire, Morocco is not as rich in classical remains as more centrally placed countries such as Algeria or Tunisia. It still boasts, however, some important sites spread mainly around the north-east of the country. Volubilis (the most impressive), Banusa and Thamusida were excavated by the French in the first half of the 19th century, and Cotta and Lixus by the Spanish in the second half.

Islamic Period In the 11th century, the Almoravid dynasty, whose empire included Andalusia, introduced the hispano-Moorish style into Morocco. The beautiful prayer hall of the Kairaouine Mosque in Fès owes a great deal to the art of the caliphs of Cordoba in Spain.

With the succession of the Almohads in the second half of the 12th century, the Spanish influence reached its peak.

Under Abd al-Mu'min, some magnificent mosques were built – the most famous of which is the Koutoubia in Marrakesh.

His son, Abu Yacoub, was responsible for the Giralda in Seville (which once formed part of an enormous mosque) and the Great Mosque at Salé.

The greatest of Al-Mu'min's successors, his grandson Yacoub al-Mansour (1184-99),

finished the kasbah at Marrakesh and added to it the Great Mosque. He was responsible for the enormous Almohad wall with its famous gates at Rabat. Yacoub also began work on what was intended to be the greatest mosque in all of the Muslim west, if not the world, the Hassan Mosque which was never completed.

Much work was continued under the Merenids. Abu Youssef Yacoub, the second of their sultans, founded a new town, Fès el-Jdid, next door to Fès el-Bali where he set up his palace complex. In the last quarter of the 13th century, many mosques were built in towns throughout the country, including Fès, Meknès, Marrakesh and Salé. Medersas (religious schools) were also built, including the two stunning examples at Fès: the Bou Inania and el-Attarine. The royal necropolis at Chellah was also constructed during this time.

As the Merenid dynasty waned, so too did the fortunes of the empire and the artistic output. A brief period of expansion occurred at the end of the 17th century under the Saadian dynasty, which included an incursion into Sudan by the sultan Moulay Ahmed el-Mansour.

Enormous booty was brought back from the wealthy city of Timbuktu and used to embellish Moulay Ahmed's capital city of Marrakesh, particularly the el-Badi palace.

Unfortunately only the ruins remain, but the Saadian Tombs give some idea of the former richness of the palace.

Of the sultans of the Alawite dynasty (which continues to this day) the second, Moulay Ismail (1672-1727), was the most prolific. He dotted his empire with kasbahs where he housed the famous black regiments and prepared for his campaigns. Meknès, his chosen capital, was encircled by over 40km of walls and embellished with a palace, barracks and enormous stables. The extraordinary Bab Mansour gate is the archetypal monument of the period.

European-Style Architecture In the 16th century, the lucrative trade in spices, slaves and gold that flourished along the Mediterranean and Atlantic coasts attracted the greedy eyes of the Spanish and Portuguese.

Having seized these coastal towns, they constructed many Christian fortresses in order to maintain control. These were characterised by vast fortified walls topped by towers and monumental gateways flanked by square bastions. Examples of this style include those at Agadir, Essaouira, Safi and Mazagan.

Towards the end of the 18th century, Sultan Sidi Mohammed ben Abdallah used the captive French architect Cornut to completely redesign the walls and street plan of the city of Essaouira. The new fortifications, characterised by *skalas* (fortresses) and batteries, was a defensive formula later adopted by many ports along the Atlantic coast. Sidi ben Mohammed, along with many of the sultans who followed him, also built a series of public buildings in a kind of neo-hispanic-Moorish style, particularly at Fès, Marrakesh and Meknès.

Contemporary Architecture During the French protectorate, the construction of the *villes nouvelles* (new administrative towns) in many of the cities not only left those cities intact, but also provided an opportunity for new architectural expression.

For several years, two French town planners, Prost and Ecochard (administrators appointed by General Lyautey), oversaw a new 'rational' policy of town planning which eventually gave rise in 1917 to a whole new school.

Initially (from around 1912 to 1920), the aims of the school were to try to marry modern living requirements with the classic hispano-Moorish style, while keeping in check the increasing numbers of unscrupulous architects and speculators.

In the 1930s, a Moroccan variant of Art Deco was developed, in which the buildings either harmonised or deliberately broke with the traditional style of the surrounding buildings. The best examples can be seen in Casablanca, where Marius Boyer, the leading architect of the movement, worked. His Hôtel de Ville is a good example.

Since the 1940s, Casablanca has been the site of further experiments in town planning, including the use of aerial photography and revolutionary building techniques, such as concrete formwork. Among the most famous disciples of the new school are the architects Bodiansky and Candilis.

Bodiansky has created three different styles of 'progressive housing' in the outskirts of Casablanca, and Candilis, attempting to tackle the serious housing problem among the poor Muslim population, developed the concept of low-rent, 'culture-specific' housing for the masses. Also well known is the architect JF Zevaco, who was responsible for a large part of the reconstruction of the town of Agadir.

Although new town planning departments have been set up in different towns across the country – most recently in Fès and Agadir in 1989 – Casablanca continues to lead the way in architectural innovation. In 1993, the great Hassan II mosque was inaugurated. Designed by the French architect Michel Pinceau, it was the culmination of five years of intensive work by over 30,000 Moroccan craftsman. It is the biggest and most impressive mosque in the world after Mecca, and is a superb and confident affirmation that Morocco has lost none of its tradition of craftsmanship.

continued on page 68

Moroccan Architecture

History

From the 7th century onwards, Morocco – like the rest of North Africa, the Middle East, northern India and Spain – fell under the control of Islam. The resulting impact on the country's culture was enormous and Morocco's architecture, like many of its arts, was dominated by Islamic influence.

With the course of time, however, Morocco developed its own style. The country's particular climate, history, social structure and natural resources all played their part in this, as did its situation on the major trade routes which brought it into contact with other foreign influences. The angular, austere style of the Moroccan mosque, for example, is in stark contrast to both the opulent buildings of the Ottoman Turks and the decorative, Persian-influenced structures found in Iraq.

Nevertheless, much of the philosophy and the basic principles behind Islamic construction remained the same throughout the Arab World, including North Africa and Morocco.

Title page: View of the Gazleane Mosque through the horseshoe arch of Bab Bou Jeloud, Fès (photograph by Frances Linzee Gordon).

Top box: Detail of Muqarna stucco work, Medersa el-Attarine, Fès (photograph by Frances Linzee Gordon).

Lower box: Mosque in silhouette at sunset, Asilah (photograph by Chris Wyness).

Below: On Friday the minbar is the place from where the sermon is delivered.

Religious Architecture

Mosques Embodying the Islamic faith, and representing one of its predominant architectural features is the mosque, or *masjid*, also known as *jamaa, jami`, djemaa, 'jama* or *jemaa*. The building was developed in the very early days of the religion and takes its form from the simple, private houses where believers would customarily gather for worship.

The very first house – that belonging to the Prophet Mohammed who began to preach the new faith in Yathrib (later Mecca) in the year 622 – is said to provide the prototype for all later designs. The original setting was an enclosed, oblong courtyard with huts (housing Mohammed's wives) along one side wall and a rough portico, or *zulla* providing shade at one end for the poorer worshippers.

This plan can be seen in almost all mosques subsequently built. The courtyard has become the *sahn*, the portico the arcaded *riwaqs* and the houses the *haram* or prayer hall.

Divided into a series of aisles which segregate the sexes, this hall can reach immense proportions in the larger mosques. Running down the centre is a broader aisle which leads to the mihrab, the vaulted niche in the qibla. Built to face Mecca, this wall indicates the direction of prayer.

It is also the site of the *minbar*, a kind of pulpit raised above a narrow staircase. As a rule, only the main community mosque, or jamaa, contains a minbar. In grander mosques, the minbar is often ornately and beautifully decorated. They are less commonly found in the smaller local mosques.

On Friday, the minbar is also the place from where the *khutba*, or the weekly sermon, is delivered to the congregation. Islam does not recognise priests as such, but the closest equivalent is the *imam*, a learned man, schooled above all in Islam and the Islamic law. Often he will double as the mosque's *muezzin*, who calls the faithful to prayer each day.

Before entering the haram and participating in the communal worship, Muslims must perform a ritual washing (ablution). Serving for this purpose and placed in the middle of the courtyard, is the mosque's fountain or basin. It's usually carved from marble, and in the older mosques, is often worn from centuries of use.

Every mosque has a mihrab – a niche in the wall facing Mecca.

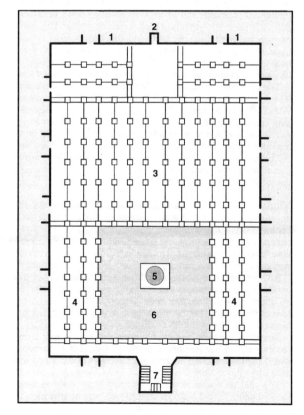

Typical Mosque

1 Qibla Wall
2 Mihrab (indicating the direction of Mecca) & Minbar (pulpit found in community mosques or jammaas, where the mosque's imam delivers the Friday sermon, or Khutba)
3 Haram (Prayer hall) which is segregated by gender
4 Riwaq
5 Fountain for ritual ablution
6 Sahn (courtyard)
7 Minaret where the muezzin calls the faithful to prayer

Beyond its obvious religious function, the mosque also serves as a kind of community centre, school, and point of social contact. You'll often see groups of children or adults, cross-legged on reed mats, being versed in some text (usually the Qur'an), people in quiet discussion, or seeking all sorts of advice from the imam. Others just choose to shelter here or pause for thought in the cool, peaceful tranquillity that the mosque invariably provides.

Minarets (from the word *menara*, meaning lighthouse), is the tower at one corner of the mosque. Usually (and based on the design of Syrian towers) it consists of a square base leading to more slender cylindrical or hexagonal stages. Most minarets have internal staircases for the muezzins to climb; the advent of the microphone saves them the effort now.

In the Maghreb and Spain, however, the dominant style of minaret is square-based all the way to the top. This is the most prominent characteristic of what is often referred to as Andalusian (from Al-Andalus) religious architecture. The comparison between such minarets and the bell-towers of many Spanish churches is revealing. Only one rather small but beautiful minaret, built in 1939 in the sacred town of Moulay Idriss near Meknès, departs from the standard – it's cylindrical.

The greatest mosque in Morocco is the Kairaouine (Qayrawin) mosque in Fès which dates from the 9th century. With its elaborate interior decoration and vaulting (developed over many centuries) it is the most impressive monument to Almoravid and Almohad power. Unfortunately, like the great majority of mosques in Morocco, it is closed to non-Muslims.

The one exception to the rule is the Hassan II Mosque in Casablanca, inaugurated in 1993 and the largest mosque in the world after Mecca. It should not be missed.

FRANCES LINZEE GORDON

Above: An intricately carved stone bracket, Rabat.

Below: Qur'anic cursive script in relief, Medersa Bou Inania, Fès.

FRANCES LINZEE GORDON

Medersas As if in compensation, there are many medersas open to view that are greatly rewarding. Originating in 10th century Persia, these beautiful buildings served as residential colleges where theology and Muslim law were taught. Some also functioned as early universities. Morocco's first medersa was built in the 13th century, following the traditional design.

An open-air courtyard, with an ablution fountain in the centre and a main prayer hall at the far end, is surrounded by an upper gallery of student cells. Generally the most impressive of them were built by the sultans of the Merenid dynasty between the 14th and 16th centuries.

The medersas are remarkable not so much for their architecture, but rather for their incredibly elaborate decoration, which includes detailed carving, zellij tile work, Kufic script and muqarna stucco work.

The master craftsmen who designed them liked to challenge visitors to find a single square inch free of artwork.

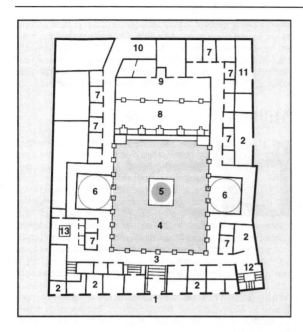

Medersa

1 Main entrance
2 Shops
3 Porticos
4 Courtyard
5 Fountain
6 Lecture rooms
7 Student cells
8 Prayer hall
9 Mihrab & Minbar
10 Mosque
11 Qua'ranic school
12 Minaret
13 Toilet

Marabouts Other religious buildings in Morocco, but in complete contrast to the medersa, include the very simple marabout. Dotted throughout the towns, villages and countryside of Morocco, these whitewashed, earth-walled huts mark the tombs of *marabouts*, Muslim holy men.

Widespread as they are, the marabouts play a very important role in the lives of the local communities. They serve not just as the site of pilgrimages (for those in search of 'baraka', a blessing), but also as weekly markets and charitable and community centres. Above all, and once a year, a moussem is held in the honour of the name-saint, and is the occasion of often very exuberant festivals.

The marabout is a shrine to holy men, or saints, and the site of a pilgrimage each year.

Mausoleums Similar to the marabouts, but on a much grander scale, are the mausoleums. Although Islam forbids the building of elaborate tombs, mausoleums erected in the memory of great sultans or kings became, after mosques and palaces, the most important structures in Islam.

For a powerful leader, a building constructed after his death was as important as one built during his life: they symbolised above all his great power.

Although Morocco has nothing in the same league as India's extraordinary Mughal tomb, the Taj Mahal, there are

nevertheless several tombs very much worth a visit. Unusually, they are open to non-Muslims. Among them are the mausoleums of Moulay Ismail in Meknès, one of the most powerful men in Moroccan history; and the more modern, but no less richly decorated, mausoleum found in Rabat. It was completed in 1971 for Mohammed V, the present king's father.

Military Architecture

Islamic military architecture is characterised by three major features: walls, gates and citadels (kasbahs).

Initially, such fortifications were only erected in frontier towns. From the late 9th and 10th centuries, however, and right up until the advent of artillery rendered them useless, vast fortified walls, mighty towers, and elaborate gates became a crucial feature of almost every city and town.

As central control weakened, political power began to be seized by the large numbers of local dynasties. Constantly at war with one another, the need for protection was paramount.

Walls & Towers Vast city ramparts are a feature of many towns in Morocco, and particularly of the imperial cities. Undistinguished architecturally, they are more impressive for their sheer size.

Typically, they were constructed of *pisé* (wet clay naturally baked by the sun), and square towers which served as barracks, granaries, and arsenals. At Meknès, the fortifications also contained water cisterns and vast stables – so providing everything necessary for long and rigorous defence.

Other features typically characterising the walls include crenellations, walkways, and machiolations. Measuring over 16km in circumference and defended by 200 gates, the red pisé walls surrounding Marrakesh are among the most impressive of Morocco's town defences.

Gates The Islamic gate, or bab, was designed above all to impress. It was a symbol of power, security and riches, and an assertion of the sultan's status far beyond any functional need. For historians, the gates are also a very useful gauge of building techniques and available building materials of the time.

In general, two crenellated, stone block towers flank the central bay in which the gate is set. The arch itself most frequently takes the horseshoe form and encloses or is enclosed by several multifoil curves. The gates are usually highly decorated with friezes, tracery or brightly coloured glazed tiles, and the spandrels, lintels and merlons are ornamented with geometric, flower and foliage or shell motifs.

Box: City ramparts designed to protect the city and its people from seizing armies (photograph by Frances Linzee Gordon).

One of the best known babs in Morocco is the Almohad Bab Oudaia in Rabat. Built in the 12th century, it is considered one of the masterpieces of Moorish architecture. The monumental Bab Mansour in Meknès was begun in the 17th century by the megalomaniac sultan Moulay Ismail, and is famous for the almost outrageously rich decoration which covers it.

Citadels The citadel, or *kasbah*, as it's commonly known in the western Islamic world, was usually constructed at the same time as the city walls and gates. It is regarded as one of the most original developments of Islamic architecture, and served as the fortified urban residence of the king, sultan or feudal lord. From the 10th century, almost any town of any significance had one.

Usually the kasbah was built astride the city's walls, or positioned in a commanding corner. Its location was designed above all to dominate both practically and symbolically the city it overlooked.

Initially, the function of the kasbah was strictly military, serving to house the army away from the city's population. Gradually, feudal rulers, keen to emphasise their elevated status, chose kasbahs as their homes and installed amenities such as reception rooms and baths. Later established as official palaces, they became a symbol of dynastic authority, arousing great respect and fear among the populace.

Domestic Architecture

Royal Palaces Also built to impress were the royal palaces. Remarkably austere on the outside, their status as symbols of power lay not so much in their architectural magnificence as in their physical presence: the huge walled enclosures separating a world of luxury within from the base world without.

In complete contrast to western extravagances like Versailles or the Winter Palace in St Petersburg, the visual impact was reserved for those granted the privilege of entering the building. For the Muslim ruler, it was the lavish furnishings and effects of the interior which made a palace and not the artificial, architectural features of the exterior.

For centuries, the extraordinary decoration and luxury of these palaces far surpassed any European vision of good living. One of the most famous palaces was the 16th century El Badi, 'the incomparable' in Marrakesh. Although in ruins now, it became a legend in its time in Europe. The sultan Ahmed al-Mansour employed the world's best craftsmen and filled the gardens, galleries and belvederes with objects of art from around the globe.

Box: Detail of chairs in the Palais de la Bahia, Marrakesh (photograph by Frances Linzee Gordon).

A typical feature of the palaces was the *mechouar* or judgement hall, a large open space used for ceremonies, parades, games and public executions. It was overlooked by an *iwan* (platform), from where the sultan would receive homage from, and dispense justice to his people.

Inside the palace, and well protected from intruders and prying eyes, was the **harem**. It was often housed in particularly luxurious and spacious apartments, and decorated with beautiful examples of geometrical zellij designs and stucco muqarna work. The Bahia Palace in Marrakesh is a good example of this. Also reserved for the ladies of the house were the gardens of the harem where exercise could be taken. These gardens are often fine monuments in themselves to the use of enclosed, sheltered space.

The Dar el-Makhzen Palace in Fès is considered one of the finest palaces in Morocco. Its 80 hectares are covered with pavilions, gardens, a private mosque, and medersa. Although it's not open to the public, many smaller, former palaces are.

Some house museums, such as the Dar Jamaï Museum in Meknès, others now serve as restaurants or luxury hotels, such as the Palais Jamaï in Fès. Those palaces in Marrakesh, in particular, can give visitors an idea – if superficially – of the former lavishness and splendour of these places.

Town Houses

The Moroccan town house has remained largely unaltered for five millennia. Known as the *dar* or interior courtyard house, it is typical of the Islamic dwellings of the Middle East and Mediterranean.

The principal feature is a central courtyard, around which are grouped suites of rooms in a symmetrical pattern. In the wealthier houses, service areas are often tacked on to one side, and these in turn might have their own courtyard as necessity and means dictate.

The interior courtyard serves a very important function as a modifier of the climate in hot, dry regions. With very few exterior windows, the courtyards function as a kind of 'light well' into which the light penetrates during the day, and a 'air well', into which the cool, dense air of evening sinks at night.

One of the great advantages of this set-up is that it permits outdoor activities, with protection from the wind, dust and sun. The system also allows natural ventilation. Because the house is surrounded by tall walls, the sun's rays cannot reach the courtyard until later in the afternoon. When they do reach the courtyard, and heated air rises, convention currents set up an air-flow that ventilates the house and keeps it cool.

While rooms in European houses are usually allotted a specific function, such as a bedroom or sitting room, the rooms in Muslim houses are more multipurpose. Rooms can be used interchangeably for eating, relaxing and sleeping.

This flexible use of living space is also reflected in the

FRANCES LINZEE GORDON

Above: Typical facade of an old Jewish house in the mellah, Fès.

Below: Ornate screen at the deep-blue Majorelle villa, Jardin Majorelle, Marrakesh.

FRANCES LINZEE GORDON

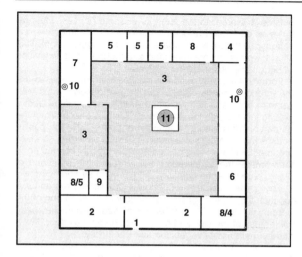

Courtyard House

1 Entrance (placed to obscure view into courtyard)
2 Men's reception room
3 Courtyard & gardens
4 Living & sleeping area (Harem)
5 Service & storage area
6 Stable
7 Formal salon
8 Kitchen
9 Toilet
10 Well
11 Fountain/pool

absence of awkward furniture such as tables and cupboards. Many Muslims take their meals on the floor, sitting on rugs, mats or cushions. When the meal is over, these can be rolled up and squirreled away.

The function of interiors can also change with the time of day. The hottest part of the day is spent in the cool of the courtyard, and at night, the roof terrace is used as a sleeping area.

Again, reflecting the Islamic architectural concern with the interior space of a building, decoration is reserved for the internal elements such as the courtyard, and not, as with the European style, the external elements. The street facade is usually just a plain wall, and the only opening is the entrance door. Any other openings are small, grilled and above the line of vision of passers-by. This reflects the strict demarcation of public and private life in Islamic society.

Sometimes the doors of houses can be elaborately decorated, marking the symbolic importance of the house entrance – the vulnerable threshold between the private world and the public world. Auspicious symbols, designs and colours are often used, such as the stylised design of the hand of Fatima, seen so commonly in the medinas of Morocco.

The importance of domestic privacy is also extended into the interior of the house also. The word for women *harim,* is related to the word haram *(harem)*, 'sacred area', which, far removed from its western connotations, denotes the family living quarters.

The harem, or domestic area of the house, is primarily the women's domain, the husband usually has his own room just

Protecting the inhabitants from evil spirits – a Hand of Fatima door hinge, Fès medina.

FRANCES LINZEE GORDON

outside this area. In the interiors of some houses, *mashrabiyya*, or perforated wooden screens, are sometimes erected in front of a harem which opens onto the reception room. This allows women to observe men's gatherings and festivities without being observed themselves.

Forming an essential part of the wealthier town houses are the interior **gardens**. These can be elaborately paved with ceramic tiles, and richly planted. Paths, often raised above ground level, divide the flower beds. Usually the centre of the garden is dominated by a fountain or pool – even the poorer houses may contain some focal point such as a tree, shrub or ornamental object. This design again is closely connected to the climate: the evaporation of water and the presence of plants both raise the humidity and keep the air cool.

The garden also has a strongly symbolic and recreational function too. To the Muslim, the beauty of creation and of the garden is held to be a reflection of god. Within the dusty wilderness of the city, and hidden behind a small door, lies a sudden paradise of vegetation and tranquillity.

The aim of many Moorish gardens is to create harmony. This is achieved through a combination of scent and colour provided by plants, with music provided by tinkling fountains and bird song. Fruit trees, laurel and cypress provide the essential shade; jasmine, rose and geranium, the scents.

Traditional gardens which are open to the public include the Dar Jamaï museum in Meknès, the Dar Batha museum in Fès and the Dar el-Makhzen museum in Tangier.

Urban Architecture

Unlike European urban centres, Islamic villages, towns and cities rarely conform to any geometric symmetry of town planning. More commonly, cities are divided into town quarters.

This ancient system is found throughout the Islamic world, and is thought to originate in 8th-century Baghdad. Again, in contrast to western towns, quarters are not divided by social status; instead, the communal mosque, hammam, fountain, oven and school, are shared by all residents, rich and poor.

Despite their chaotic appearance, the old, Islamic towns are carefully adapted to the rigours of the climate. Like the domestic house, the deep, narrow streets of the medina keep the sun's rays from the centre during the day, and draw in the cool, dense evening air during the night.

The massing of multi-storeyed structures sharing party walls also reduces the total surface area exposed to the sun. Traditional building materials such as earth, stone and wood,

Box: Aerial view of Moulay Idriss displaying typical Moroccan urban architecture (photograph by Frances Linzee Gordon).

Top four photos: Interior scenes from palaces in Marrakesh medina.

Bottom: Fireplace designed by US architect Bill Willis, Yacout Restaurant, Marrakesh.

FRANCES LINZEE GORDON

Top: The Marrakesh ramparts and High Atlas mountains at dusk.

Bottom: Kasbah in the gorges of the Dadès Valley.

FRANCES LINZEE GORDON

KARYN DUGGAN

because of capillary effect, absorb water which then evapo-
rates from their surfaces, and cools the surrounding air.

*Quintessentially Moroc-
can – a skyline view of
the old medina, Fès.*

Souqs The souq or bazaar, along with the mosque and
possibly the hammam, make up the quintessential elements
of a Muslim town. The souq is also the commercial backbone
of the city.

At first sight, it appears a hotchpotch of houses randomly
erected wherever the tiniest space allows. In reality, a very
particular order governs the layout of the souq. This pattern is
amazingly constant, and can be found repeating itself from
North Africa to India.

The standard plan consists of a network of streets covered
with vaults, domes or awnings. The streets are lit by openings
in the central bays which allow light to penetrate, but keep
the interior cool and well ventilated. The design owes much in
its form to the Classical precedent with the agora and its
surrounding buildings, and colonnaded market place.

The congregational mosque provides the focal point to the
souq, and around it the shops are grouped in a strict hierarchy. First come the vendors of candles, incense and other
objects used in the rites of worship. Next to them are the booksellers, long venerated by Muslim cultures, and the vendors
of small leather goods. These are followed by the general
clothing and textile stalls, long the domain of the richest and
most powerful merchants.

The hierarchy then descends through furnishings, domestic goods and utensils, until, with the most ordinary wares, the
walls and gates of the city are reached.

Here, on the city perimeters, where the caravans often used
to assemble, are the ironmongers, blacksmiths and the other
craftsmen and vendors serving the caravan trade. Among

them are the saddlers, suppliers of sacking and string, tents and whatever else the traveller might need in preparation for his long journey.

Furthest afield are the potteries and the tanneries, usually exiled to beyond the city walls because of the noxious odours and smoke they produce.

Qissaria Another feature of the Islamic souq is the qissaria, generally found at the heart of the medina. Its form is said to derive from the classical basilica, and consists of an oblong and colonnaded covered hall, with a large door at one end that is securely locked at night.

The quissaria serves as an internal strong-room housing the trade in valuable objects such as precious textiles, furs, gems and metals, similar to a certain degree to the covered arcades in London's Piccadilly. In recent times, this term also seems to have been coined to describe the covered shopping centres in the nouvelle ville.

Funduqs Muslim civilisations have always been mobile. Arab conquerors were originally nomadic, huge Muslim armies were constantly on the move, and students and scholars undertook long journeys to sit at the feet of famous masters. From the earliest days of Islam, pilgrims travelled long distances for the performance of the *Hajj* (pilgrimage) to Mecca. Above all, and particularly in Morocco, there was the strong tradition of trade, with merchants travelling vast distances to purchase and sell goods.

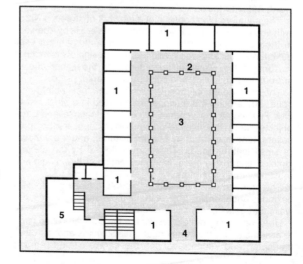

Funduq

1 Shops, Mills, Warehouses, Bakeries, Teashops & Stabling (ground floor). Pilgrim's cells (second floor)
2 Peristyle
3 Courtyard
4 Doorway
5 Mosque

With the harsh climate of some parts of Morocco, and the difficult and often dangerous terrain, many merchants and pilgrims required rest and shelter for the night. This led to the creation of caravanserais, known in North Africa as *funduqs*, which sprang up at regular intervals along the major trade routes of the entire Islamic world.

Their function can be compared to modern-day motels or motorway cafes, providing food and accommodation for both traveller and their transport, usually camels, mules or horses.

In general, they were unremarkable architecturally. An unadorned facade provided a doorway wide enough to allow camels or heavily laden beasts to enter. The central courtyard was usually open to the sky and was surrounded by a number of similar stalls, bays or niches, usually arranged over two floors. The first storey housed shops, mills, warehouses, bakeries, tea shops and stabling for the animals, and the second, the upper gallery, accommodated the pilgrims.

Funduqs can be seen in many of the larger cities. Although no longer used for accommodation, herds of animals can still sometimes be seen filling them, on their way to or from market. Many of them have fallen into a sad state of decay.

Hammams Another essential feature of Islamic towns and societies is the *hammam* or public bath. Although serving a mundane function, the hammam can be a surprisingly impressive architectural structure. Most commonly, however, they are identifiable only by the smoking chimney and low, glass-studded dome.

The Muslim hammam is directly descended from the Classical bath, although with time the emphasis altered from social and sporting purposes to the Muslim concern with ritual and cleanliness. In modern Morocco, the hammam has come to play an extremely important role in the social life of women.

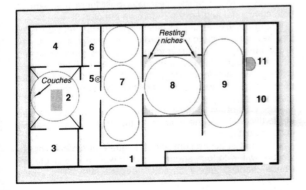

Hammam

1 Entrance (Zigzag design)
2 Disrobing room with pool plus couches to rest on with tea, coffee or sherbet after bathing
3 Attendant's room
4 Relaxing room
5 Fountain
6 Toilet
7 Cold room, traditionally with three domes
8 Warm room with niches for reclining bathers. Washing, massage and rinsing are aided by bath attendants.
9 Hot room
10 Heating room
11 Boiler & furnace

Mothers frequently use them as catching pens for potential wives for their sons.

Traditionally, the hammam consists of a spacious, domed disrobing room, with a pool in the centre. Next in the bathing sequence is the 'cold room', an elongated room with three domes, so named because of its position furthest from the heating room. Afterwards comes the warm room, larger and more elaborately constructed and decorated than the cold room, with niches in the four corners of the chamber where the bather can recline.

The hot or steam room is the next stop and is the simplest room with a low, domed ceiling. A final stop is made in the warm room where the bather can be cleansed and massaged, soaped and shampooed and rinsed by bath attendants.

Later, after returning to the disrobing room, the bather can recline and rest on couches before being served tea, coffee or sherbet.

Berber Architecture

In the central and southern regions of Morocco, just as in the north, the climate, geography and social conditions of the region have largely dictated the forms of architecture.

Formerly, in the isolated, rugged regions of the south where policing was difficult and communication nearly impossible, tribal feuds and banditry were frequently the order of the day. As recently as the late 1930s, it was considered highly dangerous to travel in these areas of Morocco. Born of these conditions, the buildings of the region – even the very poor ones – were primarily structures of defence.

In the southern valleys of the Drâa, Dadès and Ziz, the indigenous Berber communities have built large numbers of both communal and private defensive structures.

Rising out of the desert landscape, the impression is of massive, powerful and uncompromising strength and some of these buildings number among Morocco's most imposing sights. Throughout the centuries, these Berbers have adhered to their own, austere building style, unmoved by contact with other traditions, most notably those of Islam and the Arabs.

Box: A typical red-walled town in the Dadès Gorge (photograph by Frances Linzee Gordon).

Ksars One of the earliest forms of Berber architecture was the fortified village, the *ksar* (from the Arabic *qasr*, meaning castle or palace).

The basic structure consists of a square or rectangular enclosure wall with four, square corner towers and a single entrance leading into a central, covered alley. The space between this street and the wall is filled with warren-like court-yard houses and alleys, a mosque and a well.

As the village expands, more quarters are constructed around this structure, with new exterior ramparts erected along with entrance ways. The towers are used as granaries, food stores or arsenals. One of the best examples of the ksar (plural *ksour*) is the spectacular Aït Benhaddou in the valley of the Assif Mellah, which has been the setting of many Hollywood films.

Individual houses are built along these same lines, with the basic courtyard plan, high ramparts and corner towers. Both the village and the house are constructed of pisé. The lower half of the defensive walls is earthen and the upper storeys are made of baked brick, and feature characteristic mud-brick decoration. The towers taper a little towards the top, and slit windows let the light in and missiles out.

The most unfortunate thing about these ochre-coloured, starkly impressive constructions is their fragility. Permeable to water, they can withstand only a very dry climate. Rain constantly undermines the buildings and within 50 years a magnificent new kasbah can be reduced by the elements to a ruinous pile of mud and rubble. The shells of many such casualties litter the desert plains of the south.

Kasbahs Similar in style to the ksar is the kasbah. This building is most commonly an urban structure (see above), but also exists in some parts of southern Morocco and particularly along the Route des Kasbahs in the Dadès Valley.

The kasbahs were usually erected by some local potentate at key places in the region under his rule in order to give protection for his small garrisons. Like their cousins in the cities, they are generally fortified, square, pisé buildings with just a few openings on the outside.

FRANCES LINZEE GORDON

The Kasbah at Aït Benhaddou set against the spectacular High Atlas Mountains.

Agadirs One of the most curious structures of North African architecture, is the agadir, or fortified communal granary. It is generally found among the indigenous Berber communities in isolated mountain areas, and its development grew out of the social needs of these people.

The nomads of the plain needed to store grain and dates in a single place, safe from attacks and looting during their frequent absences. By contrast, the sedentary agriculturists of the valleys needed a strong defensive structure where they could safely keep food reserves, arms and valuables from the ravages of marauding tribesmen.

These requirements led to communal building efforts, in which walls, fortifications and water-cisterns were built by the whole tribe. Within the walls, each family then built their individual storehouses. These fortifications also provide a refuge for women, children and valuable livestock in times of battle. In times of peace, the agadirs on trade routes and strategic crossings serve as market-places and caravanserais.

As a result of this tribal, group effort, the building came to represent both physically and symbolically the survival and identity of the group. Unfortunately, because of these strong cultural connotations, a large number of granaries were systematically destroyed by the Glaoui overlords during their expansion in southern Morocco at the beginning of this century.

Other features of agadirs may include a miniature mosque, and, in the granaries of the Anti-Atlas and western High Atlas, a council chamber, reception room and blacksmith's workshop. Some anthropologists interpret the granary as an early, but intermediate, stage of urban organisation among the Berbers; the next evolutionary stage of which is the ksar.

Agadir

1 Entrance through Agadir wall
2 Entrance to granary
3 Courtyard
4 Cistern
5 Dwellings
6 Watch-tower
7 Council chamber
8 Room dedicated to granary's patron saint
9 Stable
10 Yard for animals
11 Water trough
12 Blacksmith's workshop
13 Mosque & religious school

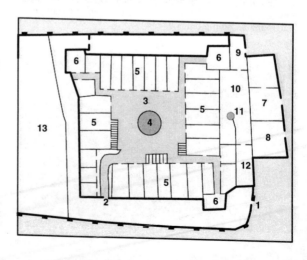

The building materials and construction techniques of Agadirs depend on the region where they are found, and the communities they serve. Generally there are two basic forms: those with an interior courtyard, and those where storehouse cells are aligned along either side of a long narrow alley.

Both types follow a common plan: there are usually two to four tiers of small storage chambers grouped around the central courtyard or alley, which is entered through a narrow door set in the bleak and impregnable exterior facade. This single entrance is guarded by watchmen. The livestock is generally kept on the first floor, the grain on the second and living quarters are on the third or fourth. The wall of the granaries are generally made of pisé in the south of Morocco and dry stone in the Atlas mountains. Good examples of agadirs in Morocco include the one at Imilchil.

Tent The tent has existed as a form of shelter throughout Islamic history and is still widely in use today in many parts of Morocco, particularly around the High Atlas. Like other forms of accommodation, the tent has been adapted to the social need of the people. Easy to put up and take down, this flexibility is well suited to the lifestyle of the nomads and herdsmen who live in them.

As in the domestic house, space is carefully divided into separate areas for the women, men and their guests. There is also space inside the exterior wall of the tent for animals and for the storage of food. The tent is made of a weave of wool and hair and is surprisingly resistant to the elements.

The interior of the tent is highly structured – and carefully divided into separate spaces.

Easy to put up and bring down, tents are ideally suited to the nomadic life of Berber herdspeople.

Berber Tent

1. Main tent panel
2. Guy rope panels
3. Wooden rack for storing cooking utensils
4. Hand mill for grinding wheat to make bread
5. Women's area
6. Fireplace
7. Sleeping area divided by carpets and filled sacks
8. Simple vertical loom (fixed to tent post)
9. Main tent support poles
10. Wooden rack for storing carpet weaves and garments.
11. Mat screen separating men's area from utility area
12. Men's section
13. Space for newly born animals, agricultural tools and storage sacks

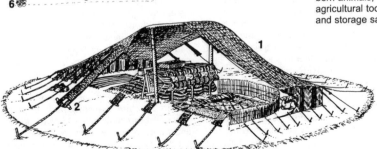

Literature

Far from the heart of Muslim Arab civilisation, and great seats of power and learning such as Cairo, Damascus, Baghdad and Jerusalem, Morocco has never really been at the forefront of Arab letters, although several greats spent some time in Morocco.

They include Ibn Khaldun and the philosopher Averroes (or Ibn Rushd). The former, who lived in the 14th century, is considered the foremost Arab historian and is best known for his remarkable *Histoire Universelle* and philosophical treatise *Muqqaddina*. Born in Algeria, he spent some time in Fès, but his travels took him on to Spain, Cairo and Syria.

Averroes, as he was known in the west, was equally known for his medical treatises and commentaries on Aristotle. Born in Cordoba, in Muslim Spain, he spent his last years in Marrakesh.

Moroccan literary genres such as the novel and drama, long taken for granted as an integral part of western culture, are a comparatively recent development in the Arab world. Until the late 19th century, the bulk of literature consisted of traditional poetry, much of it in imitation of older classics (for a full treatment of literature in the Arab world, past and present, see the three volume *Cambridge History of Arabic Literature*).

Egypt has tended to lead the way over the past 100 years, but Morocco, too, has seen a growth of modern talent. Many Moroccan authors still write in French, although more and more are turning to their native tongue, even at the risk of not gaining wider recognition for want of translation into French.

Much of the literature emerging from Morocco over the last century has appeared more political than literary, concerning itself almost exclusively with the independence movement and the construction of a post-colonial society.

Two writers of the extreme left, Abraham Serfaty and Mohammed Khaïr-Eddine, were arrested for their political writing in 1972, and the works of one of Morocco's most famous and talented writers, Driss Chraïbi (see later in this entry), were for a long time banned.

Until very recently, the bulk of Moroccan literature was not known beyond France and the Maghreb. Gradually, Moroccan writers are getting better known and, in 1987, one of the most outspoken of the country's writers and critics, Tahar Ben Jeloun, won the prestigious French *Prix Goncourt* for his novel *La Nuit Sacrée* (The Sacred Night).

Another well known writer and international prize winner is the poet Abdu Elaraki who, in 1988, won the Gold Medal at the European Academy of Arts awards for his collection of poems entitled *Rêe de Poème* (Dream of Poetry). In 1990 Mohammed Al-Haloui won the Kuweiti prize for his poem *A Sebta*.

Unfortunately, very few of these titles have been translated into English. The following books are a recommended selection of Moroccan literature which has been translated.

Most books are published in different editions by different publishers in different countries. As a result, a book might be a hardcover rarity in one country while it's readily available in paperback in another. Fortunately, bookshops and libraries search by title or author, so your local bookshop or library is best placed to advise you on their availability:

Year of the Elephant, by Leila Abouzeid, is one of a series of stories which recount the life of Zahra, a Moroccan woman who, in the face of an unsympathetic society, carves out a degree of independence for herself without abandoning the pillars of her upbringing, including the Islamic faith.

In *Si Yussef*, Anouar Majid evokes Moroccan life through the eyes of a man who looks back on his life in Tangier. The character was a bookkeeper who started his apprenticeship in survival, as did most of the port city's urchins, as a guide for foreigners.

One of Morocco's better known authors (and winner of the 1994 Prix Méditerranée) is Tahar ben Jelloun, a resident of France since 1971. At least two of his works, which he writes in French, have appeared in English. *Solitaire* explores the seemingly insurmountable difficulties encountered by a Moroccan migrant in France.

In *Silent Day in Tangier*, an elderly and bedridden man ruminates over his past. Although the book is largely a personal exploration, the many allusions to the history of Tangier and Morocco from about the time of the Rif war onwards are unobtrusively woven into the observations of an old and angry man.

Abdel Krim Ghallab, editor-in-chief of *Al-'Alam* newspaper, is considered one of Morocco's finer modern writers. Although he writes in Arabic, some of his works, including *Le Passé Enterré*, have been translated into French.

Ahmed Sefrioui, a writer of Berber origin who grew up in Fès, aims to relate the life of ordinary Moroccans through the eyes of his characters, such as little Mohammed in *La Boîte à Merveilles*. Here is all the hubbub and local colour of the Fès of half a century ago.

An important representative of Moroccan émigré literature is Driss Chraïbi, who was born in El-Jadida and now lives in France. A prolific writer, his novels tend to be politicised, which sets him at odds with Sefrioui (who prefers to deal with more essential human issues). His works include *Le Passé Simple* and *Mort au Canada*.

One work that appears in English translation is *Heirs to the Past*. A couple of other novels have also been translated into English, but are hard to come by.

Mohammed Khaïr-eddine, who writes in French and Arabic, is one of Morocco's ground-breaking authors. His poems, novels and other writings express a desire for revolt and change, not only in the context of Moroccan society and traditions, but in his own methods of writing. One of the better known anthologies is *Ce Maroc!*

For something closer to the pulse of traditional society, *Contes Berbères de l'Atlas de Marrakesh*, a series of Berber tales edited by Alphonse Lequil, might be worth perusing.

The famous American novelist and Tangier resident, Paul Bowles, has translated a series of oral tales from Moroccan Arabic into English. The tales were compiled by Mohammed Mrabet, Mohammed Choukri and Larbi Layachi (whose work was published under the pseudonym Driss ben Hamed Charhadi). Among Mrabet's works are *Love with a Few Hairs* and *M'Hashish*. His is an uncompromising account of the life of Tanjawi street lads and the sometimes irksome activities they undertook to earn a crust.

Choukri's main work is *For Bread Alone: An Autobiography*, in which he describes the seemingly unbearable saga of his family, one of many families forced by drought in the Rif during the early 1940s to seek opportunities in Tangier, only to be largely crushed by its indifference.

Layachi's best known work is *A Life Full of Holes*. As humble in origin as the other two, Layachi is said to have wanted to use a pseudonym because he didn't want anyone to know who he was: jobless and living in 'a rotten country in rotten times'.

'A gentleman without reading is like a dog without training.'
Moroccan Proverb

Crafts

Morocco has a rich and varied tradition of handicraft production, and the better souqs are crawling with items to keep the avid souvenir-hunter well occupied. See the Arts & Crafts colour section, and the Things to Buy sections in some of the major cities.

Film

Morocco's first exposure to the world of cinema was as the setting for many pre-independence films, particularly French productions. However, as a film maker, it's a relative newcomer, with its first efforts (which were little more than shorts and documentaries) not produced until the 1960s.

The first feature film was made in 1968, but during the 1970s a period of stagnation occurred. In the 1980s the Cinema Support Fund, tax benefits and film festivals at

Rabat and Casablanca were set up in order to encourage production. Films are being made again, but cinema remains a very small industry in Morocco.

In contrast to western directors, who are drawn to Morocco for its exotic locations, film makers are more interested in the exploration of contemporary issues and, in particular, the conflict that arises between ancient tradition and modern life.

The film *El-Chergui* (1970) by Moumem Smihi is a good example of this last theme. Other films include *Le Soiffeur du Quartier des Pauvres* (1985) by Mohammed Reggab, which deals with the plight of the poor in a working class suburb of Casablanca, and *Le Grand Voyage* (1980) by Abd er-Rahmane Tazi, in which the geographical and social gap between the north and the south of the country is emphasised.

Other contemporary film makers include Souheil Ben Barka, Latif Lahlou, Hassan Benjelloun, Abdellah Mesbahi and Hakim Noury.

Morocco is also keen to win back foreign directors put off in the past by Morocco's notorious bureaucracy, lack of facilities and absence of any cohesive organisation with which to deal. Tunisia continues to net far more custom than Morocco and provides the classic desert location for scenes such as those in the film *The English Patient* in 1996.

For more information on foreign films shot in Morocco, see the Film section in the Facts for the Visitor chapter.

Theatre

Morocco is one of the most theatrical places in the world. Storytellers, acrobats, clowns, musicians, dancers, and mimes have been found for centuries in public squares, private houses and palaces, transmitting from generation to generation an important part of the country's artistic heritage.

The Place Djemaa el-Fna in Marrakesh is considered the cradle of popular Moroccan theatre and is a good place to watch it in action.

In contrast to western theatre, the Moroccan *halqa* (meaning circle and in reference to the crowds it draws around it) is itinerant, spontaneous, relies on audience participation and does not confine itself to one genre; it is a mixture of farce, tragedy and history, and is often accompanied by music and dancing.

The second form of Moroccan theatre is the more classic *el-Bsat* (entertainment). It enjoyed a golden age during the reign of the Alawite sultan, Sidi Mohammed ben Abdallah, at the end of the 18th century and was essentially a critical theatre which took contemporary social and political issues as its themes.

Most performances were staged before the sultan inside the walls of the Dar el-Makhzen palace in Fès. Various companies would perform a series of short sketches, after which the second part would start. A theme was chosen and all the companies would be expected to contribute to an improvised performance.

Actors traditionally took advantage of this occasion to denounce the abuses of the administration, or the injustices committed by even the most powerful official. It was also a place for settling accounts or the enactment of revenge through the ultimate public mortification.

Egyptian troupes touring Morocco in the 1920s inspired a revival of this art form and it once again became a mouthpiece for popular protest, this time against the colonial powers.

Ironically, in order to escape censorship the plays of Molière were chosen, using particular characters to symbolise the anti-colonial struggle.

There is a tremendous number of other forms of Moroccan theatre, including the travelling puppet shows, poetry recitations of the Ilizlan, the itinerant Berber artists from the Middle Atlas, the Tuaregs from the Sahara and the 'ceremonial theatre', (consisting of ecstatic dancing and mysterious chanting) of the Zaouias.

Despite the recent onslaught of satellite television, the Moroccan theatrical tradition is still thriving.

Painting

Europeans in Morocco Since the Renaissance, the common western perception of Oriental society was one of harems, opulent palaces and all-powerful sultans. The imagination of many had been fired by the tales of explorers and travellers such as the 19th century writer, Mariano Fortuny.

With the expansion of colonialism and development of transport in the 19th century, this fascination came to a head and many artists, rejecting the traditional Grand Tour of Italy and Greece, crossed the Mediterranean in search of the exotic.

One of the first artists of this period to visit Morocco was the French Romantic painter Eugene Delacroix (1798-1863). The official court painter to Louis-Philippe, Delacroix first arrived in Morocco as part of a diplomatic mission to the sultan Abd er-Rahman. During the five months he spent in Morocco, he discovered pristine countryside, a way of life unchanged since the Middle Ages and an intensity of light and brilliance of colours he had never imagined.

After a visit to Meknès, the artist observed: 'There are paintings to made at every street corner ... which would make the fortunes of 20 generations of painters'.

The countless notebooks he filled with watercolours, sketches and minute descriptions of colour and tone were to inspire him and influence his painting for the rest of his life.

Ironically, it was Delacroix's work – and one painting in particular, the *Jewish Wedding* exhibited in the Palais du Luxembourg in Paris – which would inspire countless other French artists to visit Morocco. Some of them, including Emile Vernet-Lecomte and Alfred Dehodencq, both contemporaries of Delacroix, even reworked his Jewish wedding theme.

Two other painters greatly influenced by Delacroix's work were the French artists Henri Regnault and Georges Clairin. Visiting Tangier for the first time in 1863, they too became responsible for perpetuating the myth of the Oriental dream.

Initially, artists continued to paint purely imaginative compositions based on classical themes. Gradually a note of realism crept in as they tried to embellish their pictures with authentic, decorative detail and local colour. By the end of the 19th century, artists were recording, often straight onto the canvas, the people and the culture they came across, albeit still in rather a romanticised way.

Public squares, ceremonies, street scenes and souqs, combined with the legendary painterly qualities of the Moroccan light – its clarity, intensity and continual interplay – all provided endless inspiration for the artists who visited the country.

Other famous painters to visit Morocco included the Russian painter Elie-Anatole, the Belgium Jean-François Portaels, the Frenchman Adolphe Gumery, the Spaniard José Gallegos y Arnosa, the Englishman Edmund Aubrey Hunt and, in 1912, the father of Fauvism, Matisse.

The latter spent two periods in Tangier experimenting and developing techniques that would characterise his mature style: the use of bold, non-naturalistic and expressive colour; the abstraction rather than strict representation of the image through pure colour, flat shape and strong pattern; and the creation (rather than imitation) of light through colour. His aim was to 'express spirituality through the tangible'. Matisse was also greatly influenced by the abstract quality, subtle harmony and pure colour that he found in traditional Moroccan art.

Moroccan Artists Although in the 1940s, Moroccan 'naïve' (self-taught) artists such as Hamri in Tangier and Ben Allal in Marrakesh were exhibiting their work, it was not until the 1960s that anything like a school of painting began to develop.

Several movements resulted, with little in common except for a tendency to abstraction which has traditionally dominated Moroccan painting. This is partly explained by the fact that Islam has for centuries frowned upon the representation of living things.

Other common characteristics include inspiration sought from rural life, a return to one's roots, and the recurring theme of the conflict between ancient tradition and modern life.

One of the best known of Morocco's painters is the semiotic painter (whose works are dominated by signs and symbols), Ahmed Cherkaoui. Other well known artists include Rabi, who tries through his compositions to 'synthesise spiritual meditation with the act'; Hassani, whose pictures are a celebration of the colours of his country; Alaoui, who examines through abstraction the play of Moroccan light; and Boutaleb, Asladi and Ahardan, whose strongly imaginative work borders on surrealism.

SOCIETY & CONDUCT
Traditional & Modern Lifestyles

For the first-time visitor to a Muslim country, the curious mix of conservatism and westernised 'liberalism' never ceases to confuse. At the one end of the spectrum is the jellaba-clad Muslim fundamentalist, who rejects all things European (particularly French), new and modern. At the other end, is the very westernised Muslim, donning baseball cap and sneakers and renouncing all things Islamic, traditional and old.

However liberal some Moroccans may wish to seem, travellers will still be treated and judged by the very definite social code that governs Muslim societies. Many travellers may find this judgmental attitude a little difficult to adjust to initially. The key is trying to understand it.

For the Moroccan, the family is the most important single element in life and comes before work, friendship and sometimes even marriage. Many Moroccans live with their families before and after marriage, and some of the worst insults question one's parentage. Although strongly resembling nosiness in western eyes, it's perfectly normal for a Moroccan to inquire in detail about family relationships.

Sole women travellers are particularly prone to inquisitive interrogation. Moroccans simply cannot understand why any woman would either attempt to, or want to, travel unaccompanied by a member of her family or spouse.

Many Moroccan women won't even visit the souq without a family member and never venture outside the home after nightfall.

Coming also under close scrutiny is the traveller's conjugal status. Marriage remains an extremely well-respected institution in Morocco and no women would consider life without it. For some Moroccans, it is the woman's only purpose in life and there are abundant Moroccan proverbs to confirm this: 'a women without a husband is like a bird without a nest', for example.

For this reason, it is not considered in the least rude or presumptive to inquire about marital status and women will find that questions of this nature follow very early on in a conversation, often preceded only by: 'What's your name, where are you from?'

Although the average age for marriage has gone up, most men still marry before reaching 30 and women generally before 25. Unmarried Moroccan women above this age are often treated with much patronising sympathy (and sometimes even suspicion – of having lost the all-essential virginity). western women above the accepted age for brides will often be asked bluntly why they are not married, or even (much to the chagrin of the thirty-somethings), if they are in fact widowed!

In Moroccan society, marriage is seen less as the culmination of a romance and more as the signing of a business contract. Many marriages continue to be arranged, particularly in the rural areas, and parents play an important role in the negotiations which, like a major commercial deal, can take months to set up. Bridegrooms pay a *sedaq* (bride price) and the brides come with a dowry. The aspiration of a young couple is to produce children which will continue the family line and bring it prestige and respect.

Consequently, single women travellers should not be overly shocked or surprised by the number of marriage proposals they may attract. It wouldn't even occur to a Moroccan male that a single (and particularly older woman, possibly with her virginity in doubt), wouldn't utterly jump at the chance to be married to him.

The fact that some women may choose not to marry at all would not occur to most Moroccans, and probably wouldn't be believed anyway.

On the business side, a marriage to a westerner has become the longed-for solution for many Moroccans hoping to escape the high unemployment with a passport and visa. Interestingly, each year many of them manage it.

Religion is also a very important element in the Moroccan's life, and one that Moroccans love to discuss. Unlike in western societies where atheism or just apathy are acceptable or even fashionable, for the Moroccan a life without god would be unthinkable and blasphemous. The term *haj* or *haja* (for women), accorded to those who have made the journey to Mecca, is highly respected and often aspired to, even among the young. Muslims see Islam as the last and therefore most perfect of all religions and are proud of it.

Because of the strength of feeling involved, it may be wise for travellers to adopt a mild stance on religion if they have any views it. By the same token, Moroccans very rarely become pedantic or aggressive on the subject and will be surprised and delighted if you show even the most minimal knowledge of Islam, or any interest in learning about it. Sometimes foreigners are even encouraged to convert, and a surprising amount of expats do, such is the kudos surrounding the religion.

Moroccans love to talk. For the men, particularly, conversation forms a major part of life and hours are spent every day arguing about current issues over a coffee in the abundant cafes of the towns. Foreigners are often alarmed at the intensity and emotion of these arguments. A squabble on a bus can seem to degenerate into a life-threatening feud.

This public display of emotion is perfectly normal for the Moroccan and is often accompanied by a dramatic accompaniment of shouting, gestures and lots of acting. If you should ever become the target of these displays, you should ignore it and quietly leave.

Etiquette

Much more likely, you'll become the target of Moroccan hospitality. Hardly an hour will go by when you are not invited to talk over a coffee or tea with a Moroccan. Such invitations are perfectly normal and shouldn't in general be treated with any suspicion. One of the most attractive aspects of the country is the warmth, openness and complete lack of inhibition of the people.

Arab hospitality is legendary and invitations may well soon be extended to the home. Again, this is perfectly normal in Morocco and you may find that a invitation is earned after just a brief conversation with the driver of a taxi, with a young man or woman in the hammam, or sitting next to an old man on the bus. This is a tremendous opportunity to experience something of real Moroccan culture.

'Dine and feed your guests even if you are starving' goes the proverb, and the generosity you are shown can be nothing short of astonishing.

Sometimes etiquette can be baffling. It is customary in Muslim countries for example, to remove the shoes if there is a carpet in the house, and your compliance with this custom will be greatly appreciated.

Handshakes are always exchanged between guests and hosts and, if you can manage it, a greeting in Arabic will go down well. Sometimes a short tour of the house will follow or you will be shown to the bathroom. Conversation over tea and (usually) pastries then follows and, quite some time later and while still seated, you will be invited to carry out the pre-dinner ablution ritual. Water from a kettle is poured over your hands which are held over a basin.

Meals are usually eaten at a knee-high table (which can be excruciatingly uncomfortable for the unaccustomed westerner).

Food is served in common dishes and eaten with the hands, and you should only eat what is placed nearest to you. Stretching is considered very bad form.

The first course usually consists of various 'Moroccan salads' which are more like pickles, relishes and warm, freshly baked bread. A large main course is generally served next, such as a couscous or tajine. You will probably find that all the 'choice' morsels (often little more than gristle or fat among the poorer households) are pushed firmly and persistently towards you. It is considered impolite to decline these, but if you're really stuck, a claim to be vegetarian may alleviate the situation a little, although it should be said in passing that vegetarianism is a completely alien notion to most Moroccans. Meat, including goat or camel, remains a luxury.

Several more courses may appear, so don't feel obliged, as in the west, to finish everything on your plate. Moroccans tend to encourage, even bully, their guests into eating as much at they can and wouldn't dream of sending you home anything less than stuffed. Pacing is the secret. Guests should remember to keep their left hand firmly out of the trough (see the Taboos entry later in this section).

Body contact plays an important role in Moroccan social interaction and friendship is much more physical than westerners are used to. Handshakes, kisses and hugs are all common forms of greeting and Moroccans of the same sex can often be seen walking down the street, or sitting side by side, with hands interlocked. Women in particular shouldn't necessarily feel offended by seemingly intimate contact (unless it is).

Women in Morocco

One of the features of Moroccan society that strikes the traveller most, is the strict segregation of the sexes in public life. Characteristic of most Muslim societies, it finds its origin in the Qur'an: 'Men are in charge of women, because Allah hath made the one of them to excel the other', is an oft-quoted excerpt from the holy book.

Although passages that are equally incriminating can be found in the Bible, the majority of Moroccans (both men and women) would not think of questioning the truth of them. The role of women remains firmly in the home.

Public areas, by contrast, such as the cafes, streets, cinemas and bars, are firmly the domain of men. Any woman seen in these areas (although allowances are obviously made for foreigners) is assumed to be – and probably is – a prostitute.

Considered to be 'women's areas' are the women's public baths, the cemeteries on Fridays and the flat roofs of the medina, where many domestic tasks are carried out. Both sexes greatly respect the respective 'spaces' of the other and tension can arise when the boundaries are crossed. Women travellers can feel extremely uncomfortable in the seedy, male preserve of the bars, for example, and may wish to stick to the hotel bars.

These unwritten social rules do not apply uniformly across the country, however, and Arab and Berber traditions can vary widely. While women of Arab descent are generally discouraged from, say, selling produce in shops and markets, Berber women have no

Souqs

Souqs (markets) are a major feature of Moroccan life and are to be found in every town and village throughout the country.

The souqs originally permitted different tribes to trade products such as meat and milk for oil and grain. They were usually set up on 'neutral' territory, such as tribal borders, because of the very precarious and volatile state of relations between tribes.

Nowadays, souqs still play an essential role in Moroccan society, not only commercially, but administratively and socially. In the theatre of the souq, debts are often settled, conflicts resolved, marriage contracts drawn up and, of course, all the local gossip exchanged. ■

trouble with this. Arab women are, theoretically, not supposed to dance, especially in public. It is not, however, uncommon for Berber women to participate in communal dances with men.

The lot of women is definitely improving in Morocco. For many, the turning point – symbolically at least – came in 1947 on the occasion of the opening of a school in Tangier, when the eldest daughter of King Mohammed V appeared in public without a veil. It was not until the constitution of 1972, however, that women won the right to vote. Twenty years later, during the elections of 1993, for the first time two women were elected to parliament. In the municipal elections of the following year, 77 women candidates were selected.

Despite these advances on the political front, women still remain inferior to men in the eyes of the law. A woman's inheritance, for example, is still half that of a man's.

Nevertheless, women are now entitled to maternity benefits, widow's pension and, in theory at least, equal opportunity in the workplace. Women are entering the workforce in greater numbers (although married women still have to seek their husband's permission) and, for the first time in history, they are beginning to hold important, professional positions such as company directors, doctors, judges and even pilots.

In the last 25 years, the number of working women has risen dramatically, up from a figure of just 8% in 1973 to around 25% today. However, although entitled to equal pay in theory, women in practice earn a salary 15% to 40% less than a man's.

Social conditions over the last years have improved significantly. Polygamy has been on the decrease for some years and the minimum age of marriage has been increased by law to 16 years.

Women in Morocco, like their European neighbours to the North, are choosing to marry later and, outside the very conservative rural areas, there is now more freedom to choose a husband.

New laws have made divorce more difficult, combating at last the vicious situation in which women, often with children but without means to support themselves, could be divorced by their husbands by verbal repudiation. With little chance of finding a new husband – and without training or the opportunity to work – many of the poorer women continue to turn to prostitution.

In the school room, too, there are signs of improvement with increasing numbers of girls receiving education at both primary and secondary levels, although they are still outnumbered by their male counterparts by a ratio of around 1:3.

In 1993, a national survey revealed that 80% of girls in rural areas had never been to school at all. In January 1997, a World Bank report addressed to the Moroccan government singled out the basic education of women and girls in these rural areas as an area in need of urgent reform.

During the 1960s, centres and clubs were set up by the state for women across the country. Their establishment sprang less from altruism, however, and more from the pragmatism of a government anxious to bridle the galloping birth rate. Nevertheless, these centres have been instrumental in teaching women about health, child care, and family planning.

The media has also started to acknowledge the female half of the population and their influence and importance in society. Radio stations now broadcast programmes for women to disseminate knowledge about preventative and curative medicine. These have been particularly useful in rural areas.

Other recently established organisations include needlework workshops for widowed or divorced women, kindergartens, multi-purpose work cooperatives and vocational centres.

On an international level, Morocco has participated in women's conferences, including the UN's Women's Decade conference at Nairobi in 1985, which set out various agendas to be put in action by the year 2000.

At the Los Angeles Olympic Games of 1984, Nawal el-Moutawakil became Morocco's first female gold medallist, for her performance in the 400m hurdles, and has become an idol for African and Moroccan woman alike. At the Ministry of Youth and Sport, a special department now exists with the aim of encouraging women's participation in sport.

Changes are occurring slowly, but it will take several decades for any significant progress to be achieved. For the present, the large majority of women remain in low status, menial jobs and are victims of considerable social prejudices, at least by western standards.

If you want to read more about women in Morocco, see the recommendations in the Books section of the Facts for the Visitor chapter. Among the more famous feminist writers of Morocco is Fatima Mernissi.

If you would like more general information, you can contact the following organisations in Morocco: The *Union Nationale des Femmes Marocaines* (☎ (7) 727937; fax 201029) at 3 Rue Al-Afghani, Quartier des Orangers, Boîte Postale 30, Rabat, or the *Union de l'Action Féminine* (☎/fax (7) 727222) at Appartement Diour Jamaâ, 425 Ave Hassan II, Rabat.

Helping to promote women in business is the: *Association Marocaine pour la Promotion de l'Entreprise Féminine* (☎/fax (2) 989790) at 19 Blvd du 9 Avril, Maarif, Casablanca.

Taboos

Unfortunately, mosques in active use, including some of the most impressive, are off limits to non-Muslims. You may be able to get the odd glimpse through the doors, but don't push it if people make it known that your curiosity is not appreciated. The same applies to most other religious monuments still in use. Cemeteries are also close to being no-go areas and many Muslims don't appreciate westerners taking shortcuts through them.

As much as Moroccans love to talk, there are certain subjects that, if not outright taboo, are best left alone, particularly in group discussion. One of these is the Royal Family.

With the possible exception of the more radical students, Moroccans are incredibly averse to criticising, or even discussing, their Royal Family. Although many may in reality feel anti-monarchist, it's not the done thing to be seen to be so. It may even be foolish and dangerous.

Photos and posters of the Royal Family are displayed, almost big-brother-like, in every public space and place, as is the striking, red Moroccan flag.

Many Moroccans feel genuinely patriotic and, with the King's claim to direct descent from the Prophet, criticism of him could be regarded as blasphemous. This may well explain the Moroccans' reluctance to discuss their royals.

Other taboo subjects include Islam and

Body Language

One of the most common sounds you will probably hear coming from the mouths of Moroccans will be a hiss. This is an all-purpose noise that can easily get on a newcomer's nerves. It is perhaps most commonly used by people riding bicycles or pushing carts to warn people to move out of the way; you will also often here the word *ba'alak!*, which means the same thing.

A hiss can also simply be a means of getting your attention. Sometimes there is little doubt that it is the equivalent of the wolf whistle.

When well-acquainted people meet on the street, they will often shake hands and then fleetingly kiss the back of their fingers. It is not recommended you try this one out for yourself, as it requires a depth of acquaintance travellers are unlikely to build up with locals.

If someone draws a finger up and down their chin while trying to explain something to you, they are almost certainly telling you something about Berbers (nine times out of 10 it'll be some fellow telling you there is a Berber market on today, and that this is the only chance you'll have to see it – a tale not to be believed). ■

the Prophet, Israel and Palestine, the issue of the Western Sahara (see the History section earlier in this chapter) and the topic of sex and sexual etiquette (although you may find that Moroccans of the same gender will quiz you in private and with great relish about this).

The left hand in Muslim societies is also taboo as it is used for personal hygiene after visiting the toilet. It should not be used to eat with or to touch any common source of food or water, nor to hand over money or presents or for unnecessary contact with others, such as patting children on the head.

Avoiding Offence

As a rule, a high degree of modesty is demanded of both sexes in dress as well as behaviour. None of the rules is adhered to uniformly and, in the bigger cities, especially Casablanca, the veil and the *hijab* (head covering) are more the exception than the rule. Nevertheless, for the outsider it pays to err on the side of modesty, particularly in the more conservative countryside.

Women, in particular, are well advised to keep their shoulders and upper arms covered and to opt for long trousers or skirts. Stricter Muslims consider excessive display of flesh, whether male or female, offensive.

Women who disregard such considerations risk arousing the ire of the genuinely offended and attracting unwanted attention (see the Women Travellers entry in the Facts for the Visitor chapter). Obviously a little common sense goes a long way. You can get away with a lot more on the beaches of Agadir than in a Berber village in the Atlas Mountains.

Public displays of affection, although very common among friends of the same sex, is much frowned upon between couples, even married ones.

RELIGION
Islam

'Allahu akbar, Allahu akbar ... Ashhadu an la Ilah ila Allah ... Ashhadu an Mohammedan rasul Allah ... Haya ala as-sala ... Haya ala as-sala...'.

Of all the sounds that assault the ears of the first time visitor to Morocco, it is possibly that of the call to prayer that leaves the most indelible impression. Five times a day, Muslims are called, if not to enter a mosque to pray, at least to take the time to pray where they are. The midday prayers on Friday, when the imam of the mosque delivers his weekly sermon, or khutba, are considered the most important.

Islam shares its roots with the great monotheistic faiths that sprang from the harsh land of the Middle East – Judaism and Christianity – but is considerably younger than the former two.

The holy book of Islam is the Qur'an. Its pages carry many references to the earlier prophets of both the older religions – Adam, Abraham (Ibrahim), Noah, Moses and others – but there the similarities begin to end. Jesus is seen merely as another in a long line of prophets that ends definitively with Mohammed.

What makes Mohammed different from the rest is that the Qur'an, unlike either the Torah of the Jews or the Christian Gospels, is the word of God, directly communicated to Mohammed in a series of revelations.

For Muslims, Islam can only be the apogee of the monotheistic faiths from which it derives so much. Muslims traditionally attribute a place of great respect to Christians and Jews as *ahl al-kitab*, the People of the Book. However, the more strident will claim Christianity was a new and improved version of the teachings of the Torah and Islam was the next logical step and therefore 'superior'. Do not be surprised if you occasionally run into someone wanting you to convert!

Mohammed was born into one of the trading families of the Arabian city of Mecca (in present-day Saudi Arabia) in 570 AD. He began to receive revelations in 610 AD and, after a time, started imparting the content of Allah's message to the Meccans. The essence was a call to submit to God's will (the word 'islam' means submission), but not all Meccans thought a much of it.

Mohammed gathered quite a following

in his campaign against Meccan idolaters, but the powerful families of the city became so angry with him that he felt forced to flee to Medina (Islam's second most holy city, also in Saudi Arabia) in 622. Mohammed's flight from Mecca or *hijra* (migration) marks the beginning of the Muslim calendar.

In Medina he continued to preach and increased his power base. Soon he and his supporters began to clash with the Meccans, led by powerful elements of the Quraysh tribe, possibly over trade routes.

By 632, Mohammed had been able to revisit Mecca and many of the tribes in the surrounding area had sworn allegiance to him and the new faith. Mecca became the symbolic centre of the faith, containing as it did the Ka'aba, which housed the black stone supposedly given to Abraham by the archangel Gabriel. Mohammed determined that Muslims should face Mecca when praying outside the city.

Upon his death in 632, the Arabs exploded into the Syrian desert, quickly conquering all of what makes up modern Syria, Iraq, Lebanon, Israel and Palestine. This was accomplished under the caliphs (successors), or Companions of Mohammed, of whom there were four. They in turn were succeeded by the Umayyad (661-750) dynasty in Damascus and then the Abbassid line (749-1258) in the newly built city of Baghdad.

Islam quickly spread west, first taking in Egypt and then fanning out across North Africa. By the end of the 7th century, the Muslims had reached the Atlantic and thought themselves sufficiently in control of the Gezirat al-Maghreb ('the Island of the West', or North Africa beyond Egypt) to consider marching on Spain in 710.

Islam is now the religion of about 99% of Moroccans. In order to live a devout life, the Muslim is expected to carry out at least the Five Pillars of Islam:

shahada – This is the profession of faith, the basic tenet of the Muslim faith. 'There is no God but Allah, and Mohammed is His Prophet.' It is a phrase commonly heard as part of the call to prayer and at many other events, such as births and deaths. The first half of the sentence has virtually become an exclamation – useful for any time of life or situation. People can often be heard muttering it to themselves, as if seeking a little strength to get through the trials of the day.

sala – Sometimes written 'salat', this is the obligation of prayer, done ideally five times a day, when muezzins call the faithful to pray. Although Muslims can pray anywhere, it is considered more laudable to pray together in a mosque (masjid or jami'). The important midday prayers are on Friday (the loose equivalent of Sunday Mass for Catholics) and are held in a special kind of mosque, the *jami'*.

zakat – Alms-giving to the poor was, from the start, an essential part of the social teaching of Islam. It was later developed in some parts of the Muslim world into various forms of tax to redistribute funds to the needy. The moral obligation towards one's poorer neighbours continues to be emphasised at a personal level, and exhortations to give are often posted up outside mosques.

sawm – Ramadan, the ninth month of the Muslim calendar, commemorates the revelation of the Qur'an to Mohammed. In a demonstration of the Muslims' renewal of faith, they are asked to abstain from sex and from letting anything pass their lips from dawn to dusk every day of the month. This includes smoking. For more on the month of fasting (Ramadan), see the Holidays entry in the Facts for the Visitor chapter.

haj – The pinnacle of a devout Muslim's life is the pilgrimage to the holy sites in and around Mecca. Ideally, the pilgrim should go to Mecca in the last month of the year, Zuul-Hijja, and join Muslims from all over the world in the pilgrimage and the subsequent feast. The returned pilgrim can be addressed as *Haj* and, in simpler villages at least, it is still quite common to see the word *Al-Haj* and simple scenes painted on the walls of houses showing that its inhabitants have made the pilgrimage.

Sunnis & Shiites The power struggle between Ali, Mohammed's son-in-law and the last of the four caliphs of Mohammed, and the emerging Umayyad dynasty in Damascus, caused a great schism at the heart of the new religion.

The succession to the caliphate had been marked by considerable intrigue and bloodshed. Ali, the father of Mohammed's male

Islam & The West

Ignorance abounds in the west about the nature of Islam and Muslims, who are associated all too readily with a fearful image of unpredictable, gun-toting, unreasonable terrorists. Ever since the Crusades, this sort of image has tended to stick in the western subconscious, and has been fuelled by the intractable conflict in the Middle East between Israel and its Arab neighbours and the determined campaign of demonisation of Arab leaders who are considered a menace to western interests.

Many Muslims point to conflicts in the heart of the west, such as the horrors perpetrated in Northern Ireland, and ask whether they make everyone living in Ireland and the UK bloodthirsty extremists.

It also has to be said that, although perhaps more familiar with western ways than westerners are with Arab ways, people in the Arab world, Muslims or otherwise, sometimes have a startlingly contorted picture of the west and what makes it tick.

A combination of grudging respect for, and envy of, its wealth and technological advantages and occasionally a disdain for its perceived moral decadence colour the way many Muslims, including Moroccans, deal with westerners. The soap operatic drivel of western TV does little to help.

For all this, visitors to Morocco find that – hustlers, hasslers and touts aside – the reality could not be further from the truth. That a gulf separates east and west in terms of mentality and world view few would dispute, but the warmth accorded to outsiders by the average Moroccan belies any stereotypes of the typical Muslim. After all, Islam demands of its faithful a sense of community and hospitality to strangers.

Much is made of religious fundamentalism in Muslim countries, but it should be considered in the light of the role that religion plays in these countries. Islam is not just a religion that can be separated from daily life and government, as is now the case with the Christian churches in the west. Islam is, for want of a better word, more holistic in that it provides a framework for both secular and spiritual life. Calls for an Islamic state therefore do not sound as strange to Muslims as they do to westerners.

Having said that, it is probably fair to observe that the majority of ordinary Muslims do not favour such a development, and that the popular following of fundamentalist groups is not as great as some imagine. Much of the success they do have is less a result of religious fervour than a reflection of the frustrated hopes of many classes in countries grappling with severe economic difficulties.

Morocco is not exempt from this, although neither the social stresses nor the fundamentalist movements are as great an issue as in, say, neighbouring Algeria. ■

heirs, lost his struggle and the Umayyad leader was recognised as the legitimate successor to the caliphate. Those who favoured the Umayyad caliph became known as the Sunnis. They are the majority of Muslims and are considered the orthodox mainstream of Islam.

The Shiites, on the other hand, recognise only the successors of Ali. Most of the Shiites are known as Twelvers, because they believe in 12 *imams* (religious leaders), the last of whom has been lost from sight, but who will appear some day to create an empire of the true faith. The rest are called the Seveners because they believe that seven imams will succeed Ali.

The Sunnis have divided into four schools of religious thought, each lending more or less importance to various aspects of doctrine. In Morocco, where the population is virtually entirely Sunni, it is the Maliki school that predominates. The Malikis, along with the Hanafi school, are somewhat less rigid in their application and interpretation of the Qur'an than the other schools. An illustration of this emerged by the 15th century, when *qadis* (community judges) were recorded as having applied *shari'a*

(Qur'anic law) in accordance with local custom rather than to the letter.

Saints & Mysticism Morocco is not alone in the Muslim world in hosting a strongly mystical offshoot of Islam, but perhaps is so in the weight this carries with a large part of the population.

From an early point in the life of Islam, certain practitioners sought to move closer to God through individual effort and spiritual devotion, rather than simply living by God's laws. These people came to be known as Sufis (from *suf*, meaning wool and referring to the simple woollen cord they tended to wear as a belt for their garments). Various orders of Sufis emerged throughout the lands where Islam held sway, and this was as true of Morocco as of anywhere else.

Orthodox Muslims regarded (and still regard) such groups with suspicion, particularly as the orders tend to gather in the name of a holy man (or *wali*, which has come to be loosely translated as 'saint', although saints in the Christian sense play no role in Islam). Public gatherings take many forms, from the dances of the 'whirling dervishes' to more ecstatic and extreme demonstrations of self-mutilation (where participants may, for instance, push skewers into their cheeks without feeling any pain).

The orders generally gather at the mosque or tomb of their 'saint' and follow a particular *tariqa* (path), or way of worshipping. Various orders acquired permanence over the centuries. 'Membership' might run through generations of the same families, who trace their lineage back to the original saint or spiritual master and through him to the Prophet; the veracity of such links is of secondary importance.

This mystic tendency found particularly fertile ground in the traditions and superstitions of the Berbers. There is little doubt that the cults that prosper in Morocco do so mostly in rural Berber areas. The focal point of gatherings of such groups is generally a *zawiyya*, which could be a small meeting place or a big complex grouping mosque,

school and hostels around the tomb of the saint, or marabout. Marabout, from the Arabic *muraabit*, is a word used more by French scholars than the locals and has come to designate the saint *and* the tomb.

For orthodox Muslims, veneration of a saint is tantamount to worship of an idol, although Sufis would not see it that way. According to them, the wali is a 'friend' (the more literal meaning of wali) of God and so an intermediary, and marabouts are regarded in a similar fashion. The great *moussems* (pilgrimages) to the tombs of such saints are as much a celebration of the triumph of the spirit as an act of worship of a particular saint.

Possibly the best known of these saints in Morocco is Moulay Idriss, whose tomb stands in the town of the same name outside Meknès. He died in 791 and is one of a number of equally venerated figures across the Muslim world, who include Ahmed al-Badawi in Tanta (Egypt) and Abdal Qadir in Baghdad.

In Morocco as elsewhere, such cults and their individualistic approach to Islam were considered by the mainly city-dwelling orthodox Muslims as deviant and by their leaders as politically dangerous.

And so, armed with imprecations against heresy, various attempts have been made to put an end to the phenomenon in Morocco, starting with the Almoravids. In more recent times, concerted efforts were made again in the 1930s, but there are two obstacles to such campaigns: the territory of the rural Berbers is difficult to control, and the people who follow the cults make up a big chunk of the total populace – you cannot simply get rid of them all!

Islamic Customs When a baby is born, the first words uttered to it are the call to prayer. A week later this is followed by a ceremony in which the baby's head is shaved and an animal is sacrificed.

The major event of a boy's childhood is circumcision, which normally takes place sometime between the ages of seven and 12.

Marriage ceremonies are colourful and

noisy affairs which usually take place in summer. One of the customs is for all the males to get in their cars and drive around the streets in a convoy making as much noise as possible. The ceremony usually takes place in either the mosque or the home of the bride or groom. After that, the partying goes on until the early hours of the morning, often until sunrise.

The death ceremony is simple: a burial service is held at the mosque and the body is then buried with the feet facing Mecca.

When Muslims pray, they must follow certain rituals. First they must wash their hands, arms, feet, head and neck in running water before praying; all mosques have an area set aside for this purpose. If they are not in a mosque and there is no water available, clean sand suffices; where there is no sand, they must just go through the motions of washing.

They must always face towards Mecca – all mosques are oriented so that the *mihrab* (prayer niche) faces the correct direction – and follow a set pattern of gestures and genuflections. Photos of rows of Muslims kneeling in the direction of Mecca with their heads touching the ground are legion. You regularly see Muslims praying by the side of the road or in the street, as well as in mosques.

In everyday life, Muslims are prohibited from drinking alcohol and eating pork, which is considered unclean, and must refrain from gambling, fraud, usury, and slander.

Christianity

There are precious few Moroccan Christians and the existence of the odd church is due more to the presence of Europeans over the centuries than local need. Nevertheless, there is evidence that Christianity made some inroads in North Africa during the period of Roman rule. How far it went beyond the Roman or Romanised population and upper classes is a matter of debate, although it appears that some Berber tribes turned, for a time at least, to the imported faith.

For whatever reason, the departure of the Romans and later of the Byzantines was followed by the virtual disappearance of Christianity from North Africa.

LANGUAGE

The official language in Morocco is Arabic, although French, the legacy of the protectorate, is still widely used in the cities (much less so among rural Berbers) and remains surprisingly important in education, business and the press. Morocco's close ties to France also help to explain the continued importance of French.

There are three main Berber dialects in use, mainly in the Rif and Atlas Mountains. Modern means of communication have left only a minority of Berbers monolingual – most speak at least some Arabic.

To a lesser extent than French, Spanish has maintained some hold in northern parts of the country, where Spain exercised administrative control until 1956. You may also come across it in the territory of the former Spanish Sahara, over which Madrid relinquished control in 1975, and the former enclave of Sidi Ifni. In towns like Tetouan, for instance, Spanish is more likely to be understood than French and a little knowledge of it can be a great asset.

In the main cities and towns you will find plenty of people, many of them touts you may not necessarily want to hang around with, who speak a variety of other languages, including English, German and Italian.

Arabic

Moroccan Arabic *(darija)* is a dialect of the standard language, but is so different in many respects as to be virtually like another tongue. It is everyday language that differs most from that of other Arabic-speaking peoples. More specialised or educated language tends to be much the same across the Arab world, although pronunciation varies considerably. An Arab from Jordan or Iraq will have little trouble discussing politics or literature with an educated Moroccan, but might have more trouble ordering lunch.

The influence of French is seen in some

of the words that Moroccan Arabic has taken on. An example is the use of the French word for 'coach' (intercity bus), *car*.

The spread of radio and TV has increased Moroccans' exposure to and understanding of what is commonly known as Modern Standard Arabic (MSA). MSA, which has grown from the classical language of the Qur'an and poetry, is the written and spoken lingua franca of the Arab world, and in fact not so far removed from the daily language of the Arab countries of the Levant. It is the language of radio and TV presenters and the press, and also of the great majority of modern Arabic literature.

Foreign students of the language constantly face the dilemma of whether first to learn MSA (which could mean waiting some time before being able to talk with shopkeepers) and then a chosen dialect, or simply to acquire spoken competence in the latter.

Dialects supposedly have no written form (the argument goes it would be like writing in Cockney or Strine), although there is no reason why they could not avail themselves of the same script used for the standard language. If this leaves you with a headache, you will have some idea of why so few non-Arabs or non-Muslims embark on the study of this complex tongue.

If you do take the time to learn even a few words and phrases, you will discover and experience much more while travelling through the country. Just making the attempt implies a respect for local culture that Moroccans all too infrequently sense in visitors to their country.

Pronunciation Pronunciation of Arabic can be tongue-tying for someone unfamiliar with the intonation and combination of sounds. Pronounce the transliterated words and phrases slowly and clearly.

The following guide should help, but it is not complete because the rules governing pronunciation and vowel use are too extensive to be covered here.

For a more comprehensive guide to the Arabic spoken in the Maghreb, get hold of

Lonely Planet's *Moroccan Arabic Phrasebook*, by Dan Bacon with Abdennabi Benchehda & Bichr Andjar.

Vowels In spoken Moroccan Arabic, there are at least five basic vowel sounds that can be distinguished:

a like the 'a' in 'had' (sometimes very short)
e like the 'e' in 'bet' (sometimes very short)
i like the 'i' in 'hit'
o like the 'o' in 'hot'
u like the 'oo' in 'book'

The **ā** symbol over a vowel gives it a long sound.

ā like the 'a' in 'father'
ē like the 'e' in 'ten', but lengthened
ī like the 'e' in 'ear', only softer, often written as 'ee'
ō like the 'o' in 'for'
ū like the 'oo' in 'food'

Long vowels are also informally transliterated as double vowels, eg 'aa' (**ā**), 'ee' (**ī**), 'oo' (**ū**).

Combinations (Diphthongs) Certain combinations of vowels with vowels or consonants form other vowel sounds (diphthongs):

aw like the 'ow' in 'how'
ai like the 'i' in 'high'
ei ay like the 'a' in 'cake'

These last two are tricky, as one can slide into the other in certain words, depending on who is pronouncing them.

Consonants Most of the consonants used in this section are the same as in English. However, a few of the consonant sounds must be explained in greater detail.

Three of the most common are the glottal stop ('), the 'ayn' sound ('), and the 'rayn' (**gh**). These are two of the most difficult sounds in Arabic, so don't be discouraged if you aren't understood at first, just keep trying. Both can be produced by tightening your throat and sort of growling, but the (**'gh'**) requires a slight **'r'** sound at the beginning – it is like the French 'r'.

When the (**'**) comes before a vowel, the vowel is 'growled' from the back of the throat. If it is before a consonant or at the end of a word, it sounds like a glottal stop. The best way to learn these sounds is to listen to a native speaker pronounce their written equivalents.

The glottal stop is the sound you hear between the vowels in the expression 'oh oh!', or the Cockney pronunciation of 'water' (wa'er). It is caused by a closing of the glottis at the back of the throat so that the passage of air is momentarily halted. It can occur anywhere in the word – at the beginning, middle or end.

Other common consonant sounds include:

j   more or less like the 'j' in 'John'

g   for those who read some Arabic, it is worth noting that the Moroccans have added a letter for the hard 'g' (as in Agadir) – a kaf (letter'k') with three dots above it

H   a strongly whispered 'h', almost like a sigh of relief

q   a strong guttural 'k' sound. Often transcribed as 'k', although there is another letter in the Arabic alphabet which *is* the equivalent of 'k'

kh a slightly gurgling sound, like the 'ch' in Scottish 'loch'

r   a rolled 'r', as in the Spanish 'para'

s   pronounced as in English 'sit', never as in 'wisdom'

sh like the 'sh' in 'shelf'

ẑ   like the 's' in pleasure

Double Consonants In Arabic, double consonants are both pronounced; for example the word *istanna*, which means 'wait', is pronounced 'istan-na'.

Transliteration What you read and hear

will as often as not be two or three entirely different things. Even after many attempts there is still no satisfactory system of transcribing the 'squiggles' of Arabic into Latin script.

Some semblance of standard 'rules' have been loosely agreed upon, but one big problem remains who has made the running. Where Anglo-Saxons have had the most influence, a transliteration system reflecting English phonemics has emerged, but where France held sway, and this means particularly in the Maghreb, Lebanon and Syria, quite another way of rendering Arabic emerged.

In addition, the same word may be written in Latin script in all manner of ways, depending on, say, a sign-writer's own feelings about how the Arabic should appear in 'European'. The high rate of illiteracy among Moroccans does not help. Reliable standardisation is therefore an elusive goal. Names of hotels, restaurants and the like spelled in this guide as they appear, however bizarre the variations.

Since most modern maps, books and the like dealing with Morocco tend to reflect French usage, this guide generally goes along with it.

There is only one word for 'the' in Arabic – *al* (before certain consonants, it modifies). In Arabic, Saladin's name is Salah ad-Din – 'righteousness of the faith'. Here, *al* has been modified to 'ad' before the 'd' of Din), but in Morocco *el* is more commonly used. In Moroccan Arabic, the pronunciation is such that the initial **a** or **e** is hardly heard at all, and many language guides simply prefix words with **l** to indicate this.

The letters **'q'** and **'k'** have long been a problem, and have been interchanged willy-nilly in transliteration. For a long time, Iraq (which in Arabic is spelled with what can only be described as its nearest equivalent to the English 'q') was written, even by scholars, *Irak*. Another example of an Arabic 'q' receiving this kind of treatment is the word for market, *souq* (often written as 'souk').

The word for castle or palace, *qasr*, is another example. In fact, the most common transliteration for it in Morocco is *ksar*, reflecting local pronunciation. The plural *qusour* is usually given as *ksour*.

It may be useful, especially to travellers who have been elsewhere in the Arab world and become accustomed to certain transliterations, to consult the following list of common sounds and words and their 'standardised' equivalents:

ou as in oued; it is the French equivalent of **w** in wadi (a usually dry, seasonal river bed). You may see references to the Alaouites (the dynasty of Hassan II) or, alternatively, to the Alawites. The name Daoud can also be written Dawud.

dj as in djebel; it is the French equivalent of simple **j** in jebel – mountain.

k often corresponds to the Arabic letter qaf, or the English **q**. Ksar versus qasr (castle) is an example.

e often appears where some would prefer to see an **a**. Vowels in Arabic are not as important as in other languages. Vowel and consonant order are sometimes at variance. The common word for school, hich also refers to older religious learning institutions, is madrassa, which most commonly appears as medersa.

Speaking Arabic When Arabic speakers meet, they often exchange more extensive and formalised greetings than westerners are used to. How and when they are used varies from country to country, time to time and depends often on the social status of the people concerned. Even an attempt to use a couple of them (whether correctly or not) will not go astray.

As in all the Arabic vocabulary in this section, some expressions tend to be more standard than Moroccan Arabic, but will be understood and often used. Occasionally both MSA and Moroccan versions are given. (The Moroccan version is followed by (M).)

When addressing a man or woman, the polite terms more or less equivalent to Mr and Mrs or Ms are *Si* or *Sidi* and *Lalla*, followed by the first name. You may be addressed as 'Mr John' or 'Mrs Anne'. A few basic greetings follow:

Greetings & Civilities

Hello. (literally, 'peace upon you')	*as-salaam 'alaykum*
Hello. (in response – 'and upon you be peace')	*wa 'alaykum as-salaam*
Goodbye. ('go in safety')	*ma' as-salaama*
Good morning.	*sabaH al-khēr*
Good morning. (in response)	*sabaH an-nūr*
Good evening.	*masa' al-khēr*
Good evening. (in response)	*masa' an-nūr*
Please. (to m/f/pl)	*'afak/'afik/'afakum*
Thank you (very much).	*shukran (jazilan)*
You're welcome.	*la shukran 'ala wajib*
Yes.	*eeyeh/na'am*
Yes, OK.	*wakha* (M)
No.	*la*
No, thank you.	*la, shukran*
Excuse me.	*smeH leeya*
How are you?	*kayf Haalek? la bas?* (M)
Fine, thank you.	*la bas, barak Allah feek* (M)
Fine, thanks be to God.	*bikhēr, al-Hamdu lillah*

Basics Here are some nuts and bolts to get you through the simple encounters:

I	*ana*
you (m/f/pl)	*inta/inti/intum*
he/she	*huwa/heeya*
we	*eHna*
they	*huma*
Why?	*laysh?*
now	*allaan/daba* (M)
Is there ...?	*wash kayn ...?* (M)

big/small	*kabeer/sagheer*	bus	*al-otobīs*
open	*meHlool*	intercity bus	*al-kar*
Do you speak (English)?	*tatakallem (ingleezee)?*	train	*al-qitar al-masheena* (M)
	wash kt'aref ngleezeeya? (M)	boat	*as-safeena al-baboor* (M)
Who is that?	*meen hadha?*	Where is (the) ...?	*fein ...?*
	shkoon had? (M)	bus station for ...	*maHattat al-otobīs li ...*
I understand.	*fhemt*		
I don't understand.	*ma fhemtesh*	train station	*maHattat al-masheena/ al-qitar*
Go ahead/move it/ come on!	*zid!* (M)	ticket office	*maktab al-werqa/ at-tazkara*

Emergencies

Call the police!	*'eyyet al-bolis!*	street	*az-zanqa*
Call a doctor!	*'eyyet at-tabeeb!*	city	*al-medīna*
Help me please!	*'awenee 'afak!*	village	*al-qarya*
Thief!	*sheffar!*	bus stop	*mawqif al-otobīs*
They robbed me!	*sheffaroonee!*	station	*al-maHatta*
		Which bus goes to ...?	*ey kar yamshee ila ...?*

Small Talk

What's your name?	*asmeetak?*	Does this bus go to ...?	*yamshee had al-kar ila ...?*
My name is ...	*ismee ...*		
	smeetee ... (M)	How many buses per day go to ...?	*fi/kayn kam kar kul yūm ila ...?*
How old are you?	*shaHak fi 'amrak?*		
I'm 25.	*'aandee khamsa wa ashreen*	Please tell me when we arrive in ...	*qulnee emta nassil ...*
Where are you from?	*min een inta/inti/ intum?(m/f/pl)*	Stop here.	*qif hena, 'afak*
I/We are from ...	*ana/eHna min ...*	Please wait for me	*intazarnee 'afak*
America	*amreeka*	May I/we sit here?	*(wash) yimkin ajlis/najlis hena?*
Australia	*ustralya*		
Canada	*kanada*	Where can I rent a bicycle?	*fein yimkin ana akra beshkleeta?*
England	*inglaterra*		
France	*fransa*	address	*'anwān*
Germany	*almanya*	air-conditioning	*kleemateezaseeyon*
Italy	*itaaliyya*	airport	*matār*
Japan	*al-yaban*	camel	*jamal*
The Netherlands	*holanda*	car	*tomobeel, sayara*
Spain	*isbanya*	daily	*kull yūm*
Sweden	*as-sweed*	donkey	*Humār*
Switzerland	*sweesra*	horse	*Husān*
		number	*raqm*
		ticket	*werqa/tazkara*
		Wait!	*tsanna!*

Getting Around

I want to go to ...	*ureed/bgheet amshee ila ...*	
What is the fare to ...?	*bshaHal at-tazkara ila ...?*	
When does the ... ... leave/arrive?	*emta qiyam/wus uul .?*	

Directions

How far is ...?	*kam kilo li ...?*	
left/right	*yasar/yameen leeser/leemen* (M)	

here/there	*huna/hunak*
next to	*bi-janib*
opposite	*muqabbal*
behind	*khalf/mor* (M)
Which?	*ash men?*
Where?	*fein?*
north	*shamal*
south	*janoob*
east	*sharq*
west	*gharb*

Around Town

Where is (the) ...?	*fein ...?*
bank	*al-banka*
barber	*al-Hallaq*
beach	*ash-shaatta' al-plāẑ* (M)
embassy	*as-sifāra*
market	*as-sūq*
mosque	*al-jāmi'*
museum	*al-matHaf*
old city	*al-medīna*
palace	*al-qasr*
pharmacy	*farmasyan*
police station	*al-bolīs*
post office	*al-bōsta/maktab al-barīd*
restaurant	*al-mat'am*
university	*al-jami'a*
zoo	*Hadīqat al-Haywān*

I want to change ...	*ureed/bgheet asrif ...*
money	*fulūs*
US$	*dolār amreekānī*
UK	*jinay sterlīnī*
A$	*dolār ustrālī*
DM	*mārk almānī*
travellers cheques	*shīkāt siyaHiyya*

Accommodation

Where is the hotel?	*fein (kayn) al-otēl?*
Can I see the room?	*(wash) yimkin lee nshūf al-bayt?*
How much is this room per night?	*bshaHal al-bayt lilayl?*
Do you have any cheaper rooms?	*wash kayn bayt rakhees 'ala had?*
That's too expensive.	*ghaalee bazyaf*

This is fine.	*had mezyan*
bed	*namooseeya*
blanket	*bataneeya*
camp site	*mukhaym*
full	*'amer*
hot water	*ma skhūn*
key	*saroot*
roof	*staah*
room	*bayt*
sheet	*eezar*
shower	*doosh*
toilet	*bayt al-ma, mirHad*
youth hostel	*oberẑ, dar shabbab*

Shopping

Where can I buy ...?	*fein yimkin as ashteree ...?*
How much?	*bi-kam? bish-hal?* (M)
Too much.	*ghalee*
Do you have ...?	*wash 'andkum ...?*
stamps	*tawaaba tanber* (M)
newspaper	*al-jarida*

Time

When?	*emta?*
today	*al-yūm*
tomorrow	*ghaddan*
yesterday	*al-bareh*
morning	*fis-sabaH*
afternoon	*fish-sheeya*
evening	*masa'*
day/night	*nahar/layl*
week/month/year	*usbu'/shahr/'am*
What is the time?	*sa'a kam?* *shahal fessa'a?* (M)
At what time?	*fi sa'a kam?* *fooqtash?* (M)
after	*min ba'd*
on time	*fil-waqt*
early	*bakrī*
late	*mu'attal*
quickly	*dgheeya*
slowly	*bishwayya*

Days of the Week

Monday	*(nhar) al-itnēn*
Tuesday	*(nhar) at-talata*
Wednesday	*(nhar) al-arba'*

Thursday	*(nhar) al-khamīs*
Friday	*(nhar) al-juma'*
Saturday	*(nhar) as-sabt*
Sunday	*(nhar) al-ahad*

Months of the Year The Islamic year has 12 lunar months and is 11 days shorter than the Gregorian calendar, so important Muslim dates fall about 10 days earlier each (western) year. It is impossible to predict exactly when they will fall, as this depends on when the new moon is sighted.

The Islamic, or Hijra (referring to the year of Mohammed's flight from Mecca in 622 AD), calendar months are:

first	*Moharram*
second	*Safar*
third	*Rabi' al-Awal*
fourth	*Rabi' al-Akhir* or *Rabi' at-Tani*
fifth	*Jumada al-Awal*
sixth	*Jumada al-Akhir* or *Jumada at-Taniyya*
seventh	*Rajab*
eighth	*Sha'aban*
ninth	*Ramadan*
tenth	*Shawwal*
eleventh	*Zuul Qe'da*
twelfth	*Zuul Hijja*

In the Levant, as well as the Hijra calendar, there's another set of names for the Gregorian calendar.

Luckily, in Morocco, the names of the months are virtually the same as in English and are easily recognisable:

January	*yanāyir*
February	*fibrāyir*
March	*maaris*
April	*abrīl*
May	*māyu*
June	*yunyu*
July	*yulyu*
August	*aghustus/ghusht*
September	*sibtimbir/shebtenber*
October	*uktoobir*
November	*nufimbir/nu'enbir*
December	*disimbir/dijenbir*

Arabic Numbers Arabic numerals are simple enough to learn and, unlike the written language, run from left to right across the page.

An added bonus is that you won't need to recognise the Arabic numerals, as the European ones are commonly used in Morocco.

0	*sifr*
1	*wāHid*
2	*itneen/jooj* (M)
3	*talata*
4	*arba'a*
5	*khamsa*
6	*sitta*
7	*saba'a*
8	*tamanya*
9	*tissa'*
10	*'ashara*
11	*wāHidash*
12	*itna'ash*
13	*talattash*
14	*arba'atash*
15	*khamastash*
16	*sitt'ash*
17	*saba'atash*
18	*tamantash*
19	*tissa'atash*
20	*'ashreen*
21	*wāHid wa 'ashreen*
22	*itneen wa 'ashreen*
30	*talateen*
40	*arba'een*
50	*khamseen*
60	*sitteen*
70	*saba'een*
80	*tamaneen*
90	*tissa'een*
100	*miyya*
101	*miyya wa wāHid*
125	*miyya wa khamsa wa 'ashreen*
200	*miyyateen*
300	*talata mia*
400	*arba'a mia*
1000	*alf*
2000	*alfeen*
3000	*talat alāf*
4000	*arba'at alāf*

Ordinal Numbers

first	'awwal
second	tānī
third	tālit
fourth	rābi'
fifth	khāmis

French

The most commonly spoken European language in Morocco is French, so if the thought of getting your tongue around Arabic is too much, it would be a good investment to learn some French.

An inability on the part of westerners to speak French is seen by some French-speaking (and therefore at least bilingual) Moroccans as the height of ignorance.

The following words and phrases should help you communicate on a basic level in French:

Greetings & Civilities

Hello	Bonjour.
Good morning Good day.	
Goodbye.	Au revoir/Salut.
Good evening.	Bonsoir.
(Have a) good evening.	Bonne soirée.
Good night.	Bonne nuit.
Please.	S'il vous plaît.
Thank you.	Merci.
You're welcome.	De rien/Je vous en prie.
Yes.	Oui.
No.	Non.
No, thank you.	Non, merci.
Excuse me.	Excusez-moi/Pardon.
How are you?	Comment allez-vous/Ça va?
Well, thanks.	Bien, merci.

Basics

I	je
you	vous
he/she	il/elle
we	nous
they	ils/elles (m/f)
Why?	Pourquoi?
now	maintenant

Is/Are there ...?	(Est-ce qu')il y a ...?
big/small	grand/petit
open/closed	ouvert/fermé
Do you speak English?	Parlez-vous anglais?
Who is that?	C'est qui, celui-là/celle-là? (m/f)
I understand.	Je comprends.
I don't understand.	Je ne comprends pas.

Emergencies

Call the police!	Appelez la police!
Call a doctor!	Appelez un médecin!
Help me please!	Au secours/Aidez-moi!
Thief!	(Au) voleur!

Small Talk

What's your name?	Comment vous appelez-vous?
My name is ...	Je m'appelle ...
How old are you?	Quel âge avez-vous?
I'm 25.	J'ai vingt-cinq ans.
Where are you from?	D'où êtes-vous?
I/We are from ...	Je viens/Nous venons ...
America	de l'Amérique
Australia	de l'Australie
Canada	du Canada
England	de l'Angleterre
Germany	de l'Allemagne
Italy	de l'Italie
Japan	du Japon
The Netherlands	des Pays Bas
Spain	de l'Espagne
Sweden	du Suède
Switzerland	de la Suisse

Getting Around

I want to go to ...	Je veux aller à ...
What is the fare to ...?	Combien coûte le billet pour ...?
When does the ... leave/arrive?	À quelle heure part/arrive ...?
bus	l'autobus
intercity bus/coach	le car
train	le train
boat	le bateau

ferry	*le bac*
Where is the ...?	*Où est ...?*
bus station for ...	*la gare routière pour ...*
train station	*la gare*
ticket office	*la billeterie/le guichet*
street	*la rue*
city	*la ville*
village	*le village*
bus stop	*l'arrêt d'autobus*
Which bus goes to ...?	*Quel autobus/car part pour ...?*
Does this bus go to ...?	*Ce car-là va-t-il à ...?*
How many buses per day go to ...?	*Il y a combien de cars chaque jour pour ...?*
Please tell me when we arrive in ...	*Dîtes-moi s'il vous plaît à quelle heure on arrive ...*
Stop here, please.	*Arrêtez ici, s'il vous plaît.*
Please wait for me.	*Attendez-moi ici, s'il vous plaît.*
May I sit here?	*Puis-je m'asseoir ici?*
Where can I rent a bicycle?	*Où est-ce que je peux louer une bicyclette?*
address	*adresse*
air-conditioning	*climatisation*
airport	*aéroport*
camel	*chameau*
car	*voiture*
crowded	*beaucoup de monde*
daily	*chaque jour*
donkey	*âne*
horse	*cheval*
number	*numéro*
ticket	*billet*
Wait!	*Attendez!*

Directions

How far is ...?	*À combien de kilomètres est ...?*
left/right	*gauche/droite*
here/there	*ici/là*
next to	*à côté de*
opposite	*en face*

behind	*derrière*
Which?	*Quel?*
Where?	*Où?*
north	*nord*
south	*sud*
east	*est*
west	*ouest*

Around Town

Where is the ...?	*Où est ...?*
bank	*la banque*
barber	*le coiffeur*
beach	*la plage*
embassy	*l'ambassade*
market	*le marché*
mosque	*la mosquée*
museum	*le musée*
old city	*le centre historique*
palace	*le palais*
pharmacy	*la pharmacie*
police station	*la police*
post office	*la poste*
restaurant	*le restaurant*
university	*l'université*
zoo	*le zoo*

I want to change ...	*Je voudrais changer ...*
money	*de l'argent*
US$	*des dollars américains*
UK	*des livres sterling*
A$	*des dollars australie*
DM	*des marks allemands*
travellers cheques	*des chèques de voyage*

Accommodation

Where is the hotel?	*Où est l'hôtel?*
Can I see the room?	*Peux-je voir la chambre?*
How much is this room per night?	*Combien est cette chambre pour une nuit?*
Do you have any cheaper rooms?	*Avez-vous des chambres moins chères?*

That's too expensive.	C'est trop cher.
This is fine.	Ça va bien.
bed	lit
blanket	couverture
camp site	camping
full	complet
hot water	eau chaude
key	clef or clé
roof	terrasse
room	chambre
sheet	drap
shower	douche
toilet	les toilettes
washbasin	lavabo
youth hostel	auberge de jeunesse

Shopping

Where can I buy ...?	Où est-ce que je peux acheter ...?
How much?	Combien?
How much does it cost?	Ça coûte combien?
more/less	plus/moins
too much	trop cher
Do you have ...?	Avez-vous ...?
stamps	des timbres
newspaper	un journal

Time

When?	Quand?
today	aujourd'hui
tomorrow	demain
yesterday	hier
morning	matin
afternoon	après-midi
evening	soir
day/night	jour/nuit
week/month/year	semaine/mois/an
What is the time?	Quelle heure est-il?
At what time?	À quelle heure?
after	après
on time	à l'heure
early	tôt
late	tard
quickly	vite
slowly	lentement

Days of the Week

Monday	lundi
Tuesday	mardi
Wednesday	mercredi
Thursday	jeudi
Friday	vendredi
Saturday	samedi
Sunday	dimanche

Months of the Year

January	janvier
February	février
March	mars
April	avril
May	mai
June	juin
July	juillet
August	août
September	septembre
October	octobre
November	novembre
December	décembre

Numbers

0	zéro
1	un
2	deux
3	trois
4	quatre
5	cinq
6	six
7	sept
8	huit
9	neuf
10	dix
11	onze
12	douze
13	treize
14	quatorze
15	quinze
16	seize
17	dix-sept
18	dix-huit
19	dix-neuf
20	vingt
21	vingt-et-un
22	vingt-deux
30	trente
40	quarante
50	cinquante

60	soixante
70	soixante-dix
80	quatre-vingts
90	quatre-vingt-dix
100	cent
101	cent un
125	cent vingt-cinq
200	deux cents
300	trois cents
400	quatre cents
1000	mille
2000	deux milles
3000	trois milles
4000	quatre milles

Ordinal Numbers

first	premier
second	deuxième
third	troisième
fourth	quatrième
fifth	cinquième
sixth	sixième
seventh	septième
eighth	huitième
ninth	neufième
tenth	dixième
twentieth	vingtième
thirtieth	trentième
fortieth	quarantième
fiftieth	cinquantième

Berber

There are three main dialects commonly delineated among the speakers of Berber, which in a certain sense also serve as loose lines of ethnic demarcation.

In the north, centred on the Rif, the locals speak a dialect which has been called Riffian and is spoken as far south as Figuig on the Algerian frontier. The dialect that predominates in the Middle and High Atlas and the valleys leading into the Sahara goes by various names, including Braber or Amazigh.

More settled tribes of the High Atlas, Anti-Atlas, Souss Valley and south-western oases generally speak Tashelhit or Chleuh. The following phrases are a selection from the Tashelhit dialect, the one visitors are likely to find most useful:

Greetings & Civilities

Hello.	la bes darik/darim
(m/f)	
Hello (in response).	la bes
Goodbye.	akayaoon Arbee
Please.	barakalaufik
Thank you.	barakalaufik
Yes.	eyeh
No.	oho
Excuse me.	semhee
How are you?	meneek antgeet?
Fine, thank you.	la bes,
	lhamdulah
Good.	eefulkee/eeshwa
Bad.	khaib
See you later.	akrawes dah
	inshallah

Basics

Is there ...?	ees eela ...?
big/small	mqorn/eemzee
today	zig sbah
tomorrow	ghasad
yesterday	eegdam
Do you have ...?	ees daroon ...?
a lot/little	bzef/eemeek
food	teeremt
mule	aserdon
somewhere to	kra lblast
sleep	mahengwen
water	amen
How much is it?	minshk aysker?
no good	oor eefulkee
	mqorn/eemzee
too expensive	nuqs emeek
give me	feeyee
I want ...	reeh ..?

Getting Around

I want to go to ...	reeh ...
Where is (the) ...?	mani heela ...?
village	doorwar
river	aseet
mountain	adrar
the pass	tizee
Is it far/	ees yagoog/
close?	eeqareb?
straight	neeshan
to the right	fofaseenik
to the left	fozelmad

Numbers

1	*yen*	10	*mrawet*
2	*seen*	11	*yen d mrawet*
3	*krad*	12	*seen d mrawet*
4	*koz*	20	*ashreent*
5	*smoos*	21	*ashreent d yen d mrawet*
6	*sddes*	22	*ashreent d seen d mrawet*
7	*sa*	30	*ashreent d mrawet*
8	*tem*	40	*snet id ashreent*
9	*tza*	50	*snet id ashreent d mrawet*
		100	*smoost id ashreent/meeya*

Berber Lion's paw symbol
The lion symbolises strength and its claw acts as protection from evil forces.

Facts for the Visitor

PLANNING

When to Go

The most pleasant seasons to explore Morocco are spring (April to May) and autumn (September to October). Midsummer can be lovely on the coast, but viciously hot in the interior. Likewise, winter can be idyllic in Marrakesh and further south during the day, but you can be chilled to the bone at night. Don't underestimate the extremes of heat in the summer and cold in the winter, particularly in the High Atlas where some peaks can remain snow-capped for much of the year. Along the north coast and in the Rif Mountains, it can get very chilly and is frequently wet and cloudy in winter. For weather information (24 hour answering machine), call ☎ 364242 in Casablanca.

Travel during Ramadan – the traditional month of fasting and purification that takes place during the ninth month of the Islamic calendar – may present some difficulties for those intent on traditional holiday activities. Some restaurants and cafes close during the day and general business hours are usually reduced. See the Holidays entry in the chapter for more information.

For an entertaining and informative overview of what Morocco has to offer, and the season that appeals most, you may like to look at Lonely Planet's new *Morocco* video (contact your nearest Lonely Planet office).

What Kind of Trip?

Morocco can be a rewarding destination for the lone traveller. Getting around (whether by public or private transport) is straightforward and Moroccan people are some of the most hospitable and helpful you're likely to meet. Women travelling alone needn't feel nervous. Provided you understand local codes of conduct, you'll find most of Morocco to be safer then the average western city (see the Women Travellers entry later in this chapter).

Travelling solo is a guaranteed way of meeting and getting to know local people, not to mention being invited to share some of the best food to be had in the country.

If you're thinking of trekking, it may be wise to look for a small group of like-minded travellers. Though you can hire a guide and mule for a lone trek, it's likely to be much more economical (for traveller and guide alike) to go in a bunch.

Travelling with a small group of friends opens up a huge range of possibilities in Morocco, mainly because hiring a car or taxi becomes economical and one of the best things the country has to offer is its incredible diversity of landscape. Hotel costs also will be substantially cheaper for four or five people travelling together.

There are numerous travel companies offering adventure-based holidays (mostly mountain trekking and desert expeditions) in Morocco. Prices vary, but are generally more expensive than arranging a trip yourself. For those with little time, however, organised holidays can be excellent value. They take away the hard work of hiring guides, finding accommodation and so on, leaving you free to enjoy some of the most fabulous parts of the country. For more information see the Organised Tours entry in the Getting Around chapter.

Maps

Few decent maps of Morocco are available in the country itself, so you are advised to get one before leaving home if you require any degree of detail and accuracy.

There are several reasonable maps covering all of north-western Africa and taking in parts of Egypt and the Sudan in the east. Kümmerley & Frey publish one called *Africa, North and West* (US$16.50) on a scale of 1:4,000,000. Michelin map number 953 (US$8) covers much the same area and is perfectly adequate.

There are several possibilities for maps

of Morocco itself and the choice depends partly on what you want from the map. Michelin's map number 959 (US$8) is the best. In addition to the 1:4,000,000 scale map of the whole of Morocco, which includes the disputed territory of Western Sahara, there is a 1:1,000,000 enlargement of Morocco proper and 1:600,000 enlargements of the Marrakesh, Casablanca, Rabat, Middle Atlas and Meknès areas.

Hildebrand's *Morocco* (US$9.75) covers the entire country, at a scale of 1:900,000 and includes seven small city maps. Kümmerley & Frey's *Morocco* (US$11.50) includes six small city maps, but its main 1:1,000,000 scale map doesn't cover all of the Western Sahara.

GEOprojects, based in Beirut, produces *Maroc* (US$9.75), a very basic map of the country which includes six detailed city plans and some information about the country and major cities. The 1:2,000,000 scale main map and the 1:500,000 area enlargements are thin on detail.

Hallwag's *Morocco* (US$6.50) is distinguished by its comparatively detailed maps of the Canary Islands. The main map is on a scale of 1:1,000,000.

Survey Maps & Air Charts The Cartography Division of the Conservation & Topography Department (☎ 705311; fax 705191), at 31 Ave Moulay Hassan in Rabat, produces highly detailed survey maps on a scale of 1:100,000, as well as a range of other maps. It's not easy to get hold of them – you need to go to the office and apply for them by filling in an official application form (in French). Maps cost around Dr80 each. See the Rabat section for more information.

The topographical maps of the Toubkal region (UK£15 for a set of four) and the M'Goun massif can usually be found at Stanford's bookshop (☎ 0171 836 1915) at 12-14 Long Acre, London WC2E 9LP.

If travelling from the US, you might try Rand McNally in New York (☎ 212-758-7488) at 150E, 52nd St, or in San Francisco (☎ 415-777 3131) at 595 Market St.

Australians can contact Mapland (☎ 03-9670 4383) at 372 Little Bourke St in Melbourne, or The Travel Bookshop (☎ 02-9241 3554) at 20 Bridge St in Sydney.

In France see Ulysse (☎ 01.43.25.17.35) at 26 rue Saint Louis en l'ile, or IGN (☎ 01.43.98.80.00) at 107 rue de la Boetie.

What to Bring
Pack the minimum. There is nothing worse than having to lug loads of excess stuff around. If it's not essential, leave it at home.

A backpack is far more practical than an overnight bag and more likely to stand up to the rigours of Moroccan travel. It is worth paying for a good one, as buckles and straps soon start falling off cheap backpacks.

In summer, a hat, sunglasses and sunscreen are a must. For women, a large cotton scarf is useful to have (though there are plenty to buy in Morocco). Shorts are a bit of a no-no – they may be OK on the beach and unavoidable when hiking in midsummer, but elsewhere you're better off wearing long, loose, lightweight skirts and cotton shirts that cover the shoulders and upper arms (see the Women Travellers entry later in this chapter for more on appropriate dress in Morocco). Moroccan men never wear shorts – male travellers will feel more comfortable and will be a lot better received if they do likewise.

If you plan to hike in the Atlas Mountains, it really is worth having decent hiking clothing. Sturdy walking boots are essential and a water bottle and purification tablets are recommended. You may well have to sleep out, so a sleeping bag (good down sleeping bags are lightweight and take up very little room) and groundsheet are worth considering. A silk sleeping bag sheet is an excellent multi-purpose travel item.

It gets chilly and wet in the mountains, even in summer, so bring a warm jacket and waterproof clothing. Serious trekking above the snow level requires more specialised equipment. For more information, see the trekking sections in the High Atlas chapter.

Other handy items include a Swiss army knife, a universal sink plug (a tennis ball cut in half will often do the trick), a torch (flashlight), a small calculator (for bargaining in markets) a few metres of nylon cord, a handful of clothes pegs, earplugs (for successful sleeping in the noisier cheapies), a small sewing kit and a medical kit (see the Health section later in this chapter).

Condoms, the pill and other contraceptives are available in the big cities, but you are better off bringing your own. You should also bring any special medication.

SUGGESTED ITINERARIES
One Week
Itinerary A If you fly into **Marrakesh**, you could do a pleasant seven day loop taking in both Atlantic beaches and mountain scenery. About 176km west of Marrakesh is the colourful former Portuguese port of **Essaouira**. From here you could trundle a further 173km down the coast to the modern beach resort of **Agadir**, stopping at some of the less crowded beaches on the way.

A worthwhile excursion from Agadir is to the village of **Immouzzer des Ida Outanane** 60km to the north-east. A superb drive east of Agadir will take you on to the

attractive town of **Taroudannt** and then over the breathtaking **Tizi n'Test** pass (don't miss the beautiful **Tin Mal Mosque** just north of the pass) and back to Marrakesh.

Itinerary B Avoiding the major cities altogether, you could fly into Agadir and head 90km south to the small town of **Tiznit** and then further down the coast to the quirky former Spanish Saharan town of **Sidi Ifni**.

A lovely drive east from Tiznit will take you through the stunning landscape of the Anti-Atlas via the pretty Berber town of **Tafraoute** and back up to Agadir.

Itinerary C Starting from **Casablanca**, a seven day tour of the north could take you up the coast as far as **Tangier** and then south via **Tetouan** to **Chefchaouen** in the wild **Rif mountains**.

From Chefchaouen you could continue south towards **Ouezzane** and from there you could travel onto the remarkable Roman ruins of **Volubilis** and back to Casablanca.

Itinerary D If you have just four or five days, but want to fit in a bit of countryside

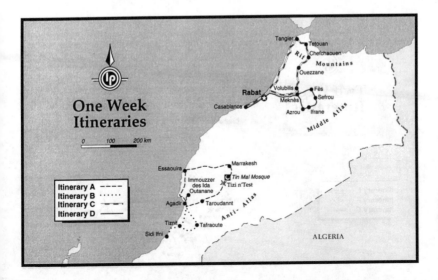

and some Berber towns, as well as seeing something of the major cities, you could travel from Casablanca directly to **Rabat**, and then on to **Meknès**, **Fès** and Volubilis. The town of **Sefrou**, 28km south of Fès, makes a good day trip. A little further south, the French-built Alpine town of **Ifrane** is surrounded by some magnificent cedar forests. Just 17km away is the very Berber town of **Azrou**, a good base also from which to explore some of the most attractive country in the Middle Atlas. From Azrou, you could return via Meknès to Rabat and Casablanca.

Two Weeks

A tour of Morocco's Imperial Cities (Fès, Meknès, Rabat and Marrakesh) could be accomplished in one week if necessary, although you should set aside about two weeks to do them any justice.

If you're around in spring, you could combine the cities with some travelling in the north, a lovely region at this time of year. It's best avoided in winter, however, as heavy rain tends to sweep away bridges and many of the roads become impassable.

Itinerary E Casablanca is a reasonable starting point from which to explore the north. If you're arriving by air, there are frequent, direct charter flights from Europe which are also among the cheapest around.

From Casablanca, you could head 133km up the Atlantic coast to the port town of **Kenitra** where, if you're into ornithology, you could visit the excellent bird sanctuary. Better still are the wetlands and peaceful lagoon of **Moulay Bousselham** around 80km further north. There are good, unspoilt beaches in the area too.

A little further north, you'll pass the old Spanish town of **Larache** and the picturesque port town of **Asilah** before reaching Tangier at the furthest northern point. Turning eastwards, the town of Tetouan makes a good stop. The journey towards Chefchaouen, 61km further east, will take you through some of the most spectacular mountain scenery in Morocco.

You could spend a couple of days in Chefchaouen, trekking in the hills or exploring its charming medina.

The 222km drive east from Chefchaouen to **Al-Hoceima** will take you deeper into

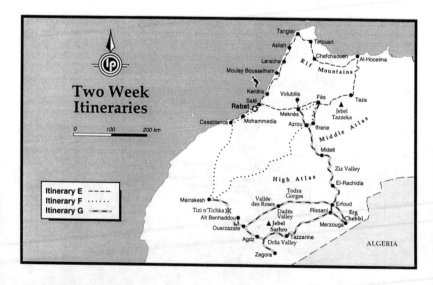

the Rif mountains and into the heart of kif country. Those brave enough to face the hustlers will be rewarded by the views.

From Al-Hoceima and the Mediterranean coast you could loop back south for 173km to **Taza**, a good base for the **Jebel Tazzeka** circuit. Fès, the first of the Imperial Cities, is 120km to the west. From Meknès, we highly recommend a day trip to the fabulous Roman ruins of Volubilis. From Rabat, 136km west of Meknès, you can catch the shuttle train directly to the Mohammed V international airport south of Casablanca.

Itinerary F For those wishing to take on all of the Imperial Cities, the obvious tack is to start with Meknès, then loop around to Marrakesh via Fès, before making the trip to Tangier via Rabat by train.

The entire train journey time from Marrakesh to Tangier is 10 to 12 hours, so a couple of days in Rabat along the way would break it up nicely.

Itinerary G Two weeks would allow ample time to explore central Morocco, the fascinating sub-Saharan area south of the High Atlas. The best starting point is probably Marrakesh. A 200km road journey takes you south to **Ouarzazate** (for a price, there are direct flights from Paris to Ouarzazate) over the **Tizi n'Tichka** pass. Along the way it's worth taking a short side trip to see the fabulous kasbah of **Aït Benhaddou**.

From Ouarzazate you can head south along the **Drâa Valley** to **Zagora** and/or east along the **Dadès Valley** to **Erfoud**, stopping to explore the **Vallée des Roses** and the **Dadès** and **Todra gorges**. A short drive east of Erfoud is the **Erg Chebbi**, an area of real Saharan dunes worth more than the glimpse most tourists see.

From Erfoud you could loop back to Marrakesh via the villages of **Rissani** and **Tazzarine**, skirting the volcanic peaks of the **Jebel Sarhro**. Alternatively, you could head north from Erfoud along the **Ziz Valley** to **Midelt** and from there travel up into the Middle Atlas and on to Meknès or Fès, if you had time.

One Month
Though you'd be pushing it to see the entire country in four weeks, you could cover a fair old chunk in that time.

Travelling by public transport may mean that you cover less territory than you would by car, but you could then afford to stop for longer in places that took your fancy and spend time trekking between destinations.

Itinerary H In four weeks you could comfortably combine a tour of the Imperial Cities with a trip around the southern river valleys, as described above in Itineraries F and G. You could also combine a tour of the valleys with a trek out of **Boumalne du Dadès** through the rugged Jebel Sarhro.

From the Dadès or Todra gorges you could head up into the High Atlas mountains; and from Zagora or **M'Hamid**, 100km south of Zagora, you could organise a camel trek through the desert.

Itinerary I If you're not particularly interested in the ancient monuments and history (not to mention hassle) of the cities (two or three days in any of them is probably enough), you could combine a coastal trip with forays into the mountains. Starting from Casablanca you could snake slowly down the Atlantic coast, stopping at the former Portuguese port of **El Jadida** and at **Oualidia** for oysters and good beaches. This route would take you on through **Safi**, famous for its pottery, Essaouira, Agadir, Tiznit and Sidi Ifni. If you're into ocean fishing and long lonely stretches of road, you could continue into the Western Sahara, going as far south as **Tan Tan, Laayoune** and on another 550km to **Dakhla**.

Taroudannt, inland from Agadir, is a good base for any number of serious treks up into the Western High Atlas. Likewise, Tafraoute is the place to be based for walks in the Anti-Atlas.

It wouldn't be difficult to spend four weeks exploring the High Atlas alone, perhaps combining days of walking with travel by local *camionette* (pick-up trucks which travel between villages on market days).

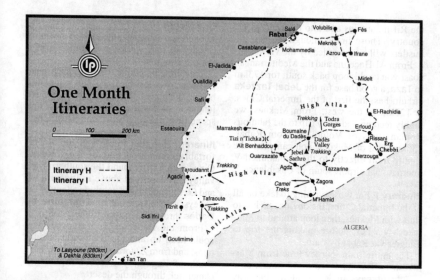

HIGHLIGHTS
The Top Ten

Morocco has so much to offer that compiling a list of highlights is almost impossible. Nevertheless, the authors have selected a handful of the not-to-be-missed and the very-much-to-be-missed (see also the Highlights Table on pages 100-101).

1. The High Atlas, Anti-Atlas and Rif mountains
2. Imperial Cities, particularly Fès, Marrakesh and Meknès
3. The Dadès Gorge
4. The desert sky and Saharan dunes of Merzouga
5. The Riffian town of Chefchaouen
6. A splurge in one of Morocco's (better) palace-restaurants
7. The quirky former Spanish town of Sidi Ifni
8. Moroccan patisseries
9. Volubilis in spring
10. Mint tea

The Bottom Ten

This list should be taken with a pinch of salt. Some people love Tan Tan in the rain.

1. Figuig's hotels
2. Agadir's discos
3. Wondering what to do in Oujda
4. Kif hustlers in the Rif mountains
5. Tan Tan in the rain
6. A splurge in one of Morocco's (poorer) palace-restaurants
7. Getting lost in Salé
8. Border controls at Spanish Melilla and Ceuta
9. The drive from Taza to Oujda
10. Mint tea

TOURIST OFFICES
Local Tourist Offices

The Moroccans rely heavily on tourism as a source of national income, and the Office National Marocain du Tourisme (ONMT) has a network of offices throughout the country.

These usually go by the name of Délégation Régionale du Tourisme. Some towns also have *Syndicats d'Initiative* which specialise in local information. The addresses and telephone numbers of tourist offices in Morocco have been listed under the entries for individual cities and towns.

Tourist Offices Abroad

The ONMT also has offices abroad. They generally stock brochures, some glossy maps and lists of tour operators running trips to Morocco.

Australia
c/- Moroccan Consulate, 11 West St, North Sydney, NSW 2060 (☎ 02-9922 4999; fax 9923 1053)
Canada
2001 Rue Université, Suite 1460, Montreal H3A 2A6 (☎ 514-842 8111; fax 842 5316)
France
161 Rue Saint Honoré, Place du Théâtre Français, 75001 Paris (☎ 01.42.60.63.50; fax 01.40.15.97.34)
Japan
Owariya Building 4F 8, Banchi LP Chome, Kanda Ogawa KU, Tokyo 101 (☎ 03-251 7781; fax 251 7797)
Spain
Calle Quintana No 2, 28008 Madrid (☎ 91-541 2995; fax 559 4534)
UK
205 Regent St, London W1R 7DE (☎ 0171-437 0073; fax 734 8172)
USA
Suite 1201, 20 East 46th St, New York 10017 (☎ 212-557 2520; fax 949 8148)

VISAS & DOCUMENTS
Passport

Your most important travel document is your passport. It should be carried with you at all times and guarded carefully. To enter Morocco, your passport must be valid for six months from the date of entry.

If you need to renew your passport, allow plenty of time as it can take anything from an hour to several months. Bureaucracy usually grinds faster if you do everything in person rather than relying on the mail or agents, but check first what you need to take with you: photos of a certain size, birth certificate, exact payment in cash etc.

Holders of British Visitors passports should note that the Moroccan authorities do *not* accept them. People aged 16 and over must have their own passport. Children under the age of 15 must have their photo attached to their parents' passports if they do not carry their own.

Visas

A visa is a stamp in your passport or on a separate piece of paper permitting you to enter the country and stay for a specific period of time. Most visitors to Morocco do not require visas and are allowed to remain in the country for 90 days on entry. Exceptions to this rule include nationals of Israel, South Africa and Zimbabwe, who can apply for a one month single-entry visa (US$23) or a three month double-entry visa (US$33).

Visa requirements can change, so check with the Moroccan Embassy in your country or a reputable travel agent before travelling.

People requiring a visa who are contemplating travelling to and fro between Morocco and, say, Spain should consider getting a double-entry visa to avoid the hassle of applying for new visas. If you need a visa, you'll have to fill in three forms and provide three photos. A first-time visa can take up to four weeks to be issued; subsequently it generally takes 48 hours.

In Spain, visas are available at consulates in Barcelona, Málaga, Las Palmas de Gran Canaria and Madrid. In Algeria, it is possible to get a Moroccan visa at Morocco's consulates in Algiers or Oran.

Visa Extensions Should the standard 90-day stay be insufficient, it is possible to apply for an extension or even for residence (but the latter is difficult to get).

It is probably easier to simply leave the country and try to re-enter after a few days. Your chances improve if you enter by a different route the second time.

People on visas may prefer to try for the extension. Go to the nearest police station with your passport, three photos and, preferably, a letter from your embassy requesting a visa extension on your behalf. If you are in Rabat go to the Sûreté Nationale office, off Ave Mohammed V in the centre of town. It should take a maximum of four days to process.

Visas for Ceuta & Melilla These two enclaves are Spanish territory, so anyone requiring a visa to enter Spain will need one

HIGHLIGHTS Title	Region	Comments
Activities		
Bird-Watching Besides the many resident species, Morocco boasts vast numbers of migrant birds.	Atlantic Coast	Best viewing times are March, April, September and October.
Desert Safaris The Tafilalt region offers excursions with 4WDs, camels, tents and bivouacs.	Central Morocco	Organise your trip in the towns closest to the desert.
Skiing The town of Oukaïmeden, in the Ourika Valley, is Morocco's premier skiing spot.	High Atlas	Long cross-country trips are possible with specialist guides.
Trekking Morocco's unexplored ranges offer dramatic scenery and traditional Berber villages.	Morocco's ranges	Short or long walks are possible. You may need guides and mules.
Windsurfing The top spot is Essaouira, also known as 'Windy City'.	Atlantic Coast	Hire gear for around Dr120 an hour.
Natural Beauty		
Anti-Atlas Pink mountains and pretty valleys surround the Berber village of Tafraoute.	South-east of Agadir	Best visited in the spring and autumn.
Erg Chebbi Drifting Saharan sand dunes near the town of Merzouga in the Tafilalt region – don't miss it.	Central Morocco	There's plenty of cheap accommodation by the dunes.
Drâa, Dadès & Ziz Valleys Rich river valleys full of palmeries and beautiful ruined kasbahs.	Central Morocco	If you can, this is the time to hire a car.
Rif Mountains A wild, isolated and very unexplored landscape.	Around Chefchaouen	Among the most dramatic landscapes in Morocco.
Holy Places		
Hassan II Mosque Inaugurated in 1993, it is the second largest mosque in the world after Mecca.	The city of Casablanca	Rich decoration is proof of the mastery of Morocco's craftsmen.
Moulay Idriss Morocco's holiest town with the tomb of Moulay Idriss, Morocco's most revered saint.	Just north of Meknès	For centuries, the town was out of bounds to non-Muslims.
Tin Mal Mosque Built in 1155 in memory of the founder of the Almohad dynasty, Mohammed ibn Toumert.	Tizi n'Test pass	Non-Muslims are permitted entry every day except Friday.

Museums & Medersas

Archaeological Museum
An excellent museum, it has the most important finds from Roman sites across Morocco.

The city of Rabat

Don't miss the two stunning bronze busts of Cato and Juba II.

Bou Inania Medersa
This is the most extravagant, elaborate and perfect of all the Merenid dynasty monuments.

The city of Fès

Superb zellij tilework, sculpted plaster and carved cedar ceilings.

Dar Batha Museum
A former palace that houses antique Fassi embroidery, tribal carpets and ceramics.

The city of Fès

Some excellent examples of the famous blue pottery of Fès.

Dar Jamaï Palace
Houses an excellent collection of Moroccan artefacts, particularly from the Meknès region.

The city of Meknès

Beautiful Andalusian gardens in the grounds of the museum.

School of Traditional Arts & Crafts
For 50 years, it has taught ancient professions such as woodwork, weaving and zellij-making.

The city of Rabat

A wonderful chance to observe Moroccan craftsmen at work.

Cultural Experiences

A Visit to the Doctor
Every souq has an apothecary for ancient cures for illnesses of the body, mind and soul.

Moroccan souqs

Try the carob fruit commonly prescribed for unhappy stomachs.

Culinary Treats
Among the best cuisine in the world. Have at least one splurge at a palace-restaurant.

Imperial cities

Exclusive restaurants are excellent value by western standards.

Entertainers
Morocco has many brilliant musicians, spectacular acrobats and spell-binding storytellers.

The city of Marrakesh

The arts have been passed from father to son for generations.

Henna Hands
Women travellers may like to go local and have their feet or hands decorated with henna.

Herb/spice markets

This decoration is the traditional mark of newlyweds.

Hot from the Hammam
Public baths offer a fascinating insight into Moroccan society (and can be a nice treat too).

All towns & cities

Good substitute for cold (or nonexistent) showers in some hotels.

Moroccan Hospitality
Don't pass up the chance to share a cup of tea with the locals.

Anywhere

In homes, remove your footwear and accept at least three cups.

Music
There's plenty of opportunity to enjoy exciting Berber music in informal surroundings.

Central Morocco

The Berbers' hypnotic music is an ancient tradition.

Roman Morocco
The ruins at Volubilis are remarkably well preserved and feature beautiful mosaics.

North of Meknès

Try and catch the ruins in the last rays of the setting sun.

to get into the enclaves too. For more details on who needs visas and other requirements, see the Foreign Embassies entry in the Information section of the Rabat chapter.

Photocopies

The hassles created by losing your passport can be greatly reduced if you have a record of its number and issue date or, even better, photocopies of the relevant pages. A copy of your birth certificate can also be useful.

Also keep a record of the serial numbers of your travellers cheques (cross them off as you cash them) and photocopies of your credit cards, airline ticket and other travel documents. Keep all this emergency material separate from your passport, cheques and cash, and leave extra copies with someone you can rely on back home.

Add some emergency cash, say US$100, to this separate stash as well. If you do lose your passport, notify the police immediately (make sure you get a statement), and contact your nearest consulate.

Travel Insurance

You should seriously consider taking out travel insurance. This not only covers you for medical expenses and luggage theft or loss, but also for cancellation or delays in your travel arrangements. Cover depends on the insurance and your type of ticket, so ask both your insurer and the ticket-issuing agency to explain where you stand. Ticket loss is also covered by travel insurance.

Buy travel insurance as early as possible. If you buy it the week before you fly, you may find, for instance, that you're not covered for delays to your flight caused by strikes or other industrial actions that may have started or been threatened before you took out the insurance.

Paying for your airline ticket with a credit card often provides limited travel accident insurance and you may be able to reclaim the payment if the operator doesn't deliver. Ask your credit-card company what it's prepared to cover.

Some policies offer lower and higher medical expense options; the higher ones are chiefly for countries such as the USA which have extremely high medical costs. Some policies specifically exclude 'dangerous activities' which can include scuba diving, motorcycling, even trekking. A locally acquired motorcycle licence is not valid under some policies.

You may prefer a policy which pays doctors or hospitals direct rather than you having to pay on the spot and claim later. If you have to claim later make sure you keep all documentation. Some policies ask you to call back (reverse charges) to a centre in your home country where an immediate assessment of your problem is made.

Check that the policy covers ambulances or an emergency flight home.

Driving Licence & Permits

Although technically you need an International Driving Permit to drive in Morocco, most national licences are recognised. If bringing your own car, you will need all the appropriate documentation, including a Green Card (for details see the Getting There & Away chapter).

Hostel & Student Cards

You can stay at most hostels without a membership card, usually for a couple of dirham extra. To get a Hostelling International card, ask at any hostel or contact your local or national hostelling office.

International student cards do not seem to open many magic doors (eg in museums) in Morocco, but if you're under 31 they do entitle you to a 25% discount on internal travel with Royal Air Maroc (RAM).

International Health Certificate

If you're coming to Morocco from certain parts of Asia, Africa and South America, where outbreaks of yellow fever or cholera have been reported, you'll need this yellow booklet.

It is a record of your recent vaccinations and is available from your physician or government health department. See the Health section later in this chapter for general information on immunisations.

EMBASSIES
Moroccan Embassies Abroad

Algeria
   Embassy: 8 Rue des Cèdres, Parc de la Reine, Algiers (☎ 02-607408, 02-691737)
   Consulate: 5 Ave de l'ANP, Sidi Bel Abbès, Algiers (☎ 02-243470)
Australia
   Consulate: Suite 2, 11 West St, North Sydney, NSW 2060 (☎ 02-9922 4999, 02-9957 6717)
Canada
   Embassy: 38 Range Rd, Ottawa K1N 8J4 Ontario (☎ 416-236 7391/2)
   Consulate: Suite 1510, 1010 Rue Sherbrooke West, Montreal H3A 2R7 (☎ 514-288 8750, 514-288 6951)
Egypt
   10 Sharia Salah Eddine, Zamalek, Cairo (☎ 02-340 9677)
France
   Embassy: 5 Rue Le Tasse, Paris 75016 (☎ 01.45.20.69.35)
   Consulate: 19 Rue Sauliner, Paris 75009 (☎ 01.45.23.37.40)
Japan
   Silva Kingdom 3, 16-3, Sendagaya Shibuya-KU, Tokyo 151 (☎ 03-478 3271, 03-478 3272, 03-478 3273)

Mauritania
   Tevragh Zeina 634, BP 621, Nouakchott (☎ 02-51411)
Spain
   Embassy: Calle Serrano 179, 28002 Madrid (☎ 91-563 1090)
   Consulates: Calle Leizaran 31, 28002 Madrid (☎ 91-561-2145); Rambla de Cataluña 78, Barcelona 08008 (☎ 93-215-3470/4); Ave de Andalucia 15, Málaga 29002 (☎ 953-29950/62)
UK
   Embassy: 49 Queen's Gate Gardens, London SW7 5NE (☎ 0171-581 5001)
   Consulate (visas): 97-99 Praed St, Paddington, London SW2 (☎ 0171-724 0719)
USA
   Embassy: 1601 21st St NW, Washington DC 20009 (☎ 202-462 7979)
   Consulates: 30th floor, 767 Third Avenue, New York, NY 10017 (☎ 212-421 1580); 437 Fifth Ave, New York, NY 10016 (☎ 212-758 2625)

Foreign Embassies in Morocco

Foreign embassies are concentrated in the capital, Rabat. In addition, many countries have consulates and vice-consulates in other major cities. All are listed under the

---

Your Own Embassy

As a tourist, it's important to realise what your own embassy – the embassy of the country of which you are a citizen – can and can't do.

Generally speaking, they won't be much help in emergencies if the trouble you're in is remotely your own fault. Remember that you are bound by the laws of the country you're in. Embassies will not be sympathetic if you end up in jail after committing a crime locally, even if such actions are legal in your own country.

In genuine emergencies you might get some assistance, but only if other channels have been exhausted. For example, if you need to get home urgently, a free ticket home is exceedingly unlikely – the embassy would expect you to have insurance. If you have all your money and documents stolen, they might assist with getting a new passport, but a loan for onward travel is out of the question.

Embassies used to keep letters for travellers or have a small reading room with home newspapers, but these days the mail holding service has been stopped and even their newspapers tend to be out of date.

On the more positive side, if you are heading into very remote or politically volatile areas, you might consider registering with your embassy so they know where you are, but make sure you tell them when you come back too. Some embassies post useful warning notices about local dangers or potential problems. The US embassies are particularly good for providing this information and it's worth scanning their notice boards for 'travellers' advisories' about security, local epidemics, dangers to lone travellers and so on. ■

appropriate city or town entry. Visa information for various countries appears in the Rabat section (with the exception of Senegal, for which see Casablanca).

Australians should note that the Canadian Embassy handles consular affairs in Morocco for the Australian government.

Algeria
   46 Rue Tarik Ibn Ziyad, Rabat (☎ 07-765474)
   16 Rue Khemisset, Rabat (☎ 07-762312)
France
   3 Rue Sahnoun, Rabat (☎ 07-777822)
Italy
   2 Rue Idriss al-Azhar, Rabat (☎ 07-706598)
Japan
   39 Ave Ahmed Balafrej Souissi, Rabat (☎ 07-631782)
South Africa
   34 Rue des Saadiens, Rabat (☎ 07-706760)
Spain
   3 Rue Madnine, Rabat (☎ 07-768989)
UK
   17 Ave de la Tour Hassan, Rabat (☎ 07-720905)
USA
   2 Ave Marrakesh, Rabat (☎ 07-762265)

CUSTOMS

Visitors are permitted to import up to 200 cigarettes and a litre of spirits. A *Customs Guide for Tourists* is sometimes available from ONMT offices and consulates.

MONEY
Costs

For westerners, Morocco isn't an expensive country to travel through. Those hoping to push their travelling funds the furthest will save most money by staying in cheap, unclassified hotels (for around Dr30 per night). Cooking for yourself or buying fresh foods from local markets will stretch your budget.

There's not much difference in price between trains and buses. Local buses are a bit cheaper than CTM (the main national carrier) services.

You can get by on the equivalent of about US$20 to US$25 a day. If you'd like more freedom to sample a range of restaurants, take the occasional taxi ride and enjoy a few comforts (hot showers, European newspapers, the odd bottle of wine and so on), count on paying US$35 to US$45.

The following prices will give you some idea of what to expect. A 100km bus or train journey costs about Dr17. Super and unleaded petrol costs Dr7.50 a litre and diesel is Dr4.50 a litre.

A meal in a lower-end restaurant costs as little as Dr25. In a medium-range restaurant you'd pay up to Dr70 and in a more upmarket place, around Dr150, including wine.

Stall food can provide a filling meal for about Dr15. A loaf of bread costs just over Dr1, a kilogram of olives around Dr12, a kilogram of tomatoes about Dr6 and a kilogram of bananas about Dr10.

A pot of mint tea is worth Dr2 to Dr3 – more in very touristy places. Coffee tends to be a little more expensive. One litre of bottled water costs about Dr5. A 500ml bottle of Coca-Cola will set you back around Dr6. Juice stands can be good value – a big, freshly squeezed orange juice goes for as little as Dr2.50.

The two main local brands of beer, Flag Spéciale and Stork, cost about Dr12 and Dr15 respectively in restaurants and bars, but about half that from liquor stores.

Local wines, too, are much cheaper in liquor stores, where you'll pay from Dr28 to Dr35 for a decent drop that could easily cost you Dr80 in a restaurant.

A packet of American cigarettes costs Dr25. You can, as many locals do, buy them one at a time for Dr1. Local brands, such as Marquise, cost Dr10 for 20.

Although you can buy many foreign newspapers and magazines in the bigger cities, they're not cheap; papers often start at Dr25.

The exception is the French press, which costs pretty much the same as it does in France and generally arrives on the same day.

Local telephone calls are cheap, but a call to Europe will cost at least Dr17 per minute. Practically all museums and monuments charge a standard Dr10 entry fee.

Carrying Money

Nothing beats cash for convenience ... or risk. If you lose it, it's gone forever and very few travel insurers will come to the rescue. You'll certainly need to carry some cash with you, though. Keep a handful of small denomination notes in your wallet (but never carry it in a back pocket) for day to day transactions and put the rest in a money belt or another safe place. If you're travelling in out of the way places, make sure you have enough cash to last you until you get to a decent sized town.

Travellers Cheques

The main reason for carrying travellers cheques rather than cash is the protection that they offer from theft, although they are losing their popularity as more travellers simply withdraw money from ATMs or get cash advances on credit cards as they go.

American Express and Thomas Cook cheques are widely accepted and have efficient replacement policies. Keeping a record of the cheque numbers and those you have used is vital when it comes to replacing lost travellers cheques. Make sure you keep this separate from the cheques themselves. Before changing cheques, ask the bank whether they charge a commission.

American Express is represented by the travel agency Voyages Schwarz at the following locations:

112 Rue Prince Moulay Abdallah, Casablanca (☎ 222947, 278054)
Immeuble Moutaouakil, 1 Rue Mauritania, Marrakesh (☎ 433022)
54 Blvd Pasteur, Tangier (☎ 933459)

Thomas Cook has one office in Morocco: c/- KTI Voyages (☎ 398572; fax 398567), 4 Rue des Hirondelles, Casablanca.

Credit Cards & ATMs

If you're not familiar with the options, ask your bank to explain the workings and relative merits of credit, credit/debit, charge and cash cards.

A major advantage of credit cards is that they allow you to pay for expensive items (eg airline tickets) without your having to carry great wads of cash around. They also allow you to withdraw cash at selected banks or ATMs (*guichets automatiques*).

All major credit cards are widely accepted in the main cities and even in many small towns, although their use often incurs a commission of 5%. You can get cash advances on Visa and MasterCard in various banks, including the Banque Populaire, the BMCE, the BMCI and Wafabank. Though Morocco's network of ATMs is increasing and improving all the time, ATMs can be unreliable when it comes to foreign cards. If you don't want to risk having your card swallowed, stick to cash advances.

The amount of money you can withdraw from an ATM generally depends on the conditions attached to your particular card, although the daily ATM limit on most cards is around Dr3000.

If you want to rely on plastic cards, the best bet is to take two different cards. Better still is a combination of credit card and travellers cheques so you have something to fall back on if an ATM swallows your card or the banks in the area are closed.

International Transfers

Transferring money from your home bank will be easier if you've authorised someone back home to access your account. If you have the option, find a large bank and ask for the international division.

Most banks charge a minimum of around US$30 to send money by telegraphic transfer and it can take up to 14 working days (possibly longer if there are cock-ups) to reach you.

If you have a Giro or other postal account and can have international postal cheques issued on it, these can be changed in the main post offices.

Currency

The Moroccan currency is the dirham (Dr), which is divided into 100 centimes. You will find notes in denominations of Dr5, Dr10, Dr20, Dr50 and Dr100 and coins of

Dr1, Dr2, Dr5 (these are becoming pretty rare), as well as 10, 20 and 50 centimes.

Currency Exchange

The importation or exportation of Moroccan currency is prohibited, but any amount of foreign currency – cash or cheques – may be brought into the country. Hang on to any exchange receipts as you will need them to re-exchange leftover dirham on the way out of Morocco.

Most currencies are readily accepted, but the Irish punt, Scottish pound and Australian and New Zealand dollars are not recognised at all. This goes for cash and cheques.

Exchange Rates

Algeria	AD100	=	Dr16.66
Australia	A$1	=	Dr7.19
Canada	C$1	=	Dr7.11
France	1FF	=	Dr1.68
Germany	DM1	=	Dr5.42
Japan	¥100	=	Dr8.11
New Zealand	NZ$1	=	Dr6.25
Spain	100pta	=	Dr6.42
UK	UK£1	=	Dr15.59
USA	US$1	=	Dr9.82

Changing Money

You have a choice of banks where you can change money in Morocco, which is generally a quick process. The currency, although not yet fully convertible, operates in a largely free market, virtually eliminating any black market. Rates vary little from bank to bank, but it can't hurt to look around. Remember to have your passport, as you will need it to change travellers cheques and get cash advances; some banks will want to see it when you change cash, too.

Banks are generally open Monday to Friday from 8.30 to 11.30 am and 2.30 to 4.30 pm with the midday break on Friday being slightly longer.

The Banque Populaire seems to be the most efficient of the Moroccan banks. They don't charge a commission on travellers cheques and some branches have exchange facilities open on weekends. Wafabank is planning to open for Saturday trading in the major cities.

The main Mohammed V airport outside Casablanca has two BMCE branches and a couple of ATMs. If you are arriving from, or heading for, the enclaves of Ceuta and Melilla, the Moroccan banks on the border will exchange cash only. It is difficult to obtain Moroccan currency in mainland Spain and not worth the effort. The banks in Melilla and Ceuta, however, deal in dirham at rates inferior to those in Morocco. Another option in the enclaves and on the borders is the black market (see below) – check the bank rates first, which are usually just as good.

As importing and exporting Moroccan currency is illegal (though it's unlikely anyone will bother you if you take out a little as a souvenir), the best thing is to wind down to nothing as you approach the end of your trip.

Should you find yourself stuck with un-seemly amounts of the stuff when you're about to leave, you can exchange it for hard currency at most Moroccan banks (including on the borders and at the airports) if you can present bank receipts proving exchange in Morocco – so hang on to these as you go.

Black Market

The near convertibility of the dirham leaves little room for a black market, but you will find people in the streets asking if you want to exchange money, especially in Tangier and Casablanca. There is no monetary benefit to be had from such transactions and, unless you are desperate for cash when the banks are closed, it is wiser to avoid these characters.

There is also a frontier black market. You will find plenty of Moroccans dealing in dirham and hard currency on the Ceuta frontier and inside the Melilla enclave. In Ceuta itself and on the actual Melilla border there seems to be less activity.

Check bank rates before dealing with black marketeers. In Melilla, ignore the stories about disastrous bank rates and huge commissions – check the exact details with a bank first and then see what the street dealers have to say.

In Oujda and Figuig it is possible to buy and sell Algerian dinar for dirham (in Oujda, you can also get hard currency). Discretion is the word, although the authorities seem to turn a blind eye to such transactions. When dealing in dinar, shop around before concluding an exchange. You can get dinar in Melilla, too, though the rates are unlikely to be as good as in the two Moroccan frontier towns.

Tipping & Bargaining

Tipping and bargaining are an integral part of Moroccan life. Although you needn't feel obliged to part with your change at the drop of a hat, the judicious distribution of a few dirham for a service willingly rendered will certainly make your life a lot easier.

Expect to pay a tip of 10% in a restaurant; in addition, it's usual to leave a few coins on the table (unless the service has been poor, of course). Museum guides, *gardiens de voitures* (car park attendants), porters, baggage handlers and petrol pump attendants expect to be tipped (between Dr3 and Dr5) and it's polite to offer the same to people for permission to take their photograph.

Souq Survival

Bargaining in the souqs is essential, although when souvenir-hunting some western visitors may sometimes get the impression it is a game reserved for them. Nothing could be further from the truth, as the following extract from *La Boîte à Merveilles*, by the Fès author Ahmed Sefrioui, demonstrates. Some of the merchant's lines may ring a bell and the purchaser's replies are a neat introduction to basic souq survival tactics:

The shopkeeper asked: 'So you like this vest, Madame?'
'That depends entirely on how much it costs', my mother replied.
'Ah well, in that case I'll start wrapping it up right away. I'm always happy to give serious customers a discount. Now this vest usually sells for five rials, but I'll let you have it for just four.'
'Let's cut out all the chitchat – I'll give you two rials.'
'You're offering less than what it cost me to buy it in the first place, I swear. I can't possibly let you have it for that price – I'd have to go begging in the streets tonight to feed my children.'
The shopkeeper had finished carefully folding up the vest and was looking for a sheet of paper to wrap it in.
'Listen', said my mother, 'I've got kids and things to do at home; I haven't got time to hang around here bargaining with you. Would you let me have the vest for two and a quarter rials? I'm ready to make a sacrifice for my son, who would like so much to wear this on the day of Achoura.'
'I like the lad, so I'll make every effort for his sake – give me three and a half rials.' The shopkeeper held out his hand for the money, but my mother turned around, took me by the hand and started to walk off.
'Come on,' she said. 'There are plenty of vests in the Qissaria. We'll soon find a shopkeeper who talks sense.'
The shopkeeper cried out: 'Come back Madame! Do come back! Your son likes this vest ... take it ... pay me what you think is fair ...'.
She pulled out two and a half rials, which she handed to the shopkeeper without a word. Not waiting long enough to hear his protests, she seized the package and dragged me off.

Translated from the French by Damien Simonis
Copyright Éditions du Seuil (1978)

Try to judge each situation on its merits, and pay accordingly. It's also worth bearing in mind that the average daily wage in Morocco is equivalent to about US$3.25.

Some people love it, others hate it, but whatever your view, bargaining is a central part of Morocco's commercial culture. Bargaining applies mainly to the souqs, with hotels, restaurants and transport prices generally fixed. Taxi fares can sometimes be negotiated.

Just about everyone has a personal modus operandi for dealing with merchants. The best advice is to enter into the spirit of the thing and *enjoy* the process. By refusing to bargain where it is expected, you almost appear to be robbing the vendor of one of the pleasures of the trade (and yourself of cash).

When on the hunt for souvenirs and the like, look around, indulge in the banter over prices and get a feel for what people are asking. You'll be invited for tea and countless samples of their wares will be laid out before you, along with countless reasons for buying them. Despite this and the sometimes overbearing tactics of some less scrupulous shopkeepers, there's never an obligation to buy.

On the art of bargaining, one reader (Julian Ash of Canberra, Australia) suggests the following tactics:

'Above all, know clearly in advance what your upper offer for an item is and stick to it (you need to have some idea of the value of the item). Knock off about 10% for final haggling and, starting at about 50 to 60%, approach your limit slowly and leave if that offer is not accepted. I noted that the vendor's initial prices dropped very slowly at first, testing the customer's determination to hold their offer down; sometimes only after much bargaining would the price collapse rapidly to just above my final offer. I suspect that many customers respond to the maintained high price by raising their offers much more that they intended. However, to be finally accepted you may need to make some token increase (say 5%): that way the vendor feels good about the deal.'

Never embark on a discussion of prices if you are not really interested, as Moroccans attach a good deal of importance to your last word. If they accept one you name, they can get understandably shirty if you turn around and say you're not interested.

Do not allow yourself to be intimidated into buying anything you don't want at a price you don't like. Whatever they tell you, no one can *make* you buy.

You may not have to part with any money at all. A lot of western goods, such as decent jeans and printed T-shirts, can easily be traded against local products. It's up to you what value you attach to whatever you're trading and haggle accordingly.

Begging
Whatever advances Morocco may be making economically, great chunks of the population are still being left behind. Although it is noticeable that well-heeled Moroccans are not always so willing to part with donations, it is hard to find a reason for not giving the elderly and infirm something.

You'll also see a fair number of women of all ages, apparently abandoned by their husbands, begging on the streets. They're in a difficult position and it goes without saying that there is no such thing as a single mother's benefit in Morocco.

Wherever you go, children will hound you for dirham, *bonbons* and *stylos*. The best policy is not to encourage them at all. If you'd like to provide children in a poor village with something, go to the local school and ask the teacher if the school needs a supply of pens or notebooks.

POST & COMMUNICATIONS
Postal Rates
Although the postal system is fairly reliable, it is not terribly fast. It can take about a week for letters to get to their European destinations and two weeks or so to get to Australia and North America. Occasionally you get lucky and mail moves faster. It's about the same going in the other direction.

Standard letters and postcards to Europe and the UK cost Dr5.50; to Australia and North America they cost Dr11. In the main tourist centres you may be charged above the standard rates.

Post offices are distinguished by the 'PTT' sign or the new 'La Poste' logo.

You can buy stamps at some *tabacs*, the small tobacco and newspaper kiosks you see scattered about the main city centres. This is useful, as post office counters are often besieged.

Sending Mail

The parcel office (indicated by the sign 'Colis postaux') is generally in a separate part of the building. Take your parcel unwrapped for customs inspection. To be on the safe side, bring your own wrapping materials, as more often than not there is nothing in the parcel office. There is a 20kg limit and parcels should not be longer than 1.5m on any side.

A 10kg parcel to Australia will cost Dr780 by surface mail and Dr1500 by air. The same parcel to the UK is Dr270 by surface mail and Dr420 by air.

There is usually an Express Mail Service (EMS), or Poste Rapide, in the same office as parcel post. You can send up to 500g to France, Spain and Portugal for Dr160, to the rest of Europe for Dr200, to the Americas for Dr300 and to Australia for Dr400. Your letter or package should arrive within 24 hours in Europe and within two to three days elsewhere, but don't rely on it.

Receiving Mail

Having mail addressed to 'Poste Restante, La Poste Principale' of any big town should not be a problem. There is generally a small charge for picking up any items you receive. Note, however, that some offices don't hang on to parcels for more than a couple of weeks before returning them to the sender. Remember to take your passport as proof of identity, as no other document will be accepted.

Possibly a more reliable way to receive mail is American Express, which has three branches in Morocco (see the earlier Money section for addresses). To qualify for the client mail service, you are supposed to have American Express travellers cheques

or an Amex card. In practice, you are usually asked only to produce a passport for identification. There is no charge for any letters you receive.

Telephone

The telephone system in Morocco is now very good thanks to the hundreds of millions of dollars that have been poured into it in recent years.

Most cities and towns have at least one phone office (increasingly known by its Arabic title – Itissalat al-Maghrib) and in the main centres they are open round the clock, seven days a week.

For overseas calls you can either book a call at the office and pay at the counter, or dial direct.

Private sector *téléboutiques* have recently mushroomed throughout the country and are much quicker than the official phone offices. You can buy *télécartes* (phone-cards) for Dr93.50 (70 units) and Dr156 (120 units) here for use in card phones or the attendant can provide as much change as you might need. Télécartes are also available at phone offices as well as from tabacs.

Domestic Dialling For telephone purposes, Morocco is divided into eight regions. Roughly from north to south, the area codes are as follows (remember to dial 0 first when calling from within Morocco):

9 – Tangier, Tetouan, Al-Hoceima, Larache, Asilah

6 – Nador, Oujda, Bouarfa, Figuig

5 – Fès, Meknès, Taza, Er-Rachidia

7 – Rabat, Kenitra, Ouezzane

2 – Casablanca and immediate vicinity

3 – El-Jadida, Beni Mellal

4 – Marrakesh, Essaouira, Safi, Ouarzazate

8 – The rest of the country, including Agadir, Taroudannt, Tata and all of the Western Sahara

The police can be reached on ☎ 19; the fire service on ☎ 15; and the highway emergency service on ☎ 177.

To make a local call with a coin-operated phone, you must insert a minimum of Dr1.50. Costs are worked out in units (one unit equals 80 centimes) and your initial Dr1.50 gets you about 12 minutes.

For long-distance calls within Morocco, one unit gets you from two minutes (35km or under) to 12 seconds (300km or more). Calls are half-price from midnight to 7 am, 40% off at any other time on Sunday and holidays, as well as from 12.30 pm to midnight on Saturday and 8.30 pm to midnight on other days. There is a 10% discount from 12.30 to 2 pm on weekdays.

International Dialling When calling overseas from Morocco, dial ☎ 00, your country code and then the city code and number. To call Morocco from abroad, dial the international access code, then 212 (Morocco's country code), the regional code and the local number.

International calls from Morocco are expensive. The cheap rate (40% off) operates all day Sunday and on holidays, all day Saturday except from 7 am to 12.30 pm and from midnight to 7 am on weekdays. On weekdays the rate is 20% off from 10 pm to midnight.

There are six international zones for telephone purposes, and rates range from Dr8.20 a minute in Zone 1 (just under US$1) to Dr32 (just over US$3) in Zone 6. France, for instance, lies in Zone 2 (Dr13.70 a minute), as do most other Western European countries.

Calling London from Morocco
London telephone numbers currently have two codes (☎ 0171 or ☎ 0181) before a seven-digit number, but as of Easter Saturday 2000, the area code will change to 020. Subscribers will also have to put a 7 in front of numbers that used to have an 0171 code and an 8 in front of those with an old 0181 code. Please modify the London numbers given throughout this book accordingly.

It makes no difference whether you use a phonecard or place a call through a telephone office. There is, thankfully, no three-minute minimum, but in the telephone offices you'll pay for every minute or part thereof.

Reverse Charges It is possible to make reverse-charge (collect) calls from Morocco (except to Australia), but it can involve painfully long waits in phone offices. If you want to do this, say 'Je voudrais téléphoner en PCV' (pronounced peh-seh-veh) – the French expression for this service.

A popular international service known as 'country direct' or 'home direct' is barely acknowledged as yet in Morocco, but before you leave home it might be worth investigating whether such a link exists between your country and Morocco. It involves calling a toll-free number (usually from phone offices only) that connects you with operators in your home country, through whom you can then request reverse-charge calls and the like. Countries providing this service include the UK, Spain and Holland.

Calling from Hotels You can make local calls from hotels, but you will generally be charged a minimum of about Dr5. The bigger hotels usually offer international phone and fax services should you want to avail yourself of them. Remember that it can easily cost double the normal amount, depending on the type of call you make, so it is really only for the desperate or those on expense accounts.

Telephone Directories There is one standard phone book for all Morocco in French – the *Annuaire des Abonnés au Téléphone*. Most phone offices have a copy lying around. There is a slimmer volume containing fax numbers only. Look up the city first and then the person you want.

A kind of Yellow Pages, *Télécontact*, is available in some bookshops. If your French is OK, you could dial ☎ 16 for information *(renseignements)*.

Fax, Telegraph & Email

Most téléboutiques offer fax services. Prices per page vary, but you can expect to pay about Dr50 to Europe and Dr100 to Australia and North America. Only the main post offices in any given town have telex and telegraph services. Few, if any, post offices offer fax services.

Email access is available at the Sheraton hotels in Casablanca and Fès and there is an Internet cafe in Tangier. See individual entries for addresses.

Ceuta & Melilla

Although situated in North Africa, the two enclaves of Ceuta and Melilla are Spanish territory and so their post and phone services are part of the Spanish system.

Post Post offices are called *Correos y Telégrafos*. Don't expect a superfast service. Post can take a good week or more to arrive from just about anywhere – distance seems to make little difference.

Postcards and letters up to 20g cost 60pta to other countries of the European Union, 114pta to North America and 156pta to Australia.

Parcels Parcels up to a maximum weight of 20kg can also be sent from the post office. It costs 2052pta to send a 2kg parcel to Europe by air. Charges for larger packages vary considerably.

The Express Mail Service also goes by the name of *postal exprés*. You can send up to one kilogram for 3300pta to Europe, Turkey and the countries of the Maghreb. The same parcel would cost 5500pta to North and Central America and most Middle Eastern countries, and 7000pta to the rest of the world.

Receiving Mail Poste restante is in the main post office of each of the enclaves. Ask for the *lista de correos*.

Telephone The Telefónica is a separate organisation from the Correos y Telégrafos. Phoning is generally no problem. Telefónica either has its own phone office or has contracted the service out to bureaux known as *locutorios*, which are generally open from 10 am to 10 pm, with a three hour afternoon break from 2 pm.

You can buy phonecards in post offices and selected newsstands and kiosks. They cost 1000 and 2000pta. Most phones accept cards and coins.

There is nothing cheap about the phone in Spain (and hence its enclaves). The standard day rate for international calls will make that clear. A three minute call costs 350pta to other EU countries, 600pta to North America, and 1100pta to Australia. There is no minimum call time, but you pay for every minute or part thereof. The cheap rate (about 15% off) for international calls is from 10 pm to 8 am, after 2 pm on Saturday and all day Sunday and during holidays.

For calls within Spain, there are three different bands: urban, provincial and inter-provincial calls. There are three rates: morning, evening and night. The latter is the cheapest and runs from 10 pm to 8 am on weekdays and from 2 pm on Saturday until 8 am on Monday.

Making reverse-charge calls is possible from phone offices, but a growing number of countries are linked to Spain in the *país directo* (home direct) service. Home direct numbers are listed on the newer telephones.

To call outside Spain dial ☎ 07, then the country code and number. Spain's country code is 34. Ceuta's area code is 56 (same as Algeciras) and Melilla's is 5 (same as Málaga). If calling from Spain, dial 9 first.

Fax & Telegram Fax and telegram services are available in the post office. A one page fax to Europe costs 950pta, and 1700 to 2000pta to other countries.

BOOKS

Most books are published in different editions by different publishers in different countries. As a result, a book might be a hardcover rarity in one country while it's readily available in paperback in another. Fortunately, bookshops and libraries search by title or author, so your local bookshop or library is best placed to advise you on the availability of the following selections.

Because of Morocco's colonial heritage under the French, and the continued importance of French in Moroccan society, works in French have been added to the suggested reading list that follows. For information on Moroccan literature see the Arts section in the Facts about the Country chapter.

Lonely Planet

For an introduction to the complexities of Moroccan Arabic, pick up a copy of Lonely Planet's *Moroccan Arabic phrasebook*. And for an armchair glimpse of the splendours that await you, Lonely Planet also produces a video *Morocco Experience*. Contact your nearest Lonely Planet office to find out where you can purchase it.

Guidebooks

Michelin's *Guide de Tourisme – Maroc* is an excellent route guide to Morocco. The bad news is that it's only available in French. If this is not an obstacle, you can find it outside the Francophone world in some London bookstores, including Stanford's bookshop (see the Bookshops entry later in this section).

For people planning any desert driving in Morocco, the *Sahara Handbook* by Simon Glen offers detailed advice on how to plan such adventures. The same publishers have put out another book in a similar vein called *Africa Overland*.

The Adventure Motorbiking Handbook by Chris Scott is a comprehensive guide to off-road motorcycling, containing advice on planning a trip and preparing your bike, plus sections on biking off the beaten track in Morocco and a selection of first-hand travellers' tales.

Travel

Morocco – The Traveller's Companion by Margaret & Robin Bidwell is a compilation of writing by westerners who in one way or another have come into contact with Morocco. The line-up ranges from the likes

of Leo Africanus to Samuel Pepys and George Orwell.

By Bus to the Sahara by Gordon West tells of an eventful journey made by the author and his wife Mary across Spanish Morocco in the 1930s. Their travels take them to Rabat, Meknès and Marrakesh, as well as to tiny oases villages where they are met and befriended by fire-eaters, sorcerers, slave dealers, holy men and descendants of the prophet.

Edith Wharton's *In Morocco* chronicles the three years she spent in the country from 1917.

An entertaining account of a westerner's travails in Morocco more than a century ago is *Morocco – Its People & Places* by Edmondo de Amicis, which first appeared in 1882. Equally interesting, but potentially very irritating for modern readers, is Frances Macnab's *A Ride in Morocco*, a British woman's rather strident account of her adventures on horseback from Tangier to Marrakesh at the turn of the century.

Islamic, Arab & North African History

For those wanting to become generally acquainted with the wider Arabic-speaking world, there are several books to recommend. Philip Hitti's very readable *History of the Arabs* is regarded as a classic.

A more recent, but equally acclaimed, work is Albert Hourani's *A History of the Arab Peoples*. It is as much an attempt to convey a feel for evolving Muslim Arab societies as a straightforward history, with extensive, if largely generalised, treatment of various aspects of social, cultural and religious life.

If you want a more comprehensive reference source on the whole Muslim world (although it's weak on more recent history), you could try delving into the two hardback or four paperback volumes of *A Cambridge History of Islam*. Volume 2A has a section devoted to North African history.

Maghreb: Histoire et Société is one of a number of studies by Jacques Berque, who is regarded as one of the better historians of the region in the French language.

In an attempt to get away from a French interpretation of Maghreb history, Abdallah Laroui wrote *The History of the Maghreb* (translated from the French by Ralph Manheim). He strives to assert an indigenous view and is regarded by some Moroccans as the best there is. Unfortunately, the book is out of print and hard to track down. It is as much an analysis of how historians have dealt with Maghreb history as an account of events and so not as useful an introduction to the country.

For a completely different perspective, Gabriel Camp's *L'Afrique du Nord au Féminin* presents stories of famous women of the Maghreb and the Sahara from 6000 BC to the present. Camps has written several works dealing with various aspects of Maghreb history.

History

Histoire du Maroc by Bernard Lugan is a reasonable potted history of the country, although it rather falls back into the category Abdallah Laroui was combating.

Les Almoravides by Vincent Lagardare traces the history of this great Berber dynasty from 1062 to 1145.

The Conquest of the Sahara by Douglas Porch describes France's attempts to gain control of the Sahara and subdue the Tuaregs. His *Conquest of Morocco* examines the takeover of Morocco by Paris, which led to the establishment of the protectorate.

A Country with a Government and a Flag by CR Pennell is an account of the anticolonial struggle in the Rif from 1921 to 1926 which threatened the French and Spanish hold over their respective protectorates.

In *Lords of the Atlas: the Rise and Fall of the House of Glaoua 1893-1956* Gavin Maxwell recounts the story of Thami el-Glaoui, the Pasha of Marrakesh. The book relates some of the more extraordinary events linked with this local despot, who even after WWII ordered that the heads of his enemies be mounted on the city gates.

The Western Sahara desert region, which Morocco claims and to all intents and purposes now controls, remains a contentious issue. Claiming the territory has been an important feature of the government's policy and if you want to read its side of the story you could try *Hassan II présente la Marche Verte*. The title refers to the Green March, when Moroccan troops and civilians moved in to take control of the territory in 1975 as Spain pulled out.

The Western Saharans by Virginia Thompson & Richard Adloff takes a less government-friendly view of the conflict.

Other books on the issue include *Conflict in North-West Africa – The Western Sahara Dispute* by John Damis, *Spanish Sahara* by John Mercer and *Western Sahara – The Roots of a Desert War* by Tony Hedges.

On contemporary Morocco, the French writer Gilles Perrault caused a diplomatic storm with his none-too-complimentary *Notre Ami Le Roi*. Don't be seen carrying this one around with you in Morocco!

People & Society

Patience and Power – Women's Lives in a Moroccan Village by Susan Davies is a fascinating and very readable book which does away with much of the myth surrounding women in Islamic society. Davies maintains that Moroccan women are not in a position subordinate to men, but rather in possession of both patience and power.

Further insights into the lives of Moroccan women can be found in Elizabeth Warnock Fernea's personal view of women, *A Street in Marrakesh*, and Leonora Peets's *Women of Marrakesh* which has been translated from the Estonian. Although she is not Muslim, Peets became very close to the women she met in the 40 years she spent in Morocco from 1930.

Moroccan Dialogues by Kevin Dwyer discusses various sociological issues, such as marriage and circumcision, in a series of interviews with Moroccans of different generations, backgrounds and social positions.

Peter Mayne's highly readable *A Year in Marrakesh*, first published in 1953, is his account of time spent living among the people of the city and observations on their lives.

The House of Si Abdallah – The Oral History of a Moroccan Family, recorded, translated and edited by Henry Munson Jr, gives a unique insight into the daily lives and thoughts of Moroccans, mainly seen through the eyes of a traditional peddler in Tangier and his westernised cousin, a woman living in the USA. Munson's *Religion and Power in Morocco* provides an equally good insight into Islam in Morocco.

The Structure of Traditional Moroccan Rural Society by Bernard Hoffman is a good title for detailed information about the Berber population of Morocco. *Les Berbères* by Gabriel Camps and *Berbères Aujourd'hui* by Salem Chaker cover the same subject.

The Mellah Society by Shlomo Deshen looks at Jewish community life in Morocco.

Foreign Writers

Of foreigners who have written in or about Morocco, Paul Bowles, who still lives in Tangier, is probably the best known. *The Sheltering Sky*, made into a film by Bernardo Bertolucci in 1990 (in which Bowles makes a cameo appearance), tells the story of an American couple who arrive in North Africa shortly after WWII and try to put their relationship back together. The early stages of the film were shot in Morocco, although in the novel the action takes place in Oran (Algeria).

The film served to bring the author back to public prominence. Other books by Bowles include *The Spider's House* and *Let It Come Down*, the latter of which is set in Tangier. *Their Heads Are Green* is a collection of travel tales set in several countries, including Morocco, and provides some interesting insights to the country.

Iain Finlayson's *Tangier – City of the Dream* is an intriguing look at some of the western literati who found a new home in Morocco at one time or another. The single greatest entry deals with Paul and Jane Bowles and those around them, but there is interesting material on William Burroughs,

Beat writers, Truman Capote, Joe Orton and others. It is a highly readable account of the life of this 'seedy, salacious, decadent, degenerate' city.

Elias Canetti, a foremost novelist in the German language, ended up in Marrakesh in 1954 in the company of a film team and penned his recollections in a slim but moving volume of short and elegantly simple stories entitled *Die Stimmen von Marrakesch*. It has appeared in English as *The Voices of Marrakesh*.

From the 1890s to the early 1930s, *The Times'* correspondent Walter Harris lived through the period in which Morocco fell under the growing influence of France. His whimsical and highly amusing, if not always totally believable, *Morocco That Was* first appeared in 1921.

At the beginning of the century, Budgett Meakin made one of the first serious attempts by a westerner at an overall appraisal of Moroccan society and history. First published in 1901, Darf Publishers in London thought *The Land of the Moors* interesting enough to bring out again in 1986.

If the writing on Morocco from this period appeals, another book of casual interest, mainly for its reflection on the ideas of the more zealous westerners living in the Orient, is Donald Mackenzie's *The Khalifate of the West*, first printed in 1911.

Arts & Architecture

A Practical Guide to Islamic Monuments in Morocco by Richard Parker is exactly what its title suggests and is full of town maps, pictures and ground plans of important monuments.

Titus Burckhardt's *Fès, City of Islam* is a pictorial treasure, including many of the art historian's own black and white shots of the city from his visits in the 1930s.

Islamic Architecture – North Africa by Antony Hutt is a pictorial overview of the great buildings of the Maghreb.

Rome in Africa by Susan Raven discusses all the Roman sites of Morocco.

Zillij – The Art of Moroccan Ceramics, by John Hedgecoe & Salma Sanar Damluji, is a decent study of an important aspect of Moroccan decoration, also often known as *zellij*.

Les Tapis has all you ever wanted to know (in French) about Moroccan carpets and rugs.

Living in Morocco, by Lisl & Landt Dennis, is a sumptuous coffee table book with a lot of material on Moroccan arts and crafts.

Arts and Crafts of Morocco by James Jereb provides excellent information on textiles, jewellery, leatherwork, woodwork, metalwork and ceramics. There is also a good section on collecting Moroccan arts and crafts.

For an aerial approach, have a look at *Maroc Vu d'en Haut* by Anne & Yann Arthus-Bertrand.

If traditional Moroccan dancing fascinates you, a look at *Danses du Maghreb* by Viviane Lièvre will give you a deeper insight into the meaning and history behind it.

Musique du Maroc by Ahmed Aydoun and *La Musique Arabo-Andalouse* by C Poché both deal with the rich traditions of music in Morocco.

Food

The Taste of Morocco by Robert Carrier is an excellent illustrated guide to Moroccan cuisine.

Also worth dipping into is *Good Food From Morocco* by Paula Wolfert. The best way to learn the joys of the cuisine, she writes, is to try home cooking or get invited to a banquet.

There are several good cookery books in French, including *Ma Cuisine Marocaine* by Mina El Glaoui, *Gestes et Saveurs du Maroc* by Fatima Hal and *La Cuisine Marocaine Familiale* by Khadidja Kfita.

Bookshops

Morocco Morocco is not exactly bursting with good bookshops and you will certainly be much better served if you can read French, as the better stores have a far wider selection both on Morocco and general subjects.

Branches of the American Language Center in Rabat, Marrakesh and Casablanca have small bookshops dedicated mainly to English literature and learning the English language (the one in Rabat has a very good selection).

In addition, there is an English bookshop in both Rabat and Fès. Rabat probably has the best general bookstores (which mostly stock works in French, although you'll find the occasional book on Morocco in English), but there are one or two good bookshops in Casablanca, Tangier, Marrakesh and Fès. For details, see the relevant chapters.

Outside Morocco Most of the books in French are not readily available outside France, although one exception is the small Maghreb Bookshop (☎ 0171-388 1840; fax 837 4988) at 45 Burton St, London WC1H 9AL, which leans towards the academic side.

For a good range of travel guides, literature and maps, Stanford's (☎ 0171-836 1915), 12-14 Long Acre, London WC2E 9LP, is one of the best shops of its kind in the UK.

Some of the bigger mainstream bookstores also have a range of material on Morocco. Another good source of travel literature is The Travel Bookshop (☎ 0171-229 5260) at 13 Blenheim Cres, London W11 2EE.

If you are interested in literature on Islam, Moroccan history and politics, or a wide range of subjects pertinent to the Muslim world, Al Hoda (☎ 0171-240 8381; fax 497 0180) at 76-78 Charing Cross Rd, London WC2, is a useful resource.

A couple of specialist shops in Paris are worth exploring if you have more than a passing interest in things North African. L'Harmattan (☎ 01.46.34.13.71) at 21 Rue des Écoles in the Latin Quarter is probably the best. They publish a lot of Maghreb literature in French.

Another place worth trying nearby is Le Tiers Mythe (☎ 01.43.26.72.70) at 21 Rue Cujas.

ONLINE SERVICES

If you have access to the Web, there is a good site about Morocco (http://maghreb. net/countries/morocco/index.html). This site also has links to cities, culture, entertainment and history. You also might like to try Lonely Planet's entry (http:/www. lonelyplanet.com) or another location with general information about a number of Moroccan towns and cities (http://i-cias.com/ m.s/morocco/index.htm).

FILMS

Morocco has been the setting, both real and imagined, for countless films. The most famous is probably *Casablanca* starring Humphrey Bogart and Lauren Bacall (shot completely on location in Hollywood). Others having little to do with the country itself and more to do with western images of exotic North Africa include the hilarious *Road to Morocco* starring Bing Crosby and Bob Hope, the Marx Brothers' *One Night in Casablanca* and *Ali Baba & The Forty Thieves* starring Yul Brynner.

Orson Welles shot much of his acclaimed *Othello* in the former Portuguese ports of Essaouira, Safi and El Jadida, while Alfred Hitchcock chose the chaotic medinas of Marrakesh for *The Man Who Knew Too Much*, which starred James Stewart and Doris Day.

Lawrence of Arabia, directed by David Lean in 1962 and starring Peter O'Toole, Alec Guinness, Anthony Quinn, Anthony Quayle and Omar Sharif, includes scenes filmed on location in the fabulous kasbah of Aït Benhaddou (much of the village was later rebuilt for the making of *Jesus of Nazareth*). Recently restored to its full glory, 'Lawrence' contains some stupendous shots of central Morocco.

The country features strongly in Bernardo Bertolucci's *The Sheltering Sky*, based on Paul Bowles famous 1949 novel of the same name. John Malkovich and Debra Winger star as the American couple wandering ever further from the familiar in postwar North Africa. At one point, the film shows the 80-year-old Bowles watching his characters from a seat in a Tangier cafe. The 1970 film *In the Land Where the Jumblies Live* is an interview with Bowle at home in Tangier. For information on Moroccan films, see the Film entry in the preceding Facts about the Country chapter.

NEWSPAPERS & MAGAZINES

Morocco possesses a diverse press in both Arabic and French. The bulk of the daily papers owe their allegiance to one or other

---

Orson Welles' Othello

As Othello lies dead, a horrified Iago is hoisted above the crowd in an iron cage and the play begins.

Orson Welles filmed much of his adaptation of Shakespeare's classic tale of jealousy and retribution in Essaouira, including this opening scene; a dramatic panoramic shot of the town's ramparts where Iago is suspended above the rocks and sea.

Considered by many as Welles' most dazzling visual work, *Othello* includes the murder of Rodrigo in a local hammam and a riot scene in the Citerne Portugaise in El-Jadida. The reflection of the roof and the 25 arched pillars in the water covering the citerne's floor created a stunning and memorable effect.

Othello was perhaps Welles' most chaotic shooting schedule with production spanning three years. Despite being hampered by a host of difficulties – he left the set regularly to traipse around Europe to borrow money, and during the course of the film went through four Desdemonas (including his fiance who then had an affair with one of the crew) – *Othello* won the Grand Prix (now Palme d'Or) at Cannes in 1952.

At the time of Welles' death, *Othello* was the only one of his films he owned. It was restored by his daughter in 1992 and re-released to huge acclaim.

At an open-air performance in Essaouira, a square on the sea front was officially renamed Place Orson Welles in his honour. ∎

political party or grouping. Although censorship does not take the form of blobs of black ink appearing in your morning paper, none of the papers rocks the boat much. Even those run by opposition parties rarely, if ever, say anything that could be construed as antimonarchist. It is quite all right for the parties to attack one another, and for the opposition to criticise the government, but the country's real power – the royal family – is another kettle of fish.

None of the newspapers make riveting reading and none has a huge circulation.

The pro-government, French-language daily *Le Matin du Sahara et du Maghreb* (which also appears in Arabic and Spanish) is an extremely turgid read, yet sometimes manages a print run of 100,000. Most papers publish fewer than 50,000 copies.

Among the French papers (most of which have an Arabic equivalent), *l'Opinion*, which is based in Rabat and attached to the opposition Istiqlal Party, is perhaps the most interesting for getting an idea of some of the points of contention in Moroccan society.

Libération, the Union Socialiste des Forces Populaires' daily, produced in Casablanca, is similar if less punchy. *Al Bayane*, another opposition daily, is not too bad for foreign news. All have listings for the Casablanca and Rabat cinemas, airport shuttle timetables, Royal Air Maroc arrivals and departures and a list of late-night pharmacies that work on a rotating roster.

There is a plethora of sports papers, fashion magazines and the like, and a surprising number of weeklies dedicated to economics, as well as political and social themes.

For readers of French who happen to be trying to learn Arabic, the monthly *La Tribune du Maroc* is worth getting hold of. It culls the local Arabic and French language press to cover the main events of the month and runs articles in both languages.

There is virtually nothing produced locally in English. A tiny monthly put out in Fès, *The Messenger of Morocco* (Dr3), is of minimal interest.

Foreign Press

In the main centres, a reasonable range of foreign press is available at central newsstands and in some of the big hotels. News magazines such as *Newsweek* and *Time* are usually fairly easy to find, along with the *International Herald Tribune* and a range of UK papers, including the *International Guardian*, and their Continental European equivalents. The French press is about as up-to-date and easy to obtain as in France itself and is by far the cheapest – there seems to be virtually no added charge for import costs.

Tourist Publications

A useful booklet loaded with practical information, listings and the like is called *La Quinzaine du Maroc*, which appears every fortnight. It's available in the main cities (look in the bigger hotels and tourist offices) and is usually free.

RADIO & TV

Local radio is an odd mix. There is only a handful of local AM and FM stations, the bulk of which broadcast in Arabic and French. At least one of the FM stations plays quite reasonable contemporary music. The frequencies change from one part of the country to another.

Throughout northern Morocco and along much of the Atlantic coast you can pick up a host of Spanish stations, especially on the AM band. In fact, you can usually tune into Spanish radio just about anywhere in Morocco, although reception can be patchy.

None of this is much use if you don't understand Spanish, but it may give you a choice in terms of music.

On the north coast around Tangier, and across to Ceuta, you can often pick up English-language broadcasts from Gibraltar.

The Voice of America has long had a presence just outside Tangier, and in September 1993 opened its biggest transmitter outside the USA at a cost of US$225 million. You can tune into VOA on various short-wave frequencies.

The other short-wave option in English is

the BBC. It broadcasts on MHz 15,070, 12,095 and 9410, and several other frequencies. The bulk of the programmes are broadcast from about 8 am to 11 pm.

Satellite dishes constitute a striking phenomena in Moroccan cities and even in villages. There are dozens of foreign stations – Arabic, French, German and English (CNN, NBC and even Cartoon Network). Thanks to satellite dishes, Algerian TV can be watched everywhere in Morocco. Spanish networks dominate in the north of the country due to their proximity to the Iberian Peninsula – the more risqué stations like Télé 5 are extremely popular.

Apart from the above, there are two government-owned stations, TVM and 2M, which broadcast in Arabic and French (TVM also has the news in Spanish at 7 pm) and TV5 which is basically a European satellite import from the Francophone world with programs from France, Belgium, Switzerland and Canada.

VIDEO SYSTEMS

If you want to record or buy video tapes to play back home, you won't get a picture if the image registration systems are different. Morocco and France use the SECAM system, which is incompatible with the PAL system used in Australia and most of Western Europe and the NTSC system used in North America and Japan.

PHOTOGRAPHY & VIDEO
Film & Equipment

Kodak and Fuji colour-negative film, as well as video tapes, are readily available in the big cities and towns, but are marginally more expensive than in Europe. Slide film (particularly good quality film) is more difficult to come by, even in larger cities. If you buy film in Morocco, be sure to check expiry dates. A 36 frame roll of Kodak 100 ASA print film will cost around Dr45 to Dr50. A 36 frame roll of Kodak Ektachrome slide film (100 ASA) goes for about Dr80.

There are quite a few processing shops in the cities and larger towns. Photolabs offer the most professional services. It costs Dr72 to have a 36 frame roll of colour prints developed, and as little as Dr55 to have unmounted slides done.

Photography

For most daylight outdoor shooting, 100 ASA is quite sufficient. Generally it is best to shoot in the morning and afternoon, as the light in the middle of the day is harsh and can give your pictures a glary, washed-out look.

It is worth keeping a few rolls of 200 and even 400 ASA handy for lousy weather (especially in the north in winter) and for shots in the medinas, which tend to let in a minimum of sunlight.

Video

Properly used, a video camera can give a fascinating record of your holiday. As well as videoing the obvious things – sunsets, spectacular views – remember to record some of the ordinary everyday details of life in the country. Often the most interesting things occur when you're actually intent on filming something else.

Video cameras these days have amazingly sensitive microphones and you might be surprised how much sound will be picked up. This can also be a problem if there is a lot of ambient noise – filming by the side of a busy road might seem OK when you do it, but viewing it back home might simply give you a deafening cacophony of traffic noise.

One good rule to follow for beginners is to try to film in long takes and not to move the camera around too much. Otherwise, your video could well make your viewers seasick! If your camera has a stabiliser, you can use it to obtain good footage while travelling on various means of transport, even on bumpy roads.

And remember, you're on holiday – don't let the video take over your life and turn your trip into a Cecil B de Mille production.

Make sure you keep the batteries charged and have the necessary charger, plugs and transformer for Morocco's electrical system.

It is usually worth buying at least a few cartridges duty free to start off your trip.

Finally, remember to follow the same rules regarding people's sensitivities as for still photography – having a video camera shoved in their face is probably even more annoying and offensive for locals than a still camera. Always ask permission first.

Restrictions

Morocco is full of photo opportunities, but don't point your camera at anything that is vaguely military or that could be construed as 'strategic'. This includes airports, bridges, government buildings and members of the police or armed forces.

Photographing People

It is common courtesy to ask permission before taking photographs of people. Urban Moroccans are generally easy-going about it, but in the countryside locals are not so willing to have cameras pointed at them. In particular, women and older people very often do *not* want to be photographed. Respect their right to privacy and don't take photos.

Taking photographs of your new-found friends is usually a different story and sending copies back to Morocco will be greatly appreciated.

Airport Security

Moroccan airports use X-ray scanning machines for security which should pose no problems for most films. However, any given roll should not be scanned more than half a dozen times to be on the safe side. For some specialised film, for example film with an ASA (ISO) rating of 400 or higher, X-ray damage is a danger.

For those who do not want to take a chance with any film, good camera shops sell light-weight lead-lined pouches which can hold several rolls of film and which provide total protection.

TIME

Morocco is on GMT/UTC all year-round. So (not taking account of daylight-saving time elsewhere) when it's noon in Morocco it's 8 pm in Perth and Hong Kong, 10 pm in Sydney, midnight in Auckland, 4 am in Los Angeles, 7 am in New York, noon in London and 1 pm in Western Europe. Remember if travelling between Morocco and Spain that the latter is two hours ahead in summer, which can affect plans for catching ferries and the like.

On the subject of time, Moroccans are not in nearly as much of a hurry to get things done as westerners. Rather than letting yourself be frustrated by this, it helps to learn to go with the flow a little. It may even lengthen your life. Moroccans are fond of the saying, 'He who hurries has one foot in the grave!'.

ELECTRICITY

Throughout most of the country, electricity supply is 220V at 50Hz AC, although in some places you'll still find 110V; check before plugging in any appliances. Sockets are the European two pin variety.

WEIGHTS & MEASURES

Morocco uses the metric system. There is a standard conversion table at the back of this book.

LAUNDRY

Self-service laundrettes are few and far between. You are more likely to come across establishments called *Pressings;* they look like dry-cleaners, but will happily wash (the living daylights out of) a pile of backpacker's kit. They take about 48 hours to wash and iron clothes. Prices generally range from about Dr2 for socks up to Dr15 for jackets. Pressings are usually open from 8 am to 12.30 pm and from 2.30 to 7.30 pm every day.

Most hotels, even the more basic ones, will do washing for you for a few dirham. Clothes invariably will be washed by hand and dried in the sunshine, so allow plenty of time. The simplest option is to hand-wash your clothes as you go. Most hotels have rooftop terraces where you can hang your washing out to dry.

HAMMAMS

Visiting a *hammam* (public steam bath) is an excellent alternative to cursing under a cold shower in a cheap hotel. They're busy, social places where you'll find gallons of hot water (although you may have to jealously guard your bucket) and staff available to scrub you squeaky clean and massage your travel-weary bod. They're good places to chat to the locals, too.

Every town has at least one hammam, usually tucked away in the medina. Often there are separate hammams for men and women, while others are open to either sex at different hours or on alternate days. They can be difficult to find; some are unmarked and others simply have a picture of a man or woman stencilled on the wall outside. Local people will be happy to direct you to one. You'll need to bring your own toiletries and towels. The handfuls of clay you'll see people buying in hammams is *ghassoul*, used to remove grease and for washing the hair.

Hammams usually cost Dr5 with a massage costing an extra Dr15 or so.

HEALTH

Travel health depends on your predeparture preparations, your daily health care while travelling and how you handle any medical problem that does develop. While the potential dangers can seem quite frightening, in reality few travellers experience anything more than upset stomachs.

Predeparture Planning

Immunisations There are no immunisations officially required for Morocco. All travellers, however, should be up to date with polio and tetanus and you may want to consider some of the other immunisations listed below. Be aware that there is often a greater risk of disease with children and in pregnancy. Discuss your requirements with your doctor and plan ahead for getting any vaccinations: some of them require more than one injection, while some vaccinations should not be given together.

It is recommended you seek medical advice at least six weeks before you travel. Record all vaccinations on an International Health Certificate, available from your doctor or government health department.

Hepatitis A This is the most common travel-acquired illness after diarrhoea which can put you out of action for weeks. Havrix 1440 is a vaccination which provides long term immunity (possibly more than 10 years) after an initial injection and a booster at six to 12 months.

Gamma globulin is not a vaccination, but a ready-made antibody collected from blood donations. It should be given close to departure because, depending on the dose, it only protects for two to six months.

Typhoid This is an important vaccination to have where hygiene is a problem. It's available either as an injection or oral capsules.

Diphtheria & Tetanus Diphtheria can be a fatal throat infection and tetanus can be a fatal wound infection. Everyone should have these vaccinations. After an initial course of three injections, boosters are necessary every 10 years.

Meningococcal Meningitis Healthy people carry this disease; it is transmitted like a cold and you can die from it within a few hours. Although throughout most of Morocco it is not a problem, sub-Saharan Africa is within the 'meningitis belt'. A single injection will give good protection for three years. The vaccine is not recommended for children under two years because they do not develop satisfactory immunity from it.

Hepatitis B This disease is spread by blood or by sexual activity. Travellers who should consider a hepatitis B vaccination include those visiting countries where there are known to be many carriers, where blood transfusions may not be adequately screened or where sexual contact is a possibility. It involves three injections, the quickest course being over three weeks with a booster at 12 months.

Polio Polio is a serious, easily transmitted disease, still prevalent in many developing countries. Everyone should keep up to date with this vaccination. A booster every 10 years maintains immunity.

Rabies Vaccination should be considered by those who will spend a month or longer in a country where rabies is common – especially if they are cycling, handling animals, caving, travelling to remote areas – or for children (who may not report a bite). Pre-travel rabies vaccination involves having three injections.

Medical Kit Check List

Consider taking a basic medical kit including:

- **Aspirin** or paracetamol (acetaminophen in the USA) – for pain or fever.
- **Antihistamine** (such as Benadryl) – useful as a decongestant for colds and allergies, to ease the itch from insect bites or stings, and to help prevent motion sickness. Anti histamines may cause sedation and also interact with alcohol so care should be taken when using them; take one you know and have used before, if possible.
- **Antibiotics** – useful if you're travelling well off the beaten track, but they must be prescribed; carry the prescription with you.
- **Loperamide** (eg Imodium) or Lomotil for diarrhoea; prochlorperazine (eg Stemetil) or metaclopramide (eg Maxalon) for nausea and vomiting.
- **Rehydration** mixture – for treatment of severe diarrhoea; particularly important for travelling with children.
- **Antiseptic** such as povidone-iodine (eg Betadine) – for cuts and grazes.
- **Multivitamins** – especially for long trips when dietary vitamin intake may be inadequate.
- **Calamine lotion** or **aluminium sulphate spray** (eg Stingose) – to ease irritation from bites or stings.
- **Bandages** and **Band-aids**.
- **Scissors, tweezers** and a **thermometer** (note that mercury thermometers are prohibited by airlines).
- **Cold and flu tablets** and **throat lozenges**. Pseudoephedrine hydrochloride (Sudafed) may be useful if flying with a cold to avoid ear damage.
- **Insect repellent, sunscreen, chap stick** and **water purification tablets**.

Health Insurance Make sure that you have adequate health insurance. See the Travel Insurance entry in the Visas & Documents section earlier in this chapter for details.

Travel Health Guides If you are planning to be away or travelling in remote areas for a long period of time, you may like to consider taking a more detailed health guide.

Staying Healthy in Asia, Africa & Latin America, by Dirk Schroeder, Moon Publications, 1994. Probably the best all-round guide to carry, it's compact, detailed and well organised.

Travellers' Health, by Dr Richard Dawood, Oxford University Press, 1995. It's comprehensive, easy to read, authoritative and highly recommended, although it's rather large to lug around.

Where There is No Doctor, by David Werner, Macmillan, 1994. A very detailed guide intended for someone, such as a Peace Corps worker, going to work in an underdeveloped country.

Travel with Children, by Maureen Wheeler, Lonely Planet Publications, 1995. Includes advice on travel health for younger children.

There are also a number of excellent travel health sites on the Internet. From Lonely Planet's home page there are links at (http://www.lonelyplanet.com/health/health.htm/h-links.htm) to the World Health Organisation, the US Center for Diseases Control & Prevention and Stanford University Travel Medicine Service.

Other Preparations Make sure you're healthy before you start travelling. If you are going on a long trip make sure your teeth are OK. If you wear glasses, take a spare pair and your prescription.

If you require a particular medication, take an adequate supply as it may not be available locally. Take part of the packaging which shows the generic name, rather than the brand, which will make getting replacements easier. To avoid any problems, it's a good idea to have a legible prescription or letter from your doctor to show that you legally use the medication.

Basic Rules

Food There is an old colonial adage which says: 'If you can cook it, boil it or peel it you can eat it ... otherwise forget it'. Vegetables and fruit should be washed with purified water or peeled where possible. Beware of ice cream which is sold in the street or anywhere it might have been melted and refrozen; if there's any doubt (eg a power cut in the last day or two) steer well clear. Shellfish such as mussels, oysters and clams should be avoided, as well as undercooked meat, particularly in

the form of mince. Steaming does not make shellfish safe for eating. If a place looks clean and well run and the vendor also looks clean and healthy, then the food is probably safe. In general, places that are packed with travellers or locals will be fine, while empty restaurants are questionable. The food in busy restaurants is cooked and eaten quite quickly with little standing around and is probably not reheated.

Water The number-one rule is *be careful of the water* and especially ice. If you don't know for certain that the water is safe, assume the worst. Reputable brands of bottled water or soft drinks are generally fine, although in some places bottles may be refilled with tap water.

Only use water from containers with a serrated seal – not tops or corks. Take care with fruit juice, particularly if water may have been added. Milk should be treated with suspicion as it is often unpasteurised, though boiled milk is fine if it is kept hygienically. Tea or coffee should also be OK, since the water should have been boiled.

Water Purification The simplest way of purifying water is to boil it thoroughly. Vigorously boiling it should be satisfactory, however, at high altitude water boils at a lower temperature, so germs are less likely to be killed. Boil it for longer in these environments. Consider purchasing a water filter for a long trip.

There are two main kinds of filter. Total filters take out all parasites, bacteria and viruses, and make water safe to drink. They are often expensive, but they can be more cost effective than buying bottled water. Simple filters (which can even be a nylon mesh bag) take out dirt and larger foreign bodies from the water so that chemical solutions work much more effectively; if water is dirty, chemical solutions may not work at all.

It's very important when buying a filter to read the specifications, so that you know exactly what it removes from the water and what it doesn't. Simple filtering will not

---

Nutrition

If your food is poor or limited in availability, if you're travelling hard and fast and therefore missing meals, or if you simply lose your appetite, you can soon start to lose weight and place your health at risk.

Make sure your diet is well balanced. Cooked eggs, beans, lentils and nuts are all safe ways to get protein. Fruit you can peel (bananas, oranges or mandarins for example) is usually safe and is a good source of vitamins (although melons can harbour bacteria in their flesh and are best avoided). Try to eat plenty of grains (including rice) and bread. Remember that although food is generally safer if it is cooked well, overcooked food loses much of its nutritional value. If your diet isn't well balanced or if your food intake is insufficient, it's a good idea to take vitamin and iron pills.

In hot climates make sure you drink enough – don't rely on feeling thirsty to indicate when you should drink. Not needing to urinate or small amounts of very dark yellow urine is a danger sign. Always carry a water bottle with you. Excessive sweating can lead to loss of salt and therefore muscle cramping. Salt tablets are not a good idea as a preventative, but in places where salt is not used much adding salt to food can help. ∎

remove all dangerous organisms, so if you cannot boil the water it should be treated chemically.

Chlorine tablets (Puritabs, Steritabs or other brand names) will kill many pathogens, but not some parasites like giardia, which is common in Morocco, and amoebic cysts. Iodine is more effective at purifying water and is available in tablet form (such as Potable Aqua). Follow the directions carefully and remember that too much iodine can be harmful.

Medical Problems & Treatment

Self-diagnosis and treatment can be risky, so you should always seek medical help. Although we do give drug dosages in this section, they are for emergency use only. Correct diagnosis is vital. An embassy, consulate or five-star hotel can usually recommend a good place to go for advice.

Antibiotics should ideally be administered only under medical supervision. Take only the recommended dose at the prescribed intervals and use the whole course, even if the illness seems to be cured earlier. Stop immediately if there are any serious reactions and don't use the drug at all if you are unsure that you have the correct one.

Some people are allergic to commonly prescribed antibiotics such as penicillin or sulpha drugs – if you are, carry this information when travelling (eg on a bracelet).

Environmental Hazards

Altitude Sickness Lack of oxygen at high altitudes (over 2500m) affects most people to some extent. In Morocco, people trekking in the High Atlas mountains are most likely to be affected, although there are mountains in the Middle and Anti-Atlas ranges that reach high enough for altitude sickness to be a potential problem.

The effect may be mild or severe and occurs because less oxygen reaches the muscles and the brain at high altitude, requiring the heart and lungs to compensate by working harder. Symptoms of Acute Mountain Sickness (AMS) usually develop during the first 24 hours at altitude, but may be delayed up to three weeks. Mild symptoms include headache, lethargy, dizziness, difficulty in sleeping and loss of appetite. AMS may become more severe without warning and can be fatal. Severe symptoms can include breathlessness, a dry, irritative cough (which may progress to the production of pink, frothy sputum), severe headache, lack of coordination and balance, confusion, irrational behaviour, vomiting, drowsiness and unconsciousness. There is no hard-and-fast rule as to what is too high: AMS has been fatal at 3000m, although 3500 to 4500m is the usual range.

Treat mild symptoms by resting at the same altitude until recovery – usually a day or two. Paracetamol or aspirin can be taken for headaches. If symptoms persist or become worse, however, *immediate descent is necessary*; even 500m can help. Drug treatments should never be used to avoid descent or to enable further ascent.

The drugs acetazolamide (Diamox) and dexamethasone are recommended by some doctors to prevent AMS, however, their use is controversial. They can reduce the symptoms, but they may also mask warning signs; severe and fatal AMS has occurred in people taking these drugs. In general we do not recommend them for travellers. To prevent acute mountain sickness:

- Ascend slowly – have frequent rest days, spending two to three nights at each rise of 1000m. If you reach a high altitude by trekking, acclimatisation takes place gradually and you are less likely to be affected than if you fly directly to high altitude.
- It is always wise to sleep at a lower altitude than the greatest height reached during the day, if possible. Also, once above 3000m, care should be taken not to increase the sleeping altitude by more than 300m per day.
- Drink extra fluids. The mountain air is dry and cold and moisture is lost as you breathe. Evaporation of sweat may occur unnoticed and result in dehydration.
- Eat light, high-carbohydrate meals for more energy.
- Avoid alcohol as it may increase the risk of dehydration.
- Avoid sedatives.

Fungal Infections Fungal infections occur more commonly in hot weather and are usually found on the scalp, between the toes or fingers, in the groin and on the body (ringworm). You get ringworm (which is a fungal infection, not a worm) from infected animals or other people. Moisture encourages these infections. To prevent fungal infections wear loose, comfortable clothes, avoid artificial fibres, wash frequently and dry carefully. If you do get an infection, wash the infected area at least daily with a disinfectant or medicated soap and water, and rinse and dry well. Apply an antifungal cream or powder like tolnifate (Tinaderm). Try to expose the infected area to air or sunlight as much as possible and wash all towels and underwear in hot water, change them often and let them dry in the sun.

Heat Exhaustion Dehydration and salt deficiency can cause heat exhaustion. Take time to acclimatise to high temperatures, drink sufficient liquids and do not do anything too physically demanding. Salt deficiency is characterised by fatigue, lethargy, headaches, giddiness and muscle cramps; salt tablets may help, but adding extra salt to your food is better.

Anhydrotic heat exhaustion, caused by an inability to sweat, is quite rare. It is likely to strike people who have been in a hot climate for some time, rather than newcomers.

Heat Stroke This serious, occasionally fatal, condition can occur if the body's heat-regulating mechanism breaks down and the body temperature rises to dangerous levels. Long, continuous periods of exposure to high temperatures and insufficient fluids can leave you vulnerable to heat stroke.

The symptoms are feeling unwell, not sweating very much (or at all) and a high body temperature (39° to 41°C or 102° to 106°F). Where sweating has ceased the skin becomes flushed and red. Severe, throbbing headaches and lack of coordination will also occur and the sufferer may be confused or aggressive. Eventually the victim will become delirious or convulsive. Hospitalisation is essential, but in the interim get victims out of the sun, remove their clothing, cover them with a wet sheet or towel and then fan continually. Give fluids if they are conscious.

Hypothermia Too much cold can be just as dangerous as too much heat. If you are trekking at high altitudes or simply taking a long bus trip over mountains, particularly at night, be prepared. Hypothermia occurs when the body loses heat faster than it can produce it and the core temperature of the body falls. It is surprisingly easy to progress from very cold to dangerously cold due to a combination of wind, wet clothing, fatigue and hunger, even if the air temperature is above freezing. It is best to dress in layers; silk, wool and some of the new artificial fibres are all good insulating materials.

A hat is important as a lot of heat is lost through the head. A strong, waterproof outer layer (and a 'space' blanket for emergencies) are essential. Carry basic supplies, including food containing simple sugars to generate heat quickly and fluid to drink.

Symptoms of hypothermia are exhaustion, numb skin (particularly the toes and fingers), shivering, slurred speech, irrational or violent behaviour, lethargy, stumbling, dizzy spells, muscle cramps and violent bursts of energy. Irrationality may take the form of sufferers claiming they are warm and trying to take off their clothes.

To treat mild hypothermia, first get the person out of the wind and/or rain, remove their clothing if it's wet and replace it with dry, warm clothing. Give them hot liquids – not alcohol – and some high-kilojoule, easily digestible food. Do not rub victims, instead allow them to slowly warm themselves. This should be enough to treat the early stages of hypothermia. The early recognition and treatment of mild hypothermia is the only way to prevent severe hypothermia, which is a critical condition. If they don't respond, place them in a sleeping bag and get in with them. If possible, place them in a warm (not hot) bath.

Jet Lag Jet lag is experienced when a person travels by air across more than three time zones (each time zone usually represents a one hour time difference). It occurs because many of the functions of the human body (such as temperature, pulse rate and emptying of the bladder and bowels) are regulated by internal 24 hour cycles, called circadian rhythms.

When we travel long distances rapidly, our bodies take time to adjust to the 'new time' of our destination and we may experience fatigue, disorientation, insomnia, anxiety, impaired concentration and loss of appetite. These effects will usually be gone within three days of arrival, but to minimise the impact of jet lag:

- Rest for a couple of days prior to departure.
- Try to select flight schedules that minimise sleep deprivation; arriving late in the day means you can go to sleep soon after you arrive. For very long flights, try to organise a stopover.
- Avoid excessive eating (which bloats the stomach) and alcohol (which causes dehydration) during the flight. Instead, drink plenty of non-carbonated, non-alcoholic drinks such as fruit juice or water.
- Avoid smoking.
- Make yourself comfortable by wearing loose-fitting clothes and perhaps bringing an eye mask and ear plugs to help you sleep.
- Try to sleep at the appropriate time for the time zone you are travelling to.

Motion Sickness Eating lightly before and during a trip will reduce the chances of motion sickness. If you are prone to motion sickness, try to find a place that minimises movement – near the wing on aircraft, close to midships on boats, near the centre on buses. Fresh air usually helps; reading and cigarette smoke don't. Commercial motion-sickness preparations, which can cause drowsiness, have to be taken before the trip commences. Ginger (available in capsule form) and peppermint (including mint-flavoured sweets) are natural preventatives.

Prickly Heat Prickly heat is an itchy rash caused by excessive perspiration trapped

---

Everyday Health
Normal body temperature is up to 37°C or 98.6°F; more than 2°C (4°F) higher indicates a high fever.

The normal adult pulse rate is 60 to 100 per minute (children 80 to 100, babies 100 to 140). As a general rule the pulse increases about 20 beats per minute for each 1°C (2°F) rise in fever.

Respiration (breathing) rate is also an indicator of illness. Count the number of breaths per minute: between 12 and 20 is normal for adults and older children (up to 30 for younger children, 40 for babies). People with a high fever or serious respiratory illness breathe more quickly than normal. More than 40 shallow breaths a minute may indicate pneumonia. ■

---

under the skin. It usually strikes people who have just arrived in a hot climate. Keeping cool, bathing often, drying the skin and using a mild talcum or prickly heat powder or resorting to air-conditioning may help.

Sunburn In the desert or at high altitude you can get sunburned surprisingly quickly, even through cloud. Use a sunscreen, hat, and barrier cream for your nose and lips. Calamine lotion or Stingose spray are good for mild sunburn. Protect your eyes with good quality sunglasses, particularly if you will be near water, sand or snow.

Infectious Diseases
Amoebic Dysentery Similar to diarrhoea, this disease is more gradual in the onset of symptoms, with cramping abdominal pain and vomiting less likely; fever may not be present. It will persist until treated and can recur and cause other health problems.

Diarrhoea Simple things like a change of water, food or climate can all cause a mild bout of diarrhoea, but a few rushed toilet trips with no other symptoms is not indicative of a major problem.

Dehydration is the principal danger with any diarrhoea, particularly in children or the elderly as dehydration can occur quite quickly. Under all circumstances fluid replacement (at least equal to the volume being lost) is the most important thing to remember. Weak black tea with a little sugar; soda water; or soft drinks allowed to go flat and diluted 50% with clean water are all good.

With severe diarrhoea a rehydrating solution is preferable to replace minerals and salts lost. Commercially available oral rehydration salts (ORS) are very useful; add them to boiled or bottled water. In an emergency you can make up a solution of six teaspoons of sugar and a half teaspoon of salt to a litre of boiled or bottled water.

You need to drink at least the same volume of fluid that you are losing in bowel movements and vomiting. Urine is the best guide to the adequacy of replacement – if you have small amounts of concentrated urine, you need to drink more. Keep drinking small amounts often. Stick to a bland diet as you recover.

Lomotil or Imodium can be used to bring relief from the symptoms, although they do not actually cure the problem. Only use these drugs if you do not have access to toilets – for example, if you *must* travel. For children under 12 years Lomotil and Imodium are not recommended. Do not use these drugs if the person has a high fever or is severely dehydrated. In certain situations antibiotics may be required: diarrhoea with blood or mucous (dysentery); any fever; watery diarrhoea with fever and lethargy; persistent diarrhoea that does not improve after 48 hours; and severe diarrhoea. In these situations gut-paralysing drugs like Imodium or Lomotil should be avoided.

A stool test is necessary to diagnose which kind of dysentery you have, so you should seek medical help urgently. Where this is not possible the recommended drugs for dysentery are norfloxacin 400mg twice daily for three days or ciprofloxacin 500mg twice daily for five days. These are not recommended for children or pregnant women. The drug of choice for children would be co-trimoxazole (Bactrim, Septrin or Resprim) with dosage dependent on weight. A five day course is given. Ampicillin or amoxycillin may be given in pregnancy, but medical care is necessary.

Giardiasis Giardiasis is another type of diarrhoea. The parasite causing this intestinal disorder is present in contaminated water. The symptoms are stomach cramps; nausea; a bloated stomach; watery, foul-smelling diarrhoea; and frequent gas.

Giardiasis can appear several weeks after you have been exposed to the parasite. The symptoms may disappear for a few days and then return; this can go on for several weeks. Tinidazole, known as Fasigyn, or metronidazole (Flagyl) are the recommended drugs. Treatment is a 2g single dose of Fasigyn or 250mg of Flagyl three times daily for five to 10 days.

Hepatitis Hepatitis is a general term for inflammation of the liver. It is a common disease worldwide. The symptoms are fever, chills, headache, fatigue, feelings of weakness , aches and pains, followed by loss of appetite, nausea, vomiting, abdominal pain, dark urine, light-coloured faeces, jaundiced (yellow) skin and possible yellowing of the whites of the eyes.

Hepatitis A is transmitted by contaminated food and drinking water. The disease poses a real threat to the western traveller. You should seek medical advice, but there is not much you can do apart from resting, drinking lots of fluids, eating lightly and avoiding fatty foods. People who have had hepatitis should avoid alcohol for some time after the illness, as the liver needs time to recover.

Hepatitis E is transmitted in the same way and it can be very serious in pregnant women.

There are almost 300 million chronic carriers of Hepatitis B in the world. It is spread through contact with infected blood, blood products or body fluids, such as sexual contact, unsterilised needles and blood transfusions, or contact with blood via small breaks in the skin. Other risks include having a shave, tattoo, or your body pierced with contaminated equipment. The symptoms of type B may be more severe and may lead to long term problems.

Hepatitis D is spread in the same way, but the risk is mainly in shared needles.

Hepatitis C can lead to chronic liver disease. The virus is spread by contact with blood, usually via contaminated transfusions or shared needles. Avoiding these is the only means of prevention.

HIV & AIDS HIV (Human Immunodeficiency Virus) can develop into the fatal disease AIDS (Acquired Immune Deficiency Syndrome).

AIDS (or SIDA in French) is an increasing problem in Morocco, as everywhere – in 1996 the worldwide figure of reported AIDS cases was 25.5 million, double the figure reported in 1990. As yet there is a little public awareness of the disease in Morocco, despite the efforts of the medical profession.

Any exposure to blood, blood products or body fluids may put the individual at risk.

The disease is often transmitted through sexual contact or dirty needles – vaccinations, acupuncture, tattooing and body piercing can be potentially as dangerous as intravenous drug use. HIV/AIDS can also be spread through infected blood transfusions; some developing countries cannot afford to screen blood used for transfusions.

If you do need an injection, ask to see the syringe unwrapped in front of you, or take a needle and syringe pack with you. Fear of HIV infection should never preclude treatment for serious medical conditions.

Intestinal Worms Different worms have different ways of infecting people. Some may be ingested on food, including undercooked meat, and some enter through your skin. Infestations may not show up for some time and, although they are generally not serious, if left untreated some can cause severe health problems later. Consider having a stool test when you return home to check for these and determine the appropriate treatment.

Bilharzia (Schistosomiasis)

Bilharizia, or 'schisto', is a disease caused by tiny blood flukes. The worms live in snails found on the edge of lakes or slow moving rivers. Inside the snail, they multiply and emerge as free-swimming creatures and, like heat-seeking missiles, they hone in on humans and other mammals in the water. In as little as five minutes, they can bore painlessly through the skin.

Once inside you, most of the blood flukes take up residence in the intestines, where they produce eggs for seven to 30 years. If the eggs end up in the liver or spleen, they can disrupt blood flow and cause the organs to swell. In that case, the disease will be mildly painful and have a very debilitating effect over the years.

Anyone in the mud or shallow water along the edge of a lake or river is vulnerable. Even brief contact can lead to infection, so if you fall in accidentally, towel yourself off as quickly and as briskly as possible. However, don't let this scare you from missing out on every opportunity for a cooling dip. Since the disease requires a human host to complete the cycle, rivers in uninhabited areas are at low risk.

The first indication that you're infected is a tingling and sometimes a light rash around the area where the worm entered. Weeks later, when the worm is busy producing eggs, a high fever may develop. A general feeling of being unwell may be the first indication, but once the disease is established, abdominal pain and blood in the urine are other signs.

The infection often causes no symptoms until the disease is well established (several months to years after exposure) and damage to internal organs irreversible, which is why anyone living overseas for a few years must get checked for schisto upon return.

There is no vaccine and, until recently, the only cure was a dangerous treatment with strong doses of arsenic which killed the worms, but hopefully not you. Now a new drug, praziquantel (brand name Biltracide in the USA), clears it up with a single dose of pills. ■

Meningococcal Meningitis Sub-Saharan Africa is considered the 'meningitis belt' and the meningitis season falls at the time most people would be attempting the overland trip across the Sahara – the northern winter before the rains come. Although in Morocco it is not an issue, people penetrating to the very south of the country or going beyond should be aware of the potential danger. The disease is spread through close contact with people who carry it in their throats and noses and spread it through coughs and sneezes, although they may not be aware that they are carriers.

This very serious disease attacks the brain and can be fatal. A fever, severe headache, sensitivity to light and neck stiffness which prevents forward bending of the head are the first symptoms. There may also be purple patches on the skin. Death can occur within a few hours, so urgent medical treatment is required.

Treatment is large doses of penicillin given intravenously, or chloramphenicol injections.

Sexually Transmitted Diseases Gonorrhoea, herpes and syphilis are among these diseases. Sores, blisters or rashes around the genitals and discharges or pain when urinating are common symptoms. In some STDs, such as wart virus or chlamydia, symptoms may be less marked or not observed at all, especially in women. Syphilis symptoms eventually disappear completely, but the disease continues and can cause severe problems in later years.

While abstinence from sexual contact is the only 100% effective prevention, using condoms is also effective. The treatment of gonorrhoea and syphilis is with antibiotics. The different sexually transmitted diseases each require specific antibiotics. There is no cure for herpes or AIDS.

Typhoid Typhoid fever is a dangerous gut infection caused by contaminated water and food. Medical help must be sought.

In its early stages sufferers may feel they have a bad cold or flu on the way, as early symptoms are a headache, body aches and a fever which rises a little each day until it is around 40°C (104°F) or more. The victim's pulse is often slow proportional to the degree of fever present – unlike a normal fever where the pulse increases. There may also be vomiting, abdominal pain, diarrhoea or constipation.

In the second week the high fever and slow pulse continue and a few pink spots may appear on the body; trembling, delirium, weakness, weight loss and dehydration may occur. Complications such as pneumonia, perforated bowel or meningitis may occur.

The fever should be treated by keeping the victim cool and giving them fluids as dehydration should also be watched for. Ciprofloxacin 750mg twice a day for 10 days is good for adults. Chloramphenicol is recommended in many countries. The adult dosage is two 250mg capsules, four times a day. Children aged between eight and 12 years should have half the adult dose; and younger children one-third the adult dose.

Cuts, Bites & Stings
Rabies is passed through animal bites. See the Less Common Diseases entry later in this section for details of this disease.

Bedbugs & Lice Bedbugs live in various places, but particularly in dirty mattresses and bedding, evidenced by spots of blood on bedclothes or on the wall. Bedbugs leave itchy bites in neat rows. Calamine lotion or Stingose spray may help.

All lice cause itching and discomfort. They make themselves at home in your hair (head lice), your clothing (body lice) or in your pubic hair (crabs). You catch lice through direct contact with infected people or by sharing combs, clothing and the like. Powder or shampoo treatment will kill the lice and infected clothing should then be washed in very hot, soapy water and left in the sun to dry.

Insect Bites & Stings Bee and wasp stings are usually painful rather than dangerous.

However, people who are allergic to them may experience severe breathing difficulties and require urgent medical care. Calamine lotion or Stingose spray will give relief and ice packs will reduce the pain and swelling. Scorpions are found in Morocco and their stings are notoriously painful. Scorpions often shelter in shoes or clothing. There are some spiders with dangerous bites, but antivenenes are usually available.

Cuts & Scratches Wash well and treat any cut with an antiseptic such as povidone-iodine. Where possible avoid bandages and Band-aids, which can keep wounds wet.

Snakes To minimise your chances of being bitten always wear boots, socks and long pants when walking through undergrowth where snakes may be present. Don't put your hands into holes and crevices, and be careful when collecting firewood.

Snake bites do not cause instantaneous death and antivenenes are usually available. Immediately wrap the bitten limb tightly, as you would for a sprained ankle, and then attach a splint to immobilise it. Keep the victim still and seek medical help, if possible with the dead snake for identification. Don't attempt to catch the snake if there is a possibility of being bitten again. The use of tourniquets and the sucking out of the poison are now comprehensively discredited methods.

Women's Health
Gynaecological Problems STDs (sexually transmitted diseases) are a major cause of vaginal problems. Symptoms include a smelly discharge, painful intercourse and sometimes a burning sensation when urinating. Sexual partners must also be treated. Medical attention should be sought and remember in addition to these diseases HIV or hepatitis B may also be acquired during exposure. Besides abstinence, the best thing is to practise safe sex using condoms.

Use of antibiotics, synthetic underwear, sweating and contraceptive pills can lead to fungal vaginal infections when travelling in hot climates. Maintaining good personal hygiene and wearing loose-fitting clothes and cotton underwear will help to prevent these infections.

Fungal infections, characterised by a rash, itch and discharge, can be treated with a vinegar or lemon-juice douche, or with yoghurt. Nystatin, miconazole or clotrimazole pessaries or vaginal cream are the normal treatment.

Pregnancy Most miscarriages take place during the first three months of pregnancy. Miscarriage is not uncommon and can occasionally lead to severe bleeding.

The last three months should also be spent within reasonable distance of good medical care.

A baby born as early as 24 weeks stands a chance of survival, but only in a good modern hospital.

Pregnant women should avoid all unnecessary medication and vaccinations. Malarial prophylactics should still be taken where needed. Additional care should be taken to prevent illness and particular attention should be paid to diet and nutrition. Alcohol and nicotine, for example, should be avoided.

Less Common Diseases
The following diseases pose a small risk to travellers in Morocco and so are only mentioned in passing. Seek medical advice if you think you may have any of these diseases.

Malaria Malaria is a minimal problem in Morocco and highly unlikely to affect travellers, except in the extreme south during high summer.

If you expect to be in southern Morocco at that time, or plan to continue moving south into the 'malaria belt' of equatorial Africa, get expert advice on what sort of antimalarial drug is appropriate for you.

Remember that avoiding being bitten by the malaria-carrying mosquitoes is the best method of protection. Wear light-coloured clothing; long pants and long-sleeved shirts;

use mosquito nets where possible; and don't use highly scented perfumes or aftershave.

Cholera This is the worst of the watery diarrhoeas and medical help should be sought. Outbreaks of cholera are generally widely reported, so you can avoid such problem areas. *Fluid replacement is the most vital treatment* – the risk of dehydration is severe as you may lose up to 20 litres a day.

If there is a delay in getting to hospital then begin taking tetracycline. The adult dose is 250mg four times daily. It is not recommended for children under nine years nor for pregnant women. Tetracycline may help shorten the illness, but adequate fluids are required to save lives.

Rabies Rabies is a fatal viral infection that is found in many countries. Many animals can be infected (such as dogs, cats, bats and monkeys) and it is their saliva which is infectious. Any bite, scratch or even lick from a warm-blooded, furry animal should be cleaned immediately and thoroughly. Scrub with soap and running water, and then apply alcohol or iodine solution.

Medical help should be sought promptly to receive a course of injections to prevent the onset of symptoms and death.

Tetanus Tetanus occurs when a wound becomes infected by a germ which lives in soil and in the faeces of horses and other animals. It enters the body via breaks in the skin. All wounds should be cleaned promptly and adequately and an antiseptic cream or solution applied. Use antibiotics if the wound becomes hot, throbs or pus is seen. The first symptom may be discomfort in swallowing, or stiffening of the jaw and neck; this is followed by painful convulsions of the jaw and whole body. The disease can be fatal.

Tuberculosis Tuberculosis (TB) is a bacterial infection usually transmitted from person to person by coughing, but may be transmitted through consumption of unpas-

teurised milk. Milk that has been boiled is safe to drink, and the souring of milk to make yoghurt or cheese also kills the bacilli. Travellers are usually not at great risk as close household contact with the infected person is usually required before the disease is passed on.

Moroccan Hospitals & Doctors

The standards of health care in Morocco vary considerably and some hospitals are quite off-putting. Nevertheless, the better doctors are generally well trained.

If you must go to hospital, the Hôpital Avicenne (☎ 672871) in Rabat is one of the better options and is fully functional around the clock. The French-language newspapers publish lists of hospitals with 24 hour emergency services ('les urgences') in Rabat and Casablanca. The best advice, where possible, is to seek recommendations from a foreign consulate.

TOILETS

Outside the major cities, public toilets are rare and usually require your own paper *papier hygiénique*, a tip for the attendant, stout-soled shoes and very often a nose clip. They are mostly of the 'squatter' variety.

If you get caught short, duck into the nearest hotel or cafe. People are very unlikely to refuse you. Basic hotels and cafes

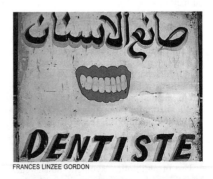

FRANCES LINZEE GORDON

Peddling the pearly whites, Larache medina.

often don't have toilet paper either so it's worth keeping a supply in your backpack.

WOMEN TRAVELLERS
Attitudes to Women

Strangely enough, Moroccan men have pretty much the same attitudes towards women as do males everywhere else in the world. Prior to marriage, Moroccan men have very little opportunity to meet and get to know women, which is one reason why western women travelling in Morocco receive so much attention. Western women exist outside the Moroccan social structure and are seen as almost a different species – not bound by the laws of Islam, excitingly independent, somewhat exotic and possibly even available! (Notice those posters for cheap western movies with titles like *Fair Game* featuring huge breasted blond women.)

Female visitors will find they have constant male company at various times during their stay in Morocco. This may go no further than harmless banter or proposals of marriage and declarations of undying love (or considerably less noble suggestions). Harassment usually takes the form of leering, sometimes being followed and occasionally being touched up. Physical harassment is, however, very rare; it may happen in a crowded medina or in a major city, but is extremely unlikely to occur in the countryside.

Generally speaking, Morocco is a very safe country for female travellers. Moroccans live in close-knit communities, the positive attributes of Islam are strong and alcohol is a minor presence. If a woman feels threatened by the behaviour of a man or group of men, she should look out for a policeman (in the cities there are plenty of them about), go into the nearest shop or hotel and tell an older, responsible-looking person she has a problem, or even stop a passer-by. She is much less likely to encounter the indifference such a situation would elicit in the west.

Ignoring or being rude to the spirited banter of young men usually has a worse effect than an open, good-humoured response.

Women travelling with male companions are likely to encounter a different problem altogether – that of being invisible. Conversation and transactions will be directed towards the man or men in the party, leaving any women involved feeling superfluous to say the least.

Safety Precautions

To help avoid potentially risky and ambiguous situations, women should bear in mind the following common sense precautions. Don't hitchhike. Don't go into 'bunker-style' all-male bars (the only women you'll find in here will be prostitutes). Be aware that many bottom-end hotels double as brothels. In cafes and local restaurants sit at a table in the 'family section' – usually upstairs or towards the back of the establishment.

Don't wander about alone, anywhere, beyond nightfall (after dark all women are at home). If you want to go to a restaurant late at night it's perfectly acceptable to ask someone from your hotel, say a porter, to walk you there. Likewise, if you're nervous about walking home from a restaurant, ask a waiter to accompany you. A tip isn't necessarily expected for this service, but will certainly be appreciated.

A wedding ring can be a useful accessory for discouraging unwelcome attention. Moroccans of both sexes wear these (someone once defined a prostitute as a 'woman without a wedding ring'). A photo of some unsuspecting boyfriend or male friend also helps and, for extra kudos, you could carry a picture of your 'child' – perhaps a niece or nephew.

It's very important, particularly in the countryside, to dress modestly. If you do not, you will arouse unwanted attention, not to mention the ire of the genuinely offended. If you do dress modestly, you will treated with respect, largely left alone and helped a great deal more. Even in the height of summer, cover the shoulders, upper arms and legs – and not with skin-tight apparel.

Western women needn't cover their heads, but it's worth bringing along a scarf anyway – if nothing else, it'll protect you from the African sun.

MEN TRAVELLERS

If you're travelling with your wife or girlfriend, Moroccan men will expect you, like them, to put up a good macho display. You must play very protective and jealous; if you don't, some Moroccans will assume that your friend or wife is available for all to appreciate.

All 'decent' women are safely at home by nightfall. Consequently, almost all the women in bars, discos, cafes and nightclubs are working as prostitutes. They are young, attractive and often soberly dressed. It is frequently impossible to differentiate between 'those who are and those who are not', but any woman who approaches you is certainly a prostitute. Even if you just chat, you will be expected to pay for her drinks.

In the main, Moroccans dress conservatively and it's wise for travellers – men included – to cover themselves up. Day to day transactions, serious bargaining sessions and general conversation will go better if you slip those hairy legs into a pair of trousers.

GAY & LESBIAN TRAVELLERS

Homosexual acts are officially illegal in Morocco, with article 489 of the penal code prohibiting any 'shameless or unnatural act' with a person of the same sex. Penalties are six months to three years imprisonment and a fine of up to Dr1200. There are higher penalties for more serious offences such as the corruption of minors. Though not openly admitted or shown, male homosexuality remains relatively common. Male homosexuals are advised to be discreet – aggression towards gay male travellers is not unheard of.

The *Spartacus International Gay Guide*, published annually, includes information about Morocco and lists 'gay' bars and clubs in the bigger cities, as well as health clinics and places to stay.

Lesbians shouldn't encounter any particular difficulties beyond the usual attentions that female visitors receive (see the earlier Women Travellers entry). Mind you, announcing that you're gay probably won't make would-be Romeos magically disappear. For Moroccan men it may simply confirm their belief that western men don't measure up in the sexual department.

Platonic affection is freely shown in Morocco. You'll often see men, more so than women (probably because they're too busy working), holding hands. However, heterosexual public affection isn't freely shown – it's difficult for single men and women even to meet.

DISABLED TRAVELLERS

Morocco has few facilities geared for the disabled. But that doesn't necessarily make it out of bounds for those who do have a physical disability (and a sense of adventure). Not many hotels have lifts, so booking ground-floor hotel rooms well ahead of time would be one essential. Travelling by car is probably the best transport option.

Get in touch with your national support organisation (preferably the 'travel officer' if there is one) before leaving home. They often have travel literature to help with holiday planning and can put you in touch with travel agents who specialise in tours for the disabled.

In the UK the Royal Association for Disability & Rehabilitation (☎ 0171-250 3222; fax 250 0212), 12 City Forum, 250 City Rd, London EC1V 8AF, produces three holiday fact packs for disabled travellers. They cost UK£2 each and cover planning, insurance, useful organisations, transport, equipment and specialised accommodation.

In the USA, contact the Society for the Advancement of Travel for the Handicapped (SATH; ☎ 212-447 7284), 347 Fifth Ave No 610, New York, NY 10016. Or you could try Access – The Foundation for Accessibility by the Disabled (☎ 516-887 5798), PO Box 356, Malverne, NY 11565.

In France contact the CNFLRH (☎ 01. 53.80.66.66) at 236 bis rue de Tolbiac.

Australians can contact NICAN (☎ 02-6285 3713; fax 6285 3714) at PO Box 407, Curtin, ACT 2605.

No Limits Adventure Tours (☎ 01372-452419), Manda Lodge, 67 Eastwick Drive, Great Bookham, Surrey KT23 3PU, UK, organises camping expeditions around Morocco, including the Atlas Mountains, the Northern Sahara and the Atlantic coast. Disabled people in good health are welcome to participate (the company is part-owned by a wheelchair user).

The four-star Hôtel Le Tafilalet in Marrakesh and the Holiday Inn in Casablanca have facilities for wheelchair users.

TRAVEL WITH CHILDREN

Moroccan people are very welcoming and open towards children and there are no particular reasons for not taking young children on holiday with you. It's probably wise to avoid travelling in the interior of the country during midsummer and it's essential to bring any special foods etc with you. There's little in the way of Disney-type attractions in Morocco, but the exotic sights and scents of the country itself should make up for it. Lonely Planet's *Travel with Children* by Maureen Wheeler contains detailed information about planning successful family holidays.

DANGERS & ANNOYANCES

When all is said and done, Morocco is a comparatively safe place to travel and the great majority of people are friendly and honest. Nevertheless, the country does have a few traps for the unwary.

Theft & Violence

On the whole, theft is not a huge problem in Morocco. Travellers can minimise any risk, however, by being particularly vigilant in the major cities and in general following a few basic precautions.

When wandering around the streets, keep your valuables to a minimum and what you must carry around with you well hidden.

External money pouches attract attention, but neck pouches or money belts worn under your clothes do not; that's where you should keep your money, passport and other

---

Travelling with Children

Geoff Crowther, who did several trips into Morocco for earlier editions of Lonely Planet's guides to the region, has some useful observations for those wanting to take younger children (of one to two years of age) into Morocco.

The three biggest considerations with children of this age are finding suitable food and bathroom facilities and keeping them amused on long journeys. Where your child is already eating solids, you shouldn't have too much trouble.

Certain things will be out though, such as street stall food, if you want to minimise the risks of diarrhoea and the like. Soups, tajines (stews), couscous, fried or grilled fish, omelettes/boiled eggs and fruit (washed and peeled, of course) should all be OK. For liquids, you can get powdered milk in many places to mix with bottled mineral water. Where this isn't possible, on long journeys for example, you may have to stick to the mineral water alone.

As for nappies (diapers), it's impractical to take along more than half a dozen of the washable variety. Disposable nappies, despite their environmentally unfriendly nature, are the only practical solution. These are readily available all over Morocco, but they aren't cheap. Babidou is the only decent brand.

Keeping infants and their clothes clean is the biggest constraint. You may find you have to take rooms in hotels with private showers and hot water most of the time.

Geoff Crowther

important documents. Pouches made of cotton are much more comfortable than nylon ones.

In some of the medinas – such as in Marrakesh and Tangier, which have a particular reputation for petty theft – a common tactic is for one guy to distract you while another cleans out your pockets. There is no point walking around in a state of permanent alert, but it is worth keeping an eye open.

Other valuables such as cameras should be left with the hotel reception when you don't want to use them. If you prefer to keep things in your room, nine times out of 10 you'll have no trouble. Where you can, lock everything up. Leaving anything in a car, even out of sight, is asking for grief.

In places like Tangier, physical attacks on foreigners are not entirely unheard of. There are some desperate people in the bigger cities and some feel no compunction about trying to extract money from tourists. Treat the medinas with particular caution at night.

Drugs & Dealers

For some people, Morocco means only one thing – lots of drugs. There's certainly plenty of dope about and of course it's much cheaper than in Europe, where the bulk of it ends up. But stories abound of travellers being led down Tangier alleyways, lured by offers of large quantities of hashish, only to find themselves paying off unpleasant characters not to denounce them to the police (a threat they'd be highly unlikely to carry out).

Tangier's lowlife is for the initiated only. If you feel you know the lie of the land, fine. New arrivals should ignore late-night offers of hashish and grass – these dealers have a sixth sense for greenness, and won't miss an opportunity to squeeze ridiculous amounts of money out of frightened people. Much the same goes for Tetouan and care should be taken in places such as Casablanca and Marrakesh, too.

It doesn't matter where you go, offers are a part of the daily routine. More often than not, hashish is referred to as 'chocolate', the Spanish slang. You may also have offers of 'shit', which Moroccans apparently feel refers to the same substance.

At the other end of the scale is Ketama and the Rif Mountains – kif-growing heartland. If you don't want trouble, don't hang about here. The standard game consists of going to great lengths to sell vast amounts of the stuff to people, especially those in their own vehicles. The buyers then find themselves at the mercy of the next police roadblock. At best the kif will be confiscated and you'll get a hard time before being sent on your way, but westerners are doing time for trafficking in Morocco; who knows how many of them simply got unlucky in this way.

Always bear in mind that it is illegal to sell or consume hashish in Morocco – although in practice, except for the Ketama capers, this usually means little if you're discreet.

Smoking it in public is inviting trouble. According to a recent report by the UK organisation Fair Trials Abroad, any possession of drugs leads to automatic conviction. There are currently about 400 EU citizens imprisoned in Morocco and at least 95% are alleged to have committed offences concerning the trafficking or possession of cannabis.

Many have been found guilty 'by association' – this includes drivers giving lifts to

---

Munching Majoun

You may occasionally come across someone offering you *majoun*, a kind of sticky, pasty mass (not unlike molasses) made of crushed seeds of the marijuana plant.

A small ball of this can send your head into a bit of a spin (see Paul Bowles' *Their Heads Are Green* or *Let It Come Down* for descriptions).

Anyone with a slight tendency to paranoia when smoking dope should be aware that this is a common reaction among first time majoun-munchers. ■

people carrying cannabis in their hand luggage. Fair Trials Abroad believes that up to 10% of those imprisoned may be innocent.

If you find yourself arrested by the Moroccan police, you won't have much of a legal leg to stand on. Unless you speak fluent Arabic, it is unlikely that any interpreter to hand will be of sufficient standard to translate an accurate statement.

Any statement obtained will play a vital part in subsequent judicial proceedings. According to Fair Trials, physical abuse while in custody is commonplace.

As for taking personal supplies of drugs through customs into Spain – plenty of people take the risk, but it is hardly recommended. Although the police attitude in Spain is relaxed in respect of small amounts of cannabis, Spanish Customs will come down hard on people entering the country from Morocco if they find any.

If you're taking a car across, the chances are high that it will be searched. Possession of small amounts of cannabis for personal use was made legal in Spain in 1983, but that law was later revoked.

Touts, Guides & Hustlers

The legendary hustlers (or *faux guides* – false guides) of Morocco remain an unavoidable part of the Moroccan experience.

In the major cities and tourist centres you'll be confronted by numerous guides and hustlers wanting to guide you through the medina, take you to the kasbah, show you a good hotel etc, etc.

In places like Marrakesh and Fès, harassment of visitors was beginning to have such an adverse effect on tourism that the Moroccan government recently cracked down on unofficial guides, making it a criminal offence for people other than registered guides to be seen with tourists.

This has made a noticeable difference (as being slung into prison might) and hustlers are less persistent than they were. Nevertheless, travellers will still have to deal with the phenomena to some degree.

To make life easier for all concerned, it helps to understand why so many people are so intent on offering you their services. Reasons include large families to support, a massively high unemployment rate and no social security system. You shouldn't allow yourself to be bullied, but there's no point arriving with a siege mentality, either. These people are desperate to make a living, that's all.

When arriving in a place for the first time it is worth considering whether you might benefit from the services of a guide – official or otherwise. Faux guides are not necessarily complete impostors. Most are very experienced and many will speak half a dozen languages. They charge around Dr50 per day compared to the Dr150 charged by official guides. A few dirham will suffice if you want to be guided to a specific location (like a medina exit). Whatever you give, you'll often get the you-can't-possibly-be-serious look. The best reply is the I've-just-paid-you-well-over-the-odds look.

Official guides can be hired through tourist offices or bigger hotels, although you'll sometimes find them hanging around in the medina. Ask to see their brass badge.

Guides can be very helpful when it comes to local knowledge and employing one means that you won't be hassled by all the other hopefuls. The most important thing is to be clear about where you want to go and agree a price beforehand. Many guides still make commissions by delivering you into the clutches of some of the best carpet salesmen in the world. If you're not out to buy goods, make this clear.

To avoid being hounded to within an inch of your life, there are various tactics that can be employed. None is guaranteed to work, but they may help to prevent nervous breakdowns and embarrassing incidents of 'medina rage'.

Politely decline all offers of help and exchange a few good humoured remarks, but don't shake hands or get involved in lengthy conversation. Don't ignore them entirely – there's nothing they hate more than the brush-off.

Give the impression that you know exactly where you're going or explain that you

How to Spot a Faux Guide

For many travellers in Morocco, it is a constant puzzle how to tell a good Moroccan from a bad one – or rather, one interested in you from one more interested in your wallet.

In general, be suspicious of any one who approaches you unasked. A real give away are those who claim to be students. Unfortunately, knowledge of English also is often an unfavourable indication. English is not widely taught at schools and some have learned it in order to exploit what are considered the most lucrative nationalities.

Apart from the more obvious approaches to start up a friendship such as showing you around town, taking you to a cheap shop, helping you find a hotel etc, other classic approaches include wanting to practise English, help with the reading or deciphering of official documents, medical prescriptions and, more commonly, letters from friends abroad.

Motorists should look out for false hitchhikers and false breakdowns. ■

employed a guide on your first day and now you'd like to explore the town on your own.

Pretend to be a foreigner from an incredibly obscure place and speak in a suitably unintelligible language. Alternatively, speak extremely politely in Arabic. Wear mirrored sunglasses. Retreat to a cafe or restaurant if you're beginning to lose your cool. In extreme situations, use the word 'police' and look like you mean it.

After two or three days in one place the hassle does tend to lessen. People will recognise you and leave you alone. In the meantime other prey will have arrived anyway. If you have maintained your good humour you may well be rewarded for it.

Drivers should note that motorised hustlers operate on the approach roads to Fès and Marrakesh. These motorcycle nuisances are keen to find you a hotel, camp site and so on, and can be just as persistent as their colleagues on foot.

Streets & Medinas

A minor irritation is the ever-changing street names in Moroccan cities. For years now, there is a slow process of replacing old French and Spanish names with Arabic ones. The result so far is that, depending on whom you talk to, what map you use or which part of the street you are on, you are likely to see up to three different names.

The general Arabic word for street is *sharia* (*zankat* for smaller ones). You'll still find the Spanish *calle* quite often in the north and, more commonly, the French *avenue*, *boulevard* or *rue*.

In some cases the Arabic seems to have gained the upper hand. This is reflected in this guide, in which some streets appear as 'sharia' or 'zankat' if local usage seems to justify it.

Street names won't help much in the labyrinthine medinas, but one rule might help if you feel you are getting lost. If you stick to the main paths (which generally have a fair flow of people going either way), you will soon reach a landmark or exit.

It's really only when you dive into the maze of little alleys that it becomes more difficult – some would say more fun!

False Hitchhikers

Professional hitchhikers operate on some of the more popular tourist routes. They get in your car and oblige you to accept their thanks for your help with a glass of tea at their house and the inevitable carpet-sales session – or something worse.

See the Car & Motorcycle section of the Getting Around chapter for more information.

Moroccan Plumbing

Patience is required when it comes to Moroccan plumbing. In the cheap, unclassified hotels, cold water is often the norm.

Sometimes hot water is enthusiastically promised, but doesn't come close to the steaming, powerful shower you'd hoped for. In many hotels, hot water is only available at certain times of the day. In country areas, water is sometimes heated by a wood fire – and wood can be an expensive commodity.

Hammams (public steam baths) are everywhere, but not particularly obvious if you don't read Arabic – local people will be happy to point you in the right direction. See the section on Hammams earlier in this chapter.

BUSINESS HOURS

Although it's a Muslim country, for business purposes Morocco adheres to the western Monday to Friday working week.

In Muslim countries, Friday is the equivalent of Sunday for Christians, and hence is usually the main day off during the week. During Ramadan, office hours are generally 8 am to 3 or 4 pm.

Banks

In the bigger centres, at least, banks tend to be open Monday to Thursday from 8.30 to 11.30 am and 2.30 to 4.30 pm. On Friday, the midday break generally runs from 11.15 am to 3 pm to take the main Friday prayers into account. These hours can vary slightly from bank to bank, but usually not more than by a quarter of an hour or so either way.

The Banque Populaire usually maintains an exchange bureau open out of normal banking hours at its main branches in the big cities. These booths are good for currency exchange and cash advances on Visa and MasterCard.

They open from 10 am to 2 pm and 4 to 8 pm seven days a week (usually). Wafabank is planning to open branches in major cities on Saturdays.

Offices

Government offices, should you have any need to tangle with Moroccan bureaucracy, are generally open Monday to Thursday from 8.30 am to noon and 2 to 6.30 pm. On Fridays, the midday break lasts from about 11.30 am to 3 pm.

As with the banks, these times are gener-

ally adhered to in the main centres, but should be taken with a pinch of a salt.

Museums & Monuments

Most museums are closed on Tuesdays and otherwise loosely follow office hours, which means they are usually closed from about 11.30 am to 3 pm. Not all of the sights follow this rule, however. Some of the medersas (former Qur'anic schools) close at noon on Friday.

Shops & Souqs

Shops tend to be open from about 8 am to 6 pm, often closing for a couple of hours in the middle of the day, but there are no strict rules about this. Most shops, apart from grocery stores and the like, tend to close over the weekend.

Medina souqs and produce markets in the villes nouvelles of the bigger cities tend to wind down on Thursday afternoon and are usually dead on Fridays, but there is no law fixing this.

HOLIDAYS
Secular Holidays

There are 10 national secular holidays:

New Year's Day	1 January
Independence Manifesto	11 January
Feast of the Throne	3 March
Labour Day	1 May
National Day	23 May
Young People's Day	9 July
Allegiance of Wadi-Eddahab	14 August
Anniversary of the King's and People's Revolution	20 August
Anniversary of the Green March	6 November
Independence Day	18 November

Islamic Holidays

Of more significance to the majority of people are the principal religious holidays tied to the lunar Hijra calendar. The word 'hijra' refers to the flight of Mohammed from Mecca to Medina in 622 AD, which marks the first year of the Islamic calendar (so the year 622 AD is the year 1 AH).

The calendar is about 11 days shorter than the Gregorian calendar, meaning that the holidays fall on different days each year (see the Table of Holidays below). Although most business hours and daily life are organised around the Gregorian calendar, the religious rhythms of Muslim society are firmly tied to the lunar calendar. Predicting the exact day the holidays will begin is impossible, as this depends on when the new moon is sighted – the decision rests with the religious authorities in Fès.

Ras as-Sana This means New Year's day and is celebrated on the first day of the Hijra calendar year, 1 Moharram.

Achoura This is a day of public mourning observed by Shiites on 10 Moharram. It commemorates the assassination of Hussein ibn Ali, the grandson of the Prophet Mohammed and pretender to the caliphate, which led to the schism between Sunnis and Shiites. But for children it can be a joyous occasion. They receive toys and sweets and parade through the streets to the beating of drums.

Mawlid an-Nabi Achoura This is a lesser feast celebrating the birth of the Prophet Mohammed on 12 Rabi' al-Awal. For a long time it was not celebrated at all in the Islamic world. In the Maghreb this is generally known as Mouloud.

Ramadan & Aïd al-Fitr Most Muslims, albeit not all with equal rigour, take part in the fasting that characterises the month of Ramadan, a time when the faithful are called upon to renew their relationship with god as a community.

Ramadan is the month in which the Qur'an was first revealed. From dawn until dusk, Muslims are expected to refrain from eating, drinking, smoking and sex. This can be a difficult discipline and only people in good health are asked to participate. Children, pregnant women and people who are travelling or are engaged in exacting physical work are considered exempt.

Every evening is, in a sense, a celebration. Iftar or ftur, the breaking of the day's fast, is a time of animated activity when the people of the local community come together not only to eat and drink, but also to pray.

The Arabic for fasting is *sawm*. You may find yourself being asked *inta sa'im?* – 'Are you fasting?' – and encouraged to do so if your answer is *la, ana faatir* – 'No, I am breaking the fast'. Non-Muslims are not expected to participate, even if more pious Muslims suggest you do. Sharing the suffering involved is an important symbolic social element of Ramadan. The peer pressure on unenthusiastic Muslims is considerable.

Restaurants and cafes that are open during the day may be harder to come by and, at any rate, you should try to avoid openly flouting the fast.

The end of Ramadan – or more accurately the first days of the following month of Shawwal – mark the Aïd al-Fitr, the Feast of the Breaking of the Fast (also known as the Aïd as-Sagheer, the Small Feast). It generally lasts four or five days, during which just about everything grinds to a halt. This is not a good time to travel, but it can be a great experience if you are invited to share in some of the festivities with a family. It is a very family-oriented feast, much in the way Christmas is for Christians.

Table of Holidays

Hijra Year	New Year	Prophet's Birthday	Ramadan begins	Eid al-Fitr	Eid al-Adha
1418	09.05.97	17.07.97	31.12.97	29.01.98	08.04.98
1419	28.04.98	06.07.98	19.12.98	18.01.99	28.03.99
1420	17.04.99	26.06.99	09.12.99	08.01.00	16.03.00
1421	06.04.00	14.06.00	27.11.00	27.12.00	06.03.01

The Hajj & Aïd al-Adha The fifth pillar of Islam, the sacred duty of all who can afford it, is to make the pilgrimage to Mecca – the *hajj*. It can be done at any time, but at least once it should be accomplished in Zuul-Hijja, the 12th month of the Muslim year. At this time, thousands of Muslims from all over the world converge on Islam's most holy city.

The high point is the visit to the Ka'aba, the construction housing the stone of Ibrahim (Abraham) in the centre of the *haram*, the sacred area into which non-Muslims are forbidden to enter. The faithful, dressed only in a white robe, circle the Ka'aba seven times and kiss the black stone. This is one of a series of acts of devotion carried out by pilgrims.

In the past, great caravans set out from Cairo and Damascus, their ranks swollen by pilgrims from all over the Muslim world, to converge on Mecca amid great circumstance and fanfare. Now the national airlines of Muslim countries put on hundreds of extra flights to jet in the faithful, although many Arabs still head for the sacred city overland. Moroccans often drive or take the bus all the way across North Africa to Cairo and the Red Sea, where they take a boat to Aqaba in Jordan and then continue on into Saudi Arabia. Some get boats direct to Jeddah from Suez. It can be a long and frustrating journey.

The hajj culminates in the ritual slaughter of a lamb (in commemoration of Ibrahim's sacrifice) at Mina. This marks the end of the pilgrimage and the beginning of the Aïd al-Adha, or Feast of the Sacrifice (also known as the 'grand feast' or Aïd al-Kabeer). Throughout the Muslim world the act of sacrifice is repeated and the streets of towns and cities seem to run with the blood of slaughtered sheep. The holiday runs from 10 to 13 Zuul-Hijja.

CULTURAL EVENTS
Moussems & Amouggars

Festivals are commonly held in honour of *marabouts* (local saints). Sometimes no more than an unusually lively market day,

quite a few have taken on regional and even national importance. These festivals are common among the Berbers and are usually held during the summer months.

This is one of those religious frontiers where orthodoxy and local custom have met and compromised. The veneration of saints is frowned upon by orthodox Sunni Muslims, but Islam (no less than Christianity) is made up of many parts and sects (see the Religion section in the Facts about the Country chapter). Thus these festivals, which take some of their inspiration from a mix of pre-Islamic Berber tradition and Sufi mystic thought, continue.

Some of the more excessive manifestations, such as self-mutilation while in an ecstatic trance, were once not an unusual sight at such gatherings. Today they have all but disappeared in the face of official disapproval of such 'barbarism'.

It's worth making enquiries to determine when moussems and other such festivals are due to happen. Some of the most important, in chronological order, are as follows:

March
  Moussem of Moulay Aissa ben Driss in Beni Mellal.
May
  Moussem of Moulay Abdallah ben Brahim in Ouezzane.
  Fête des Roses (Rose Festival) at Kélâa des M'Gouna in the Dadès Valley. It is held late in the month.
  Moussem of Sidi Bou Selham near Larache. This festival sometimes takes place in June.
  Moussem of Sidi Mohammed M'a al-'Ainin at Tan Tan is an occasion where you may see the so-called blue people, the Tuareg nomads from the Sahara. It also acts as a commercial gathering of tribes and is usually held at the end of May or in early June.
June
  National Folklore Festival in Marrakesh. This festival runs for 10 days and is held early in the month.
  Moussem at Goulimime. With its big camel market, this is as much a trade affair as a religious get-together.
  Fête des Cerises (Cherry Festival) in Sefrou.

July
  Moussem at Mdiq, north-west of Tetouan. This festival takes place early in the month.
August
  Moussem of Moulay Idriss in Zerhoun, north of Meknès.
  Moussem of Moulay Abdallah south of El-Jadida. The festival takes place late in the month.
  Moussem of Sidi Ahmed in Anti-Tiznit. This celebration of prayer is held towards the end of the month.
  Moussem of Setti Fatma in the Ourika Valley, south of Marrakesh.
  International Arts Festival in Asilah.
September
  Fête des Fiancés in Imilchil, where women choose prospective husbands. The festival is held late in the month.
  Moussem of Sidi Moussa or *Quarquour* near El-Kelas du Straghna, north of Marrakesh.
  Moussem of Moulay Idriss in Fès. It is sometimes held in early October.
  Moussem of Sidi-Allal in Arbaoua, north of Meknès.
October
  Fête du Cheval (Horse Festival) in Tissa, north-east of Fès. This is held in early October.
  Fête des Dattes (Date Festival) in Erfoud. This takes place in late October.

The Folklore Festival at Marrakesh, usually held around the end of May or early June, is essentially a tourist event, although it attracts many Moroccans. Nevertheless, it's colourful and well worth attending as groups of dancers, musicians and other entertainers are invited from all over the country.

ACTIVITIES
Bird-Watching
Morocco is a bird-watchers' paradise. A startling array of species lives in the varied habitats of the country year-round and thousands of birds pass through Morocco during spring and autumn.

Birds who have spent winter south of the Sahara head northwards to breed in Europe during the spring and return through Morocco in the autumn. Other species fly south to Morocco to avoid the harsh northern European winter.

Prime bird-watching sites include the dunes, marshes and freshwater lagoon systems which begin about 40km east of Nador on the Mediterranean coast; the 70km stretch of Atlantic coastline between Sidi Moussa (36km south of El Jadida) and Cap Beddouza; the Massa Lagoon, 40km south of Agadir; and the stony desert and grassy plains to the south of Boumalne du Dadès. For more information see the special section on Morocco's birdlife or individual town entries. A couple of tour operators which specialise in bird-watching trips to Morocco are listed in the Organised Tours entry in the Getting There & Away chapter.

Camel Treks
For those prepared to sacrifice their bottoms for the ultimate desert experience, several places in the south of the country offer camel expeditions ranging from a couple of days to two weeks.

Autumn and winter are the only seasons worth considering. Prices start at around Dr200 to Dr300 per person, but vary depending on the number of people involved, the length of the trek and your negotiating skills.

Places to head for include Zagora and Tinfou in the Vallée du Drâa; M'Hamid, 95km further south; and the Saharan dunes of Merzouga, south-east of Rissani. See the entries under individual towns for more information.

Climbing
Rock climbing is becoming an increasingly popular pursuit everywhere these days and Morocco has some sublime opportunities for the vertically inclined.

As yet it's an undeveloped activity and anyone contemplating routes should have plenty of experience under their belt and be prepared to bring all their own equipment.

The beautiful Dadès and Todra gorges provide almost endless climbing possibilities; areas in the Anti-Atlas and High Atlas also offer everything from bouldering to very severe routes.

Fishing

Freshwater fish to be found in Morocco include pike, black bass, perch, roach and carp. In the Mediterranean and Atlantic you'll find bonito, sea perch, mullet, chad and sea bream. Beach fishing in the area around Dakhla, in the south, has been recommended. Some of the creeks around Marrakesh provide good fishing, but the artificial lake created by the Moulay Youssef dam, stocked with fish such as black bass, is better. Individuals don't require a fishing permit.

For information on freshwater fishing contact the Water and Forest Department at 11 Rue du Devoir in Rabat. For details on deep sea fishing contact the National Fisheries Office (☎ 240551; fax 242305), BP 20300, in Casablanca.

Golf

Golf is high on the list of Morocco's advertised attractions (the honorary president of the Moroccan Golf Federation is King Hassan himself) and there are some excellent courses in the country. There are currently 14, with another 16 expected to be established by the end of the century.

The oldest course, laid out in 1917, is the Royal Country Club of Tangier (☎ 944484; fax 945450), an 18 hole course that one golfing writer has described as 'adventurous'. The Royal Dar es-Salaam (☎ 755864; fax 757671), 10km out of central Rabat, is the most modern course – the Hassan II Challenge Cup is held here annually.

Some of the other courses are to be found in Marrakesh (Royal Golf Club; ☎ 444341; fax 430084), Ben Slimane, Casablanca (Royal Golf d'Anfa; ☎ 365355; fax 393374), Mohammedia and Agadir (12km out of town).

For further information contact the Royal Moroccan Golf Federation (☎ 755960; fax 751026) at the Dar es-Salaam Golf Club in Rabat.

Mountain Biking

Ordinary cycling is possible in Morocco, but mountain biking opens up the options considerably. Roads are well maintained, although very often narrow. For the very fit, the vast networks of *pistes* (dirt tracks) and even the footpaths of the High Atlas offer the most rewarding biking.

Any bike tour should be well planned and you'll need to ensure that you have enough supplies, particularly water, for each leg of the journey.

Some outside adventure holiday companies and a few operators in Marrakesh and elsewhere offer organised mountain bike trips.

Skiing

Although somewhat rough and ready in comparison to Europe's alpine offerings, skiing is a viable option in winter. The higher slopes and peaks of the High Atlas usually have decent cover from February to early April. Oukaïmeden, about 70km south of Marrakesh, is a popular ski station and boasts the highest ski lift in north Africa. A day lift pass costs around Dr80 and full equipment hire is usually around Dr100 a day. There are a few other spots dotted around the Middle Atlas equipped for snow sport, the best known and equipped being Mischliffen and Ifrane.

Off-piste skiing is gaining popularity in some areas of the High Atlas, mainly around Toubkal and even in some less accessible spots such as the Tichka plateau in the Western High Atlas.

A useful organisation to contact is the Royal Moroccan Ski and Mountaineering Federation (☎ 203798; fax 474979) at Parc de la Ligue Arabe, BP 15899, Casablanca.

Surfing

With thousands of kilometres of ocean coastline, Morocco isn't a bad place to take your board. Surfing has had little or no attention in Morocco, but you wouldn't be the first to abandon the chill of the European Atlantic for something a little warmer.

The beaches around Kenitra are a safe and enjoyable bet; Media Beach, just a few kilometres north of Rabat, is said to have a reliable year-round break; and Anchor Point in Agadir has also been recommended, although it can be very inconsistent. Essaouira, too, has been singled out by some surfers.

For more information on surfing and windsurfing in Morocco, contact the Royal Moroccan Surfing Federation (☎ 259530; fax 236385) in Casablanca.

Trekking

Morocco is a superb destination for mountain lovers, offering a variety of year-round trekking possibilities. There are quite a number of outside adventure travel companies which organise treks in Morocco to suit all abilities (a list of tour operaters offering such holidays can be found under the Organised Tours entry in the Getting There & Away chapter). If you'd rather do it on your own, it's relatively straightforward to organise guides, porters and mules for a more independent adventure. Look at paying a minimum of Dr200 per person plus food.

Jebel Toubkal (4167m), the highest peak in the High Atlas mountain range, tends to attract the lion's share of visitors. Toubkal itself is a fairly easy two day climb and there's no need to hire a guide. But if you're willing to hire guides and mules, you can trek for days through the Toubkal area (see the High Atlas chapter), enjoying stunning mountain views and friendly Berber hospitality.

The Western High Atlas, to the north of Taroudannt, is a much less developed mountain destination and offers any number of challenging walks, including a rewarding 13 day trek all the way across to Toubkal (see the Taroudannt entry in The Atlantic – South of Casablanca chapter).

The High Atlas is primarily a summer destination, but plenty of lower level walks are possible in the winter.

The pink and ochre-coloured mountains of the Anti-Atlas range, south of the High Atlas, also offer wonderful trekking possibilities and, according to some, the blue-black volcanic peaks of the Jebel Sarhro, which rise up to the south-east of Ouarzazate, have some of the best walking of all.

White-Water Rafting

Some specialist adventure companies organise rafting trips, particularly on some of the rivers in the High Atlas near the Bin el-Ouidane lake in the area around Azilal and Afourer. People do it here as much for the setting as for the sport itself.

For more information contact the Royal Moroccan Federation of Canoeing (☎/fax 770281), at the National Sports Centre, Ave Ibnou Sina, BP 332, Rabat.

Windsurfing

The windy conditions at Essaouira make it an even better spot for windsurfers than for their wax-and-board colleagues. There are two places along the beach where you can hire equipment.

Dar Bouazza, south of Casablanca, is another popular spot for windsurfing.

COURSES
Arabic

The business of learning Arabic is fairly undeveloped in Morocco and the possibilities for doing so are strictly limited.

Apart from possible summer courses at the university in Rabat, your best bet would be to head for the Arabic Language Institute (☎ 624850; email alif@mbox.azure.net) at 2 Rue Ahmed Hiba in Fès.

The institute has been going since 1983 and is affiliated to the American Language Center.

Classes are generally quite small, so each student can expect a reasonable amount of individual attention.

The institute offers courses over three and six weeks which cost Dr3300 or Dr6200 (Dr3500/6700 in the summer). Individual tuition is available for Dr135 per hour.

The institute can also help with accommodation, either in hotels or on a homestay basis with Moroccan families.

Some branches of the Institut Français (formerly the Centre Culturel Français) run Arabic courses – this is the case in Tangier. The Ecole Assimil (☎ 312567) is a private school offering language courses in Casablanca.

WORK

Morocco is not the most fruitful ground for digging up work opportunities. A good command of French is usually a prerequisite and a knowledge of Arabic would certainly not go astray. If you do secure a position, your employer will have to help you get a work permit and arrange residency, which can be an involved process. There is some very limited scope for teaching English and voluntary work.

Teaching English

It is technically possible to get this kind of work here, but the openings are limited. The British Council has only one branch in Morocco, in Rabat, but as a rule it recruits all its staff directly from London. You could try them for supply work and they might have suggestions on smaller local outfits.

The only really credible alternatives are the American Language Center and the smaller International Language Centre. The former has schools in Rabat, Casablanca, Kenitra, Tetouan, Marrakesh, Tangier and Fès (see the individual entries for addresses). Don't get your hopes up though. These are all fairly small operations and the chances of just walking into a job are not high. Obviously, qualified teachers of English as a Foreign Language (TEFL) will have a better chance.

The best time to try is around September-October (the beginning of the academic year) and, to a lesser extent, early January. Casablanca has about half a dozen outfits and so is the best hunting ground.

Voluntary Work

There are several organisations in Morocco that organise voluntary work on regional development projects. They generally pay nothing, sometimes not even lodging, and are aimed at young people looking for something different to do for a few weeks over the summer period. A couple of possible sources of information in Morocco are:

Les Amis des Chantiers Internationaux de Meknès, BP 8, Meknès

Chantiers Jeunesse Maroc, BP 1351, 31 Rue du Liban, Rabat
Chantiers Sociaux Marocains (☎ 791370), BP 456, Rabat

ACCOMMODATION
Camping

Provided you have the site owner's permission, you can camp practically anywhere in Morocco. There are also quite a few official camp sites dotted around the country. Most of the bigger cities have one, often located well out of town and of more use to people with their own transport. Some of them are brilliantly located and worth the extra effort to get to them, but many offer little shade and are hardly worth what you pay. Most have water, electricity, a small restaurant and grocery store.

As a rule, you'll be up for Dr10 per person, plus a fee for pitching your tent (also often around Dr10), along with fees for cars, motorbikes and caravans. Electricity generally costs another Dr10 and a hot shower about Dr5. For two people travelling by car, the total can easily come to nearly Dr30 a head, so there are times when it will be better to spend a little more for a hotel.

Hostels

Hostelling International (HI) recognises about a dozen hostels in the country (Asni, Azrou, Casablanca, Chefchaouen, Fès, Laayoune, Marrakesh, Meknès, Oujda, Rabat and Tangier). The head office of the Royal Moroccan Federation of Youth Hostels (☎ 220551; fax 226777) is at Parc de la Ligue Arabe, BP 15988, Casablanca.

Beds cost from Dr15 to Dr30 (a little more without a membership card). The hostels in Marrakesh, Meknès and Casablanca are among the better ones. Some hostels have kitchens and family rooms.

Hotels

About the cheapest hotel rooms you're likely to find anywhere will cost around Dr30/50 for a single/double. As a rule you get what you pay for and most of these unclassified hotels tend to be clustered in certain parts of the medinas of the bigger cities. For a little more, you can often find better unclassified or one-star hotels outside the medinas. This is especially the case in the high season, when the unclassified hotels tend to crank up prices as high as they think possible.

It is always worth looking around. Most of the unclassified places are clean, if basic, and rooms often tend to be on the small side. Hot water is either not available or costs Dr5 per gas-heated shower. Where there is no hot water at all, hotel staff can point you in the direction of a local public shower (*douche*) or hammam. Don't get too excited by claims of hot water in the cheapies either, as this sometimes amounts to little more than a warm trickle.

You can dig up some very good hotels in the one and two star range from around Dr100/130 for a single/double with private shower and shared toilet in a one star hotel. In the better cases, you are looking at good, clean rooms with comfortable beds and, with a bit of luck, a decent shower. Hot water tends to be available only at certain times. Rooms in the one and two star categories tend to vary more than in the lower and higher brackets so, if you have the time, it may be worth looking at a few.

In the three and four star bracket you will sometimes come up with a gem of an older place left over from more elegant days and which may have been tastefully renovated. In the upper bracket you're more likely to be confronted with more modern and sterile places.

Although many unclassified places in the most popular locations increase their prices in the high season, it is fair to say that cities like Marrakesh offer a reasonable choice of places to stay. Not-so-popular destinations like Tetouan offer little and the quality of what's there is poor.

If you are resident in Morocco, you are entitled to a 25% discount on the classified hotel rates in some establishments.

You will need to record your passport details and so on when filling in any hotel register.

Classified Accommodation Costs		
Category	Price (Dr) Single	Price (Dr) Double
1 Star	68 - 138	89 - 160
2 Star	124 - 194	146 - 226
3 Star	205 - 382	252 - 475
4 Star	317 - 950	396 - 1138
5 Star	650 - 1470	800 - 1650

A third bed in these rooms costs from around Dr45 (one-star) to Dr100 (four or five-star). Breakfast is also extra, costing from Dr15 a person (one-star) to Dr40 (five-star). There is also an additional tourist tax, which ranges from Dr3 to Dr8 per person.

Self-Catering
If you're travelling in a small group or as a family, it may be worth considering self-catering options, particularly in the low season when prices can drop substantially. Agadir has a fair number of residences which offer apartments with self-catering facilities.

You'll find apartments available in quite a few other places along the Mediterranean and Atlantic coasts and in the bigger tourist centres.

Houses can sometimes be found to rent, but tend to be pretty basic. Official prices for self-catered apartments start at Dr110 per person, going up to as much as Dr750 per person.

Village Accommodation
If you are trekking in the High Atlas or travelling off the beaten track elsewhere, you may be offered accommodation in village homes; many won't have running water or electricity, but you'll generally find them to be a great deal more comfortable than basic hotels (and even middle and top-range hotels when it comes to warmth and hospitality).

You should be prepared to pay what you would in an unclassified hotel or mountain refuge.

FOOD

Moroccan cuisine has been described by food writer Robert Carrier as among the most exciting in the world, and it very much reflects the country's rich cultural heritage. The Berber influence remains strong – many standard Moroccan dishes, such as couscous, *tajines* and *harira*, are Berber in origin.

The Bedouin Arabs introduced dates, milk, grains and bread, which are staples still. They are credited, too, with inventing dried pasta as a way of preserving flour on their long caravan treks across the desert.

The Moors introduced Andalusian foods (olives, olive oil, nuts, fruits and herbs) and the Arabs brought back a wealth of spices from the Spice Islands (modern Indonesia). Added to all this is the more recent influence of the French (a common breakfast, particularly in the cities, is milky coffee with a croissant).

The best cooking is to be enjoyed in the palace restaurants of the major cities and in private homes throughout the country. Moroccans are extremely hospitable and most

FRANCES LINZEE GORDON

Found in markets and on menus
all over Morocco – escargot.

travellers will find themselves invited to share in a home-cooked meal at least once during their stay.

There may be little variety of dishes in out-of-the-way places, but almost everywhere you'll find plenty of deliciously fresh bread, tajines, fruits and nuts. Budget travellers should keep a look out for the weekly markets which are excellent for stocking up on picnic foods. It's also possible to buy fresh meat or fish and have it cooked for you in a local restaurant.

It's usual in many restaurants to order your meal an hour or two in advance, particularly if you'd like couscous. Moroccans tend to eat their evening meal fairly early so, if you're outside the major cities and set out for a feed after 8 or 9 pm, you may not find a great deal of choice.

Menus are generally in French and/or Arabic, so a smattering of either or both will be useful in the eating department.

A cheap meal in a cafe/restaurant can cost as little as Dr20. A good three course meal in a mid-range restaurant will set you back about Dr60 to Dr80. Moving up a little or indulging in non-Moroccan cuisine (at the occasional Italian or Asian) will generally cost around Dr80 to Dr100.

If you want to eat in one of the cavernous restaurants decorated like some of the monuments you have visited – and be treated to a folk music show or Egyptian-style belly -dancing – the bill per person will be Dr200 plus. Alcohol will substantially up your bill.

Grocery Stores

In cities, towns and even villages you will come across tiny grocery stores brimming with all sorts of foods and household necessities. You'll find fresh bread, biscuits, French processed cheese (the only type you'll find in Morocco), tins of sardines and packets of teabags here. They are good places to buy a little basic food for bus journeys or if you're not feeling well.

Grocery stores generally stock toilet paper, soap, shampoo, washing powder and sanitary towels, too. They tend to be open every day until late in the evening.

Street Food

Morocco's cities and bigger towns offer quite an array of cheap food stalls where dishes are freshly cooked and eaten outdoors at simple wooden tables (dining at night in among the musicians and fire eaters of the Place Djemaa el-Fna in Marrakesh is a treat).

You'll also find basic snack stands selling fresh baguette-style sandwiches and wandering vendors selling various Moroccan finger foods.

A good, popular meal-in-itself consists of brochettes of *kefta* (seasoned mince lamb) or lamb with salad, fried potatoes and hot sauce all wrapped in bread (about Dr15).

In some places you'll see people selling little pots of steaming snails and others offering hard boiled eggs, hot chick peas or fava beans served with a sprinkling of salt and cumin.

In coastal places, the catch of the day can be found at stalls in the port area.

Markets

The outdoor street markets of Morocco are a wonderland of fresh fruit and vegetables, mouth-watering preserves, and colourful, vital spices. Look out for the following typically Moroccan foods and ingredients.

Ras el-hanout is a warming mixture of many spices added to winter tajines – ingredients include cardamom, mace, nutmeg

FRANCES LINZEE GORDON

Unique food packaging at the spice souq, Marrakesh.

and belladonna berries. Salt-preserved lemons, sold in tall jars, are often used in Moroccan cooking. *Limouns*, which look like limes, are small green Moroccan lemons.

Among the amazing variety of olives on display, you'll discover delicious violet-coloured olives preserved with the juice of bitter oranges.

Rich golden argan oil, found mainly in the Anti-Atlas region, has a distinctive peppery flavour. It is extracted from argan tree nuts and used by the Berber people to cook with.

High in vitamin E, it is said to be good for the skin and for treating infertility.

Soups & Starters

Harira, a thick soup made from lamb stock, lentils, chick peas, onion, garlic, chopped tomatoes, fresh herbs and spices, is popular as a first course in the evening, but is substantial enough to make a meal on its own.

During Ramadan, harira (accompanied by dates or honey cakes) is the dish Moroccans traditionally break the day's fast with. There are variations on the traditional harira, including *marrakchia* harira which is made without meat.

Other soups you may be offered include couscous soup, vegetable soup (usually made with lamb broth) and chicken soup with vermicelli.

Mid-range restaurants will generally offer a choice of salads as a first course. A typical Moroccan salad you'll come across is one made from finely diced green peppers, tomatoes and garlic. This is sometimes served as a side dish with grilled brochettes or fish.

Briouats – which you'll probably only find in smart city restaurants – are small envelopes of flaky pastry stuffed with fillings such as minced meat, fish, nuts and rice cooked in milk.

Main Dishes

Couscous and tajines are the staples and you'll find them everywhere. Couscous is a dish traditionally consisting of coarsely ground wheat, but today it is more usually made with rolled grains of semolina pasta.

The grains are steamed in the top container of a *coucoussier* (a large, two tiered pot used specifically to make couscous), while underneath, in the bottom container, meat or vegetables (or both) simmer away for hours in an aromatic broth. Couscous is often served on huge wooden or ceramic platters (to enable large groups to share in the meal) with the tender stew served on the mounded pile of fluffy semolina, accompanied by a fiery hot sauce called *harissa*.

The preparation of couscous is a long and laborious process, so the dish tends to be served only in the family home. At restaurants, for authentic (and good) couscous, you will probably need to order hours in advance. The quality of couscous offered in restaurants varies hugely. Any opportunity to try the home-cooked variety, however, is not to be missed.

Tajines, delicious slow-cooked stews of meat and vegetables flavoured with herbs and spices, are named after the pot they are cooked in – a round shallow earthernware dish with a tall conical lid. The stew is usually cooked over an individual charcoal brazier and is served in the tajine. Typically it's placed in the centre of the table and everyone dips into this with small pieces of bread rather than using knives and forks. The juice is mopped up first, then the vegetables are gathered up and finally the meat is divided up and eaten with the fingers.

There are endless varieties of tajines; some are very simple, others come with the addition of olives or eggs, prunes and almonds or other dried fruits.

Another Berber speciality is *m'choui*, a whole lamb roasted in the open air, often seasoned with saffron and hot red pepper, and traditionally served with by brochettes of lamb's heart and liver. It's often cooked to celebrate festivals.

The most fabulous Moroccan dish of all may well be *pastilla* (*bastaila* in Arabic). It is a delicious and incredibly rich mixture of pigeon meat and lemon-flavoured eggs, plus almonds, cinnamon, saffron and sugar, encased in layer upon layer of very fine *ouarka* pastry. Even though pastilla is difficult to find outside the major cities (it's common in Fès where you can buy it from stalls as well as restaurants), try not to leave Morocco without tasting it.

A much simpler dish, popular just about everywhere, is roast chicken served with crispy chips (the chips are often served cold, so you may have to ask for them to be warmed up), fresh bread and sometimes a Moroccan salad.

Brochettes – pieces of meat on a skewer barbecued over hot coals – are also available everywhere and are usually very good.

You'll find a wealth of seafood, straight from the day's catch, along the coast, particularly in El Jadida, Oualidia, Essaouira,

---

Harissa

A condiment made from hot red peppers, olive oil and garlic, *harissa* is widely used throughout the Maghreb for flavouring tajines, couscous and soups.

- Remove the seeds and stems from 100g of hot, dried red chilli peppers and soak them in hot water until soft.

- Meanwhile, peel six cloves of garlic and pound with two tablespoons of course salt in a mortar and pestle until smooth.

- Set aside and then do likewise with the drained peppers and another two tablespoons of salt.

- Add to the garlic paste.

- Put six tablespoons of coriander seeds and four tablespoons of cumin seeds in the mortar and pound to a powder.

- Add the garlic and pepper paste and a little olive oil and pound until smooth.

- Continue this process, adding up to 10 tablespoons of olive oil, until the sauce is well blended.

Safi and Agadir. The culinary traditions of Portugal and Spain have long been assimilated into the art of preparing seafood, so you're looking at something more exotic than plain fish and chips. Seafood you're likely to be offered includes sardines, sole, sea bass, prawns, *calamaris* (squid), oysters, mussels and occasionally lobster.

No Moroccan meal is complete without a round or two of fresh bread, the 'staff of life'. In the countryside, you can't beat a breakfast of bread dipped in olive oil and washed down with hot, sweet mint tea. A delicious alternative is bread dipped in argan or almond oil (nicer than the standard offering of bread with margarine and apricot jam!). In Berber homes you'll sometimes be offered bread with a bowl of oil and honey combined – the oil sits on top of the thick sweet honey – the ultimate dunking experience.

Bread-making is a central activity in most Moroccan homes. In the cities and towns, bread is made each morning and baked in a wood fire by the local neighbourhood baker. You may see children carrying the uncooked loaves through the streets. If you're lucky enough to be invited into a Berber home, you'll find the women of the house busy in the smoky kitchen kneading dough and attending to a simmering tajine. The leftover dough is sometimes pressed onto the back wall of the brick fireplace and comes out crispy and boat shaped.

Desserts & Pastries

Dessert often consists of a platter of fresh fruit. In summer there is a huge variety to choose from – all sorts of melons, fresh dates and figs, yellow and red plums, peaches, grapes, pears, bananas, Barbary figs (the fruit of the prickly pear cactus), pomegranates, mandarins, tangerines and oranges.

Beghrir, very light pancakes cooked on a griddle or earthenware dish, and *rghaif*, flaky pancakes which are deep-fried in oil, are sometimes served in restaurants as a dessert with melted butter and honey, but are more traditionally eaten for breakfast.

FRANCES LINZEE GORDON

Pyramid of almond pastries – a familiar sight at the patisseries.

The delicious deep-fried doughnuts *sfenj* are more like a snack food – you'll often find them sold at little booths at the centre of a *souq*, or near open markets or bus stations.

Those with a sweet tooth are in for a double treat in Morocco – in the cities and bigger towns you'll find both Moroccan and French pastries. Moroccan patisseries tend to be family-run affairs and have often been going for generations.

Two famous sweets are *kaab el ghzal* (gazelle's horns), crescent-shaped pastries stuffed with delicately flavoured almond paste and coated with icing sugar, and *m'hancha* (coiled serpent cake), a flat round of baked almond-stuffed pastry coated with icing sugar and cinnamon.

English	Arabic	French
Vegetables & Pulses		
artichoke	*qooq*	*artichaut*
cucumber	*khiyaar*	*concombre*
garlic	*tooma*	*ail*
green beans	*loobeeya*	*haricots verts*
haricot beans	*fasooliya*	*haricots blancs*
lentils	*'aads*	*lentilles*

lettuce	khess	laitue
mushrooms	feggee	champignons
olives	zeetoun	olives
onion	besla	oignon
peas	zelbana	petits pois
		bisila
potatoes	batatas	pommes
		de terre
tomato	mataisha	tomate
		tamatim
vegetables	xôdra	légumes

oil	zit	huile
pepper	filfil/	poivre
	lebzaar	
salt	melha	sel
soup	chorba	potage
spicy lentil	harira	...
soup		
sugar	sukur	sucre
yoghurt	zabadee	yaourt
	laban/	
	danoon	

Fish

anchovies	shton	anchois
cod	lamooree	morue
lobster	laangos	homard
sardine	serdeen	sardine
shrimp	qaimroon	crevette
sole	sol	sole
tuna	ton	thon
whiting	merla	merlan

Meat

beef	begree	bouef
camel	lehem jemil	chameau
chicken	farooj/dujaj	poulet
kidneys	kelawwi	rognons
lamb	lehem	agneau
		ghenmee
liver	kebda	foie
meat	lehem	viande

Fruit

apple	teffah	pomme
apricot	mesh-mash	abricot
banana	banan/moz	banane
dates	tmer	dattes
figs	kermoos	figues
fruit	fakiya	fruits
grapes	'eineb	raisins
orange	leemoon	orange
pomegranate	remman	grenade
watermelon	dellah	pastèque

Miscellaneous

bread	khubz	pain
butter	zebda	beurre
chips	ships	frites
cheese	fromaj	fromage
eggs	bayd	œufs

DRINKS
Tea & Coffee

Morocco's national beverage, sometimes referred to as 'Moroccan whisky', is freshly brewed mint tea (atay in Arabic, thé à la menthe in French) made with Chinese green gunpowder tea, sprigs of fresh mint (nanaa') and vast quantities of sugar. Moroccans adore it and tend to drink it all day long, at every opportunity they get.

Traditionally it's served in elegant Moroccan teapots and poured (from a height to make it frothy on top) into small glasses. In restaurants it may be just served by the glass. English tea is usually served black and is invariably known as thé Lipton.

Coffee is available everywhere and is generally very good. It's made in varying strengths depending on how much milk is added.

You can order black coffee (qahwa kehla/cafe noir), coffee 'broken' with a spot of milk (qahwa mherresa/cafe cassé), half coffee and half milk (ness-ness), standard coffee with milk (qahwa hleeb/café au lait) and very weak coffee which is mostly milk 'broken' with a little coffee (hleeb mhers). If you ask simply for coffee you'll get café au lait.

Coffee served in Moroccan homes is sometimes flavoured with cinnamon, cardamom, black pepper, ginger or other spices.

Juices

The best places to get freshly squeezed juices are in the occasional small shops that do nothing else, although most cafes and restaurants can make them for you. Orange juice is popular, but you may also come across pomegranate, watermelon and grape juice. Drinks are also made with a mixture of milk or buttermilk and the juices of fresh fruits and almonds.

Soft Drinks & Bottled Water

Coca-Cola, Pepsi and other soft drinks are well established in Morocco, but remember that in hot weather, they don't do an awful lot to quench your thirst. Several brands of bottled water are available, including Sidi Harazem (still) and Oulmes (sparkling).

Alcohol

Islam forbids the drinking of alcoholic beverages, but they are nonetheless widely available. Some of the better (or at least more expensive) restaurants are licensed, but many are not. The cheapest places are rarely licensed unless they have a bar attached.

There are more bars around than is at first obvious. They tend not to advertise themselves and most are basic set-'em-up-and-knock-'em-down places. The bigger cities have the occasional liquor store, where you can get beer, wine and spirits for considerably less than in the bars or restaurants.

Beer The two main locally produced beers, Flag Spéciale (brewed in Tangier) and Stork (brewed in Fès & Casablanca) are quite drinkable without being anything to write home about. Smallish bottles cost between Dr6 and Dr8 in the liquor stores and Dr12 to Dr15 in the bars and restaurants.

Amstel and Heineken are also produced in Morocco under licence and you can come across the odd imported brand, such as US Budweiser, in the liquor stores.

Wine Some quite reasonable wines are produced in Morocco. Vieux Papes is the best known red table wine and Valpierre, made near Rabat, is a popular dry white wine.

Recommended reds include Guerrouane and Aït Souala, both from the Meknès region, and the more expensive Beau

Vallon. Toulal, both red and white, has received favourable reviews and a rosé worth trying is Gris de Boulaouane. In the liquor stores, wine prices start at about Dr35.

Spirits Various spirits can be had, although they are hardly cheap. There is a French emphasis, especially in the northern half of the country.

If you like the aniseed-based *pastis*, one of the more well known brands sells in Morocco for around Dr120.

ENTERTAINMENT

Morocco isn't exactly the last word in night life. The major cities do have some good cinemas and there are bars, discos and nightclubs to be found (though prostitution features heavily in these places).

You may find that the best Moroccan night life is to be enjoyed in the countryside – it's difficult to beat listening to the hypnotic music of the Berbers or drinking in the immense desert sky of the sub-Sahara.

Cinemas

The best cinemas are in Rabat and Casablanca. It's pretty cheap entertainment, with seats costing from Dr7 to Dr12, depending on where you want to sit.

The better cinemas get some quite up-to-date films, but if they're not French films, they are almost invariably dubbed into French.

Every town has at least one cinema specialising in kung fu movies, often with a sprinkling of the vague Indian equivalent of the genre.

Bars

These come in two varieties. The majority are pretty basic, tend to be discreet about their existence and close fairly early. Many have a Flag Spéciale sign outside – push the door open and there you are. In Casablanca, some go by the name of *drogueries*. The local punters will probably be surprised to see you – particularly if you are a woman.

The other version is the expensive hotel bar. These stay open a little later and are considerably more expensive. Some mid-range hotels and a few of the top-end places have comfortable, atmospheric bars that are worth seeking out.

Discos & Nightclubs
The difference between discos and nightclubs is not always clear. Generally you'll have to pay at least Dr50 to get in, which usually includes a drink, and subsequent drinks cost an average of Dr50. Many discos are decidedly overpopulated with local lads; a couple of the more chic jobs in the Casablanca suburbs are better, but very dear.

Some of the sleazier nightclubs, particularly in central Casablanca, put on a cabaret or floor show, usually of the bellydancing variety.

Cultural Shows
Some of the big hotels and tourist restaurants put on folk performances. Those in the restaurants are probably preferable, since the settings are often quite sumptuous.

The shows themselves can be a mixed bag, but are entertaining enough if reasonable musicians have been engaged to play traditional Andalusian or Berber music.

The dancing is more often than not Egyptian-style bellydancing (it is not really a Moroccan genre). A few of the top hotels opt for western-style cabarets.

SPECTATOR SPORT
With more than 60 per cent of the population aged under 25, sport plays a large role in Moroccan life. Moroccan's biggest passion by far is football (soccer) which seems to be played at every opportunity. You won't have to go far to find a game in progress and you'll know when a big match (local or international) is on because the streets will be deserted and every male worth his salt will be sitting in a cafe glued to the television.

There are some 320 football stadiums across the country, with the biggest being the Complexe Mohammed V in Casablanca and the Complexe Moulay Abdellah in Rabat.

The Moroccan national team, nicknamed the 'Lions of the Atlas', play at these stadiums to crowds of 80,000 or more. The Lions played in the World Cup in 1970, 1986 and 1994, and in the 1986 competition, the Lions became the first Arab and African national team to qualify for the second round.

Many Moroccan footballers also play abroad, mainly in France, Portugal and the Arab Gulf States.

Morocco began to distinguish itself in the field of athletics in the mid 1980s when Said Aouita (a native of Kenitra) and Nawal El Moutawakil burst on to the international scene. At the 1984 Los Angeles Olympics, Aouita won the gold medal in the 500m and Moutawakil became the first Arab woman to achieve a gold by winning the 400m hurdles.

The most famous Moroccan athlete is the young Hicham El Guerrouj who looks set to succeed the Algerian Noureddine Morcelli as number one in the world for middle distance running. In 1996 he established two world indoor records by a large margin. Another Moroccan athletics star, Salah Hissou, holds the 10,000m world record.

One of the most gruelling marathons in the world, *Le Marathon des Sables*, takes places every April across the desert terrain of the Moroccan sub-Sahara. Held over seven days, the course covers 220km altogether – 78 of them non-stop. Participants also carry everything they need for the week with them, including their food.

The 1997 marathon attracted a field of 370 participants, 34 of them women, and included competitors from as far away as Hong Kong, Japan and New Zealand. The youngest runner was Jallal Sefraoui, a Moroccan student aged 16, and the eldest participant a 74-year-old retired osteopath, Claude Compain.

Golf is becoming increasingly popular, thanks largely to the Moroccan Federation for Golf whose honorary president is none other than King Hassan himself.

The Hassan II Challenge Cup is held annually at the Dar es-Salaam golf course in Rabat and is one of the biggest competitions in the world. Morocco expects to have 30

FRANCES LINZEE GORDON
Potpourri for sale, Spice Markets, Marrakesh

golf courses throughout the country by the end of the century.

Morocco boasts a handful of tennis players who are making a name for themselves on the international circuit. One player, Karim Alami, has beaten big names like Pete Sampras and Boris Becker.

The best Moroccan female tennis player is Bahia Mouhtacine who won the recent African championships.

Other popular sports in Morocco include cycling, basketball and handball.

THINGS TO BUY

The souvenir hunter could spend weeks trawling through the souqs of Morocco. From silver jewellery to copper and brassware, and myriad rugs and carpets, there is an enormous choice. Obviously items of inferior quality are produced as well as higher quality objects – it pays to take your time before buying. For a better idea of what to look for, see the colour Arts & Crafts section.

For some people the big attraction is the herbs and spices. Besides the cumin, saffron, ginger and so on that are usually displayed in huge colourful mounds, you'll find all sorts of obscure things for medicinal purposes.

The Djemaa el-Fna in Marrakesh is a good place for this. If you've got a cough, cold or other ailment, point to the part that hurts and you'll soon have a small plastic bag with the wonder herb in your hand.

Directions for use vary, so try to get an explanation of how to take your herbal remedy. The locals swear by these *'ashaab* (herbs).

Markets

In common with most African and Middle Eastern countries, Moroccan towns and villages have a weekly market day (sometimes twice a week) when people from the surrounding area come to sell their wares and buy goods they do not produce themselves.

These markets are different from the permanent covered markets you'll find in most towns and usually provide a lively opportunity to observe the distinctive customs and clothing of local tribespeople. Some of the most interesting include:

Agadir	Saturday, Sunday
Figuig	Saturday
Ifrane	Sunday
Larache	Sunday
M'Hamid	Monday
Midelt	Sunday
Moulay Idriss	Saturday
Ouarzazate	Sunday
Ouezzane	Thursday
Oujda	Wednesday, Sunday
Sefrou	Thursday
Tafraoute	Wednesday
Taroudannt	Friday
Tinerhir	Monday
Tinzouline	Monday
Zagora	Wednesday, Sunday

|◁| |◁| |◁| |◁| |◁| |◁| |◁|

Berber nose or beak symbol
Traditionally, Berbers hung crows' beaks around their children's necks to protect them from the evil eye.

Moroccan
Arts & Crafts

Since the 16th century, merchant ships have been leaving Moroccan shores laden with exotic goods bound for Europe. Maroquinerie (leatherware) was the single most prized item and the word became synonymous with quality leather goods throughout the fashionable courts and houses of Europe.

That tradition lives on, accompanied by a rich heritage in the production of all sorts of goods – from carpets to fine pottery, heavy silver jewellery to elegant woodwork.

The traditional crafts of Morocco are the living embodiment of its pre-industrial manufacturing industry. Although much of what is made today is aimed at tourists and is for decorative use, it has its roots in the satisfaction of the everyday needs of people – from the humblest person to the most elevated.

The government goes to some lengths to keep these arts alive because they are as important to the economy as phosphates and agriculture. As far back as 1918, the then resident-general of the French protectorate over Morocco, General Lyautey, set up the Office des Industries d'Art Indigène to promote craft sales abroad. No doubt some of what is produced today is garbage – quick, cheap souvenirs that end up in the hands of tourists too impatient to look around for quality – but there is plenty of decent stuff to be found.

Moroccan tourism took a battering during the Gulf War, recovered to prewar levels on 1993, then suffered a three-year recession until 1996. Currently it seems to be showing strong signs of growth, with an 8% increase from 1995.

Nevertheless, the figures are still not what they were during the boom a decade ago, and inconsiderate as it sounds, this can be good news for the patient bargainer, as shopkeepers are still keen to make a sale.

Many of the products that attract visitors, such as rugs and chased brass and copperware, owe at least some of their visual appeal to a meeting of religious precept and traditional tribal design. Considering the depiction of all living beings an affront to God, Islam imposed strictures on the artist. There was no question of art imitating life (let alone life imitating art). Consequently, public art had little choice but to follow an abstract and decorative path which inspired the serene contemplation of seemingly endlessly repeated and interlaced motifs.

Alongside variations on floral designs, geometry developed as a prime tool of the artist. In Morocco and throughout the Islamic world, artisans have, over the centuries, perfected the creation of intricate geometrical patterns, many of which are elaborations on tribal themes long known in Morocco.

Added to this came calligraphy, which made of the Arabic language, and particularly the sacred words of the Qur'an, an artistic medium in itself. For although it was sacrilegious to portray the image of God, it was praiseworthy to have His words on display for all the world to see. The calligraphy you

Title Page: Berber flat weave fabric (photograph by Glenn Beanland).

Below: Detail of mausoleum in the garden of the Saadian tombs, Marrakesh.

DAMIEN SIMONIS

FRANCES LINZEE GORDON

FRANCES LINZEE GORDON

see in great religious buildings in Morocco is generally composed of extracts from the Qur'an or such ritual declarations as *la illah illa Allah* ('There is no god but Allah').

An artistic peak was reached in the 13th century under the Merenids (see the Art & Architecture entry in the Facts About the Country chapter). This dynasty seemed to specialise in sponsoring the construction of theological colleges (*medersas*) in all the great cities, and they are the most richly decorated of all of Morocco's historical buildings. The base of the medersa walls is covered in zellij tiles – fragments of ceramic tiles in hues of green, blue and yellow, interspersed with black, on a white background.

Above these tiles, the stylised decoration is continued in lacework stucco, topped finally by carved wooden (often cedar) panels, which are continued on the ceiling.

Geometric finesse and harmony in design (much of it introduced by Arabs from Muslim Spain) spread through all levels of artisanal handicrafts, although the origins of many Berber designs, especially in textiles and jewellery, predate the emergence of Islam. Carpets and rugs almost always feature some geometric decoration; today you will find items depicting animals and the like, but they have nothing to do with traditional artistic norms.

Most of the popular copper and brass trays boast flurries of calligraphic virtuosity. The beauty of the most intricate jewellery is in the sum of its many simply shaped parts.

Although much craftwork is now aimed at tourists, little of it has been specifically designed *for* them. Rugs, trays, silver jewellery and swords were being made for local use long before tourism became a phenomenon. There are exceptions. Much of the leatherware is more inspired by an attempt to imitate popular European tastes than it is by tradition.

The same can be said of most woollen products, such as caps, multicoloured coats, sweaters and the like – you'll be

Left: Working the loom to produce fabric for hats, jackets and bags, Fès medina.

Right: Traditional, handcrafted teapot being welded, Fès medina.

lucky to see a Moroccan wearing any of these items. A lot of woodwork, especially thuya-wood carvings from the Essaouira region, is a reaction to the influx of tourists hungry for original souvenirs.

Shopping in the Souq

The most useful tool when hunting for crafts is patience. Morocco is crawling with craft souqs, and tourists often find themselves subjected to heavy sales pressure. Before you even get to the shops in many cities you will have to deal with 'guides' and touts of various types. Once inside the shops, you will, in the best circumstances, be caught up in the age-old mint tea ritual, in which gentle but persistent pressure is applied to you to purchase something.

Less scrupulous (or more desperate) shopkeepers tend to go for more strong-arm tactics and badger unsuspecting visitors into buying things they barely even wanted to look at – this species is a minority and mainly inhabits the bigger tourist cities like Marrakesh. Most shopkeepers are perfectly all right, although some can put on rather long faces if you leave with your hands empty and wallet full.

Before buying anything, you should look around. If you buy the first items you see, you may well be disenchanted with them by the time you leave. Every big city has an Ensemble Artisanal. These are government-run 'supermarkets'. Prices are generally higher than those you would pay if you bargained in the souqs, but here you can check out the goods in peace and get an idea of what good-quality items are like.

It is also a good idea to visit some of the various Moroccan traditional arts museums, where you can admire classical pieces of work, be they rugs or rings.

Carpets & Rugs

Opposite Page: Berber carpets and fabrics are generally flat woven with wools that are thicker and dyed with less lustrous colours than Islamic urban carpets. Strong geometric patterns are their signature.

Above Box: Moroccan jewellery, elaborate and exquisite, is among the most highly prized in Africa (photograph by Karyn Duggan).

Bottom Box: Hexagonal motif typical of the Rabat style in the urban Islamic carpet tradition (photograph by Damien Simonis).

Carpet shops. The words themselves evoke for many the sum total of their Moroccan experience. All Moroccan touts seem to assume the first (and only) thing tourists want is a carpet.

The selling of carpets is exclusively men's business and the same can be said for practically all arts and crafts. The big difference between carpets and other crafts is that making them is the women's preserve. Making good carpets and rugs can take months, but the women see little cash for their labours.

The heavy woollen carpets and throw rugs vary greatly in design and colouring from region to region. Rabat is the centre of the Moroccan urban Islamic carpet making traditon, which is inspired by the carpet-makers of the Middle East.

The style is very formal, characterised by its use of rich yarns in lustrous colours, and normally features a central motif and an intricate border. As a rule of thumb, the wider and more complicated the work in the border, the more the carpet is worth.

The value of a carpet is based not only on the intricacy of design, but also on its age, the number of knots and, perhaps most importantly, the strength of the wool. The tougher and more wiry the wool, the longer the rug will last – many Moroccan soft-wool carpets will not stand up well to much foot traffic.

A handmade carpet can become something of an antique if it's well made, and those done by masters are much sought after by connoisseurs and are hard to come by. A square metre of carpet contains tens of thousands of knots and it's basically a case of the more the better, as they indicate a product is more likely to last. Top-class examples can have 36,000 to 38,000 knots per square metre. These are comparatively rare, and glib claims that the item in front of you has several hundred thousand knots per square metre can, as a rule, be confidently discounted.

For decades, chemical colours have been used instead of vegetable dyes, but despite what you may be told, they tend to fade too, sometimes quite dramatically. Vegetable dyes are still used, and tend to fade more slowly. A wide range of products are used to create different colours, including almond leaves, bark, iron sulphate and cow urine.

For the locals, carpets are utilitarian as much as works of art, and the brilliant colours of a new rug are not expected to retain their intensity. If you find a genuinely old piece (of 40 or so years), you can be fairly confident that it *won't* change colour significantly.

Hanbels, Shedwis & Zanafis Outside Rabat, most of the carpets and rugs are the work of hundreds of different Berber as well as Arab tribal groups, who each employ their own quite distinctive designs, techniques and use of colour, according to tradition.

Most of the rugs made by these tribal groups are flatwoven (though many do make pile rugs) and feature zigzag, diamond and lozenge designs as well as strong, simple geometric patterning, such as deep horizontal bands or abstract symbols of the evil eye. Colours are more natural than in Rabat rugs of the Islamic urban style.

Moroccan flatweaves used as blankets, coverings for the floor or for general domestic use are called *handels*. A *zanafi*

ALL PHOTOS BY GLENN BEANLAND

DAMIEN SIMONIS

Above: Elaborate geometric patterns and many colours in flat weave rugs, photographed in Tangier.

Box: Detail of leatherwork on bag, Marrakesh (photograph by Glenn Beanland).

is a rug with a combination of flatweave and pile, and a *shedwi* is a flatwoven rug of black and white bands, tapestry weave and twining.

Buying Carpets You will hear many absurd asking prices while bargaining in Morocco. A high, but not insane, starting price for good wool carpets is Dr150 to Dr200 per square metre. If you hold out and the item is not of great quality, the price will come down.

Flatwoven pieces require more work and are generally more expensive. From Dr800 to Dr1200 for two square metres is a not unreasonable price, but insistent bargaining would bring it down to Dr600 to Dr1000 or perhaps less.

Again, much depends on the quality of the handiwork and the eagerness of the shopkeeper to sell.

Other Wool Products

Plenty of other good woollen purchases can be made. Chefchaouen and Ouezzane are in flourishing wool country and, in the former especially, all manner of garments can be found. Perhaps the best are thick sweaters, which cost from around Dr80-Dr100 (depending on quality and thick-

ness). Jackets, head gear and woven bags are also available.

Inspect the goods closely. The most attractive coats made of superb wool can look great, but if they're of poor quality, you'll find them unravelling within weeks. Another popular item is the heavy, hooded cloak (*burnouse*), worn by Berbers from all over the country. They are practical in the cold mountain weather, but westerners can look a little silly in them.

Textiles

Although Morocco does not have Egypt's reputation for producing cotton products, many visitors are tempted by *jellabas*, the full-length cotton garments traditionally worn by men.

Similar items are worn by women and both types of garment are very cool and comfortable in hot climates.

Various materials are used to produce a whole range of, what for Berber households, are useful floor covers and the like. Depending on the designs, they can be as attractive a buy as the carpets.

Fès is reputedly Morocco's great silk and brocade centre, but both these artforms are apparently heading for extinction and so are increasingly hard to find.

Box: Multi-coloured thread for sale at the Haberdashers' souq, Fès (photograph by Frances Linzee Gordon).

Below: Colourful dyes, embroidery and embossing – Tuareg bags, Taroudannt.

DAMIEN SIMONIS

Leatherwork

The bulk of contemporary leatherware is aimed solely at tourists. The tanneries of Fès provide raw material for about half the country's total production in leather goods, but several other big cities maintain their own tanneries.

The most 'authentic' of these items are *babouches* (around Dr25), slippers that are still the most common footwear among Moroccans of both sexes. Men wear yellow or white ones, while bright colours and ornate styles are reserved for women.

A whole range of products designed for westerners in search of leather goods more affordable than in the designer stores at home can be found in Fès, Marrakesh, Rabat and Tetouan. They include jackets, bags of all descriptions, wallets, belts and stools. The latter are a genuinely traditional item and are made of goat leather. If camel saddles are your thing, try Marrakesh.

Some of the best shoulder bags are made in the Rif and find their way into the markets of Tetouan and Chefchaouen. Tiny bags designed to carry around personal copies of the Qur'an are popular souvenir items.

The leather is often of a high quality, and to this extent the fame of maroquinerie remains justified. Unfortunately, the artisanship of many items leaves a lot to be desired – check the links, stitching and so on of anything you're interested in.

Pottery & Ceramics

The potteries of Safi have long been touted as the main centre of ceramic production in Morocco, but smaller cooperatives are springing up in other parts of the country, and the cities of Fès and Meknès have a centuries-old heritage of ceramics production. A lot of it is prosaic, such as the ubiquitous green roof tiles that are largely made in these two Middle Atlas cities and to some extent in Safi.

Top Box: Babouches (slippers) in the Fès medina (photograph by Maria Rainone).

Bottom Box: Detail of a large plate with popular Fès design: brown, blue and black against white background (photograph by Glenn Beanland).

Safi's pottery-makers have taken their inspiration from the ceramics once produced in Málaga (southern Spain), which are identified by a characteristic metallic sheen. The arrival of many potters from Fès has led to an increasing mixture of that city's traditional designs, which were mostly handed down by artisans exiled from Al-Andalus.

Fès' ceramics are dominated by browns, blues or yellows and greens on white backgrounds. You can see excellent examples of jars, pots and other household items (for wealthy

GLENN BEANLAND

DAMIEN SIMONIS

GLENN BEANLAND

Top: Tajine bowls – the essential crockery for Moroccan cuisine – and a vase.

Middle: Spoilt for choice in the potters' souq, Safi.

Bottom: Catche-pots (flowerpot holders) and candlestick.

households!) in most of the museums of Moroccan art in the big cities. Meknès inherited much of its skills from Fès, and its pottery industry only began to flourish in the 18th century.

Among the handiest commercially available souvenirs are decorative ceramic plates or coffee and tea sets. The rougher examples can sell for as little as Dr80, but expect to pay several hundred for a decently made plate.

A uniquely Moroccan item is the *tajine*, the casserole dish with the conical cover used to cook the meal of the same name (and indeed other meals, too). You can get a smarter decorative tajine, or settle for the locally used product. One of the latter can cost as little as Dr15 (for a two person dish) or Dr35 (for a dish serving up to nine people).

One way to tell the difference between something of value or production-line tourist trash is the gaudiness of colour and brightness of finish. The more precious pottery tends to be muted in colour, decoration and finish. This doesn't make the other stuff intrinsically bad, but it *does* mean you should not pay an arm and a leg for it.

In contrast to the largely urban and sophisticated pottery are the rougher, rustic products of the Berbers. Although simpler, they have their own charm and are characteristic of the regions in which they are made. In the High Atlas south of Marrakesh, ochre is the dominant colour, the exception being down by Zagora, where you can find pots, jars and cups with a green finish. Water vessels are often decorated with a mysterious black substance that is said to purify the water.

Combining the domestic and the decorative: beaten copper utensils (below) and an ornamental brass candle stick (box: photograph by Frances Linzee Gordon).

Brass & Copperware

One of the best things about brass and copperware is that it is comparatively hard to cheat on quality. Probably the most commonly bought items are plates and trays of chased copper and sometimes brass. You can start at about Dr15 for saucer-sized decorative plates of low quality to around Dr600 for large, heavy trays. The latter are lavishly decorated and can be used in coffee tables or hung on the wall as decoration.

There are plenty of other souvenirs. Candlesticks and lamp bases come in all shapes and sizes, and are best looked for in Marrakesh, Fès and Tetouan. Tetouan can be quite a good place to pick up these products, provided you are not accompanied by guides and hangers-on. Also worth buying are brass mirror frames, often with patterns and designs reminiscent of those found in the best Moroccan Islamic architecture.

For hammered rather than chased copper items, Taroudannt is about the best place.

ADRIENNE COSTANZO

GLENN BEANLAND

Jewellery

Much of the jewellery around is not what it is claimed to be. Gold and silver are more often than not plated, and amber is plastic (put a lighted match to it and smell). Unless you are sure of your stuff, you should be cautious about what you buy and be prepared for disappointment.

This is not to say that genuinely good jewellery cannot be found, but you have to look for it. The making of jewellery in Morocco was once the preserve of the Jewish population, and it is said that Muslims at one stage had a superstitious aversion to metalwork. Whatever the truth of that, the Jews have left and Muslims have been fashioning jewellery for centuries.

Above: The Islamic influence embossed in brass – detail of plate, Fès.

Box: Jewellery detail, Taroudannt (photograph by Damien Simonis).

Below: Genuine silver jewellery can be found, if you put in the time and research.

DAMIEN SIMONIS

Delicate filigree and engraved silver in Berber brooch fasteners, Taroudannt.

DAMIEN SIMONIS

Gold Fès is traditionally *the* place to buy gold jewellery, as much because of the sophisticated, urban and well-off clientele as anything else. Some of the city's artisans started a minor migratory wave to Essaouira a century ago, making the Atlantic town a secondary centre for the production of gold. Gold markets are to be found in various other big cities too – the one in Meknès, which is not overwhelmed by gold-hunting tourists, is worth investigating.

Classic jewellery made in Fès and Tangier remains largely faithful to Andalusian recherché lines, and is often ostentatious and beyond the means of most. The Meknès products are generally more modest.

Essaouira, apart from the contribution made by the jewellers from Fès, boasts a local style dominated by floral designs and enamel work, although little of the jewellery produced has any gold content.

Silver You can find cheap silver-plated jewellery just about anywhere. If you're looking for slightly more valuable and characteristically Moroccan items, you should head south to Tiznit, Rissani, Tan Tan or Taroudannt. Silver has long been highly prized by Berber women – a look in some of the museums of Moroccan art will soon convince you of that. The reason for this is that few peasant families, however powerful in their own stamping ground, could afford the luxury of gold.

Silver necklaces, bracelets, rings and earrings are invariably quite chunky, and often enlivened with pieces of amber or comparatively cheap precious stones. A particular item you will see in jewellery souqs is the hand of Fatima. The open palm is supposed to protect its wearer from ill fortune.

Other Metalwork

While down around Tiznit and Taroudannt, you might be interested in other silverwork. Specialities in both towns are silver-encrusted sabres and muskets. You can also come across silver daggers and silver (or silver-plated) scabbards.

For wrought iron, the place to hunt around is the ironsmiths' souq in Marrakesh. Here you can find frames for mirrors, fire screens, lanterns and the like. There is little of this sort of work outside Marrakesh, and it is generally classed among those artisanal arts originally imported from Muslim Spain.

GLENN BEANLAND

Box: Chickens on display behind delicate wrought iron, market day, Poultry souq, Fès (photograph by Frances Linzee Gordon).

Left: Usually worn as a pendant by women of the Atlas, a small engraved Qur'an case in silver.

Woodwork

The artisans of Tetouan, Salé and Meknès continue to produce veritable works of art in wood. Painted and sculpted panels for interior decoration are commonplace, and the infinitely more intricate work required to produce the stalactite-like decoration that graces the interior of various medersas, religious buildings and private homes of the rich also survives.

Nor has the *mashrabiyya* (sometimes also spelled *mousharabiyya*) been consigned to history. These screens were and are designed to allow women to observe the goings-on in the street without being seen themselves. Fès and Meknès are the main centres of production.

While these items don't make likely candidates for souvenirs, they do serve to show that Moroccan crafts are not completely dependent on floods of tourists.

Pleasantly perfumed cedar is used for most woodwork, and in some of the better workshops you will find beautiful bowls, candlesticks, painted cribs, chests, jewellery boxes and the like. Fès is particularly good for this sort of work. Tetouan produces some interesting pieces too.

Box: Detail of an intricately carved cedar door at the Hassan II Mosque, Casablanca (photograph by Frances Linzee Gordon).

Below: Distinctly rural – colourful and naive Berber painted wooden box found in Rabat.

For marquetry, inlaid chessboards, caskets and all sorts of trinkets, you should wait until you get to Essaouira. The artisans here mainly use thuya wood *(Tris articuta)*, the most common tree in Essaouira's hinterland, but virtually unknown outside Morocco. The wood is so coveted that it is valued like a precious metal.

From little jewellery boxes right through to enormous wooden statues, the range of thuya products is almost unlim-

GLENN BEANLAND

ited. The remarkable natural patterns that show up in the grain of better-quality items are found in the roots of the thuya tree.

Stone & Precious Stones

In Taroudannt you can pick up lamps, paperweights and boxes made of stone. Various kinds of softer stone are also sculpted into all sorts of shapes and sold for a pittance.

Throughout the Middle and High Atlas you'll pass roadside stands with people offering clumps of all sorts of semiprecious stones such as quartz and amethyst.

In the desert around Erfoud are black marble quarries that furnish the base element for that town's souvenir industry. There are several stores there selling everything from statues to paperweights in black marble, as well as plenty of kids trying to unload more modest trinkets.

Fossils in rock (especially ammonite) are sometimes offered alongside the semiprecious stones. Morocco is full of fossils, and enterprising merchants convert them into all sorts of things, including bowls and superb table-top sections.

Box: Scallop motif on carved stone spandrel, Ali ben Youssef Medersa, Marrakesh (photograph by Frances Linzee Gordon).

Middle: Stone Statue, Er-Rachidia.

Bottom: Stone masks, also from Er-Rachidia.

GLENN BEANLAND

GLENN BEANLAND

Basketware

Throughout Morocco you will come across basketware, a wide term that covers everything from the Rif-style straw hats of the north to baskets with cone-shaped covers used by Berbers to carry dates and other merchandise. They make cheap souvenirs and are obviously not made to last forever.

Musical Instruments

Top Box: Baskets holding potpourri, Herb & Spice souq, Marrakesh (photograph by Frances Linzee Gordon).

Middle Box: Handmade Tambourine (photograph by Photo Younis).

Bottom: Wooden bendir and ceramic darbukas (drums) with goatskin heads.

It is possible to pick up traditional Moroccan instruments in various places. One good place to look around is in the Bab el-Jedid area of the Meknès medina, where you'll find various string, wind and percussion instruments.

Probably the best place, however, is the medina of Fès (see the Things to Buy section under that city), where small, medium and large drum sets go for around Dr20, Dr50 and Dr80 respectively. For more information on Moroccan music and instruments see the Music entry in the Arts section of the Facts about the Country chapter.

GLENN BEANLAND

Getting There & Away

AIR

Airports & Airlines

As far as flying into Morocco is concerned, the highest season is considered to be July through to the end of August, and mid-December to the end of December. The lowest season is November to mid-December, and January to mid-February.

Morocco is well served by air from Europe, the Middle East and West Africa. Morocco's main international entry point is the Mohammed V airport, 30km south-east of Casablanca, which also services most flights to Rabat. Shuttle trains and buses link Casablanca and Rabat to the airport.

Passport control and customs formalities are straightforward. You will find representatives of the main international car rental agencies in the arrivals hall, along with representatives for some of the big hotels.

The tourist office has a desk on the 1st floor, just inside the departure lounge, which is open daily from 8.30 am to 7 pm. The BMCE bank has offices in the arrivals and departures lounges, as well as ATMs.

There are several cafes and newsstands dotted around the airport. For details on getting to and from the airport, see the Getting Around entries under Casablanca and Rabat.

International flights also land at Marrakesh, Tangier and Agadir, and occasionally at several other airports, including Fès, Laayoune, Oujda and Ouarzazate.

Marrakesh's airport is 5km south-west of town and the No 11 bus runs irregularly into the city centre. The taxi fare (per cab not per person) shouldn't exceed Dr50.

Shuttle trains run between Tangier and the tiny airport 16km south-west of the city. The taxi fare should not exceed Dr100.

Agadir's modern airport is about 28km south-west of the town. A taxi will cost about Dr100. Otherwise there are a couple of possibilities by bus: see the Getting Around entry under Agadir for more details.

Air France and Morocco's national carrier, Royal Air Maroc (RAM), take the lion's share of flights, but other airlines operating to Morocco include Lufthansa, KLM, Iberia, GB Airways (a subsidiary of British Airways), Swissair, TAT European Airlines, Sabena, Alitalia, Air Algérie, Royal Jordanian, EgyptAir and Tunis Air.

Oujda is linked to Paris and several other French cities, as well as to Amsterdam, Brussels, Düsseldorf and Frankfurt.

There are connections from the USA to Casablanca. You can get direct flights from various cities including Paris, Geneva, London, Rome and Frankfurt to Marrakesh and, less frequently, Fès. There are direct flights between Paris and Ouarzazate.

Laayoune, capital of the Western Sahara, is linked to Abidjan (Côte d'Ivoire) and Libreville (Gabon) by RAM and also to the Canary Islands.

Most Middle Eastern capitals can be reached from Casablanca.

Air Travel Glossary

Apex (advance purchase excursion) This is a discounted ticket which must be paid for in advance. There are penalties if you wish to change it.

Baggage Allowance This will be written on your ticket and usually includes one 20kg item to go in the hold, plus one item of hand luggage.

Bucket Shop This is an unbonded travel agency specialising in discounted airline tickets.

Budget Fare These can be booked at least three weeks in advance, but the travel date is not confirmed until seven days prior to travel.

Bumped Just because you have a confirmed seat doesn't mean you're going to get on the plane (see Overbooking).

Cancellation Penalties If you have to cancel or change an Apex ticket there are often heavy penalties involved; insurance can sometimes be taken out against these penalties. Some airlines impose penalties on regular tickets as well, particularly against no show passengers (see No Shows).

Check-In Airlines ask you to check in a certain time ahead of the flight departure (usually one to two hours on international flights). If you fail to check in on time and the flight is overbooked, the airline can cancel your booking and give your seat to somebody else.

Confirmation Having a ticket written out with the flight and date you want doesn't mean you have a seat until the agent has checked with the airline that your status is 'OK' or confirmed. Meanwhile you could just be 'on request' (see Reconfirmation).

Discounted Tickets There are two types of discounted fares – officially discounted (see Promotional Fares) and unofficially discounted. The lowest prices often impose drawbacks like flying with unpopular airlines, inconvenient schedules or unpleasant routes and connections. A discounted ticket can save you other things than money – you may be able to pay Apex prices without the associated Apex advance booking and other requirements. Discounted tickets only exist where there is fierce competition.

Full Fares Airlines traditionally offer 1st class (coded F), business class (coded J) and economy class (coded Y) tickets. These days there are so many promotional and discounted fares available from the regular economy class that few passengers pay full economy fare.

ITX An 'independent inclusive tour excursion' (ITX) is often available on tickets to popular holiday destinations. Officially it's a package deal combined with hotel accommodation, but many agents will sell you one of these for the flight only. They'll give you phoney hotel vouchers in the unlikely event that you're challenged at the airport.

Lost Tickets If you lose your airline ticket an airline will usually treat it like a travellers cheque and, after enquiries, issue you with another one. Legally, however, an airline is entitled to treat it like cash and if you lose it then it's gone forever. Take good care of your tickets.

MCO A 'miscellaneous charge order' (MCO) is a voucher that looks like an airline ticket, but carries no destination or date. It is exchangeable with any International Association of Travel Agents (IATA) airline for a ticket on a specific flight. Its principal use for travellers is as an alternative to an onward ticket in those countries that demand one, and it's more flexible than an ordinary ticket if you're not sure of your route.

No Shows No shows are passengers who fail to show up for their flight. Full-fare passengers who fail to turn up are sometimes entitled to travel on a later flight. The rest of us are penalised (see Cancellation Penalties).

On Request This is an unconfirmed booking for a flight (see Confirmation).

Open Jaws This is a return ticket where you fly out to one place, but return from another. If available, this can save you backtracking to your arrival point.

Overbooking Airlines hate to fly empty seats and since every flight has some passengers who fail to show up (see No Shows), airlines often book more passengers than they have seats. Usually the excess passengers make up for those who fail to show up, but occasionally somebody gets bumped. If this happens, guess who it is most likely to be? The passengers who check in late.

Point-to-Point This is a discount ticket that can be bought on some routes in return for passengers waiving their rights to stopover.

Promotional Fares These are officially discounted fares like Apex fares, available from travel agents or direct from the airline.

Reconfirmation At least 72 hours prior to departure time of an onward or return flight, you must contact the airline and 'reconfirm' that you intend to be on the flight. If you don't do this the airline can delete your name from the passenger list and you could lose your seat. You don't have to reconfirm the first flight on your itinerary or if your stopover is less than 72 hours. However, it doesn't hurt to reconfirm more than once.

Restrictions Discounted tickets often have various restrictions on them – advance purchase is the most usual one (see Apex). Others are restrictions on the minimum and maximum period you must be away, such as a minimum of 14 days or a maximum of one year (see Cancellation Penalties).

Round-The-World An RTW ticket is just that. You have a limited period in which to circumnavigate the globe and you can go anywhere the carrying airlines go, as long as you don't backtrack. These tickets are usually valid for one year, the number of stopovers or total number of separate flights is worked out before you set off and they often don't cost much more than a basic return flight.

Standby A discounted ticket where you only fly if there is a seat free at the last moment. Standby fares are usually only available on domestic routes.

Tickets Out An entry requirement for many countries is that you have an onward or return ticket, in other words, a ticket out of the country. If you're not sure what you intend to do next, the easiest solution is to buy the cheapest onward ticket to a neighbouring country or a ticket from a reliable airline which can later be refunded if you do not use it (see also MCO).

Transferred Tickets Airline tickets cannot be transferred from one person to another. Travellers sometimes try to sell the return half of their ticket, but officials can ask you to prove that you are the person named on the ticket. This is unlikely to happen on domestic flights, but on an international flight tickets may be compared with passports.

Travel Agencies Travel agencies vary widely and you should choose one that suits your needs. Some simply handle tours, while full-service agencies handle everything from tours and tickets to car rental and hotel bookings. A good one will do all these things and can save you a lot of money, but if all you want is a ticket at the lowest possible price, then you really need an agency specialising in discounted tickets. A discounted ticket agency, however, may not be useful for other things, like hotel bookings.

Travel Periods Some officially discounted fares, Apex fares in particular, vary with the time of year. There is often a low (off-peak) season and a high (peak) season. Sometimes there's an intermediate or shoulder season as well. At peak times, when everyone wants to fly, not only will the officially discounted fares be higher, but so will unofficially discounted fares and there may simply be no discounted tickets available. Usually the fare depends on your outward flight – if you depart in the high season and return in the low season, you pay the high-season fare. ■

Buying Tickets

Your plane ticket will probably be the single most expensive item in your budget and buying it can be an intimidating business. It is worth putting aside a few hours to research the state of the market. Start early: some of the cheapest tickets have to be bought months in advance, and popular flights sell out early.

Talk to other travellers, look at the ads in newspapers and magazines, consult reference books and watch for special offers. Then phone around travel agents for bargains.

Airlines can supply information on routes and timetables, however, except at times of inter-airline war, they do not supply the cheapest tickets. Find out the fare, the route, the duration of the journey and any restrictions on the ticket (see the Air Travel Glossary in this section). Then sit back and decide which is best for you.

The fares quoted in this book are intended as a guide only. They are approximate and based on the rates advertised by travel agents at the time of going to press.

These quoted airfares do not necessarily constitute a recommendation for the particular carrier.

Travellers with Special Needs

If you have special needs of any sort – you have a broken leg, you're a vegetarian, are travelling in a wheelchair, taking the baby or terrified of flying – you should let the airline know as soon as possible so that they can make arrangements accordingly.

You should remind them when you reconfirm your booking (at least 72 hours before departure) and again when you check in at the airport. It may also be worth ringing around the airlines before you make your booking to find out how they can handle your particular needs.

Airports and airlines can be surprisingly helpful, but they do need advance warning. Most international airports will provide escorts from the check-in desk to the plane if necessary and there should be ramps, lifts and accessible toilets and phones.

Toilets in aircraft, on the other hand, are likely to present a problem. Travellers should discuss this with the airline at an early stage and, if necessary, with their doctor.

Guide dogs for the blind will often have to travel in a specially pressurised baggage compartment with other animals, away from their owner, though smaller guide dogs may be admitted to the cabin. All guide dogs will be subject to the same quarantine laws (six months in isolation etc) as any other animal when entering or returning to countries currently free of rabies, such as Britain or Australia.

Deaf travellers can ask for airport and inflight announcements to be written down for them.

Children under the age of two travel for 10% of the standard fare (or free, on some airlines) as long as they don't occupy a seat. They don't get a baggage allowance either. 'Skycots' should be provided by the airline if requested in advance; these will take a child weighing up to about 10kg.

Children between two and 12 can usually occupy a seat for half to two-thirds of the full fare, and do get a baggage allowance. Pushchairs can often be taken as hand luggage.

North America

The *New York Times*, the *LA Times*, the *Chicago Tribune* and the *San Francisco Examiner* produce weekly travel sections in which you'll find any number of travel agents' ads. Council Travel and STA Travel have offices in major cities nationwide.

The magazine *Travel Unlimited* (PO Box 1058, Allston, Massachusetts 02134) publishes details of cheap air fares.

In Canada, Travel CUTS has offices in all major cities. The *Toronto Globe & Mail* and the *Vancouver Sun* carry travel agents' ads.

The cheapest way from the USA or Canada to Morocco and North Africa is usually a return flight to London or Paris and an onward ticket from there. Flights are more numerous and generally better value from Paris.

RAM flies from New York to Casablanca. It also has flights from Montreal to Casablanca, via New York. The standard one way fare from New York is US$854, or US$1121 return. Youth fares are 25% cheaper. From Montreal the standard one way fare is C$1545, or C$2800 for a return excursion fare valid for six months.

The UK
For the latest fares, check out the travel page ads of the Sunday newspapers, *Time Out*, *TNT* and *Exchange & Mart*. A good source of information on cheap fares is the magazine *Business Traveller*.

Most British travel agents are registered with the Association of British Travel Agents (ABTA). If you have paid for your flight with an ABTA-registered agent who then goes out of business, the ABTA will guarantee a refund or an alternative. Unregistered bucket shops are sometimes cheaper, but are also riskier.

The Globetrotters Club (BCM Roving, London WC1N 3XX) publishes a newsletter called *Globe* that covers obscure destinations and can help in finding travelling companions.

One of the most reliable London agents is STA Travel which has offices at 86 Old Brompton Rd (☎ 0171-581 4132) and 117 Euston Rd (☎ 0171-465 0484).

Another is Trailfinders (☎ 0171-938 3366, 938 3939) at 42-50 Earls Court Rd, London W8. It has another office around the corner at 194 Kensington High St, London W8. The latter offers an inoculation service and a research library for customers.

The US agent, Council Travel (☎ 0171-287 3337), has an office at 28a Poland St, London W1V 3DB.

At the time of writing, RAM's cheapest Superpex fares in the low season from London to Tangier were UK£231 for one month and UK£285 for two. RAM also has direct flights from London to Casablanca, as well as flights to Marrakesh and Agadir via Casablanca. RAM offers various other fares, including a special youth ticket.

Many travellers use GB Airways, a sub-sidiary of British Airways, which flies from London via Gibraltar to three Moroccan destinations: Casablanca, Marrakesh and Tangier.

At the time of writing, return tickets, valid for one month, started at UK£219. GB Airways has daily flights to Casablanca from London (Heathrow). There's a weekly flight to Tangier and two others from London (Gatwick) to Marrakesh.

At the time of writing, there were no charter flights operating between the UK and Morocco. This situation is certain to change, however, so check the current charter status carefully before considering the options.

If you only want to go for a short time, consider taking a hotel or fly-drive package. Three nights (in, say, Marrakesh) in a reasonable hotel near the medina, with half-board, optional escorted tours, flights and transfers can cost well under UK£300.

If you are not in too much of a hurry and counting pennies, the most efficient way to get to Morocco is generally to fly to Málaga in southern Spain and either get a boat from there to the Spanish enclave of Melilla or a bus around to Algeciras and from there a boat across to Ceuta or Tangier (refer to the Sea section later in this chapter for details).

There are any number of flights virtually all year round to Málaga and many other Spanish destinations. It is feasible to get a one way ticket to Málaga for around UK£60. Return fares generally start at about UK£150 for scheduled flights, but deals on charters and the like abound, so look around.

Agents specialising in travel to Spain often have ridiculously cheap return flights for short breaks in early November and early December. These are in the range of UK£40 to UK£60 for practically any destination. You'll forfeit the return half, but it's still cheap.

Continental Europe
France There is no shortage of flights from Paris (and many other French cities) to Casablanca, Agadir, Rabat, Tangier, Fès,

Marrakesh, Oujda and Ouarzazate. Most travel agents can do deals, and fly-drive arrangements are an attractive option. Given the sheer volume of traffic from France, deals here are often better than in traditional bucket-shop paradises such as London or Amsterdam.

RAM has three flights a day from Paris to Casablanca. Air France operates at least 12 weekly flights between France and Morocco.

Various agencies sometimes offer charter flights at very low prices and it is possible to get one way flights or deals including accommodation.

At the time of researching, some of the cheapest return charter flights from Paris were to Marrakesh (1490FF) and Agadir (1850FF), with a maximum stay of four weeks, but in general prices are somewhat higher.

You could try looking at Sélection Informations Vacances (☎ 01.42.60.83.40) at 9 Rue de l'Échelle, 75001 Paris, or Nouvelles Frontières (☎ 01.41.41.58.58) at 87 Blvd de Grenelle, 75015 Paris.

If you are looking for something more organised on the ground, one place worth investigating is Explorator (☎ 01.53.45. 85.85) at 16 Rue de la Banque, 75002 Paris. For a couple of other suggestions see the Organised Tours entry later in this chapter.

The possibilities are much more limited from Morocco. Despite the plethora of travel agents in central Casablanca, there is little discounting. A standard one way fare to Paris costs Dr4790.

Spain Despite its proximity, Spain is not the ideal place from which to fly to Morocco, unless perhaps you have little time and want to take an organised tour (for details see the Organised Tours entry later in this chapter).

At the time of writing, a standard return flight with Spain's national carrier, Iberia Airways, from Madrid to Tangier cost 41,000pta. Iberia operates five weekly flights between Madrid and Casablanca and two between Madrid and Tangier. In the high season there are flights from numerous Spanish cities direct to Agadir.

About the only scheduled flights worth a serious look are those between Málaga and the Spanish enclave of Melilla. One way costs 10,450pta, and there are quite a few daily flights.

Travel agents in Madrid tend to be clustered in the vicinity of the Gran Vía. Budget travellers should try Viajes Zeppelin (☎ 547 79 03) at Plaza Santo Domingo 2, or TIVE (☎ 543 02 08), the student and youth travel organisation, at Calle Fernando el Católico 88.

The options *from* Morocco are more limited still. A one way ticket from Casablanca to Madrid, regardless of the airline, comes to about Dr3290.

Gibraltar Few travellers will want to fork out large sums of money to fly from 'the Rock' across the strait to Morocco, but it can be done. GB Airways has five weekly direct flights to Casablanca, three to Tangier and one to Marrakesh. A return flight to Marrakesh, valid for one month, costs UK£155.

There are plenty of travel agents in Gibraltar (and Algeciras) through which you can book tickets. For reservations with GB Airways in Gibraltar, call ☎ 79300.

GB Airways has various agents in Morocco (noted under the city entries). A return ticket from Tangier costs Dr1050.

Germany In Munich, a great source of travel information and equipment is the Darr Travel Shop (☎ 089-282032) at Theresienstrasse 66. Aside from producing a comprehensive travel equipment catalogue, they also run an Expedition Service with current flight information available.

In Berlin, Alternativ Tours (☎ 030 8812089), Wilmersdorfer Strasse 94 (U-Bahn: Adenauerplatz), specialises in discounted airfares worldwide.

Netherlands Amsterdam is a popular departure point for Morocco. Some of the best fares are offered by the student travel agency NBBS Reiswinkels (☎ 020-620 5071), which has seven branches throughout the city.

The fares are comparable to those of London bucket shops. NBBS Reiswinkels also has branches in Brussels, Belgium.

Australasia
There are no direct flights between Australia or New Zealand and Morocco. Your best bet is to get a flight to Europe and make your way to Morocco from there. Most people tend to head for London or Amsterdam first.

STA Travel is one of the more reliable travel agents and has branches around Australia. The Sydney branch (☎ 02-9212 1255) is at 855 George St, Ultimo, NSW 2007, and the Melbourne branch (☎ 03-9349 2411) is at 222 Faraday St Carlton, 3053. Flight Centre (131 600) is another reasonable place to check out.

Asia
Hong Kong and Bangkok are the main two centres for cheap air tickets in South-East Asia, although there's not a huge market for Morocco. If you can't find anything direct, get a cheap ticket to Europe and head down from there.

Mauritania
Return flights between Morocco and Mauritania with RAM or Air Mauritanie cost around Dr4245.

South Africa
Royal Air Maroc has a direct weekly flight from Johannesburg to Casablanca for around US$1300.

LAND
Taking your own vehicle to Morocco is comparatively straightforward. There is no need for a *carnet de passage en doune* when taking your car to Morocco, or indeed into Algeria or Tunisia, but this is a document required in many other African countries and worth getting if you think you'll be driving on beyond the Maghreb.

The UK Automobile Association (and most other such organisations) requires a financial guarantee for the carnet, which effectively acts as an import-duty waiver, as the vehicle could be liable for customs and other taxes if its exit is not registered within a year. The deposit they require can be well in excess of US$1000.

The carnet costs UK£62.50 to UK£72.50 in the UK, depending on the number of countries you want to cover (up to 25). It is essential to ensure that the carnet is filled out properly at each border crossing, or you could be up for a lot of money. The carnet may also need to list any expensive spares you plan to carry, such as a gearbox.

In addition to such obvious papers as vehicle registration and an International Driving Permit (although many foreign licences are acceptable), a Green Card is required from the car's insurer.

Not all insurers will issue one to cover Morocco. If yours does not, you must arrange insurance at the border. You can do this in Spain before embarkation on a ferry in Algeciras or on arrival in Morocco.

If you must arrange the insurance on arrival in Morocco, note that the liability limits on such policies are often absurdly low by western standards and if you have any bad accidents you could be in deep water.

It may be advisable to arrange more comprehensive and reliable cover before you leave. If you're starting from the UK, a company often recommended for insurance policies and for detailed information on carnets is Campbell Irvine Ltd (☎ 0171-937 9903) at 48 Earls Court Rd, London, W8 6EJ.

The UK & Europe
Bus It is possible to get a bus ticket to destinations in Morocco from as far away as London. In the high season, a return ticket with Eurolines (in conjunction with CTM, Morocco's national line) costs UK£190 to Tangier and UK£200 to Marrakesh.

The service leaves Victoria coach station (☎ 0171-730 3466) at 164 Buckingham Palace Rd, London SW1, four to six days a week, depending on the season (summer is the high season). It departs at 10 pm and arrives in Paris at 7 am the next day. The service leaves Paris at 1 pm, arriving in Tangier at 9.50 pm and Marrakesh at 8.30 am the following day.

The Eurolines office in London (☎ 0171 730 8235) is at 52 Grosvenor Gardens, London SW1W 0AU; in Paris (☎ 01.49.72. 51.51) it's at 3-5 Ave Porte de la Villette.

From Paris the fares vary according to the final destination and the season. One way tickets to Tangier, Kenitra, Rabat and Casablanca cost 730FF in the low season and 880FF in the high season. The return fares are 1350FF and 1500FF respectively.

To Marrakesh, Agadir, Taroudannt, Tiznit and other destinations in between, the one way/return fares in the low season are 880/1650FF and 1030/1800FF in the high season.

To Meknès, Fès, Taza, Oujda, Nador and Ouarzazate the one way/return fares are 930/1720FF and 1080/1870FF for low and high season respectively.

Children between the ages of four and 12 are eligible for discounted fares.

Whether you're starting in Paris or coming from elsewhere (such as London), you must pay a 30FF embarkation tax. Passengers are allowed to carry 30kg of luggage free. Each extra kilogram is another 10FF.

One of the big drawbacks with this trip is that the ticket is for a through trip without stops, whereas travellers taking the train have two months to use the ticket and can stop along the way.

If you're in Madrid, you can take a train (see the Train entry in this section) south to Algeciras or a bus from the Estación sur de Autobuses Sur (☎ 1-468 4200), which is not too far from Atocha train station.

From Algeciras you can take a boat to Ceuta (Spanish Morocco) or Tangier (refer to the Sea section later in this chapter).

With Enatcar (Spain's national bus line), the bus goes via Málaga, Torremolinos, Fuengirola, Marbella and Estepona and takes about 10 hours.

The one way fare is around 3500pta. For more detailed information, call Enatcar in Madrid on ☎ 527 99 27.

From Morocco, CTM operates buses from Casablanca and most other main cities and towns to France (Paris, Toulouse, Marseille, Lyon and several other cities) and Belgium (Brussels and one or two other stops).

Most of the services originate in Casablanca and pass through various other Moroccan cities before crossing the Strait of Gibraltar. You must book at least a week in advance to get a seat.

Frequency varies depending on your starting point, but on average there are four or five runs to Paris every week. Buses to Belgium leave once a week as a rule.

Fares vary little, regardless of your point of departure. To most of France (including Paris) you pay about Dr1530. To Belgium and northernmost France fares are around Dr2040.

Train It is possible to get a train/ferry ticket all the way from London to Morocco via Paris and Madrid. It is more expensive than the bus, but the tickets are good for two months, which means you could make Morocco part of a wider trip through France and Spain.

You can buy tickets in London through Campus Travel (☎ 0171-730 3402) at 52 Grosvenor Gardens, opposite Victoria Station. One way/return tickets to Tangier cost UK£129/252; tickets to Casablanca cost UK£145/277.

Morocco is part of the Inter-Rail network. For UK£279, travellers under the age of 26 can purchase an Inter-Rail ticket entitling them to a month of free unlimited 2nd class travel on trains in up to 28 countries in Europe, including Morocco.

To do this, they have to be able to prove they have been resident in a European country for at least six months. In practice this rule is often interpreted leniently.

Train travel is not that expensive in Morocco, so buying an Inter-Rail pass just for Morocco would be of dubious value.

Although people over 26 can now also

buy Inter-Rail passes, they are not valid in Morocco.

From Paris, your best bet is probably to take the TGV from the Gare Montparnasse, changing at Irun for Madrid and on to Algeciras. The trip takes at least 25 hours and the standard adult 2nd class fare is 755/1510FF one way/return.

From Madrid, RENFE, the Spanish rail network, has a daily train (the Estrella del Estrecho) going from Chamartín station to Algeciras, which leaves at 10 pm and arrives at about 9 am the following day. The one way 2nd class fare is 5300pta.

Alternatively, you could depart from Atocha station at 3.25 pm, changing at Bobadilla and arriving in Algeciras at 10.25 pm. The fare, including a 1000pta supplement, is 6900pta.

From there you can connect for the boat ride to Ceuta or Tangier. Going in the other direction, the direct train to Chamartín leaves at 9 pm and arrives in Madrid at around 8.45 am.

The Estrella Media Luna also leaves at 9 pm for Hendaye on the Spanish-French border. There are a couple of morning trains to Bobadilla, from where you can get connections to other destinations.

Alternatively, you could head for Málaga or Almería and take the boat from there to the Spanish Moroccan enclave of Melilla. There are four trains a day from Chamartín station to Málaga, taking from seven to nine hours and costing 4600pta. The luxury Talgo 200 train runs three times daily between Madrid and Málaga, taking just four hours and forty minutes. The fare is 6000pta to 9700pta, depending on what class you choose and when you travel.

Two trains a day run between Madrid and Almería. The faster (Talgo) takes about seven hours to/from Madrid's Atocha station and costs 5700pta. The slower train leaves from Chamartín station in Madrid, takes 10 hours and costs 4000pta. From Almería, the Talgo to Madrid leaves at 2.15 pm and the slower train at 10.05 pm. There are also three trains a day to Granada (1065pta).

Again, those under 26 could invest in a Wasteels ticket. The trip from Madrid to Marrakesh, including the Algeciras ferry crossing, is 8710/16,030pta one way/return.

You can book international tickets in Morocco up to two months ahead.

Mauritania

Car Although a UN ceasefire has kept the Western Sahara quiet since September 1991, crossing the border into Mauritania isn't straightforward.

Since early 1994, the Moroccans have been issuing travel permits in Dakhla and escorting civilian convoys to the border (through minefields).

The Mauritanian embassy in Rabat can issue visas for overland travel, but you are strongly advised to get one before arriving in Africa.

SEA
Spain

For ferry travel to Morocco, the high season is 1 July to mid-September.

Various car ferries are operated by the Spanish government-run company Transmediterranea in tandem with Islena de Navigación SA, Comarit and Limadet. There are plans to privatise the company in spring 1998, which may cause all the following prices to change substantially. At the time of writing, jetfoils also made the crossing from Algeciras to Tangier and Ceuta, but the continuation of this service was in some doubt.

The most popular service is the Algeciras-Tangier route, although for car owners the service to Ceuta might be more worthwhile because of the availability of tax-free petrol in the enclave. The others are Tarifa-Tangier, Almería-Melilla (Spanish Morocco) and Málaga-Melilla. The majority are car ferries of the drive-on and drive-off type.

On most routes, more boats are put on in the high season, which is from 15 June until 15 September.

For detailed information on Trasmediterranea's services, contact Southern Ferries

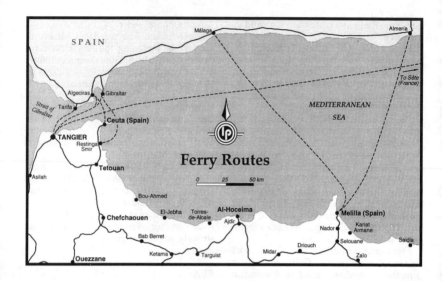

(☎ 0171-491 4968) at 179 Piccadilly, London W1V 9DB, or the Trasmediterranea offices in Madrid (☎ 1-431 0700) at Calle Pedro Muñoz Seca, 2, and in Barcelona (☎ 3-412 2532) at the Estación Marítima, Muelle Barcelona, 1.

Various reductions are available on some of the services. Pensioners of EU nations and people under 26 should enquire about them before buying tickets.

Algeciras-Tangier Trasmediterranea runs at least nine daily car ferries between Algeciras and Tangier. Depending on demand, the number of boats can increase to about 20.

It doesn't matter whose boat you end up on, the fares are generally the same with a few variations: on Comarit's boats children up to the age of four go for free, whereas the limit is two on Trasmediterranea's boats (in both cases children up to 12 years pay half-fare).

In addition to each line's official outlet at the Estación Marítima, there is a plethora of other ticket offices at the port and along the waterfront.

The one way adult fare is 4000pta. If you are considered a Moroccan resident, the fares are reduced. The fee for cars is between 1500pta and 30,000pta, depending on the dimensions of the car. Motorcycles and bicycles cost 4000pta. The crossing takes 2½ hours.

Eurail and Inter-Rail pass holders are entitled to a 20% discount on ferry tickets between Algeciras and Tangier and should make a point of asking for it. This can prove more problematic on the Moroccan side. You can usually pay for your ticket with a credit card on the Spanish side.

The fare per person from Tangier is Dr210. Cars up to 6m long cost Dr648, and Dr290 for every metre extra. Bikes and motorcycles cost Dr200.

The continuation of Trasmediterranea's jetfoil service was in some doubt at the time of writing. There was, however, a jetfoil leaving Algeciras daily at 9.30 am and Tangier at 3.30 pm. The run took an hour and the cost of the fare was the same as for the ferry.

Spanish passport control is quite straightforward if you're leaving Algeciras, but customs can be slow if you're coming from Morocco. Leaving Tangier, you must fill in an exit form before getting your passport stamped and boarding. You should be given one when you buy your ticket.

There are lot of people pretending to be officials of one sort or another – most of them *écrivains publics* (public scribes) – who will try to get one last dirham out of you before you leave. One of their services is to give you an exit form and lend you a pen to fill it out.

If you approach the port at Tangier on foot, there'll usually be a few of them around trying to create a sense of urgency and bustling you about, or guiding you to a boat (not all dock at the main port). All these characters want money, so if you're not feeling overly generous, watch out for them.

You can buy tickets in the main port building, although the booths are not always open (this is when the public scribes come into their own, producing tickets as if from nowhere). You must pay for the ticket in cash. There are a few banks represented just outside the terminal.

Tangier is swamped with agencies where you can buy tickets, but as a rule, you are probably best advised to go to the port early and get a ticket on the spot.

Algeciras-Ceuta (Spanish Morocco) At least six ferry crossings operate on this route in either direction, except on Sundays when there are only four. Around Easter and Christmas the number of services can rise to 10 each way.

The ferry trip takes 1½ hours and the fare is 1625pta (1700pta in the high season; children between two and 12 pay half-fare). Vehicles between 2.5m and 6m in length cost from 7500pta to 13,650pta, depending on dimensions.

The fee for motorcycles is from 1700pta to 2550pta depending on engine size.

At the time of writing, there were also six or more weekly jetfoils (2700pta one way and double return) running, but the future of this service was in doubt.

Tarifa-Tangier There is a daily ferry from Tarifa to Tangier. Costs for cars are identical to those for the Algeciras-Tangier ferries.

In Tarifa, you can buy your tickets on the morning at the dock or from Viajes Marruecotur (☎ 681821; fax 680256), Calle Batalla del Salado, 57.

Almería-Melilla (Spanish Morocco) The timetable for services between Almería and the Spanish enclave of Melilla is not quite so straightforward. In the low season there is generally a ferry from Almería at 1 pm Tuesday to Saturday and at 11.30 pm on Sunday. Going the other way, there is a departure every day at 11.30 pm except Sunday.

In the high season (from mid-June to mid-September) ferries run twice daily four days a week and once on the other days, but these days alternate weekly.

The trip takes 6½ to eight hours. The cheapest fare *(butaca turista* or deck) fare is 3050pta (3150pta in the high season) each way. You can also get beds in cabins of four or two, some with toilets. Prices range from 5000pta a head for four to 8500pta for single occupation of a twin berth. Fares are a little higher in the high season. Children from two to 12 years of age travel for half-price (infants go free).

A car can cost from 7550pta to 22,650pta in the low season, depending on its dimensions. You also pay to take across motorbikes. You can buy tickets at the Estación Marítima (about a 10 to 15 minute walk from the train and bus stations) or at travel agents in the centre of town. You can pay by credit card.

If you arrive in Almería from Morocco, you can push on into Spain by train or bus. The train station is about a 10 minute walk off to the right from the port. The bus station is a five minute walk further down the road in front of the train station.

Málaga-Melilla (Spanish Morocco) Also operated by Trasmediterranea, ferries leave Málaga from Monday to Saturday in the low season at 1 pm and Melilla at 11 pm. A Sunday service is occasionally put on. In the high season, in addition to the above fares, the Sunday service is permanent. The journey time is 7½ to 10 hours and fares are the same as for the Almería-Melilla ferry.

As in Almería, you can buy tickets most easily at the Estación Marítima, which is more or less directly south of the town centre.

Málaga is a good point from which to proceed to other destinations in Spain and the rest of Europe. Check out charter flight possibilities for London and other European capitals.

The main bus and train stations are within a five minute walk of each other to the west of the town centre (about a 20 minute walk).

Gibraltar

Gibraltar-Tangier The *Idriss I* ferry links Gibraltar with Tangier three times a week. The voyage (which takes about two hours) costs UK£18/30 one way/return. The ferry can carry up to 30 cars (the charge is UK£40) and runs all year, leaving Gibraltar at 8.15 am on Mondays and Wednesdays and 6.30 pm on Fridays.

The Gibraltar agents are Tourafrica Int Ltd (☎ 79140; fax 76754) at 2a Main St. The ferry departs from the nearby North Mole. Several Tangier travel agents can sell you tickets for the Gibraltar ferry.

Gibraltar-Tetouan Jasmine Lines sometimes runs a catamaran to Restinga Smir (a little north of Tetouan), usually in the summer, but inclement weather often leads to cancellations.

When the going is good (in summer), it runs four or five times a week, costing around UK£16.50/27.70 one way/return. The agents are Parodytur (☎ 76070; fax 70563) in the Cazes Arcade at 143 Main St.

Leaving Gibraltar If you arrive in Gibraltar from Morocco, you will probably want to continue on soon after going through the British enclave's passport and customs con-

trol (and perhaps a quick look around). Apart from flights to the UK, your only choice is to cross into Spain. It's a 15 minute walk to the border (La Linea) across the airstrip, or you can get the No 9 bus from Casemates Square.

Passport control and customs are pretty much a formality on the Gibraltar-Spanish border, but remember that citizens of some countries who have no trouble entering Gibraltar may require a visa to proceed into Spain.

Once through Spanish customs, it's a five minute walk to the Estación de Autobuses (bus station), from which there are buses to various destinations in Spain.

France

Sète-Tangier With a swimming pool and night club (of sorts) on board, this car ferry service is considerably more luxurious than those linking Spain and Morocco, and commensurately more expensive.

It's operated by the Compagnie Marocaine de Navigation (Comanav). The crossing is made six or seven times a month, usually once every four to five days. As a rule the *Marrakesh*, which can carry 634 passengers, leaves Sète at 7 pm and Tangier at 6 pm (local time).

The trip takes 36 to 38 hours and the fare, depending on the class, is between 1250FF and 2100FF one way (or 2130FF and 3570FF return) in shared cabins of two to four people.

If you want to have a cabin to yourself, you'll be up for about another 1000FF. There are sometimes supplements to be paid on top of the fare. Children between two and 11 travel for half price. Cars under 4m in length cost 1540FF. There is room for 220 vehicles on board.

There are special reduced fares, per passenger and vehicle, for students and people under 26. A berth in a cabin of four costs 880FF to 950FF.

You can book tickets for this service at Southern Ferries (☎ 0171-491 4968; fax 491 3502) at 179 Piccadilly, London W1V 9DB, or in France at the SNCM Ferryterranée office (☎ 01.43.43.43.27; fax 01.43.43.45.20) at 12 Rue Godot de Mauroy, Paris 75009.

The Sète office (☎ 67.46.68.00; fax 67.74.93.05) is at 4 Quai d'Alger, 34202 Sète. There are agents in Germany, Italy, Belgium, Holland, Switzerland and several other European countries.

In Morocco, Comanav's main office (☎ 303012; fax 300790) is in Casablanca, at 7 Blvd de la Résistance. In Tangier, the office (☎ 932649; fax 943570) is at 43 Ave Abou al-Alaa al-Maari.

DEPARTURE TAXES

There is no departure tax upon leaving Morocco, and departure formalities are straightforward. You must fill in an exit card and have your passport stamped before exiting.

ORGANISED TOURS

There are plenty of travel and tour agents scattered around the big cities, but Marrakesh is probably the best place for a range of options – from here you can make excursions into the desert and up into the High Atlas.

Agadir is another centre for package excursions. For more information, see the Organised Tours entries under Marrakesh and Agadir in their respective chapters.

A growing number of operators are putting more effort into organised trips to Morocco. More than 50 agencies operate out of the UK alone. The Moroccan Tourist Office (ONMT) in your country is a good place to begin and it should be able to provide you with a comprehensive list of tour operators.

Possibilities range from the more traditional style of tour of the Imperial Cities (Rabat, Marrakesh, Fès and Meknès) to beach holidays, golf trips, trekking, birdwatching and desert safaris.

The following information is intended as a guide only, and not as a recommendation of these over other operators.

Remember that the programmes on such trips are usually tight, leaving little room for roaming around on your own, but they do take much of the hassle off your plate.

Shop around and check itinerary details, accommodation, insurance and tour conditions carefully. Also find out who will arrange the ticketing, visas and other documentation.

Tours from The UK

Best of Morocco (☎ 01380-828533; fax 828630), Seend Park, Seend, Wiltshire SN12 6NZ, is one of the better established tour operators for Morocco. It offers horse and camel trekking tours, 4WD safaris in the Sahara and walking and skiing holidays.

Exodus Travels (☎ 0181-5550; fax 6730779), 9 Weir Rd, London SW12 0LT, is a well established adventure travel operator offering short or long treks in the High Atlas, Central Atlas, Anti-Atlas and Jebel Sarhro as well as trips to the Sahara and the Imperial Cities.

Explore Worldwide (☎ 01252-319448; fax 343170), 1 Frederick St, Aldershot, Hants GU11 1LQ, specialises in year-round mountain trekking trips and tours of the Imperial Cities and the Sahara.

Encounter Overland (☎ 0171-3706951; fax 2449737), 267 Old Brompton Rd, London SW5 9JA, is one of a number of adventure companies offering lengthy trans-African expeditions which include Morocco.

Discover Ltd (☎ 01883-744392; fax 744913), Timbers, Oxted Rd, Godstone, Surrey RH9 8AD, offers High Atlas trekking, mountain biking and bird-watching trips.

Dust Trails (☎ 01985-841184), Unit 11, Deverill Rd Trading Estate, Sutton, Veny Nr Warminster, Wiltshire BA12 7BZ, organises 15 day motorcycle tours across Morocco which take in the Rif Mountains, the High Atlas, the Drâa Valley and the Anti-Atlas.

Wildwings (☎ 0117-9848040; fax 967 4444), International House, Bank Rd, Kingswood, Bristol BS15 2LX, specialises in bird-watching holidays in Morocco.

Tours from France

There are any number of agencies and tour operators to turn to in France. A couple of travel agencies and an adventure specialist appear in the Air section earlier in this chapter.

In addition, a number specialise in trekking tours to Morocco. Terres d'Aventure (☎ 01.53.73.77.77), 6 Rue Saint-Victor, 75005 Paris, has been running walking trips to various parts of Morocco, including the High Atlas and the southern oases, since 1976. It can also organise special family trips. Allibert (☎ 01.40.21.16.21), 14 Rue de L'Asile Popincourt, 75011 Paris, offer trekking holidays in the Atlas mountains.

Tours from Spain

If you're in Spain, the best way to experience Morocco is simply to head down yourself through southern Spain (see the Land section earlier in this chapter). However, if your time is limited, it might be worth considering a package tour, of which there are plenty on offer, particularly through the summer.

Solafrica (☎ 91-532 00 13) and Juliatours (☎ 91-559 96 05) both offer package trips to Morocco ranging from long weekends in Marrakesh to 15 day tours of the country.

Mundojoven (☎ 91-521 86 01) and Akali Joven (☎ 91-559 33 18) are among the operators offering bus trips for younger people into Morocco from Madrid and other Spanish cities. Some of them concentrate on less challenging elements like the beaches, while others follow what are becoming fairly well trodden routes around the imperial cities, into the Atlas mountains or the Sahara.

Berber chessboard symbol
Believed to point the way to celestial existence.

Getting Around

AIR

If time is limited, it's worth considering the occasional internal flight offered by Royal Air Maroc (RAM). Several reductions are available. If you buy a return ticket (valid for no longer than a month and including a Saturday night stay), you are entitled to discounts on normal one way fares.

If you're under 22 or a student under 31, you are entitled to 25% off all fares. There are group reductions and children aged two to 12 travel at half price. These discounts are normally only available through RAM.

For an idea of what you'll pay, the standard one way fare from Casablanca to Fès is Dr466 (about US$56). Fès to Agadir (via Casablanca) is Dr1140 (US$137) and Casablanca to Marrakesh is Dr390 (US$46).

Internal airports serviced by RAM and RAI are Agadir, Al-Hoceima, Casablanca, Dakhla, Er-Rachidia, Laayoune, Oujda, Goulimime, Fès, Marrakesh, Ouarzazate, Rabat, Smara, Tangier, Tetouan and Tan Tan. About the longest flight you could take is the weekly Dakhla-Tangier run via Casablanca, which takes six hours 50 minutes (the return flight is shorter because there's no stop in Marrakesh).

The bulk of internal flights involve making a connection in Casablanca.

Among direct flights, there are at least two daily runs between Marrakesh and Casablanca (35 minutes). There are two flights a week from Marrakesh to Agadir (45 minutes), and one to Fès (1¼ hours). Agadir is also connected by two weekly flights to Laayoune and Dakhla, and one to Tan Tan. Flights connect Tangier with Casablanca six days a week (55 minutes). You can pick up a free timetable at most RAM offices.

BUS

A dense network of buses operates throughout Morocco, and many private companies compete for business alongside the main national carrier, Compagnie de Transports Marocains (CTM). The latter is the only firm to have a truly national service. In most cities or towns there is a single central bus station *(gare routière)*, but in some places CTM maintains a separate terminal.

Occasionally there are other stations for a limited number of fairly local destinations. CTM tends to be a little more expensive than the other lines, but often by only a few extra dirhams. Bus fares work out to about Dr1 for every 4 or 5km, and are comparable to 2nd class fares on normal trains.

Supratours runs a subsidiary bus service in conjunction with the railways (see the Train section later in this chapter).

Traveller's Code of Etiquette

When travelling on public transport, it's considered both selfish and bad manners to eat while those around you go without. Always buy a little extra that can be offered round to your neighbours. A bag of fruit makes a great choice.

Next comes the ritual. If you have offered the food, etiquette dictates that your fellow passengers should decline it. It should be offered a second time, this time a little more persuasively, but again will be turned down. On the third offer and now quite insistent, your neighbours are free to accept the gift if they wish to.

If, conversely, you are offered food, but you don't want it or it even repulses you, it's good manners still to accept a small piece. At the same time, you should pat your stomach contentedly to indicate that you are full.

In return, for participating in this elaborate ritual, you will be accorded great respect, offered protection and cared for like a friend, which means fewer worries about leaving your luggage when going to the toilet. ■

Compagnie de Transports Marocains

CTM is the best and most secure bus company in Morocco and serves most destinations of interest to travellers. As part of Morocco's programme of economic reform, CTM was privatised in May 1994.

CTM offers both 1st and 2nd class buses, but the distinction seems to be made mostly on longer routes away from the big centres.

Always ask about different fares, but where there is only one the official line is usually that you are getting a 1st class bus. On CTM buses, children four years old and up pay full fare.

Where possible, and especially if services are infrequent or do not originate in the place you want to leave, it is not a bad idea to book ahead.

CTM buses are fairly modern and comfortable. The 1st class buses have videos (a mixed blessing) and heating in winter (they sometimes overdo this).

The first 20 seats are theoretically reserved for nonsmokers.

Some 1st class CTM fares are as follows:

From	To	Fare (Dr)	Hours
Casablanca	Agadir	136	10
	Marrakesh	63	4½
	Fès	78	5
Marrakesh	Agadir	67	4
	Fès	123	9
	Ouarzazate	49	3
	Tangier	166	11

There is an official charge for baggage on CTM buses. Once you have bought your ticket you get a baggage tag, which you should hang on to, as you'll need it when you arrive. The charge for an average backpack is about Dr5.

In the main cities both bus and train stations have left-luggage depots which are usually open 24 hours. They charge Dr2.50 to Dr3 per item, but bags must be padlocked.

CTM also operates international buses from all the main Moroccan cities to Paris, Brussels and other destinations abroad. See the Getting There & Away chapter for more information.

Other Companies

The other bus companies are all privately owned and only operate regionally. The biggest of them is SATAS, which operates from Casablanca south and is just as good as CTM. Some of the others are two-bit operations with one or two well worn buses, so the degree of comfort can be pot luck.

Some of the stations seem like madhouses, and touts run about screaming out any number of destinations for buses about to depart. Occasionally, you will find would-be guides anxious to help you to the right ticket booth – for a small consideration of course.

Some companies offer 1st and 2nd class, although the difference in fare and comfort is rarely great. On the secondary runs you can often buy your tickets on the bus, but if you do you'll probably have to stand. The buses also tend to stop an awful lot. More often than not you'll be charged a couple of dirham for baggage, especially if it's going on top of the bus.

These buses rarely have heating in winter, even when crossing the High Atlas, so make sure you have plenty of warm clothing with you. Occasionally, buses are held up by snow drifts in mountain passes; then you'll really feel the cold. The Marrakesh-Ouarzazate road is prone to this.

TRAIN

Morocco has in its Office National des Chemins de Fer (ONCF) one of the most modern rail systems in Africa, linking most of the main centres. The trains, mostly Belgian-made, are generally comfortable, fast and preferable to buses. Present lines go as far south as Marrakesh.

Buses run by Supratours link up with trains to further destinations with no rail line, so that the ONCF can get you as far south as Dakhla.

Classes

There are two types of train (normal and *rapide*) and two classes on each (1st and 2nd), giving four possible fares for any given trip.

The main difference between the normal and the rapide trains is not, as the name suggests, speed (there is rarely any difference), but comfort and air-conditioning. Second class is more than adequate on any journey, and on normal trains 2nd class fares are commensurate with bus fares.

Tickets & Fares
You are advised to buy tickets at the station as a supplement is charged for doing so on the train.

A ticket is technically valid for five days, so that you can use it to get off at intermediate stops before reaching your final destination. You need to ask for a *bulletin d'arrêt* at the intermediate stop. Always hang on to tickets, as inspectors check them on the trains and they are collected at the station on arrival.

Children under four travel free. Those up to 12 years old get a reduction of 10% to 50%, depending on the service.

Couchettes are available on the overnight trains from Marrakesh to Tangier and are well worth the extra Dr50 or so.

Some sample 2nd class fares in normal and rapide trains are as follows:

From	To	Fare (Dr)	Hours
Tangier	Casablanca	87/110	6
	Fès	71/90	6
	Marrakesh	142.50/179.50	10
Casablanca	Fès	72.50/92.50	4
	Marrakesh	54/70	4
	Rabat	18/25	1¼

Shuttles
In addition to the normal and rapide trains, there are express shuttles (TNR) which operate regularly between Kenitra, Rabat, Casablanca and Mohammed V airport.

From Rabat to Casablanca you pay Dr20 in 2nd class normal and Dr25.50 in 2nd class for rapide and TNR. The 1st class fares are Dr28 (normal), Dr34 (rapide) and Dr43 (TNR). For more detailed information on airport connections, see the Getting Around sections under Casablanca and Rabat.

Supratours Buses
The ONCF runs buses through Supratours to widen its network. Thus Nador, near Melilla on the Mediterranean coast, is linked to the Oujda-Casablanca lines by a special bus to Taourirt station.

Tetouan is linked to the main line from Tangier by bus to Tnine Sidi Lyamani. Train passengers heading further south than Marrakesh link up with buses at Marrakesh station for Essaouira, Agadir, Smara, Laayoune and Dakhla.

Timetables
Timetables for the whole system are posted in French at most stations. A handy pocketbook timetable called the *Horaires des Trains*, covering all destinations, can usually be picked up at train stations.

TAXI
The elderly Mercedes you'll see belting along Moroccan roads and gathered in great flocks near the bus stations are shared taxis (*grands taxis* or *taxiat kebira* in Arabic). They're a big feature of Morocco's public transport system and link towns to their nearest neighbours in a kind of leapfrogging system. They take six passengers and leave when full.

The fixed-rate fares (listed in individual city entries) are generally a little higher than bus fares, but are still very reasonable. Attempts to extract more from foreigners, however, do sometimes occur – try to see what other passengers are paying.

When asking about fares, make it clear you want to pay for a *place* in a *taxi collectif* (shared taxi). Another expression that helps explain that you don't want to hire a taxi for yourself is that you wish to travel *ma'a an-nas* ('with other people').

Taxis are much faster than buses because they don't make as many stops – they also travel at a fair rate of knots.

You can hire an entire grand taxi. If you are travelling with a small group of people this option can be well worthwhile – you can take your time on the road and stop whenever you want.

Before setting off, negotiate patiently for a reasonable fare and make sure plans for stopping on route are clear. The Ziz and Drâa valleys and the Tizi n'Test Pass are particularly good to visit in a shared taxi.

PICK-UP TRUCK & 4WD

In some of the more remote parts of the country, especially in the Atlas mountains, about the only way you can get around from village to village is by local Berber *camionettes* (pick-up trucks), which is how the locals do it.

This is a bumpy, but adventurous, way to get to know the country and people a little better, but can mean waiting days at a time for the next lift. Trucks travel between villages on market days, which is generally only once or twice a week. 4WD taxis also operate on more remote *pistes* (rough dirt tracks) that would destroy normal taxis.

CAR & MOTORCYCLE

The roads connecting the main centres of Morocco are generally very good, and increasing numbers of visitors are bringing their own cars and motorcycles into the country. There are many places that you simply cannot reach without private transport, so a vehicle can be an enormous advantage.

Road Rules & Hazards

In Morocco you drive on the right, as in Continental Europe. Daylight driving is generally no problem, and even in the bigger cities it is not too stressful in the villes nouvelles. Having said that, you do need to keep your wits about you at all times – the traffic accident rate in Morocco is high.

Night driving can be particularly hazardous: it is legal for vehicles travelling up to 20km/h to drive without lights, and in the early evening roads are often very busy with pedestrians (including large groups of schoolchildren), bicycles, horse-and-carts, donkeys and so on.

When in towns note that you should give way to traffic entering a roundabout from the right when you're already on one, which

Road Distances Between Cities & Towns

Distances in kms

	Ad-Dakhla (Dakhla)	Agadir	Al-Hoceima	Casablanca	Er-Rachidia	Essaouira	Fès	Figuig	Marrakesh	Meknès	Nador	Ouarzazate	Oujda	Rabat	Safi	Smara	Tangier	Tan Tan	Tarfaya	Tetouan
Ad-Dakhla (Dakhla)	-																			
Agadir	1173	-																		
Al-Hoceima	2264	1091	-																	
Casablanca	1684	511	536	-																
Er-Rachidia	1854	681	616	545	-															
Essaouira	1346	173	887	351	745	-														
Fès	1920	756	275	289	364	640	-													
Figuig	2249	1076	669	920	395	1081	719	-												
Marrakesh	1448	273	758	238	510	176	483	905	-											
Meknès	1913	740	335	229	346	580	60	741	467	-										
Nador	2260	1095	175	628	510	979	339	516	822	399	-									
Ouarzazate	1548	375	992	442	306	380	687	701	204	652	816	-								
Oujda	2272	1099	293	632	514	983	343	326	826	403	104	820	-							
Rabat	1775	602	445	91	482	442	198	877	321	138	535	528	541	-						
Safi	1467	294	792	256	683	129	545	1078	157	486	884	361	888	347	-					
Smara	746	551	1642	1062	1232	724	1307	1627	824	1291	1646	926	1650	1153	845	-				
Tangier	2053	880	323	369	608	720	303	988	598	287	1086	811	609	278	625	1431	-			
Tan Tan	842	331	1422	842	1012	504	1087	1407	504	1071	1426	705	1430	933	625	220	1211	-		
Tarfaya	633	544	1635	1055	1225	517	1300	1620	817	1284	1639	919	1643	1146	838	331	1424	213	-	
Tetouan	2065	892	278	385	604	736	281	931	675	258	437	820	555	294	641	1443	57	1223	1436	-

Car Rental					
Type	Model	Per Day (Dr)	Per Km (Dr)	Three Days Unlimited Km (Dr)	Seven Days Unlimited Km (Dr)
A	Fiat Uno	260	2.70	1200	2400
B	Renault 5	290	3.50	1500	2985
C	Fiat Tipo	370	3.90	1680	3370
D	Peugeot SL	450	4.50	3000	6006
E	Peugeot XR	525	5.25	3290	6566

is quite a departure from prevailing rules in Europe. Speed limits in built-up areas range from 40km/h to 60km/h.

Outside the towns there is a national speed limit of 100km/h, rising to 120km/h on the only stretch of motorway, which lies between Casablanca and Kenitra. There is a Dr15 toll on the section between Casablanca and Rabat and a Dr10 toll on the section to Kenitra. The motorway is being extended to Tangier.

It is compulsory for drivers and passengers to wear seat belts.

Many minor roads are too narrow for normal vehicles to pass without going onto the shoulder. You'll find yourself hitting the dirt a lot in this way. Stones thrown up by oncoming vehicles present a danger for windscreens – locals (drivers or front-seat passengers) press their hands against the inside of the windscreens to reduce the chances of debris shattering the glass.

Driving across the mountain ranges in winter can easily involve driving through snow and ice. This kind of driving is obviously dangerous. If a strong chergui wind is blowing and carrying a lot of dust, you'll have to wait until it eases off if you don't want to do your car considerable damage.

The High Atlas passes can often be closed altogether due to snow in the winter: check the road conditions with the police or call the Service des Travaux Publiques on ☎ 07-711717 before travelling.

Some of the pistes in Morocco can be negotiated by ordinary car, many are passable in a Renault 4 and some are 4WD territory only. Whatever vehicle you have, the going will be slow. Many stretches of mountain piste will be impassable in bad weather: the Michelin 959 map generally has these sections marked.

Whatever the season, inquire about road conditions with locals before setting off, check your tyres, make sure you have a useable spare and carry an adequate supply of water and petrol with you.

Rental

Renting a car in Morocco isn't cheap, but it is possible to strike very good bargains with some of the smaller dealers, and if there are four of you it becomes affordable.

There are plenty of local agencies to choose from – many have booths at the airports and this is a good place to haggle – moving from one to another until you reach a price that suits you.

Most of the international rental companies have representatives throughout Morocco, too, including Hertz, Avis, Budget and Europcar, but note that rates can vary substantially between them and there is little room for bargaining.

The best cities in which to hire cars are Casablanca and Agadir, where the competition is greatest. There are also many agencies in Marrakesh, Tangier and Fès. The cheapest cars are the Renault 4 and Fiat Uno, and both are well adapted to tackling Moroccan pistes.

Addresses of the international companies and a couple of local ones appear under individual city entries.

Cars rented from such companies are not necessarily better than those from a local company; what differs is the degree of service or help you can get in the event of a breakdown. Major companies will replace a car from their nearest depot if there are problems, whereas local companies often don't have branch offices so there isn't much they can do. In any event, make an effort to get a look at the car yourself before you sign up.

In many cases you can hire the car in one place and leave it elsewhere, although this usually involves a fee if you want to leave it in a city where the company has no branch.

You should take out Collision Damage Waiver insurance (around Dr50 to Dr100 a day, depending on the make of car and the company), otherwise you'll be liable for the first Dr3000 to Dr5000 (depending on the company) in the event of an accident. It's also a good idea to take out personal insurance (around Dr30 a day). When bargaining, make sure that prices include collision damage, insurance and tax.

Most companies demand a (returnable) deposit of Dr3000 to Dr5000 in cash when you hire the car, unless you pay by credit card, in which case the deposit is waived. Minimum age for drivers is usually 21 years (this varies depending on the make of car), with at least one year's driving experience. An International Driving Permit is technically required, but most agencies will accept your national licence.

All companies charge from Dr35 to more than Dr100 (depending on make) per hour that you go over time on the return date. After two or three hours this becomes a full extra day's rent.

If you intend driving from Morocco to the Spanish enclaves of Ceuta or Melilla, you must have a letter from the car hire company authorising you to take the car out of the country.

Virtually all cars take premium petrol (super). Keep receipts for oil changes and any mechanical repairs, as these costs should be reimbursed.

Some companies offer motorcycle and scooter hire. Agadir is a good place to look – you'll find plenty of rental booths in among the big hotels. Scooters cost from around Dr160 per day and motorcycles from around Dr200 per day for a DT 125 Yamaha.

The preceding Car Rental table is intended as a general guide only and does not include the 20% government tax that you must pay on all rentals.

Neither is there any point differentiating between international and local companies. Advertised rates vary hugely – some being more expensive than the biggies, and others being cheaper. Bargaining means that the price you end up with generally bears little relation to advertised rates.

Fuel

Petrol is readily available in all the main centres. If you're travelling off the beaten track, however, it's not a bad idea to fill the tank up at every opportunity. Super and unleaded (*sans plomb* – found only sporadically) cost Dr7.30 a litre, and diesel is Dr4 a litre. Regular petrol *(essence)* is not so commonly available.

Costs rise the further you go from the north-west of the country. The big exception is the territory of Western Sahara, which is still awaiting a UN-administered plebiscite on whether it is to be integrated into Morocco, but to all intents and purposes already is. Petrol here is sold by the Atlas Sahara service station chain, is tax free and costs about a third less than in the rest of Morocco.

Heading south, the first of these stations is just outside Tarfaya, on the road to Laayoune. If you're heading north, stock up as much as you can here.

The same situation applies in the Spanish enclaves of Ceuta and Melilla, so drivers heading to Morocco and mainland Spain via the enclaves should do their best to arrive there with a near-empty tank.

Road Blocks

Morocco's roads are festooned with police and customs road blocks. Be sure to stop at all of them and put on your best smile – with luck you should be waved through in about half the time. Generally you'll need to show your passport, state your profession, the purpose of your visit, the place you are travelling from and your destination.

Parking Attendants

In every town there are parking zones watched by *gardiens de voitures*. The going rate is Dr6 for a few hours and Dr10 overnight. The parking attendants are not a guarantee of safety, but they do provide some peace of mind.

Mechanics & Repairs

Moroccan mechanics are generally extremely good and all decent-sized towns will have at least one garage. If you need help and are in a position to do so, get a Moroccan sufficiently well disposed towards you to help with buying parts, such as replacement tyres, as this may help to keep the price closer to local levels.

Warning

When driving into Fès, Marrakesh and one or two other spots you are likely to be accosted by hustlers on motorbikes. They will try to direct you to hotels and the like and are every bit as persistent as their colleagues on foot; dodging around these guys can be downright dangerous.

There have been reports of hitchhiking hustlers too. You pick them up and they try to lead you to their 'home' – a carpet factory or the like. The road south from Ouarzazate is particularly bad, as is the road from Asni to Imlil in the High Atlas.

In the Rif Mountains around Ketama, stories abound of tourists being stopped and having large wodges of hash foisted on them by particularly unpleasant characters, only to land in the poo when they reach the next police road block.

BICYCLE

Mountain biking is becoming an increasingly popular way of travelling in Morocco.

There's plenty of opportunity for getting off the beaten track, with thousands of kilometres of remote pistes to be explored. You do need to be pretty fit, though. Distances are great and you'll need to carry all supplies with you (including any spare parts you may need, food and plenty of drinking water).

Surfaced roads are generally well maintained, but they tend to be narrow and dusty and the traffic none too forgiving.

You can transport bikes on both buses and trains. On trains, bicycles travel in the goods van. The minimum charge is Dr20. Most camp sites charge between Dr3 and Dr5 for bicycles.

Morrocan cities and towns are better explored on foot, though you will find bicycles for hire in the bigger places (from around Dr40 per day).

Quite a few external tour operators (and some hotels in Marrakesh) offer organised mountain biking trips.

HITCHING

Hitching is never entirely safe in any country in the world, and we certainly don't recommend it. Travellers who decide to hitch should understand that they are taking a small, but potentially serious risk.

However, many people do choose to hitch, and the advice that follows should help to make their journeys as fast and safe as possible.

Hitching in Morocco is possible, but demands a thick skin and considerable diplomatic expertise in the north because of aggressive hustlers. They simply won't take no for an answer and feign outrage if you express lack of interest in whatever they're trying to sell you – usually drugs.

It's particularly bad on the road between Tetouan and Tangier. Giving lifts to people in these areas is similarly a bad idea. See the previous entry under Warning in the Car & Motorcycle section.

Drivers usually expect some money for picking you up, so it's as well to offer a little – it may be refused, but it's more likely not to be.

Keep public transport fares in mind so that, should you strike someone trying to extort silly amounts from you, you'll know what not to give.

WALKING

The beautiful mountains of Morocco offer almost endless possibilities for walking and trekking.

For those with plenty of time, it's worth considering a combination of trekking and travelling by the local trucks that ply regularly between villages on market days. See the High Atlas Trekking section for details on walking in the Toubkal area, which is the highest and most popular region of the High Atlas.

Other areas include Taroudannt, which provides access to the little-developed western High Atlas region, Tafraoute for access to the Anti-Atlas, Beni-Mellal for possibilities in the both the Middle Atlas and the High Atlas and Boumalne du Dadès for walks in the Dadès Gorge and access to the isolated peaks of the Jebel Sarhro area. You'll find guides in all of the above places.

See the Organised Tours entry in the Getting There & Away chapter for a list of adventure travel companies offering a variety of treks in Morocco.

LOCAL TRANSPORT
Bus

The bigger cities, such as Casablanca, Rabat, Marrakesh, Fès and Meknès, have public bus services. They are especially good for crossing from the ville nouvelle of a city to the medina, and there are a few other useful runs. Tickets usually cost around Dr3 to Dr4.

Taxi

Cities and bigger towns have local *petits taxis*, which are a different colour for every city. They are licensed to carry up to three passengers and are usually metered. They are not permitted to go beyond the city limits. Where they are not metered (or don't use the meter), you'll have to set a price in advance.

It's like everything else: many of the drivers are perfectly honest and some are rotten. Multiple hire is the rule rather than the exception, so you can get half-full cabs if they are going your way. From 8 pm, there is a 50% surcharge.

Berber saw symbol
Metal and metalworking is revered by the Berbers because of the belief, dating back to the stone age, that metal wards off ghosts.

The Mediterranean Coast & the Rif

From those two bastions of Spanish tenacity, the enclaves of Ceuta and Melilla, to the cosmopolitan hustle and hassle of Tangier and the contrasting laid-back ambience of Chefchaouen in the Rif Mountains, northern Morocco offers a diverse range of experiences for the independent traveller.

East of Chefchaouen, the Rif presents a spectacular mountain crest trip through the unfortunately dodgy Ketama area – the heartland of kif cultivation. Those who brave the hustlers will be rewarded by the views and by a couple of modest Mediterranean resorts where the Rif makes a rare concession and gives way to beaches – Al-Hoceima and Saidia.

Tangier

For more than 2500 years, people have inhabited this strategic point on the straits separating Europe from Africa. And just about every race or power that ever had any interests in this corner of the Mediterranean has left its mark. The world-weary port has seen them all come and go: Phoenicians, Romans, Visigoths, Arabs, Portuguese, British and Spaniards among others. For some 40 years under the dubious control of an international council, Tangier (Tanja to the locals) today is like an ageing libertine – propped up languidly at a bar, he has seen it all.

In the days of what legendary author William Burroughs called Interzone, every kind of questionable activity was carried on. Smugglers, money launderers, currency speculators, gunrunners, prostitutes and pimps formed a good part of the Moroccan and foreign population. And in its way, Tangier (often erroneously referred to as Tangiers) flourished.

Since its incorporation into the rest of independent Morocco, the city has lost much

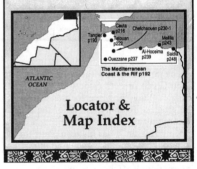

Locator & Map Index

of its attraction. But the odd cruise ship still calls in and new activities are always to be discovered. Alongside the exploding business of drug-running (including a growing contribution from South American cocaine barons), there is the commerce in people, many of whom come from sub-Saharan Africa.

Moroccan and Spanish boat captains charge these people as much as US$1000 per person to smuggle them into Spain (an enormous sum for the average Moroccan worker). Often the boats are so small and overcrowded that they don't make it – bodies of those who have risked all, and lost, frequently wash up on the Spanish and Moroccan coasts.

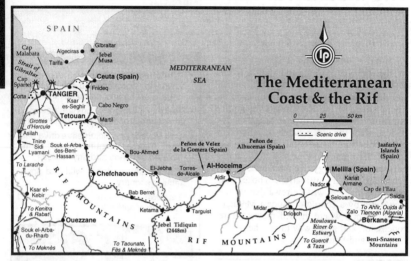

The Socco Chico (also known as the Zoco Chico or Petit Socco) in the heart of Tangier, long *the* place for transactions of the greatest diversity, is one of the centres for organising this nasty trade.

King Hassan II has his own plans for the port, and has poured money into infrastructure programmes and set the city up as an international offshore banking zone. His hope is that it will compete for international funds with Gibraltar, Tunis and Cyprus. Only the big banks need apply, for, as the king said: 'We don't want banks that create scandals. We do not want banks that come here to launder drug money'.

Little of this may be obvious to travellers passing through, but they are soon aware of what makes the place tick – money. From shoeshine boys up, everyone is on the make, and for the small-time hustlers in this city of half a million, the main trade is in tourists, especially those newly arrived from Europe.

It is a difficult city for first-time visitors; many can't wait to get out, but if you give it time and learn to handle the hustling, you'll find it a likeable, lively place that's never for a minute dull. Tangier is a unique city – hardly truly Moroccan, nor European, nor even African. Stay a few days and absorb the faded atmosphere of this mongrel creation.

History

Tangier has been coveted for millennia as a strategic site commanding the Strait of Gibraltar. The area was settled by the ancient Greeks and Phoenicians, for whom it was a trading port, and its early days are shrouded in myth. Paradise on earth, the Garden of the Hesperides, supposedly lay nearby.

It was here that Hercules slew the giant Antaeus and fathered a child, Sophax, by the giant's widow, Tinge – no prizes for guessing where the city's original name, Tingis, comes from. The name has changed little since, and also gave rise to the name of the citrus fruit tangerine, although the tree was imported by either the Romans or Arabs at a later date.

Since those early days, the port has been one of the most contested in the Mediterranean. During the period of the Roman Empire, Diocletian made it the capital of the province of Mauretania Tingitana, garrisoned by British (ie Celtic) cavalry. Not long after, it became part of the Christian Episcopal See of Spain, and in fact may have been the seat of the bishops.

Following the break-up of the Roman Empire, the Vandals arrived from Spain in 429 AD. Whether they ever took Tangier is uncertain. The Byzantines took an erratic interest in the port, but for the most part they contented themselves with their strongly fortified outpost at Ceuta. Apart from them, and scant reports suggesting

that the Visigoths from Spain occupied it for a time in the 7th century, little was recorded about the area until the arrival of the Arabs in 705 AD.

This may have been partly due to a smallpox epidemic that swept through Europe and North Africa not long after the Byzantines left the scene, but continual warfare between the indigenous Berber tribes and the conquering Arabs may not have helped.

Once Arab supremacy had been established, however, Tangier became a bone of contention between the Umayyads of Spain

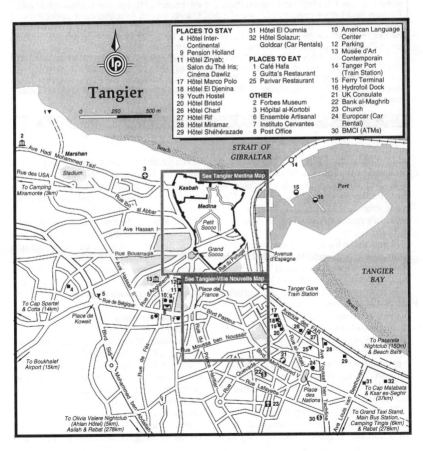

PLACES TO STAY
4 Hôtel Inter-Continental
9 Pension Holland
11 Hôtel Ziryab; Salon du Thé Iris; Cinéma Dawliz
17 Hôtel Marco Polo
18 Hôtel El Djenina
19 Youth Hostel
20 Hôtel Bristol
26 Hôtel Charf
27 Hôtel Rif
28 Hôtel Miramar
29 Hôtel Shéhérazade
31 Hôtel El Oumnia
32 Hôtel Solazur; Goldcar (Car Rentals)

PLACES TO EAT
1 Café Hafa
5 Guitta's Restaurant
25 Parivar Restaurant

OTHER
2 Forbes Museum
3 Hôpital al-Kortobi
6 Ensemble Artisanal
7 Instituto Cervantes
8 Post Office
10 American Language Center
12 Parking
13 Musée d'Art Contemporain
14 Tanger Port (Train Station)
15 Ferry Terminal
16 Hydrofoil Dock
21 UK Consulate
22 Bank al-Maghrib
23 Church
24 Europcar (Car Rental)
30 BMCI (ATMs)

Tangier

0   250   500 m

STRAIT OF GIBRALTAR

See Tangier Medina Map

Kasbah

Medina

Petit Socco

Grand Socco

See Tangier-Ville Nouvelle Map

Port

TANGIER BAY

Beach

Ave Hadi Mohammed Tazi

Marshan

Rue des USA

Stadium

To Camping Miramonte (3km)

Rue Ibn al Abbar

Ave Hassan I

Rue Bouarraqia

Ave Hassan II

To Cap Spartel & Cotta (14km)

Rue d'Angleterre

Rue de Belgique

Place de Koweit

Bld Sidi

To Boukhalef Airport (15km)

Rue Fas

Mohammed ben Abdallah

To Olivia Valere Nightclub (Ahlan Hôtel) (5km), Asilah & Rabat (278km)

Place de France

Blvd Pasteur

Rue du Portugal

Rue Moussa ben Noussair

Rue de la Liberté

Quevada

Rue Hassan

Rue Lafayette

Place des Nations

Avenue d'Espagne

Tanger Gare Train Station

Avenue des FAR

Rue Mohammed V

Ave ben Youssef

Ave Louis van Beethoven

Ave Louis van Beethoven

Mohammed V

Rue Tachfine

Beach

To Pasarela Nightclub (150m) & Beach Bars

To Cap Malabata & Ksar es-Seghir (37km)

To Grand Taxi Stand, Main Bus Station, Camping Tingis (6km) & Rabat (278km)

Ibn Battuta

Sheikh Abu Abdallah Mohammed bin Abdallah bin Mohammed bin Ibrahim al-Lawati became known as the 'voyager of Islam' and is arguably Tangier's most famous son, though little known in the west. Born in 1304 in the bustling port city, Ibn Battuta, as he became known, spent 30 years criss-crossing the Muslim world from one end to the other. There is a saying in the east that he who travels much comes to know more than he who lives long.

No sooner were his studies over than, in 1325, Ibn Battuta set off for Egypt. 'I left Tangier, my birthplace, on the 2nd day of Rajab in the year 725 (14 June 1325) ... I decided to leave behind my friends, men and women, and abandoned my home as birds leave the nest ...'

His adventures took him on several pilgrimages to Mecca and the holy places in Arabia, and beyond across Iraq and Iran into India and China. On his initial journey, after crossing North Africa and visiting Syria, he made his first pilgrimage to Mecca in 1326. He did so again the following year, after travelling to Mosul in Iraq and Isphahan, Chiraz and Tabriz in Iran. In the following years he explored the east coast of Egypt, the Arabian coast and Persian Gulf before heading into Anatolia and touring around Asia Minor. He spent seven years at the court of the sultan at Delhi in India before setting off again in 1342. From there he headed south for the Maldives and travelled on as far as Sumatra. He supposedly ended up in Peking at one point but his own accounts seem shaky at best.

In 1349 he was back in his native territory, staying in Fès, but only after more travels into the Sudan, Niger, Mali and Muslim Spain did he finally stay put and dictate his adventures, the manuscript of which now lies in the Bibliothèque Nationale de Paris. Appropriately enough, one of the ferries plying the Strait of Gibraltar between Morocco and Spain today bears his name. ■

and the Idrissids of Morocco, and was even occupied by the Fatimids of Tunis in 958. A little over 100 years later, it was taken by the Almoravids as they swept across Morocco from their Mauretanian desert strongholds; it eventually passed to the Almohads in 1149.

When the Almohad regime reached its nadir, the city elected to be ruled by the Hafsids of Tunis, but passed to Merenid control shortly afterwards in 1274.

Following the victories of the Christian armies in the Iberian peninsula, the Portuguese attempted to take Tangier in 1437. Unsuccessful at first, they finally made it in 1471. The city passed to Philip II of Spain in 1580 when Spain and Portugal were united. It reverted to Portugal when that country regained its independence, only to be passed to England in 1661 as part of Catherine of Braganza's dowry to Charles II.

The English were not to remain long. Tangier was besieged by Moulay Ismail in 1679 and the English abandoned the city seven years later (after destroying the port and most of the city), following a dispute between parliament and the king in which the former refused to fund the reinforcement of the garrison in Tangier.

The Moroccans were left in control until the mid-19th century, when Tangier became the object of intense rivalry between the French, Spanish, Italians, British and Germans. The situation was partially resolved by the Treaty of Algeciras in 1906, whereby the British were bought off with Egypt and the Italians with Libya, leaving the remaining three European powers intriguing for the spoils.

The status of the city was finally resolved only in 1923, when Tangier and the surrounding countryside was declared an 'international zone' controlled by the resident diplomatic agents of France, Spain, Britain, Portugal, Sweden, Holland, Belgium, Italy and the USA.

Even the Moroccan sultan was represented by an agent, although the latter was appointed by the French resident-general (by this time France and Spain had divided Morocco into protectorates). In fact, much of the administration of Tangier had been in European and American hands since the late 19th century, and their hold had been progressively tightened by the Treaties of Madrid (1880) and Algeciras.

Tangier was to remain an international zone until a few months after Morocco became independent, when it was reunited with the rest of the country (although it was some years before all its economic and financial privileges were removed). In the meantime it became one of the most fashionable Mediterranean resorts, and a haven for freebooters, artists, writers, refugees, exiles and bankers; it was also renowned for its high-profile gay and paedophile scene.

Each of the countries represented in Tangier maintained its own banks, post offices and currency, and took a share in the policing of the city. Banks, in particular, made fortunes out of manipulating the currency markets. All this ended in 1956, but the legend of notoriety lingers on.

Orientation

The square known as the Grand Socco (officially renamed Place du 9 Avril 1947) is the centre of things and the link between the medina and the ville nouvelle. The small and rather hilly medina lies to the north. Rue Semmarine leads off the Grand Socco almost immediately into Rue as-Siaghin, which takes you to the modest central square inside the medina – the Petit Socco (also known as the Zoco Chico, and officially Place Souq ad-Dakhil).

The kasbah occupies a dominating position on top of the cliff in the north-western corner of the medina.

East of the medina lie the port and ferry terminal. A little to the south of the port is the main train station (Tanger Gare) and the CTM bus station.

The ville nouvelle spreads out west, south and south-east of the medina, but the heart of it (Blvd Pasteur, Blvd Mohammed V and the immediate surrounding area) is compact and close to the medina. It contains the main post office, banks, some of the consulates, many of the restaurants and bars and the bulk of the middle and top-end accommodation.

Further south is the main bus station (Gare Routière) and grand taxi stand. They are on Place Jamia el-Arabia, at the end of Ave Louis van Beethoven. It's a good half-hour walk to the Grand Socco and the bulk of the cheap hotels.

Further out, to the north-west, is the Marshan, a modestly elevated plateau where the rich once maintained (and in some cases still maintain) their palatial villas. Dominated by 'the Mountain', it has a prominent place in the legends surrounding the colourful band of expatriates that has lived here.

Information

Tourist Office The Délégation Régionale du Tourisme (☎ 938239), at 42 Blvd Pasteur (see the Tangier map), has the usual limited range of maps and brochures. The staff speak several languages including English, French and Spanish, and the office is open Monday to Friday from 8.30 am to noon and 2.30 to 6.30 pm.

Foreign Consulates Quite a few countries have diplomatic representation in Tangier, including the following:

Belgium
    Consulate: Immeuble Jawara (apartment 5a), 83 Place al-Medina (☎ 943234; fax 935211) Visa office: 97 Blvd Sidi Mohammed Abdallah (☎ 933163)
France
    2 Place de France (☎ 932039/40)
Germany
    47 Ave Hassan II (☎ 938700)
Italy
    35 Rue Assad ibn al-Farrat (☎ 931064). The consulate is open Monday to Friday from 9.30 am to noon.
Netherlands
    Immeuble Miramonte, 47 Ave Hassan II (☎ 931245; fax 932684)
Spain
    85 Ave Président Habib Bourghiba (☎ 935625, 937000; fax 932381)
UK
    4 Blvd Mohammed V (☎ 941563)

Money There are plenty of banks along Blvd Pasteur and Blvd Mohammed V. Mid-range hotels can also change money at much the same rate as the banks.

The BMCE head office is on Blvd Pasteur and has ATMs. It also has an exchange booth where you can change cash or cheques and get cash advances on Visa and MasterCard. The booth is open seven days a week from 10 am to 2 pm and 4 to 8 pm.

The Crédit du Maroc, south of the Hôtel Tanjah-Flandria on Blvd Mohammed V, has taken over from Voyages Schwarz as the American Express agent. Its opening hours are the same as the BMCE bank.

Post & Communications The main post office is on Blvd Mohammed V, a 15 to 20 minute walk south from the Grand Socco. Go to the right-hand end of the counter for poste restante services.

The office is open from 8.30 am to 12.15 pm and 2.30 to 6.45 pm.

The telephone and fax office is around the corner to the right of the main post office entrance and keeps roughly the same hours. If you have a phonecard, there are card phones outside both the phone and post offices.

There are a few late-night phone offices dotted about the ville nouvelle. One, on the corner of Blvd Pasteur and Rue du Prince Moulay Abdallah, is open daily from 7.30 am to 10.30 pm. They don't have card phones, but you can book overseas phone calls. They also have telex and fax services.

Cybernet (☎ 334370) at 23 Blvd Pasteur, close to the tourist office, offers access to the Internet for Dr50 per hour. If you just want to send a message home, or check your own messages, you can do so for just Dr10.

The office is open from Monday to Friday from 8.30 am to noon and 2.30 to 6.30 pm. The helpful owner, Mr Bricha, sometimes opens the place on Saturday and Sunday from 9 am to noon.

Travel Agencies Opposite the CTM office near the port entrance is Voyages Wasteels

(☎ 938185; fax 931681). It's open every day from 6 am to 7 pm.

Carlson Wagonlits is Rue de la Liberté, just off Place du France. It's open from 9 am to noon and 3 to 7 pm Monday to Friday, and from 9 am to 12.30 pm on Saturday.

Bookshops & Books The *Rogue's Guide to Tangier* is (or was) a humorous alternative guide to the city. At best it was only ever sporadically available from some of the larger hotels, and now seems to have disappeared altogether.

A much better guidebook is the thoroughly enjoyable and well written *Tangier – City of the Dream* by Iain Finlayson, which dwells on some of the 'luminaries' that have graced Tangier since 1923.

By far the best bookshop in Tangier is the Librairie des Colonnes (☎ 936955), on Blvd Pasteur. It keeps largely Francophone literature, although there is quite a good selection of English novels.

It also stocks material on the city itself, including Finlayson's book and some Moroccan Arabic course books and grammars.

The shop was founded in the interwar years and taken over by the prestigious French publisher Gallimard. It was run for a long time by a couple of august French women, Yvonne and Isabelle Gerofi, who played host to pretty well all the high and low-life of European Tangier – most of whom found their way into the bookshop at one time or another.

Film & Photography Studio Flash at 79 Rue de la Liberté is probably the best photography shop in town and has a good selection of both print and slide film. They have a decent one hour developing service, and do repairs if you're having problems with your camera. In the ville nouvelle, there are plenty of film processing shops along Blvd Pasteur.

Cultural Centres The Institut Français (☎ 942589; fax 940937), in the Galerie d'Exposition Delacroix at 86 Rue de la Liberté, puts on a good variety of films, exhibitions and the like. It's open every day except Monday from 11 am to 1 pm and 4 to 8 pm.

The Spanish are well represented here. The Instituto Cervantes and its Biblioteca Española (☎ 931340; fax 947630) are at 9 Rue de Belgique (see the Tangier map).

The library was founded in 1941 and has a varied collection of material on Tangier (some in English), as well as Moroccan, Spanish and Gibraltarian phone books.

The complex is open Monday to Friday from 10 am to 1 pm and 4 to 7 pm. On Saturdays it's open only in the morning.

Laundry The Paris Pressing on Rue Moussa ben-Noussair, close to the Hôtel Ritz, will take around 48 hours to wash and iron a good load of dirty clothes.

In the medina, there is a Pressing close to the Hôtel Mamora. There are a few other laundries marked on the Medina and Ville Nouvelle maps.

Medical Services The *Journal de Tanger* usually lists the day's 'pharmacies de garde', which are open late, if not all night. The pharmacies in Morocco operate a rotating roster for late-night service. One that seems to be open permanently at night is the Depôt de Nuit, opposite the Cinéma Paris through the Galerías Fès, on Rue de Fès in the ville nouvelle.

Emergency The police can be contacted in an emergency on ☎ 19 and the fire brigade on ☎ 15. A doctor is on call 24 hours a day (☎ 333300).

Dangers & Annoyances Tangier is home to some of the most adept hustlers and pickpockets in the country. Those arriving by ferry, in particular, will be met by a barrage of multilingual 'friends' and 'guides'.

Expect a whole repertoire of colourful stories too – that your hotel is full, closed or in ashes after a fire; that the medina is unsafe for foreigners; that all taxis, buses and trains are on strike; and that the only way you will possibly survive all this is under your new friend's protection. The best way to deal with this is to arrive well prepared and above all, with a good sense of humour.

Before disembarking, try to change your money on the boat and decide exactly where you're headed, or you'll find yourself being led to any number of hotels, banks or places you didn't want to go to, *and* having to pay for it. Some hustlers will follow you anyway in order to try to claim commission on your hotel room; if that fails, they will then renew their offers for services every time you emerge from the hotel.

After disembarking, the best approach is to look knowledgeable, claim that you already know the city and politely decline the offers for assistance. Once you're out of the main port area you can peacefully ask for directions.

Some travellers have reported problems embarking at the ferry terminal. Hustlers dressed as officials like to claim that your ferry is about to leave. In order to 'help you catch it', they will hurriedly obtain a boarding card and departure form for you, then refuse to hand back your passport until you have shown your gratitude for this service with a large tip.

Keep hold of your ticket and if you're in any doubt about the time of departure of your ferry, check at the ticket office.

Don't hand over your ticket or passport to anyone until you're right inside the customs area.

Keep an eye on your belongings at all times. The author met one well-travelled woman who sat down at a street-side cafe after a long flight from the USA. In the time it took to drink her coffee, her hat disappeared, then her camera bag and finally her coat!

Street Names As in many other Moroccan cities, street names are being changed in Tangier, largely to replace French names with Moroccan ones. Not all of these have caught on, and the process seems somewhat haphazard. You may well come across more than one name for the same street.

Grand Socco

The Grand Socco was once as full of life as the Djemaa el-Fna in Marrakesh, with makeshift shops, snake charmers, musicians, storytellers and food stalls filling the night air with cacophonous activity. It is still a busy place, especially on Thursday and Sunday, when Riffian peasants come to market, and the area comes alive.

Medina

You enter the medina from the Grand Socco by Rue Semmarine and quickly veer right onto Rue as-Siaghin. This was once Tangier's main gold market (some jewellery stores remain), located on the northern flank of the old Jewish quarter, or mellah.

On your right, you soon pass the Spanish **Church of the Immaculate Conception** (closed), which was built in 1880 at a time when Spaniards made up one-fifth of the city's population. A few doors down is what used to be the residence of the sultan's agent *(naib)*, who was the point of contact between the Moroccan leader and European legations until 1923. From here you emerge on to the **Petit Socco**.

Gone are the days when William Burroughs could cheerfully write of the endless stream of louche offers from young boys and men around the Petit Socco, but it is still a busy little square and a great place to sit over a mint tea, watch the world go by and contemplate its colourful past.

If you feel disappointed about the passing of Tangier's sleazy era, don't despair – there's enough still going on to give you a taste of what it was like. Whispers of 'something special, my friend' are a feature of the area, and one of the cheap pensions overlooking the square, the Fuentes, doubles as a brothel.

It is perhaps difficult to imagine now, but at the end of the 19th century the Fuentes was one of Tangier's luxury hotels. At that time there was little more to the town than the medina and, as the Europeans became more influential, the city's administration was established here, including the Spanish postal service and the main banks.

If you head down Ave Mokhtar Ahardan (ex-Rue de la Poste), you will probably find it hard to believe that some of the little pensions here were classy hotels squeezed in among such important offices as the Spanish Legation and French post office. (From here you can descend a series of stairways and walk down to the train station and port.)

The grand era came to an end as the ville nouvelle was built and the administration was transferred out of the medina in the early 20th century.

At the end of Rue Jemaa el-Kebir (ex-Rue de la Marine) you come to a small belvedere overlooking the port. You could easily miss the **Great Mosque** on the corner. The building itself is of little interest, but it is said to have been the site of a Roman temple and at one time housed a church built by the Portuguese.

From the Petit Socco, Rue des Almohades (ex-Rue des Chrétiens) takes you north past some very determined shopkeepers and a hammam, to the kasbah.

Kasbah The kasbah is on the highest point of the city and isolated from the rest of the medina by its walls; you enter from Bab el-Assa (one of four gates) at the end of Rue Ben Raissouli in the medina. The gate gives onto a large open courtyard, to the right of which once stood the fort's stables.

Around to the right of them is Bab Haha, which leads back into the medina. Directly in front of you is Bab er-Raha (Gate of Rest) which leads onto a windswept, but impressive, viewpoint across to Spain.

Off to the left is the **Dar el-Makhzen**, the former sultan's palace and now an excellent museum devoted to Moroccan arts. As with many museums in Morocco, the building is as attractive and interesting as the exhibits.

The palace was built by Moulay Ismail in the 17th century and enlarged by later sultans, including Moulay Hafid – the last sultan to live here in 1912, along with his four wives and 40 concubines.

The private apartments were arranged around an inner courtyard, and still contain beautiful examples of carved wood ceilings and doors, *zellij* tilework and *muqarnas* plasterwork.

Displayed in the salons are good examples of Moroccan crafts, including musical instruments, pottery (from Fès and Meknès), textiles (including Berber kilims and embroidery from Chefchaouen), leatherwork, metalwork and weapons.

There is also a small archaeological collection. Most of the exhibits come from Volubilis, including the well preserved Roman mosaic, *Voyage of Venus*. Also look out for the ancient and mysterious Phoenician stellae.

Before leaving the museum, take a stroll around the **Sultan's Gardens** designed in the Andalusian fashion with a central fountain, fragrant herbs and shrubs, and orange and lemon trees providing welcome shade.

If you feel in need of a refreshment, the Café Détroit on the 2nd floor in the walls can be reached through these gardens. It was set up by Brion Gysin, the 1960s writer and friend of the Rolling Stones, and was called The Thousand & One Nights. It became famous for the trance musicians who played here in the 1960s and released a record produced by Brian Jones. Musicians still play here, but it has become a bit of a tourist trap.

The tour groups are all brought here, and after the obligatory mint tea they file out to songs like 'Roll Out the Barrel'. The cafe is generally open to cater for tour groups, in other words from 10 am to 2 pm, and although the views are good, the tea is expensive. The museum itself is open from 9 am to 12.30 pm and 3 to 5.30 pm in winter and 9 am to 3.30 pm in summer (closed Tuesday). Entry is Dr10.

Quite a few of the houses inside the kasbah are owned by wealthy foreigners, only some of whom live here for much of the time. Just outside the kasbah is the Calle Amrah, where expatriate American author Paul Bowles bought himself a small house in 1947.

Not far away was the Sidi Hosni Palace where Barbara Hutton, the Woolworth heiress, lived and gave some of her grandest parties. It is said that when things were going well, she had an annual income of US$3 million, but by the time she died in 1979 in Los Angeles, she had less than US$4000 in the bank.

Old American Legation Museum An intriguing relic of the international zone is the former US legation, now a museum funded by America. The three storey building was donated to the USA in 1820 by Sultan Moulay Suleyman. The Americans had sent a representative late in the previous century, as Morocco was the first nation to recognise the new country.

The museum houses archives and interesting material on the history of Tangier, and it was here that American and British agents did much of the local planning for the 1942 Allied landings in North Africa.

The easiest way to find the museum is to turn into Rue du Portugal from Rue Salah ed-Din el-Ayoubi and enter the medina at the first gate on your left. The museum is a little way down the lane, after the dogleg turn.

Getting in might prove harder. It is supposedly open on Monday, Wednesday and Thursday from 10 am to 1 pm and 3 to 5 pm, or by appointment (☎ 935317). It may not be open even at the advertised times, but knock on the door to be sure. Entrance is free.

Musée d'Art Contemporain
Housed in the former British Consulate on Rue d'Angleterre (see the Tangier map), this art gallery is devoted to modern Moroccan art.

It is the first of its kind in the country and includes work by the contemporary Moroccan painters Abdallah Hariri, Farid Belkahia and Moulay Ahmed Drissi. It's open from 8.30 am to noon and 2 to 6.30 pm (closed Tuesday). Entry is Dr10.

Forbes Museum
A half-hour walk from the Grand Socco, heading north-west from town along the coast, is the villa (a former palace of the Mendoub, or sultan's representative in

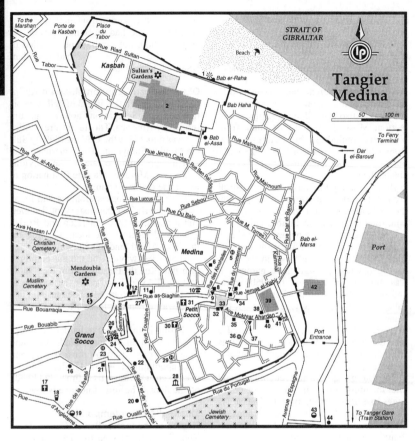

Tangier) owned by the family of the American tycoon Malcolm Forbes (of Forbes Magazine), who died in 1990.

The villa, which is still occasionally used by the Forbes family, houses what is claimed to be the largest collection of toy soldiers in the world – an 'army' of 120,000 miniatures and dioramas depicting all sorts of unrelated conflicts, from the Battle of the Three Kings (1578) to the Green March (1975), with stops in the Sudan, various WWI battlefields and several sea engagements along the way.

The scenes depicted are surprisingly engaging and dramatic, with panicking horses, women rushing for buckets of water, cavalry charging and lots of limbless, headless corpses; if the displays weren't in glass cases, the temptation to sneeze would be almost unbearable. You can also wander around the gardens outside, which offer good views, but the swimming pool is out of bounds.

The museum is open from 10 am to 5 pm and entry is free, although the Spanish-speaking attendant will expect a tip.

PLACES TO STAY	14	Restaurant Hamadi	20	Covered Market
3 Hôtel Continental	26	Pâtisserie Charaf	22	Covered Market
4 Hôtel Larache	27	Turrón Attaïk	23	Hammam
6 Pension Agadir	33	Café El Manara	24	Banque Populaire
7 Pension Becerra	34	Cheap Snack Bar	25	Telephones
8 Pension Mauritania	37	Restaurant Ahlan	28	Old American
21 Hôtel du Grand Socco				Legation Museum
32 Pension Fuentes	**OTHER**		29	Hammam
35 Pension Palace	1	Lookout	30	Spanish Church
38 Hôtel Mamora;	2	Dar el-Makhzen Museum	31	Church of the
Pressing (Laundry)	5	Hammam		Immaculate Conception
40 Hôtel Olid	10	Telephones	36	Douche
41 Pension Victoria;	11	Shamalabo Photo Shop		(Public Shower)
Hammam	13	Pharmacy Anegax	39	Great Mosque
	15	BMCE (ATMs)	42	Customs
PLACES TO EAT	16	Cinéma Rif	43	CTM Bus Station
9 Café Central	17	St Andrew's Church	44	Voyage Wasteels
12 Restaurant	18	Dean's Bar		(Travel Agency)
Mamounia Palace	19	Local Bus Terminal		

Apparently the Forbes family gets to see the visitors' book – so maybe you should sign it so that they don't shut the place down for want of visitors.

If you feel like a refreshment after visiting the museum, don't miss Café Hafa (see Cafes under Places to Eat later in this section). Ask the attendant for directions.

Ville Nouvelle

The core of the ville nouvelle, largely unchanged since its heyday in the 1930s, is worth a wander. The area around Place de France and Blvd Pasteur, with its cafes and patisseries, still retains something of that decade's glamour.

The aptly named **Terrasse des Paresseux** (Idlers' Terrace) just up from Place de France, provides lovely panoramic views of the port, Gibraltar and Spain. It's a favourite spot with the locals who come for an evening promenade.

There is a lively **market** along a lane down from Rue de la Liberté near the Hôtel El Minzah. It is not a tourist market, but rather concentrates on food, household products and all sorts of bits and bobs.

A remnant of the days when Spaniards formed the largest non-Moroccan community in Tangier is the **Gran Teatro de Cervantes**, in a side street off Rue Salah ed-Din el-Ayoubi (also known as Rue de la Plage). Opened in 1913, the theatre enjoyed its heyday in the interwar years. You can't miss the dazzling Art Deco facade. The building has long been in decline, but is now being restored, with Spanish funding.

Ever since Tangier passed to British control for about 20 years in 1661, Britons have had a special relationship with the city, immortalised by some of the literary figures who have graced the city.

There was a small English church in Tangier as far back as the 1660s. The present church, **St Andrew's**, is on Rue d'Angleterre, just outside the medina (see the Tangier Medina map). It was consecrated in 1905 on ground donated by the Sultan Moulay al-Hassan in the 1880s.

The caretaker, Mustapha Chergui, will be pleased to show you around the building, which was constructed in the Moroccan style, with the Lord's Prayer in Arabic atop the chancel.

At the western end of the church is a plaque to the memory of Emily Kean, an English woman who married the sherif of Ouezzane and spent many years of her life introducing vaccination to the people of northern Morocco.

Others buried here include Walter Harris, the British journalist who chronicled Tangier's goings-on from the late 19th century, and 'Caid' Maclean, a military adviser to the sultans who, like Harris, was at one time imprisoned and held to ransom by the Rif bandit Raissouli.

Virtually across the road stands the closed **Grand Hôtel Villa de France**. The French impressionist painter Henri Matisse stayed here in the early years of this century, his imagination captured and his brush driven by the African light. He had been preceded in 1831 by Delacroix, although the latter mainly produced sketches during his time in Tangier.

There is a story that the **Great Mosque** on Place de Koweit was built after a rich Arab Gulf sheikh sailed by Tangier and noticed that the modern cathedral's spire overshadowed all the minarets of Tangier. Shocked, he paid for the mosque and now the spire plays second fiddle to the new minaret.

Beaches

The beaches of Tangier, although not bad, are hardly the best in Morocco. They are relatively clean, but in some areas raw sewage is still pumped into the sea. There are various beach bars strung along the sand which offer changing cabins (officially compulsory), showers, deck chairs, and food and drink.

The much reduced European gay population still frequents certain of these bars, some of which can be fun in summer. As with many beaches in Morocco, women will not feel at ease sunning themselves here. The beach is not a good place to be in the evening, as muggings are common.

Language Schools

The American Language Center (☎ 933616) is at 1 Rue M'sallah. You might be able to pick up work here teaching English.

Places to Stay – bottom end

Camping Campers have a choice. The more convenient of the two sites is *Camp-*

ing Miramonte (☎ 937133), or *Camping Marshan* as it's also known. It lies 3km west of the centre of town near Jews' Bay. It's rather run down and not good value, but is close to the beach. Bring food, as its restaurant is no longer operating.

To get there, take bus Nos 12, 21 or the combined 12/21 (Dr2) from the bus terminal near the Grand Socco and get off at the Café Fleur de la Montagne. Don't leave valuables unattended here – things disappear. It costs Dr15 per person, plus Dr10 to pitch a tent and Dr8 for a car. There is hot water, and they have some low quality rooms for Dr100/150.

The other site is *Camping Tingis*, about 6km east of the town centre. It is much more expensive, but includes a tennis court and swimming pool. To get there, take bus No 15 from the Grand Socco.

Hostel The *youth hostel* (☎ 946127) is at 8 Rue al-Antaki, just up past the hotels Marco Polo and El Djenina (see the Tangier map). It's a very clean, secure and well run place, and the welcoming manager, Mohssine Laroussi, speaks English, French and Spanish.

A dormitory bed will cost you Dr25 with an ID card and Dr27.50 without. Hot showers are an extra Dr5. The hostel is open Monday to Saturday from 8 to 10 am, noon to 3 pm and 6 to 10.30 pm. On Sunday, it's open from 8 to 10 am and 6 pm to midnight.

Hotels Outside July and August, you shouldn't have trouble finding a room in Tangier. As in most Moroccan cities, you have the choice between the medina and the ville nouvelle. The hotels in the ville nouvelle have the edge on comfort, and are probably the best bet for the new arrival.

Most of the traditional Moroccan-style hostelries are in the medina around the Petit Socco and on Ave Mokhtar Ahardan, which connects the Petit Socco with the port area. They run the gamut from flophouses to two-star hotels.

If you arrive by ferry, walk out of the port until you reach the main train station on your left. Then take the road on the extreme right-hand side, which goes uphill until you get to a set of steps just past the junction with Rue du Portugal. Go up the steps and you'll find yourself at the bottom of Ave Mokhtar Ahardan.

Alternatively, once out of the port gates, carry on past the train station and take the first street on your right, Rue Salah ed-Din el-Ayoubi, which has a string of cheapies. Better are some of the unclassified one and two-star hotels further along or just back from the waterfront, as well as up the narrow Rue Magellan a couple of hundred metres to the south.

Some unclassified places simply charge per head, and singles often mean getting a small double to yourself. People travelling in pairs who want a bit of extra space might want to try turning up separately to one of these places and each asking for a single, rather than paying the same price to share a room. There is the risk, however, of finding that there's only space for one of you.

Hotels – Medina There are plenty of cheap pensions to choose from here. Most are basic and you won't get much more than a bed and shared bathroom facilities, although some have hot water (for a small extra charge). The absence of showers in some of the hotels is not a huge problem, as there are various hammams around the Petit Socco.

Prices vary slightly and you're looking at Dr30 to Dr50 for singles and Dr60 to Dr100 for doubles. Standards vary considerably, so it's worth looking around.

One of the best places on the Petit Socco is the *Pension Mauritania* (☎ 934674) on Rue as-Siaghin. Immaculate rooms with newly installed washbasin and bidet cost Dr50/80 for singles/doubles. Showers are shared, but are free. The entrance is just off the Socco. Try to get a room which looks out on to the Socco. The hotel is popular with gay travellers.

Also clean, and just around the corner up a lane, is the *Pension Agadir* (☎ 938084). Rooms are arranged around an attractive central courtyard and are good value at Dr30 per person. A hot shower costs an extra Dr5. You'll be given a warm welcome by Allal, a charming old Moroccan who speaks good Spanish.

Back on the square, up some worn, marble steps, the *Pension Fuentes* (☎ 934669) has reasonably clean, but rather overpriced, rooms for Dr70/100 (hot/cold showers cost an extra Dr5/8). There is a lively cafe on the 1st floor which can be rather noisy.

Across the Petit Socco from the Fuentes, and better value, is the *Pension Becerra* (☎ 932369). The rooms are clean and cost Dr40/60.

The main street for accommodation is Ave Mokhtar Ahardan. In the lower range, two of the best options are the *Pension Palace* (☎ 936128), at No 2, and the *Hôtel Olid* (☎ 931310), at No 12. The Palace's rooms are small but spotless, and many of them front on to a quiet, verdant courtyard. There are 39 rooms without shower which cost Dr50/100 (Dr5 for a hot shower in the shared bathrooms), and four double rooms with shower for Dr120.

The Olid has seen better days, but is fairly clean and most rooms come with private cold shower. Rooms cost Dr40/80.

One of the best of the others along this street is the *Pension Victoria* (☎ 931299) at No 22. It has reasonably clean and pleasant rooms, around a rather garish fountain and covered courtyard, for Dr30/60 with cold shared showers. It's a peaceful place and is quite good value. There is also a hammam here.

Worth checking out is the *Hôtel du Grand Socco* (☎ 933126), just outside the medina on the square of the same name. It has fairly basic singles, doubles and triples with shared bathroom facilities for Dr50, Dr80 and Dr120 respectively. They have great views of the square.

Hotels – Ville Nouvelle First up are the unclassified hotels and pensions along Rue Salah ed-Din el-Ayoubi, but most are no better than the cheapies in the medina and some are decidedly characterless. Most offer basic accommodation with shared bathroom and toilet facilities for Dr30 to Dr40 for singles and Dr50 to Dr60 for doubles. Some have hot water.

Heading up from the waterfront you strike several in a row on the left-hand side – they seem to improve as you climb. One offering better value is *Pension Le Détroit* (☎ 934838) at 130 Rue Salah ed-Din el-Ayoubi, which offers very clean, but smallish rooms for Dr40/60 and hot showers for Dr8.

One of the best deals in this category is the *Pension Miami* (☎ 932900) at No 126 which offers very clean decent rooms, some with balcony, for Dr50/80/120. Shared hot showers cost Dr10.

On the right side of the street, the *Pension Atou* (☎ 936333) is a place really only for the desperate. Its 136 rooms are very basic and a bit grubby, but it does boast two terraces with wonderful, sweeping views of the city. Some travellers have reported that the hotel is sometimes used as a brothel. Singles, doubles and triples cost Dr30, Dr60 and Dr90 respectively.

There's a public shower, *Douche Cléopatra*, just by the Hôtel Valencia. A shower costs Dr5.

If none of these appeals, or you just want to be a bit further away from the medina walls, you could try some of the places along Ave d'Espagne. One of the best value is the peaceful *Hôtel L'Marsa* (☎ 932339) at No 92, which has very clean and comfortable rooms for Dr60/100, although some look straight on to a cafe, which can be noisy.

Slightly better are the front rooms with balcony in the *Hôtel Cecil* (☎ 931087) at 112 Ave d'Espagne. The rooms could do with a lick of paint, but are furnished pleasantly enough. They charge Dr60 to Dr83 (singles) and Dr120 to Dr166 (doubles).

The little lane heading uphill between these last two is Rue Magellan. Here there are a couple of good-value places a little further up, including the *Hôtel L'Amor* and the *Hôtel Magellan* (☎ 372319). They have rather shabby but clean rooms for Dr40/80 (Dr50/100 in high season), some with views. Hot showers are available at the Magellan for Dr10.

Further up around to the left, you strike two more places opposite each other. Both the *Hôtel Ibn Batouta* (☎ 937170) and the British-run *Hôtel El Muniria* (☎ 935397), have spotless rooms with shower, and terraces with excellent views. The latter is probably a better bet, although on the expensive side for the budget wallet at Dr100/120. This is where William Burroughs wrote *The Naked Lunch*. Ask for room Nos 7 and 8 which have lovely views over the harbour.

Close by and also with good views (if you can get a front room) is the one-star *Hôtel Panoramic Massilia* (☎ 370703) on the corner of Rue Ibn Joubair and Rue Targha. The staff here are friendly; clean singles/doubles with private shower, toilet and hot water (in the morning) cost from Dr90/140. This is definitely one of the better deals in Tangier.

Heading back down the price scale, there are a number of cheap pensions scattered about the ville nouvelle, but they are not overly convenient.

The *Pension Holland* (☎ 937838), is located in a pleasant shady spot in a backstreet behind the French Consulate at 139 Rue Hollanda (see the Tangier map). It charges Dr60/100 for simple, but very clean, singles/doubles. Three rooms come with shower (cold) for no extra charge, and two rooms (Nos 3 and 11) have nice balconies; there's also space for parking. Unfortunately, the manager seems to speak only Moroccan Arabic and a Berber dialect.

A little more accessible, but less pleasant, are the pensions *Atlal* (☎ 937299) and *Al Hoceima* (☎ 933063) on Rue al-Moutanabi. Both charge Dr50/80 (Dr8 for a hot shower) and are reasonable value. For the truly desperate, there are a few more south of Rue Moussa ben-Noussair, but you shouldn't need them.

Places to Stay – middle

Medina If you prefer a modicum of luxury, but still want to stay in the medina area, then one place to try is the two-star *Hôtel Mamora* (☎ 934105), at 19 Ave Mokhtar

Ahardan, which offers spotlessly clean rooms with shower for Dr147/180 in the low season and Dr197/230 in the high season.

Some of the rooms have beautiful views of the Great Mosque, which means an early morning wake-up call unless you're a sound sleeper.

The pick of the crop, and a good choice by any standard, is the *Hôtel Continental* (☎ 931024; fax 931143). Used for some scenes in the film version of Paul Bowles' *The Sheltering Sky*, it is full of character and atmosphere, even if it is a bit ragged around the edges. Some of the long-term residents are a little ragged themselves, but what stories they could tell.

The best of the 56 rooms are those overlooking the port. Singles/doubles cost Dr161/210 during the low season and Dr186/240 during the high season. It's popular with tour groups and film crews, so book ahead if possible. You'll be given a warm welcome from Abdesselom and the rest of the staff.

The entrance is off Dar Barhoud, and the best way to get there from the port is to head *up* the street past the Great Mosque and veer right at the fork (don't take the covered lane). The entrance is about 100m up on the right.

Ville Nouvelle There are a few possibilities at the lower end of this scale (where a single will cost a little more than Dr140). One of the better ones is the *Hôtel de Paris* (☎ 931877), virtually opposite the tourist office at 42 Blvd Pasteur. Good, comfortable rooms with private shower cost Dr147/180 in the low season and Dr197/236 in the high season.

Another good deal is the *Hôtel Ritz* (☎ 322443; fax 941002) at 27 Rue Moussa ben-Noussaïr. Singles/doubles with shower cost Dr134/164; there are also two rooms without shower for Dr119/140. Prices go up by Dr50 in the high season.

Back along the waterfront, you could try the popular *Hôtel Valencia* (☎ 930770) at 72 Ave d'Espagne. It's not the most salu-

brious location, but it's a reasonable place and close to transport. It's often booked solid. Singles/doubles with showers cost Dr147/180 or Dr197/230 for low or high season. There are also some rooms without shower for Dr80/100. A garage is available for hotel clients and costs Dr20 per day.

Another reasonable one is the *Hôtel Biarritz* (☎ 932473) at 102-104 Ave d'Espagne. For Dr149/170 you can get comfortable, spacious old rooms with shower that overlook the sea.

At the junction of Ave des FAR and Ave Youssef ben Tachfine (see the Tangier map), the *Hôtel Miramar* (☎ 941715) is definitely on the tatty side, but is very clean and offers quite good value. Singles, doubles and triples with private shower are Dr119, Dr140 and Dr198 respectively.

Rooms with private toilet cost Dr134, Dr165 and Dr223. Some rooms have views. The bar seems to attract prostitutes.

Where Rue al-Antaki heads up from Ave d'Espagne (and where Ave d'Espagne becomes Ave des FAR) is the pleasant *Hôtel Marco Polo* (☎ 941124; fax 942476). The rooms are so clean, they smell of disinfectant.

This hotel used to be popular with gay travellers, and its bar and restaurant still seems to serve as a meeting point. It charges Dr154/178 for singles/doubles. Room Nos 4 and 5 have their own terrace and good views.

Next door is the recently refurbished, two-star *Hôtel El Djenina* (☎ 942244) at 8 Rue al-Antaki. It also has decent rooms for Dr150/180, along with a restaurant and bar. A couple of doors up is the two-star *Hôtel Bristol* (☎ 942914) at 14 Rue al-Antaki. It has rooms without shower for Dr87/106, with shower for Dr121/150 and with shower and toilet for Dr180 (singles and doubles). The hotel has a restaurant and bar.

At 25 Rue al-Farabi is the pricey, two-star *Hôtel Charf* (☎ 943340). If you can afford it, the self-contained rooms are very good and have magnificent views, as does the 4th floor restaurant. Singles/doubles are Dr171/203.

MEDITERRANEAN COAST

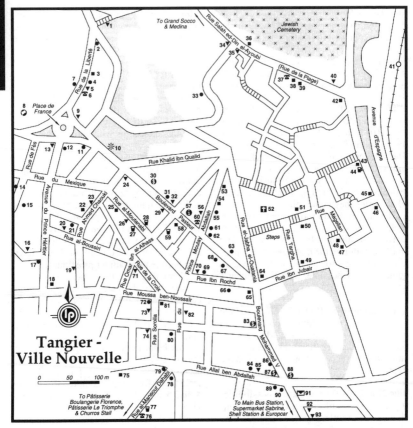

Tangier -
Ville Nouvelle

0   50   100 m

To Grand Socco
& Medina

Jewish
Cemetery

Place de
France

To Pâtisserie
Boulangerie Florence,
Pâtisserie Le Triomphe
& Churros Stall

To Main Bus Station,
Supermarket Sabrine,
Shell Station & Europcar

In the heart of the ville nouvelle are some more expensive alternatives to the Hôtel de Paris. The *Hôtel Astoria* (☎ 937201), at 10 Rue Ahmed Chaouki, offers 27 reasonable rooms for Dr109/140 in the low season and Dr136/180 in the high season.

At 3 Rue du Prince Moulay Abdallah is the fairly popular *Hôtel Lutetia* (☎ 931866). Rooms with shower and toilet cost Dr101/124 (Dr24 more during the high season). The hotel has parking facilities.

The *Hôtel Atlas* (☎ 936435; fax 933095), at 50 Rue Moussa ben-Noussaïr, is a little

out of the way, but not bad in its class. Singles/doubles with shower cost Dr191/249 while rooms with complete bathroom are Dr243/302. During the high season, prices go up by around Dr35.

Heading into what most people would consider the top range is the rather inconveniently located *Hôtel Chellah* (☎ 943388; fax 945536) at 47-49 Rue Allal ben Abdallah.

They have characterless, but perfectly comfortable, rooms for Dr386/474, including breakfast.

PLACES TO STAY

3 Hôtel El Minzah;
   Restaurant El Korsan
18 Hôtel Atlas
22 Hôtel Astoria
25 Pensions Atlal &
   Al Hoceima
36 Pension Atou
38 Pension Miami
39 Pension Le Détroit
42 Hôtel Valencia; Douche
   Cléopatra (Public
   Shower)
43 Hôtel L'Marsa;
   Restaurant L'Marsa
45 Hotel Biarritz
46 Hôtel Cecil
47 Hôtel L'Amor
48 Hôtel Magellan
49 Hôtel Panoramic Massilia
50 Hôtel Ibn Batouta
51 Hôtel El Muniria;
   Tanger-Inn
53 Hôtel Lutetia
54 Hôtel Bar
   Restaurant Maroc
58 Hôtel de Paris
64 Hôtel Rembrandt
65 Hôtel Tanjah-Flandria;
   Le Palace Disco
75 Hôtel Chellah
81 Hôtel Ritz

PLACES TO EAT

1 Restaurant Populaire
5 Pâtisserie La Española
9 Café de Paris
13 Café de France
16 Restaurant Andalou
19 Restaurant Las Conchas
20 La Pagode
23 Restaurant Raihani
24 Big Mac
26 Pâtisserie
29 Pâtisserie Le Petit
   Prince
32 Café Metropole
34 Sandwich Genève
35 Sandwich Cervantes
40 Restaurant Africa;
   Restaurant Hassi Baida
56 Romero's Restaurant
70 Rubis Grill
71 Pizzeria Piazza Capri
73 The Pub
74 Cafe
82 Pâtisserie Rahmouni
85 Churros Stall
92 Pâtisserie Oslo
93 Salon du Thé Oslo

OTHER

2 Studio Flash
4 Carlson Wagonlits
   (Travel Agency)
6 Telephones; Fax
7 Institut Français; Galerie
   d'Exposition Delacroix
8 French Consulate
10 Terrasse des Paresseux
   (Lookout)
11 Pharmacy
12 Royal Air Maroc
14 Depôt de Nuit
   (Night Pharmacy)
15 Cinéma Paris
17 Cinéma Mauritania
21 Stop Pressing (Laundry)
27 Scott's Nightclub
28 Gospel Nightclub
30 BMCE (Late Bank &
   ATMs)
31 Cybernet
33 Gran Teatro de
   Cervantes
37 Telephones
41 Tanger Gare
   (Train Station)
44 Samir Petrol Station
52 Church
55 Budget (Car Rental)
57 Tourist Office
59 The Ranch Club
60 Telephone; Fax
61 Limadet Boat Ticket
   Office
62 Studios Samar
   (Photo Shop)
63 Iberia Airlines
66 Cinéma Flandria
67 Avis (Car Rental)
68 Librairie des Colonnes
69 Casa Pepé
72 Paris Pressing (Laundry)
76 Telephone; Fax
77 London Pub
78 Cinéma Roxy
79 Pharmacy du Lycée
80 Cinéma Goya
83 Crédit du Maroc
   (American Express)
84 Pressing Dallas
   (Laundry)
86 Pharmacy
87 Banque Populaire
88 Wafabank
89 Cady & Douka
   (Car Rental)
90 Hertz (Car Rental)
91 Main Post Office

Places to Stay – top end

With a tourist trade the size of Tangier's, there is a good choice of top-range hotels.

In the four-star category with some character is the ageing *Hôtel Rif* (☎ 941731; fax 941794) at 152 Ave des FAR (see the Tangier map). Singles, doubles, and triples cost Dr447, Dr575 and Dr694 respectively.

A cheaper option is the *Hôtel Rembrandt* (☎ 937870; fax 930443), at the junction where Blvd Pasteur becomes Blvd Mohammed V. They charge Dr375/467 in the low season and another Dr100 in the high season. Across the road, the *Hôtel Tanjah-Flandria* (☎ 933279; fax 934347) offers all the mod cons including its own hammam (Dr40) for Dr538/657 (there's a 30% reduction in winter).

Another four-star joint is the *Hôtel Solazur* (☎ 940164; fax 945286), down on Ave des FAR (see the Tangier map). It charges Dr297/407, or Dr397/507 in the high season.

Not far away, the three-star *El Oumnia* (☎ 940366; fax 940677), on Ave Louis van Beethoven, has rooms for Dr274/330 (add another Dr100 in the high season).

The *Hôtel Shéhérazade* (☎ 940502; fax 940801) on Ave des FAR, is another four-star hotel. It has singles/doubles which go for Dr380/542.

The *Hôtel Inter-Continental* (☎ 936053; fax 930151), near Place de Koweit, charges Dr409/618 (Dr559/718 in the high season).

The *Hôtel Ziryab* (☎ 331812; fax 331823) at 42 Rue de Hollande is a relatively new four-star hotel offering singles/doubles for Dr398/506 in the low season, and Dr498/606 in the high season. The rooms and roof terrace have stunning panoramic views of the Bay of Tangier, the medina and the kasbah. The hotel has its own cinema, patisserie, bank, several restaurants and a tennis court.

The only five-star hotel in Tangier that deserves this ranking is the *El Minzah* (☎ 935885; fax 934546) at 85 Rue de la Liberté. A well maintained reminder of the 1930s, when it was patronised by anyone who was anyone in the transient and not-so-transient European community, the hotel is beautifully conceived along the lines of a Moroccan palace.

In 1931 the US businessman Ion Perdicaris, who at one point spent an uncomfortable spell as a prisoner of the Rif bandit Er-Raissouli, converted what had been the Palmarium casino into a hotel. The building was also once the mansion of a certain Lord Bute. During WWII, as Tangier turned into a vipers' nest of spies and mercenaries of all types, the hotel hosted a mainly American clientele.

It has all the amenities you would expect of a hotel in this category, including a swimming pool, fitness centre and a babysitting service. Golf, horse-riding and tennis are all possible in grounds nearby the hotel. The hotel hopes to have Internet facilities installed by the end of 1997. Single rooms go from Dr850 to Dr1250, and doubles from Dr1100 to Dr1500. Add another Dr100 to prices during the high season.

Swimming Pools
The Hôtel Ziryab is one of the very few hotels in Tangier with a pool. It is small, but pleasantly set with views over the Bay of Tangier. It is usually open to non-residents (unless very full) and charges Dr40/25 per adult/child.

Hammams
There are several hammams around the Petit Socco, including one close to the Pension Victoria on Ave Mokhtar Ahardan. There is another at 80 Rue des Almohades. Both cost Dr5 and are open from 8 am to 8 pm.

Places to Eat
Medina There are several cheap eating possibilities in and around the Petit Socco, in between the cafes. The *Restaurant Ahlan* at 8 Ave Mokhtar Ahardan is a good value place with decent tajine, couscous and kebabs for around Dr25. A bowl of harira soup will set you back just Dr3. It's a clean, pleasant restaurant and is open every day from 10 am to 10 pm.

There are a few *food stalls* at the bottom of the steps at the end of Ave Mokhtar Ahardan. They serve up fried fish and one or two other things for a few dirham.

On Rue as-Siaghin is the more expensive *Restaurant Mamounia Palace* (☎ 935099), which offers the usual 'Moroccan feasts' in more sumptuous surroundings. It is definitely geared towards the tour groups, however. The two set menus (Dr100) are not bad, but it's a much better place to come for a peaceful cup of tea or coffee (avoid lunch time or you might not get in). There's a great view over the medina from one of the salons where you can take it all in from very comfortable surroundings. It's open daily from 9 am to 10 or 11 pm.

The restaurant *Hamadi* (☎ 934514), at 2 Rue d'Italie, just outside the medina walls, is another Moroccan palace-restaurant. The food is not bad and reasonably cheap (Dr40 to Dr45 for a main course), but watch out for the 20% tax. They normally have a musician and a couple of shows if you're after that sort of thing. You can get a beer/wine with your meal for Dr20/70.

Don't miss *Turrón Attaïk*, the nougat seller whose stall can be found diagonally opposite the Mamounia Palace. A decent bag costs Dr2 and is to die for.

Ville Nouvelle Two good, cheap places are the *Sandwich Cervantes* and *Sandwich Genève* close to each other on Rue Salah ed-Din el-Ayoubi, just south of the Jewish cemetery. They are both popular with the locals, have seating and charge around Dr7 for a large roll filled with meat or fish and salad.

Down Rue Salah ed-Din el-Ayoubi towards Ave d'Espagne, are two reasonably priced sit-down restaurants, the *Africa* (No 83) and, next door, the *Hassi Baida*. Both offer set meals for around Dr45, main courses for Dr25 to Dr35, salads for around Dr8 and a bowl of soup for Dr4. The Hassi Baida also offers options for vegetarians. Both are open every day until 11 pm.

Perhaps the best value place of all is the *Restaurant Populaire* down the steps from Rue Liberté. It's a local favourite, and serves excellent, fresh food at reasonable prices (around Dr40 for a main course). Try the house speciality, the fish tajine. Some food is cooked on coals in front of you.

If you're desperate for western-style fare, *Big Mac* on the corner of Blvd Pasteur and Rue Ahmed Chaouki, isn't bad. The *Pizzeria Piazza Capri* (☎ 937221), at 2 Rue de la Croix, is a new place which does good pizza served on a wooden platter for around Dr18 to Dr30. It's open every day from 11 am to midnight, and also has a free delivery service.

For barbecued meat or fish, you could try the *Rubis Grill*, at 3 Ibn Rochd, where mains cost from Dr40 to 85. It's decorated like a hunter's lodge and is a cosy place for a beer (Dr15) and *tapas* (snacks served in Spanish bars) during the winter.

The stretch of Rue du Prince Moulay Abdallah around the corner from the tourist office is laden with eating possibilities. *Romero's*, at No 12, is considered one of

the best fish restaurants in Tangier. The seafood paella is a popular speciality. Mains cost from Dr50 to Dr75, and wine/ beer from Dr60/18.

The Pub, opposite the Hôtel Ritz at 5 Rue Sorolla, caters for homesick Brits hungry for pub grub. Chalked up on the blackboard each day, you'll find (for around Dr50 to Dr60) all the old favourites such as scampi and chips, liver and onions and even shepherd's pie.

Not far from the Hôtel Astoria, at 10 Rue Ahmed Chaouki, is the restaurant *Raihani* (☎ 934866), generally considered one of the best places for Moroccan fare. It's done out in a pseudo-palace style, and is a bit touristy, but the food and service are good. Main courses such as couscous and tajine cost from Dr55 to Dr60, and a three course set menu, Dr80.

On the same street at No 30 is the restaurant *Las Conchas* (☎ 931643), which is regarded as the best French restaurant in Tangier. It has an extensive menu including Italian dishes, but prices reflect its reputation: main courses cost around Dr75 to Dr85 and wine from Dr70. It's open every day except Sunday.

If you're craving Asian food, you could try the pleasant *La Pagode* restaurant at 3 Rue al-Boussiri, just off Rue du Prince Héritier. Main dishes cost around Dr65 and a bottle of wine from Dr75.

The *Parivar Restaurant* (☎ 340389) at 33 Rue Farabi (see the Tangier map), claims to be the only Indian restaurant in Morocco. The extensive menu has been adapted to suit local taste, but is still excellent. Mains cost from Dr70 to Dr85 (Chinese ones are also available for bickering couples who can't agree where to eat). It's open daily from noon to 2.30 pm and 7.30 to 11 pm.

Along Ave d'Espagne at No 92 is the unlicensed *Restaurant l'Marsa* near the hotel of the same name. It has a very pleasant terrace and serves reasonable set menus for Dr70, pizza for Dr28 to Dr43 and salads from Dr14. It's also a great place for a coffee, milkshake or, in summer, home made ice cream.

The *Restaurant Andalou*, in a side street between Rue de Fès and Rue du Prince Héritier, serves tapas.

For a big splurge, you could try the *Restaurant El Korsan* (☎ 935885) in the El Minzah hotel. It serves expensive but high quality Moroccan food (main courses cost around Dr130) and there is usually traditional dancing in the evening.

Cafes In the heart of the medina, the *Café Central* on the Petit Socco was a favourite hangout for William Burroughs and others, and today is quite a good place to have a glass of tea and watch the world go by. Like all the cafes on the square, it's rather male-dominated.

Blvd Pasteur is lined with elegant, European-style cafes, with their tables spilling out onto the footpaths. Of these the pick of the crop has to be the *Café de Paris*, an ageing grande dame of Tangier coffee society. Take a seat inside and you're likely to have an odd assortment of characters for company – remnants of the Spanish population, genteel Moroccans and the odd ageing northern European – all in all an atmosphere redolent of bygone days. Your Dr5 coffee will be served by the most correct of waiters, making it well worth the little extra.

The *Café Hafa*, about a ten minute walk from the Forbes Museum (see the Tangier map), is hidden away in a tiny street behind the stadium. Ask for directions from the museum. It's well worth the search and is a simple but delightful place to while away the hot afternoon over a cup of mint tea or a lemonade (Dr4).

The cafe is set within shaded and terraced gardens overlooking the Straits of Gibraltar. Traditionally, it's the favourite haunt of Paul Bowles, the American novelist, but you're more likely to have cats for company, snoozing among the flower pots, or the seagulls over head. It's also a popular place with locals who come for a quiet smoke.

Patisseries & Ice Cream In the medina,

the *Pâtisserie Charaf* at 28 Rue Semmarine just off the Grand Socco, is a great place to start the day with its delicious almond croissants and coffee. During the rest of the day, it's a useful refuge from the bustle of the medina.

In the ville nouvelle, the *Pâtisserie Rahmouni*, at 35 Rue du Prince Moulay Abdallah, is run by Hassan Rahmouni and his family who pride themselves on high quality, traditional Moroccan pastries.

The *Pâtisserie Boulangerie Florence* at 33 Rue al-Mansour Dahabi, has a good selection of both French and Moroccan pastries, sweet as well as savoury (including bastilla and briouats). They also sell freshly baked bread. It's a good place to prepare a picnic.

Close by at 30 Ave Lafayette, is the *Pâtisserie Le Triomphe* which does ice cream in summer. Opposite the patisserie on the same street, there's a stall selling churros (doughnuts) in the early morning, which are traditionally eaten for breakfast.

More central is the *Pâtisserie Le Petit Prince* at 34 Blvd Pasteur. It's regarded as the best cake shop in town and has an excellent selection of sweet and savoury pastries. Try the house speciality, polvorones, a kind of powdery, cinnamony shortbread. It also does fruit juice and ice cream in summer.

The *Pâtisserie Oslo* at 41 Blvd Mohammed V, is run by a Moroccan and his Norwegian wife. They have a mouthwatering selection of cakes and pastries, which you can take next door to the *Salon du Thé Oslo*, a good place for breakfast if you're staying in the ville nouvelle. It's open every day from 5 am to midnight.

At the *Salon du Thé Iris*, in the Istiraha complex beside the Hôtel Ziryab (see the Tangier map), you can sip tea while admiring the wonderful panoramic views over the bay. It's not cheap, however, and a tea/coffee and pastry will set you back Dr18.

Self-Catering The liquor store *Casa Pepé*, at 9 Rue Ibn Rochd in the ville nouvelle, stocks a decent selection of delicatessen foods such as French and Spanish salami, paté and cheese. It's probably the best place to stock up for a picnic.

There's a good supermarket (*Sabrine*), at the southern end of Blvd Mohammed V at No 143, which is open every day.

Entertainment

Bars Anyone who has done any reading about Tangier will have come across *Dean's Bar*, on Rue Amérique du Sud, south of the Grand Socco (see the Tangier Medina map).

Hardly a westerner of any repute did not prop up this bar at some time. It's a bit of a dump now, but may be worth a drink if you've steeped yourself in Tangier mythology. Women will feel uncomfortable here. Other places of the same ilk, such as the Parade Bar (a favourite haunt of Jane Bowles), have long since disappeared.

For something a little more upmarket, or if you're thirsting for a Guinness or Heineken (Dr30), you could try *The Pub*, at 5 Rue Sorolla, in the ville nouvelle. It styles itself on a typical English pub and even smells of wood and ale. It's open from noon to 3 pm and 6 pm to 2 am.

An excellent place for a civilised drink is the *London Pub*, at 15 Rue al-Mansour Dahabi (also in the ville nouvelle), which despite its name is more like a jazz bar. There is live music every night, and a happy hour from 7 to 9 pm, when your second drink is free. Beers, spirits and cocktails cost Dr25, Dr40 and Dr50.

The place is a favourite with local professionals and intellectuals, including, it is said, the writer Mohammed Choukri. It's by far the best bet for women too; any problems ask for Youssef, the owner!

A place well worth investigating is the *Tanger-Inn*, next to the Hôtel El Muniria in the ville nouvelle. It's open from 9 pm to about 1 am (until 3 am if there are plenty of people); knock on the heavy wooden door to get in. It's a tiny place and one of the last remnants of the Tangier of yesteryear where the clientele can give you a taste of Interzone.

Many of the middle and top-range hotels have bars. *Le Caid's Piano Bar* in the Hôtel El Minzah is good for an expensive tipple (spirits/cocktails for around Dr50/60). It's open from 9 pm to 1 am. The *Wine Bar* in the same hotel, is a great place if you fancy tasting some Moroccan wine; they have a selection of about 20, sold by the bottle or glass.

Nightclubs Currently the most fashionable nightclub is *Pasarela* in the southern part of the ville nouvelle on Ave des FAR. It is a large complex with several bars, an attractive garden and outdoor swimming pool. The music is a western mix. It's open from 11.30 pm to 3 am.

Another popular place is the *Olivia Valere* nightclub in the Ahlan Hôtel, about 5km outside the city on the road to Rabat. Number three in the popularity ratings is *Le Palace* disco in the Hôtel Tanjah-Flandria. It's open from 9 pm to 3 am. Entry for all the nightclubs is Dr100; drinks usually cost Dr40 to Dr50.

Gay Bars & Clubs The gay scene is not what it was in Tangier. The few places barely sustaining any reputation as meeting places for gays include *Scott's* nightclub on Rue al-Moutanabi (open from 11 pm until 2 am), and sometimes the *Tanger-Inn*, next to the Hôtel El Muniria.

You can also try the cafes around the Petit Socco, and particularly the *Café Central* and *Café de Paris* in the ville nouvelle. During the summer months, certain bars along the beach such as the *Macumba*, *Miami Beach* and *Coco Beach* are a much better bet.

Cinema The best cinema in town is the *Cinéma Dawliz* in the Istiraha complex beside the Hôtel Ziryab (see the Tangier map). The *salles* are air-conditioned and entry to the French-dubbed films is Dr20.

Things to Buy

Tangier is not the best place for souvenir hunting. The variety is quite wide, but the quality can be variable and prices are inflated for the hordes of unwary day-trippers who come here. As in all Moroccan towns, the best bargains are to be found in the medina, though be prepared to haggle hard.

Ensemble Artisanal, the government-backed arts and crafts centre on Rue de Belgique (see the Tangier map), makes a good first stop to get an idea of what crafts you might like to buy in the souqs, the quality to expect and, above all, the maximum prices to offer.

The Parfumerie Madini (☎ 934388), at 14 Rue Sebou in the medina, is run by the Madini family who have passed down the secrets of their trade – the distillation of essential oils – through 14 generations. The

---

Reddy-Made

One of the most common sights in the herb and spice souqs throughout Morocco is the large pyramids of a deep, olive green powder.

The crushed leaves of the henna plant are greatly valued for their health-giving properties and women use it for the care and beautification of their skin and hair. Mixed with egg, milk or the pulp of fruit, it is applied to the hair to lend it a vibrant reddish tone, much admired by Berber women. ■

FRANCES LINZEE GORDON

Colourful spices for sale,
Spice Souq, Marrakesh.

---

little shop attracts Muslims from all over the world and is definitely worth the olfactory experience.

Madini is said to be capable of reproducing perfectly any scent you care to give him.

To get there, walk east from the Grand Socco down Rue as-Siaghin, take the first left after passing Rue Touahine (the photo shop Shamalabo is on the corner) and follow the signs. Keep a look out for the wonderful spice shops in this part of the medina.

Getting There & Away

Air Royal Air Maroc (RAM; ☎ 935501; fax 932681) has an office on Place de France in the ville nouvelle. With the exception of one weekly flight to Al-Hoceima and to Fès (Wednesday), all RAM's internal flights from Tangier go via Casablanca. The one way fare to Casablanca is Dr557. To Marrakesh it's Dr852, Dr1067 to Agadir and Dr457 to Fès. The office is open from 9 am to noon and 3 to 6 pm.

RAM has connections to several European destinations, as do the following airlines:

Air France
    7 Rue du Mexique (☎ 936477)
British Airways
    Rue de la Liberté (☎ 935211)
GB Airways
    83 Rue de la Liberté (☎ 935877). GB Airways has flights to Gibraltar leaving at weekends. They go on to London's Heathrow airport. The one way fare is Dr950. They also have a same-day return fare for Dr1040.
Iberia
    35 Blvd Pasteur (☎ 936177/8/9). Iberia has two flights a week from Tangier to Madrid.
KLM
    7 Rue du Mexique (☎ 938926)
Lufthansa
    7 Rue du Mexique (☎ 931327)

Bus – CTM The CTM office is near the port entrance, near the Tanger Gare train station, although some buses pass through the main bus station (Gare Routière), on Place Jamia el-Arabia, a good half-hour walk south of the Grand Socco.

There are six departures for Casablanca from 11 am to midnight (Dr105; seven hours). They stop at Rabat (Dr78; 5½ hours) and Kenitra (Dr67). There are four buses a day to Fès (Dr82; six hours), the first at noon, the last at 9 pm; two to Meknès (Dr68) at 3 and 9 pm; and two to Marrakesh (Dr166) at 11 am and 4.30 pm. The latter also goes to Agadir (Dr233) and Tiznit (Dr260).

There are also buses every half hour to Tetouan (Dr15), and around 10 buses that stop in Larache (Dr24; about 2½ hours) and Asilah (Dr17, one hour) on their way to other destinations, but only if they're not already full.

At noon, a bus leaves for Chefchaouen (Dr27) and Ouezzane (Dr40).

Bus – Non-CTM The other companies run buses from the main bus station. They have departures for Casablanca, Rabat, Fès, Meknès, Tetouan, Larache and Asilah. Some put on 'deluxe' buses for a few extra dirham.

Fares vary, but tend to be lower than the CTM fares (in some cases as much as Dr25 lower, as with the fare to Casablanca).

Transports L'Étoile du Nord offers buses to Ketama (Dr52) that go on to Al-Hoceima (Dr77) and Nador (Dr109).

Train There are two train stations – Tanger Gare and Tanger Port. Almost all trains leave from the Tanger Gare station, although many seem to proceed to the Port station on arrival from elsewhere. All trains leaving from the port stop at Tanger Gare on the way out.

There's one direct train to Marrakesh which runs overnight and leaves from Tanger Port at 10.15 pm (about 10 hours).

It also stops in Rabat (around six hours) and Casablanca (about seven hours). Two other trains head for Casablanca and Rabat, departing at 8.40 am and 4.50 pm.

There are five daily trains to Fès (about five hours) via Meknès (about four hours). They depart at 6 and 8.40 am, and 2.20, 4.50 and 10.15 pm. Only the last of these starts at Tanger Port. The 6 and 8.40 am,

and 10.15 pm trains also go on to Taza (about eight hours) and Oujda (about 12 hours).

The 2nd class fares to Casablanca are Dr87 in the normal trains and Dr110 in the rapide. Other fares include Fès (Dr71/90), Rabat (Dr66.50/84), Marrakesh (Dr142.50/179.50) and Oujda (Dr151.50/191).

All trains from Tangier stop at Asilah (Dr10.50/13.50).

Taxi Grands taxis leave from a lot next to the main bus station. The main destinations are Tetouan (Dr25) and Asilah (Dr26). You may have to wait a while for Asilah-bound taxis to fill up. The bus is a better bet given that it's half the price.

Car The following are among the car rental agencies in Tangier:

Avis
    54 Blvd Pasteur (☎ 938960)
Budget
    7 Ave Prince Moulay Abdallah (☎ 937994)
Europcar
    87 Blvd Mohammed V (☎ 941938)
Goldcar
    Hôtel Solazur, Ave des FAR (☎ 940164, 946568)
Hertz
    36 Blvd Mohammed V (☎ 709227, 707366)

If your French is up to it, you can get information on the current state of the roads (important in winter when roads east towards Tetouan and Chefchaouen are often closed) from the *Services des Travaux Publiques* on ☎ 711717.

Reasonably secure parking is possible beside the Hôtel Ziryab for both residents and non-residents; it costs Dr2 per hour, Dr12 per day, Dr15 per night and Dr22 for 24 hours.

Boat If you're heading to Spain or Gibraltar by boat you can buy tickets from the company offices down at the hydrofoil dock (closed weekends), in the ferry terminal building (unreliable on weekends), or from virtually any travel agency around town.

The Voyage Wasteels agency by the port entrance is popular, but prices shouldn't vary much from agent to agent. If someone tries to add on extras, go elsewhere.

There are ferries to Algeciras, Málaga and Tarifa (Spain), Gibraltar and Sète (France). When the weather is calm, hydrofoils also make the run to Algeciras. For more details see the Getting There & Away chapter.

Getting Around
The Airport Tangier's tiny Boukhalef airport is 15km south-east of the town centre. From here you must arrange taxis into town, as there is no direct bus service.

Bus The local bus terminal is just up from the Grand Socco on Rue d'Angleterre.

Petit Taxi The price for a standard petit taxi journey around town is about Dr6. Remember that fares go up by 50% after 8 pm.

AROUND TANGIER
Cap Spartel
Fourteen kilometres west of Tangier lies Cap Spartel, the north-western extremity of Africa's Atlantic coast, marked by a lighthouse and fish restaurant. It's a dramatic drive and if you have your own transport, take Rue de Belgique, cross Place de Koweit and head west for La Montagne, an exclusive suburb of royal palaces and villas. The road beyond this to Cap Spartel is heavily wooded.

By public transport, the cheapest option is to take a *boughaz* minibus which runs throughout the day from the port entrance in Tangiers. The alternative is to charter a taxi (around Dr150) for the round trip, also from the port entrance.

If you're keen on **birds**, the area around Cap Spartel is a great place for watching flocks of birds migrating to Europe in late March to early April or returning to Africa from Europe in October.

Below Cap Spartel, **Robinson Plage** stretches off to the south. Four kilometres away are the **Grottes d'Hercule** (about

100m from the Robinson Hotel) which since the 1920s have been in turn quarried for millstones, worked by prostitutes and used as a venue for private parties by rich celebrities from Tangier.

There is usually a small entry fee for entering the chambers, but there is a good view overlooking the Atlantic from one of the windows. The caves have long been something of a tourist attraction and there are several rather overpriced cafes around the entrance to the grotto.

About 1km inland on a rough farm track are the remains of a tiny Roman settlement, **Cotta**. Like the more important town of Lixus further south, it was a centre for producing *garum* – a kind of fish-paste delicacy much prized by the Romans. Walk about 200m down the road (which continues 7km south-east to the main Tangier-Rabat highway) past the camp site on the left and you'll find a track with a barrier. Ignore the latter and proceed down the track – the scattered ruins are about 800m in front of you.

You can stay at the *Hôtel Robinson* (☎ 938765) near the caves or *Camping Robinson*. The former is pleasant enough, but pricey, with rooms with bathroom for Dr332 in the low season and quite a bit more in the high season. The camp site is a bit spartan, but OK, and costs Dr15 per person, Dr20 per tent and per car, and Dr10 for electricity. Guests can use the hotel showers for Dr10. Simple meals are available.

The *Restaurant Mirage* (☎ 333332) by the grotto is rather overpriced and charges around Dr80 for fish dishes, but there are good views across the sea from the restaurant's terrace. Alcohol is very expensive.

Fishing tackle can be hired from the shop in the Hôtel Robinson, and both golf and riding excursions can be organised to nearby clubs.

Cap Malabata & Ksar es-Seghir
The bay east of Tangier has recently seen the development of new tourist complexes, including a Club Med. The beaches are excellent and a much better choice than those

of Tangier. It's a good place to spend an afternoon, and there are some decent cafes and restaurants around if you fancy a bite of lunch.

At Cap Malabata, a curious Gothic folly, there are wonderful views of Tangier and the Straits. Bus No 15 comes here from the Grand Socco in Tangier.

Ksar es-Seghir, 37km east of Tangier, is a small fishing port still largely surrounded by high Portuguese walls and dominated by the remains of a castle. It's a picturesque place and its good, unspoilt beaches attract locals in the summer. The town makes a very pleasant day trip from Tangier. The No 15 bus also runs past here.

Road to Ceuta
If you have your own transport, the drive south from Ksar es-Seghir along the wild and hilly 'coast' road to Fnideq and Ceuta is an attractive alternative route if you are thinking of heading to Tetouan and Chefchaouen from Tangier, although it will add a couple of hours to the trip.

The road climbs up to **Jebel Musa**. Migrant birds in their thousands use the thermal currents from the Jebel Musa and Gibraltar peaks to reach a good height before embarking on the crossing of the straits between Africa and Europe. In spring or autumn, around 200 species can be spotted making the crossing.

Spanish Morocco

For hundreds of years, Spain has controlled the two North African enclaves of Ceuta and Melilla. It has also controlled five islets that have served as military bases and prisons: the three Jaafariya Islands off the Cap de l'Eau, about 25km west of Saidia; the Peñon de Alhucemas, just off the coast near Al-Hoceima; and the Peñon de Velez de la Gomera, some 50km west of the same town.

Moroccan independence in 1956 brought no change, as Spain claims a historical right to the enclaves. Curiously, it does not recognise any such historical British right to control Gibraltar. Morocco has made several half-hearted attempts to have the enclaves returned, however, Rabat is not keen to rock the boat as Spain is an increasingly important trading partner.

By the end of 1993, a process of granting Spain's regions a large degree of political autonomy was complete, except in the enclaves, which were still waiting to have their statutes approved.

In March 1995, a change to Spanish *Ley Organica* (Constitutional Law) gave Melilla limited self-government without legislative powers.

Moroccans fear that complete autonomy would mean Rabat could no longer negotiate the enclaves' future with Madrid, but would have to talk directly to the enclaves' political leaders, who will have no interest in restoring Moroccan rule.

Indeed, many of the enclaves' Muslim inhabitants, mostly of Rif Berber origin, would themselves regard such a transfer with mixed feelings.

Because of its distance from Ceuta, Melilla has been included in the East Coast section later in this chapter.

CEUTA (SEBTA)
Ceuta has a population of 75,000, about a third of which is made up of 'Spanish Muslims'. The island is devoted to the military (almost half of its 19 sq km is owned by the army), duty-free shopping and a lot of very shady cross-border commerce. Although Spanish citizens get huge tax breaks for residing in Ceuta (and Melilla), the enclave's uncertain future has led some to migrate to the Spanish mainland.

Ceuta has an Andalusian feel to it, but the presence of so many Muslims (clearly treated as second class citizens) gives it an other-wordly air. Just as it is odd to hear the bobbies of Gibraltar speaking English and Spanish, so it strikes you to hear the bus drivers of Ceuta speaking Spanish and Arabic.

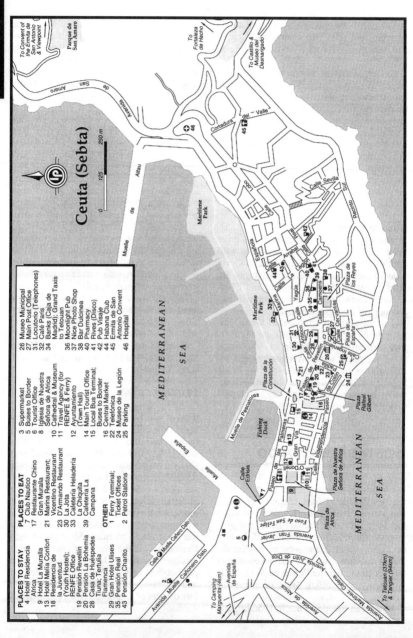

PLACES TO STAY
4 Hotel Residencia
   Africa
9 Hotel La Muralla
13 Hotel Meliá Confort
18 Residencia de
   la Juventud
   (Youth Hostel);
   RENFE Office
19 Pensión Revellín
20 Pensión La Bohemia
28 Casa de Huéspedes
   Tiuna; Tertulia
   Flamenca
29 Gran Hotel Ulises
35 Pensión Real
43 Pensión Charito

PLACES TO EAT
7 Club Náutico
17 Restaurante Chino
21 Gran Muralla
   Marina Restaurant;
   Vicentino Restaurant
23 D'Armando Restaurant
30 La Jota
33 Cafetería Heladería
   La Chiquita
39 Cafetería La
   Campana

OTHER
1 Ferry Terminal;
   Ticket Offices
2 Petrol Stations
3 Supermarket
5 Buses to Border
6 Tourist Office
8 Iglesia de Nuestra
   Señora de Africa
10 Cathedral & Museum
11 Travel Agency (for
   RENFE & Ferry)
12 Ayuntamiento
   (Town Hall)
14 Main Tourist Office
15 Local Bus Terminal;
   Buses to Border
16 Central Market
22 Telefónica
24 Museo de la Legión
25 Parking
26 Museo Municipal
27 Main Post Office
31 Locutorio (Telephones)
32 Café París
34 Banks (Caja de
   Madrid); Grand Taxis
   to Tetouan
36 Moonlight Pub
37 Nice Photo Shop
38 Bar Dulcinea
40 Pharmacy
41 Rives (Disco)
42 Pub Visaje
44 Habana Club
45 Ermita de San
   Antonio Convent
46 Hospital

Much maligned by guidebooks, and long used merely as a port of entry for Morocco, Ceuta is keen to detain many of the travellers planning to just pass through. In 1995, an extravagant new park was built on the sea front designed by the Spanish architect, César Manrique.

Certainly the town doesn't offer a great deal for the visitor, but it's a pleasant enough place to relax for a day or two, particularly if you're a bit travel-fatigued – it's like momentarily stepping back into Europe.

Ceuta is certainly not a cheap town by Moroccan standards. Many travellers may still prefer to catch an early ferry from Algerciras in Spain and push straight on from Ceuta to Tetouan or to Chefchaouen in the same day. If you're driving, stock up on duty-free petrol before leaving. The duty-free liquor is also worth a look before heading on to Morocco.

History

Ceuta's Arabic name, Sebta, stems from the Latin Septem. Two heroes of Greek mythology, Hercules and Ulysses, are both supposed to have passed through here, but more certainly it served as one of the Roman Empire's coastal bases.

The city later passed into the control of the Byzantine empire and, in 931, was taken by the Arab Umayyad rulers of Muslim Spain. In 1083 it fell to the Almoravids and remained under direct Moroccan control until 1309, when James II of Aragon took it. In 1415 Portugal grabbed Ceuta and, when Portugal and Spain united under one crown in 1580, it passed by default to Spain.

When the two countries split in 1640, Ceuta remained Spanish, as it has ever since.

Orientation & Information

Ceuta is on a peninsula jutting into the Mediterranean. Most of the hotels, restaurants and offices of interest are gathered around the narrow spit of land linking the peninsula to the mainland. The port and ferry terminal are a short walk to the west.

Tourist Offices There are two tourist offices: the main one is in the middle of town by the local bus stop; the other is not far from the ferry terminal (☎ 509275).

The latter was closed at the time of writing, but there are plans to open it again in the future. A brochure, small map and an out-of-date accommodation list are available. The town office is open Monday to Friday from 8 am to 3 pm.

Money There are plenty of banks along the main street, Paseo de Revellín, and its continuation, Calle Camoens. It's sometimes possible to buy Moroccan dirham, but there's no need as you can easily change money at the border (so long as you have cash).

Banks are open from 8 am to 2 pm. Outside business hours you can change money at the Hotel La Muralla. If you have a credit card, there are plenty of ATMs around.

If you are just passing through Ceuta, wait until you get to Morocco to change cash, as the rate of exchange is much better. Most of the banks in Ceuta also charge about 1% commission on travellers cheques, with a minimum of 650pta per transaction.

At the border you'll find a few informal moneychangers on the Spanish side and branches of the BMCE bank and Banque Populaire (which change cash only) on the Moroccan side.

The moneychangers don't offer good rates, and are only useful for changing leftover dirhams for which you have no exchange receipts.

Post & Communications The main post office (Correos y Telégrafos) is the big yellow building on Plaza de España, a square just off Calle Camoens, in the centre of town.

For letters it's open Monday to Friday from 9 am to 8 pm. You can send telegrams Monday to Friday from 8 am to 9 pm and on Saturday from 9 am to 7 pm.

Spanish public servants take the siesta seriously, so it may be hard to get anyone's attention from 2 to 4 pm.

There are plenty of blue public phones around. They accept coins and cards. A *locutorio*, from where you can book overseas calls, is on Calle Antioco. It's open from 10 am to 10 pm daily, but is closed from 2 to 5 pm.

Duty Free Ceuta is a duty-free zone, although nothing seems extravagantly cheap. If you are heading to mainland Spain, duty of 10% to 14% may be slapped on items worth more than 6840pta. Going to Morocco, the main attraction is petrol. Normal and diesel cost 55pta a litre, super 74pta and unleaded 70pta.

If you want to stock up on goodies, there are a couple of supermarkets on Avenida Muelle Cañonero Dato (Dumaya and Eurospar) which are worth a browse. A couple of service stations are on the same street.

Dangers & Annoyances Many people enter Morocco via Ceuta to avoid the touts who hang around in Tangier. Ceuta is not completely hustler-free, however – some travel all the way from Tetouan especially to meet the ferry debarkations.

Certain Spanish citizens are not beyond reproach either. Women travellers should expect to attract considerable attention from bored military conscripts. The author experienced more problems here than during her three months in Morocco put together!

The border crossing between Ceuta and Morocco is notoriously subject to long, bureaucratic delays. If you are driving, try to arrive at the frontier either early in the morning or late at night.

The Spaniards barely take any notice of you going out, but are more meticulous if you're going the other way.

On the Moroccan side you must collect, fill in and re-present a yellow card at the passport window and, if you have a car, a green one at the vehicle registration window (beware of touts who try to sell you these free cards). If you have a hired car in Morocco, you will be required to show proof of authorisation to take the vehicle out of the country.

If there's more than one of you travelling, you can save a lot of time by sending one person (preferably female!) ahead to collect the forms while the other queues. A smile, good humour and, even better, a greeting in Arabic at the window and at the barriers, will speed things up miraculously.

Museums
The **Museo de la Legión**, on Paseo de Colón, is perhaps the most intriguing of the few museums in Ceuta. It is dedicated to and run by the Spanish Legion, an army unit set up in 1920 as Spain's answer to the French Foreign Legion.

It is full of memorabilia of battles, commanders and the fallen brave, including a large collection of medals and some blood-stained flags which the guides will point out with relish. These guys are a little on the fanatical side, and the reverence with which Franco's bits and pieces are treated is a reminder of how strong the Right remains in certain quarters of Spain.

Most of the Legion's actions have been in North Africa – the Rif war of 1921-26 being the most disastrous campaign. One room is dedicated entirely to Africa, the other to Spain. The museum is open every day except Wednesday from 10 am to 2 pm (until 1 pm on Sunday; and on Saturday from 4 to 6 pm only). Entry is free.

The **Museo Municipal**, which contains a tiny room with local archaeological finds from Palaeolithic times on, is on the corner of Paseo del Revellín and Calle Ingenieros. It's open from Monday to Friday from 10 am to 2 pm and 5 to 8.30 pm. On Saturday, it's open only in the morning.

The **Museo de la Catedral** in the cathedral, has a small collection of ecclesiastical paraphernalia and paintings, but opens erratically on certain Saturday afternoons and Sundays. Check with the tourist office first.

The **Museo del Desnarigado** is a small military museum at the Castillo del Desnarigado on the south-eastern tip of the peninsula. It is open on weekends and public holidays only, from 10 am to 1 pm and 5 to 8 pm.

Maritime Park

The Maritime Park (Parque Marítimo del Mediterráneo) is a huge new complex on the sea front, complete with manufactured beach, pools and waterfalls, bridges, sculptures and even a mock-castle.

It was designed by the Catalonian architect, César Manrique, and was opened in May 1995. There is a casino in the park, several restaurants, children's playground, cafes and bars, and changing rooms for the pools. It is an agreeable, though rather expensive, place to while away an afternoon.

Entry costs 500pta per adult and 300pta per child (less in winter). The complex is open from 11 am to 8 pm in summer (from 10 am at weekends) and noon to 6 pm in winter. The swimming pools are open from May to September only.

To get to the park, take the road in front of the local bus station down to the sea front, then follow the signs.

Peninsula

If you have a couple of hours to spare, it's easy to walk around the peninsula (the No 4 bus goes part of the way), which is capped by Monte Hacho, said by some to be the southern Pillar of Hercules (Jebel Musa, west of Ceuta, is the other contender; Gibraltar is the northern pillar). From the **Convent of the Ermita de San Antonio** there is an excellent view towards Gibraltar.

The convent, originally built in the 17th century and reconstructed in the 1960s, is the venue for a large festival held annually on 13 June to mark Saint Anthony's Day.

Monte Hacho is crowned by the **Fortaleza de Hacho**, a fort first built by the Byzantines and added to since by the Moroccans, Portuguese and Spanish.

The **Castillo del Desnarigado** on the south-eastern end of the peninsula was built as a coastal battery in the 19th century, but there are remnants of earlier Spanish and Portuguese fortifications.

City Walls

The most impressive leftovers of the city walls and the navigable, walled moat of **Foso de San Felipe** date back to Almohad times, although they were largely reconstructed by the Spaniards at the end of the 17th century.

Places to Stay – bottom end

Camping Camping Marguerita (☎ 503840) is a good 4km west of the town centre. If you have your own transport, take Avenida de España then follow the signs. Camping costs around 600pta. There are hot showers and a restaurant, but no shop in the vicinity.

Hostel The Residencia de la Juventud is not an HI hostel and, at 1700pta a bed, is hardly cheap. It is nevertheless often full.

Tucked away on Plaza Rafael Gilbert, it opens in the early morning and late afternoon (no precise time). Go up the stairs off Paseo de Revellín by the Restaurante Chino Gran Muralla. The hostel is on your right as you enter the square. Ring the doorbell.

Hotels There is no shortage of fondas and casas de huéspedes, easily identifiable by the large blue-and-white 'F' or 'CH' on the entrances.

The cheapest of these is the small Pensión Charito (☎ 513982), on the 1st floor at 5 Calle Arrabal, about a 15 minute walk along the waterfront from the ferry terminal. The only indication that it is a guesthouse is the 'Chambres' sign, and the 'CH' sign on the wall. Basic singles and doubles cost 800pta and 1400pta respectively. There are no hot showers. Occasionally, it seems to close for no reason.

There are quite a few others in this category. If you're having trouble finding one, pick up a list from the tourist office.

Conveniently situated in the centre, the Pensión Revellín (☎ 516762) is on the 2nd floor at 2 Paseo de Revellín (opposite the Banco Popular Español). The doorway is in the middle of the busy shopping street and, again, can be identified by the 'CH' sign. Singles/doubles cost 1200/2200pta, and hot showers (300pta) are available in the morning. It's definitely seen better days, but the rooms are clean.

If you can afford a little more, the two best deals in town are the *Casa de Huéspedes Tiuna* at 3 Plaza Teniente Ruiz (☎ 517756) and the *Pensión La Bohemia* (☎ 510615) on the 1st floor at 16 Paseo de Revellín (look for the small sign in the shopping arcade). The Casa charges 2000/3000pta for good singles/doubles (add 1000pta in summer). It is undergoing renovation, so its rooms are newly furnished and very clean.

The Bohemia charges 2000/4000 officially, but you can usually negotiate a room for 1750/3500pta. It is even better value, but is often full, so reserve in advance. Both hotels have piping-hot showers (free) in shared bathrooms.

Should you be stuck, the *Pensión Real* (☎ 511449), at 1 Calle Camoens a few doors down from the Caja de Madrid bank, offers basic but very clean rooms (doubles only) for 3000pta in winter and 4000 in summer. There are hot showers.

Places to Stay – middle

A conveniently located place near the ferry terminal is the *Hotel Residencia Africa* (☎ 509467; fax 507527) at 9 Avenida Muelle Cañonero Dato.

In the low season it has singles and doubles for 4056pta and 7280pta respectively (breakfast 500pta), but in summer prices go up to 5720/8840pta. Credit cards are accepted.

The *Gran Hotel Ulises* (514540; fax 514546), at 5 Calle Camoens, charges about the same. Singles and doubles for 5200pta and 7280pta, plus 500pta for breakfast.

Places to Stay – top end

Just east of the square at 2 Calle Alcalde Sanchez Prados is the *Hotel Melía Confort* (☎ 511200; fax 511501), recently taken over by the Melía group.

Singles go for 8892pta to 11,388pta and doubles for 10,192pta to 13,832pta, depending on the season.

The premier establishment is the comfortable, but rather characterless, four-star *Hotel La Muralla* (☎ 514940; fax 514947) at 15 Plaza de Africa. It'll set you back 10,800/13,500pta for singles/doubles with private bath in the low season, and 12,000/15,000pta in the high season. It has a restaurant, bar, parking and swimming pool.

Places to Eat

There are a few cheap tapas and snack bars along Calle Real. Closer to the centre, the *Marina* and *Vicentino* restaurants have two/three course set menus for 1350/1800pta (including bread, fruit and wine/beer). The Vicentino also does pizza (700pta), and bocadillos or pulgas (rolls with one or two fillings in them) for 275pta to 350pta. The Marina has a good selection of tapas. They are in a side street connecting the Paseo de Revellín and Marina Española.

The restaurant *Club Nautico* (☎ 514440), on Calle Edrisis, is a simple but decent place overlooking the fishing port. It offers solid fish meals for about 1400pta, and a couple of vegetarian options.

The *Restaurante Chino Gran Muralla* at 4 Plaza de la Constitución, is the cheaper option of Ceuta's two Chinese restaurants. It's still rather pricey with fixed menus for around 1300pta per head. Mains start at 530pta.

Close to the Museo de la Legión at 25 Paseo Colón, is one of the most popular restaurants in town. *D'Armando* (☎ 514749) serves excellent pizza (from 575pta to 775pta), salads, meat and pasta dishes. If you arrive much after 9 pm, you'll probably have to queue to get in.

For a splurge, you could try the *Restaurant La Torre* in the Hotel La Muralla.

Cafes *Cafetería La Campana* at 15 Calle Camoens is probably the best place in town for breakfast (around 350pta for coffee, a juice and tostada (toast). It also does reasonably priced cakes, pastries, snacks and tapas. It's a very popular place with the locals and is open all day.

La Jota, on the corner of Calle Mendez Nuñez and Calle Antioco, is another good place for breakfast. They also have a great selection of tapas and (in summer) ice cream. It's open every day from 8 to 1 am.

The new *Cafetería Heladería La Chiquita* inside the maritime park, serves up good ice cream and delicious waffles on a pleasant terrace by the pool. They also do snacks such as hot dogs and hamburger, if you're craving for fast food, though prices are quite high.

Entertainment

Bars & Pubs The licensed *Café Paris* in the maritime park is an in-place for a drink (around 225pta). It's open every day from 4 pm to 4 am (6 am on weekends). Also at the park are special *espectáculos* (evenings of music or dance) put on during the summer; check with the tourist office for details.

The *Bar Dulcinea* on Calle Sargento Coriat is popular with an older crowd. A caña (small glass of beer) costs 200pta.

If you're into Spanish dancing, try the *Tertulia Flamenca* below the guesthouse Casa de Huéspedes Tiuna at 3 Plaza Teniente Ruiz. It's a flamenco club with a lively bar and there's usually dancing every Friday and Saturday. They generally let non-members in, particularly if you're staying at the guesthouse.

Nightclubs If you're after a late night, the disco *Rives* is Ceuta's most fashionable. It starts up around midnight and keeps going 'for as long as you can'. Entry and drinks cost 600pta. You'll find it off Calle Real (just past Pastelería Argentina at No 21), down some steps to the right.

Moonlight Pub on Calle Camoens has a kind of beer garden-cum-disco out the back. Other places you might try include the *Habana Club* on Calle Arabal or the *Pub Visaje*, which has a disco next door.

Getting There & Away

Morocco There are several buses (including the No 7) which run to the border. They leave every 15 minutes from Plaza de la Constitución, cost 75pta and takes 20 minutes. Look for the *Frontera del Tarajal* sign on the front of the bus.

If you arrive by ferry and want to head straight for the border, there is a bus stop just past the tourist booth and off to the right opposite the ramparts.

Just beyond the banks, on Calle Comoens, there are plenty of grands taxis to Tetouan. A seat costs Dr20. The whole trip from Ceuta to Tetouan should take no more than two hours and it often takes a good deal less.

Occasional buses run from various towns, such as Chefchaouen, to the Ceuta border, but it's a matter of luck whether any happen to be there when you arrive. You're best off taking a taxi and arranging further transport from Tetouan. If you set off early enough, you could conceivably make it to Fès or Meknès, and certainly to Chefchaouen, in the one day.

Mainland Spain The Estación Marítima (Ferry Terminal) is west of the town centre on Calle Muelle Cañonero Dato, and there are frequent ferry and jetfoil departures to Algeciras. See the Getting There & Away chapter for details.

You can purchase direct train tickets to European destinations at the RENFE office on Plaza Rafael Gilbert, or at one of the travel agencies dotted about town. The bus between the ferry terminal and the centre is marked 'Puerto-Centro'. Don't forget that Ceuta and Melilla keep Spanish not Moroccan time; a fact many travellers learn too late when trying to catch ferries to mainland Spain.

The Rif Mountains

TETOUAN

Established in 1912, and for more than 40 years the capital of the Spanish protectorate, Tetouan is unique for its mixed Hispanic-Moroccan look and feel.

The medina, a conglomeration of cheerfully whitewashed and tiled houses, shops and religious buildings set against the

RIF MOUNTAINS

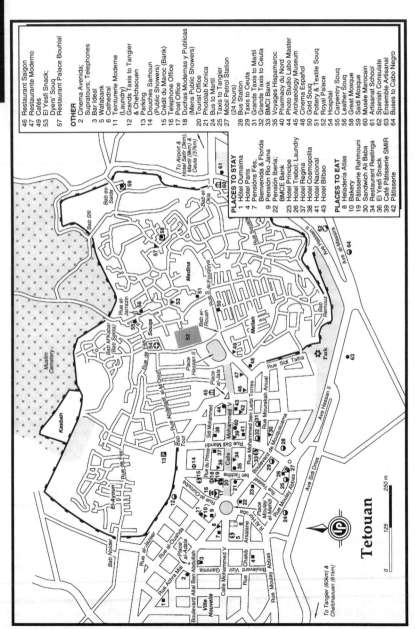

Tetouan

0   125   250 m

To Tangier (60km) &
Chefchaouen (61km)

OTHER
46 Restaurant Saigon
47 Restaurante Moderno
49 Cafés
53 El Yesfi Snack;
     Dyers' Souq
57 Restaurant Palace Bouhlal
2   Cinema Avenida;
     Supratours; Telephones
3   Bar Ideal
5   Wafabank
6   Cathedral
11 Teinturerie Moderne
     (Laundry)
12 Grands Taxis to Tangier
     & Chefchaouen
13 Parking
14 Douches Sarhoun
     (Public Showers)
15 Crédit du Maroc (Bank)
16 Telephone Office
17 Post Office
18 Duchas Modernas y Publicas
     (Mens Public Showers)
20 Tourist Office
21 Photolab Konica
24 Bus to Martil
25 Taxis to Tangier
27 Mobil Petrol Station
     (24 hours)
28 Bus Station
29 Taxis to Ceuta
31 Grands Taxis to Martil
32 Grands Taxis to Ceuta
33 BMCI Bank
35 Voyages Hispamaroc
40 Pharmacy du Nord
44 Photo Studio Labo Master
45 Archaeology Museum
48 Cinema Español
50 Gold Souq
51 Pottery & Textile Souq
52 Royal Palace
54 Hospital
55 Carpentry Souq
56 Leather Souq
58 Great Mosque
59 Saidi Mosque
60 Musée Marocain
61 Artisanat School
62 Spanish Consulate
63 Ensemble Artisanal
64 Buses to Cabo Negro

PLACES TO STAY
1   Hôtel Oumaima
4   Hôtel Paris
7   Pensions Fès,
     Bienvenida & Florida
9   Pension Rio Jana
22 Pension Iberia;
     BMCE Bank
23 Hôtel Principe
26 Hotel Trebol; Laundry
37 Hôtel Regina
38 Hotel Cosmopolita
41 Hotel Nacional
43 Hotel Bilbao

PLACES TO EAT
8   Heladeria Atlas
10 Bakery
19 Pâtisserie Rahmouni
30 Sandwich Ali Baba
34 Restaurant Restinga
36 El Yesfi Snack
39 Café Pâtisserie SMIR
42 Pâtisserie

To Airport &
Hotel Safir (3km),
Martil (9km) &
Ceuta (37km)

brooding Rif Mountains, shows off its Andalusian heritage. The Spaniards added the new part of town, where even now you can buy a bocadillo and more people speak Spanish than any other foreign language.

Unfortunately for both travellers and Tetouan's shopkeepers, the town is quite a painful introduction to Morocco (most visitors come from Ceuta).

Although not as bad as it once was, Tetouan is an active hive of touts, *faux guides* and hustlers. Wandering around the medina at night is a definite no-no – you can stumble across some decidedly inhospitable individuals.

Many visitors simply stop here to change buses and push on, which is a shame, because the medina is interesting and even the modern part of the city, although neglected, is worth a quick look.

History

Tetouan's ancient predecessor was Tamuda, a Mauretanian city founded in the 3rd century BC. Destroyed in the 1st century AD after a local revolt, the Romans built a fortified camp in its place, the unremarkable remnants of which are visible about 5km from the modern town.

In the 14th century, the Merenids created the town of Tetouan as a base from which to control rebellious Rif tribes, but the city was destroyed by Henry III of Castile in 1399.

Reoccupied in the 16th century by Muslim and Jewish refugees from Granada,

Tetouan prospered, and was the last of the Muslim kingdoms in Spain to fall to the Christians. Part of that prosperity was due to piracy, to which the Spanish put an end by blockading Tetouan's port at Martil. They succeeded in stopping the piracy, but legitimate trade suffered too.

Moulay Ismail built Tetouan's defensive walls in the 17th century, and the town's trade links with Spain improved and developed on and off until 1859, when Spanish forces occupied it for three years during a punitive campaign against Rif tribes aimed, it was said, at protecting Ceuta.

In 1913 the Spanish made it the capital of their protectorate, which they only abandoned in 1956 when Morocco regained independence.

Orientation & Information

The medina makes up about two-thirds of the city, while the modern town is tucked into the south-western corner. It is in the latter that you'll find the hotels, banks, most of the restaurants and cafes, bus station and taxi stands.

Many streets, called 'calles', still advertise the town's Spanish heritage, but this is changing as, alongside Arabic, French takes over as Morocco's semi-official second language.

Tourist Office The Délégation Régionale du Tourisme (☎ 964407, 967009) is at 30 Calle Mohammed V, just near the corner of Rue Youssef ben Tachfine. The staff here are helpful, but don't be talked into hiring a guide (unless, of course, you want one) as the medina is manageable on your own. If you get lost, it's never far to the walls or a gate.

The office is open from 8.30 am to noon and 2.30 to 6.30 pm Monday to Thursday. On Friday, it's open the same hours, but closes from 11.30 am to 3 pm.

Foreign Consulates Spain has a consulate in Tetouan at Avenida al-Massira (☎ 973941/2; fax 973946). It is open Monday to Friday from 9 am to noon.

Beware the Man on a Camel

Dream interpretation in Morocco forms an important part of life.

The snake in dreams is considered a herald of good fortune. A man on a camel augurs imminent death; a man on a mule, riches. To dream of a thief means good fortune and safety.

But dreams of corn, of grapes or of beans are omens of disaster. ■

Money There are plenty of banks along Calle Mohammed V. The most useful is the BMCE, which has a branch with ATMs on Place Moulay el-Mehdi, in the ville nouvelle.

Post & Communications The post office is also on Place Moulay el-Mehdi, and is open from 8.30 am to 12.15 pm and 2.30 to 6.45 pm. The telegram section is open from 7 am to 9 pm. The main telephone office is around the corner from the main entrance to the post office, on Rue al-Ouahda.

Film & Photography The Photo Studio Labo Master on Calle Mohammed V is probably the best place in town for film and developing. The Photolab Konica on Rue Youssef ben Tachfine is another good one.

Laundry There is a Pressing next door to Hotel Trebol. Another, the Teinturerie Moderne, is just off Rue al-Ouahda.

Medical Services & Emergencies There is a night pharmacy (☎ 966777) on Rue al-Ouahda. The police can be called on ☎ 19 and the fire brigade on ☎ 15.

Medina & Around

Place Hassan II, which links the medina to the ville nouvelle, is the heart of the city. It has traditionally served as the city's meeting place, and there are a couple of cafes where you can sit and watch the world go by. Heading west, Calle Mohammed V is a pedestrian zone right up to Place Moulay el-Mehdi, and is lined with shops, cafes, restaurants and the odd hotel.

The main entrance into the medina is Bab er-Rouah (Gate of the Winds), to the right of the former Spanish consulate. The medina is a bustling place, great for just wandering around. It is quite unlike the great medinas further south, as the Spaniards had a hand in some of the building in the 19th century. In any case, most of its inhabitants

HUGH FINLAY

Heavy traffic in the bustling Tetouan medina.

from the 16th century on were refugees from what had been Muslim Spain.

There are some 20 **mosques** within the medina, of which the Great and Saidi mosques stand out a little more than the others. As is usual in Morocco, non-Muslims are not welcome.

The north-eastern area of the medina, north of Bab el-Okla, was the upmarket end of town. Some of the fine houses built by the city's residents in the last century still stand here and several have been turned into carpet showrooms and extravagant tearooms. You'll probably stumble across them yourself, but there are plenty of touts around who will gladly take you to one, particularly the carpet shops.

Although the shopkeepers don't do a roaring tourist trade here, wood and leatherwork are two local artisanal specialities. It might be worth wandering up towards Bab M'Kabar (or Bab Sebta) for a look. You'll also come across other shops dedicated to the tourist trade, selling copper and brassware, babouches and a limited selection of souvenirs. If you're interested in Tetouan carpets, go first to the Artisanat school to get an idea of what to look for.

Musée Marocain Also known as the Museum of Moroccan Art, it is an interesting collection of traditional clothing, musical instruments, jewellery, carpets, arms and household implements. The museum is built in a bastion in the town wall, just south of Bab el-Okla – cannons are still in place in the garden.

Look out for the Jewish wedding robes beautifully embroidered with gold thread, and the very elaborate iron door knockers and key hole covers. Captions are in French and Arabic. Ask the guardian if you can get onto the terrace where there are good views of the Rif Mountains.

The museum is open Monday to Friday from 8.30 am to noon and 2.30 to 6 pm. The entry fee is Dr10.

Artisanat School Just opposite Bab el-Okla is the artisan school, where you can watch children at enormous wooden benches being taught the traditional crafts such as carpet-weaving, leatherwork, woodwork and the making of enamel zellij tiles.

The school has around 40 pupils; the youngest are 10 years old. After seven or eight years under a master craftsman, the students will sit the diploma in their chosen craft and eventually, if they are successful, open their own studio.

The 14 or so studios around the courtyard offer an excellent and fascinating opportunity to see Moroccan craftsmen at work, and to appreciate the intensity of labour and high skill still required for many of these ancient professions.

The pupils' work is on display (but not for sale) in a palatial exhibition room – which is worth a visit in itself. The school is open from 8.30 am to noon and 2.30 to 5.30 pm (closed weekends). Entry is Dr10.

Archaeology Museum The small archaeology museum just off Place al-Jala houses various artefacts from the Roman ruins of Lixus, including a good collection of Roman coins, brooches and even buttons, and a number of small but well executed mosaics.

There's also a little garden filled with old Iberian and Jewish gravestones, mosaics and some 16th century Arab stellae found in the Andalusian cemetery in Tetouan. The garden makes a pleasant and peaceful stop; it's open Monday to Thursday from 8.30 am to noon and 2.30 to 6.30 pm. On Friday it's open from 8.30 to 11.30 am and 3.30 to 6.30 pm. It's closed weekends.

Entry costs Dr10, but the enclosed gardens in front of the museum, where many of the larger exhibits have been set up, are free.

Ensemble Artisanal On Ave Hassan II, south of the town walls, is a large government-sponsored emporium of Moroccan arts and crafts. It is not a bad place to get an idea of the upper range of prices of Moroccan crafts without the pressure of souq sales tactics. It is open Monday to Friday from 9 am to 12.30 pm and 3.30 to 6.30 pm.

Language Courses The American Language Center has a branch at 1 Rue Maerakate Zelaka.

Places to Stay – bottom end

Camping The nearest camp site is by the beach at Martil, about 8km north-east of town (see the Around Tetouan section). There's also a site to the north, not far from Club Med, about halfway between Tetouan and the Ceuta border.

Hotels There are plenty of cheap, very basic pensions available in Tetouan, most of which charge from Dr50 for a single. Standards vary considerably, so have a good look around.

Some of the pensións could be straight out of Spain, with their wrought-iron balconies overlooking the street. Others are flophouses or straight-out brothels. The pensións *Fès, Bienvenida, Florida* and *Rio Jana* all fall into the latter two categories.

The *Hôtel Cosmopolita* (☎ 964821), at 5 Rue du Prince Sidi Mohammed, is one of the best deals in Tetouan, with simple but spotless singles/doubles for Dr35/70. The showers are shared and cold.

Also excellent value, and with probably the best views in town, is the *Pensión Iberia* (☎ 963679), on the 3rd floor above the BMCE at 5 Place Moulay el-Mehdi. Although there are only a few rooms, it has a homey atmosphere and is very clean. Room Nos 10, 11 and 12 get the views over the square, but the terrace is just as good if you're not in luck. Singles/doubles with shared bathroom are good value at Dr40/70. Hot showers are an extra Dr5.

The *Hotel Bilbao* (☎ 964114), at 7 Calle Mohammed V, has a lot of character, especially if you can get one of the front rooms. It costs Dr51 for a room (regardless of whether one or two people occupy it) with shared bathroom and cold showers.

The *Hotel Trebol* (☎ 962018), close to the bus station, is also good value, particularly if you can get a room with a private shower (cold). Clean singles/doubles with or without shower cost Dr50/70.

Another possibility is the *Hotel Príncipe* (☎ 962795) at 20 Rue Youssef ben Tachfine. Clean singles/doubles without shower are Dr60/74, with shower Dr70/100. There is hot water from 6.30 to 11 in the mornings and evenings.

Places to Stay – middle

The *Hotel Nacional* (☎ 963290), at 8 Rue Mohammed ben Larbi Torres, has singles/doubles without shower for Dr50/67 and with shower and toilet for Dr70/90. The rooms are a little gloomy, but are otherwise quite good.

Not quite so spotless, but with a bathroom in each room, is the *Hotel Regina* (☎ 962113) at 8 Rue Sidi Mandri. Singles/doubles cost Dr90/108 in the low season and Dr101/132 in the high season. There's hot water from 6 am to noon.

Better, but considerably more expensive, is the *Hotel Paris* (☎ 966750) at 11 Rue Chakib Arsalane. Singles/doubles with private hot shower and toilet are Dr166/198 in the low season and Dr176/207 in the high season.

The *Hotel Oumaima* (☎ 963473), at 10 Rue Achra Mai, has spotless though rather gloomy rooms for Dr161/188 in the low season and Dr168/197 in the high season (plus Dr5 tax per person). There are telephones in the rooms and little plastic chairs in the showers.

Places to Stay – top end

The four-star *Hotel Safir* (☎ 970144/77), on Ave Kennedy, is the only top-range hotel in Tetouan. It has 98 rooms, a swimming pool, tennis courts and a nightclub, but is 3km from the centre of town on the road to Ceuta. It charges Dr380/484 for singles/doubles in the low season and Dr410/530 during the high season.

Hammams

Given that so few of the cheaper hotels offer hot water, you might find that the public baths come in handy.

The public shower *Douches Modernas y Publicas* on Rue Youseff ben Tachfine (across the road from El Yesfi Snack) is for men only.

On the same street at No 3 is the *Douches Sarhoun*, open to both men and women. A shower at all of these places costs around Dr5.

Places to Eat

The best place to get a cheap, filling and nutritious meal is *El Yesfi Snack* on Rue Youseff ben Tachfine. They do great baguette sandwiches with various meats, potato salad, chips and salad for Dr15.

Another good, cheap snack place is *Sandwich Ali Baba* at 19 Rue Mourakah Anual. They do chicken (Dr20), salads (Dr8), harira (Dr3) and tajine (Dr15). It's popular with the locals so you'll have to grapple with the crowd at the front to get to the seating area in the back.

A place well known in town for serving excellent and good value fare is the *Restaurant Saigon* at 2 Rue Mohammed ben Larbi Torres. Despite its name, it serves Moroccan rather than Vietnamese dishes and you can get a big bowl of chunky harira soup for Dr4, followed by a huge serving of tasty couscous, brochettes or paella for around Dr25 (plus 10% tax). It's a friendly place and a good option for women travellers: there's seating in a tranquil gallery upstairs.

Close by, down a lane opposite the Cinema Español, is the *Restaurante Moderno*. It's a bit more down to earth, but the prices are much the same. It, too, is a popular place with the locals.

Also good is the *Restaurant Restinga*, which you get to through a small alley off Calle Mohammed V. You can eat inside or in a partly open courtyard. The staff are friendly and serve much the same fare at the Saigon; the big plus, however, is that they serve beer. A bottle of Amstel costs Dr13.

For a splurge, the *Restaurant Palace Bouhlal* in the medina is about the best place. They serve a decent four course set lunch (including couscous) for Dr72. It's attractively decorated in the traditional way, but the place is popular with groups who come for the 'spectacles' (musicians and

dancing). If you want to avoid them, come around 2 pm.

The restaurant is open every day from 10 am to 5 pm. To get there, look for the large iron gates in a tiny alley off the route around the Great Mosque. You'll probably need to ask a local for directions.

Patisseries & Ice Cream If you're keen on your cakies, you'll be spoilt for choice in Tetouan.

Generally considered the best in town and with an excellent selection of Moroccan and French goodies is the *Café Pâtisserie SMIR* at 17 Calle Mohammed V. There's a large seating area upstairs where you can have breakfast. It's also a good place for women travellers looking for a bit of peace and quiet. It's open every day from 6 am to 9.15 pm. If you're appreciative enough, Hassan, the unsmiling but charming manager, is quite likely to give you a little something *pour goûter* (to try).

The patisserie opposite Pâtisserie SMIR, though no rival for cakes, does a good cup of coffee and delicious freshly squeezed fruit juices; the almond juice is to die for.

The *Pâtisserie Rahmouni*, at 10 Youssef ben Tachfine, is the sister shop of the one in Tangier. The Rahmouni family has established a reputation for high quality, traditional (largely Moroccan) sweets. It's open every day from 6 am to 11 pm and makes a wonderful last stop in the evening.

If you're after ice cream, you could try the *Heladería Atlas* on Rue Achra Mai.

Entertainment

The bar in the Hôtel Safir is about the best bet for a drink, though it's not cheap. The alternative is the bar *Ideal*, – look for the Flag Spéciale sign off Rue Achra Mai, but it's the usual men-only (and prostitutes), spit-and-sawdust place.

Getting There & Away

Bus The bus station is at the junction of Rue Sidi Mandri and Rue Moulay Abbas.

CTM has five buses to Chefchaouen a day, starting at 5 am and finishing at 8 pm.

They cost Dr16.50 and take about an hour and a half. Buses for Tangier leave at 5.30 am and 4.15 pm (there's another at 4.45 pm from Fès, but sometimes it's already full). The trip takes an hour and costs Dr13.

There are buses for Casablanca via Rabat at 6.30 am and 10.30 pm. There's a *rapide* bus (stopping only at Rabat) at 11 pm. The trip takes about seven hours and costs Dr105. There are two buses to Fès at 11.30 am (Dr55) and at 1.45 pm (Dr63). Both stop in Ouezzane and take about five hours.

Three buses a day head for Al-Hoceima (about eight hours) at 5 am, 9 and 10 pm (Dr62.50). For Nador, there are two buses at 5 am and 7 pm. It costs Dr97.50 and takes around 11 hours.

If you can't get on a CTM bus, there are plenty of other private lines. These buses are often not in such great shape, but the competition means you have quite a few choices. There are regular departures for Chefchaouen and Tangier, and some of these companies cover destinations CTM doesn't. Transports AMA, for instance, goes to Oujda for Dr157. It also has a bus every three hours to Cabo Negro for Dr3.

A local bus to Martil (Dr3) leaves from Rue Moulay Abbas, not far from the bus station.

Train There is no train station at Tetouan, but the ONCF runs two Supratours buses to Tnine Sidi Lyamani, just south of Asilah, at 7.30 am and 4 pm to link up with trains to and from Tangier. The Supratours office is on Rue Achra Mai, near the Cinema Avenida.

Taxi Grands taxis for the Spanish enclave of Ceuta leave frequently from the corner of Rue Mourakah Anual and Rue Sidi Mandri, just up from the bus station. A seat costs Dr14 for the 20 minute trip to Fnideq on the Moroccan side. Although the border is open 24 hours a day, transport dries up from about 7 pm to 5 am.

On the Spanish side of the border, the No 7 public bus runs every half hour or so to the centre for 60pta.

Local grands taxis to the beach at Martil leave from further up Rue Mourakah Anual and cost Dr3.50.

Grands taxis to Chefchaouen leave frequently from a taxi rank on Rue al-Jazeer (Dr20). There are less frequent departures from the same rank for Tangier (Dr30).

Getting Around
Taxi It's unlikely you'll need one, but a petit taxi ride around town should not be more than about Dr6. If you need to get to or from the airport (also fairly unlikely), you'll pay Dr15 for the 4km run.

AROUND TETOUAN
Martil & Cabo Negro
About 8km north-east of Tetouan is the beach town of Martil. Once Tetouan's port and home to pirates, it's an altogether quieter place now, but has a reasonable beach and some pleasant waterfront cafes.

Further north up the coast is Cabo Negro (or Ras Aswad in Arabic), a headland jutting out into the Mediterranean clearly visible from Martil beach.

Places to Stay & Eat *Camping Martil* is the closest camp site to Tetouan, but it's not a well-maintained place. It costs Dr6 per person and car, and Dr10 for pitching a tent. Cold showers are available, and electricity costs an extra Dr3.

Camping Ch'bar, on the road from Martil up to Cabo Negro, is a little better for much the same price.

As Martil is so close to Tetouan, there is hardly any need to stay here, but you could try the *Charaf Pensión*. In summer they charge a fairly hefty Dr70/90/120/160 for a room with a bed and basin. Another place is the *Pensión Badia*, near the bus stop.

A more upmarket place is the *Hotel Estrella del Mar* (☎ 979276), which has modern rooms for Dr165/215/285 including breakfast. In summer, it's half-board only; doubles cost Dr350.

Getting There & Away The local bus to Tetouan leaves from a dirt patch near the camp site, but it'll stop for you on the main road back to Tetouan.

CHEFCHAOUEN

Also called Chaouen, Chechaouen and Xauen, this delightful town in the Rif Mountains is a favourite with travellers for obvious reasons: the air is cool and clear, the people are noticeably more relaxed than in Tangier or Tetouan, there's more kif than you can poke a stick at, and the town is small and manageable. All this makes it a great place to hang out for a few days.

Founded by Moulay Ali ben Rachid in 1471 as a base from which to attack the Portuguese in Ceuta, the town prospered and grew considerably with the arrival of Muslim refugees from Spain. It was these refugees who built the whitewashed houses with blue painted doors and window frames, tiny balconies, tiled roofs and patios (with a citrus tree planted in the centre) that give the town its distinctive Hispanic flavour. The obvious intention was to re-create at the base of Jebel al-Qala'a (1616m) that they had been forced to leave behind in Spain.

The town remained isolated, and almost xenophobic, until occupied by Spanish troops in 1920, and the inhabitants contin-

ued to speak a variant of medieval Castilian. In fact, Christians were forbidden entry to the town and only did so on pain of death. Two managed to do so in disguise: the French adventurer Charles Foucauld in 1883 and, five years later, the British wanderer and journalist Walter Harris (disguised as a Jew).

The Spanish were briefly thrown out of Chefchaouen by Abd el-Krim between 1924 and 1926 during the Riffian rebellion, but returned to stay until independence in 1956.

Despite being firmly on the tourist circuit, Chefchaouen (Chaouen means 'peaks', referring to the Rif heights around the town, and Chefchaouen 'look at the peaks') is remarkably easygoing, with only a few touts around.

The new bus station is a 20 minute hike south-west of the town centre, which is downhill when you leave, but a rather steep incline on arrival. The main street in the ville nouvelle is Avenida Hassan II. At Bab al-'Ain it swings south and follows the medina wall around towards Oued Laou.

Information

Tourist Office There is a Syndicat d'Initiative office in a lane just north of Plaza Mohammed V, but it has been closed for years. No one seems sure why or for how long. If you're after local information, you'd be best asking at some of the larger hotels such as the Hotel Rif which has a knowledgeable and helpful crew.

Money The BMCE and the Banque Populaire are both on Avenida Hassan II. You can change cash and travellers cheques and get cash advances on Visa and MasterCard at both. There are no ATMs.

Post & Communications The post office is on Avenida Hassan II, about 50m west of the Bab al-'Ain entrance to the medina. It's open from 8.30 am to 12.15 pm and 2.30 to 6.45 pm Monday to Saturday (on Friday it is closed for noon prayers from 11.30 am to 3 pm). You can make international phone calls from here, but there are no card phones.

Kif, *n.* **another name for marijuana. [C20: from Arabic *kayf*, pleasure]**

The smoking of kif (cannabis) is an ancient tradition in northern Morocco. In the Rif mountains around the Ketama region, its cultivation is tolerated until another crop can be found that will grow as successfully.

Discreet possession and use is also, in practice, tolerated. Travellers should never be tempted, however, to buy more than small quantities for personal use. Never travel in possession with it, avoid buying it in Tetouan and Tangier, and mistrust all dealers: many double as police informers. ∎

RIF MOUNTAINS

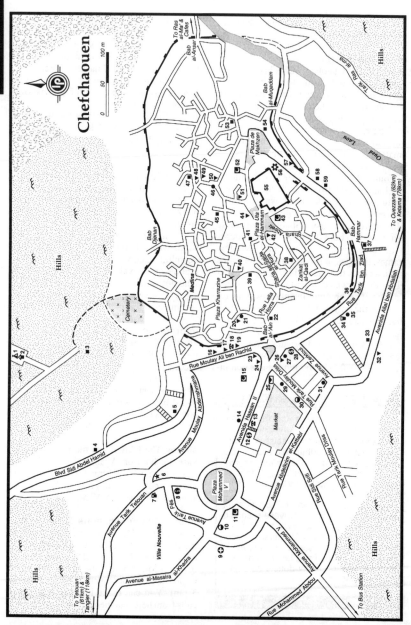

Chefchaouen

PLACES TO STAY
1 Camping Azilan
2 Youth Hostel
3 Hotel Asma
4 Residencia La Estrella
5 Auberge Granada
22 Hotel Bab el-Ain
33 Hotel Sevilla
36 Hotel Rif
37 Hotel Madrid
38 Pensión Mauritania
39 Hotel Andaluz
41 Pensión La Castellana & Hammam
45 Pensión Znika
47 Pensión Valencia
53 Pensión al-Hamra
54 Hotel Parador
58 Hotel Marrakesh
59 Hotel Salam

PLACES TO EAT
16 Restaurant Zouar
17 Restaurant Moulay Ali Berrachid
19 Sandwich Store
20 Restaurant Assada
23 Pâtisserie Diafa
24 Café & Terrace
26 Pâtisserie Magou
32 Café Ahlan
40 Restaurant El-Baraka
42 Cafes
44 Cafes
48 Restaurant Granada
49 Restaurant Chez Fouad
50 Restaurant Marbella
51 Restaurant Tissemlal
57 Restaurant Chefchaouen

OTHER
6 Police
7 Mobil Petrol Station
8 Tourist Office
9 Hospital
10 Grands Taxis North (Tetouan, Tangier etc)
11 Mosque
12 BMCE Bank
13 Telephones
14 Newsstand
15 Sidi Ali ben Rachid Mosque
18 Telephones
21 Food Store
25 Post Office
27 Librairie Al-Nahj
28 Banque Populaire
29 Pharmacy Chefchaouen
30 Grands Taxis South (Ouezzane, Ketama, Al Hoceima etc)
31 Kodak Shop
34 Bar Oum-Errabii
35 Voyage Wasteels (Travel Agency)
43 Great Mosque
46 Fountain
52 Mosque
55 Kasbah
56 Kasbah Garden

Newspapers & Bookshops There is a newsstand across the road from the BMCE bank on Avenida Hassan II, which normally has French newspapers.

The *Librairie Al-Nahj*, next door to the Pâtisserie Magou on Avenida Hassan II, has a small collection of books including the odd publication in French, English, Spanish and occasionally German.

Market
The market near Plaza Mohammed V is the centre of things on Monday and Thursday, when merchants come from all over the Rif to trade. The emphasis is on food and second-hand clothes, although there are sometimes a few interesting souvenirs.

Medina
The old medina is small, uncrowded and easy to find your way around in. For the most part, the houses and buildings are a blinding blue-white and, on the northern side especially, you'll find many with tiny ground-floor rooms crowded with weaving looms. These are a legacy of the days when silkworms were introduced by Andalusian refugees and weaving became the principal activity of families living here.

You can still hear the sound of looms in Chefchaouen, but most of the weaving done now is of wool, which is one of the biggest products of the area. The people working these looms are friendly and may well invite you in for tea and a chat.

There is also a fair smattering of tourist shops, particularly around Plaza Uta el-Hammam and Plaza de Makhzen – the focal points of the old city.

Plaza Uta el-Hammam & Kasbah The shady, cobbled Plaza Uta el-Hammam, with the kasbah along one side, is at its busiest in the early evening, when everyone starts to get out and about after the inactivity of the afternoon. It's a great time to sit in one of the cafes opposite the kasbah and relax. The atmosphere is sedate and almost medieval, except for the cars and, unfortunately, the tour buses.

The red-hued ruins of the 17th century kasbah dominate the square and its walls enclose a beautiful **garden**. The kasbah was built by Moulay Ismail to defend the town against unruly Berber tribes, as well as outsiders such as the Spaniards. For a time it was Abd el-Krim's headquarters, but, in one of those twists of history, he ended up being imprisoned here by the Spaniards.

To the right of the entrance to the kasbah are the cells – complete with neck chains at floor level – where Abd el-Krim was imprisoned in 1926. To the left is a small **museum** containing a collection of traditional arms, instruments, textiles and some old photos of the town. It also houses a small Andalusian studies centre. You can climb up a couple of storeys onto the roof for some good views of the town.

The kasbah is open from 9 am to 1 pm and 3 to 6.30 pm, and entry costs Dr10.

Great Mosque Next door to the kasbah is Chefchaouen's Great Mosque, built in the 15th century by the town's founder, Ali ben Rachid. Non-Muslims are not welcome.

Plaza de Makhzen The Plaza de Makhzen is the lesser of the two town squares; it has a large old gum tree in the centre. Instead of cafes, it has mostly tourist shops. However, on market days you still get people squatting under the tree selling bundles of mint and vegetables grown in the district.

If you take the lane heading north-east from the square, you'll eventually come out at Bab al-Ansar; after this comes the river, Oued Laou, with a couple of shady cafes on its banks. Off to the left is Ras al-Ma', the spring at the source of the Oued Laou's clear, fresh water. This is also where women come to do the washing while the men busy themselves drinking tea.

Hiking
The Rif Mountains, bordering the Moroccan coast for about 200km, are the highest peaks in the north. Though rarely reaching above 1800m, they are also the best watered and offer very attractive mountain scenery

for the hiker. Cedars dominate the hillsides, and forests of pine and holm oak the higher slopes.

The hills around Chefchaouen provide some good opportunities for exploring the region. If you want to do anything ambitious, you should consider engaging a guide. Mules can also be hired, though you will need to give at least a day's notice. Guides cost around Dr100 per day, mules Dr140 to Dr175, though prices vary and are open to negotiation (particularly outside the high season).

The Hotel Rif is a good source of information and can suggest and help you organise excursions. Ask for Younes who co-manages the hotel and is very helpful.

Hikes particularly recommended include the three day excursion from El-Kalaa to Beni Ahmed via Talasmetane National Park, Arhermane (a typical Riffian village), and the *Pont de Dieu*, (God's Bridge) a local landmark, shaped naturally in the rock by the elements.

A four day hike to Azilane will also take you past the Jebel Tazout peak, Lac d'Akchour and through good cedar and pine forests. Accommodation (tents or shelters) and meals are arranged with the locals in the hill villages.

Special Events
Chefchaouen occasionally hosts a modest festival of traditional Andalusian music in July or August.

Places to Stay – bottom end
Camping & Hostel Right up on the side of the hill behind the Hotel Asma is *Camping Azilan* (☎ 986979) and the *youth hostel* (☎ 986031). They are only really worth considering if you have your own vehicle, as it's quite a hike to get to them. It's a steep 30 minute walk by the road (follow the signs to the Hotel Asma), or a 15 minute scramble up the hill through the cemetery; you shouldn't attempt the latter on a Friday, as the locals don't take kindly to it.

Camping Azilan, although popular with shady foreigners 'holidaying' in caravans, is reasonably well maintained. It costs Dr5 per person and car (children under 12 go free), Dr15 for a caravan, Dr5 to pitch a tent, Dr5 for electricity, and Dr5 for a hot shower. It's open the whole year round.

The hostel is only open March to August and costs Dr5. It is extremely basic and best avoided.

The *Auberge Granada,* just down the hill from Camping Azilan, is worth avoiding.

Hotels If you've arrived from Tetouan, you'll find the standard of accommodation considerably better and cheaper here. There are plenty of places around, but in peak periods especially, they can all fill up fairly quickly. It's a good idea to make a reservation, or arrive here early.

In winter (when it can be very cold) the main problem is that few hotels have heating. Be sure to ask for lots of extra blankets.

The cheapest places are the pensions in the medina. For the most part they are OK, if a little gloomy and claustrophobic at times. It all depends on what you are offered, but some of them are very popular with budget travellers so, if you want a good room, get there early in the day.

The *Pensión La Castellana* (☎ 986295), just off the western end of Plaza Uta el-Hammam at 4 Sidi Ahmed el-Bouhali, is a popular travellers' hang-out, with beds for Dr25 a person and hot showers for Dr5 more. The rooms are small and not bad, but a lot more fun is the terrace where you can stay for just Dr5. The panoramic views are great. Guests also get free use of the kitchen.

Also with kitchen facilities and charging the same price for rooms, is the *Hotel Andaluz* (☎ 986034) on Rue Sidi Salem. Rooms on the upper floor are lighter and airier than those below. Hot showers are available for Dr5.

Another place travellers zero in on is the *Pensión Mauritania* (☎ 986184) at 15 Zankat Qadi Alami, which offers singles/ doubles for Dr25/50 and hot showers for Dr5. The rooms are a bit dark and cell-like, but the staff are friendly and there's an attractive, traditional lounge area.

Also good value is the pleasant *Pensión Znika* (☎ 986624) at 4 Rue Znika, north of the kasbah. Rooms are spotlessly clean, light and airy and cost Dr25 per person. Hot showers are available on the ground floor.

Up in the higher reaches of the medina, with good views and the chance of a breeze, is the *Pensión Valencia* (☎ 986088) at 1 Rue Hassan I. The doubles and triples are basic, with white-washed walls and moth-eaten sheets, but they're clean and good value at Dr25/45.

Don't come here for a single; they're glorified cupboards. The communal showers (hot) and toilets are well maintained.

To find the Valencia, take the lane off to the north from Plaza Uta el-Hammam; it twists back and forth up the hill, but after a few minutes you come to the Restaurant Granada. From there take the left fork and follow it around to the right.

North-east of Plaza de Makhzen at 39 Rue Ibn Askar is the *Pensión al-Hamra* (☎ 986362). It's a quiet place away from the bulk of the tourist trade and has clean, reasonable rooms decorated in the traditional style with arched doorways and wooden ceilings. The rooms cost Dr30/50 and a hot shower Dr5.

Outside the medina is the *Hotel Salam* (☎ 986239) on Rue Tarik Ibn Ziad. It's basic and a bit dusty, but at Dr30/60, a pretty good deal. It has hot water most of the time and its own terrace restaurant. Rooms No 12, 13 and 14 have good views over the valley to the south. If you're not in luck, then the terraces are just as good.

Places to Stay – middle

The *Hotel Sevilla* (☎ 987287), on Avenida Allal ben Abdallah, is one of the best deals in town. Simple but pleasantly decorated modern rooms with shower cost Dr41 per person, and breakfast just Dr8. The only problem seems to be with the hot water which is not forthcoming.

Just inside the Bab al-'Ain, on the right at 77 Rue Lalla Horra, is the *Hotel Bab El Ain* (☎ 986935), with seven rooms without bathroom for Dr40/70, and 20 rooms with bathroom for Dr50/80-100. It was reno-vated in 1996, and is a well furnished, spot-less place. The terrace is a peaceful spot with good views, and a nice place for break-fast (Dr15).

The *Hotel Marrakesh* (☎ 987113), virtu-ally next door to the Salam, has singles/doubles without private shower for Dr50/100 and with shower and toilet for Dr80/120. The rooms are on the small side, but modern, very clean and comfortable. Six rooms have views, as does the very pleas-ant terrace where you can spend the night, if you fancy, under the stars. It's also a great place to come for breakfast (Dr15) or for coffee (Dr5), even if you're not staying at the hotel.

A long-time favourite with travellers is the *Hotel Rif* (☎ 986982), just below the city walls Avenida Hassan II.

Singles/doubles without shower cost Dr50/80 and with hot shower cost Dr80/120 (Dr87/125 in the high season). Try to get a room with valley views. They also have a tea-room and a licensed restaurant. Credit cards are accepted.

Off to the north-west of town on the long and winding road to the Hotel Asma is the *Residencia La Estrella* (☎ 986526) at 130 Blvd Sidi Abdel Hamid. It's some way out, but the rooms, at Dr50/80 (Dr70/100 in the high season), are peaceful and quite com-fortable and the place has a homey atmos-phere. There are hot showers and a kitchen which guests are free to use. Groups may prefer an apartment. There are three to let for Dr400 per day (they accommodate up to ten people).

Another mid-range hotel on Avenida Hassan II is the *Hotel Madrid* (☎ 987496). The rooms are spotless and have heaters in winter. You pay Dr160/230/320, though outside the high season, you can negotiate this down by at least 30%.

Places to Stay – top end

The cheapest of the top-end hotels is the three-star *Hotel Asma* (☎ 986002), a huge concrete structure overlooking the town, above the cemetery. It has 94 reasonable rooms (if you don't mind the 70s style), a bar and a pricey restaurant. The rooms cost Dr255/312. The views are good, but you're some way away from town. Avoid having laundry done here, however, as the rates are extortionate.

The most expensive hotel in Chefchaouen is the four-star *Hotel Parador* (☎ 986324; fax 987033), on Place de Makhzen inside the medina. It costs Dr312 for singles and Dr397 for doubles. The hotel has its own bar, restaurant and swimming pool, and good views overlooking the valley.

Swimming Pools

The Hotel Parador has a pool, but it's not very large, and is only open from mid-May to the end of October. Non-residents can generally use it free of charge. The only other option is the small and not very well maintained pool at the Hotel Asma. They charge non-residents Dr50.

Hammams

The best hammam in Chefchaouen is the one next door to Pensión La Castellana, just off Plaza Uta al-Hammam. It's open to men from 6 am to noon and 7 to 11 pm, and to women from noon to 7 pm. It costs Dr5.

Places to Eat

Among the cafes on Plaza Uta el-Hammam are a number of small restaurants that serve good local food. You are looking at about Dr20 for a full meal with soft drink.

Near the Pensión Valencia, the *Restau-rant Granada* is run by a cheery character who cooks a variety of dishes at reasonable prices.

Look out for the village oven opposite the restaurant, where the local women bring enormous trays of doughy delicacies to be baked. The heavenly smells will follow you all over the medina.

A block back down is a simple but ex-cellent place, popular with the locals, the *Restaurant Chez Fouad*. Prices are roughly the same as in the Granada and the food is equally good. Also in the area is the *Restau-rant Marbella*, opposite the fountain on the tiny square, where it sometimes sets up a couple of tables.

The *Restaurant Assada*, just inside the Bab al-'Ain to the left, is a friendly little place with lots of character. It serves decent food at modest prices and during the summer sets up a small terrace outside. It's a favourite with the locals who come here to play board games.

Outside the medina, just up the hill from the Bab al-'Ain, are Chefchaouen's two best-value eateries: the *Restaurant Moulay Ali Berrachid* and the *Restaurant Zouar* – take your pick. They are simple but very good places and charge just Dr2 for harira soup, Dr3.50 for salads and Dr16 to Dr23 for main courses of meat or fish. The Zouar has a filling set menu for Dr25.

For something more upmarket, you could try the *Restaurant Chefchaouen* on the street leading up to Plaza de Makhzen. It's pleasantly designed in the traditional Andalusian style. A full meal (soup, tajine or couscous and fruit) for lunch or dinner costs Dr50.

Similar in price is the *Restaurant Tissemlal* at 22 Rue Targui, just up from Plaza Uta el-Hammam and off to the right. Like the Chefchaouen, this restaurant has been beautifully conceived, and has an upstairs balcony running the whole way around. The food *can* be very good, though it caters largely for the tour groups who stay here.

The restaurant *El-Baraka* (☎ 986988), just off Plaza Kharrazine, also serves traditional Moroccan fare and the place is done up in a pseudo-palace style.

In the past, the quality of food has been rather erratic, but Didi Fès, the owner, is keen to make amends. He, his wife and son offer a good value, four course set menu for Dr45. With enough notice (at least half a day), they will prepare for you any Moroccan dish you care to taste (including pastilla and mechoui).

If you're vegetarian, get Didi to run up the delicious couscous de Chefchaouen (vegetables only). The restaurant is open daily from noon to 2 pm and 7 to 11 pm.

For a splurge, you could try the restaurant at the Hotel Parador. They do a good three course *menu touristique* for Dr130, or for a real treat, the four course *menu gastronomique* (Dr145). A bottle of wine costs from Dr60.

Cafes Most of the cafes on Plaza Uta el-Hammam are little more than seedy smoking dens. They're worth a peek, however, and you can just about cut the air with a knife in some of them. Women will definitely not be made to feel welcome here.

Patisseries The *Pâtisserie Magou*, at 10 Avenida Hassan II, is the best cake shop in town. If you want to enjoy your sweet with a coffee, you can take it to the terrace across the road, a very pleasant spot with parasols and a fountain.

The terrace actually belongs to the *Pâtisserie Diafa* up the road on Rue Moulay Ali ben Rachid, but they don't seem to mind. It's a lovely place to start the day, and a full breakfast (coffee, orange juice and croissant or toast and jam) will cost you Dr11. Pâtisserie Diafa is open every day from 6.30 am to midnight and the Pâtisserie Magou, from 7 am to 10 pm.

Self-Catering Do what the locals do and seek out some fresh hobs dial makla (a type of bread) from the *food store* close to the Restaurant Assada. Next head for the *market stalls* on Plaza Kharrazine, where you can stock up on delicious local butter, ewe's cheese and fragrant mountain honey – ingredients for a heavenly picnic.

If you're keen on olives, this is a great place to indulge yourself. At the market, you'll find a whole range: the black ones are from the north of the country, the green are from the west, and the brown are from the Atlas.

Entertainment

In the centre of kif country, Chefchaouen is as laid-back a place as you could imagine. There's no cinema, no nightclub and only one bar, the *Bar Oum-Errabii*, on Avenida Hassan II, which closes at 7 pm!

A beer here will cost you Dr14 and is served with tapas. Some of the larger hotels also serve alcohol, including the *Hotel Parador*. The terrace, with its panoramic views, is a pleasant place for a beer or two (Dr15) while watching the sun go down.

Getting There & Away

Bus The bus station is about a 20 minute walk south-west of the town centre. CTM and all other buses leave from here, but be warned: many of them are through services from elsewhere and are often full on arrival. It's a very good idea to make a reservation (free) in advance. You'll have to go in person to the station and collect the ticket.

CTM has a bus to Casablanca (Dr89; seven hours) via Ouezzane (Dr16.50), Kenitra (Dr52; nearly four hours) and Rabat (Dr64; five hours) at 7 am. There are buses to Fès (Dr42; four hours) via Ouezzane at 1.15 and 3.15 pm.

The easiest place to get to is Tetouan (departures at noon, 3, 4 and 7.30 pm). The fare is Dr16.50 and the trip takes an hour and fifteen minutes. There is a bus at 3 pm to Tangier (Dr31; 2½ hours).

There are two buses a day to Nador (Dr84; 10½ hours), via Ketama (Dr20; two hours) and Al-Hoceima (Dr49; seven hours). They leave at 6.30 am and 8.30 pm.

Other companies are represented at three other windows. The timetables are generally posted up outside and are quite easy to follow. Fares are usually between 15% and 30% cheaper than the CTM prices depending on the length of the journey (though tickets to Fès cost the same).

Buses to Fès run at 8.45 and 9.30 am, to Casablanca (via Rabat and Kenitra) at 6 and 7.30 am, and to Ceuta (Dr22) at 6, 9.45 and 11 am and 12.30 pm. There are also buses to Meknès at 6 and 11 am, noon and 4 pm (Dr45; four hours).

For Tangier, there are at least nine buses a day, and at least 16 for Tetouan (the first bus for both destinations leaves at 6.45 am and the last at 6 pm). Seven buses a day make the journey to Ouezzane, with the first leaving at 6 am and the last at 4 pm.

Taxi There are two collection points for grands taxis. For journeys north, they depart from just beyond the Plaza Mohammed V. Destinations include Tetouan (Dr25) (the most common run) and Tangier (Dr80).

For trips south, the little square next to the Pharmacy Chefchaouen on Rue Tariq Moulay Driss is the departure point. A trip to Ouezzane costs Dr25, to Ceuta Dr35, to Rabat Dr75 and to Fès Dr100. It's best to arrive early for all trips. The longer journeys are expensive and infrequent; you might have to head for Ouezzane first (it's more of a transport hub) and pick up something from there.

OUEZZANE

Lying in the plains at the southern edge of the Rif, Ouezzane (pronounced 'wazane') is another town to which Andalusian refugees, many of them Jews, fled in the 15th century. Muslims regard it as a holy city, with a zawiyya dedicated to the memory of Moulay Abdallah ben Brahim, one of several contenders for supremacy in the chaotic Morocco of the early 18th century. His moussem is celebrated in late March.

Jews, too, make an annual pilgrimage (around May) to visit the tomb of Rabbi Amrane ben Diwan, an Andalusian 'miracle worker' who died in about 1780 and whose tomb lies 9km north-west of Ouezzane off the road to Rabat, in the Jewish cemetery of Azjem.

The bus and grand taxi station is a huge dirt patch to the north-west of the central Place de l'Indépendance. The small medina, the southern half of which forms the old Jewish quarter (the mellah), lies to the south-east. North of the medina are the **Moulay Abdallah Sherif Mosque** and the **Mosque of the Zawiyya** (which is also known as the Green Mosque).

If you enter the Bab ash-Shurfa, the main gate in the south-eastern corner of the square, you'll find yourself walking through the metalworkers' market and soon after across into the woodworkers' market.

There are a few places where rugs and the like can be bought, and you're bound to

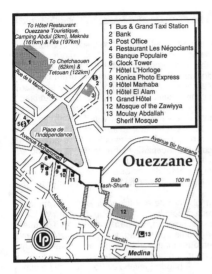

To Hôtel Restaurant
Ouezzane Touristique,
Camping Abdul (2km), Meknès
(161km) & Fès (197km)

To Chefchaouen
(62km) &
Tetouan (122km)

Rue de la Marche Verte

Place de
l'Indépendance

Avenue Mohammed V

Avenue Bir Inzarane

Ouezzane

Bab
ash-Shurfa

0   50   100 m

Abdallah

ben

Lamlih

Medina

1 Bus & Grand Taxi Station
2 Bank
3 Post Office
4 Restaurant Les Négociants
5 Banque Populaire
6 Clock Tower
7 Hôtel L'Horloge
8 Konica Photo Express
9 Hôtel Marhaba
10 Hôtel El Alam
11 Grand Hôtel
12 Mosque of the Zawiyya
13 Moulay Abdallah
   Sherif Mosque

meet one of the town's two or three guides pretty soon. With so few travellers coming through, you could well strike a good bargain for a carpet.

Information
There is a bank and post office on the main road leading north off Place de l'Indépendance.

Places to Stay & Eat
Of the three hotels on the southern end of Place de l'Indépendance, the *Hôtel El Alam* (☎ 907182) is probably the best bet. It has basic but clean rooms around an open courtyard on the top floor for Dr35/50/70. Room Nos 1 to 4 have wonderful views over the Place to the mountains, and No 6 bridges the medina.

The *Grand Hôtel* (☎ 907096) is a cavernous old place with rooms for Dr30, Dr60 and Dr90. Cheapest of all is the *Hôtel L'Horloge*, with rooms for Dr15/30/45. The rooms are a bit pokey, but some have views and it's not bad for the price. All the hotels have shared cold showers and toilets.

Around 2km from the centre on the road

to Fès, is the more expensive *Hôtel Restaurant Ouezzane Touristique* (☎ 907154) at Place Lalla Amina. The rooms have seen better days, but are clean and cost Dr80/94 for singles/doubles with shower (hot).

Camping Abdul is close to the hotel and charges Dr7 per person, Dr5 per caravan and Dr3 per car. Facilities are basic, but it's a pleasant, tranquil spot amid olive trees. It's open the whole year around. For information and directions, ask for Samir at the hotel.

There are a few cafes and snack stands on the square. For a good view of the northern plains, head through Bab ash-Shurfa and after a couple of hundred metres you'll come to the *Café Bellevue* on your right.

Getting There & Away
Bus There is one CTM bus a day to Casablanca (Dr72), to Rabat (Dr47) and to Fès (Dr33). There are frequent non-CTM buses from 7.30 am to 5.30 pm to Meknès (Dr30), and to Chefchaouen (Dr15). There are also buses to Tetouan (Dr30) and Tangier (Dr45).

Ouezzane is a bit of a crossroads and if you are losing hope of getting out of Chefchaouen to head south, it might be worth trying your luck here. There is no guarantee, and the earlier you start the better. There are virtually no buses after 5 pm.

Taxi Grands taxis run from the bus station to Chefchaouen (Dr25), Fès (Dr60) and Rabat (Dr60). They are not that frequent, but if you get there in the morning you should be able to pick up something, as most people just pass through Ouezzane.

KETAMA
Instead of heading south out of the Rif from Chefchaouen towards Ouezzane and on to the coast or the Middle Atlas, you could turn east instead and plunge into the heart of the Rif and on to a couple of minor Mediterranean resorts.

Buses head right across to Al-Hoceima and Nador via Ketama, and the ride along what is virtually the backbone of the Rif

Car Chases in Kif Country

If you've ever fantasised about car chases, or dreamt about donning disguises in a foreign land, then here's your chance. The 100km or so between Ketama and Chefchaouen in the heart of Kif country will take you along one of the most dramatic routes in Morocco.

Unfortunately, the scenery does not provide the only spectacle; equally dramatic and certainly more memorable is the sudden appearance of the kif dealers, who line the road almost the whole length of the journey. Generally the assault takes two forms. The motorised attack comprises a couple of large, dark Mercedes which loom up out of nowhere, tooting horns, flashing lights and sitting on your bumper. One vehicle will attempt to overtake you in order to sandwich you between it and the colluding car behind, so forcing you to pull over.

Strong-arm tactics are next on the agenda in an attempt to persuade you to buy huge quantities of kif on the spot, or at least to accept the 'hospitality' of a dealer at his house or kif farm. Alternatively, these shady characters might metamorphose into 'shepherds' attempting to hitch a lift back home, 'victims' of car breakdowns or even of accidents. The rule is never stop, not for anyone. And don't bother trying to enlist the help of the local police; they will just turn a blind eye.

A few useful precautions before setting off might include a quick vehicle check (particularly the tyres, and water and petrol levels – which should be full). Wind up all windows, lock all doors (including the boot of the car), fasten seat belts and prepare for take off. The best getaway tactic is to drive at some speed in the middle of the road, though this clearly carries considerable risk. The drive is not for the nervous or inexperienced. The roads are windy and narrow, and you are very likely to meet cars driving fast the other way.

The alternative is to try and pass off as a local. A hooded *jellaba* or (for the girls) a simple head scarf should do the trick, but don't dawdle or try the same ploy twice. After all is said and done, many travellers may prefer just to go on fantasising ... ∎

---

is among the most breathtaking trips to be experienced in Morocco.

You could stop in Ketama, but there is little reason to do so, and you could be inviting hassles. This is the centre of kif country and it will be assumed you've come to buy a load, which might have unpleasant consequences (see Dangers & Annoyances in the Facts for the Visitor chapter).

AL-HOCEIMA

Set on a bay at one of the rare points along the coast where the Rif drops away and makes a little room for beaches, Al-Hoceima is a relaxed and largely modern town. Founded in 1920 by a Spanish officer, General Sanjuro, it was known initially as Villa Sanjuro.

The fact that the Rif rebel Abd el-Krim had, from 1921 to 1926, one of his main bases only 10km away at Ajdir shows how tenuous was Spain's hold over this part of its protectorate after 1912.

Orientation

Al-Hoceima only began to grow in the wake of Moroccan independence, and now has about 62,000 inhabitants. The Spanish influence remains – all the streets seem to be 'calles' here – but all new construction is resolutely cheap North African style.

The main attraction is the couple of small beaches, making Al-Hoceima a pleasant stop while en route east or west through the Rif. In high summer it fills up with Moroccan holiday-makers and even some European charter tourists. What attracts the latter is hard to guess; although it is a pleasant enough place to rest up while touring the country, it's hardly one of the Mediterranean's great package resorts.

Most of the banks, better hotels and restaurants are on or near Calle Mohammed V, the main road in from Nador. Just east of this road, as you enter the town proper, is the old village centre, with the budget hotels and eateries, as well as all transport.

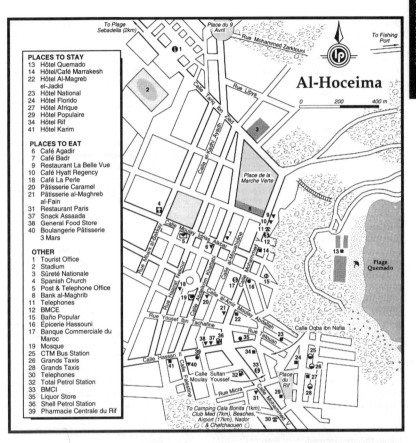

Al-Hoceima

PLACES TO STAY
13 Hôtel Quemado
14 Hôtel/Café Marrakesh
22 Hôtel Al-Magreb el-Jadid
23 Hôtel National
24 Hôtel Florido
27 Hôtel Afrique
29 Hôtel Populaire
34 Hôtel Rif
41 Hôtel Karim

PLACES TO EAT
6 Café Agadir
7 Café Badr
9 Restaurant La Belle Vue
10 Café Hyatt Regency
18 Café La Perle
20 Pâtisserie Caramel
21 Pâtisserie al-Maghreb al-Fain
31 Restaurant Paris
37 Snack Assaada
38 General Food Store
40 Boulangerie Pâtisserie 3 Mars

OTHER
1 Tourist Office
2 Stadium
3 Sûreté Nationale
4 Spanish Church
5 Post & Telephone Office
8 Bank al-Maghrib
11 Telephones
12 BMCE
15 Baño Popular
16 Épicerie Hassouni
17 Banque Commerciale du Maroc
19 Mosque
25 CTM Bus Station
26 Grands Taxis
28 Grands Taxis
30 Telephones
32 Total Petrol Station
33 BMCI
35 Liquor Store
36 Shell Petrol Station
39 Pharmacie Centrale du Rif

Apart from the town beach, Plage Quemado, there are a couple of quieter ones just out of town on the Nador road. From some vantage points you can see the Spanish-controlled islet of Peñon de Alhucemas off the coast. It may look pretty, but it has served mainly as a prison and military base.

Information

Tourist Office The Délégation Régionale du Tourisme (☎ 982830), on Calle Tariq ibn Ziad, is open Monday to Thursday from 8.30 am to noon and 2.30 to 6.30 pm, and Friday from 8.30 to 11 am and 3 to 6.30 pm. They have some brochures, but little else.

Money There are plenty of banks along Calle Mohammed V where you can change cash and travellers cheques. You can get cash advances on Visa and MasterCard at the BMCE and BMCI.

Post & Communications The post and telephone office is on Calle Moulay Idriss Alkbar, a few blocks west of Calle Mohammed V.

Beaches

The town beach, Plage Quemado, is OK, but with the large ugly hotel of the same name forming the main backdrop, it is a little off-putting. Better are the small beaches at **Cala Bonita** (where there is a camp site), before the southern entry into town, and **Plage Sebadella**, about a 2km walk to the north-west.

Plage Espalmadero, 4km from the centre of town along the road to Nador, and **Plage Asfiha**, 5km further on, are usually fairly quiet, especially in late spring. Local buses to Ajdir run by the turn-offs for both. Neither will win beautiful beach prizes, but they're OK.

Places to Stay – bottom end

Camping About a kilometre from the town centre on the road to Ajdir, is the *Camping Cala Bonita*. Although it's right on what is probably the prettiest little beach in Al-Hoceima (the name is Spanish for 'beautiful cove'), there is rather an expensive flat fee (Dr45) for a place which includes tent space, car and amenities.

The *Club Med* (☎ 802013; fax 802014), around 7km out of town, past Ajdir, down a track off the Ketama-Nador road, is an altogether grander affair, with all the usual facilities. It's a popular place, and you'll need to book at least a week in advance. It costs a little more than the Camping Cala Bonita.

Hotels There is no shortage of budget hotels in the area immediately around Place du Rif, but things can still get crowded in midsummer. The *Hôtel Populaire* (☎ 985750) has basic but OK rooms for Dr35/40/60.

Away from the chaos of the square, a better choice is the *Hôtel Rif* (☎ 982268) at 13 Calle Sultan Moulay Youssef. Simple, clean rooms with a washbasin cost Dr30, Dr45 and Dr60. There are cold communal showers.

On the square itself is a curious Art Deco building, the *Hotel Florido* (☎ 982235). At the time of writing it was closed for renovation and applying for a two-star rating, so prices may go up.

Perhaps the best place of all is the nearby *Hôtel Afrique* (☎ 983065). Rooms with sink are very clean and bright and cost Dr30/40/55 (add Dr5 to Dr6 during the high season). Each floor has its own hot, communal shower (Dr6).

Places to Stay – middle

About the cheapest of the mid-range hotels and good value is the *Hôtel Marrakesh* (☎ 983025) on Calle Mohammed V. Rooms with comfortable beds, sea glimpses and en suite bathroom (24 hour hot water) cost Dr114/135.

For the same price, the *Hôtel Karim* (☎ 982184; fax 984340), at 27 Calle Hassan II, has rooms with simple en suite bathrooms. It's clean, but has definitely seen better days.

More expensive, but closer to public transport, is the *Hôtel National* (☎ 982681) at 23 Rue Tetouan. Its rooms cost Dr157/187/243 and are pleasant enough.

Not spectacularly better than the others, but considerably pricier, is the *Hôtel Al-Maghreb el-Jadid* (☎ 982505; fax 982504) at 56 Calle Mohammed V. It has self-contained rooms for Dr200/245 in the low season and Dr230/281 in the high season.

If you want to pay that much, you could head for the *Hotel Quemado* (☎ 983315; fax 983314) on the beach, which has 102 rooms and some attractive bungalows with good sea views.

Hammams

The Baño Popular, off Calle Mohammed V, is open to women from 10 am to 5.30 pm, and to men from 6 to 9.30 am and 5.30 to 10.30 pm. It costs Dr5.

Places to Eat

Restaurants There are numerous little restaurants serving up the usual fare for about Dr25 to Dr30 on or near Place du Rif. One of the cheapest is *Snack Assaada* on Calle Hassan II, which serves various meats by weight. A filling meal with salad, chips and a soft drink will cost about Dr25.

One of the best restaurants in town is the

modest but attractive *Restaurant Paris* at 21 Calle Mohammed V. You'll get a terrific welcome from Ahmed, the ebullient owner who also does the cooking. Main courses cost around Dr30 and there are good value set menus for Dr47/58 with a choice of chicken, beef or fish. If you give him some notice, he'll run you up a veggie option too. For pud, ask for Ahmed's speciality, the delicious, lemony crème caramel.

The *Restaurant La Belle Vue*, also on Calle Mohammed V, is attractively decorated and justifies its name with a good view. You could also try one of the better hotels; the *Hôtel Al-Magreb el-Jadid* serves a set menu for Dr75 and there is a bar.

Patisseries & Self-Catering The *Pâtisserie al-Maghreb al-Fain*, on Calle Mohammed V, is OK for breakfast (Dr12) and is open from 5 am to 10 pm. The *Café La Perle* has an agreeable terrace at the roundabout off Calle Abdelkrim Khattabi. They also do breakfast, and have good fruit juices for Dr3.50.

The *Pâtisserie Caramel*, on Calle al-Amir Moulay Abdallah, does a good selection of Moroccan goodies. A great place to stock up for a picnic on the beach is the *Boulangerie Pâtisserie 3 Mars* at 3 Calle Falestine. It has a mouth-watering selection of cakes and savouries, and delicious crusty bread (including wholemeal). It is open from 6 am to 11 pm every day.

There is a general food store, *Épicerie Hassouni*, on Calle Mohammed V, and a *liquor store* around the corner from the Hôtel Rif on Calle Hassan II.

Getting There & Away
Air Royal Air Maroc (RAM) has one or two weekly flights from Al-Hoceima to Tangier, Tetouan and Casablanca. There is also a weekly flight to Amsterdam (I wonder why?). In summer the airport, 17km to the south-east, plays host to charter flights, mainly from France.

Bus All the bus companies have their offices on or near Place du Rif. CTM has buses to Nador at 5.30 am and 12.30 pm (Dr35.50; 3½ hours); the 5.30 pm bus goes on to Oujda (Dr59).

Its services to Tetouan (Dr62.50; seven hours) via Chefchaouen (Dr50; about 5½ hours) leave at 1, 9 (summer only) and 10 pm. At 8 pm, a bus leaves for Casablanca (Dr157; 10 hours) via Fès (Dr79; five hours), Meknès (Dr95; 5½ hours) and Rabat (Dr132; 6½ hours).

There are three or four other small companies. As always, it's best to turn up in the morning and check timetables.

Nador is the most frequently served destination, with at least five departures a day (the first at 6 am, the last at 9 pm) for around Dr30.

There are three buses to Fès (Dr63.50) at 7 and 10 am and 10 pm, and seven to Ketama (Dr25) and Taounate (Dr46). They travel along the Route de l'Unité highway (a spectacular drive over the Rif).

There is one bus a day for Oujda at 9 am (Dr55; about six hours). Alternatively, go to Nador and pick up further transport there.

Buses to Tetouan (Dr62) via Chefchaouen leave at 7, 8 and 11.30 am and 7 pm. Another goes through to Tangier at 8 am (Dr74; about 8½ hours). Buses to Targuist (1¼ hours) leave four times a day and cost Dr16.50. There are two buses to Rabat at 12 and 8.30 pm (Dr100 to Dr120).

Taxi The best time to try to get a grand taxi is the morning, but you may find yourself hanging about for one to fill up. They line up a block east of the Place du Rif. The fare to Taza and Nador is Dr55.

The East Coast

MELILLA
With about 70,000 inhabitants, a third of whom are Muslims of Rif Berber origin, Melilla (pronounced Melee-ya) is marginally smaller than its Spanish sister enclave to the west, Ceuta.

The presence of 10,000 troops provides a boost to the local economy, but Melilla lives mainly on contraband trade. Anything up to 80% of the goods that arrive in the enclave end up not only in Morocco, but countries throughout north-west Africa.

Some people within Melilla's business community worry that a free-trade agreement between the EU and Morocco could kill this business, leaving Melilla in deep trouble – it already has an unemployment rate higher than any city in the EU.

Relations between the Muslim population, worst hit by the unemployment, and the rest of the enclave's inhabitants are strained. The ill-feeling bubbled over into violent protests in the 1980s when new citizenship laws threatened to leave in limbo many Muslims without proper papers.

Spaniards in the enclave also worry that the Muslims will one day push for the enclave to be handed over to Morocco. Most of the Muslims say this is rubbish, that as Rif Berbers they owe no allegiance to the Moroccan king and that in any case they would prefer to be under Spanish rule. Other Spaniards fear that, with their big families, the Muslims will eventually outnumber the Christians and gain power. Melilla, like Ceuta, lives under a cloud of uncertainty.

The city also leaves the visitor with equally ambiguous impressions. Uncompromisingly Spanish in look and feel, and not a little run down, the presence of so many Muslims (some of them Moroccans who have slipped across the border), most of whom are underemployed or jobless, lends it an atmosphere quite unlike that of any city on the peninsula.

History

The port and peninsula of Melilla have been inhabited for more than 2000 years. The Phoenicians and Romans both counted it among their network of Mediterranean coastal bases – it was then known as Russadir. After the departure of the Romans, the city fell into obscurity until it was captured by Abd ar-Rahman III of Cordova.

In 1496 it was taken by a Spanish raiding party and has remained in Spain's hands ever since, although Abd el-Krim's rebels came close to taking the town during the Rif war in 1921. It was from here that Franco launched the Spanish Civil War in 1936.

Its excellently preserved medieval fortress gives the city a lingering fascination. Right up until the end of the 19th century virtually all of Melilla was contained within these massive defensive walls.

This old part of town has a distinctly Castilian flavour, with its narrow, twisting streets, squares, gates and drawbridges, and the area has been declared a national monument.

Orientation

Plaza de España is the heart of the new part of town, which was largely designed by Don Enrique Nieto, a contemporary of Gaudí. Most of the hotels are in the grid of streets leading north-west of the plaza. In the same area you'll find the banks and most of the restaurants and bars.

East of Melilla la Vieja (the old town) lies the ferry terminal; the frontier with Morocco is a 20 minute bus ride south, over the trickle of effluent inappropriately known as the Río de Oro.

Information

Tourist Office This office (☎ 684013) is close to Plaza de Toros (the bullring). It's well stocked and the staff are helpful. Opening hours are roughly from 9 am to 2 pm Monday to Friday, and to noon on Saturday.

Money You'll find several banks along or near Avenida de Juan Carlos I Rey, starting with the Central Hispano on Plaza de España, which is as good as any.

They buy and sell dirham at a slightly inferior rate to that found in Morocco, but as good as anything you'll get from the Moroccan dealers in the streets. The latter hang about Plaza de España and deal in Algerian dinar as well. Don't believe their stories about the atrocious bank rates – check them first.

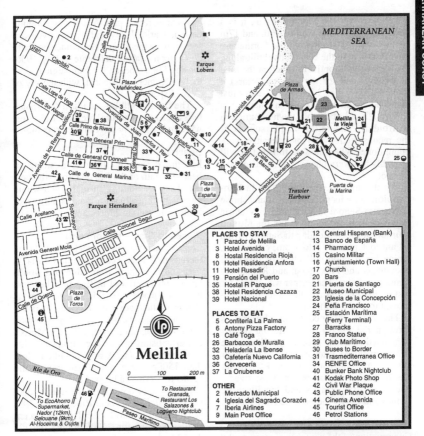

PLACES TO STAY
1   Parador de Melilla
3   Hotel Avenida
8   Hostal Residencia Rioja
10 Hotel Residencia Anfora
11 Hotel Rusadir
19 Pensión del Puerto
35 Hostal R Parque
38 Hotel Residencia Cazaza
39 Hotel Nacional

PLACES TO EAT
5   Confitería La Palma
6   Antony Pizza Factory
18 Café Toga
26 Barbacoa de Muralla
32 Heladería La Ibense
33 Cafetería Nuevo California
36 Cervecería
37 La Onubense

OTHER
2   Mercado Municipal
4   Iglesia del Sagrado Corazón
7   Iberia Airlines
9   Main Post Office

12 Central Hispano (Bank)
13 Banco de España
14 Pharmacy
15 Casino Militar
16 Ayuntamiento (Town Hall)
17 Church
20 Bars
21 Puerta de Santiago
22 Museo Municipal
23 Iglesia de la Concepción
24 Peña Francisco
25 Estación Marítima
    (Ferry Terminal)
27 Barracks
28 Franco Statue
29 Club Marítimo
30 Buses to Border
31 Trasmediterranea Office
34 RENFE Office
40 Bunker Bank Nightclub
41 Kodak Photo Shop
42 Civil War Plaque
43 Public Phone Office
44 Cinema Avenida
45 Tourist Office
46 Petrol Stations

Post & Communications The post office (Correos y Telégrafos), on Calle Pablo Vallescá, is open Monday to Friday from 9 am to 8 pm for ordinary mail, and a little longer for telegrams. It is also open on Saturday morning.

The main public telephone office is on Calle Sotomayor, on the western side of the Parque Hernández (open daily from 9 am to 2 pm and 6 to 9 pm).

There are plenty of public phones that accept coins and cards; you can also make reverse-charge calls.

Petrol & Supplies Remember that Melilla is a duty-free zone. If you are driving it is worth waiting to fill up here, as the petrol is about a third cheaper than in Morocco or Spain. The EcoAhorro supermarket, on the road to the border post of Beni-Enzar, is open from 10 am to 10 pm if you need supplies before heading south.

Melilla la Vieja
Under normal conditions, Old Melilla (or, according to some guides, the Medina Sidonia) is well worth exploring.

Perched over the Mediterranean, it is a good example of the kind of 16th and 17th century fortress stronghold the Portuguese (and in this case the Spaniards) built along the Moroccan littoral. However, at the time of writing (and for the last four years) it looked like the Moroccans had just launched an attack to retake the place.

Virtually all of the old town is buried in scaffolding, and rattles to the sounds of the reconstruction and maintenance work being done. When they've finished, it will probably be a very pleasant, if sanitised, little spot.

Worth a look are the **Iglesia de la Concepción**, with its gilded reredos and shrine to Nuestra Señora la Virgen de la Victoria (the patroness of the city), and the **Museo Municipal** (open Monday to Saturday from 10 am to 1 pm and 5 to 7 pm; entry free), which has a good collection of historical documents and Phoenician and Roman ceramics and coins. The former was closed for restoration in 1994 and the latter had been moved to a new building.

The main entrance to the fortress is through the Puerta de la Marina on the Avenida de General Macías (you'll also see a monument to Franco here). After your visit, you could leave by the **Puerta de Santiago**, which takes you west over a couple of drawbridges and the Plaza de Armas and out by the Foso de Hornabeque.

New Town

Construction of the new part of town, to the west of the fortress, was begun at the end of the 19th century.

It was laid out by Don Enrique Nieto who, following Gaudí's lead, is considered by some to have made Melilla Spain's 'second modernist city' after Barcelona; this may be rather on the generous side.

Unfortunately the general decay of the city, and the proliferation of shiny duty-free shopfronts, have not helped the case. Nevertheless, the contrast with Moroccan towns like Nador, next door, never fails to impress travellers.

A walk around can be instructive in the city's more recent past. A statue on Avenida de Juan Carlos I Rey and a plaque you can see opposite the Parque Hernández on Calle de General Marina celebrate 7 July 1936, the day Franco began the campaign against the government in Madrid, with the cry of 'Viva España'.

The **Casino Militar**, on Plaza de España, has a Centro Cultural de los Ejércitos, which occasionally stages little art exhibits.

Beaches

For the desperate, there is a string of beaches south of the Río de Oro to the border. They are nothing special – you would be better off heading for mainland Spain or continuing on into Morocco.

Places to Stay – bottom end

Contrary to what some guidebooks tell you, there is no longer a camp site in Melilla.

If you're coming from Morocco, you'll know you've arrived in Europe when you look for a place to stay. Hotels at all levels charge a little more in the high season (summer and Easter week). The cheapest option is the *Pensión del Puerto*, a largely Moroccan establishment just back from Avenida de General Macías. A bed should cost less than 1500pta, but it's a little rough and seems to serve as a brothel too.

Easily the best place for the tight budget is the *Hostal Residencia Rioja* (☎ 682709) at 10 Calle Ejército Español. It has decent singles/doubles for 2400/3400pta outside the high season, with communal hot showers. It's a fairly basic place, but is clean and well run. It's often full, so make a reservation.

Another decent alternative, but a little more expensive, is the *Hostal R Parque* (☎ 682143) which fronts the Parque Hernández. It's often full and costs 3000/5275pta for recently renovated singles/doubles with telephone and bathroom.

Not such good value, but acceptable, is the *Hostal Residencia Cazaza* (☎ 684648) at 6 Calle Primo de Rivera. Shabby, but reasonably clean, singles/doubles with bath cost 2750/4620.

A block west is the recently refurbished *Hotel Nacional* (☎ 684540; fax 684481) at 10 Calle Primo de Rivera. It has pleasant singles/doubles with bathroom for 3744/5200pta.

Places to Stay – middle

Heading up the price scale is the *Hotel Avenida* (☎ 684949; fax 683226) at 24 Avenida de Juan Carlos I Rey. It has singles/doubles for 4503/7176pta. However, there are plans to renovate it in 1997, and prices are expected to rise by 1000pta.

More expensive still is the *Hotel Residencia Anfora* (☎ 683340), at 8 Calle Pablo Vallescá, with rooms with air-con and TV for 7100/10,460.

Places to Stay – top end

Across from the Hotel Residencia Anfora, at No 5, is the *Hotel Rusadir* (☎ 681240; fax 670527) with rooms for 11,220/14,190pta plus tax.

The *Parador de Melilla* (☎ 684940; fax 683486) on Avenida de Candido Lobera, is part of a top-class Spanish hotel group and is probably top of the tree in Melilla, with a pool and views over the Mediterranean. Unfortunately, the concrete exterior is less inspired. Rooms start at 8500pta (for a single without a sea view) to 14,500pta for one of the better doubles.

Swimming Pools

The Parador's pool is open to non-residents, but you pay 1500pta per day for the privilege. It costs 50% less if you eat at the restaurant (3500pta for lunch/dinner). The pool is open from June to September.

Places to Eat

Restaurants The best area to search for good cheap bocadillos (sandwiches) and the like is along Calle Castelar, not far from the Mercado Municipal (food market).

There are countless bars and the odd restaurant where you can get a meal in the streets around Avenida de Juan Carlos I Rey. A very popular place with the locals is the *Antony Pizza Factory* which serves

good pizza for 650pta to 850pta. You can buy slices to take away for 300pta.

The *Restaurant Granada* at 36 Marqués Montemar in the Barrio Industrial (Industrial Quarter) to the south of town, serves seafood and fish dishes in a traditional setting. Set menus cost between 3000pta to 4000pta.

Another restaurant with a good reputation for seafood is the *Restaurante Los Salazones* off the Paseo Marítimo at 15 Calle de Alcaudete. The set menu (three courses and wine) costs 2500pta. It's open every day except Monday.

For a splurge, you can't beat the *Barbacoa de Muralla*, at Calle Fiorentina in the southernmost corner of Melilla la Vieja. There's a three course set menu for 4000pta.

Cafes & Tapas Bars For a traditional breakfast of churros (doughnuts) and hot chocolate (so thick it's like soup), head for *Café Toga* on Plaza de Don Pedro de Estopiñán. They also have a selection of around 20 different tapas. It's open every day from 8 am to 5 pm.

A very popular meeting place for young and old alike is the *Cafetería Nuevo California* on Avenida de Juan Carlos I Rey. There is a cafe and bar downstairs, and a restaurant upstairs where you can get traditional Spanish food at reasonable prices.

If you're looking for a traditional tapas bar, probably the best is the attractive *La Onubense* bar at 5 Calle General Pareja. It's run by the Hernández family who prepare an excellent selection of classic tapas including callos (tripe), and the speciality bollito de Pringá (a kind of meatball).

For something altogether more modern, you could try the *Cervecería* at 23 Calle General O'Donnell, done out in a Gaudiesque fashion by the Melillan architect Carlos Baeza. Both bars are open from 7.30 pm to midnight (closed Monday).

Patisseries & Ice Cream The *Heladería La Ibense* on Calle General O'Donnell is the best place in town for ice cream. It has around 35 different flavours (cones cost

125/200/250pta, and cups 225/275/500pta depending on the size). Try the delicious nougat speciality. In winter, they do hot waffles (150pta) covered in chocolate or cream – or both, if you're feeling really piggy. It stays open late (from 10 am to 3.30 or 4 am every day).

The *Confitería La Palma*, on Avenida de Juan Carlos I Rey, has a good selection of sweet and savoury goodies, including the best calatraba (a type of poached cake) in town. It's open from 9 am to 9 pm.

Entertainment

Apart from exploring the many bars and cafes around the centre of town and joining in the evening *paseo* (promenade), you could try a folk-music club such as the *Peña Francisco* inside the fortress (see the Melilla map). Of the various discos and disco-pubs (a Spanish speciality), *Logüeno*, on the Carretera de Alfonso XIII, is the best bet.

For gay travellers, the *Bunker Bank* on Calle General Prim, is recommended by locals. All nightclubs are open from around 11 pm to 3 am; admission is usually free and drinks cost around 450pta.

Getting There & Away

Air Iberia, the Spanish national carrier, has an office on Avenida de Juan Carlos I Rey. The one way fare to Málaga is 10,200pta, and there are numerous daily flights (except in bad weather) on 46 seat Fokkers. There's one flight a day to Almería (9900pta one way). To Madrid there are up to five daily flights (only one direct) and tickets cost 27,100pta one way.

Bus & Taxi Local buses (catch the one marked for 'Aforos') run between Plaza de España and the Beni-Enzar border post about every half hour from around 7.30 am to 10 pm. From where the buses stop, it's about 150m to Spanish customs and another 200m to Moroccan customs. Spanish checks seem largely cursory, but the Moroccans can hold things up for quite a while.

Remember that some nationalities require visas to enter Spain (see the Foreign Embassies entry under Rabat in the North Atlantic Coast chapter). If they don't stop you here, they will when you try to move on to the mainland.

Don't give in to Moroccan customs officers suggesting that you'd like to give them a few hundred of your excess dirham 'for a coffee'. Just change it at the bank (if you have an exchange receipt) or deny having any and change it to pesetas in Melilla. You can buy dirham in Melilla or at the Moroccan side of the border (the latter accepts cash only).

From Beni-Enzar there are Moroccan local buses (No 19; Dr2) and grands taxis (Dr4) to Nador, from where you can catch other buses and grands taxis to a host of destinations further inside the country (see the Nador entry later in this section).

If driving into Morocco, remember to retain the green customs slip, which you must present when you (and your vehicle) leave Morocco.

Boat Trasmediterranea ferries leave Melilla every night but Sunday for Málaga and Almería. For details, see the Getting There & Away chapter. Buy your tickets at the Trasmediterranea office on Plaza de España (open Monday to Friday from 9 am to 1 pm and 5 to 7 pm, and 9 am to noon Saturday), or direct at the port (Estación Marítima).

You can also buy rail tickets for mainland Spain and beyond at the RENFE office on Calle de General O'Donnell. Ferries are sometimes cancelled because of bad weather.

There are fairly thorough passport and Customs checks at Melilla (although technically you're travelling inside Spain). All cars are searched, and the process can delay departure considerably. Similar, but less rigorous, checks are carried out on arrival in Málaga and Almería.

AROUND MELILLA

About 15km south of Melilla is the unremarkable little town of **Selouane**. For those who enjoy a splurge, and can afford it, the place might still be worth a stop.

The *Restaurant Brabo* (☎ 609033), next door to the Banque Populaire at 110 Ave Mohammed V, is considered one of the best restaurants in northern Morocco. It's run by a Moroccan and his Belgian wife, and they do all the cooking. Main fish and meat courses from an extensive menu cost around Dr100 (wine from around Dr75). If you're very lucky, you might even get a Belgian chocolate with your coffee. The restaurant is open every day (except Sunday evening and Monday) from noon to 4 pm and from 8 pm to midnight.

If you are driving, watch the stretch of road from Melilla to Nador. It is notorious for police controls, where heavy fines (up to Dr400) are levied on the spot for the slightest infraction. Don't break the 40kmp/h town speed limit by even 1kmp/h.

NADOR

Only the traveller with plenty of time and a love of unloved places would want to do more than catch the first bus or grand taxi out of Nador, a sprawling town set on a lagoon 13km south of Melilla and earmarked, officially at least, for development as a business centre.

Luckily, most of the transport is located in the one place, which makes arriving and leaving comparatively painless. Should you get stuck and have to stay overnight, there is no shortage of hotels of all classes. Many of them are near the bus and grand taxi lots.

One of the best cheapies is the *Hôtel Anoual*, at 16 Rue Hay Khatabi, which charges from Dr50/80 for singles/doubles. The best value restaurant in town (according to the Moroccan Customs Chief in Melilla), is the *Restaurant Majid* at 3-5 Blvd Kaid Ahmed Riffi, near the Central Market.

The *Pizzeria/Heladeria Villanapoli* at 124 Blvd Ibn Khaldoun serves excellent pizza and ice cream.

Information

The tourist office (☎ 606518) is at 80 Blvd Ibn Rochd. Spain has a consulate in Nador at 12 Rue Mohammed Zerktouni (☎ 606136; fax 606152).

Getting There & Away

Bus The bus station (Gare Routière) is down by the lagoon, south of the city centre. CTM and other lines run from here. Basically there are three lines. The first is to Casablanca (Dr162) via Rabat (Dr139). Buses leave twice daily at 8 am and 8.30 pm.

The second line is to Tangier (Dr172). One bus departs daily at 7 pm; stops include Asilah (Dr168), Larache (Dr156), Meknès (Dr105), Fès (Dr89) and Taza (Dr28).

The third line is to Tetouan (Dr97.50), with two buses setting off at 9.30 am and 6 pm. Stops en route include Chefchaouen (Dr84), Ketama (Dr64) and Al-Hoceima (Dr35.50). There is also a bus to Oujda (Dr23.50) at 9 am.

The non-CTM buses offer many more services to these destinations from around 5.30 am to 9 pm; fares are around 30% cheaper. Ten buses a day go to Al-Hoceima, eight to Tetouan, four to Casablanca and five to Tangier. There's also buses every hour to Fès and Meknès, and every half hour to Oujda.

If you're going to Melilla, the local bus station is next to the main bus station. The No 19 regularly makes the 20 minute run to Beni-Enzar for Melilla, but stops operating by about 8 pm.

Train It is possible to get a Supratours bus to Taourirt to catch connecting trains going west to Fès and beyond or east to Oujda. The bus leaves Nador at around 7 pm and you buy a ticket for the bus and train to the destination you want. The same trip can be done in the other direction (leaving Taourirt around 5 am). As a rule, it's easier to use buses and grands taxis.

Taxi The main grand taxi station is across from the bus station. Taxis cost Dr35 to Oujda, Dr55 to Taza and Al-Hoceima, Dr100 to Fès, Dr120 to Meknès, Dr150 to Rabat and Dr200 to Tetouan.

There are usually grands taxis available to most of these and other destinations until about 8 pm.

If you're going to Melilla, the grands

taxis to the border (Dr4 for a place) use a lot that is a fair distance from the main grand taxi station. The best way to get between the two is by petit taxi.

SAIDIA

A couple of kilometres short of the Algerian border (you can't cross here) is the little seaside town of Saidia. In summer it is often packed with Moroccans, especially during the August traditional music festival, but out of season it's empty and offers a fine sandy beach and crystal-clear water.

There are a few hotels in the town, but they're all on the expensive side, and they mainly open for the summer season from mid-June. Saidia's distance from the main Moroccan cities thankfully makes it a spot unlikely to become a huge resort.

Places to Stay & Eat

There are three camp sites in and around town, and the best of these is the *Camping al-Mansour* (☎ 625165), about 3km from town on the road to Moulouya Estuary. It is well kept with good facilities. Camping costs Dr15 per person/car and Dr30 for a

site, including electricity. They also rent bungalows for up to five people (Dr250, but rising to Dr450 in June and July and Dr600 in August!).

Of the hotels, the *Hôtel Paco* (☎ 625110; fax 625555) is one of the cheapest options and charges Dr120/160 (Dr160/200 in the high season) for pleasant singles/doubles. Try to get a room with a shower (which costs the same).

The *Hôtel Atlal* (☎ 625021), across the road at 44 Blvd Hassan II, is awaiting classification, but should charge around Dr150/ 200. For the same price is the *Hôtel Hannour* (☎ 625115) in the centre of town.

Around the corner from the Hôtel Paco is the *Hôtel Rimal* which should open towards the end of 1997. It looks to be the best hotel in town (two or three-star) with good sea views, and will charge around Dr200/250. It's a good idea to make advance reservations for the period from mid-July to the end of August.

There are quite a few little restaurants in the centre of town. The unmarked *Restaurant Saïd*, close to the police station, is well known for good, fresh fish, and is a popular

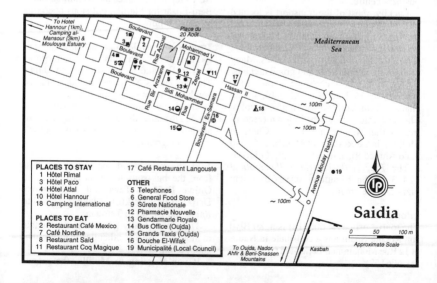

PLACES TO STAY	17 Café Restaurant Langouste
1 Hôtel Rimal	
3 Hôtel Paco	OTHER
4 Hôtel Atlal	5 Telephones
10 Hôtel Hannour	6 General Food Store
18 Camping International	9 Sûrete Nationale
	12 Pharmacie Nouvelle
PLACES TO EAT	13 Gendarmarie Royale
2 Restaurant Café Mexico	14 Bus Office (Oujda)
7 Café Nordine	15 Grands Taxis (Oujda)
8 Restaurant Saïd	16 Douche El-Wifak
11 Restaurant Coq Magique	19 Municipalité (Local Council)

Saidia

place with Spaniards over for the day. A main course costs around Dr55. A cheaper place is the new *Restaurant Café Mexico* on Rue Zerktouni, which specialises in fish and barbecued meat. It charges around Dr35 for a main course.

The *Café Nordine*, not far from the Hôtel Atlal, is the best place for breakfast. You can get a drink in a couple of bars, and such nightlife as there is in summer seems to revolve around the *Hôtel Hannour* and the *Kiss* disco, which is about a kilometre west along the beach.

Getting There & Away

Without your own transport, the easiest access to Saidia is from Oujda by bus (Dr15; at least four a day throughout the year) or grand taxi (Dr20). See also the Oujda entry in the Middle Atlas & the East chapter.

AROUND SAIDIA

The coast west of Saidia presents some good opportunities for **bird-watching**.

The area around the **Moulouya Estuary** in particular attracts rich birdlife; from the shore further west you can get a reasonable view of the Spanish-owned **Jaafariya Islands** just off the coast, which is said to support the Mediterranean's largest seabird colony. There are hopes that it will soon be declared a nature park. Audouin's gull breeds here, but the slender-billed curlew, once a drawcard for region, has disappeared over the past few years.

Further west still, at the tiny town of **Kariat Arkmane**, you can spot a host of other birdlife inhabiting the salt marshes, including the greater flamingo and various terns and gulls.

If you have your own transport (preferably a 4WD), or are prepared to hire a taxi, there are some very scenic routes into the **Beni-Snassen Mountains**.

One of the best is the S403 which you can pick up from the town of Berkane, south-west of Saidia. It passes through the remote hill village of **Taforalt**, several **grottes** (caves; which you can explore with a good torch), and the **Zegzel Gorge**.

The circuit will take you back down to Ahfir and the road to Saidia. The Morocco Michelin map is the best reference to the region.

Berber finger symbol
Believed to be a double cross enclosing a diamond – a protective symbol.

The Middle Atlas & the East

A visit to the Middle Atlas region can take in such diverse activities as snow skiing in the mountain resort of Ifrane, visiting Morocco's best preserved Roman ruins at Volubilis, trekking in the Middle Atlas mountains around Azrou and Midelt, wandering through the labyrinthine medina of Fès, and visiting Moulay Ismail's huge palace complex at Meknès.

From Fès, a natural route leads via Taza and Oujda on the border to Algeria. The road south from Oujda is the easiest way to get to the frontier oasis town of Figuig, reputedly the hottest place in Morocco.

Meknès

The city of Meknès is known by some as the Versailles of Morocco. Had the enormous building projects of the Alawite sultan, Moulay Ismail, survived the ravages of time, then this metaphor might not seem so extravagant.

Although on the tour programmes, Meknès ranks third behind its more famous sisters, Marrakesh and Fès. It was for a time the heart of the Moroccan sultanate, and boasts some impressive buildings.

Meknès is also a quieter, smaller and more hassle-free place and, with the beauty of its sights, it has a habit of imperceptibly growing upon you.

Not quite so tourism-dependent, it has an air of quiet self-sufficiency and authenticity unlike the other Imperial cities. It's worth at least a couple of days exploration. You may well choose to stay longer; many travellers do.

Meknès also makes a convenient base for visiting the remarkable Roman ruins of Volubilis. It's an excursion that shouldn't be missed, even if you're not normally into Roman relics.

Next door and perched on a hill top is the

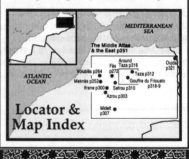

intriguing village of Moulay Idriss, a holy site that contains the tomb of the founder of Morocco's first imperial dynasty. From the town there are beautiful views of the surrounding country.

Encircled by the rich plains that precede the Middle Atlas Mountains, Meknès is blessed with a hinterland that provides abundant cereal crops, olives, wine, citrus and other agricultural products that have long been the city's economic backbone. The comparative prosperity of the city and the surrounding countryside continues to fuel its population – at last count 740,000 and growing.

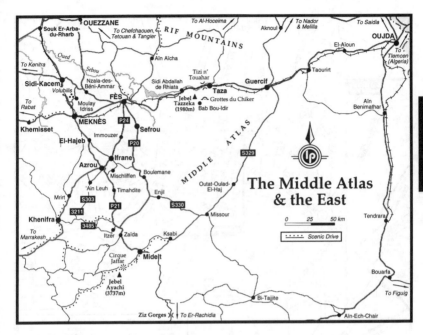

History

Meknès is a good thousand years old. The Berber tribe of the Meknassis (hence the city's name) first settled here in the 10th century. Under the Almohads and Merenids, the medina was expanded and some of the city's oldest remaining monuments were built. The fall of the Merenids brought a hiatus in the city's fortunes.

It was the accession to power of Moulay Ismail in 1672 (on the death of his brother and founder of the Alawite dynasty, Moulay ar-Rashid) that yanked Meknès back from obscurity. He reigned for 55 years and made Meknès his capital, which he endowed with an enormous palace complex (which was never finished) and 25km of imposing walls with monumental gates. That he was able to devote so much energy to construction was partly due to his uncommon success in subduing all opposition in Morocco and keeping foreign meddlers well at bay.

His death in 1727 also struck the death knell for Meknès, as his grandson Mohammed III (1757-90) moved back to Marrakesh. Meknès again became a backwater; its monuments, as so often happened in the course of Moroccan history, were stripped for materials to build elsewhere. The 1755 earthquake that devastated Lisbon had already dealt Meknès a heavy blow.

The arrival of the protectorate in 1912 gave the town a fillip, as the French made it their military headquarters. The army was accompanied by a corps of French farmers, attracted by the good land around the city. Most of their properties were taken over by the Moroccan government after independence in 1956 and leased out to local farmers.

It's only in the past few decades, as the tourist potential of the city has become obvious, that any serious attempts at restoration have taken place.

MIDDLE ATLAS

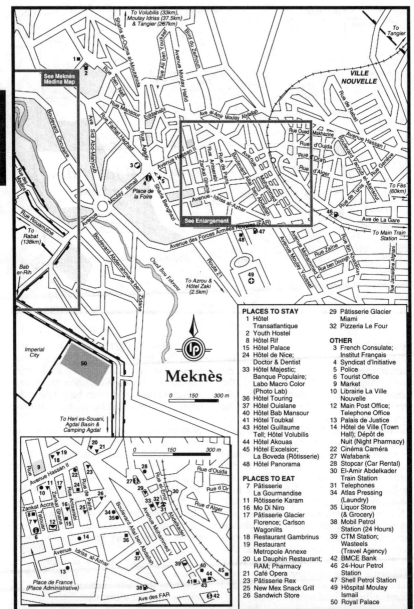

To Volubilis (33km),
Moulay Idriss (37.5km)
& Tangier (267km)

To Tangier

VILLE NOUVELLE

See Meknès
Medina Map

See Enlargement

To Rabat
(138km)

Bab
er-Rih

Imperial
City

Meknès

0   150   300 m

To Heri es-Souani,
Agdal Basin &
Camping Agdal

To Azrou &
Hôtel Zaki
(2.5km)

To Fès
(60km)

To Main Train
Station

Place de France
(Place Administrative)

0   150   300 m

PLACES TO STAY
1 Hôtel Transatlantique
2 Youth Hostel
8 Hôtel Rif
15 Hôtel Palace
24 Hôtel de Nice; Doctor & Dentist
33 Hôtel Majestic; Banque Populaire; Labo Macro Color (Photo Lab)
36 Hôtel Touring
37 Hôtel Ouislane
40 Hôtel Bab Mansour
41 Hôtel Toubkal
43 Hôtel Guillaume Tell; Hôtel Volubilis
44 Hôtel Akouas
45 Hôtel Excelsior; La Boveda (Rôtisserie)
48 Hôtel Panorama

PLACES TO EAT
7 Pâtisserie La Gourmandise
11 Rôtisserie Karam
16 Mo Di Niro
17 Pâtisserie Glacier Florence; Carlson Wagonlits
18 Restaurant Gambrinus
19 Restaurant Metropole Annexe
20 Le Dauphin Restaurant; RAM; Pharmacy
21 Café Opera
23 Pâtisserie Rex
25 New Mex Snack Grill
26 Sandwich Store
29 Pâtisserie Glacier Miami
32 Pizzeria Le Four

OTHER
3 French Consulate; Institut Français
4 Syndicat d'Initiative
5 Police
6 Tourist Office
9 Market
10 Librairie La Ville Nouvelle
12 Main Post Office; Telephone Office
13 Palais de Justice
14 Hôtel de Ville (Town Hall); Dépôt de Nuit (Night Pharmacy)
22 Cinéma Caméra
27 Wafabank
28 Stopcar (Car Rental)
30 El-Amir Abdelkader Train Station
31 Telephones
34 Atlas Pressing (Laundry)
35 Liquor Store (& Grocery)
38 Mobil Petrol Station (24 Hours)
39 CTM Station; Wasteels (Travel Agency)
42 BMCE Bank
46 24-Hour Petrol Station
47 Shell Petrol Station
49 Hôspital Moulay Ismail
50 Royal Palace

Orientation

The old medina and the French-built ville nouvelle are neatly divided by the valley of the Oued Bou Fekrane. The (usually dry) riverbed also marks an administrative boundary. The Wilayat Ismailia covers the medina side and the Wilayat al-Menzah the modern side.

Train and CTM bus connections are in the ville nouvelle, as are most offices and banks. All the more expensive hotels and most of the better restaurants are also in the ville nouvelle.

All the private bus lines and the main inter-city grands taxis use a station on the west side of the medina. The cheap hotels, campgrounds and sights are in the old city. It's a 20 minute walk between the old and new cities, but there are regular (and very crowded) local buses, as well as petits taxis.

Information

Tourist Offices The Délégation Régionale du Tourisme (☎ 524426) is next to the main post office facing Place de France (or Place Administrative). A simple city map is available and the staff are quite helpful. It's open Monday to Friday from 8.30 am to noon and 2.30 to 6.30 pm; on Friday it's closed from 11.30 am to 3 pm.

The Syndicat d'Initiative (520191) is on Place de la Foire, but is not the mine of information it might be.

Money Most banks are concentrated in the ville nouvelle (mainly on Ave Hassan II, Ave Mohammed V and Blvd Allal ben Abdallah). Rates do seem to vary between banks, so you could check out a couple.

As usual, the BMCE is a good bet. Its main branch operates an out-of-hours change office on Ave des FAR, opposite the Hôtel Excelsior; it's open daily from 10 am to 2 pm and 4 to 8 pm. It also has a couple of ATMs.

In the medina, there's a string of five banks along Rue Sekkakine, including the Banque Populaire. It's open from Monday to Friday from 8.15 to 11.30 am (11.15 on Friday) and from 2.15 to 4.30 pm (from

2.45 to 4.45 pm on Friday). There's also a branch on Rue Dar Smen. Other banks are marked on the map.

Post & Communications The main post office is in the ville nouvelle on Place de France. It's open from 8.30 am to 12.15 pm and 2.30 to 6.45 pm. The phone office is in the same building and is open daily from 8.30 am to 9 pm. The parcel post and EMS department is around the corner to the left.

There is another large post office in the medina, on Rue Dar Smen, near the corner of Rue Rouamzine.

French Consulate & Institut Français The Institut Français (☎ 524071) is on the corner of Ave Moulay Ismail and Rue Farhat Hachad in the ville nouvelle. It has a programme of films and lectures, and a small library. It's open Monday to Saturday from 9 am to noon and 3 to 7 pm.

The consulate (☎ 522227) does *not* issue visas – you'll have to go to Fès.

Travel Agencies Carlson Wagonlits (☎ 521995) has an office at 1 Zankat Ghana. Wasteels (☎ 523062) is at 45 Ave Mohammed V next to the CTM bus station.

Bookshops & Newsstands The Librairie La Ville Nouvelle on Ave Hassan II is one of the better French-language bookshops, but stocks mainly novels.

There are several newsstands where you can get hold of English-language press, as well as the usual full range of French press. There's one virtually across the road from the Hôtel Majestic on Ave Mohammed V.

Film & Photography There are several places around the ville nouvelle where you can have film developed. The Labo Macro Color at 21 Ave Mohammed V, next to the Hôtel Majestic, is a good place. In the medina, try the Studio el-Almal on 131 Rue Rouamzine, close to the Hôtel Maroc.

Laundry In the medina, the pressing El-Fath at 46 Rue Rouamzine is open every day from 10.30 am to 8.30 pm (Friday until 1 pm only).

In the ville nouvelle, Atlas Pressing at 26 Blvd Allal ben Abdallah is open every day except Sunday from 8 am to 8 pm.

Medical Services & Emergencies There are three hospitals in Meknès. The most centrally located is the Hôpital Moulay Ismail (☎ 522805), south of Ave des FAR.

The Depôt de Nuit (night pharmacy) is diagonally opposite the Hôtel de Ville.

If you want to see a doctor, Dr Abdelilah Mechti has a surgery (☎ 515885) close to the Hôtel de Nice at 8 Zankat Accra. He can be contacted in emergencies at home on ☎ 530024. In the same building on the second floor, Dr Mohammed Dahani has a dental surgery (☎ 526838; 527587 at home). Both doctors trained in France and are recommended.

Old City

From the ville nouvelle, you get to the old city by crossing Oued Bou Fekrane along Ave Moulay Ismail.

On the other side, you follow the street as it veers to the right, up into a little square. This is Rue Rouamzine, which you take until you get to the post office, at which point you turn left into Rue Dar Smen. Follow this until a great square opens up on your right, Place el-Hedim.

The heart of the old medina lies to the north (with the old Jewish quarter, the mellah, to the west). On your left (to the south) Moulay Ismail's imperial city opens up through one of the most impressive monumental gateways in all Morocco, the Bab el-Mansour. Although not nearly as bad as, say, Fès, if the *faux guides* are going to get you, it will most likely be around Rue Dar Smen and Place el-Hedim.

Medina

Dar Jamaï Museum On the far north side of Place el-Hedim is the Dar Jamaï, a palace built in 1882 by the powerful Jamaï family. Two of their number were viziers to Sultan Moulay al-Hassan I in the late 19th century.

When the sultan died in 1894, the Jamaï family fell into disgrace, as so often happened in the fickle political atmosphere of the Moroccan court. They lost everything, including their Meknès palace, which went to Al-Maidani al-Glaoui. The French turned it into a military hospital in 1912 and since 1920 it has housed the Administration des Beaux Arts, and is one of the best museums in the country.

As is often the case in Morocco, the museum building is as interesting as the exhibits. The exhibits consist of a good collection of traditional ceramics, jewellery, rugs, textiles, embroidery and woodwork. Keep an eye out for the silver *sebsi* for smoking kif and the beautiful, 17th century cedar *minbar* (pulpit).

There are also some impressive items of jewellery, including some very decorative ankle bracelets. Fully decked out for a ceremony, a woman might traditionally carry up to 20kg of jewellery. There is also a reconstructed Berber tent.

The *koubba* (domed reception room) upstairs is furnished in the style of a traditional *grand salon*, complete with luxurious rugs and cushions. Despite the rather sad state of the building (under-funding is a major problem for museums in Morocco), the exhibition has been well put together, though explanations are in French and Arabic only.

When you've finished, the museum's charming Andalusian garden and courtyard make a good pause for breath. It's a shady, peaceful spot amid overgrown orange trees and twittering sparrows. The museum is open daily, except Tuesday and holidays, from 9 am to noon and 3 to 6.30 pm. Entry costs Dr10.

Souqs Before plunging into the heart of the old medina from Place el-Hedim, you might want to take a look at the food hall west of the square (behind the rows of barber shops), which borders on the old mellah. The food displays are a sight in themselves. If you like olives, you'll think you've died and gone to heaven.

The Place itself once attracted itinerant street entertainers rather like the Place Djemaa-el-Fna in Marrakesh. Unfortunately, the square has been ruined by modern attempts (against local wishes) to 'grandify' it. The ugly fountains no longer even work and collect litter instead. *Caleches* (horse-drawn carriages) are available for hire opposite the Bab el-Mansour gate.

The easiest route into the medina proper is through the arch to the left of the Dar Jamaï. If you plunge in here, you will quickly find yourself in among the **carpet shops**. As you walk along the streets, you will occasionally notice covered market areas (or *qissariat*) off to your right or left. A couple of these are devoted to carpets, and the hard sell is not as hard here as elsewhere.

Keeping more or less to the lane you started on, you will emerge at Rue Najarine. Here the carpets give way to textiles and to quite a few shops specialising in *babouches* (slippers).

If you follow the street west and veer with it left into Rue Sekkakine, you will find yourself at an exit in the west wall of the medina. Virtually opposite it is the **Qissariat ad-Dahab**, the gold and jewellery souq.

If you take the exit and follow the lane north hugging the city wall on the outside, you'll go past the colourful **spices and nuts souq**, a **flea market** and, a bit further to the west, Meknès' **tanneries**.

Enter the city again at Bab el-Jedid, and as you pass inside the gate you'll find yourself in a small **musical instruments souq**. Turning left up Rue el-Hanaya, the local-produce markets open up in front of you – this is a cheap place to do your grocery shopping.

Eventually, if you continue north, you will arrive at the **Berdaine Mosque** and, just beyond it, the city's northernmost gate, **Bab Berdaine**. Outside is a Muslim cemetery, in which is located the tomb and **koubba** (sanctuary) of Sidi ben Aissa, who gave rise to one of the more extreme religious fraternities in Morocco.

At his moussem, entranced followers would cheerfully digest anything from glass to snakes, but nowadays such practices have been all but suppressed.

You could then proceed straight back down Rue Zaouia Nasseria (which becomes Rue Souika) to get to the Great Mosque and the nearby Medersa Bou Inania.

Medersa Bou Inania The Great Mosque is, of course, closed to non-Muslims, but you can enter the medersa, which was built in the 14th century during the reign of the Merenids.

Completed in 1358 by Bou Inan (after whom a more lavish medersa in Fès is also named), the Meknès version of the Qur'anic school is typical of the exquisite interior design that distinguishes Merenid monuments from those of other periods. For some ideas on the use and layout of medersas, see the special section on Moroccan architecture in the Facts about the Country chapter.

The standard zellij-tile base, stucco middle and carved olive-wood top of the interior walls (only the ceiling is made of cedar) is repeated here in all its elegance.

Students aged eight to 10 once lived two to a cell on the ground floor, while older students and teachers lived on the 1st floor. You can climb on to the roof and see the green-tiled roof and minaret of the Great Mosque next door.

The medersa is open daily from 9 am to noon and 3 to 6 pm. Entry is Dr10. A guide will probably want to show you around for a fee. It's a quick walk back to Place el-Hedim.

Imperial City
Bab el-Mansour The focus of the old city is the massive gate of Bab el-Mansour, the main entrance to Moulay Ismail's 17th century imperial city that stands opposite Place el-Hedim. The gate is well preserved and lavishly decorated, with (faded) zellij tiles and inscriptions that run right across the top. The gate was completed by Moulay Ismail's son, Moulay Abdallah.

Moulay Ismail

Moulay Ismail, the second sultan of the Alawite dynasty (which still rules today), marked his ascent to power at the age of 25 in 1672 in an unforgettable manner. As a warning to unruly tribes, he sent the heads of 10,000 slain enemies to adorn the walls of the two great imperial capitals, Fès and Marrakesh. He had presumably collected these earlier during battles against insurgents in the north of Morocco.

It was the beginning of a particularly gruesome period of rule, even by Moroccan standards, but Moulay Ismail is one of the few Moroccan sultans ever to get the whole country under his control. His cruelty was legendary, and the cheerful ease with which he would lop off the heads of unfortunate servants who displeased him or labourers not working hard enough probably contributed much to his hold over the country.

His first 20 years of rule were taken up with bloody campaigns of pacification. It is difficult to know just how much blood was spilt, but more than 30,000 people are said to have died at his hands alone.

The core of his military success lay in the infamous Black Guard. Having brought some 16,000 slaves from Black Africa, Moulay Ismail guaranteed the continued existence of his elite units by providing the soldiers with women and raising their offspring for service in the guard. By the time of his death, the Black Guard had grown tenfold and resembled a huge family whose upkeep was paid for by the treasury.

In addition to quelling internal rebellion, he chased the Portuguese and English out of Asilah, Larache, Mehdiya and Tangier. Spain managed to hang on to Ceuta, Melilla and Al-Hoceima in spite of unrelenting sieges. Moulay Ismail disposed of the Ottoman Turk threat from Algeria, securing a stable eastern frontier with a string of fortifications centred on Taza, and established a virtual protectorate over modern Mauritania.

A contemporary of Louis XIV of France, the Sun King, Moulay Ismail was at least partly inspired by descriptions of Versailles when he planned the construction of his imperial palace and other monuments in Meknès. For decades he tried to secure an alliance with France against Spain, but continued attacks by the corsairs of Salé on French merchant shipping effectively scuppered his hopes.

Although both monarchs bestowed presents on each other, Louis XIV stopped short of acceding to Moulay Ismail's request to marry one of his daughters, the Princess of Conti. Not that the sultan was in need of more female company – it is reckoned he had 360 to 500 wives and concubines (depending on which source you believe) and 800 children by the time he died.

To carry out his building plans, he needed plenty of labour, and it is said he used 25,000 Christian prisoners as slave labour in Meknès, in addition to 30,000 common criminals. His great stables (Heri as-Souani) could house 12,000 horses. ■

Koubbat as-Sufara' After passing through Bab el-Mansour and along the *mechouar* (parade ground), where Moulay Ismail reviewed his famed Black regiments, the road runs straight ahead and then round to the right. On the right is an open grass area with a small building, the Koubbat as-Sufara', which was once the reception hall for foreign ambassadors. It's hardly worth visiting, but beside it is the entrance to an enormous underground granary complete with vents that open onto the surface of the lawn.

The popular story has this as a huge prison in which thousands of Christians (most captured by corsairs operating out of Salé) were held captive as slave labour on Moulay Ismail's building schemes. This story has largely been discredited, but it dies hard.

Entry to the vaults and the reception hall, open daily from 9 am to noon and 3 to 6 pm, costs Dr10. Almost directly opposite are the royal gardens, which form part of what was Moulay Ismail's imperial city complex. The gardens are off-limits.

Impressive Portals

As with most of Morocco's great artistic expressions, the best of the *maallem's* (woodworker's) art is reserved for mosques and medersas. The feature most characteristic of Moroccan woodwork is the door.

Throughout Morocco, you can see huge doors with elaborate detailing, decorated with an ornamental vocabulary that includes calligraphy, geometrical motifs and the ubiquitous talismanic images. Hands of Fatima, ancient fertility symbols, star patterns and necklaces are often carved into doors as protection against *djinn* (evil spirits). This is particularly true of the massive doors to *agadirs* (fortified granaries) which were built to protect lives and possessions during times of fierce tribal warfare.

Metalwork also features on Moroccan doors, often studded with iron and nails made of brass. Traditionally, iron door handles were found on the doors of poorer rural people, while those in brass and bronze, often in the shape of Fatima's hand, adorned the doors of the urban wealthy.

Another common feature of Moroccan doors is the colour blue. Doors and shutters are painted in shades of eye-catching blue in keeping with traditional practise (believed to originate in ancient Egypt) of using the colour to ward off evil spirits.

Martin Hughes

Box: Decorative iron door handle, Chefchaouen.

Left: Door at Majorelle's villa, Jardin Majorelle, Marrakesh.

Right: Typical blue doorway, Chefchaouen.

ALL PHOTOS BY FRANCES LINZEE GORDON

*Clockwise from right:
Painted wooden door,
medina palace,
Marrakesh;
Detail of the brass
door of King Hassan
II's palace, Rabat;
Decorative door latch,
medina palace,
Marrakesh;
Elaborate door handle,
Chefchaouen medina.*

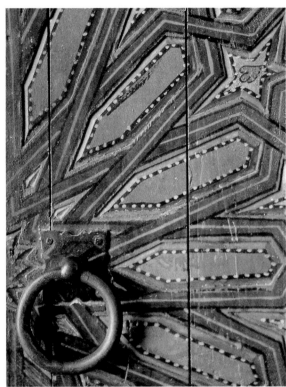

FRANCES LINZEE GORDON

FRANCES LINZEE GORDON

FRANCES LINZEE GORDON

KARYN DUGGAN

Mausoleum of Moulay Ismail To the left of the gardens is a more imposing gateway, through which you proceed to the resting place of the man who elevated Meknès to a capital in the 17th century. He is generally considered one of the greatest figures in Moroccan history, and perhaps because of this non-Muslims are allowed in to the sanctuary (although only Muslims can visit the tomb itself). Visitors should make the most of this opportunity; the mausoleum is a peaceful and beautifully designed place, and is a good example of Moroccan architecture and craftsmanship.

The mausoleum is open every day from 9 am to noon and 3 to 6 pm (3 to 6 pm only on Friday) and entry costs Dr5. On the opposite side of the road are a number of craft and carpet shops belonging to a cooperative of artisans. There's a good selection of Meknassi specialities, but prices are fairly high and salesmen are persistent.

Heri es-Souani & Agdal Basin If you turn left on leaving the mausoleum and pass under the Bab er-Rih (Gate of the Wind), you have about a 20 minute walk around what remains to this day an official royal residence (no visitors). The complex was once known as the Dar el-Makhzen ('the House of the Government').

Follow the street to the end and turn right (you have no choice) and head straight down past the main entrance of the Royal Palace (on the right) and on past the campground (on the left). Virtually in front of you are the impressive Heri es-Souani granaries and vaults.

The storerooms are immense and brilliantly designed for the storage of grain. There are small windows in the walls and water was circulated below the floor in order to keep temperatures cool and the air circulating.

The wells for drawing water can still be seen. The first few vaults have been restored, but the stables, which once housed 12,000 horses, stand in partial ruin with no roof, seemingly stretching forever. If you position yourself correctly, you can appreciate the incredible symmetry of the structure. Such is the atmosphere here that the place vies with Aït Benhaddou (near Ouarzazate) as one of the country's favourite film sets and poster subjects. It is open daily from 9 am to noon and 3 to 6 pm. Entry costs Dr10.

Another doorway further around to the Agdal Basin leads upstairs to a charming rooftop cafe, from where you have sweeping views back towards the Royal Palace and of the Agdal Basin below.

The basin is an enormous stone-lined lake about 4m deep that was once fed by the Oued Bou Fekrane and served as both a reservoir for the sultan's gardens and a pleasure lake.

Places to Stay – bottom end
Camping There is a good, shady camp site near the Agdal Basin on the southern side of the imperial city. It's a long walk to *Camping Agdal* (☎ 551828) and a taxi from the train, CTM or private bus stations will cost about Dr12.

Camping costs Dr17 per person (Dr12 for children), Dr10 to pitch a tent, Dr17 for a car or caravan (Dr20 for a camper van), Dr7 for a hot shower and Dr10 for electricity. There is a food store, bar, restaurant and cafe at the site.

Hostel The *youth hostel* (☎ 524698) is close to the large Hôtel Transatlantique in the ville nouvelle, about 1km north-west of the centre. It's a clean and reasonably well kept place.

In summer, it's open from 8 to 9 am, from noon to 4 pm and from 7 pm to midnight. During the rest of the year, it's open from 8 to 10 am, noon to 3 pm, and 6 to 10 pm. On Sunday, it's open all day from 10 am to 6 pm. A dormitory bed costs Dr25.

They also have family rooms for three and four people, which come to Dr30 per person. Hot showers cost an extra Dr5, and there is a communal kitchen and washing room. You can also have meals there if you want (breakfast costs Dr15; lunch or dinner Dr50).

Hotels – Medina Most of the cheapest places are clustered together in the old city along Rue Dar Smen and Rue Rouamzine.

One of the best places, though no longer the value it was since its recommendation in the last edition, is the *Hôtel Maroc* (☎ 530075) on Rue Rouamzine. Rooms are quiet, clean, and pleasantly furnished (all rooms with a washbasin) and face a verdant courtyard. The (cold) showers and toilets are reasonably well maintained. It costs Dr50/100 for singles/doubles.

Not quite as good, but cheaper, is the *Hôtel de Paris*, also on Rue Rouamzine at No 58. This is an older hotel with large singles/doubles, with a table, chair and washbasin, for Dr30/50. There are no showers and the place smells oddly of sour milk, but if you can put up with that, it's not a bad deal.

The rest of the cheapies are nothing special, and many don't have showers. The *Hôtel de Meknès* on Rue Dar Smen, is about the best of the lot, if you can get a room – the owner is stone deaf and his French is on the limited side.

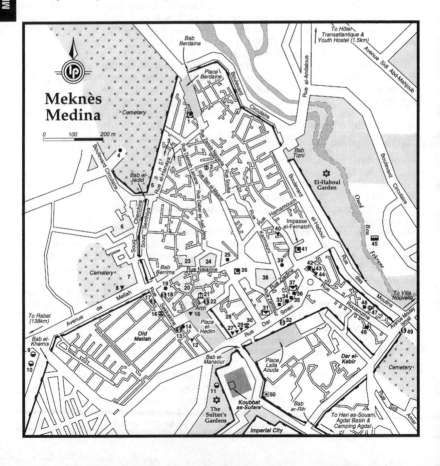

The rooms come with sinks and are clean and fairly spacious; they cost Dr30/60. There are no showers.

A few doors away is the *Hôtel Regina* (☎ 530280) which was closed at the time of writing for renovation. It should charge around Dr40/80 and should be worth checking out. Nearby, too, is the *Hôtel Nouveau* (☎ 533139), opposite the Banque Populaire. It's a little dusty with peeling walls, but is OK and charges Dr30/50.

Hotels – Ville Nouvelle Probably the cheapest place in town is the *Hôtel Guillaume Tell* (☎ 521203) on 51 Rue de la Voûte, down an alleyway next to the Hôtel Volubilis. The rooms are cell-like, but reasonably clean, and cost Dr20/30.

However, it rarely gets western guests; you may find the Arabic language crib at the beginning of the book more useful than you imagined!

The one-star *Hôtel Touring* (☎ 522951), at 34 Blvd Allal ben Abdallah, is clean, though a bit dark, gloomy and frayed around the edges. Rooms cost Dr87/107 with shower and Dr100/130 with shower and toilet.

Recently renovated and awaiting classification is the *Hôtel Panorama* (☎ 522737), just off Ave des FAR.

When it reopens it should be good value with rooms with bathroom going for around Dr90/130.

Virtually overlooking the train line is the *Hôtel Excelsior* (☎ 521900) at 57 Ave des FAR. Very clean, decent rooms without shower cost Dr65/88, while those with shower are Dr95/121. Add a few dirhams for taxes.

Also good value is the *Hôtel Majestic* (☎ 522035; fax 527427) at 19 Ave Mohammed V. It has lots of character and the staff, led by the manager Majid, are very friendly and eager to please.

Rooms come with washbasin and a bidet and some have a balcony. Singles/doubles without private shower cost Dr102/137. The shared showers are clean and the water piping hot. Rooms with shower cost Dr137/164, and with bathroom Dr172/205. In summer, you can have breakfast (Dr22) on the terrace.

Slightly more expensive, but very good value, are two recently declassified hotels

MIDDLE ATLAS

PLACES TO STAY	OTHER	22 BMCI Bank
33 Hôtel Nouveau	1 Berdaine Mosque	23 Textiles Souq
34 Hôtel de Meknès	2 Hammam (Men Only)	24 Slipper Souq
35 Hôtel Regina	3 Fruit & Vegetable	25 Medersa Bou Inania
36 Hôtel Agadir	Market	26 Great Mosque
46 Hôtel de Paris	4 Koubba of Sidi	30 Telephones
48 Hôtel Maroc; Studio	Ben Aissa	31 Post Box
el-Almal (Photo Lab)	5 Musical Instrument	32 Banque Populaire
	Souq	37 Post Office
PLACES TO EAT	6 Flea Market	38 Haberdashers' Souq
8 Moroccan Pâtisserie	7 Spices & Nuts Souq	39 Mansour Palace
12 Food Hall	9 Main Bus Station	41 Mosque
15 Café El-Hedim	10 Grands Taxis	42 Pressing El-Fath
27 Restaurant Bab	11 Local Buses	(Laundry)
Mansour;	13 Wafabank	45 Public Swimming Pool
Fruit Juice Bars	14 Pharmacy El-Fath	47 Douche (Men) &
28 Restaurant	16 Telephones	Bain (Hammam -
Économique	17 Banque Populaire	Men & Women)
29 Café Asila	18 BMCE Bank	49 Crédit du Maroc
40 Restaurant Zitouna	19 Qissariat ad-Dahab	(Change)
43 Sfinj (Doughnut)	(Gold & Jewellery Souq)	50 Mausoleum Moulay
Shop	20 Carpet Shops	Ismail
44 Café Mamounia	21 Dar Jamaï Museum	

(from three stars to two), the *Hôtel de Nice* (☎ 520318), at 10 Zankat Accra, and the *Hôtel Palace* (☎ 525777), at No 11 Zankat Ghana. Both have spotless, well furnished singles, doubles and triples with private bathroom for Dr135, Dr166 and Dr227 respectively.

Places to Stay – middle

At the lower end of this category is the two-star *Hôtel Ouislane* (☎ 521743), at 54 Ave Allal ben Abdallah, which has clean, but rather gloomy, singles/doubles with bathroom for Dr168/197.

Older, and a bit on the tired side, is the recently declassified (from three stars) *Hôtel Volubilis* (☎ 525082) at 45 Ave des FAR. Rooms go for Dr172/205/270, but are quite good value. Unfortunately, it is on a noisy intersection.

There are two three-star hotels within a stone's throw of each other around Ave des FAR and Ave Mohammed V. The *Hôtel Bab Mansour* (☎ 525239; fax 510741), at 38 Rue El-Amir Abdelkader, has clean and modern, if somewhat sterile, rooms with carpet and phone. Rooms with bath or shower cost Dr255/312.

Quieter and very pleasant is the *Hôtel Akouas* (☎ 596768; fax 515994) on 27 Rue El-Amir Abdelkader. It's a modern, comfortable place and a popular choice with business people; there is access to office facilities and a decent bar and a restaurant. Rooms cost Dr255/312/413 and are good value, but some are definitely better than others; ask to see a few. It's a good idea to make a reservation during the summer.

Places to Stay – top end

The four-star *Hôtel Rif* (☎ 522591; fax 524428), on Zankat Accra, and the *Hôtel Zaki* (☎ 521140), on Blvd al-Massira on the road to Azrou, have similar facilities, including swimming pool, restaurant, bar and air-con throughout, and cost Dr375/474 with shower or bath and toilet.

A little more expensive and top of the line is the *Hôtel Transatlantique* (☎ 525051; fax 520057), on Rue el-Meriniyine, which

has 120 air-con rooms, tennis courts, and a swimming pool. Rooms go for Dr450/580.

Swimming Pools

There is a nice pool at the Hôtel Transatlantique, but non-guests pay a steep Dr100. It's open from May to October. The pool at the Hôtel Rif is open all year and is a cheaper option at Dr30. There is a municipal pool (not much fun for women) across the Oued Bou Fekrane to the east of the medina.

Hammams

There are several hammams in the medina. You'll find a reasonable one down an alley near the Hôtel de Paris. Look for the yellow signs marked 'Douche' and 'Bain'. The showers are for men only (7 am to 9 pm); there are small towels and soap if you forget your own. The baths are open to men from 7 am to 1 pm, and from 8 pm to midnight. For women, they are open from 1 to 8 pm.

Another hammam for men only is at the northern end of Rue Ben el-Maacer. Showers and baths cost Dr5.

Places to Eat

Medina If you are staying in the old town, there are a few simple restaurants along Rue Dar Smen between the Hôtel Regina and Place el-Hedim.

Two of the best are the *Restaurant Économique*, at No 123 (one of the few with a sign) and, a little closer to Place el-Hedim, *Restaurant Bab Mansour* at No 127. Tajine costs around Dr25, or you can simply point to a range of dishes on display and put together your own meal for about the same price.

Next door to the cafes are a couple of good fruit juice bars (Dr4 to Dr6 for a glass). There's also a mass of cheap-eat stalls spilling out in the lanes just outside the Bab el-Jedid.

The best value restaurant of all is the *Collier de la Colombe* (☎ 555041) hidden away in the southern part of the medina at 67 Rue Driba. It's a well run, upmarket place with good panoramic views over the city. It has a selection of excellent four course set menus (Moroccan and international) with mint tea and patisserie for Dr70 to Dr75. Call them and they'll have someone guide you through the narrow streets to the restaurant.

Worth avoiding is the better known *Restaurant Zitouna* at 44 Jamaa Zitouna. It's done up in the usual palace-restaurant style, but is geared exclusively towards the large tour groups who are herded through here. Many travellers have complained about the poor food and service, and it was no better when the author visited.

Ville Nouvelle There are a few cheap eats along Ave Mohammed V, plus a roast-chicken place *La Boveda*, close to the Hôtel Excelsior on Ave des FAR.

There are two good little restaurants around the corner from the Hôtel Majestic on the road leading to the El-Amir Abdelkader train station. A filling meal of brochettes, salad and a drink costs about Dr30.

One place that stands out is the justifiably popular *Rôtisserie Karam*, at 2 Zankat Ghana, near the corner of Ave Hassan II. The food is cheap and good; filled rolls cost from Dr12 and main meals (typically tajine or brochettes and chips) cost from Dr23 to Dr25. There are a few tables upstairs where you can take your food, if you can find a place.

If you're desperate for western-style fast food, by far the best place in town is the new and trendy *Mo Di Niro* at 14 Rue Antserabi. They serve decent hamburgers with chips (Dr14.50 to Dr21.50), salads, pizzas and milk shakes and there's even a non-smoking area. The upstairs section is a good place for lone women travellers looking for some peace.

Another new and fun place is the American-style *New Mex Snack Grill*, at 20 Rue de Paris, with very edible Tex-Mex meals for around Dr35 to Dr45; they also have hot dogs, burgers and the like for under Dr20. It's designed to look like an American bar and is open all day from 11.30 am to 11 pm. It's also a popular place with students.

Pizzeria Le Four on Rue Atlas is a pleasant place decorated in an Italian style with timbered roof and whitewashed walls. Excellent pizzas are served on a wooden platter and cost Dr34 to Dr46. Meat dishes, pasta and decent salads (Dr22 to Dr45) are also available, as are wine and beer (Dr14). Watch out for the 19% taxes. It's a popular place with trendy locals.

For traditional Moroccan food, many travellers head for the *Restaurant Metropole Annexe* (☎ 525223), 11 Rue Charif Idrissi, around the corner from the junction of Ave Hassan II and Ave Mohammed V. A three course, Moroccan-style set meal costs Dr90. If you just want one dish, ask for the 'la carte'. Mains cost from Dr60. The food is good and the restaurant is licensed. Tajine is the speciality; if you want to try something else such as pastilla or mechoui, you'll need to order it in advance.

Next door on the corner is the *Restaurant Gambrinus*. It's probably better value than the Metropole and is very popular with the locals. Abdullah, the elderly owner, will give you a warm welcome, though he's really only conversant in German. It's a very simple place, but the food is good and very reasonably priced. There is a three course set menu for Dr60 (mains cost around Dr40).

Le Dauphin restaurant (☎ 523423) at 5 Ave Mohammed V has a reputation for its fish dishes. It's not cheap though – mains cost between Dr85 and Dr110. Alcohol is available. The entrance to the restaurant is through a side door down the street off Ave Mohammed V.

Cafes The cafes on Place el-Hedim in the medina are good for people-watching. The *Café Mamounia* on Rue Rouamine is also not bad, and just down from it is a hole-in-the-wall selling freshly fried sfinj – a kind of light, deep-fried doughnut great for dunking in coffee. You buy a few at a time and they are tied together with a strand of palm frond. Get there before 11 am (it opens at 5 am), or they'll all be sold out.

The ville nouvelle, especially on and

MIDDLE ATLAS

FRANCES LINZEE GORDON
Draughts players in Place el-Hedim, Meknès

around Ave Mohammed V, is full of French-style cafes. The *Café Opera* at 7 Mohammed V has a very peaceful upstairs section which is good for women travellers tired of street attention. *The Café* at the Institut Français is a popular with students.

Patisseries & Ice Cream If you fancy something sweet and sticky, follow the smell of baking to the *Pâtisserie Glacier Florence* opposite the Rôtisserie Karam on Zankat Ghana. A breakfast of orange juice, chocolate croissant and coffee/tea costs Dr12. If you haven't yet tried a Moroccan jus d'amande (almond juice), this is the place to do it – it's heavenly. The patisserie is open every day from 7 am to 9.30 pm.

For very early starters, there's the *Pâtisserie Glacier Miami* at 15 Ave Mohammed V, which opens at 4 am (until 9.30 pm) every day. It has wonderful, fresh almond croissants most mornings. For lovely sweets, head for the *Pâtisserie La Gourmandise* near the Hôtel Rif at 8 Rue Tetouan. It's open daily from 8 am to 8 pm.

Both places have ice cream in summer.

Entertainment

Bars The piano bar inside the restaurant *La Coupole*, on Ave Hassan II, opened in October 1996 and is seemingly the best place in town for a drink. Don't confuse it – as the author did – with the Bar Le Coupole just around the corner which is a very seedy affair. Beers cost Dr15, and it's open from 7 to 11 pm.

You may prefer the highly discreet *liquor store* (disguised as a grocery store) further up Blvd Allal ben Abdallah for some take-home alcohol. As noted, some of the restaurants in the ville nouvelle are licensed. All the bigger hotels have bars.

Nightclubs & Cinemas Meknès is quite a conservative little town; bars close by 11 pm and nightclubs by 1 am. The two best discos are currently those in the *Hôtel Zaki* and *Hôtel Bab Mansour*. Entry and drinks each cost Dr50 during the week and Dr70 over the weekend.

There are a few cinemas around town which are marked on the map; the best of these is the *Cinéma Camera* which charges Dr12/15, depending on your seat. There are shows (in French) at 3 and 9 pm.

If you have time before the show, nip across the road to the Pâtisserie Rex which has wonderful strawberry tarts and good ice cream.

Getting There & Away

Air Royal Air Maroc has several representatives, including Wasteels and Carlson Wagonlits (see the Travel Agencies entry under Information earlier in this section).

It also has an office (☎ 523606) at 7 Ave Mohammed V. There is a small airstrip just outside Meknès, but no regular flights.

Bus The CTM station is on Ave Mohammed V near the junction with Ave des FAR. There are eight departures daily to Casablanca and Rabat (Dr63/37; the first at 5.30 am and the last at 8 pm); eight to Fès (Dr13; the first at 10.30 am and the last at 11 pm); two to Er-Rachidia (at 10 and 11.30 pm – the first continues on to Rissani); two to Ifrane and Azrou (at 6.30 am and 4.30 pm); two to Tangier (Dr68; at 1.30 and 7 pm); and three to Taza (Dr49).

CTM also operates international buses to Paris and Brussels – for details see the Getting There & Away chapter.

The main bus station for all other companies is just outside Bab el-Khemis on the northern side of the new mellah along Ave du Mellah (see the Meknès Medina map). There is a left-luggage office (Dr5 per item per 24 hours), a cafe and phone office.

There are two buses a day to Marrakesh (Dr96) at 5.30 am and 6.30 pm (Window 9). For Moulay Idriss (Dr6) buses leave every hour from 7 am to 6 pm (Window 8). There are also five buses a day to Kenitra, 13 to Rabat and 10 to Casablanca. Most buses run between 5 am and 4 pm, and tickets for these buses can be bought at Window 5.

Four buses a day depart for Tetouan (Dr56), Chefchaouen (Dr45), and Ouezzane (Dr30). For Tangier (Dr50; six hours) there are five buses a day. All tickets for these buses can be bought from Window 6.

The first buses generally leave between 4 to 6 am and the last between noon and 2.30 pm.

Fès tickets (Dr11) can be purchased at Window 7. Buses leave every hour or so from 6 am until 7 pm, after which there are a few more at uncertain times in transit from Rabat.

There are five buses a day to Taza (Dr35), two to Sefrou (Dr18), and eight to Oujda (Dr74.50) and Nador (Dr75).

Train The main train station is some way from the centre of the new city, on Ave du Sénégal. It's much more convenient to use the El-Amir Abdelkader station, one block away from and parallel to Ave Mohammed V, as all trains stop here. All trains to or from Fès also stop in Meknès.

A total of eight trains go to Fès (one hour), four of which go on to Oujda (6½ hours), and at least nine to Casablanca (4¼ hours) via Rabat (3½ hours). There are eight services to Marrakesh, three of them direct (7½ hours).

Second class fares on normal and rapide services include: Fès (Dr12.50/15); Tangier (Dr59/70); Casablanca (Dr60/72.50) and Marrakesh (Dr116/137.50).

Taxi All the grands taxis leave from a dirt lot between Bab el-Khemis and the main bus station. You can't miss it.

There are regular departures to Fès (Dr15), Rabat (Dr35), Moulay Idriss (for Volubilis, Dr7), Sidi Kacem (Dr12) and Beni Slimane (Dr44). As always, it's best to arrive in the morning.

Car Zeit (☎/fax 525918) has an office at 4 Rue Anserabi. Stopcar (☎ 525061) is at 5 Rue de la Voûte.

Getting Around

Bus There are local buses between the medina and the new city, but they are invariably crowded and hard to get on.

Useful routes include the No 2 (Bab el-Mansour to Blvd Allal ben Abdallah, returning to the medina along Ave Mohammed V) and No 7 (Bab el-Mansour to the CTM bus station).

Taxi A useful urban grand taxi route, which connects the new and old cities, starts in the new city from Zankat Ghana near the corner of Ave Hassan II, directly opposite the Rôtisserie Karam.

The grands taxis are silver Mercedes with black roofs. The fare is Dr5 per person. Pale-blue petits taxis covering the same distance would cost about Dr10. A petit taxi ride from the main bus station to El-Amir Abdelkader train station is Dr12.

AROUND MEKNÈS
Volubilis

About 33km from Meknès is the site of the largest and best preserved Roman ruins in Morocco.

Volubilis dates largely from the 2nd and 3rd centuries AD, although excavations have revealed that the site was originally settled by Carthaginian traders in the 3rd century BC.

Volubilis

Detail from the mosaic in the House of Orpheus, depicting a variety of wild and domesticated animals (photograph by Frances Linzee Gordon).

Volubilis (*Oualili* in Arabic) was one of the Roman Empire's most remote outposts, after the area was annexed in about 40 AD. According to some historians, Rome imposed strict controls on what could, or could not, be produced in its North African possessions, according to the needs of the empire. One result was massive deforestation and the large-scale planting of wheat. The sweep of largely treeless plains around Volubilis certainly makes such a thesis plausible.

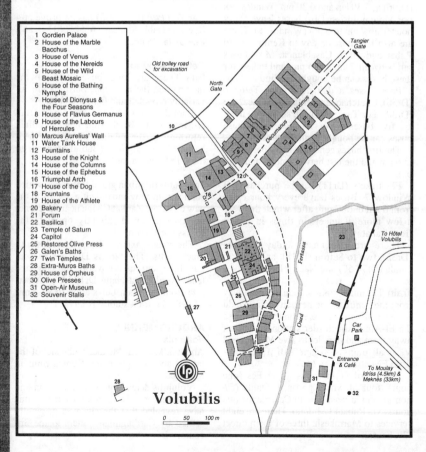

1 Gordien Palace
2 House of the Marble Bacchus
3 House of Venus
4 House of the Nereids
5 House of the Wild Beast Mosaic
6 House of the Bathing Nymphs
7 House of Dionysus & the Four Seasons
8 House of Flavius Germanus
9 House of the Labours of Hercules
10 Marcus Aurelius' Wall
11 Water Tank House
12 Fountains
13 House of the Knight
14 House of the Columns
15 House of the Ephebus
16 Triumphal Arch
17 House of the Dog
18 Fountains
19 House of the Athlete
20 Bakery
21 Forum
22 Basilica
23 Temple of Saturn
24 Capitol
25 Restored Olive Press
26 Galen's Baths
27 Twin Temples
28 Extra-Muros Baths
29 House of Orpheus
30 Olive Presses
31 Open-Air Museum
32 Souvenir Stalls

Tangier Gate

Old trolley road for excavation

North Gate

Decumanus Maximus

Fertassa

Oued

To Hôtel Volubilis

Car Park

Entrance & Café

To Moulay Idriss (4.5km) & Meknès (33km)

Volubilis

0   50   100 m

Volubilis' population of Berbers, Greeks, Jews and Syrians continued to speak Latin and practise Christianity right up until the coming of Islam. Unlike Lixus, to the north-west, which was abandoned shortly after the fall of the Roman Empire, Volubilis continued to be inhabited until the 18th century, when its marble was plundered for the building of Moulay Ismail's palaces in Meknès.

Volubilis is an easy day trip from Meknès and shouldn't be missed, even if you're not normally into Roman remains. You can also take in the nearby town of Moulay Idriss.

The site's most impressive monuments were built in the 2nd and 3rd centuries AD, including the triumphal arch, capitol, baths and the basilica. Its most attractive feature without doubt is the stunning mosaics, made even more so by the fact that they have been left *in situ*.

The site is open daily from sunrise to sunset and entry is Dr20. The best time to visit is during the early morning (ideally just after sunrise) or at sunset, when you'll share the place with just the guardian's donkey grazing among the ruins. The coach parties start arriving in late morning, and the midday sun on the open plain can seem very fierce. At dusk, with the last rays of the sun on the ancient columns, the place can seem almost magical.

If there are several of you, or you can find others, you might want to share a guide. They do good 45 to 60 minute tours for

The ruins of the Capitol in the last rays of the setting sun.

FRANCES LINZEE GORDON

Dr80 to Dr100. Unfortunately no other information about the place is available on the site.

Major Points of Interest

The best known monuments are in the northern part of the site, although it's more convenient to start in the south. Once over the Oued Fertassa, the path from the entrance takes you through an unremarkable resi-

Right: Detail of the mosaic in the Gordien Palace.

Below: The dolphin mosaic is one of many featuring aquatic animals at the site.

ALL PHOTOS BY FRANCES LINZEE GORDON

dential quarter. The **House of Orpheus**, a little higher up and identifiable by the three pine trees growing in the corner, was a sumptuous mansion for one of the city's wealthier residents. Its two mosaics, one representing the Orpheus myth and the other the chariot of Amphitrite, are still in place.

The basilica, capitol and forum are, typically, built on a high point. The **capitol** dates back to 217 AD; the **basilica** lies to the north of it.

On the left, just before the Triumphal Arch, are a couple of roped-off **mosaics**. One depicts an athlete being presented with a trophy for winning a *desultor* race, a competition in which the rider had to dismount and jump back on his horse as it raced along. Opposite these mosaics are the remains of an aqueduct and fountain.

The **Triumphal Arch** on the Decumanus Maximus road, built in 217 AD in honour of Emperor Caracalla and his mother, Julia Domna, used to be topped with a bronze chariot. The arch was reconstructed in the 1930s, and the mistakes made then were rectified in the 1960s.

The **Decumanus Maximus** stretches up the slope to the north-east. The houses lining either side of the road contain the best mosaics on the site. The first house on the far side of the arch is known as the House of the Ephebus and contains a fine mosaic of Bacchus in a chariot drawn by panthers.

The marble Triumphal Arch of Volubilis was built in 217 AD to honour the Roman Emperor Caracalla.

FRANCES LINZEE GORDON

FRANCES LINZEE GORDON

The large Basilica, with its five aisles, served as the law courts and trading centre.

Next along is the **House of the Columns** (so named because of its columned facade), and adjacent to this is the **House of the Knight** with its incomplete mosaic of Bacchus and Ariadne.

Behind these houses you can still see the trolley tracks laid to cart away excavated material. The size of the pile of waste moved to uncover the site is astonishing – there's a sizeable artificial hill out there.

In the next couple of houses are excellent mosaics entitled the *Labours of Hercules* and *Nymphs Bathing*. However, the best collection on the whole site is in the **House of Venus**, one block further up and one block to the right. Although some of the house is roped off, there is a viewing platform built along the southern wall that gives you a good vantage point over the two best mosaics – the *Abduction of Hylas by the Nymphs* and *Diana Bathing*.

The Decumanus Maximus continues up the hill to the Tangier Gate, past the uninteresting Gordien Palace, which used to be the residence of the city's administrators.

At the time of writing, just 18 of the 40 hectares comprising the site of Volubilis had been excavated. A Moroccan-French team of three archaeologists is working on the site, and new and exciting discoveries are made every day. Recently, a formal request was made to UNESCO to declare Volubilis a World Heritage site.

There are also plans to make more information available at the site. In 1998, explanatory panels should be in place, and eventually a museum will open displaying the objects unearthed here (many are now in the archaeology museum in Rabat). Brochures and books should also be available soon.

Places to Stay & Eat The *Camping Zerhoune* (☎ 517756), 9km from Volubilis (14km from Meknès) is a pleasant, shady and well-run place with swimming pool, cafe and restaurant. It costs Dr15 per person, Dr10 per child and tent and Dr7 per car (Dr20 for a caravan or camping van). The pool is open from June to August only and costs Dr15/10 per adult/child. El-houcine, the charming son of the owner, speaks a little of various languages and will look after you.

The only hotel in the area is the four-star *Hôtel Volubilis* (☎ 544405; fax 636393), about 500m further on from the site coming from Meknès. It's a peaceful and extremely pleasant place with a pool, tennis court, two restaurants and a bar. It charges Dr368/506 (Dr100 supplement for rooms with a view) for singles or doubles with balcony and bathroom, TV, fridge, and telephone, and is good value for what you get. If you want to have just one night of luxury in Morocco, this might be the place for it.

It's also a good spot for a splurge. The set menu (lunch or dinner) in a restaurant designed like a Berber tent costs Dr154 (main courses from Dr90). If you can't afford a room or a meal here, then you could always come for coffee (Dr6) and a cake (Dr6). There is a very pleasant, shaded terrace with wonderful views of the ruins and the plain stretching below.

Coffee, mint tea or a soft drink (Dr5) is also available at the cafe near the entrance to the site. They usually offer a fixed meal too (tajine, salad and fruit) for around Dr70.

Getting There & Away To get to Volubilis from Meknès, take one of the infrequent buses from the bus station outside Bab el-Khemis. Get off at the turn-off to Moulay Idriss. From there it's about a 30 minute walk – extremely pleasant when it's not too hot – and follow the turn-off to the left for Oualili.

Alternatively, you can take a grand taxi to Moulay Idriss. These leave fairly frequently from near the bus station.

Getting back, the best thing to do is to try and hitch a lift with the many tourist coaches, minibuses or private vehicles heading back to Meknès, or at least to Moulay Idriss (a good hour's walk) from where you can catch a bus or grand taxi to Meknès. Don't leave it too late in the afternoon however, as transport tends to dry up.

The last option is to get a group together and a hire a grand taxi for half a day. You should pay no more than Dr300.

The Roman ruins of Volubilis perch on a small plateau in a treeless plain.

FRANCES LINZEE GORDON

Moulay Idriss

The other main place of interest outside Meknès is Moulay Idriss, about 4.5km from Volubilis. The town is named after Morocco's most revered saint, a great-grandson of the Prophet Mohammed and the founder of the country's first real dynasty.

Moulay Idriss fled Mecca in the late 8th century AD in the face of persecution at the hands of the then recently installed Abbassid Caliphate, which was based in Baghdad. Idriss settled at Volubilis, where he managed to convert the locals to Islam and made himself their leader. From there he went on to establish Morocco's first imperial dynasty.

Moulay Idriss is an attractive town, nestled in a cradle of verdant mountains, and for Moroccans it's a place of pilgrimage. For non-Muslims, the place has been open to them only for the past 70 years or so. You still cannot visit any of the mosques or shrines and you are not supposed to stay overnight.

Things to See Although the twin hill town is a veritable maze of narrow lanes and dead ends, it is not hard to get around to the few points of interest.

The first is the **Mausoleum of Moulay Idriss**, the object of veneration and the reason for the country's greatest annual moussem in late August.

From the main square (where buses and grands taxis arrive), walk up the street that starts to the left of the bus ticket booths. This brings you into the main street, which is lined on both sides by cafes and cheap food stands; those on the right overlook the square from which you have just emerged.

Proceed straight down this street and under the arch – the number of guides (unnecessary) and tourist groups should reassure you that you're getting warm.

About 50m on to your left you'll see a three-arched gateway. Go through it and continue straight ahead – you'll soon come up against the barrier that marks the point beyond which non-Muslims may not pass. The mausoleum that stands here today was built by Moulay Ismail, although various additions have since been made.

You can now head left into the maze of streets and try to find your way to a couple of vantage points that give you a good **panoramic view** of the mausoleum, the town and the surrounding country – plenty of guides will offer to help.

If you don't feel like being guided, there is an alternative. Head back to the beginning of the main street, which you reached coming up from the bus station square. Looking again in the direction of mausoleum, you'll notice a side street heading uphill to your left and signposted 'Municipalité'. Follow it, and just before the Agfa photo shop on the left take the cobbled street to the right.

As you climb up you'll notice the only **cylindrical minaret** in Morocco. The green tiles spell out in stylised script the standard Muslim refrain, *la illah illa Allah* – 'There is no god but Allah'.

Proceed another 200m and you're close. This is where you have to ask a local for the 'grande' or 'petite terrasse' – this should produce no problem. The terraces provide vantage points high above the mausoleum and a good part of the town.

Saturday is market day and so a more lively time to be in Moulay Idriss; it's also easier to get there on a Saturday.

Places to Eat There is nowhere to stay in Moulay Idriss. The main battery of cheap restaurants and cafes is in the main street above the bus station.

The best restaurant in town (even with a minor international gastronomy award) is the *Restaurant Baraka* at 22 Aïn Smen-Khiber, which has two excellent though pricey menus for Dr95/110. Main courses are available for around Dr65.

There are a few cafes on the square and its approaches too. It's open from noon to 3 pm only.

Getting There & Away Occasional buses and more frequent grands taxis run from the bus station outside Bab el-Khemis in

Meknès. The ride costs Dr7. Note that it can be extremely difficult getting out of Moulay Idriss after about 3 pm. There are few services and often a lot of customers. The occasional bus stops here en route to or from such places as Casablanca.

If you have your own transport, you might consider taking an alternative route back either to Fès or to Meknès. Both routes are really only possible in summer, unless you have a 4WD. The road surfaces are very rough, but there are some wonderful views to be had along the route. Both roads eventually join up with the principal roads to these two towns.

To Meknès, ask for the road towards the village of El-Merhasiyne; towards Fès, ask for the road to Nzala-des-BéniAmmar.

If you're taking the usual road to Meknès, watch the police control just out of sight as you roll down the hill from Moulay Idriss. They have a reputation for fining tourists large sums for the slightest infraction (especially speeding or not wearing seat belts).

Fès

The oldest of the Imperial cities, Fès is arguably the symbolic heart of Morocco.

Founded shortly after the Arabs swept across North Africa and Spain, it quickly became the religious and cultural centre of Morocco. Even in those periods when it was not the official capital of the whole country, Fès could not be ignored and never really ceased to be considered the northern capital.

All the great dynasties left their mark on the city, but it owes much of its magnificence to the people who from the start made up its cosmopolitan population. In the early days, thousands of families from Muslim Spain came, followed by Arabs from further east along the North African littoral. Despite the arrival over the centuries of some Berbers from the interior, Fès has retained a distinctly Arab identity.

It has also long considered itself the centre of Islamic orthodoxy, and its allegiance, or at least submission, has always been essential to Morocco's rulers.

With such symbolic importance attached to their city, Fassis (the people of Fès) have always been conscious of the power they wield.

The city has, up until the present day, acted as a barometer of popular sentiment. Morocco's independence movement was born in Fès, and when there are strikes or protests, they are always at their most vociferous here.

The medina of Fès el-Bali (Old Fès) is one of the largest living medieval cities in the world and the most interesting in Morocco. With the exception of Marrakesh, Cairo and Damascus, there is nothing remotely comparable anywhere else in the Arab world.

Its narrow winding alleys and covered bazaars are crammed with every conceivable sort of craft workshop, restaurant, meat, fruit and vegetable market, mosque and medersa, as well as extensive dye pits and tanneries – a veritable assault on the senses as you squeeze past recalcitrant donkeys and submit to the sounds and smells of this jostling city.

The gates and walls that surround the whole are magnificent. The expanding population has filled out the ville nouvelle to the south-west and spread to the hillsides in an arc stretching principally north and south of the new city.

But Fès is a city in trouble. Its million or so inhabitants are straining it to the utmost, and the old city, some experts have warned, is slowly falling apart. UNESCO has done a lot to stop this deterioration, and is working on a cultural heritage plan for the city, but in the long term it will need huge investment if its unique beauty is to be preserved.

For now, it still represents an experience you are unlikely to forget. You could easily spend a week wandering through this labyrinth and still not be ready to leave.

In spite of the hordes of tourists that pile

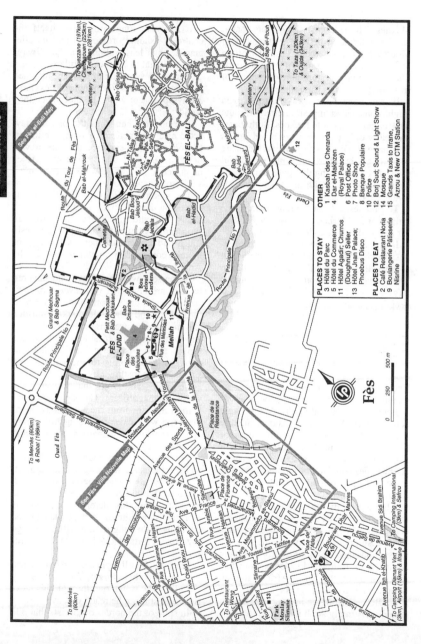

Fès

0   250   500 m

PLACES TO STAY
3   Hôtel du Parc
5   Hôtel du Commerce
11 Hôtel Agadir; Churros
    (Doughnut) Seller
13 Hôtel Jnan Palace;
    Phoebus Disco

PLACES TO EAT
2   Café Restaurant Noria
9   Boulangerie Pâtisserie
    Nisrine

OTHER
1   Kasbah des Cherarda
4   Dar el-Makhzen
    (Royal Palace)
6   Post Office
7   Photo Shop
8   Banque Populaire
10 Police
12 Borj Sud; Sound & Light Show
14 Mosque
15 Grands Taxis to Ifrane,
    Azrou & New CTM Station

through, Fès gives the impression of living largely in the centuries-old traditions that have shaped it.

The ville nouvelle and its chic, cafe-lined avenues provide a jarring contrast – the modern flipside to the ancient city. Sipping coffee and watching the passers-by along Blvd Mohammed V, you could just about be forgiven for thinking you're in a southern French city.

Young Fassis, like young Moroccans in the other big cities, appear to have cast aside the trappings of their parents' lives, instead adopting fashions and lifestyles more readily identified with the west. The downside is that many are without work. The smart, clean centre of the ville nouvelle disguises the sad lot of the poorer people living on the periphery.

This aspect of the city's life will be most evident to travellers in the touts, hustlers and beggars who will undoubtedly be encountered.

History

There is some dispute over who founded Fès. Some say that Idriss I, who founded Morocco's first imperial dynasty, decided Oualili (Volubilis) was too small for the role of capital and began work on a new one here in 789 AD. Others claim his son, Idriss II, was responsible.

In any event, a town was well established here by 809. The town's name is believed to come from the Arabic word for 'axe', and one tale relates that a golden pickaxe was unearthed at the beginning of construction around Oued Fès.

The city started off modestly enough as a predominantly Berber town, but its complexion changed with the arrival on the east bank of 8000 families fleeing Al-Andalus. They were later joined by Arab families from Kairouan (or Qayrawan – in modern Tunisia), who set up home on the west bank – the quarter of the Kairaouine (people from Kairouan).

They brought with them the religious, cultural and architectural heritage of two great Muslim centres, thereby forming a solid foundation for future greatness. Just as his father is venerated still in the village of Moulay Idriss, so the memory of Idriss II is perpetuated in his zawiyya in the heart of Fès el-Bali.

Idriss II's heirs split the kingdom up, but for a while Fès continued to enjoy peace and prosperity. In the 10th century, Berber tribes descended on the city, which was torn by a bitter civil war and was also experiencing a famine.

The chaos continued until the arrival of the Almoravids in 1070. For 80 years they ruled the city, which was second in importance only to Marrakesh, the chosen capital of their greatest leader, Youssef bin Tachfin.

The Almoravid stay was short, however, for a still more ascetic movement arose to take their place – that of the Almohad dynasty.

In their conquest of Fès in about 1154, the Almohads destroyed the walls of the city and only replaced them when they were assured of the inhabitants' loyalty. Large sections of the walls of Fès date from this period.

Although Marrakesh remained the imperial capital, Fès continued to be a crucial crossroads and, with the importance of the Kairaouine mosque and university already well established, it became *the* centre of learning and culture in an empire that stretched from Spain to Senegal.

Fès recovered its political status only much later, with the arrival of the Merenid dynasty. They took the city around 1250, but it took them another 20 years to wrest control of Marrakesh from the Almohads and so definitively remove their predecessors from power.

Never sure of his subjects' loyalty, the second Merenid sultan, Abu Youssef Yacoub (1258-86), built a self-contained walled city outside the old one – Fès el-Jdid (New Fès) – and there stationed loyal troops, most of whom were Syrian and Christian mercenaries.

In the 14th century, the Jewish community was relocated from Fès el-Bali to the new city. In this way the first Jewish ghetto,

MIDDLE ATLAS

Fès in the 19th Century

Entering Fès el-Bali today is like stepping into a time warp back to the Middle Ages, not so different from the city discovered by Edmondo De Amicis on a diplomatic visit from Italy in the 1880s. He described his experiences in *Morocco: Its People & Places* and had this to say about Fès:

The first impression is that of an immense city fallen into decrepitude and slowly decaying. Tall houses, which seemed formed of houses piled one upon the other, all falling to pieces, cracked from roof to base, propped up on every side, with no opening save some loophole in the shape of a cross; long stretches of street, flanked by two high bare walls like the walls of a fortress; streets running uphill and down, encumbered with stones and the ruins of fallen buildings, twisting and turning at every thirty paces; every now and then a long covered passage, dark as a cellar, where you have to feel your way; blind alleys, recesses, dens full of bones, dead animals, and heaps of putrid matter; the whole steeped in a dim and melancholy twilight. In some places the ground is so broken, the dust so thick, the smell so horrible, the flies so numerous, that we have to stop to take breath.

In half an hour we have made so many turns that if our road could be drawn it would form an arabesque as intricate as any in the Alhambra. Here and there we hear the noise of a mill, a murmur of water, the click of a weaver's loom, a chanting of nasal voices, which we are told come from a school of children, but we see nothing ... We approach the centre of the city; people become more numerous; the men stop to let us pass, and stare astonished; the women turn back, or hide themselves; the children scream and run; the larger boys growl and shake their fists at a distance ... We see fountains richly ornamented with mosaics, arabesque doors, arched courts ... We come to one of the principal streets, about six feet wide, and full of people who crowd about us ... There are a thousand eyes upon us; we can scarcely breathe in the press and heat, and move slowly on, stopping every moment to give passage to a Moor on horseback, or a veiled lady on a camel, or an ass with a load of bleeding sheep's heads.

To the right and left are crowded bazaars; inn courtyards encumbered with merchandise; doors of mosques through which we catch a glimpse of arcades and figures prostrate in prayer ... The air is impregnated with an acute and mingled odour of aloes, spices, incense and kif; we seem to be walking in an immense drug-shop. Groups of boys go by with scarred and scabby heads; horrible old women, perfectly bald and with naked breasts, making their way by dint of furious imprecations against us; naked, or almost naked, madmen, crowned with flowers and feathers, bearing a branch in their hands, laughing and singing ... We go into the bazaar. The crowd is everywhere. The shops, as in Tangier, are mere dens opened in the wall ... We cross, jostled by the crowd, the cloth bazaar, that of slippers, that of earthenware, that of metal ornaments, which altogether form a labyrinth of alleys roofed with canes and branches of trees ...

Essentially, the only way in which Fès has changed since then is that the moderate affluence Fassis now enjoy has enabled them to restore many of the buildings and clean up the streets. However, that hasn't radically altered the atmosphere; Fès is still worlds apart from anything you will find north of the Strait of Gibraltar. ■

or *mellah*, was created in Morocco. Although regarded as second class citizens, the Jews were important economically in the life of the nation and were to become increasingly so.

The records suggest that the move was partly inspired by a desire to offer the Jews greater protection from pogroms. Whatever the truth of this, they enjoyed the protection of the sultan, and could be relied upon to side with him in the event of an insurrection.

Few Jewish families remain in Fès. Most left for Israel during the 1950s and 60s, and their synagogues have been converted into carpet warehouses and the like.

The Merenids' single greatest gift to posterity, in Fès as in several other cities, is the exquisite medersas they built.

As the Merenids in their turn collapsed, two dynasties vied for power – the Saadians in the south and the Fès-based Wattasids in the north. Although the latter won, they did not last long. Saadian rule was short-lived too, and the Alawites arrived on the scene in 1664.

The second of their sultans, Moulay Ismail, shifted the capital to Meknès in 1672; however, his successors chose to move back to Marrakesh. Fès never really lost its importance, however, and successive sultans made a point of residing there at intervals in order to maintain some control over the north.

As central power crumbled and European interference increased over the 19th century,

the distinction between Marrakesh and Fès diminished – they effectively both served as capitals of a fragmented country.

If anything, Fès retained its status as the 'moral' capital and it was here that the treaty introducing the French and Spanish protectorates over Morocco was signed on 30 March 1912. On 17 April, three days of rioting and virtual revolt against the new French masters proved a reminder of the city's volatile history.

Largely because of the insurrection, France moved the political capital to Rabat, where it has remained ever since, but Fès is still a constituency to be reckoned with. The Istiqlal (Independence) Party of Allal al-Fassi was established here, and many of the impulses towards ejecting the French came from Fès.

Fès was also the scene of violent strikes and riots in the 1980s, showing that Morocco's rulers, wherever they make their capital, must still reckon with Fès.

In 1916, following the establishment of

The 1912 Insurrection

The insurrection of 17-19 April 1912 caught the French somewhat by surprise, although in the wake of the violence it appeared a fairly predictable reaction to the signing of the Treaty of Fès, which ushered in the protectorate. Several French journalists were in Fès at the time. *L'Illustration* reported:

The Mellah, the Jewish quarter, was the first to be sacked – still a Moroccan tradition. How many corpses have been swallowed up in its ruins?

There were only some 1400 to 1500 troops to bring the situation under control, colonial infantry and sharpshooters camped at Dar Debibagh, some of whom were still engaged in operations around Sefrou.

Throughout the afternoon the struggle between the rebels and our soldiers continued in the streets. By nightfall, all the Europeans who had escaped the insurgents' assaults were safe. Our officers and non-commissioned officers had many an occasion to display their courage and sangfroid ...

The following day, however, the rebels dared attack Dar Debibagh. They were pushed back, but Captain Bourdonneau was mortally wounded.

It was only on the 18th that the uprising was brought under control; General Dalbiez's troops, called in from Meknès, arrived and quickly overcame the last sparks of resistance... By the time General Moinier had arrived at a forced march beneath the ramparts of Fès, it was all over.

Losses among the rebels have been estimated at 800 dead. For our part, we can only deplore the deaths of nine civilians ... Among the military, it has been a bloodbath. ∎

the protectorate, the French began construction of the ville nouvelle on the plateau to the south-west of the two ancient cities. That Fès, in common with most Moroccan cities, did not experience the wholesale destruction and rebuilding that characterised colonial practice in Algeria is largely due to General (later Marshal) Lyautey.

Orientation

Fès comprises three distinct parts: Fès el-Bali, Fès el-Jdid and the ville nouvelle. The first two form the medina, while the last is the administrative area built by the French.

Fès el-Bali is the original medina and the area of most interest to visitors. Its walls encircle an incredible maze of twisting alleys, blind turns and souqs. Finding your way around, at least at first, can be difficult, but this is no problem: you can either take a guide or, if you do get lost, pay an eager kid a couple of dirham to guide you at least as far as a familiar landmark. In spite of what you'll hear, it is not at all necessary to take a guide to find your way around if you don't want to.

The wall has a number of gates, of which the most spectacular are Bab Bou Jeloud, Bab el-Mahrouk and Bab Guissa. Bab Bou Jeloud, in the south-western corner of the old part of the city, is the main entrance to the medina. You will probably pass through it many times during your stay, and there is a cluster of cheap pensions in the area. For a good view over the medina, walk up to the Merenid tombs on the hill north of the Bab.

Next to Fès el-Bali is the less interesting Merenid city of Fès el-Jdid, which houses the *mellah* (old Jewish quarter). There are a couple of hotels here, where you can stay if you want to be close to the medina and if the hotels around Bab Bou Jeloud are full.

The ville nouvelle lies south-west of Fès el-Jdid and is laid out in typical French colonial style with wide, tree-lined boulevards, squares and parks. Here you'll find the majority of restaurants and hotels, as well as the post office, banks and most transport connections.

It lacks the atmosphere of the medina,

but pulses to the rhythm of modern Morocco and is where you'll stay if you're looking for something other than a medina cheapie.

There are local buses connecting the ville nouvelle with various parts of the old city. They run regularly and don't take long, so there's no great disadvantage in staying here. It is also possible to walk between the two – set aside about half an hour to go from Place de Florence in the ville nouvelle to Bab Bou Jeloud.

Information

Tourist Offices ONMT (☎ 623460; fax 654370) is on Place de la Résistance (Immeuble Bennani) in the ville nouvelle. It has little of interest other than the usual brochures. There is also a Syndicat d'Initiative on Place Mohammed V. You can hire official guides to the medina here at a fixed price of Dr120/150 for a half/full day.

Unfortunately, the guides in Fès, the official no less than the unofficial ones, have a reputation for taking tourists on a compulsory shopping tour (in the hope of gaining some commission). If you don't want one, make it very clear before setting out. Try to work out in advance the sights you're most interested in seeing. This will avoid any other misunderstandings, and perhaps save you having to hire a guide all over again the following day. A half-day tour is adequate to give you an introduction to Fès el-Bali, though a whole day will do the city more justice.

One guide that can be recommended and that speaks good English is Mr Nour-Eddine Masrour, who can be contacted on ☎ 741052; and for French speakers, Mlle Amina Lebbar (☎ 630456). The Syndicat should be able to put you in touch with both.

While the government has done much to combat the problem of unofficial guides (see the Dangers & Annoyances entry later in this section), it has also unwittingly encouraged them.

The prices for hiring an official guide have gone up quite significantly, and although a rise in their wages was long overdue, the fact remains that unofficial guides are considerably more attractive economically. Some travellers, and particularly those on a tighter budget, may still choose to try their luck with the unofficial type.

If you do, don't go looking for one; they will soon find you. Initially, its best to feign a lack of interest until you come across a guide who seems reliable. You can always have a tea together and decide afterwards. Unfortunately, the guides who speak English tend to be the most variable. Many have learnt English as a means to tapping the richest resources: unwary Japanese and American tourists. If you're French is up to it, you'll have a much wider and more reliable choice.

Both offices are open Monday to Friday from 8.30 am to noon and 2.30 to 6 pm. The Syndicat is also open on Saturday morning.

Foreign Consulates France maintains a consulate (☎ 625547) in the ville nouvelle at Ave Obaid Bnou el-Jarrah.

Money Most of the banks are in the ville nouvelle on Blvd Mohammed V. The Wafabank is a good bet. Several other banks have branches in the ville nouvelle and the medina.

The Royal Air Maroc office has a booth where you can change cash and cheques. Some travellers have reported problems with the ATMs on weekends. If you're stuck, try one of the bigger hotels such as the Sheraton Fès Hôtel on Ave des FAR.

Post & Communications The main post office is in the ville nouvelle on the corner of Ave Hassan II and Blvd Mohammed V. It is open Monday to Friday from 8.30 am to 6.45 pm, and on Saturday from 8 to 11 am. Poste restante is at window No 9. The parcels office entrance is on Ave Hassan II. There is another post office in the medina near the Dar Batha.

The telephone office next to the post office on Blvd Mohammed V is open daily from 8.30 am to 9 pm.

There is access to the Internet at the *Cyber C@fé El Boustan* (☎ 930909), in the

Sheraton Fès Hôtel on Ave des FAR. It's open every day from 10 am to 8 pm, and access costs Dr50 per hour.

Travel Agencies Carlson Wagonlits (☎ 622958; fax 624436) is close to the Restaurant Chamonix near Blvd Mohammed V. It's open from Monday to Friday and Saturday morning.

Bookshops Close to Place de la Résistance at 68 Ave Hassan II, the English Bookshop (☎ 620842) is a good place if you need to stock up on holiday reading. Its main market is students of English, so it doesn't have too many books on Morocco and the emphasis is literary. It has a fairly broad range of classic novels, drama and poetry, and will sometimes exchange books. It's open from 9 am to 12.30 pm and from 3 to 7 pm.

The best place to find foreign newspapers and magazines is along Blvd Mohammed V. The stand virtually across the road from the police building is not bad.

There are a few decent bookshops if you read French. One of the best is the Librairie Papeterie du Centre (☎ 622569) at 134 Blvd Mohammed V.

Cultural Centre The Institut Français (☎ 623921) at 2 Rue Loukiki puts on films, lectures and occasional classes in Arabic.

Film & Photography There are quite a few places around the ville nouvelle and the well trodden parts of the medina where you can buy film. For developing film, two places with good reputations are the Photomagic Kodak store on Blvd Mohammed V, a block in from Ave Hassan II, or the Labo Couleur Florence (☎ 620449) at 52 Ave Hassan II.

Language Schools The American Language Center (☎/fax 624850) and its affiliated Arabic Language Institute (same ☎/fax No; email alif@mbox.azure.net) are at 2 Rue Ahmed Hiba in the ville nouvelle, near the youth hostel.

MIDDLE ATLAS

This is one of the few places in Morocco set up for the systematic teaching of Arabic to foreigners. They can also organise accommodation for you either in the school itself, with a family, or in an apartment.

Courses are for three/six weeks and cost from Dr3300/6200 (Dr3500/6700 in summer), though private tuition can also be arranged (Dr135 per hour). If there are several of you, the group rate is cheaper.

For more details, refer to the Activities section in the Facts for the Visitor chapter. If you're interested in teaching English, you could look up the International Language Centre rep, Mme Bassou (☎ 641408), at 15 Blvd el-Joulan.

Laundry The Pressing Nationale at 47 Ave Mohammed es-Slaoui, just off Place Mohammed V, is open every day from 8 am to 12.30 pm and from 2.30 to 7.30 pm. Shirts cost Dr6, jeans/trousers Dr8, skirts Dr10 and jackets Dr15.

Medical Services & Emergencies. If you need to visit a doctor, Dr Annie Burg has a surgery (☎ 650647) on the 1st floor at 13 Rue Imam Ali, close to the French Consul's Residence.

If you have dental problems, you can visit Mr Leblond's practice (☎ 624030) next door to the Café Zanzibar at 91 Blvd Mohammed V. Both are French and come recommended by the American Language Center. You will need to make an appointment at both places, unless it's urgent.

The Garde Medicale (all-night pharmacy) (☎ 623380) is on Blvd Moulay Youssef in the nouvelle ville. One of the biggest hospitals is the Hôpital Ghassani (☎ 622776) in the Dhar Mehraz district, east of the ville nouvelle. For the police, call ☎ 19.

Dangers & Annoyances Morocco's notorious *faux guides* (see the Touts, Guides & Hustlers entry in the Facts for the Visitor chapter) used to be a big problem in Fès.

Interview with a Faux Guide

Ahmed is one of ten children; he has four brothers and five sisters. They live with their mother and aunt in the medina of Fès.

Ahmed's father, a bus driver, had a heart attack one morning in 1987 at the age of 46. Ahmed, aged 15, was the eldest, so he left school in order to help his mother. He had hoped to learn the wood carver's trade, but Dr700 had to be found each month to pay the rent.

Sometimes he helped his uncle who owned a clothes stall in the medina. Occasionally he sold cigarettes or ran errands for his neighbours and friends. Then he got to know the tourists who gave him sweets and pens, and did the same for them, guiding them through the medina when they got lost. Sometimes he'd get tips as well which he'd take home to his family.

Spurred on by his mother, he learnt to repeat what the official guides told the tourists – the history, the places, the stories. Later, and encouraged by his progress, he began to borrow basic school language books from his cousin, Ali. Things began to improve for the family. The best times, he remembers, were always in June, July and August when he could find work amongst the tourists all day and sometimes in the evening too. Then the new law came and they weren't allowed to guide any more.

Ahmed was caught by the police one day leading a German tourist to the Medersa Bou Inania in Fès. He got three months in prison. Many of his friends – the older ones – have now given up guiding. It's the shock, he says, 'C'est la mort là', and doesn't want to talk about it. Ahmed will continue, he says, he can take it – he's still young, and so are his brothers and sisters who need him. What else will he do, anyway? He's never learned any other profession and there are no jobs. Prison won't kill him and, if it does, at least he's done his duty and taken care of the family. ■

After Marrakesh, it was the worst city in the country for tourist harassment. The situation has definitely improved, however, since the promulgation of a new law in March 1996, which severely penalises offenders (heavy fines and up to three years imprisonment).

A Brigade Touristique has also been set up; plain-clothed policemen patrol the medina and tourist areas, and have the power to arrest suspects at random.

However, high unemployment among young people forces many to persist. Most of them operate in the area stretching from the centre of the ville nouvelle to the old city gates. Many tend to hang about Fès train station (it's a good idea to arrive knowing exactly where you're headed), some of the hotels, and at various strategic points approaching Fès el-Jdid and Bab Bou Jeloud. On a good day, you'll hardly notice any, and once inside the medina you are generally left alone.

Drivers should note a Fès speciality: motorised hustlers and guides on the approach roads to the city. They will suggest a hotel, or offer to guide you there, and can be very persistent. The best thing is to ignore them entirely.

Fès el-Bali

According to one count, about 9400 streets and lanes twist and turn their way through the original old medina of Fès el-Bali (Old Fès). Because there are many cemeteries outside the walls, and also as a result of the enlightened policies of General Lyautey in siting the ville nouvelle well away from the old city, nothing has been built immediately outside the walls.

Finding your way around can be confusing, but it's a delightful way to get lost and found. Although it is easy to become quickly disoriented, one 'rule' is worth bearing in mind while navigating. Through the labyrinth are threaded a few main streets that will bring you to a gate or landmark sooner or later. It is not always evident whether you are on one of these, but the density of crowds moving up and down them is a clue.

The easiest stretch is from Bab Bou Jeloud down At-Talaa al-Kebir or At-Talaa as-Seghir to the Kairaouine Mosque area – it is virtually downhill all the way. Heading back therefore, you'll know you aren't far wrong if you follow the crowds and head uphill.

Similarly, if you want to get towards the Hôtel Palais Jamaï and the northern gates, keep heading *up*. If this fails, you can always ask shopkeepers for directions or pay someone a few dirham to lead you to where you want to go.

It will take you at least a couple of days to get around and appreciate the city's sights to any degree. And, even though notable buildings such as mosques and medersas are interesting, they form only part of the essence of Fès. You're much more likely to find the real Fès by letting your senses lead you slowly through the crowded bazaars, pausing wherever the mood takes you to watch something of interest, rummage through the articles for sale, or simply sit down with a glass of tea and take it all in. Listen out for the mule driver's cry 'barek' (look out), or you'll risk being knocked off your feet by some urgent load. The animals wear special shoes in the medina made of car tyres, which help them up the steeper slopes.

Like any Moroccan medina, Fès el-Bali is divided into areas representing different craft guilds and souqs interspersed with houses. It is replete with fascinating old buildings, mostly of a religious nature, but many are closed to non-Muslims. Because of the compact nature of this part of the city, little can be seen of them from the outside either. No-one particularly minds if you discreetly peer through the doorways, but that's the limit.

What follows can be interpreted as a suggested itinerary for an excursion into the medina, taking you from Bab Bou Jeloud to the area around the Kairaouine Mosque and finishing with several options for exiting the medina. The medina's souqs are virtually empty on Thursday afternoon and Friday.

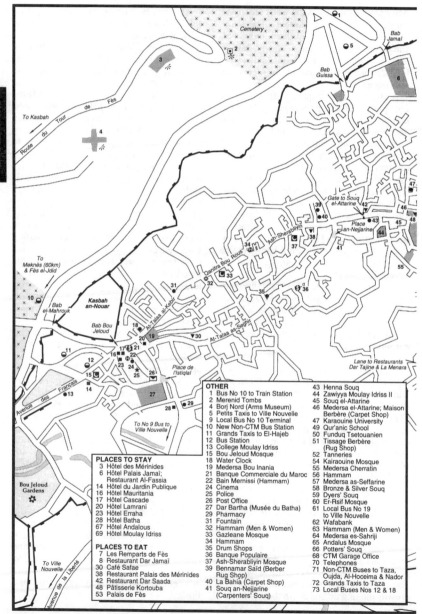

OTHER
1 Bus No 10 to Train Station
2 Merenid Tombs
4 Borj Nord (Arms Museum)
5 Petits Taxis to Ville Nouvelle
9 Local Bus No 10 Terminal
10 New Non-CTM Bus Station
11 Grands Taxis to El-Hajeb
13 College Moulay Idriss
15 Bou Jeloud Mosque
18 Water Clock
19 Medersa Bou Inania
21 Banque Commerciale du Maroc
22 Bain Mernissi (Hammam)
24 Cinema
25 Police
26 Post Office
27 Dar Bartha (Musée du Batha)
29 Pharmacy
31 Fountain
32 Hammam (Men & Women)
33 Gazleane Mosque
34 Hammam
35 Drum Shops
36 Banque Populaire
37 Ash-Sherabliyin Mosque
39 Bennamar Saïd (Berber
   Rug Shop)
40 La Bahia (Carpet Shop)
41 Souq an-Nejjarine
   (Carpenters' Souq)
43 Henna Souq
44 Zawiyya Moulay Idriss II
45 Souq el-Attarine
46 Medersa el-Attarine; Maison
   Berbère (Carpet Shop)
47 Karaouine University
49 Qur'anic School
50 Funduq Tsetouanien
51 Tissage Berbère
   (Rug Shop)
52 Tanneries
54 Kairaouine Mosque
55 Medersa Cherratin
56 Hammam
57 Medersa as-Seffarine
58 Bronze & Silver Souq
59 Dyers' Souq
60 Er-Rsif Mosque
61 Local Bus No 19
   to Ville Nouvelle
62 Wafabank
63 Hammam (Men & Women)
64 Medersa es-Sahriji
65 Andalus Mosque
66 Potters' Souq
68 CTM Garage Office
70 Telephones
71 Non-CTM Buses to Taza,
   Oujda, Al-Hoceima & Nador
72 Grands Taxis to Taza
73 Local Buses Nos 12 & 18

PLACES TO STAY
3 Hôtel des Mérinides
6 Hôtel Palais Jamaï;
   Restaurant Al-Fassia
14 Hôtel du Jardin Publique
16 Hôtel Mauritania
17 Hôtel Cascade
20 Hôtel Lamrani
23 Hôtel Erraha
28 Hôtel Batha
67 Hôtel Andalous
69 Hôtel Moulay Idriss

PLACES TO EAT
7 Les Remparts de Fès
8 Restaurant Dar Jamaï
30 Café Safae
38 Restaurant Palais des Mérinides
42 Restaurant Dar Saada
48 Pâtisserie Kortouba
53 Palais de Fès

MIDDLE ATLAS

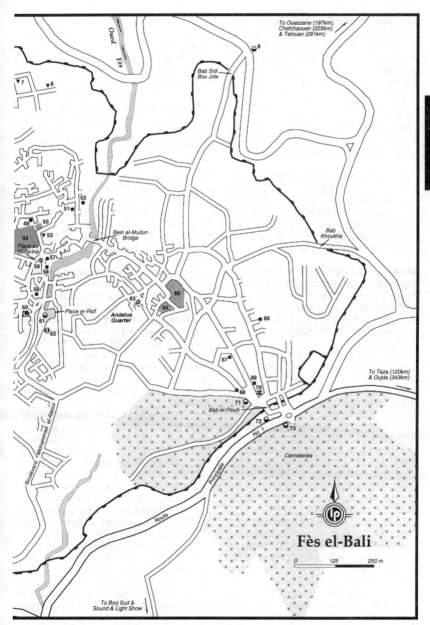

Fès el-Bali

Bab Bou Jeloud Bab Bou Jeloud is the main entrance to Fès el-Bali. Although you will probably encounter people offering to be guides, they are not nearly as bad here as they can be further out from the medina. You are bound to be warned by would-be guides in the ville nouvelle, for instance, that you should accept their services now to avoid the packs of man-eating guides circulating by the Bab and inside the medina. Should they be persistent, tell them you're staying at one of the cheap hotels just inside the gate.

Bab Bou Jeloud, unlike much of the rest of the city walls and gates, is a recent addition, which was built in 1913. When you pass through it you come upon a cluster of cheap hotels and cafes – this area is a hive of activity and a great place to sit and watch people's comings and goings.

Medersa Bou Inania Not far from the Bab Bou Jeloud is the Medersa Bou Inania, built by the Merenid sultan Bou Inan between 1350 and 1357. It is said to be the finest of the theological colleges built by the Merenids, and represents the building style at its most perfect.

The zellij, *muqarna* (plasterwork) and wood carving is stunning, and should not be missed. The entrance is on At-Talaa al-Kebir. It's easy to find, as the minaret is visible from the moment you enter the city by Bab Bou Jeloud.

The medersa has been restored in recent years with a degree of skill that proves that Moroccans have lost none of the talents for which they are justly famous. The carved woodwork and stucco are magnificent. There are excellent views over Fès from the roof (closed at the time of writing for further restoration work).

This medersa differs in a number of ways from others you may have seen already; most of those that can be visited in Morocco were built under the Merenids and all betray a common artistic inspiration. A comparison with its namesake in Meknès is sufficient to get the point across. All medersas come equipped with what we might call a prayer hall, but what Muslims would still call a mosque *(masjid)* – of admittedly modest dimensions and containing a simple *mihrab*. Here, opposite the entrance, the 'mosque' is more elaborate, and the outstanding feature is its minaret. This distinguishes it from other medersas, as they rarely come equipped with minarets.

One explanation is that the medersa required something approaching a full-scale mosque of its own because of the absence of a nearby mosque at the time it was built. As this little mosque is still in use, non-Muslims may not pass the barrier marked by a tiny tributary of the Oued Fès.

Opposite the entrance to the medersa, to your left, is a famous water clock designed by a clockmaker who was said to be a part-time magician. Unfortunately, it, too, was covered up for restoration at the time of writing.

The medersa is open between 8 am and 5 pm (except at prayer times), and closed on Friday mornings. Entry costs Dr10.

Towards the Zawiyya Moulay Idriss II

Turn right out of the medersa and head down At-Talaa al-Kebir. About 150m down the street on a bend you will pass a **fountain** on your left and a little further on a **hammam**, which precedes one of the medina's 300 or so mosques, the **Gazleane Mosque**.

At-Talaa al-Kebir continues right down to the Medersa el-Attarine, but changes its name along the way. At the Gazleane Mosque it is known as the Qanitra Bou Rous. About 100m further down, at an unmistakable dogleg (there is another **hammam** on the left just after it), it becomes Ash-Sherabliyin ('the slippermakers'); the **mosque** you pass on the right another 200 or so metres further down has taken the same name. Note on the right also, a little way past the mosque, one of the numerous 'traditional' Moroccan restaurants that Fès boasts, the Restaurant Palais des Mérinides (see Places to Eat in this section).

Another 100m on, At-Talaa as-Seghir (the parallel artery from Bab Bou Jeloud) joins this street and takes you on to an unassuming gate, beyond which it makes a slight incline into the Souq el-Attarine (the spice market).

Just past the gate on the left is another restaurant and cafe worth noting, the **Dar Saada**. It doubles as a carpet warehouse, and is a useful landmark.

Virtually across the road and down a short narrow alley is the **henna souq**, where you can buy, well, henna. It is used as a hair dye and, more importantly, to paint complex tattoo-like designs on women's hands and feet. Certain designs are associated with particular events, such as weddings.

In the jumble of back lanes and small squares just south of where At-Talaa as-Seghir and Ash-Sherabliyin meet is the **Souq an-Nejjarine** (Carpenters' Souq), through which you will find a pretty little square, **Place an-Nejjarine**, dominated by one of the city's most beautiful fountains and an impressive *funduq* – a former caravanserai for travelling merchants who would store and sell their goods below and take lodgings on the floors above.

Zawiyya Moulay Idriss II The son of the founder of Morocco's first dynasty, Moulay Idriss II is often credited with founding the city of Fès. It is more likely that his father was the founder, but there is no doubt that Moulay Idriss II brought the city to life.

He is almost as highly revered as his father, and his zawiyya is an object of pilgrimage. You can get to two gates leading into the sanctuary. From Place an-Nejjarine, a lane leads off the south-east corner to the women-only gateway.

Alternatively, from the restaurant Dar Saada you can continue a few metres east into the Souq el-Attarine and take the first alley to the right – this leads to the main entrance. Both usually have bars across them marking the point beyond which non-Muslims may not pass. With discretion, you can go up to the gates and get a look inside.

Next to the Kairaouine mosque and university, it is one of the main monuments in the heart of Fès. From vantage points overlooking the city, its green-tiled roof stands out with those of the Kairaouine against the white-grey backdrop of the surrounding houses and buildings.

MIDDLE ATLAS

Ibn Khaldoun

Although Fès cannot count him as one of its own, Ibn Khaldoun, one of the Arab world's greatest thinkers, was one of many luminaries attracted to Morocco's centre of learning, where he studied in the Kairaouine University for some years.

Considered the greatest of Arab historians, Ibn Khaldoun developed the first philosophy of history not based on religion. Called the *Muqaddimah* (Introduction to History), his book is regarded as a classic. The 20th century historian Toynbee has called it 'a philosophy of history which is undoubtedly the greatest work of its kind that has ever yet been created by any mind in any time or place'. Ibn Khaldoun also wrote a definitive history of Muslim North Africa.

He was born in Tunisia in 1332 and spent the early years of his life there, but by the age of 23, after completing his studies at the Kairaouine, he had become a secretary to the sultan of Fès. After having been imprisoned for two years on suspicion of being involved in a palace rebellion, Ibn Khaldoun moved to Granada, then Bejaia, Tlemcen, Biskra and Fès before ending up back in Granada.

In 1375 he gave up the world of business and politics and retired to the village of Frenda in Algeria where, under the protection of the local emir, he spent four years writing the *Muqaddimah*.

He spent the later years of his life teaching at the Kairaouine's eastern counterpart, the Al-Azhar in Cairo. He died in 1406. ∎

Medersa el-Attarine The street that leads through the Souq el-Attarine continues for another 200m or so (past a qissaria, or covered market, on the right) until it ends in a T-junction. Right in front of you is the Medersa el-Attarine.

It was built by Abu Said in 1325 and follows the traditional pattern of Merenid artisanship. The central courtyard is flanked by halls for teaching and the modest masjid. The zellij tile base, stucco work and cedar wood completion at the top of the walls and the ceiling cede nothing in elegance to the artistry of the Medersa Bou Inania.

It's open from 9 am to noon and 2 to 6 pm (closed Friday mornings and often Thursday afternoons, too). Entry costs Dr10. There are good views of the courtyard of the Kairaouine Mosque from the roof, but access up there seems to be limited. It's worth asking.

Kairaouine Mosque & University Emerging again from the medersa, turn left. You'll see Rue Bou Touil on the left with a few snack stalls. The walls of the great Kairaouine (or Qayrawin) mosque and university stretch down this street and ahead of you on the left-hand side (the qissaria opens up on your right).

The mosque is said to be capable of holding 20,000 people, while the university, one of the oldest in the world, has for centuries been one of the most highly regarded centres of Muslim religious learning, surpassed in reputation only by the Al-Azhar in Cairo.

It was built between 859 and 862 by Fatma bint Mohammed ben Feheri for her fellow refugees from Tunisia. It was enlarged in 956 and brought to its present size by the Almoravid sultan Ali ben Youssef. The Almohads and Saadians also contributed to its detail. The buildings include one of the finest libraries in the Muslim world, and there are usually 300 students in residence in the university. Unfortunately, non-Muslims may not enter, and it's so hemmed in by other buildings that little can be seen of it from the outside.

You can follow the walls right around it and occasionally get a look inside.

Around the Kairaouine If you head down Rue Bou Touil, following the university walls, you will be obliged to make a right turn. Just on your left is the 14th century **Funduq Tsetouanien** (Tetouan Funduq). For centuries it served as a hotel and warehouse for travelling merchants; the name suggests that it was originally the preserve of businessmen from Tetouan. Mohammed Bouzoubaa, who runs a carpet factory in the former funduq, will be happy to tell you a bit about the place, but may be a little disappointed if you don't stay a while for some tea and a look at his wares.

A little way down and still on the left is a wonderful 14th century merchant's mansion that has been converted into a carpet shop and restaurant, the **Palais de Fès**. The rooftop cafe has superb views over the Kairaouine University. Proceeding along the university walls, you emerge on another small square, Place as-Seffarine (Brassmakers' Square). With the university walls still on your right (the entrance to its library opens on to this square), there is a small and not particularly captivating **medersa**, named after the square, on your left – look for the heavy studded cedar door. Built in 1280, it is the oldest in Fès, but is in an advanced state of disrepair. Across the main street leading east off the square (away from the Kairaouine) is a **hammam**.

You could now continue to follow the walls of the Kairaouine back to where you started and head back to Bab Bou Jeloud, ideally taking At-Talaa as Seghir and perhaps winding up the day's visit with a look at the Dar Batha museum. On the way, if you're interested, you could get off the beaten track south of the Kairaouine University to have a quick look at the **Medersa Cherratin**, which was built in 1670 under Moulay ar-Rashid, the first of the Alawites. It is far less interesting than its Merenid precursors.

There are other options from Place as-Seffarine. You can head north-east to see

Fès' famous tanneries (from where you could push on over the Oued Fès towards the Andalus quarter, south to the Bab el-Ftouh and buses to the ville nouvelle) and then return to the square before setting off for the dyers' souq, Er-Rsif mosque and an alternative bus stop for rides back into the ville nouvelle.

Yet another possibility would be to return to the gateway into the Souq el-Attarine for an excursion north towards Bab Guissa, the Hôtel Palais Jamaï and perhaps beyond to the Merenid tombs (see that entry later in this section). You can also pick up a bus to the ville nouvelle from Bab Guissa.

Tanneries From Place as-Seffarine, take the lane just north of the medersa on the square. Take the left fork after about 50m and follow your nose – or the directions locals are bound to give you.

You will probably be led to a platform overlooking the tanners' pits through a leather shop. You'll be expected to leave a small tip for this, or you might be asked to give a donation (Dr10) for a 'workers' fund'.

The tanneries are best visited in the morning, when the pits are awash with the colours used in the tanning and dyeing process. It doesn't smell great, but is not quite as bad as you might be led to believe. If in doubt you can always do as the Japanese tour parties do – arrive with a small bunch of mint to press to your nose.

Dyers' Souq & Er-Rsif Mosque From Place as-Seffarine, take the main lane heading east away from the Kairaouine, and south of the medersa on the square, and you will quickly find yourself in the Dyers' Souq by the Oued Fès.

There are two small bridges over the fairly filthy-looking stream, whose water is used in the dyeing of textiles.

If you cross either one and head off to the right you will emerge on to a wide square by the Er-Rsif Mosque.

From here you can get the No 19 bus back to the ville nouvelle.

Andalus Quarter The only real attractions here are the Andalus Mosque and the Medersa es-Sahriji next door.

From Place as-Seffarine, take the lane for the tanneries, but turn right instead of left at the fork and you will reach the Bein al-Mudun ('Between the Cities') bridge over the Oued Fès. It will not be immediately obvious how to proceed from here, and you may want to enlist someone's help.

There are at least two ways to choose from. The first is as follows. As soon as you cross the bridge, turn right and then take the first left (which starts out as a covered street). At the T-junction turn right and then take the first left; about 100m up on your right is a hammam for men and women. As you head up to an archway over the street, you pass a mosque on the right.

Once through the arch (you emerge on a small square), turn left. Dead ahead is the women's entrance to the Andalus Mosque and, shortly before on the right, the entrance to the medersa. The main entrance to the mosque is around the corner to the left of the women's entrance.

The **medersa** was built in 1321. The basic structure of this college is simple, but the inside is richly decorated and there are good views from the roof. Much of the structure lay in ruins until fairly recently, but restoration work is still continuing. It is open daily from 8.30 am to 5 pm, usually with a break from noon to 3 pm. It is closed on Friday morning. Entry is Dr10.

The **mosque** was founded as a small local place of worship in the 9th century and was expanded by the Almohads in the 13th century, not long before the arrival of the Merenids, who also added to the decoration and installed a library.

If you want to leave the medina at this point, you can return to the small square, turn left and follow the wide street heading south off the square. It leads right down to Bab el-Ftouh, where you can catch local buses to the ville nouvelle.

Northern Medina The best way to reach Bab Guissa and the Hôtel Palais Jamaï in the north of the medina is to start off at the gateway to Souq el-Attarine. Take the street just on the western side of the gate. If you stick to the wider streets and keep going *up*, you really can't go wrong. You'll know you're on the right track if you pass by a little square with a cinema on its northern side.

From there you will probably arrive at Bab Guissa, from which you can easily see the Hôtel Palais Jamaï to the east. What is now a luxury hotel was built in the late 19th century by the Grand Vizier to Moulay al-Hassan I, Sidi Mohammed ben Arib al-Jamaï. (He and his brother also had a palace built in Meknès, on Place el-Hedim, which now houses a museum.)

The Jamaï brothers fell from grace at the rise of Sultan Abd al-Aziz, and lost all their property. Set in lush gardens, the palace is a wonderful place to have a refreshment – if you can afford Dr20 for a cup of coffee!

Across the road from Bab Guissa you can pick up local buses back into the ville nouvelle. There are also petits taxis.

Dar Batha

One place on the border of Fès el-Jdid and Fès el-Bali that you should not miss is the Dar Batha, now the Musée du Batha (also known as the Museum of Moroccan Arts). It is on Place de l'Istiqlal, about five minutes walk from Bab Bou Jeloud.

Built as a Hispano-Moorish palace about 100 years ago by Moulay al-Hassan and Moulay Abd al-Aziz, it houses an excellent collection of historical and artistic artefacts, including examples of fine wood carving, zellij work and sculpted plaster, much of it from ruined or decaying medersas.

There is also some fine Fassi embroidery, colourful tribal carpets and a well known ceramic collection dating from the 14th century to the present. It's a great place to see some of the famous blue pottery of Fès, and some of the exhibits number among the best examples of their kind in the country. The cobalt glaze responsible for the colour, developed from a special process discovered in the 10th century.

The museum is a good place to catch a glimpse of what better Moroccan craftsmanship is capable of. As usual, the exhibit explanations are in Arabic and French. The attractive Andalusian-style garden outside offers a pleasant temporary respite before returning to the bustle and noise of the medina. The museum is open from 8.30 am to noon and 2.30 to 6.30 pm (closed Tuesday). Entry costs Dr10.

Fès el-Jdid

Fès el-Jdid was built next to Fès el-Bali by the Merenids in the 13th century. It has some spectacular buildings and the old Jewish quarter and, although less interesting than the older city, is much easier to explore. No-one will hassle you for guide services (except perhaps to suggest that you engage a guide here to take you into Fès el-Bali).

The entrance to the Dar el-Makhzen (Royal Palace) on Place des Alaouites is a stunning example of modern restoration. The grounds cover 200 acres and house palaces, pavilions, medersas, mosques and pleasure gardens; the complex has been used to host an Arab League conference. It used to be possible to visit the palace with prior permission from the tourist office, but this is no longer the case unless you have political or cultural elbow.

At the northern end of the main street, Sharia Moulay Suleiman (formerly Grande Rue de Fès el-Jdid), is the **Petit Mechouar**, a parade ground for the sultan's troops, and the enormous Merenid gate of **Bab Dekkaken**, once the main entrance to the royal palace.

Between it and Bab Bou Jeloud are the well maintained and relaxing **Bou Jeloud Gardens** (or Jnan Sebil), though the partially dried-up lake is used as a rubbish dump. Through the gardens flows the Oued Fès, still the city's main source of water.

North of the gate is the **Grand Mechouar**, leading up to Bab Segma. Behind the western wall of the Grand Mechouar was the royal arms factory, established in 1886 by Moulay al-Hassan. It now serves as a carpet factory.

Sharia Moulay Suleiman is lined with shops and a few hotels and cafes, but lacks the atmosphere of the main streets in Fès el-Bali. South of it is the old **mellah**, the Jewish quarter. Few Jews live here now, but their houses, with windows and balconies looking into the streets, are in marked contrast to the usual Muslim practice of having windows opening on to an internal courtyard. They were transferred from the centre of the old city by the Merenids. Some say they were moved for their own protection, others maintain that it made it easier to keep an eye on their activities, and others believe it was to provide the Merenids with a loyal bulwark against possible rebellions from Fassis of the old city, whose loyalty they were unsure of.

Outskirts

For a spectacular overview of Fès, head through the Grand Mechouar and Bab Segma, cross the highway (Route Principale No 1), veer off to the left and walk around the old Kasbah des Cherarda (which now houses secondary schools, a university and hospital), following the road behind the cemetery to the **Borj Nord** (see the Fès map).

Mellah

The word *mellah* (from the Arabic for salt) appears to have referred to the area of Fès el-Jdid to which the city's Jewish population was transferred under the Merenids. Some say it was watered by a salty tributary of the Oued Fès, whereas others describe something more along the lines of a salty swamp. The word eventually took on the same meaning in Morocco as 'ghetto' in Europe – the Jewish quarter.

According to a more colourful explanation, the area in which the Jews lived derived its name from a job some were assigned by the Muslim city authorities – salting the heads of criminals, rebels and the like before they were hung up to adorn the city's gates and walls. ■

The Borj (like its counterpart on the southern side of the city) was built by the Saadian sultan Ahmed al-Mansour in the late 16th century to keep a watch on the potentially disloyal populace of Fès.

It now houses a military museum, which consists mainly of endless rows of muskets, rifles and cannon, many of them taken from Riffian rebels in 1958. Opening hours are 8.30 am to noon and 2.30 to 6.30 pm (closed Tuesday). Entry is Dr10.

Merenid Tombs

Further along, a short way past the Hôtel des Mérinides, are the Merenid tombs. These date from the time when the Merenids abandoned Chellah in Rabat as their necropolis.

Unfortunately, they're in an advanced state of ruin and little remains of the fine original decoration. There are good views over Fès from here, but watch out for stone-throwing kids.

Places to Stay – bottom end

Fès is a large city, so where you stay on arrival will depend largely on the season and the time of day you arrive. In summer, when many of the smaller hotels tend to fill up quickly, there's little point in heading for Fès el-Bali if it's getting late. Take something close to where you are for the first night and have a look around the following morning.

In summer many of the cheapies in Fès el-Jdid and Fès el-Bali hike up their prices, and you end up paying the same as you would for better accommodation in the ville nouvelle.

During this time, too, single rooms in the cheapies are almost impossible to find, as hoteliers make more money by letting them out to two or three people at corresponding double and triple prices.

Camping There are two camp sites outside the city. The *Camping Diamant Vert* at 'Ain Chkef, some 6km south of town off the Ifrane road, sits at the bottom of a valley through which a clean stream runs. There's plenty of shade, and facilities include a swimming pool and disco. Some travellers have complained that the 'traditional Moroccan evening' at the restaurant is a rip-off.

Camping costs Dr20 per person (Dr10 for children), Dr30 for a car, Dr40 for a caravan and Dr25 to pitch a tent. Motorised 'guides' tend to hang about here. Bus No 17 to 'Ain Chkef (from Place de Florence in Fès) will get you close to the camp site. You can pick it up in the ville nouvelle from Place Atlas, near the mosque.

The second place is the new and rather more luxurious Camping International (☎ 731430; fax 731554), about 3km out of town, close to the stadium on the Sefrou road.

Opened in August 1996, it is a very well maintained place set in the middle of large gardens, with a swimming pool (open May to October), tennis courts, three restaurants and bar, and various shops. It's a good place for children, who have their own pool, play park and a few organised activities such as swimming lessons.

Each camping block has its own showers, and use of a kitchen. It costs Dr50/20 per adult/child, Dr30 for a tent, and Dr40/30/15 for a caravan/car/motorbike. Bus No 38 from Place Atlas in Fès comes past here.

Hostel The cheapest place in the ville nouvelle is the youth hostel (☎ 624085) at 18 Rue Abdeslam Serghini. It costs Dr30 per person in dormitory accommodation or Dr40 with breakfast. Simple three course meals are also available for Dr40, and there are cold showers.

It's fairly scruffy, but is reasonably clean, and you can sleep on the roof if there are no beds left. They are planning to add family rooms, a communal kitchen and a cafe.

Many travellers have complained about the hostel management trying to rake in commissions by getting travellers into carpet and craft shops (sometimes in the form of a 'free crafts tour') or from hiring guides. Don't put up with this. The hostel is open from 8 to 9 am, noon to 3 pm and 6 to 10 pm.

Hotels – Fès el-Bali (Bab Bou Jeloud)
The most colourful places to stay are the bunch of cheapies clustered around Bab Bou Jeloud. They're basic and the shower situation is grim, but there are hammams all over the city.

One of the cheapest is the Hôtel Erraha (☎ 633226), just outside Bab Bou Jeloud. It has squat toilets and cell-like, but clean, singles/doubles for Dr40/60, but there is no hot water.

The Hôtel du Jardin Publique (☎ 633086) close by, down an alleyway, has definitely declined since its appearance in the last edition, but its rooms are cheap at Dr35/60.

There are a couple of rooms on the 3rd floor with windows in the outside wall, and Nos 32-4 have balconies. These are preferable to the more claustrophobic lower rooms which face the internal courtyard, although the upper ones are hotter in summer. There is no hot water and the bathrooms are pretty grubby. As with most hotels in the medina, you'll be woken in the early hours each morning by the call to prayer; it's particularly vocal here.

Just inside the Bab is the Hôtel Mauritania (☎ 633518), on Rue Serrajine, which charges Dr40 per person for clean, cell-like rooms; the bonus is the hot water in the shared showers (Dr10).

Next door, the Hôtel Cascade (☎ 638442) is one of the best deals in the medina. The rooms are simple, but spotless, and there are two roof terraces with wonderful views of the medina. The place is well run by Saïd, the friendly manager, and you can also get your washing done (Dr15 for 20 items). Rooms cost Dr40/60 and there's usually hot water. If you're badly in need of a haircut, there's a 'coiffeur' next door to the hotel, which charges Dr20/25 for men/women.

Closer to the Medersa Bou Inania is another excellent deal, the Hôtel Lamrani (☎ 634411). It has quiet, spotless rooms for Dr30/60, or for a night under the stars, you can sleep on the roof (Dr20). The shared shower is cold.

FRANCES LINZEE GORDON

DAMIEN SIMONIS

DAMIEN SIMONIS

DAMIEN SIMONIS

Top left: View of the seafront of Tangier.
Top right: Cool and clear: backstreets in Chefchaouen.
Bottom left: Lounging and people-watching in the Place el-Hedim, Meknès.
Bottom right: Mausoleum of Moulay Ismail through a gate in the classic Islamic style.

Zellij

One of the most captivating and enduring of Morocco's artistic traditions is *zellij* – the intricate mosaic designs using hand-cut tiles that adorn the walls and floors of mosques and palaces throughout Morocco.

The art of zellij is believed to have been influenced originally by the mosaics of the Byzantines, as well as techniques from Moorish Spain, but Arab influences shaped the craft in a unique Moroccan style.

Moroccan zellij is distinguished by an extraordinary colour palette and by a complex mathematical geometry. Islamic tradition forbids any depiction of living things – which is considered a decadent pagan tradition – and hence creativity relies on geometry as its expression, with spectacular results.

There are over 360 shapes or *fourmah* available to the *zlayiyyah* (craftsman) who spends the first few years of his apprenticeship endlessly drawing the multitudes of geometric configurations and committing them to memory.

Although zellij enjoyed its greatest popularity between the 10th and 14th centuries, this painstaking and expensive art form remains popular in modern Morocco. The government has helped preserve the tradition by commissioning zellij-makers to decorate public buildings and mosques. Recent examples include the Hassan II Mosque in Casablanca, one of the largest and most elaborate mosques in the Islamic world.

Martin Hughes

Intricate zellij tilework found in medersas, mosques and palaces across Morocco.

ALL PHOTOS BY FRANCES LINZEE GORDON

Hotels – Fès el-Bali (Bab el-Ftouh) If you want to be near the buses that leave from Bab el-Ftouh, or happen to be desperate for a cheapie, you could look at the handful of hotels down here.

The *Hôtel Moulay Idriss*, with rooms for Dr30/60, is about as cheap as you'll find. It's simple, but clean.

Further up the road, the *Hôtel Andalous* (☎ 648262) is even cheaper. It's also basic, but quiet, with cold showers. The toilets are a bit smelly, however. They charge Dr25/40.

You'll probably have to call into action the Arabic language section at the beginning of the book to get a room at either of these places. They're not that used to western visitors.

Hotels – Fès el-Jdid There are a few options spread out in this area, if you have no luck around Bab Bou Jeloud or don't want to be quite so close to the action.

The *Hôtel du Parc* (☎ 941698), nearest the Bab on Sharia Moulay Suleiman, is a bit dusty and shabby with cracked furniture, but it's reasonably clean, and a cheap deal at Dr30/50 for singles/doubles.

Practically in the ville nouvelle and one of the best deals in town, is the *Hôtel du Commerce* (☎ 622231) on Place des Alaouites. It has 29 pleasant and spotless rooms, most with a bit of furniture, and five with balconies; No 2 has views over the palace. Singles and doubles cost Dr40 and Dr60 respectively.

Hotels – Ville Nouvelle One of the cheapest hotels is the *Hôtel Regina* (☎ 622427) at 25 Rue Moulay Slimane, which has basic, but clean, singles/doubles for Dr40/80.

Slightly more expensive is the *Hôtel Renaissance* at 29 Rue Abdel el-Khattabi. It's an old, rather damp, cavernous place, but has clean singles, doubles and triples for Dr50, Dr80 and Dr120 respectively. There's a cold, shared shower, and the loos are the squat-type.

Slightly better, and just around the corner on Blvd Abdallah Chefchaouni, is the *Hôtel*

Savoy (☎ 620608). It has reasonably clean, airy rooms with washbasins and there are hot (usually), communal showers. Rooms cost Dr50/70/90. The Volubilis next door is used as a brothel.

Places to Stay – middle
The ville nouvelle has plenty of one and two star hotels. Among the cheapest is the *Hôtel CTM* (☎ 622811) just off Blvd Mohammed V next to the CTM bus station. It offers singles/doubles with communal shower for Dr53/73, or rooms with private shower for Dr76/96 plus taxes. The rooms are OK, but the beds are a little dodgy. They claim to have hot water all day.

Nearby is the *Hôtel Central* (☎ 622333) at 50 Rue du Nador, on the junction with Blvd Mohammed V. It's reasonably clean and secure. Rooms with private shower (hot water in the mornings and evenings), bidet and washbasin cost Dr83/106/159 plus taxes. Baggage can be safely left in reception if you're catching a late bus or train. Unfortunately, guides hang about outside the front door in the mornings.

The *Hôtel Excelsior* (☎ 625602), at 107 Blvd Mohammed V, is a bit tatty and noisy, but clean. Singles/doubles cost Dr76/94 with shower and a little furniture in the room. Hot water is sporadically available.

Closer to the train station, and quite good value in comparison with some other places in this range, is *Hôtel Kairouan* (☎ 623590) at 84 Rue du Soudan. It has spacious rooms with big clean beds, basin and bidet for Dr85/111. Rooms with private shower cost Dr109/129.

Even better is the nearby two-star *Hôtel Royal* (☎ 624656) at 36 Rue du Soudan. It has very clean singles/doubles with piping hot private shower for Dr85/111 and rooms with shower and toilet for Dr109/129.

Also in the two-star range and reasonable value, is the *Hôtel Lamdaghri* (☎ 620310) at 10 Rue Abasse el-Massadi. Though the furniture's looking the worse for wear, it's a clean, reasonably quiet place with good singles and twins (no double beds) for Dr109/129.There are showers in the rooms

Fès - Ville Nouvelle

0   100   200 m

To Merenid Tombs & Chefchaouen (225km)

Boulevard des Alaouites

To Fès el-Jdid

Agdal

To Bab el-Ftouh, Fès el-Bali & Taza (120km)

MIDDLE ATLAS

and shared toilets. The hotel also has a pleasant dining area on the first floor. Although it was not obvious at the time of researching, travellers have written in to say it is used as a brothel.

A little more expensive, but recently refurbished, is the pleasant *Hôtel Amor* (☎ 623304) at 31 Rue Arabie Saoudite. It has clean rooms with bathroom for Dr117/146, and there is a restaurant and bar. There is hot water in the mornings and evenings.

Going up in price again is the *Hôtel Olympic* (☎ 624529), around the corner

from the covered market on Blvd Mohammed V. Clean rooms go for Dr109/129/174 and come with private bathroom and toilet. There is hot water for a few hours in the evening. This place is in the process of being renovated, so may be a good (though perhaps slightly more expensive) place to try.

Moving up to the three-star range is the very pleasant *Grand Hôtel* (☎ 932026; fax 653847), on Blvd Abdallah Chefchaouni, which is also undergoing renovation. It's an older place with a bit of character, and is

PLACES TO STAY
5   Hôtel Moussafir
14 Hôtel Kairouan;
    Boulaugerie Pâtisserie
    Kairouan
21 Hôtel de la Paix;
    Papeterie Nouvelle
25 Hôtel Royal
29 Hôtel Amor
33 Hôtel Menzeh Zalagh
34 Youth Hostel
36 Hôtel Savoy
38 Hôtel Sofia
42 Hôtel Olympic
50 Grand Hôtel
52 Hôtel Excelsior
53 Hôtel Lamdaghri
62 Hôtel Splendid
63 Hôtel Renaissance
70 Hôtel Central
71 Hôtel Regina
72 Sheraton Fès Hôtel;
    Cyber C@fé
    El Boustan
75 Hôtel Volubilis

PLACES TO EAT
4   Sandwich Store
11 Restaurant La
    Cheminée
17 Pâtisserie Glacier;
    Zegzouti
    Restaurant;
    L'Empire Cinema
23 Sandwich Bajelloul
28 Venisia
40 Restaurant Fish Friture

47 Café Renaissance;
    Fruit Bars
48 Pizzeria Oliverdi
51 Restaurant Chamonix
55 Restaurant Sicilia
59 Pâtisserie L'Épi d'Or
60 Café du Centre;
    Café Zanzibar;
    Dentist
66 Sandwich Store
69 Restaurant Al-Khozama
73 Pizzeria Restaurant
    Assouan
76 Restaurant Pizzeria
    Chez Vittorio
82 Pâtisserie La Noblesse

OTHER
1   Train Station
2   Grands Taxis to Meknès
3   Petits Taxis
6   Public Swimming Pool
7   Garde Medicale
    (All-Night Pharmacy)
8   Tourist Office
9   Budget (Car Rental)
10 Supermarket La Gare
12 Telephones
13 Shell Petrol Station
15 Institut Français
16 English Bookshop
18 Royal Air Maroc Office
19 ABM (Bank)
20 Labo Couleur Florence
22 BCM (Bank)
24 BMAO (Exchange)
26 Mosque

27 Hertz (Car Rental)
30 Bank al-Maghrib
31 Main Post &
    Telephone Office
32 Europcar (Car Rental)
35 American Language
    Center
37 Police
39 Bar Lala Iris
41 Librairie Papeterie
    du Centre
43 Petrol Station
44 Newsstand
45 Wafabank
46 Photomagic Kodak
49 Carlson Wagonlits
    (Travel Agency)
54 Goldcar (Car Rental)
56 French Consul's
    Residence; Doctor
57 Church
58 Syndicat d'Initiative .
61 French Consulate
64 Cinéma Rex
65 Pressing Nationale
    (Laundry)
67 Telephones; Fax
68 Coiffeur (Hairdresser)
74 Ensemble Artisinal
77 Pharmacy
78 Grands Taxis to
    Rabat & Casablanca
79 Douche el-Fath
    (Public Shower)
80 CTM Bus Station;
    Hôtel CTM
81 Shell Petrol Station

decorated in the traditional style with a Moroccan salon and fountain. It has rooms with shower and toilet for Dr273/320. It also has a basement parking lot.

A very good choice with modern, large and comfortable rooms with en suite bathrooms is the *Hôtel Splendid* (☎ 622148; fax 654892) at 9 Rue Abdelkrim el-Khattabi. Prices are Dr222/273 plus taxes.

The hotel also has a small swimming pool and a good restaurant (four course dinner for Dr102).

The *Hôtel de la Paix* (☎ 625072; fax 626880), at 44 Ave Hassan II, has slightly more expensive, but spotless, rooms at Dr222/273/360 (the second night is 25% cheaper). The rooms are self-contained, quiet and comfortable.

Right by the train station is the *Hôtel Moussafir* (☎ 651902; fax 651909). It is part of a chain of modern hotels located at train stations, and rooms come with all the mod cons. The big plus is its proximity to the trains. Singles/doubles cost Dr256/312 plus taxes.

An excellent location within quick strolling distance of the medina is the *Hôtel Batha* (☎ 741077; fax 741078) on Place de l'Istiqlal (or Place Batha; see the Fès el-Bali map). It was temporarily shut down in 1996 after serious management problems. It seems to have sorted them out, and prices have fallen dramatically, so it might be a very good deal. Four-star singles/doubles go for three-star prices (Dr198/253). They have a pool (rather grubby) and an attractive courtyard, bar and restaurant.

Places to Stay – top end
In the four-star category is the very pleasant *Hôtel Volubilis* (☎ 621126; fax 621125) on Ave Allal ben-Abdullah. It has a lovely garden and pool and the rooms are air-conditioned. The only drawback is that it's located in the ville nouvelle at the opposite end of town, and is not really within quick strolling distance of anything. Singles/doubles cost Dr530/650, but you can quite easily negotiate a 25% to 40% discount in the low season.

Another good choice in this category is the *Hôtel Menzeh Zalagh* (☎ 625531; fax 651995), on Rue Mohammed Diouri, not far from the youth hostel. Many of the big rooms have wonderful views across to Fès el-Bali. Singles/doubles with toilet and shared shower cost Dr500/650 plus tax.

At the five-star end of the spectrum, there are two places in the ville nouvelle. On the corner of Ave Hassan II and Ave des FAR, the *Sheraton Fès Hôtel* (☎ 930909; fax 620486) has rooms ranging from Dr1400/1700 right up to Dr10,000 for a suite (plus taxes).

Further out still is the extremely posh *Hôtel Jnan Palace* (☎ 653965; fax 651917), on Ave Ahmed Chaouki, where rooms start at Dr1800/2000.

More interesting is the recently rebuilt *Hôtel des Mérinides* (☎ 645226; fax 645 225), with its sweeping views of the old medina from near the Merenid tombs (see the Fès el-Bali map). It has a swimming pool and two restaurants, and rooms start at Dr950/1100 plus tax.

If you had the money, the most interesting place to stay without doubt would be the *Hôtel Palais Jamaï* (☎ 634331; fax 635096).

Once the pleasure dome of a late 19th century grand vizier to the sultan, it's set in a lush Andalusian garden. Its rooms start at Dr900 and go up to Dr2200 for a double in the old palace. Along with the Mamounia in Marrakesh, it is a jewel of another epoch. The hotel has a swimming pool (set on a lovely terrace above the medina) and its own luxurious hammam (Dr180 with massage).

Swimming Pools
The Hôtel Menzeh Zalagh allows non-guests to use their pool for a fee of Dr40/60 per day per adult/child.

Hammams
There are many hammams in the medina; most are marked on the map, but it's not a bad idea to ask your hotel for a local recommendation.

One good one is the Bain Mernissi at Bab Bou Jeloud which is open to men from 6 am to 1 pm, and from 9 pm to midnight; for women it's open from 1 to 9 pm. It costs Dr6/15 for a bath/massage.

In the ville nouvelle, there are also various hammams and douches (public showers) dotted around. In the lane behind the CTM bus station is a modern place called Douche el-Fath. You pay Dr5 for 30 minutes. Men can go from 6 am to 8.30 pm and women from 8 am to 8 pm. Soap and towels are available.

Places to Eat
Restaurants The restaurants around Bab Bou Jeloud in Fès el-Bali remain among the most popular places to hang out in the medina. Although the quality-price relationship is not always as good as it might once have been, enough Moroccans eat here to reassure the wary diner.

The *Café Restaurant des Jeunes*, close to the gate, is a very basic place, but is cheap and convenient for a quick lunch, such as some bread and a bowl of harira soup (Dr5).

There are some great value snack stands interspersed among the restaurants and cafes in this area. For around Dr12 you can get a huge sandwich stuffed with meat, sausage, chips, salad and various other condiments – easily a satisfying lunch.

There are similar restaurants along Sharia Moulay Suleiman, close to Bab Smarine in Fès el-Jdid.

If you get hungry down around the Kairaouine Mosque, there is a small huddle of cheap food stands and an ice-cream stall between the Kairaouine and the Medersa el-Attarine.

In the ville nouvelle, there are a few cheap eats on or just off Blvd Mohammed V, especially around the municipal market. A couple of these food places are on the same side street off Blvd Mohammed V as the Hôtel Olympic.

A decent place and very popular with the locals is the *Sandwich Bajelloul* on 2 Ave Saoudia. It has a good selection of meat, including liver and sausages, which they will grill in front of you.

The *Restaurant Chamonix*, in a side street several blocks south, offers a limited range of reasonable fare. It has a set menu (salad, tajine and dessert) for Dr47.50. Unfortunately, since its inclusion in the last edition, it's become more touristy and less reliable. Across the street is the *Pizzeria Oliverdi* (☎ 620231). Pizzas are cheap, but not spectacular; it's better for sandwiches, which is what the locals come here for.

The best place in town for pizzas is the modern and clean *Pizzeria Restaurant Assouan*, 4 Ave Allal ben Abdullah. Pizzas cost from Dr30 to Dr45 and are good value, while salads are Dr25 to Dr40. They also do excellent pastries. It's open every day from 11 am to 3 pm and from 7 to 11 pm.

If you're after a drink with your meal, you could try the *Café du Centre* on Blvd Mohammed V (there's a Crédit du Maroc bank opposite). It looks rather lugubrious, but they prepare good, simple French fare which washes down nicely with some wine or beer.

The Restaurant *Al-Khozama* (☎ 622377), at 23 Avenue Mohammed es-Slaoui, is a clean, pleasant place with a terrace. It serves sandwiches from around Dr14, main

courses for around Dr35 and pizza and pasta for around Dr40. It's open from 7 am to 11pm.

The *Restaurant Fish Friture* (☎ 940699), at 138 Blvd Mohammed V, is a new fish restaurant highly recommended by some travellers. It's a bright, friendly place, decorated in a Mediterranean style and serves very tasty food.

Starters cost from Dr35 to Dr40, mains Dr35 to Dr70 and pizzas from Dr40 to Dr50. There is also a good set menu for Dr60. The restaurant is air-conditioned, and has a terrace around a fountain in thesummer. It's open every day except Sunday,and Mohammed, the multi-lingual manager, hopes to obtain a licence in the future.

Another restaurant with a good reputation for fish is *Nautilas* in the Hotel Le Paix, with dishes from Dr55 toDr80.

Further south and just opposite the Hôtel Central is another place with a good reputation. The *Restaurant Pizzeria Chez Vittorio* (☎ 624730), at 21 Rue Brahim Roudani, is decorated in a kind of Tuscan-style and has salads from Dr25, and pasta and pizza dishes from Dr45. You can get beer here (Dr15) and wine (Dr35 for half bottle).

Restaurant Sicilia (☎ 626565), at 4 Blvd Abdallah Chefchaouni opposite the Syndicat d'Initiative, is a pleasant new place which also does pizza, and at very good prices. Pizzas cost from Dr20 to Dr35 and salads (you make up your own) from Dr12 to Dr20. It's a good place for vegetarians and you can take food away. It's open every day from noon to midnight.

La Cheminée (☎ 624902), at 6 Avenue Lalla Asma (ex Rue Chenguit), is a tranquil, civilised little place with air-conditioning and waiters in bow-ties. They serve good French/Moroccan dishes for Dr60 to Dr75.

If you're craving a change of cuisine, the restaurant *Wong* (☎ 652760), at the Rèsidence Kenza in the Champ de Courses area (south of the city centre), is a good place to head.

It does Chinese, Vietnamese and Italian food, so is a good compromise for couples bickering over what to eat. Both menus are large; the Chinese one offers everything from prawn crackers to duck, seafood and even pork dishes (not bad in a Muslim country).

They also have good desserts, including tiramisu and profiteroles, and are licensed (beer from Dr20). Starters cost around Dr35 and main courses from Dr50 to Dr80. It's open every day except Monday from noon to 2 pm and from 7 pm to midnight. To get there, take bus No 14 from opposite the French Consulate in the nouvelle ville, or take a petit taxi. Ask the bus/taxi driver for the Pâtisserie Sanabil, which is opposite the restaurant.

Splurges Fès is dotted with a good half-dozen restaurants housed in old palaces and the like offering extravagant Moroccan meals in grand traditional surroundings. Many also offer stage shows, including Moroccan music and Oriental dancing.

The idea is to create something of the atmosphere of *A Thousand and One Nights*, and although it can be a bit artificial, one extravagant evening along these lines is worth the experience. Some of these restaurants are among the best in Morocco. You'll be looking at about Dr200 per person.

These places are at their best in the evening and when reasonably well patronised. In the winter, the palaces are often very cold, and very empty. If it's just you, the expensive menu and some desultory singing can seem rather depressing.

One of the cheapest of such restaurants in Fès el-Bali (and one of the least known on the tourist group circuit) is the *Restaurant Dar Jamai* (☎ 635685) at 14 Funduq Lihoudi, about 100m from the Hôtel Palais Jamaï. Ask the hotel for directions.

It's a pleasant, friendly place and there is no 'traditional' entertainment, which may be a boon for some. A three course set menu cost Dr120 and main courses such as couscous Dr70.

Also close to the hotel is *Les Remparts de Fès* (☎ 637415) which has menus from Dr150 to Dr350 and puts on a nightly music and dance show.

The *Dar Saada* (☎ 633343), down in the Souq el-Attarine in the heart of the medina is good value and offers set menus (including a superb couscous) for Dr135/185/220. It's also a great place for sampling the less standard Moroccan dishes such as trid, mechoui, dalaa, m'bakhar and pigeon tajine which cost around Dr90 to Dr135 (plus tax).

The *Restaurant Palais des Mérinides* (☎ 634028), near Ash-Sherabliyin mosque, is marginally cheaper. Although it has had bad reviews in the past, it seems to have redeemed itself. Set menus cost Dr130, Dr170 and Dr190 and main courses Dr90. It's well worth ordering in advance the excellent pastilla. Come in the evening to avoid the groups.

Possibly the pick of the crop is the *Palais de Fès*, a gracious 14th century mansion housing a restaurant and roof terrace cafe. Though the views are good, you certainly pay for them: a coke costs a steep Dr10. It is open for lunch.

The *Restaurant Al-Fassia* (☎ 637314; fax 634624) in the Hôtel Palais Jamaï, is well known both for its beautiful decoration and for the quality of its food. There's a choice of French or Moroccan cuisine and a terrace overlooking the medina, but its reputation and popularity with well heeled tourists has kept prices high (Dr390 per person for food alone).

Unfortunately the waiters are positively sycophantic here in their attempts to secure the tips they have grown to expect. There is traditional Moroccan entertainment in the evening, and it's wise to make a reservation.

Cafes There is no shortage of cafes and salons du thé. There are a few inside Bab Bou Jeloud, and an innumerable collection of them along the main streets of the ville nouvelle, particularly on Blvd Mohammed V. Take your pick. You could buy yourself some croissants or cakes in one of the patisseries and then settle down for breakfast at one of the outdoor tables and watch the morning slide by.

The *Café Restaurant Noria*, in the Bou Jeloud Gardens in the medina, is a great place to start the day, or as a midday retreat from the noise and bustle of the medina.

It's a very peaceful place, set in a cool garden beside an old *noria* (water wheel); there's also a fountain and plenty of shade provided by trellised vines. It's a popular place with Moroccan students. A cup of coffee/ tea costs Dr6 and coffee and toast Dr12; they also do main courses such as couscous (Dr40) or omelettes and salads (Dr20). The cafe is open every day from 6 am to 9 pm.

The *Café Restaurant des Jeunes* close to Bab Bou Jeloud, is a much less attractive place for breakfast, but is cheaper and more convenient. It costs Dr8 for a tea/coffee, bread, butter and jam. A better place and still cheaper is the *Café Safae* not far from the Banque Populaire right in the medina on Rue At-Talaa as-Seghir. Breakfast costs Dr7.

The *Café Renaissance* in the nouvelle ville, has the best fruit juices in town (Dr5 to Dr9), and is a popular place with students from the American Language Center. It's open every day from 7.30 to 2.30 am.

Fast Food Among the cafes and shops on Ave de France are a couple of hamburger joints. The *Venisia* is extremely popular locally. It's probably the best snack-restaurant in town and has a good range of the usual meats and sausages for sandwiches, brochettes etc. Hamburgers cost Dr15 and brochettes Dr25. It's open from 12.30 to 9.30 pm.

Patisseries & Ice Cream In the medina between the Kairaouine Mosque and the Medersa el-Attarine, the *Pâtisserie Kortouba* is a good place for an energy boost while sightseeing. They have a small, but good, selection of Moroccan and French cakes.

The *Boulangerie Pâtisserie Nisrine*, opposite the Royal Palace, is a good place for a cuppa/snack too.

There is a huge choice of patisseries in the ville nouvelle. Perhaps the best in town

for breakfast is the *Patisserie L'Epi d'Or* at 83 Blvd Mohammed V. It's a very civilised place and there's plenty of seating, including a pleasant section upstairs which is good for lone women travellers. It's open from 6 am to 9 pm every day; breakfast, which includes their delicious crusty bread, costs Dr12.

There are also several patisseries/fruit bars in a row just outside the Marché Central, some with seating. A very upmarket place, and with one of the best selections in town (though not the cheapest), is the *Pâtisserie La Noblesse* on Blvd Mohammed V. Try the wonderful florentines. It also does ice cream in summer.

The *Boulangerie Pâtisserie Kairaouan*, at 84 Rue de Soudan next door to the hotel of the same name, is a great place for preparing a picnic. It has a good selection of freshly baked bread, sweet and savoury pastries and even some chocolates. Try the chriba – the house speciality, a type of soft macaroon made with almonds, and the cornes de gazelles. It's open every day from 6 am to 9 pm.

The *Pâtisserie Glacier Zegzouti* on Ave Hassan II sells ice cream in summer.

If you've got a weak spot for the Spanish *churros* (doughnuts), there is a stall next door to the Hôtel Agadir, close to Bab Smarine. A large packet costs Dr2, but bring your own sugar to sprinkle on them.

Self-Catering There is a supermarket *La Gare* not far from the train station just off Rue Chenguit open from 8.30 am to 12.30 and from 3 to 9 pm.

For fresh fruit and veg, some spices, nuts, olives or just a parcel of delicious gooey dates, you can't beat the *Marché Centrale* (Central Market) in the ville nouvelle. It's open every day from 9 am to 1 pm.

Entertainment
Bars There are a few bars scattered around the ville nouvelle. They are generally male-only, spit and sawdust places that can get a bit rowdy towards the end of a night's drinking. Take your pick; one popular place

with the locals is the *Lala Iris* on Ave Hassan II.

Apart from these, there are bars in the middle and top-range hotels. Again, the company is more often than not all male, and any local woman there is almost certainly 'working'. The best option may be to find a licensed restaurant (see above).

Nightclubs Some of the bigger hotels have nightclubs or discos. Entry generally costs around Dr50 to Dr100, drinks around Dr80, and decent dress is expected, but after going to all that effort, you often find they are little more than a glorified version of some of the bars, except with mirror balls.

Most are open every day except Monday from 10.30 pm to 3 am. Considered the three best are *Le Phoebus* nightclub in the Hôtel Jnan Palace (entry costs Dr120, drinks Dr80), the *Volubilis Hôtel* disco (entry Dr60, drinks Dr60) and the nightclub in the *Hotel Mérinides*.

Son & Lumière Morocco's first *Son et Lumière* (Sound and Light show) opened in Fès in February 1995.

It's well done with all the usual laser, sound and even water effects. Images are projected on to the walls of the Borj Sud near Bab el-Ftouh, where its based, and on to the medina below.

It recounts 12 centuries of Fès' history and lasts 45 minutes.

Shows are run from 15 February to 15 November, every evening except Sunday. From February to May, the performance starts at 9.30 pm, from June to August at 10 pm, and from September to November at 7.15 pm.

There are versions in English, French, and Spanish, but only two are possible on the same night. You can check the schedule and buy tickets for it at the tourist office, Syndicat d'Initiative and in the larger hotels, or by phoning ☎ 931892. Entry is an expensive Dr200, but if you can afford it, it's an entertaining evening.

Some hotels try to charge a commission on the ticket; if they do, go elsewhere.

Cinema The best cinema in town is *L'Empire* at 60 Avenue Hassan II, next door to Pâtisserie Glacier Zegzouti. It has one salon and two sessions at 3 and 9 pm with tickets at Dr15/12/7.

Traditional Music The more expensive Moroccan palace-restaurants listed earlier often put on *spectacles* (traditional Moroccan music and dancing) especially for the tour groups.

This usually revolves around rather a faded belly dancer (in fact Egyptian in origin) with a fixed grin, but the musicians can be excellent (see Places to Eat – Splurges).

Things to Buy

Fès always has been, and still is, the artisanal capital of Morocco. The choice and quality of its crafts is high, and prices are about half those in Marrakesh and Tangier. As usual, it's best to seek out the little shops off the main tourist routes (principally the At-Talaa al-Kebir and At-Talaa as-Seghir). If you head for the craftsmen's workshops rather than the boutiques, you'll find much cheaper prices. You'll also learn more about the crafts themselves and the range of quality available.

The Ensemble Artisinal, next door to the Hôtel Volubilis on Ave Hassan II, is open every day from 9.30 am to 12.30 pm and from 2.30 to 6.30 pm, and is one of the best of its kind in Morocco. As usual, it's a good first stop to get your eye in regarding quality and price.

A good place for Berber kilim rugs is the Tissage Berbère at 4 Derb Taouil in the medina opposite the Tanners' Souq. La Bahia at 3 Bouakda, is a huge carpet shop in an old palace, and you'll almost certainly be led here at some stage by a guide after commission.

Even if you don't buy anything (and the 'fixed prices' are quite high), enjoy over a mint tea the beautiful carpets rolled out for you and the interesting short talk on the different styles and qualities. Don't feel pressured into buying anything.

The Carpet Buying Ritual

At some stage during your stay in Morocco, and however averse you are to the idea, you will eventually find yourself in a carpet shop. The secret is to accept the hospitality, enjoy the ceremony and not feel in the least obliged to buy.

Many of the larger stores, particularly in the bigger cities, are housed in former palaces and your brief sojourn will also provide you with a wonderful opportunity to admire one.

Just inside the shop you will be met by the manager (probably Mohammed, Ahmed or Hassan). Well groomed and multi- lingual, he will welcome you ceremoniously to his unique and superlative country, town and store. You will then be led to a seat, positioned almost throne-like at one end of the room and the obligatory glass of mint tea will soon arrive. Next you'll receive the all-you-ever-wanted-to-know-about-carpets lecture.

Five to ten minutes later, Ahmed, Mohammed or Hassan will be addressing you with newly found respect, sharing his opinions and seeking yours, as if from one great carpet connoisseur to another.

MARIE RAINONE

Overwhelming seas of patterns unfold during the carpet shop ceremony.

Unsatisfied and impatient with the rugs so far shown, and certain of your unusual, appreciative abilities, he will demand that the real stock – even his own private collection – be brought out before you. Attendants, silent and slipper-shod, will wait for the cue (anticipation is all) to send them unrolling in a flourish before you.

Carefully calculated to contrast dramatically with the tired, motley wares that came before, these 'unique, rare and genuinely antique carpets' cannot fail to impress. Carpet after carpet will be bared before you (your host now almost in a frenzy of lyrical appreciation) until a veritable sea of colour, pattern and design seems ready to overwhelm you.

All the while you will be scrutinised intently. The slightest comment, the hint of a smile, a lingering gaze, will give you away, and a whole range of similar-styled rugs will be unleashed in a torrent before you. Smelling blood, your host will go in for the kill. As the ceremony nears the end, you will be treated to the full repertoire of the famous Moroccan sales techniques, generally regarded as the most skilled, sophisticated and effective in the world. But that's a whole other story. ■

Close by and hidden away at No 13, is a much smaller place, Bennamar Saïd, run by a proud Berber and his family. It's a very good and reasonably priced place for beautiful kilims and blankets, but as with all these places, come prepared to bargain hard and don't look too interested. A blanket costs around Dr350; a kilim around Dr600 per square metre (depending on the quality), so a 4½ to 5m kilim should cost in the region of Dr2500 to Dr3000 (though baby kilims are available for Dr400 to Dr500).

Another place with a good selection at reasonable prices is the Maison Berbère

(☎ 635686), at 4 Riad Jouha near the Medersa el-Attarine.

For musical instruments, there are two excellent and very unvisited drum shops not far from Bab Bou Jeloud, near the Banque Populaire. You should pay around Dr10 for miniature set or Dr20/50/80 for the small/large/very large sets. The lutes cost around Dr500.

If you're after some of Fès' famous blue and white pottery, the best place to head is the Potter's Souq close to Bab el-Ftouh. It's up a rough track about 100m on the left. You'll probably need to get a petit taxi to take you there; negotiate a price in advance and get him to wait for you (it's difficult to find one back).

For all kinds of perfumed oils and scents, try the area around the henna souq (close to Zawiyya Moulay Idriss). The map lists more souqs that specialise in other goods.

Getting There & Away

Air The airport serving Fès is at Saiss, 15km to the south. For Casablanca, there are flights every day at 7 am (4.15 pm on Thursday) for Dr512 one way. There are three flights a week to Marrakesh via Casablanca (Dr692), nine a week to Agadir also via Casablanca (Dr927), three to Tangier via Casablanca (direct on Wednesdays, Dr457), and a weekly direct flight to Er-Rachidia every Thursday (Dr372).

There is also a weekly direct flight to Paris for Dr1776. Some flights (particularly to Agadir and Marrakesh), involve long waits at Casablanca airport for connecting flights, so it's worth checking schedules carefully.

Royal Air Maroc (☎ 625516) is at 54 Ave Hassan II. The one way fare to Casablanca is Dr512. To Marrakesh it costs Dr692 (one way), to Agadir it's Dr927 and to Tangier Dr457. The office is open Monday to Friday from 8.30 am to 12.15 pm and 2.30 to 7 pm; on Saturday mornings from 8.30 am to 12.15 pm and 3 to 6 pm; and on holidays from 9 am to noon and 3 to 6 pm. You can only use credit cards to purchase air tickets.

Bus – CTM The CTM station is in the ville nouvelle on Blvd Mohammed V. There are plans to move it (soon after this book's publication) to a brand new site not far away on Blvd Dhar Mahres, near the mosque. Tickets for CTM buses can be bought five days in advance and in the high season it's a good idea to do so, particularly on the Fès-Tangier and Fès-Marrakesh runs.

There are nine daily departures to Casablanca, starting at 7 am and finishing at 7 pm (Dr78; five hours). All but the 7 am bus call at Rabat (Dr54; 3½ hours). They also call at Meknès (Dr15; one hour), except for the 9.30 am service. There is an additional Meknès run at 6 pm.

Two buses a day depart for Marrakesh, at 6.30 am and 9 pm (Dr123; nine hours), and three for Tangier, at 11 am, 6 pm and 12.30 am (Dr82; six hours). There are two daily buses for Tetouan, which leave at 8 and 11 am (Dr63; five hours).

There are two buses each day to Oujda – a night service at 1.30 am (Dr89) and the other at 12.30 pm (Dr75). Both take around six hours, the latter goes via Taza (Dr30.50; two hours). Another bus heads for Taza at 6.30 pm.

There are international departures four times a week at 8 pm for Paris and Brussels, as well as other French and Belgian destinations (for more detailed information, see the Bus section in the Getting There & Away chapter).

Bus – Non-CTM The bulk of the non-CTM departures are from a station at Place Baghdadi, near Bab Bou Jeloud. Reservations can also be made for the most popular runs. There are various companies doing regular runs to such destinations as Meknès (around Dr12), Rabat (about Dr40) and Casablanca (Dr55). There are at least three daily departures to Tangier for Dr60 and five to Marrakesh for Dr97. It's all very higgledy-piggledy, so the best thing to do is get there as early as you can and get yourself shepherded to the right window and on to the right bus.

Three CTM buses leave from here: one to

Meknès at 3 pm, one to Ouezzane at 7.30 am and another to Taza at noon. Buses for Oujda (about Dr62), Chefchaouen, Al-Hoceima and Taza (Dr24 to Dr32) leave from the station just inside Bab el-Ftouh, the south-eastern gate. Get here early, as the runs are quite irregular.

A new bus station has been built at the foot of the cemetery next to the kasbah. Departures from here include Chefchaouen (Dr42).

Train The train station is in the ville nouvelle, a 10 minute walk from Place de Florence. Trains are the best bet if you are headed for Casablanca, Marrakesh, Meknès, Oujda, Rabat or Tangier.

There are at least 11 daily departures to Casablanca (five hours), all of which stop at Rabat (four hours) and Meknès (one hour) en route.

There are two direct runs to Marrakesh (7.20 and 9.40 am; about 8¼ hours) and four other services requiring changes at Casa-Voyageurs, Kenitra or Rabat. The longest wait is about 50 minutes.

There are two direct trains (coming from Oujda) for Tangier (1.10 and 4.10 pm; six hours). Three other trains (heading south) require changes at Sidi Kacem or Sidi Slimane. They all stop at Meknès and Asilah. Direct trains for Oujda (six hours) via Taza (two hours) leave six times a day.

Some 2nd class fares (normal/rapide) include: Casablanca (Dr72.50/91.50); Marrakesh (Dr130/163); Meknès (Dr12.50/16); Oujda (Dr79/100); Rabat (Dr53/65) and Tangier (Dr71/90).

Taxi Grands taxis on fixed-price routes leave for Rabat (Dr55) and Casablanca (Dr100) from a rank near the CTM bus station, off Blvd Mohammed V. Taxis for Meknès (Dr15) leave from Ave des Almohades in front of the train station.

Others for Taza (Dr30) leave from just outside Bab el-Ftouh.

Local ones run to places like El-Hajeb (Dr15) from a rank near the Place Baghdadi bus station and if you want to get to Ifrane (Dr20) or Azrou (Dr25), there is a rank behind the mosque on Blvd Dhar Mahres in the ville nouvelle.

For any other destination you will have to negotiate a *corsa* (special) fare.

Car The following are among the car rental agencies located in Fès:

Avis
    50 Blvd Abdallah Chefchaouni (☎ 626746)
Budget
    Corner of Ave Hassan II and Rue Bahrein (☎ 620919); Hôtel Palais Jamaï, Bab Guissa (☎ 634331)
Europcar
    41 Ave Hassan II (☎ 626545)
Goldcar
    89 Rue Abdelkrim el-Khattabi (☎ 620495)
Hertz
    Blvd Lalla Maryam (☎ 622812); Airport (☎ 651823)
Zeit
    35 Ave Mohammed es-Slaoui (☎/fax 654063)

The Grand Hôtel on Blvd Abdallah Chefchaouni, has reasonably secure car parking facilities and charges Dr10/20 for guests/non-guests.

Getting Around
The Airport There is a regular bus service between the airport and the train station. Look for No 16. The fare is about Dr4. Otherwise you'll have to get a grand taxi, which will cost around Dr80.

Bus Fès has a fairly good local bus service, although the buses are like sardine cans at certain times of the day, and are notorious for pickpockets.

The route number is usu-ally displayed on the side of the bus, near the back door, or at the front.

You get on the back and off at the front door. There's a conductor sitting at the back. Fares hover around the Dr1.90 mark. Useful routes include:

No 2
    Bab Smarine – Ave Hassan II – Hay Hussein
No 9
    Place de l'Atlas – Ave Hassan II – Dar Batha

MIDDLE ATLAS

No 10
Train station – Bab Guissa – Sidi Bou Jidda
No 12
Bab Bou Jeloud – Bab Guissa – Bab el-Ftouh
No 16
Train station – Airport
No 17
Blvd Tariq ibn Ziad – 'Ain Chkef
No 18
Bab el-Ftouh – Dar Batha
No 19 & 29
Ave Hassan II – Bab el-Jedid – Bab er-Rsif
No 47
Train station – Bab Bou Jeloud
No 50
Bab Smarine – Ave Hassan II – Soukarin

Taxi The red petits taxis are cheap and plentiful. The drivers generally use the meters without any fuss, except occasionally at the train and bus stations. Expect to pay about Dr10 to go from the train station or CTM station to Bab Bou Jeloud.

Only grands taxis will go out to the airport and although it's only 15km they're virtually impossible to beat down to less than Dr80.

SOUTH OF FÈS

For travellers heading south, there are two main options from Fès. You can take highway P24 towards Marrakesh, stopping in at the odd 'alpine' village of Ifrane and then Azrou on the way. A detour from Beni Mellal on this route would also allow you to take in the impressive Cascades d'Ouzoud (see the Around Marrakesh section in the High Atlas chapter for more on this) before finally reaching the southern imperial capital.

Alternatively, you could make a stop at Sefrou on your way along highway P20 to the southern valleys, including a tour through the Ziz Gorges before reaching Er-Rachidia. From there you could head east to Figuig, south to Erfoud or west to Ouarzazate via the still more impressive Todra and Dadès valleys.

Ifrane

Just 17km short of Azrou on highway P24 from Fès is Ifrane (altitude 1650m), where

you would be hard pressed not to do a double-take and wonder whether you hadn't just left Morocco. Built by the French in the 1930s as an Alpine resort, the red-tiled roofs of this highly un-Moroccan looking place are a bit of a shock when they come into view. The place is popular with Moroccans though, and more villas are being jerry-built in much the same style.

Outside the uncertain winter ski season and summer weekends, when the better-off flock to their holiday homes to escape the heat of the big cities, the place is a bit of a ghost town. Many of the grander villas are actually company hotels – the post office, Banque Populaire and CTM some that have 'hotels' here for staff holidays.

Information The tourist office (☎ 566822) is in a little hut on the corner of Ave Prince Moulay Abdallah and Ave des Tilleuls. It's a helpful place and can make good suggestions for activities in the area.

Things to See & Do Dominated by holm oak and cedar forests, the countryside surrounding Ifrane is a pleasant place to hike

1 Hôtel Mischliffen
2 Telephones
3 Labo Photo Ismailia (Photo Shop)
4 Hôtel/Restaurant Chamonix; Café de la Paix
5 Pharmacie Mischliffen
6 Café Restaurant Rose
7 Mobil Petrol Station
8 Alimentation Générale (Food Store)
9 Post Office
10 Cookie Craque; Résidence Squalli Inn
11 Grand Hôtel
12 Tourist Office
13 Bus & Grand Taxi Station

or enjoy a picnic. For those with their own vehicle, there is an attractive **Lake Circuit**, the ('Tour Touristique des Lacs') which starts at a turn-off 17km north of Ifrane. The five lakes are spread along the 100km or so between the P24 and P20, and attract large numbers of birds (when there's been enough rain), as do the surrounding woodlands. Keep an eye out in particular for raptors, including booted eagles, black and red kites and Egyptian vultures.

The Dayet Aoua, the first lake on the circuit, is a particularly good spot for wildlife, attracting significant numbers of ducks and waders. Sightings of crested coot are common and, if you're lucky, you may see woodpeckers, treecreepers and nuthatches, particularly among the trees around the south-eastern end of the lake.

There are several very pleasant picnic areas dotted around the lake. If you've come without provisions, you could head for the *Hôtel Restaurant Chalet du Lac* (☎ 663197), on the northern edge of the lake. It's run by a mother and daughter from Toulouse in France, who are well known in the region for their excellent cooking.

Politicians and statesmen come from as far afield as Rabat; look out for the enormous cars parked outside. If you can stretch to it, the 'menu gastronomique' for Dr170 makes a great lunch or dinner-time splurge on a day trip from Ifrane. It's a pleasant, very peaceful place and has wonderful views overlooking the lake. If you want to wake up to them, rooms without private bathroom cost Dr168/177.

If you're interested in trekking, mountain guides can be hired from the tourist office (Dr160 per day). Tents can also be rented. There is a horse-riding club next door to the Hôtel Mischliffen which organises excursions from April to October. Inquire at the hotel or the tourist office.

If you want to ski at nearby Mischliffen, you can hire equipment at the Hôtel Chamonix. It costs Dr100 per day for the whole kit (don't expect the latest technology), and lifts cost Dr3 per ride. Sledges can be hired for Dr30 to Dr40 per day.

Places to Stay & Eat Other than the *campgrounds*, west of the bus station on Blvd Mohammed V (which are not bad at all), there is no budget accommodation in Ifrane. Camping costs Dr5 a person and the same each for car, tent place and electricity. It's a pleasant, leafy spot.

If you plan to stay a few days, an apartment might be a good alternative to the hotels.

The *Résidence Squalli Inn* (☎ 567171; fax 566833) on Ave des Tilleuls, rents well equipped small, medium and large apartments for groups of two to four, five to seven, or eight to ten people for Dr500, Dr800 and Dr1100 (add Dr200 in the high season). These prices are very much open to negotiation, particularly in the low season, so you could get a very good deal.

On Ave de la Marche Verte in the centre of town, the *Hôtel/Restaurant Chamonix* (☎ 566028), is about the cheapest option, with rooms for Dr168/215.

Inside the *Grand Hôtel* (☎ 566203; fax 566407), on Ave de la Poste, you would swear you were in the Alps. Built in 1941, it's the most characterful of Ifrane's hotels and has its own bar and restaurant. Singles/doubles are Dr249/300 and you'll need to book ahead in winter.

The top of the range is the five-star *Hôtel Mischliffen* (☎ 566607; fax 566623), north of the town centre. It overlooks and dominates the town, and has rooms for Dr779/958 (extra beds cost an additional Dr179). It has a large restaurant serving Moroccan or international dishes (the set menu costs Dr230), and there is a nightclub which is open from 11 pm to 2 am.

The *Cookie Craque* on Ave des Tilleuls, is an excellent place for breakfast (Dr17) or for preparing a picnic. It has a wonderful selection of sweet and savoury delicacies (Dr5 to Dr15) including fruit tarts, crepes and chocolate mousse. There's also ice cream in summer. It's open every day from 7 am to 10 pm. They have a restaurant next door serving pizza (Dr30 to Dr49) and the like.

The *Café Restaurant Rose* (☎ 566215), at

MIDDLE ATLAS

7 Rue des Érables, is a simple but attractive place and is about the best of the few restaurants in Ifrane. It has a good set menu for Dr60 (main courses cost around Dr45). There is couscous on Friday.

A slightly cheaper option, and popular with the locals, is the *Café de la Paix* on Rue de la Marche Verte. Tajine costs Dr35 and omelettes Dr15 to Dr20.

Getting There & Away The main bus and grand taxi station is on Blvd Mohammed V, west of the town centre.

Buses for Marrakesh (Dr108) via Beni Mellal, and Casablanca (Dr81) via Rabat (Dr56) leave every day at 8 am. There are buses every hour to Fès from 6.30 am to 5.30 pm. There is also a non-CTM bus to Er-Rachidia (Dr80) every day at 11.30 am.

Grands taxis run to Azrou (Dr6), Sefrou (Dr18.50), Fès (Dr17.50) and Meknès (Dr11). They will also take you to Dayet Aouaa for Dr9.50.

Mischliffen

This is the main ski station of the Middle Atlas. The season runs from January to early March, but conditions can be very unreliable. The runs are quite good, but short, and apart from a couple of cafes and nice views, there's precious little to do. In summer, it's a popular place with walkers, though you'll need your own transport.

Azrou

The green-tiled rooftops of central Azrou are in total contrast to Ifrane, and this primarily Berber town is a cheerful, hasslefree little place – and full of life in a way that Ifrane is not.

Surrounded by pine and cedar forests, which are ideal for exploring either on foot or by car, the cool mountain air helps make this a good location to relax after the pressure-cooker of Fès.

The Tuesday market is a lively affair, and the centre of the town busy enough to hold your interest, but there's not much to do in Azrou, which is part of its charm.

The cheaper hotels and most of the little restaurants are on or near Place Mohammed V or just south of it in the narrow lanes of the old town. The banks and post office are also on Place Mohammed V. The bus and taxi stations are a five minute walk to the north, beyond the big new mosque that is (officially) due to open at the end of 1998, though it seems destined to remain forever 'under construction'.

Azrou means 'rock', and the clump of stone that gives the town its name, and below which the weekly market takes place, lies near Blvd Mohammed V, to the west of the town centre.

Information There is no tourist office in Azrou, but the Hôtel Le Panorama is a good place to go for information. The staff can suggest and help you organise one to six day excursions (or longer) into the mountains of the Middle Atlas, to the cedar forests or in search of the famous Barbary apes. Mountain guides can be hired (Dr150 per day), along with full camping gear, mules and even a cook (Dr75 per day). Permits for fishing the local trout streams and lakes can also be obtained from July to September. Speak to Ferhi Hammadi, the helpful hotel manager.

You can change money at the BMCE or Banque Populaire on Place Mohammed V. The post office is next to the Banque Populaire, just east of the square.

Places to Stay – bottom end The cheapest place to stay, and probably the least convenient, is the *youth hostel* (☎ 562496). It's a couple of kilometres east of the town centre on the Midelt road (take the first left before the Petrom petrol station). A bed in a clean dormitory costs Dr20/25 with/without card. The showers are cold and blankets seem to be in very short supply. There's no kitchen. The hostel is open from noon to 3 pm and from 6 to 10 pm.

Of the little places around Place Moulay Hachem ben Salah, the cheapest is *Hôtel Beau Séjour* (☎ 563272), at Dr25 a person. It's a bit grubby, but cold showers are available. Try for a room overlooking the square.

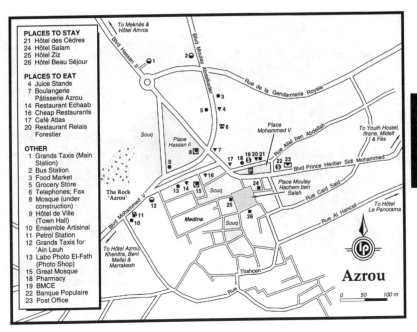

PLACES TO STAY
21 Hôtel des Cèdres
24 Hôtel Salam
25 Hôtel Ziz
26 Hôtel Beau Séjour

PLACES TO EAT
4 Juice Stands
7 Boulangerie
  Pâtisserie Azrou
14 Restaurant Echaab
16 Cheap Restaurants
17 Café Atlas
20 Restaurant Relais
  Forestier

OTHER
1 Grands Taxis (Main
  Station)
2 Bus Station
3 Food Market
5 Grocery Store
6 Telephones; Fax
8 Mosque (under
  construction)
9 Hôtel de Ville
  (Town Hall)
10 Ensemble Artisinal
11 Petrol Station
12 Grands Taxis for
  'Ain Leuh
13 Labo Photo El-Fath
  (Photo Shop)
15 Great Mosque
18 Pharmacy
19 BMCE
22 Banque Populaire
23 Post Office

MIDDLE ATLAS

Azrou

0   50   100 m

The *Hôtel Ziz* (☎ 562362) just off the square, is much the best place in this category, though you'll need to ask for a room with a window; the others are very cell-like. Basic, but spotless, singles cost Dr25/30 with/without window, while doubles are Dr40 to Dr70. The communal showers are cold.

The second best is the *Hôtel Salam* (☎ 562562) with rather scruffy, but reasonably clean, rooms for Dr30/60. The boon is the hot communal showers (Dr5).

Though OK in summer, these places don't make a great choice in winter. There's no heating and blankets are in very short supply.

Places to Stay – middle The one-star *Hôtel des Cèdres* (☎ 562326), on Place Mohammed V, has large, airy, comfortable and spotlessly clean rooms for Dr68/94/147. Rooms have a basin, bidet, table and chairs

and a balcony overlooking the square. A steaming bath or shower in the communal bathroom costs Dr10.

Even better value, particularly for those with a car, is the one-star *Hôtel Azrou* (☎ 562116), Route de Khenifra, quite a way from the centre of town and not so easy to find. It has spotless and pleasant singles/doubles without shower for Dr68/94, and rooms with shower for Dr99/129. Because it's less central, it often has rooms when its competitor, the Cèdres, doesn't, and prices can often be negotiated. They also have a bar (open until 10 pm), a restaurant (set menu Dr76) and guarded parking.

Further up the scale, and a long walk or olive-green petit taxi ride from the bus station is the pricier *Hôtel Le Panorama* (☎ 562010; fax 561804). The 40 rooms (heated in winter) cost Dr255/312 with shower and private loo. The hotel has a bar and restaurant (there's a fixed menu for

FRANCES LINZEE GORDON

Donkeys laden with radishes on the way to market.

Dr118), and offers a good, help-yourself breakfast for Dr33.

Places to Stay – top end About 5km out on the road to Meknès is the four-star *Hôtel Amros* (☎ 563663; fax 563680). It has all the amenities you would expect of a top class hotel, including a pool, tennis courts and a nightclub.

Singles and doubles cost Dr408 and Dr526 respectively, though they may try and talk you into a half-board arrangement.

Places to Eat There is no shortage of cheap eats in Azrou – a couple are scattered through the old town and there is a string of at least 10 of them across the road from the big unfinished mosque.

Of these, the *Restaurant Echaab* is good value. They usually have a huge pot of steaming harira (Dr2) by the entrance in the evenings – just the thing for a cool night or after a long hike. A big meal of harira, bro- chettes, chips, salad and a drink comes to Dr26.

The *Restaurant Relais Forestier*, on Place Mohammed V, has a fixed menu for Dr65 and main courses, including a hamburger á cheval (horse burger!) for Dr40. Most restaurants in Azrou close around 8pm to 9 pm, so don't leave dinner too late.

There are numerous cafes and a few juice stands on Blvd Moulay Abdelkader. The best of these is the *Boulangerie Pâtisserie Azrou*. The *Café Atlas* is the most pleasant place for breakfast and is good value: a coffee, orange juice and pastry cost just under Dr10.

Things to Buy A visit to the Ensemble Ar- tisanal on the road to Khenifra (signposted) is worthwhile. Here you can find work in cedarwood and wrought iron, as well as Berber carpets typical of the Middle Atlas.

Getting There & Away Azrou is a cross-roads, with one axis heading north-west to south-east from Meknès to Er-Rachidia and the other north-east from Fès to Marrakesh in the south-west. The bus station (Gare Routière) and taxi station are located just north of the mosque construction site.

Bus CTM has departures to Fès at 5 am (direct) and at 2.30 pm (Dr19). There's a direct bus to Casablanca (Dr87) at 1 am, and another via Meknès, Rabat, Ifrane and Khemisset at 7.30 am. A third bus also runs from June to September at 4 am.

For Marrakesh (Dr103), a bus leaves at 8 am and 10.30 pm. The bus to Agadir (Dr190) at 9.30 pm passes via Marrakesh and Beni Mellal (Dr63). Buses depart for Meknès (Dr16) at 7.30 am and 9 am.

The other lines have buses to these destinations at other times and for a dirham or two less. All up, there are plenty of departures for Fès and Meknès, but for places like Marrakesh you'd be advised to book ahead. There are at least two buses to Er-Rachidia (Dr72) at 11.30 pm and at 1 am; otherwise you would be better off getting one of the more frequent buses to Midelt (Dr25/30) and hooking up with transport there.

Taxi Grands taxis leave from the lot behind the bus station regularly for Fès (Dr23), Meknès (Dr18), Khenifra (Dr23), Ifrane (Dr6), Sefrou (Dr22), and Midelt (Dr35). From the last two you could arrange further transport on to Er-Rachidia and Beni Mellal (or even Marrakesh) respectively.

Around Azrou

If you have your own transport, there's a good drive from Azrou that takes you through some of the best of the Middle Atlas greenery along a forest lane to the Berber village of 'Ain Leuh. On Wednesday, there's a souq which attracts market-goers from around the region, and particularly from the semi-nomadic Beni m'Guid tribe.

Leave Azrou by the Midelt road and take the first right (the S3398). Once in the village of 'Ain Leuh, you could continue south into the heart of the Middle Atlas along the S303 – be warned that some of the tracks here are difficult and impassable in or after foul weather. A little further on (signposted to the left around 25km south of the village) are some impressive waterfalls at the **Sources de l'Oum-er-Rbia** which make a good spot for a picnic.

If you continue a further 10km south, you will come to a crossroads. Turning right along the 3485 will take you to Khenifra and the road south towards Marrakesh; turning left along the 3485 will lead you towards Midelt, Er-Rachidia and eventually the Sahara.

Along the latter, the volcanic lake **Aguelmane Sidi Ali**, formed in an extinct crater, makes a pleasant stop where you can swim. It's also a good place to camp if you've come equipped. Continuing along the road and around 5km before it joins the main P21 road to Midelt, you'll pass through the tiny Berber village of **Itzer**. It's a great place to pick up a Berber carpet or kilim, particularly at the large weekly markets on Monday and Thursday.

Midelt

Lying almost at the centre of Morocco between the Middle and the High Atlas mountains, Midelt is a kind of no-man's land between the north and the south of the country. Of little interest in itself, the town's situation makes it a convenient stopping point on the principal route south from Fès, Meknès and Azrou to Er-Rachidia and the South. It's also a useful base from which to explore both mountain ranges.

The town consists of little more than one main street (Ave Mohammed V which later becomes Hassan II), a modest souq and a number of out-sized restaurants which cater to the well-heeled tourist buses whistling through on their way south. As there's nothing to see, you're unlikely to be hassled by would-be guides. More common, though largely targeting the tour parties, are the energetic mineral and fossil sellers or the carpet-shop touts.

MIDDLE ATLAS

Carpets are probably Midelt's greatest asset. The quality is high and the attractive geometric designs are distinctive to the Berber tribes of the surrounding Middle Atlas region. Be wary of the town boutiques however, which are accustomed to the ten-minute shoppers of the coach parties. Prices are high, there's pressure to buy and any so-called 'antique' carpets will never be more than 10 to fifteen years old. The **carpet souq**, in the Souq Djedid area off Ave Mohammed V, is the best place to head. There is a special carpet market here every Sunday.

Also well worth a visit is the **Atelier de Tissage** run by some charitable, French Franciscan sisters in a convent off the road north of town to Tattiouine. Every three years, some 20 or so local Berber women are taken on for apprenticeship, during which time they will learn the trades of embroidery, weaving and sewing. The fruits of their training form a very small exhibition and some items are for sale.

Prices are high, but so also is the quality. The studio is open every day except Friday and Sunday from 8 to 11.45 am and from 2 to 5 pm. At the time of writing, a bridge connecting the convent road with the town road had been washed away. Access was from a road to the right just before another bridge at the northern entrance to the town. Look out for the sign.

While the bridge remains down (it may take years to get another built), opening times are from 8 to 11.45 am only.

If you're into **minerals** or **fossils**, there is a shop opposite the Hôtel Roi de la Bière on the road to Er-Rachidia. It's a good place to get an idea of the quality available, and maximum prices to pay the street vendors.

Information You can change money at the Banque Populaire on Ave Mohammed V, or further south at the BMCI bank on Hassan II. Both keep the usual banking hours.

Places to Stay – bottom end *Camping Municipal* (☎ 580581) is about 1km south of town. It's a bit untidy and there are few facilities, but it's cheap and friendly and there's a small pool open from June to August. It costs Dr2 per person and per tent, Dr2.50 for a car and Dr3 for a caravan.

The best of the lower-end hotels is the *Hôtel Boughafer* (☎ 583099) opposite the central market off Ave Mohammed V. Small, clean and peaceful singles/doubles without shower cost Dr35/70 (hot showers cost an extra Dr10) and with private shower, Dr80/120. There is also a restaurant which has set menus for Dr45.

The *Hôtel Atlas* (☎ 582933) is close to the main square on Rue Mohammed Amraoui. Although basic and on the small side, the rooms (without shower) are spotless and cost Dr60, Dr90 and Dr150 for two, three and four people. A hot shower costs Dr10 and there's a pleasant terrace.

You could also try the *Hôtel Mimlal* (☎ 582266), 1km out of town on the road to Meknès. The rooms are basic and could do with fresh paint, but are clean. Singles/doubles without private shower cost Dr40/80, and with shower Dr50/90. There's also a 'suite' available for four people for Dr140, and if you fancy a night under the stars, you can sleep on the terrace for Dr15. Hot showers cost an extra Dr10.

The hotel restaurant serves a decent and excellent value set menu for Dr45, or you can try the house speciality, the 'tajine Berbère' for Dr25. Brahim, the man who runs the hotel, is a very friendly Berber and will wave you off with a 'Good Lucky'.

Places to Stay – top end The *Hôtel El-Ayachi* (☎ 582161; fax 583307), on Rue d'Agadir off Ave Hassan II, is a comfortable, well run place catering largely to tour groups. Singles/doubles with bathroom cost Dr200/247 (Dr249/300 during the high season). The hotel has a pleasant garden, a bar which is open all day to 11 pm, and a licensed restaurant in a Berber tent which serves both Moroccan and international food. The set menu costs Dr93 (Dr118 in the high season), with main courses for Dr55 and wine Dr70 a bottle.

About 2km south of the centre is the

Kasbah Hôtel Restaurant Asmaa (☎ 580406; fax 580406). The building itself, opened in 1996, is a pretty hideous version of a kasbah, but it's pleasantly decorated and very comfortable inside, with several differently coloured salons arranged around a central fountain. Singles, doubles and triples cost Dr205, Dr260 and Dr315 respectively.

From March to September, you can sleep under one of the large Berber tents and sleeping bags can also be hired.

The hotel has a pleasant roof terrace and a good restaurant with a three course set menu for Dr95 (mains cost Dr50). Pony trekking can be arranged through the hotel.

Places to Eat Apart from the hotel restaurants, the best place in town by far is the *Restaurant Fès* on Rue Lalla Aicha.

It's run by a Berber family and Fatima, the grandmother who oversees the cooking, has earned quite a following for her meals.

The excellent set menu costs Dr65, main courses Dr50 to Dr60 and a bowl of hearty harira soup Dr3. Vegetarians should ask for the specially prepared tajine á sept legumes which is delicious.

Outside the high season, main courses should be ordered in advance.

The *Pâtisserie Belle Vue*, on Place el Mahkama, makes up for being the only one of its kind in town by serving as an all-purpose patisserie, boulangerie, tea salon, cafe and ice cream parlour. It's a good place for breakfast (Dr15) or for stocking up for a picnic, and is open every day from 7.30 am to 9 pm.

Getting There & Away – Bus The bus station is off the main street Ave Mohammed V. Midelt's central location makes it quite a transport hub for buses all over the country, and you may well find yourself passing through here. CTM runs

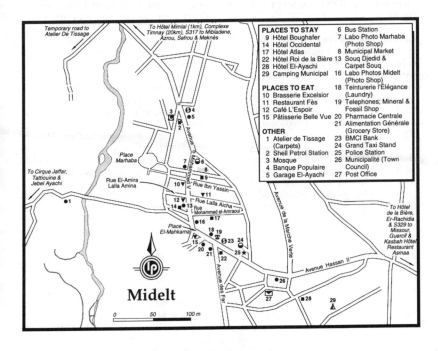

PLACES TO STAY	6	Bus Station
9 Hôtel Boughafer	7	Labo Photo Marhaba
14 Hôtel Occidental		(Photo Shop)
17 Hôtel Atlas	8	Municipal Market
22 Hôtel Roi de la Bière	13	Souq Djedid &
28 Hôtel El-Ayachi		Carpet Souq
29 Camping Municipal	16	Labo Photos Midelt
		(Photo Shop)
PLACES TO EAT	18	Teinturerie l'Élégance
10 Brasserie Excelsior		(Laundry)
11 Restaurant Fès	19	Telephones; Mineral &
12 Café L'Espoir		Fossil Shop
15 Pâtisserie Belle Vue	20	Pharmacie Centrale
	21	Alimentation Générale
OTHER		(Grocery Store)
1 Atelier de Tissage	23	BMCI Bank
(Carpets)	24	Grand Taxi Stand
2 Shell Petrol Station	25	Police Station
3 Mosque	26	Municipalité (Town
4 Banque Populaire		Council)
5 Garage El-Ayachi	27	Post Office

Midelt

0   50   100 m

an evening bus (around 9.30 pm) to Casablanca (Dr117, eight hours) via Meknès (Dr92, four hours) and Rabat (Dr54, six hours). There is also a morning bus to Meknès via Azrou (Dr33, two hours).

Other buses run once a day to Beni Mellal (Dr47, 4½ hours) and Rissani (Dr68, six hours), and twice a day to Er-Rachidia (Dr40, three hours) and Erfoud (Dr61, 3½ hours). There are no direct buses to Fès; you must change at Meknès.

There are around 30 other companies which run much more frequent buses, including four night-runs to Casablanca (Dr80/87.50 depending on the bus), five a day to Rabat (Dr70), 14 to Meknès (Dr44) and 12 to Fès (Dr40/44.50, 4½ hours) from 5 am to 5 pm. Other departures include two to Nador (Dr80) and one to Oujda (Dr6).

Heading south, there are 18 buses a day to Azrou (Dr29), two to Sefrou (Dr35), two to Kenifra (Dr30), 18 to Er-Rachidia (Dr33), seven to Erfoud (Dr45) and seven to Rissani (Dr50).

Getting There & Away – Taxi The grands taxi stand is down a little lane close to the police station, just off Ave Hassan II. Departures are also quite frequent, but it's best to arrive early in the morning.

Destinations include Azrou (Dr35), Er-Rachidia (Dr40), Meknès (Dr55), Fès and Sefrou (Dr60), Erfoud (Dr60) and Rissani (Dr70).

Getting There & Away – Car For those with their own vehicle, the Garage El-Ayachi on Ave Mohammed V is supposedly the best garage in the region, and a good place to sort out minor problems before continuing further south.

Around Midelt

For those with their own vehicle (for those without, see the Complexe Timnay below), there are some excellent excursions which will take you into the heart of the Middle Atlas mountains. The roads are rough and only negotiable during the drier months from around May to October. It's a good

idea to check the state of the roads before setting off. Some routes, such as the Cirque Jaffar, are best attempted by 4WD vehicles, though village 'guides' (such as Youness at the Restaurant Fès) claim to know a route for ordinary cars.

The 79km **Cirque Jaffar** to the west of Midelt is the best known excursion. The road winds through the foothills of Jebel Ayachi (3737m), the highest mountain in the Middle Atlas, and gives you a glimpse of traditional Berber villages, wild mountain scenery and some spectacular views.

The circuit is well signposted from town, starting just off the 3424 road to Tattiouine, passing via Miktane and Ait Oum Gam, looping back to the Midelt-Azrou road. You should allow almost a day for the circuit.

If you want to climb Jebel Ayachi, you can drive or take a taxi to Tattiouine. From a point just beyond the village near the springs, there's a mule track which leads up to the summit. It's not a difficult climb, and the descent can take you via cedar forests and various mountain villages, though you'll probably need a guide for this.

Other routes you might follow include the S317 road to Ksabi which will take you through the Moulouya gorges and some old mines around 15km to the north of Midelt.

If you have more time, you could follow the S329 road (off the Er-Rachidia road around 20km south of Midelt) towards Missour, or all the way to Guercif. The road travels through a well watered, fertile region with good flora, fauna and birdlife. The best time of year to visit this region is in the spring.

An area particularly noted for its **birds** are the plains a few kilometres south of the village of Zaïda on the main Midelt-Meknès route. The place has become synonymous among ornithologists with a rare species of bird – Dupont's lark.

Other birds more commonly spotted include species of finch, other larks and sandgrouse. The Complexe Timnay (see below) is a useful source of information for bird-watchers.

Around 20km to the north of Midelt, just

before the village of Zaïda on the main Meknès road, is the **Complexe Touristique Timnay Inter-Cultures** (☎/fax 583434). It's well signposted and is built in the style of a kasbah, so is easy to spot. The centre was the result of a joint Moroccan/Belgian venture set up in 1990 by a group of teachers with the aim of 'initiating visitors into the culture and lifestyle of the nomads and sedentary people of the mountains'.

It's a very pleasant and peaceful place, and the Berber manager, Hafid, runs the place efficiently, seriously and enthusiastically. It's an excellent place for those keen to get to know the Berber people and landscape of this part of the Atlas.

The complex includes a well equipped camp site, bungalows, tents, restaurant, cafe, grocery store and swimming pool (open from March to the end of August). It's an excellent source of information for the region, with knowledgeable staff and guides and a few reference books on the birds and flora of the region. Mountain bikes can be hired (Dr30/50 per half/ whole day) and so can horses.

Camping costs Dr18 per person, Dr15 for a car and per tent (Dr25 for a camper van), and Dr10 for electricity. Basic bungalows (with a simple bathroom) can be rented for Dr50/30 per adult/child. From March to August, you can spend the night under one of the large Berber tents for Dr15 per person, though only mattresses are available for use. If you really want to get to know the locals, you can stay *en famille* on a Berber farm for Dr50 per person.

Various excursions can be organised: on foot, with mountain bikes, mules and a cook, bivouacs, or in 4WD vehicles. The most regular trips take from a half day to two days, but there are also one week to 15 day circuits, and longer trips which could take you right across the Atlas mountains or deep into the desert in the south.

Shorter trips include various excursions to nearby lakes and cedar forests, the Outat Gorges (Dr120, half day), the Mougger Saffen gorges (Dr300, full day), the Cirque de Jaffar (Dr300, full day), the Tadroute Canyon (Dr380, full day) and the Berber villages in the upper valley of Taâraârt (Dr415, two days). All prices are per person and include meals. If the thought of an organised tour doesn't appeal, you can hire a guide, some mules and a bivouac and take off on your own. Guides cost from Dr200 to Dr300 per day and mules Dr100.

Unfortunately, the centre is becoming better known, so it's a good idea to make a reservation, particularly during the high season, and to book longer trips. For those without their own vehicle, the centre can organise an airport pick-up. Alternatively, you can get a bus to Midelt and hire a grand taxi from there.

Sefrou

Just 28km from Fès, Sefrou is much easier to contemplate as a day trip than either Ifrane or Azrou, and with virtually no accommodation at the time of writing, a dubious choice for an overnight stop on the way south to the Ziz Valley and Er-Rachidia.

About the size of Chefchaouen, this picturesque Berber town is well worth the effort. With the exception of the odd Fès-trained 'guide' hanging about the gates near the bus station, you will be left in complete peace to wander the compact medina. Sefrou once had one of the largest Jewish communities of any Moroccan city and it was here, in a nearby *ksar* (fortified stronghold), that Moulay Idriss II lived while he planned the development of Fès.

The walled medina and mellah straddle the garbage-strewn Oued Aggaï, across which there are a number of bridges. The best points of entry/exit are the Bab Taksebt, Bab Zemghila and the Bab Merba. The town walls that stand today were built in the 19th century.

Once you've visited the walled town, walk up the gorge of the river to the waterfall about 1.5km from town. To get there, follow the Ave Moulay Hassan over the bridge and turn right at the first turn-off (signposted 'Cascades'). Follow this road

MIDDLE ATLAS

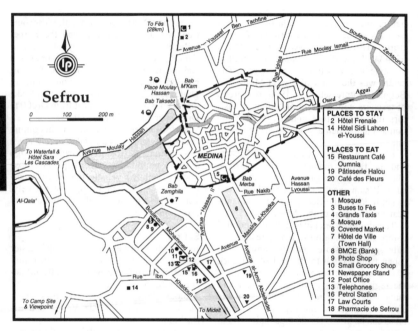

Sefrou

0   100   200 m

MEDINA

| PLACES TO STAY |
| 2 Hôtel Frenaie |
| 14 Hôtel Sidi Lahcen |
| el-Youssi |
| |
| PLACES TO EAT |
| 15 Restaurant Café |
| Oumnia |
| 19 Pâtisserie Halou |
| 20 Café des Fleurs |
| |
| OTHER |
| 1 Mosque |
| 3 Buses to Fès |
| 4 Grands Taxis |
| 5 Mosque |
| 6 Covered Market |
| 7 Hôtel de Ville |
| (Town Hall) |
| 8 BMCE (Bank) |
| 9 Photo Shop |
| 10 Small Grocery Shop |
| 11 Newspaper Stand |
| 12 Post Office |
| 13 Telephones |
| 16 Petrol Station |
| 17 Law Courts |
| 18 Pharmacie de Sefrou |

around to the right (north side) of Al-Qala‘ (a sort of semi-walled ksar) and then follow the dirt road alongside the river until you get to the waterfall.

Information The main post office and a branch of the BMCE bank are along Blvd Mohammed V.

Places to Stay There's not a huge choice of accommodation in Sefrou. There is rather a neglected *camp site* on the hill overlooking the town. It's a long, steep walk (take a taxi), but a pleasant spot. There are toilets and cold showers; it costs Dr10 per person, tent and car. If you continue a little further up the hill, you'll find a magnificent viewpoint over Sefrou and the plains below.

The cheapest place in town is the unmarked *Hôtel Frenaie* (☎ 660030) on the road to Fès. It's difficult to find (look for the building with the green tiles just after

the mosque as you approach Sefrou), and is a basic place with a broken shower. Rooms cost Dr70/100.

The two-star *Hôtel Sidi Lahcen el-Youssi* (☎ 683428) on Rue Sidi Ali Bouserghine is the only other option. It has singles/doubles for 113/136 (Dr150/179 in the high season). All rooms come with hot shower and balcony, and there's heating in winter.

The hotel also has a restaurant, a modest nightclub (open until midnight; beers cost Dr12) and a swimming pool (non-residents pay Dr15 per day), which is open from May to September.

The *Hôtel Sara Les Cascades*, right by the waterfall, was not a bad little place in a peaceful location. Even if it ever re-opens, you may not want to stay. The authorities shut it in 1993 after the bodies of a couple of young local girls were discovered there, apparently after a night's revelry with off-duty soldiers turned nasty.

Places to Eat There's a good choice of small, cheap snack bars on either side of the covered market and at the entrance to the Bab Merba.

Otherwise, pickings are slim. The only proper restaurant is town the *Restaurant Café Oumnia* up near Blvd Mohammed V. It does a good set menu for Dr60, and main courses for Dr35.

There's a string of cafes and a bar on the same street, all near the post office, and an excellent patisserie hidden away down a street off Mohammed V. *Pâtisserie Halou* is unmarked, but you'll recognise it by the bright pink-framed window and doorway, after the grocery shop. You can buy a pastry here and have it for breakfast at the *Café des Fleurs* nearby.

Getting There & Away There are regular buses between Fès and Sefrou (Dr5) which drop you off at Place Moulay Hassan in front of Bab M'Kam and Bab Taksebt.

Grands taxis (Dr7) can also be found here. Grands taxis go to Immouzer (Dr10), from where you can pick up others for Azrou.

A few taxis heading south leave from the law courts on Blvd Mohammed V.

The East

TAZA

Despite its tempestuous history, Taza is a relatively quiet city these days. Nevertheless, it is worth a visit if you are passing through the area, if only for the views and the crumbling fortifications.

If you have your own transport, there's a superb drive around Jebel Tazzeka, taking in a visit to the Gouffre du Friouato – one of the most incredible open caverns in the world.

As it was an important French military and administrative centre during the protectorate, Taza has a ville nouvelle which, as usual, is separate from the old town. The two are quite some distance from each other (3km in fact), although urbanisation is rapidly closing the gap.

History

The fortified citadel of Taza, built on the edge of an escarpment overlooking the only feasible pass between the Rif Mountains and the Middle Atlas, has been important throughout Morocco's history as a garrison town from which to exert control over the eastern extremities of the country.

The Taza Gap, as it is known, has provided the traditional invasion route for armies moving west from Tunisia and Algeria. The Romans and the Arabs entered Morocco via this pass, and the town itself was the base from which the Almohads, Merenids and Alawites swept down on Fès to conquer lowland Morocco and establish their respective dynasties.

All the various Moroccan sultans had a hand in fortifying Taza. Nevertheless, their control over the area was always tenuous since the fiercely independent and rebellious local tribes were always willing to exploit any weakness in the central power in order to overrun the city.

Never was this more the case than in the first years of the 20th century, when 'El-Rogui' (the pretender to the sultan's throne), Bou Hamra, held sway over Taza (although he was based largely in Selouan, 24km south of Melilla) and most of northeastern Morocco.

After some early successes, his claims to the throne were revealed to be a sham and he met a colourfully grisly end at the hands of Sultan Moulay Abd al-Hafiz.

The French occupied Taza in 1914 and made it the main base from which they fought the prolonged rebellion by the tribes of the Rif and Middle Atlas.

Orientation

Arriving by bus (except CTM) or train, you'll find yourself on the main Fès-Oujda road, which might appear to be in the centre of town, but is actually quite some distance away.

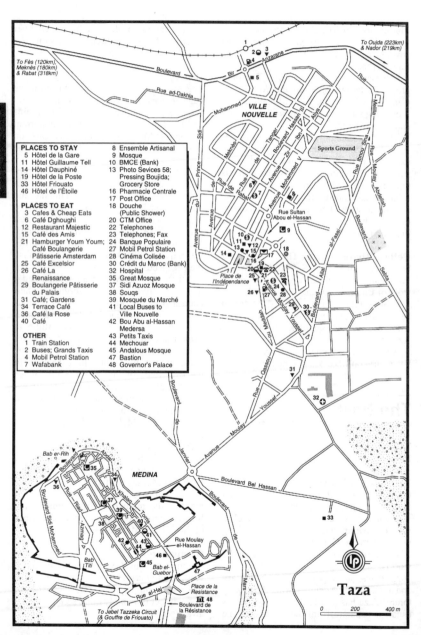

PLACES TO STAY
5 Hôtel de la Gare
11 Hôtel Guillaume Tell
14 Hôtel Dauphiné
19 Hôtel de la Poste
33 Hôtel Friouato
46 Hôtel de l'Étoile

PLACES TO EAT
3 Cafes & Cheap Eats
6 Café Dghoughi
12 Restaurant Majestic
15 Café des Amis
21 Hamburger Youm Youm;
   Café Boulangerie
   Pâtisserie Amsterdam
25 Café Excelsior
26 Café La
   Renaissance
29 Boulangerie Pâtisserie
   du Palais
31 Café; Gardens
34 Terrace Café
36 Café la Rose
40 Café

OTHER
1 Train Station
2 Buses; Grands Taxis
4 Mobil Petrol Station
7 Wafabank
8 Ensemble Artisanal
9 Mosque
10 BMCE (Bank)
13 Photo Sevices 58;
   Pressing Boujida;
   Grocery Store
16 Pharmacie Centrale
17 Post Office
18 Douche
   (Public Shower)
20 CTM Office
22 Telephones
23 Telephones; Fax
24 Banque Populaire
27 Mobil Petrol Station
28 Cinéma Coliséé
30 Crédit du Maroc (Bank)
32 Hospital
35 Great Mosque
37 Sidi Azuoz Mosque
38 Souqs
39 Mosquée du Marché
41 Local Buses to
   Ville Nouvelle
42 Bou Abu al-Hassan
   Medersa
43 Petits Taxis
44 Mechouar
45 Andalous Mosque
47 Bastion
48 Governor's Palace

Bou Hamra

Bou Hamra (the 'Man on the She-Ass'), or Jilali ben Driss as he came into the world, was one of a host of colourful and violent characters who strode across the Moroccan stage at the turn of the century as central power evaporated and the European powers prepared to take greater control.

Born in 1868 in the Jebel Zerhoun area, he became a minor government official in Fès. In 1894, he was jailed for forgery, but managed to escape to Algeria six years later.

In for a penny, in for a pound, Bou Hamra decided on a more ambitious fraud – claiming with conviction to be Sultan Abd al-Aziz's elder brother Mohammed. He acquired his name by dint of his custom of travelling around on a she-donkey and staked a claim in eastern Morocco as the legitimate pretender to the throne – 'El-Rogui'. As the British journalist Walter Harris wrote, he had learned 'a few conjuring tricks' – but surely the best was having himself proclaimed sultan in Taza in 1902.

Another character of a different style, Er-Raissouli, who at this time held sway in the Tangier area of northern Morocco, placed an each-way bet by signing a deal with Bou Hamra recognising him as sultan. In the end he needn't have worried, for in 1908 the real Mohammed stood up and the Rif tribes that had backed Bou Hamra turned on him.

He soon fell into the hands of the new sultan, Moulay Abd al-Hafiz. Bou Hamra was paraded around the country for a month in a 1m-high cage on the back of a camel before being thrown to the lions of the sultan's menagerie in Fès in March 1909. ■

Place de l'Indépendance is the heart of the ville nouvelle. On it, or nearby, are the banks, post office and most of the hotels and restaurants. If you arrive by CTM bus, you're in luck because the station is right on this square. The old town is another 3km to the south. Local buses and petits taxis run regularly between the two.

Information

Tourist Office The office (☎ 672737) was in the Immeuble des Habous, on Blvd Ave Hassan II, but seems to have closed down for good.

Money There are a couple of banks in Taza, including the BMCE on Ave Mohammed V and the Banque Populaire on Ave Moulay Youssef, on the way from the ville nouvelle to the medina.

Post & Communications The post and telephone offices are on the south-eastern corner of Place de l'Indépendance. Both are open during normal office hours only.

Film & Photography Across the road from the Café des Amis, there's a good Agfa photo shop, the Photo Services 58, where you can buy or develop print film.

Laundry The Pressing Boujida is next door to the Photo Services 58 on Ave Mohammed V.

City Walls

Most of the city walls, which are about 3km in circumference, date from the time of the Almohads (12th century). Having withstood so many sieges, they are ruined in parts.

There's also a bastion built by the Saadians in the 16th century in a part of the walls that juts out to the east of the medina.

The most interesting section of a trip around the walls is the **Bab er-Rih** (Gate of the Wind), with its superb views over the surrounding countryside. On the extreme left you can see the wooded slopes of Jebel Tazzeka and before that, across the Oued Taza, the terraced gardens and dry ravines of the foothills of the Rif. On the right, below the park, is the ville nouvelle, with the Rif Mountains in the distance.

Great Mosque

Not far from Bab er-Rih is the Great Mosque, which was begun by the Almohads in 1135 and added to by the Merenids in the 13th century. Non-Muslims are not allowed to enter, and it is difficult to get much of an impression of the outside of the building.

Stretching from here down to the far end of the old town is the main thoroughfare, known variously as Rue Kettanine, Rue Nejjarine, Rue Koubet and Rue Sidi Ali Derrar.

This is perhaps the most interesting part of town: there are many examples of richly decorated doorways and, occasionally, windows high up in the walls guarded by old, carved cedar screens.

Souqs

The souqs are about halfway down the street, around the Mosquée du Marché. Some of the souqs offer mats and carpets woven by the Beni Ouarain tribe in the surrounding mountains, and are virtually bereft of tourist shops (and faux guides). It's a great chance to observe the workings of a typical Berber market.

Most of the shops cater for household necessities and foodstuffs, as do the ones in the nearby qissaria (the commercial centre of the medina).

While in this part of the city, don't miss the minaret of the **Mosquée du Marché**, which is perhaps unique in Morocco in that its upper part is wider than its base.

Andalous Mosque

Right at the end of the main street, close to the *mechouar* (royal assembly palace), is the Andalous Mosque, constructed in the 12th century.

Nearby is a ruined house once occupied by Bou Hamra, and the Merenid Bou Abu al-Hassan Medersa. It may be possible to gain entry to the latter if you ask around and enlist the help of a guide.

Places to Stay – bottom end

Medina In the medina itself about the only choice is the fairly basic, but clean, *Hôtel de l'Étoile* (☎ 270179), inside Bab el-Guebor on the left along Rue Moulay el-Hassan.

It's a cheerful place with a shocking pink courtyard and is run by a sweet, old Spanish lady. Rooms cost Dr35.

There's no showers, but there is a public one and a hammam in the medina a couple of minutes away.

Ville Nouvelle Down by the traffic lights on the main Fès-Oujda road, more or less in front of the train station, is the *Hôtel de la Gare* (☎ 672448). It has cheap and not overly inviting rooms (some of them decidedly on the nose) without shower for Dr48/64/99, and substantially better rooms with en suite shower for Dr75/95/130. It's convenient for the transport, but not for the centre of the new town or the medina.

The remaining moderately priced hotels are around Place de l'Indépendance. About the cheapest and most reasonable is the *Hôtel Guillaume Tell* (☎ 672347) which offers simple and reasonably clean rooms for Dr41/62. There are communal showers (cold).

Just off Ave Moulay Youssef is the *Hôtel de la Poste* (☎ 672589) which has small, but clean and comfortable, rooms for Dr48/64, but no shower at all and somewhat smelly loos.

Places to Stay – middle

The *Hôtel Dauphiné* (☎ 673567) is a two-star hotel, to the left of Place de l'Indépendance, housed in an attractive colonial-style building.

It's a very clean, comfortable place to stay with balconies overlooking the square. Rooms without shower cost Dr70/ 87, with shower Dr96/120, and with shower and toilet Dr116/145. There's hot water in the evenings only.

The hotel restaurant serves a fixed menu for Dr70 and main courses for Dr40 (including couscous on Fridays). Downstairs there's a lively bar which, with the restaurant, is open from 10 am to 2 pm and from 5 to 9 pm.

Places to Stay – top end
The only top-end hotel in Taza is the three-star *Hôtel Friouato* (☎ 672593; fax 672244), set in well maintained grounds between Place de l'Indépendance and the old town.

Although it's awkwardly located and the concrete building is rather depressing, it is a quiet and pleasant enough place.

Singles/doubles with shower and toilet go for Dr246/303. The hotel has a bar, restaurant and tennis courts.

Swimming Pools & Hammams
The pool at the Hôtel Friouato is open from June until the end of August; non-guests pay a fee of Dr30 per day.

There are plenty of hammams in the medina, including a couple close to the Hôtel de l'Etoile, and in the ville nouvelle, close to the Hôtel de la Poste. Ask your hotel for directions.

Places to Eat
Medina A pleasant place to have a coffee (no food served) is the *Café La Rose* on Rue Riad Azmag.

While wandering around the medina, there are numerous small stands where you can pick up a snack, and some of the cafes sometimes do food as well.

Ville Nouvelle There is a series of cafes and cheap eateries by the grand taxi lot on Blvd Bir Anzarane (the Fès-Oujda road).

In town, probably the best choice for a meal remains the *Restaurant Majestic* on Ave Mohammed V. It's a bit basic, but popular with locals. Harira soup goes for Dr4 and main dishes such as tajine, brochettes or chicken cost Dr30.

Around the corner from the Hôtel de la Poste is the *Hamburger Youm Youm* which does a decent hamburger, egg and chips for Dr12. There are some quiet tables upstairs which are good for women travellers.

Cafes & Patisseries At 65 Blvd Allal ben Abdullah, is the *Boulangerie Pâtisserie du Palais* (which is better known by the locals as Pâtisserie Mahfoud, after the proprietor).

Its pastries are considered to be the best in town, and you can take them to have with coffee at the cafe next door. It's also a great place to prepare a picnic.

A couple of doors down from the Hamburger Youm Youm, is the *Café Boulangerie Pâtisserie Amsterdam*, which is the most pleasant place for breakfast (Dr12). It's open every day from 4 am to 9 pm.

In the medina, one of the most agreeable places is the nameless terrace cafe on the eastern side of the medina. From here you have sweeping views of the new town and the countryside.

Getting There & Away
Bus The CTM bus terminal is next to the Hôtel de la Poste on Place de l'Indépendance, but it offers only a few services. At 7 am there are two buses: one to Casablanca (Dr109, 7½ hours) via Fès, Meknès and Rabat; the other is a *mumtaz* (top class) run to Fès for Dr33. At 2 and 10 pm there are two other buses to Fès.

All other buses gather near or pass by the grand taxi lot on the main Fès-Oujda road. There are around five to Oujda (Dr50) and Nador (Dr57), a bus to Al-Hoceima (Dr121) at noon, and two buses to Tangier (Dr115) at 10 and 10.30 pm.

As there is no organised bus station as such, it can be a bit chaotic. The best bet is to turn up as early as you can and choose between the buses and grands taxis – taking whichever leaves first.

Train The train is generally a more reliable and comfortable option. There are four daily trains to Casablanca (Dr98/124 for standard/rapide trains) via Fès (Dr27/34), Meknès, Sidi Kacem, Kenitra and Rabat.

There is one direct train for Marrakesh (Dr153/196), at 4.13 pm and two others which require a change at Casablanca.

Two trains go to Tangier (Dr39.50/50), with a change at Sidi Kacem, and three to Oujda (Dr39.50/50).

Taxi Grands taxis all leave from a lot near the train station on the main Fès-Oujda road. They depart fairly regularly for Fès (Dr30). You'll be dropped off at Bab el-Ftouh and you'll need to take a local bus or petit taxi from there to Bab Bou Jeloud or the ville nouvelle.

You can also catch a grand taxi to Oujda (Dr50) throughout the day, but the morning is best. Less regular taxis go to Nador and Al-Hoceima for Dr50 a person.

AROUND TAZA
Jebel Tazzeka Circuit

If you have your own transport (hitching isn't really feasible), you can make a interesting day trip around Jebel Tazzeka, taking in the Cascades de Ras el-Oued (waterfalls), the Gouffre du Friouato (cavern), Daïa Chiker (lake) and the gorges of the Oued Zireg.

Though the road is sealed and good the whole way, it's very narrow and twisty in parts. Unaccustomed to meeting any other

traffic, grands taxis belt helter-skelter down them. Take particular care outside the summer months.

If you don't have your own transport it would be worthwhile getting a small group together and hiring a taxi for the day.

Having negotiated the long, winding road up from Taza onto the plateau, you'll find yourself in a different world.

It's almost eerie in its apparent emptiness, with small patches of farmland, a few scattered houses and, closer to Jebel Tazzeka itself, dense coniferous forests.

There are superb views from many points, including the semi-derelict hamlet of Bab Bou-Idir (this hamlet must have been a beautiful retreat at one time, with its tiled Alpine-style houses, but it appears to have been largely abandoned – weekend picnickers notwithstanding).

The **Cascades de Ras el-Oued** are the first stop. Shortly before you reach the Daïa

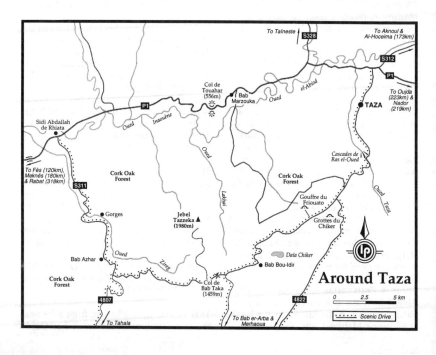

Chiker plateau, you'll see a sign on your left for Ras el-Ma ('Headwater'). The waterfalls are here, but they are really only worth a stop after the winter rains. By the summer they have usually slowed to a trickle.

A little further on, where the road flattens out, you take a right fork and have the odd depression of the **Daïa Chiker** on your left. The lake bed is usually pretty dry, but the earth is good and is used for grazing and crops. Daïa Chiker is a geological curiosity associated with fault lines in the calciferous rock structure.

It is connected to a subterranean reservoir, the water of which is highly charged with carbon dioxide. Depending on the season and the state of affairs in the subterranean reservoir, the surface of the lake can change dramatically.

The nearby **Grottes du Chiker** (Caves) at the northern end of the lake have been explored and are said to give access to a 5km-long underground river, but they are not open to casual visitors.

A little further along, the **Gouffre du Friouato** is signposted off to the right. You can drive up or take a steep, 20 minute walk to the entrance. It is the main attraction of this circuit and a must at any time of the year.

This vast cavern is said to be the deepest and possibly the most extensive in the whole of North Africa. It was first explored in 1935, and has only been partially explored to date – no one has ever reached the end of the chamber.

The main part plummets vertically some 100m to a floor below, from where various chambers break off and snake away to who knows where. There are 520 rather precipitous steps (with handrails) leading you to the floor of the main cavern (quite strenuous on the climb back up).

At the bottom of the steps is a hole through which you drop to start exploring the more interesting chambers 200 more steps below. Here you will need your own light. Some of the stalactite formations are extraordinary.

Speleologists have made explorations to a depth of 300m and it is believed a fossil river runs another 500m below. Among the most spectacular chambers are the *Salle de Lixus* and the *Salle de Draperies* which takes around 2½ hours to reach.

Entry to the cave is Dr3. Mostapha, the guardian of the caves, has a torch if you don't and though his guided tours seem pricey at Dr100, he is honest and reliable and there is no one who knows the caves better than he. His longest exploration of the caves was with a party of Germans with whom he emerged 28 hours later!

There is quite a bit of climbing and clambering to do, so wear shoes/trainers with a good grip and be prepared to get pretty grubby. If you have your own torch, you're free to explore the caves on your own, and if you don't re-emerge, Mostapha will come and look for you anyway. The caves are open from 8 am to 6, 7, or 8 pm, depending on the number of visitors.

As you leave the Daïa Chiker behind, the road begins to climb again into coniferous forests past Bab Bou-Idir. Along the way you can catch good views of the snow-capped Atlas. About 8km past Bab Bou-Idir, a poor piste branches 9km off to the right (north).

If you can get your car up the incline, you'll find the TV relay station at the top of Jebel Tazzeka (1980m) and wonderful views all around, to the Rif in the north and the Atlas in the south.

The main road continues around for another 38km back to the main Fès-Taza road at Sidi Abdallah de Rhiata. On the way you will wind your way around hairpin bends through some dense woodland and then down through the pretty **gorges** of the Oued Zireg.

From the intersection at Sidi Abdallah de Rhiata, you can take the main highway back east to Taza, pausing at Tizi n'Touahar on the way for some more views. If you're coming from Fès, take the right turn signposted for Bab Bou-Idir. This road curves round and under the main highway to head south. There is often a police checkpoint here.

EAST MOROCCO

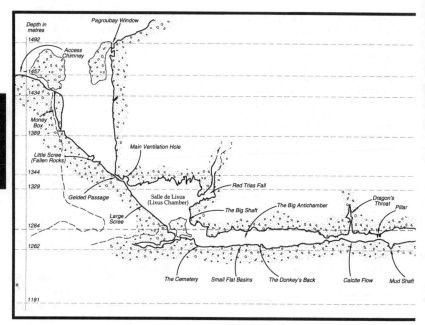

Depth in metres

1492

Pagroubay Window

Access Chimney

1457

1434

Money Box
1389

Little Scree (Fallen Rocks)

1344

1329

Main Ventilation Hole

Gelded Passage

Salle de Lixus (Lixus Chamber)

Large Scree

1284

1262

Red Trias Fall

The Big Shaft

The Big Antichamber

Dragon's Throat

Pillar

The Cemetery   Small Flat Basins   The Donkey's Back   Calcite Flow   Mud Shaft

1191

EAST MOROCCO

OUJDA

With a population of around a quarter of a million, Oujda is the largest town in the east of Morocco. It owes its size to its position close to the Algerian border. In the past, it saw floods of Algerian visitors (often buying up products unavailable at home for resale), but few westerners – a situation which ensured a relaxed and hassle-free atmosphere.

Now, with the closure of the Algerian border in 1995, it sees very few visitors at all. The devastating effect this has had on the local economy is everywhere apparent. Restaurants and hotels are empty, the cafes are filled with bored young men with long faces and the talk everywhere is of the *crise* (economic crisis).

Essentially, Oujda is rather an undistinguished sprawl of a modern city, with little to interest travellers. However, it makes a convenient stopping point for those crossing the border into Spanish Melilla (and in the future, hopefully, Algeria), or for those on their way south to Figuig and the Sahara. An added attraction is the fact that the Mediterranean beach town of Saidia is only 58km from Oujda and relatively accessible.

Oujda used to be armed to the teeth with hotels that used to accommodate visiting Algerians; now hotels are struggling just to survive and most have cut their prices by between 40% to 50%. You won't find better value anywhere in Morocco, nor get a warmer welcome. Make the most of this cheap luxury.

History

The site of Oujda has long been important, lying as it does on the main axis connecting Morocco with the rest of North Africa (the Romans built a road through here).

Like Taza, it has occupied a key position in controlling the east and often a step

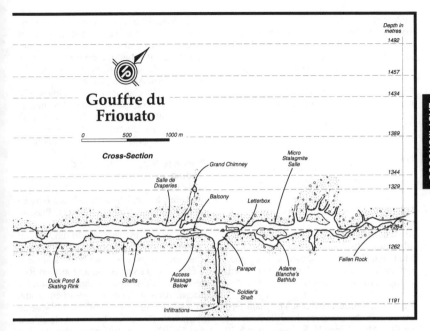

Depth in
metres
1492
1457
1434
1389
1344
1329
1264
1262
1191

Gouffre du Friouato

0   500   1000 m

Cross-Section

Micro
Stalagmite
Salle

Grand Chimney

Salle de
Draperies

Balcony

Letterbox

Duck Pond &
Skating Rink

Shafts

Access
Passage
Below

Parapet

Adame
Blanche's
Bathtub

Soldier's
Shaft

Fallen Rock

Infiltrations

towards seizing control of the heartland around Fès.

The town was founded by the Meghraoua tribe in the 10th century and it remained independent until the Almohads overran it in the 11th century. All the subsequent dynasties left their mark on its fate.

Under the Merenids, however, Algerian rulers based in Tlemcen took the town on several occasions, and in the 17th century it fell under the sway of the Ottoman administration set up in Algiers.

Moulay Ismail put an end to this in 1687, and Oujda remained in Moroccan hands until 1907 when French forces in Algeria crossed the frontier in one of a series of 'incidents' and occupied the town. The protectorate was still five years away, but the sultan was powerless to stop it.

The French soon expanded the town, which has since swelled in size as provincial capital and in its role as the main gateway for commerce with Algeria. Its industrial role rests on mining, particularly zinc, which is carried out further to the south.

Orientation

Although quite large, only the centre of Oujda is of any interest to travellers. The main street is Blvd Mohammed V, along or near which you'll find banks, the post and tourist offices, and many of the better budget and mid-range hotels and restaurants.

About a five minute walk to the west along Blvd Zerktouni is the train station. A further 15 minutes to the south-west, across Oued Nachef, is the main bus station (Gare Routière).

Also here, on the Taza exit road, are grands taxis for Taza and Fès. Buses and taxis to the Algerian border leave from Place du Maroc, just outside the medina.

Information

Tourist Office The office (☎ 689089, 684329) is on Place du 16 Août 1953 at the junction with Blvd Mohammed V. It has the usual brochures and the staff try to help out.

Foreign Consulates The following countries have foreign consulates in Oujda:

Algeria
　11 Blvd Bir Anzarane (also known as Blvd de Taza; ☎ 683740/1).
France
　3 Rue de Berkane, in the same complex as the Institut Français (☎ 68404).

Money Most Moroccan banks have branches in Oujda. The BMCE and BMCI on Blvd Mohammed V have ATMs and give cash advances. The Banque Populaire on Blvd Mohammed Derfoufi should also be good for cash advances and most banks will change cash and cheques.

Post & Communications The main post office is in the centre of the ville nouvelle on Blvd Mohammed V. It's open from 8.30 am to 12.15 pm and again from 2.30 to 6 pm.

The phone office, next door to the right of the main entrance to the post office, is open seven days a week from 8.30 am to 9 pm. There are card phones outside.

Film & Photography One good place for buying film or having it developed is the Dar Labo photo shop beside the BCM bank on Blvd Mohammed V.

Emergency The Dépôt de Médicaments de Nuit (All-Night Pharmacy) is opposite the CTM bus station.

Laundry The Central Pressing is opposite the Hôtel du 16 Août on Rue de Marrakesh.

Medina

Although hardly the most fascinating of medinas, Oujda's old centre warrants a bit of stroll at least. The most animated part is the area inside and outside the eastern gate,

Bab el-Ouahab. Also known as the Gate of Heads – local pashas had a habit of having the heads of criminals and renegades hung here – it is full of food stalls, beggars, shoppers and all the noise and bustle of a typical North African market.

Plunging deeper into the medina you'll find mainly clothes shops and a few hotels. The **Great Mosque**, built in the 14th century by the Merenids, is in bad shape and in any case is closed to non-Muslims.

Places to Stay – bottom end

Medina & Around This area has a few fairly simple places for the die-hard lovers of medina living, which include the *Ifriquia* (☎ 682095), *En-Nasr* (☎ 683932), *Rissani*, *Du Peuple* and *Al-Kasbah*. As a rule of thumb, rooms in these places cost about Dr30/60, usually with shared cold showers. They are adequate without being stunning.

Closer to the centre, on and around Rue de Marrakesh, is another bunch of similar places. Among the better ones here is the *Hôtel du 16 Août* (☎ 684197) at 128 Rue de Marrakesh. Rooms are basic, but clean, and cost Dr30/60. The communal showers are cold.

The best of the lot is the well run *Hôtel Al-Hanna* (☎ 686003) at 132 Rue de Marrakesh. Spotless and quite pleasant singles/doubles with basin cost Dr40/60. There is a communal, cold shower. Try to get one of the rooms upstairs, as the lower floors are a little gloomy.

Ville Nouvelle A better hunting ground for cheap hotels is the pedestrian zone off Blvd Mohammed V and the area nearby.

A little tatty around the edges, but probably the best value of the cheapies, is the *Hôtel Isly* (☎ 683928) at 24 Rue Ramdane el-Gadhi. It has adequate and clean rooms for Dr40/65. The hot water in the showers is hit and miss, however.

A little more money will get you a considerably better deal. The *Hôtel Simon* (☎ 686304) at 1 Rue Tarik ibn Ziad has rooms with private shower, bidet, basin and (some of them) wrought iron balcony for

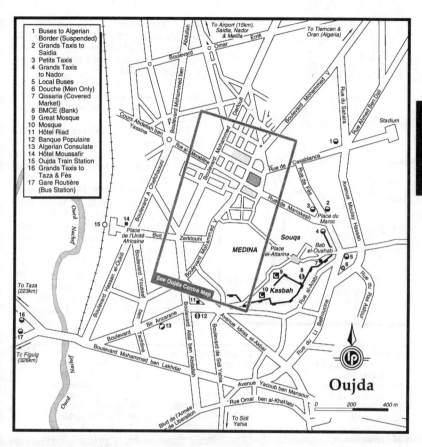

1 Buses to Algerian Border (Suspended)
2 Grands Taxis to Saidia
3 Petits Taxis
4 Grands Taxis to Nador
5 Local Buses
6 Douche (Men Only)
7 Qissaria (Covered Market)
8 BMCE (Bank)
9 Great Mosque
10 Mosque
11 Hôtel Riad
12 Banque Populaire
13 Algerian Consulate
14 Hôtel Moussafir
15 Oujda Train Station
16 Grands Taxis to Taza & Fès
17 Gare Routière (Bus Station)

Oujda

Dr70/90. It's a little run down, but a clean place and quite good value.

Better still is the *Hôtel Afrah* (☎ 686533), at 15 Rue de Tafna, which has been attractively decorated in the traditional style, with zellij (tile work), fountain, ghebs (intricate plaster work) and horse shoe arches. Rooms cost Dr70/120 and are small and comfortable and contain spotless en suite bathrooms (with hot water when there's enough demand for it).

Not far away, at 13 Blvd Zerktouni, is one of the best lower-end deals in Oujda,

the one-star *Hôtel Royal* (☎ 682284). Officially its rates are Dr73/89 for rooms without shower (Dr5 for a hot shower in the communal bathroom) and Dr116/133 with private shower and toilet (hot water more or less all day). With the current economic situation, however, you can get rooms without showers for as little as Dr45/75.

The hotel also has some guarded parking (Dr12 a night).

Places to Stay – middle

There's a small group of hotels to the north-

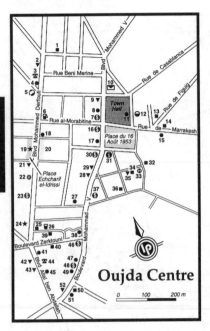

Oujda Centre

0   100   200 m

west of the post office. The *Hôtel/Restaurant Mamounia* (☎ 690072; fax 690073), has been a reliable bet in the past, but was closed for Ramadan at the time of writing. It charges Dr98/153.

Better value, but a bit further away and heading up the price scale, is the *Hôtel Riad* (☎ 688353), on Ave Idriss el-Akbar (see the Oujda map).

It has rooms for Dr163/188; those on the higher floors are quite good, with en suite bathroom, central heating in winter, and air-con in summer. The hotel bar is a haunt of local prostitutes.

The *Hôtel Al Fajr* (☎ 702293), just off Blvd Mohammed Derfoufi, offers good value. It opened in early 1994 and has 48 sparklingly clean and modern rooms (decorated by a French interior designer) with central heating, en suite bathroom and telephone and TV. Rooms cost Dr164/196, and there's a 25% discount for the second night.

One of the best value places in this category is the recently renovated *Hôtel des Lilas* (☎/fax 680840), at Rue Jamal ed-Din el-Afghani. It has 38 rooms and 10 suites.

PLACES TO STAY	52	Glacier Pâtisserie Le	19	Police
1	Hôtel/Restaurant		Printemps	20	Market
	Mamounia			22	Douche Balima
13	Hôtel Al-Hanna	**OTHER**			(Public Showers)
14	Hôtel du 16 Août	3	Telephones	23	Banque Populaire
25	Hôtel Al Fajr	4	Pharmacie Nouvelle	24	Sûreté Nationale
32	Hôtel Isly	5	Institut Français;	26	Bar Chanteclair
34	Hôtel Afrah		French Consulate	27	Cinéma Royal
36	Hôtel Simon	6	Agip Petrol Station	30	BMCI (ATM); BCME
39	Hôtel des Lilas	7	Wafabank; Pharmacie		(ATM)
40	Hôtel Royal		Ben Bakhti	31	Tourist Office
50	Hôtel Oujda	8	Hertz (Car Rental)	33	Douche Moderne
		10	Main Post Office		(Men Only)
PLACES TO EAT	11	Dépôt de Médicaments de	37	Bank el-Maghrib
2	Restaurant Paella		Nuit (All-Night Pharmacy)	38	Pharmacie L'Orientale
9	Café Le Trésor	12	CTM Bus Station	41	Avis (Car Rental)
21	Café Champs Elysées	15	Central Pressing	44	Telephones; Fax
28	Pâtisserie Colombo		(Laundry)	45	Pharmacy
29	Brasserie Restaurant	16	Crédit du Maroc (Bank)	46	Sociéte Générale
	de France	17	Carlson Wagonlits	47	Budget (Car Rental)
35	Restaurant Wassila		(Travel Agency);	48	BCM (Bank)
42	Café Bar des Anciens		Europcar (Car Rental)	49	Dar Labo (Photo Shop)
43	Sandwich	18	Maison de la Presse	51	Royal Air Maroc
	Taroudannt		(French Newspaper Stand)		

The rooms are smallish, but very comfortable with private bathroom, satellite TV and telephone, and cost Dr120/150. Parking is available.

Places to Stay – top end
There are a few hotels in the three-star bracket and up. Right near the train station (see the Oujda map), the *Hôtel Moussafir* chain (☎ 688202; fax 688208) has one of its standard and fairly reliable hotels for people who want to be near train stations. Rooms, as usual, are modern and well kept at the standard Dr256/312.

One of the two top hotels in town is the *Hôtel Oujda* (☎ 685063; fax 685064) on Blvd Mohammed V. It charges Dr244/299 and has its own restaurant and bar.

Swimming Pools
The Hôtel Oujda has a pool which is open to non-residents if it's not too full (which is unlikely), and charges Dr50 per day.

Hammams
You can take a shower at the Douche Balima on Blvd Mohammed Derfoufi. The Douche Moderne close to the Hôtel Afrah, is open to men only. Both places cost Dr5.

Places to Eat
Probably the cheapest place to eat snack food is at the stalls set up inside Bab el-Ouahab, providing you have a taste for broiled sheep heads, deep-fried intestines and very large bags of snails. Fortunately, you can also find slightly more mundane meals along the lines of cooked potatoes and omelettes.

Otherwise, there's not an oversupply of cheap eating places in Oujda. A good, simple place is *Sandwich Taroudannt*, on Blvd Allal ben Abdallah, just around the corner from the Hôtel Royal. It serves generous portions of the usual dishes such as tajine for around Dr45. If you want anything more ambitious, you'll have to order it in advance.

The *Restaurant Wassila* next door to the Hôtel Afrah, is an excellent place for good Moroccan food at reasonable prices. It does a delicious harira soup for Dr5, main courses such as tajine, brochettes and couscous (on Friday or ordered in advance) for Dr30 and salads for Dr15. There's some seating upstairs for women looking for a quiet corner.

The *Restaurant Paella*, at 85 Blvd Mohammed Derfoufi, specialises in seafood at reasonable prices (Dr45 to Dr65 for main dishes). Paella, the speciality, costs Dr100 for two people.

If you're desperate for a beer or some wine with your meal, the licensed *Brasserie Restaurant de France* (☎ 685987) on Blvd Mohammed V is a possibility.

Cafes & Patisseries There is no shortage of cafes all over the ville nouvelle and in the area around the medina. A couple of those on Blvd Mohammed V have a definitely more swish air about them.

Café Le Trésor, on Blvd Mohammed V, run by the friendly Mahdaoui brothers, is a very good place for breakfast (Dr12). It does delicious, freshly baked croissants and petits pains (pastries). It's open every day from 5 am to 9 pm, and has some seating upstairs which is good for lone women travellers.

Pâtisserie Colombo, at 80 Blvd Mohammed V, next door to the Brasserie Restaurant de France, is considered the best patisserie in town in terms of quality, and it has an excellent selection of cakes. It's also good for breakfast (Dr10). Both patisseries are open from 5 am until 9 or 9.30 pm.

Entertainment
Bars The town bars are never difficult to find (a few are marked on the map), but are the usual seedy spit-and-sawdust variety. A better bet, particularly for women, are those at the bigger hotels. These often double as discos. The bar at the *Hôtel Oujda* is open from 6 pm to midnight.

Getting There & Away
Air The airport serving Oujda is 15km north of the town (about a Dr50 petit taxi ride).

Royal Air Maroc (☎ 683909), which has an office close to the Hôtel Oujda on Blvd Mohammed V, has six flights a week to Casablanca (Dr889 one way; one hour 40 minutes). There is also a weekly direct flight to Rabat/Salé (Dr790) and a flight to Agadir via Casablanca (Dr1490).

There is one direct flight a week to Paris (Dr5978 one way) on Saturday at 8 am. Air France also has a weekly flight to Paris, departing on Sunday at 3.55 pm.

Bus CTM has a small office behind the town hall. There are only two departures from here. The first goes to Casablanca (Dr162) via Rabat (Dr139), Fès (Dr89; six hours) and Meknès (Dr103) at 8 pm. There is a mumtaz run to Fès at 8.30 pm.

Another bus leaves for Fès at 10 am (passing by the Gare Routiére at 11 am). It costs Dr75 and passes via Taza (Dr50). The SAT bus company has an office across the road for its Casablanca and Rabat runs at 6 and 8 pm.

All other buses, including CTM's other services, leave from the bus station (Gare Routière) across Oued Nachef on the south-western edge of town, about a 15 minute walk from the train station. Advance booking is available on the main runs.

Several non-CTM companies operate buses to most destinations. Around 15 buses a day run to Fès, from 5.30 am to 10 pm (more than seven of these stop at Meknès). There are at least five to Taza, seven to Figuig (Dr66) and Bouarfa (Dr49), around 20 to Nador (Dr25), seven to Al-Hoceima (Dr55) and four or five to Saidia (Dr10). There are at least 12 buses to Casablanca every day. Prices are generally 15% to 30% less than the CTM prices.

CTM has daily departures to Taza and Fès at 5 and 11 am, and to Taza and Nador at 7 and 10 am and 1 and 3.30 pm.

Train Oujda station is fairly close to the centre of town, at the western end of Blvd Zerktouni. There's a left-luggage counter which is open 24 hours and costs Dr2.50 per item, but everything must be padlocked.

There are at least three departures for the west of the country from 7.05 am to 1.15 pm; in summer there are a further three until 10.20 pm. All these trains call at Taza (four hours), Fès (6½ hours) and Meknès (7½ hours). Two morning trains continue on to Tangier, while the others continue on to Rabat and Casablanca. First and 2nd class sleepers are available on the evening trains.

Second class minimum/maximum fares (depending which service you take) include: Taza (Dr39/67), Fès (Dr59/99), Casablanca (Dr114/194), Tangier (Dr151/157), Marrakesh (Dr156/266; no direct trains), Meknès (Dr69/116) and Rabat (Dr100/168).

There are also trains to Mohammed V international airport outside Casablanca. There are no more services to Bouarfa.

Supratours has an office at the station, should you want to book rail/coach tickets to destinations south of Marrakesh.

Taxi Grands taxis to Taza and Fès (change at Taza) leave fairly regularly from outside the main bus station. The fares per person are Dr50.50 and Dr90 respectively. Taxis to Fès take you to Bab el-Ftouh (see the Getting Around section for Fès).

Grands taxis to Nador (Dr35) leave from Place du Maroc (see the Oujda map). Others travelling to Saidia on the Mediterranean coast leave from the other side of the square, but they are very infrequent outside summer (Dr15). Taxis from here also serve other regional towns.

Car The following agencies can be found in Oujda:

Avis
   Maroc Voyages, 110 Boulevard Allal ben Abdallah (☎ 683993)
Budget
   Immeuble Kada, Boulevard Mohammed V (☎ 682437)
Europcar
   Carlson Wagonlits, Place Mohammed V (☎ 682520)

Algeria With the closure of the Algerian border, services here have rather fallen into disuse. In the past, buses ran there every half-hour, as well as trains and grands taxis. Should the border open again, enquire at the relevant services.

AROUND OUJDA
Sidi Yahia Oasis
About 7km south of Oujda is the oasis village of Sidi Yahia. It is the site of an annual moussem held in September. It is one of the bigger celebrations of this type in the country, and if you're in the area at the right time, it's well worth a visit.

BOUARFA
The 376km journey south from Oujda to Figuig is long, hot and, for the most part, monotonous. Figuig itself warrants a visit – particularly for those who see the desert routes through the Sahara as the main attraction of Maghreb travel – but the towns on the way down from Oujda do not.

The administrative and garrison town of Bouarfa is no exception, and the only thing that separates it from the others is the fact that it serves as a minor transport hub for the south-eastern corner of Morocco.

Places to Stay & Eat
Should you get stuck here, the best accommodation bet is the *Hôtel Tamlalte*, on the town's main street and about 100m from the bus station. Rooms are clean and basic and cost Dr30/60. There are no showers, but there are basins in the rooms. A few cafes and snack stands are scattered around town.

Getting There & Away
Bus There are six buses daily to Oujda which cost Dr49.50, and four departures to Figuig (Dr21). Heading west to Er-Rachidia there is a bus for Dr53 at around noon.

Train The weekly service to Oujda has now stopped running.

FIGUIG
Some 100,000 palm trees are fed by artesian wells in this oasis on the edge of the Sahara. Figuig was once the last stop before crossing the Sahara for Moroccan pilgrims heading to Mecca, and until the closure of the Algerian border in 1995, was the second border post after Oujda. Like Oujda, the local economy has suffered heavily; the camping site and all but one hotel has closed.

However, if you do come all this way, there is a surprising amount of interest in the town.

If you want a guided tour (by foot or by car), you should contact Mostapha Tabou (☎ 898145), the local bicycle mechanic-turned-reluctant-guide! He does very interesting 3 to 4-hour tours which include a circuit around the ksour, the pink mosque, the old Jewish quarter and the springs, where he will explain the ancient irrigation system still in use in the *palmeraies* (palm groves).

If you're here for a couple of days, Mostapha can suggest other excursions such as visiting local tribes (including one that marries only among its own kind). You can find Mostapha working at the garage next to the now defunct Hôtel Sahara.

There is a souq held every Friday at Figuig. On Sunday, after the first prayer, but before sunrise, the unusual Souq de

EAST MOROCCO

Date palms are a common sight in the Figuig area, which is one of Morocco's principal date-producing areas.

Sand Baths

Anyone suffering from rheumatism may want to consider being buried up to their neck in the baking hot sands of the desert while they're in Morocco.

A famous doctor in Figuig came up with this form of treatment as a very effective way of drawing dampness out of the body. It can be dangerous (several people died doing this in Merzouga in 1993) and must be carefully supervised.

The time spent buried (head poking out, one presumes) is just a few minutes, but overall treatment usually takes place over several days. Despite the possibility of being cooked alive, sand baths seem to be growing in popularity. ■

Jellaba takes place, which is for the old people of Figuig only.

Figuig's greatest charm is as a place to simply unwind. It would be hard to find a more laid-back place, although in summer this is mainly due to the oppressive heat. The main road from Bouarfa goes through the oasis and on to Beni Ounif, on the Algerian side of the frontier.

Information

There is a Banque Populaire, post and phone office set back off the main road, Blvd Hassan II.

Places to Stay & Eat

A lack of accommodation is Figuig's biggest problem. The only hotel open at the time of writing was the *Hôtel El-Meliasse*. Filthy, dark rooms go for Dr30/60. It's no use asking the hotel owner to change the grubby sheets; he'll just pull off another set from a neighbouring bed.

If you haven't yet visited a Moroccan hammam, there's one next door to the now defunct Hôtel Sahara.

The only other possibility of a bed in town is at the *Maison des Jeunes*, opposite the Café La Paix on Hassan II. Just knock at the door and ask if there's space. It has just eight simple, but clean, rooms with basin which cost Dr20 per person. There are cold, communal showers.

It's rumoured that the state-run *Hôtel/Camping Diamant Vert* is going to reopen sometime in 1998. One of its 20 rooms (which come with bathroom) should cost in the region of Dr100 to Dr120.

There are no proper restaurants in Figuig, just a couple of cafes/snack bars. The best is the *Café Oasis*, just short of Moroccan customs on the border.

It does a reasonable tajine each day which costs Dr20 to Dr25, (anything else will have to be ordered in advance), and is a good place for breakfast. It's open from 6 am to 10.30 pm.

The *Café La Paix* on Hassan II is good for coffee.

Getting There & Away

Bus There are buses to Oujda at 2, 5, 6, 7 and 8 am every day. They all stop at Bouarfa (in case you want to link up with the Er-Rachidia bus there at 12.45 pm). The fare is Dr68 to Oujda.

Algeria Should the border reopen in the future, It's a 3km walk to Moroccan Customs, another kilometre to Algerian Customs and a further 3km to the first Algerian town, Beni Ounif.

Berber frog symbol
Associated with fertility and magic rites.

The North Atlantic Coast

From Tangier to the Mauritanian border, Morocco boasts an Atlantic seaboard of some 2500km (including the still-disputed territory of the Western Sahara).

Just as Tangier is a unique mix of Moroccan and European influences, the cities and towns of the coast present a very different face from those of the interior. Most of Morocco's coastal towns and cities were occupied, or even founded, by European powers, and this is reflected in their appearance and feel.

Long used to the sight of foreigners, the people of the coastal cities have been handed down a legacy quite different from that of the long-xenophobic interior. Rabat and Casablanca, the political and economic capitals since the French installed their protectorate in 1912, are cosmopolitan centres at the heart of modern Morocco. They are flanked up and down the coast by towns that at one time or another served as bridgeheads for European merchant empires.

HIGHLIGHTS

- **Rabat** – Morocco's capital and home to some of its most important monuments
- **Asilah** – a picturesque coastal town with Portuguese ramparts and white-washed houses
- **Casablanca** – with its extraordinary new Hassan II mosque
- **Moulay Bousselham** – a peaceful coastal town famous for attracting remarkable bird life
- **Salé** – for its stunning Merenid medersa

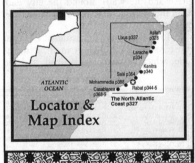

What remains is a curious combination of European and Moroccan fortifications and medinas. In between lie hundreds of kilometres of beaches, many of them crowded in summer. Foreigners tend to head still further south, to Essaouira and Agadir.

North Coast

ASILAH

A 46km drive south of Tangier, through verdant country along a stretch of beaches, lies the port of Asilah. Small it may be, but over two millennia it has had a tumultuous history far out of proportion to its size.

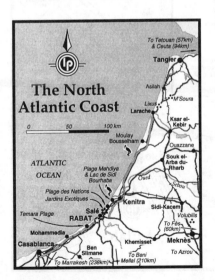

The North Atlantic Coast

To Tetouan (57km) & Ceuta (94km)
Tangier
Asilah
M'Soura
Lixus
Larache
Ksar el-Kebir
Moulay Bousselham
Ouazzane
Souk el-Arba du-Rharb
Plage Mehdiya & Lac de Sidi Bourhaba
Oued
Sebou
Plage des Nations
Jardins Exotiques
Kenitra
Sidi-Kacem
ATLANTIC OCEAN
Temara Plage
Salé
RABAT
Volubilis
To Fès (60km)
Mohammedia
Ben Slimane
Khemisset
Meknès
To Azrou
Casablanca
To Beni Mellal (210km)
To Marrakesh (238km)

0   50   100 km

The first settlers were the Carthaginians, who named the port Zilis. Next were the Romans. Forced to deal with a population that had backed the wrong side during the Punic Wars, Rome decided to move the inhabitants to Spain and replace them with Iberians.

Asilah featured again in the 10th century, when it held Norman raiders from Sicily at bay. In the following century it became the last refuge of the Idrissids.

The town's most turbulent period, however, followed the Christian victories over the forces of Islam on the Iberian peninsula in the 14th and 15th centuries.

In 1471 it was captured by the Portuguese and the walls around the city date from this period, although they have been repaired from time to time.

In 1578 King Dom Sebastian of Portugal chose Asilah as the base for an ill-fated crusade, which resulted in his death and the subsequent passing of Portugal (and its Moroccan possessions) into the hands of Spain.

Asilah was captured by the Moroccans in 1589, lost again to the Spanish and then was recaptured by Moulay Ismail in 1691. In the 19th century, as a result of pirate attacks on its shipping, Spain sent in the navy to bombard the town.

Early this century, Asilah was used as a base by one of the most colourful bandits ever produced by the wild Rif mountains – Er-Raissouli.

Shortly after the end of WWI he was forced to abandon Asilah, and within a few years had lost everything.

Asilah has found its niche in the late 20th century as a bijou resort town. Money has been poured into gentrifying the houses within the city walls by both affluent Moroccans and Europeans. Consequently, the streets gleam with fresh whitewash, ornate wrought-iron adorns windows, and chic

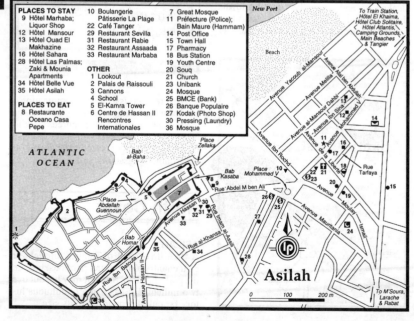

PLACES TO STAY	10 Boulangerie	7 Great Mosque
9 Hôtel Marhaba;	Pâtisserie La Plage	11 Préfecture (Police);
Liquor Shop	22 Café Tanger	Bain Maure (Hammam)
12 Hôtel Mansour	29 Restaurant Sevilla	14 Post Office
13 Hôtel Ouad El	31 Restaurant Rabie	15 Town Hall
Makhazine	32 Restaurant Assaada	17 Pharmacy
16 Hôtel Sahara	33 Restaurant Marbaba	18 Bus Station
28 Hôtel Las Palmas;		19 Youth Centre
Zaki & Mounia	OTHER	20 Souq
Apartments	1 Lookout	21 Church
34 Hôtel Belle Vue	2 Palais de Raissouli	23 Unibank
35 Hôtel Asilah	3 Cannons	24 Mosque
	4 School	25 BMCE (Bank)
PLACES TO EAT	5 El-Kamra Tower	26 Banque Populaire
8 Restaurante	6 Centre de Hassan II	27 Kodak (Photo Shop)
Oceano Casa	Rencontres	30 Pressing (Laundry)
Pepe	Internationales	36 Mosque

Asilah

Er-Raissouli

Moulay Ahmed ben Mohammed er-Raissouli (or Raisuni) began his career in the late 1800s as a petty mountain bandit, but soon progressed to murder on such a scale that the whole countryside around Tangier and Tetouan lived in fear of him.

At this time, however, he had been made *pasha* of Asilah, which was to become his main residence and base. In 1899, when Er-Raissouli was 23 years old, the sultan lost patience (or summoned up the nerve to act against the 'pasha') and had him arrested and jailed in Mogador (modern Essaouira) for several years.

When he was released he returned home, but was soon at it again. His most profitable game proved to be the kidnapping of westerners. He and his band held various luminaries to ransom, including US businessman Ion Perdicaris, who was ransomed in 1904 for US$70,000.

In return for promising good conduct, Er-Raissouli was made governor of the Tangier region. His conduct, however, was anything but good and by 1907 the European powers were sufficiently worried by his antics that they compelled the Moroccan government to attack him. It did, but failed to capture him.

Things were looking grim for Er-Raissouli, but in 1909 Moulay Abd al-Hafiz became sultan, and Er-Raissouli – whose influence over the Rif tribes was still great – proclaimed his allegiance to the new sultan immediately. In return he was made governor of most of north-west Morocco, with the exception of Tangier.

Spain, which took control of the north under the deal that cut Morocco up into protectorates in 1912, tried to make use of Er-Raissouli to keep order among the Rif tribes. Madrid invested considerable money and military hardware in the effort, but in vain. Er-Raissouli as often as not used the arms against the Spanish, inflicting several stinging defeats.

Having obtained promises from Germany that he would be made sultan after WWI, he found himself at loggerheads with everyone when Germany lost the war in 1918. The Spaniards forced him to flee Asilah, but for the following few years he continued to wreak havoc in the Rif hinterland.

The final irony was his arrest and imprisonment at the beginning of 1925 by a Rif rebel with a slightly broader political outlook, Abd el-Krim. Er-Raissouli, who had submitted to the medical attention of a Spaniard, stood accused of being too closely linked to the Spanish! He died on 10 April 1925. ∎

craft shops have sprouted along virtually every alley.

A new harbour is under construction and should soon be providing berths for both pleasure yachts and the small local fishing fleet.

A little further north along the beaches, camping resorts have mushroomed to cater to legions of European summer holiday-makers.

Despite the changes mass tourism has brought (including the arrival of a handful of touts and guides), it is worth staying in Asilah for a while, especially in the low season, when there are hardly any tourists around.

Information

Money Both the BMCE and Banque Populaire, on Ave Mauritania, will change cash and travellers cheques and issue cash advances on credit cards. There are no ATMs.

Post & Communications The post and telephone office is on the east side of town, just off the Tangier-Rabat road. It is open during regular office hours.

There are a couple of card-operated telephones outside the office.

Laundry There is a *pressing* next door to the Restaurant Sevilla on Rue Imam al-Assili.

Medical Services Asilah has several pharmacies. The easiest one to find is on Ave Mohammed V near the bus station.

Ramparts & Medina

The impressive 15th century Portuguese ramparts are largely intact, partly as a result of modern restoration work. Access is limited since many private houses abut them. The two prongs that jut out into the ocean, however, can be visited at any time and these afford the best views. It's reminiscent of the old towns enclosed behind the walls of El-Jadida and Essaouira and there are plenty of photographic opportunities.

The bright medina is worth a wander. You'll notice a lot of cheery **murals** on many of the houses. Of more historical note is the **Bab Homar** (also known as Bab al-Jebel or, to the Spaniards, Puerta de la Tierra), topped by the much-eroded Portuguese royal coat of arms.

On Place Abdellah Guennoun is an interesting-looking **tower** known as the El-Kamra. There are a few old cannons left just inside the seaward wall, although you can only see them from a distance – access has been cut off by another cement wall.

Palais de Raissouli (Raissouli Palace)

Undoubtedly one of the town's most interesting sights, this beautifully preserved, three storey building was constructed in 1909 and includes a main reception room with a glass-fronted terrace overlooking the sea. It was from this terrace that Er-Raissouli forced convicted murderers to jump to their deaths onto the rocks 30m below.

Unfortunately, all the furniture has been removed, so it's hard to get an idea of the sumptuousness of Er-Raissouli's life at the height of his power. It now houses a series of exhibitions and, if you're unlucky, you may find it closed while preparing for the next exhibition. Otherwise, it is open from 8.30 am to 12.30 pm and from 3 to 6.30 pm every day, except Friday.

Entry is free and access is through a door just inside the seaward wall; a guardian will open it up, for a small tip. The palace is also

the venue for a national arts festival held in July or August each year.

Beaches

Other than the medina, the beaches to the north of town are the main attraction. During the summer months they are awash with tourists from Europe.

A whole service industry has grown up to cater for the needs of these people, including camp sites, restaurants, discos and the like. It's a smaller-scale version of Agadir at this time of year and you can meet people from as far afield as Brisbane and Bremen.

Places to Stay – bottom end

Camping For campers, there are a number of resorts/sites along the beach – all of them north of town. The first two you come across, and among the best, are *Camping As-Saada* (☎ 917317) and, about 1km from the train station, the *Camping Echrigui* (☎ 917182).

The latter is the better of the two and charges around Dr5 to Dr10 less than the As-Saada. It costs Dr10 per person, per tent and for electricity, and Dr5 per child and for a hot shower. Caravans and camping vans cost Dr20. There are grocery stores at both sites, and both stay open all year.

The As-Saada also rents out bungalows for Dr100/150 in the winter/summer.

Closer to the Mohammed V Bridge, which lies about 10km north of Asilah, are at least three more Atlantic coast camps, *L'Océan*, the *Atlas* and the *Sahara*. They tend to be pretty full in summer and at Easter, as they are often block-booked by tour groups from Europe. At other times of the year, you'll virtually have the place to yourself. They all have guarded camping facilities, shower and toilet blocks, and restaurants and bars. They all charge around the same rates, as quoted above.

Hotels The *Hôtel Marhaba* (☎ 917144), overlooks Place Zellaka in front of the main entrance (Bab Kasaba) to the old town and is quite adequate for most travellers. It was being totally refurbished at the time of writing, but prices at Dr50/100 for singles/doubles should stay the same. Showers are communal and cost Dr5 extra. Ask for a room at the front; those at the back can be a bit poky.

The *Hôtel Asilah* (☎ 917286) at 79 Ave Hassan II is one of the best value deals in town. Small but clean rooms without shower cost Dr35/70 and rooms with shower Dr100/120. The communal showers have hot water.

Further up the price scale is the *Hôtel Sahara* (☎ 917185) at 9 Rue Tarfaya. Singles, doubles and triples cost Dr98, Dr126 and Dr186 respectively. Showers are Dr5 extra.

Places to Stay – middle

There are a few mid-range options in Asilah. Probably the best value is the *Hôtel Las Palmas* (☎ 917694) at 7 Rue Imman Asili. It has very clean, newly furnished rooms with shower for Dr130/150.

Another good bet is the *Hôtel Mansour* (☎ 917390; fax 917533) at 49 Ave Mohammed V. It's a cosy little place with spotless rooms, all with shower and toilet. The small dining area is almost reminiscent of an English tea room. Rooms cost Dr146/195 and the staff are helpful.

A rather characterless place, but with spacious and comfortable rooms, is the *Hôtel Ouad El Makhazine* (☎ 917090; fax 917500), on Ave Melilla. The rooms have carpet, showers, toilets and phones and cost Dr138/164.

Places to Stay – top end

The three-star *Hôtel El Khaima* (☎ 917428; fax 917566) is beside the road heading north, just out of town on the right-hand side. Singles, doubles and triples cost Dr274, Dr330 and Dr433 respectively in the low season and Dr374, Dr430 and Dr533 in the high season. Add Dr8 per person for tax. Breakfast costs Dr41. The hotel has 110 rooms, a restaurant, a pool and a disco.

Out near the camp sites by the Mohammed V Bridge are a couple of other hotels, the *Club Solitaire* and the *Atlantis*,

which are more important for the pools, restaurants and discos they offer campers than for their accommodation. If you would like to stay here, prices are in the same league as Hôtel El Khaima.

Apartments

Because many people have bought houses in the old town and converted them into holiday homes, it is possible to find apartments to rent. If there's a small group of you, and you plan to hang around Asilah for a while, these can be an excellent and very reasonable option, although it's wise to book well ahead during the high season.

If you're interested, contact Ali Meghraoui at *Zaki & Mounia Appartements* (☎ 917497 or 917815; fax 917497). You'll find his office next door to the Hôtel Las Palmas at 14 Ave Imam al-Assili. It's open every day (except Sunday) from 9 am to 1 pm and from 3 to 8 pm.

The apartments aren't far from the office, so get Ali to show you a couple before deciding. They are comfortable and well maintained, and have terraces. A 'large' one (for four to seven people) costs Dr300/400 per day in winter/summer, while a 'small' one (for two people) will cost Dr150/250. There are also a couple of 'medium' ones available for up to four people.

If you have no luck here, you could also try the *Hôtel Belle Vue* (☎/fax 917747), on Rue al-Khansa, which has four simple, but adequate, apartments with lounge, kitchen and refrigerator for Dr250/300 in winter/summer. It also offers larger ones (for up to five people) for Dr350/500.

Swimming Pools

The Hôtel Ouad El Makhazine has a pool which is open to non-guests for Dr25 per day.

Hammams

The best place for a good scrub is the Bain Maure hammam close to the police station. It costs Dr6 and is open from 5 to 11 am and from 7 pm to midnight for men, and from 11 am to 7 pm for women.

Places to Eat

About the cheapest option is the string of restaurants and cafes on Ave Hassan II and, around the corner, on Rue Imam al-Assili. They're simple, pretty basic places which specialise largely in fish dishes. Main courses such as fish tajine, brochettes and paella cost around Dr30. You can browse the day's suggestions (chalked up on a blackboard outside many of the restaurants) until one takes your fancy. Many of them have little terraces spilling onto the street. The *Restaurant Rabie* is one of the better ones and serves pretty edible fare.

Of the slightly more expensive restaurants across from Bab Kasaba, *Restaurante Oceano Casa Pepe* (☎ 917395), at 8 Place Zallaka, is definitely the best. The charming old owner, Pepe, inherited the restaurant from his father who came here from Almería in Spain in 1914. It specialises in Spanish-style fish dishes (all around Dr45) and the varied menu ranges from octopus and eels to shrimps and barnacles. It's a simple but very pleasant place and is good value. The place is a popular haunt with Spanish day-trippers who come all the way from Tangier.

Also good value is the little *Restaurant Sevilla* at 18 Ave Imam Ali Assili which has fish dishes and some traditional Moroccan fare for Dr30 to Dr45.

Cafes & Patisseries

The *Café Tanger*, at 52 Ave Mohammed V, is a good place for some coffee, fruit juice and toast in the morning. It's a clean, comfortable place and in summer has air-conditioning. It's open every day from 4 am to 8 pm.

The *Boulangerie Pâtisserie La Plage*, close by on Ave Ibn Rochd, is also good for breakfast (Dr12) and has some fine-quality pastries, including croissants and some heavenly almond tarts. They will also prepare sandwiches for you to take away. It's a great place for preparing a beach picnic.

Entertainment

The bar in the *Hôtel Ouad El Makhazine* is locally regarded as the most pleasant place

for a drink. It's open every day from 11 am to midnight and a beer will cost you Dr13.

The most popular discos are those at the *Hôtel El Khaima* and, on Saturdays, the *Hôtel Club Solitaire*. Entry costs Dr50 at both discos.

For a quiet tipple at your hotel, there is a small liquor shop next to the *Hôtel Marhaba*.

Getting There & Away

Bus Your best bet for getting to and from Asilah is the bus. All buses leave from the same lot (on Ave de la Liberté) which has just the one ticket window.

For Tangier (Dr10/15 for non-CTM/CTM buses) departures are every half hour from 6.30 am to 8 pm.

There are nine buses a day to Larache (Dr9/13); 10 to Meknès (Dr45/78) from 6.30 am; a bus every half hour to Casablanca (Dr60/105), via Rabat (Dr40/64), from 6 am to 11.15 pm; and four buses a day to Fès (Dr52/82) from 9.15 am to 4.45 pm. Pay on the bus.

Train This is the painful way to get to Asilah, as the station is 2.5km north of town. Rapide/2nd class ordinary fares are Dr71.50/56.50 to Rabat, Dr97/77 to Casablanca and Dr13.50/10.50 to Tangier.

Taxi Grands taxis to Tangier cost Dr20 and, if you get there early enough in the day, you might be able to get one to Larache for Dr10 a person.

AROUND ASILAH
Monoliths of M'Soura

An ancient and little-understood stone circle stands on a desolate patch of ground some 25km (by road) south-east of Asilah. The stones range from 50cm to 6m in height and some historians believe they surround the tomb of a noble, perhaps dating back to Punic times.

To get to it you must first reach the village of Souq Tnine de Sidi el-Yamani, off highway P37 which branches east off the main Tangier-Rabat road. From here, 6km of bad piste lead north to the site. You need a good vehicle, and a local guide would help.

The area just north of Asilah is a popular spot for wintering **birds**, including huge populations of common cranes (up to a 1000 have been reported at one time) and a good number of birds of prey, including black kites, lesser kestrels and, particularly, the great bustard. They often can be spotted from the main road around Briex and Pont Mohammed V, about 10km north of Asilah.

LARACHE
Most people come to Larache to visit the Roman ruins of Lixus, 4 to 5km out of town to the north, but it's worth staying a night or two just for its own sake. Bigger and scruffier than Asilah and with a more substantial fishing port, Larache is a tranquil town where you'll have few hassles.

The old town was once walled, but the kasbah and ramparts are now in almost total ruin. What remains intact is the old medina, a fortress known as the Casbah de la Cigogne and a pocket-sized, Spanish-built citadel that houses the archaeological museum.

The medina, a tumble-down affair, is worth walking around to get a feel for a typical, living Moroccan town without any of the tourist trappings and hassle. The heart of the new town is Place de la Libération (formerly the Plaza de España), a typical example of colonial Spanish urban planning.

The whitewashed town, inside the medina and out, is dominated by one other colour – the blue used on doors and window frames.

One thing that makes Larache interesting is the nightlife. Although it's a long time since the Spanish left, the social institution of the evening stroll lives on in the warmer months. Between the hours of 5.30 and 9 pm, everyone emerges from the woodwork to promenade, drink coffee or beer, play cards and talk about the day's events.

Not so Spanish, however, is the fact that by 10 pm the streets are virtually empty.

Naturally, there's some good seafood available in the restaurants.

Information
Foreign Consulates Spain has a consulate at 1 Rue Casablanca (☎ 913302). It's open from 8 am to 1 pm Monday to Friday and from 10 am to 12.30 pm on Saturday.

Money Across the road from the post office is a cluster of banks, all of which accept cash and travellers cheques. There are no ATMs.

Post & Communications The post and telephone office is on Blvd Mohammed V and is open normal office hours. There are some card-operated phones outside.

Laundry There is a pressing next door to the Pensión Malaga, in the narrow passageway.

Musée Archéologique
The tiny archaeological museum contains a small collection of artefacts, mostly from nearby Lixus, including coins, ceramics, utensils and the like from Phoenician and Roman times. The display is on two floors, but is so small that, if you are on a tight budget and want to save yourself the tenner, you could probably skip it. The explanations are in Arabic and French only.

The building itself is a former Spanish citadel and bears the arms of Charles V above the main door. It's open daily from 9 am to noon and 3 to 6 pm (closed Tuesday). Entry costs Dr10.

The Old Town
The only intact fortification here is the **Casbah de la Cigogne**, which was built by the Spaniards under Philip III in the 17th century. However, it is out of bounds to visitors.

The old city walls and ruined kasbah (the Qebibat) constructed by the Portuguese in the 16th century, while not out of bounds, are made dangerous by the possibility of falling masonry.

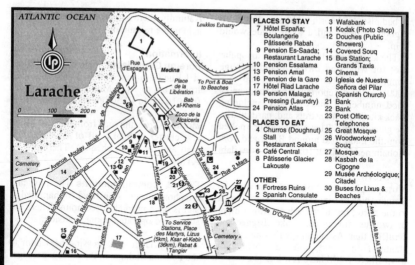

PLACES TO STAY
7 Hôtel España;
  Boulangerie
  Pâtisserie Rabah
9 Pension Es-Saada;
  Restaurant Larache
10 Pension Essalama
13 Pension Amal
16 Pension de la Gare
17 Hôtel Riad Larache
19 Pension Malaga;
  Pressing (Laundry)
24 Pension Atlas

PLACES TO EAT
4 Churros (Doughnut)
  Stall
5 Restaurant Sekala
6 Café Central
8 Pâtisserie Glacier
  Lakouste

OTHER
1 Fortress Ruins
2 Spanish Consulate
3 Wafabank
11 Kodak (Photo Shop)
12 Douches (Public
  Showers)
14 Covered Souq
15 Bus Station;
  Grands Taxis
18 Cinema
20 Iglesia de Nuestra
  Señora del Pilar
  (Spanish Church)
21 Bank
22 Bank
23 Post Office;
  Telephones
25 Great Mosque
26 Woodworkers'
  Souq
27 Mosque
28 Kasbah de la
  Cigogne
29 Musée Archéologique;
  Citadel
30 Buses for Lixus &
  Beaches

The old cobbled **medina**, on the other hand, is alive and well and, although not comparable with the medinas of the imperial cities, it is worth exploring. No-one will hassle you about guide services and there are excellent photographic possibilities.

As you enter by the large, unmistakable Hispano-Moorish arch on Place de la Libération (the Bab al-Khemis), you come immediately into a colonnaded market square, the **Zoco de la Alcaiceria**, built by the Spaniards during their first occupation of Larache in the 17th century. It is the busiest part of the medina, full of vendors displaying their wares.

You can also get into the heart of the medina through a similar arch opposite that of the Zoco and turn past the Pension Atlas down Rue 2 Mars, which will take you through, among other things, the wood-workers' souq.

Beaches

The nearest beaches are north of Larache, across the other side of the Loukkos estuary. To get there, you can take a small boat across the estuary from the port or go by the more circuitous road route (7km) using the No 4 bus, which you can also pick up from the main bus stop opposite the Casbah de la Cicogne.

The buses run approximately hourly throughout the day, but only during the summer months (June to August).

There are a number of simple restaurants at the beach, offering the usual range of seafood.

Places to Stay – bottom end

There's a good choice of budget accommodation to be found in Larache. Inside the medina there are at least three extremely basic places.

About the best of these is the *Pension Atlas* (☎ 912014) at 154 Rue 2 Mars, close to the Zoco, which charges Dr20/40 for moderately clean rooms. Really, you're better off staying in one of the places in the new part of town.

Among the cheapest here is the *Pension Essalama* (☎ 910192) at 50 Ave Mohammed ben Abdallah, which charges Dr25/50. Showers are cold.

A little more expensive, but better value,

is the *Pension Es-Saada* (☎ 913641) at 16 Ave Mohammed ben Abdallah, close to Place de la Libération. Simple but clean rooms, some with balcony, cost Dr30 per person. Try to avoid the rooms on the ground floor as they can be a bit noisy.

If you want to be near the bus station, you could try the *Pension de la Gare* (☎ 913030), on Ave de la Résistance, which has very basic but clean rooms with a sink for the pretty much standard Dr30/60, but no hot water.

The bulk of the other cheapies are on or near Ave Mohammed ben Abdallah. The *Pension Malaga* (☎ 911868) at 4 Rue de Salé is one of the best. It has small but spotless and decent rooms, some with balcony, and charges Dr40/60 for singles/doubles. It also has one double room with bathroom for Dr100.

Perhaps the top of the lot is the *Pension Amal* (☎ 912788), at 10 Ave Abdallah ben Yassine, which has smallish, but very clean, rooms for Dr40/80. The boon is that it also has hot water in the communal showers (Dr6). Outside the high season, you may well be able to negotiate a room for a few dirham less.

Places to Stay – middle
Once *the* place to stay during Spanish colonial times, the two-star *Hôtel España* (☎ 913195; fax 915638), which fronts onto Place de la Libération, is faded, but still exudes an air of grandness. It has 50 clean and well maintained rooms, including some with private bathroom and balcony.

They charge Dr165/195 for singles/doubles with private bathroom and Dr100/150 without.

Places to Stay – top end
The only top-end hotel in town is the three-star *Hôtel Riad Larache* (☎ 912626; fax 912629) on Ave Mohammed ben Abdallah. Apparently once the private home of a French noble family, it is now part of the Kasbah Tours Hotels chain.

Set in its own somewhat neglected grounds, with swimming pool, tennis courts and private parking, the hotel offers spacious, self-contained rooms at Dr260/360, plus taxes. Breakfast is included in the price. As well as a beer garden, there's an internal bar and restaurant that offers fairly pricey meals.

Hammams
There is a *douche* (public shower) next door to the Pension Amal on Ave de la Résistance.

Places to Eat
The cheapest eateries are the little places around Place de la Libération and the Zoco (inside the medina) which serve very edible Spanish-style fare.

One of the best of them is the *Restaurant Sekala*, on your right just before you enter the Zoco through Bab al-Khemis. For around Dr30 you get a big serving of paella-style rice, chicken, fish, salad and a soft drink.

The *Restaurant Larache*, at 18 Ave Mohammed ben Abdallah next door to the Pension Es-Saada, is another good-value place which serves decent seafood dishes for around Dr40. For a splurge, you could try the restaurant at the *Hôtel Riad Larache*, although it's quite pricey.

Still popular since the days of the Spanish are churros, a kind of doughnut traditionally eaten for breakfast. There's a stall selling them in the late afternoon (around 5 pm) three doors down from Bab al-Khemis.

Cafes & Patisseries The *Pâtisserie Glacier Lakouste* is right opposite the Hôtel España on Ave Mohammed ben Abdallah. It has a good selection of cake and ice cream, and is open from 6 am to 9 pm.

If you arrive too late for the restaurants, you can always head for the *Boulangerie Pâtisserie Rabah* at 5 Ibn Batouta just around the corner from the Hôtel España. It keeps later hours (until 11 pm) and has a mouthwatering selection of French and Moroccan sweet and savoury goodies to take away.

Entertainment

There are various cafes around Place de la Libération and along Ave Hassan II and Blvd Mohammed V. One that has remained almost unchanged since the days of the Spanish Protectorate is the *Café Central* on the Place. You can slouch like the locals over the old polished bar and enjoy a beer and some tapas.

Otherwise, the best place for a drink – particularly for women travellers – is the beer garden at the *Hôtel Riad*.

Getting There & Away

Bus Larache is most easily reached by bus. CTM and several private lines run buses through here. Since booking is not always possible, the best bet is to turn up in the morning and get the first service you can.

CTM runs three buses a day to Fès (Dr59) at 7.30 am, 4.30pm and 8.30 pm; six to Tangier (Dr29), the first at 11.30 am and the last at 10.30 pm; and five to Casablanca (Dr77) via Rabat, the first at 8.15 am and the last at midnight. There is also a daily bus to Tiznit in the south (Dr231; 18 hours) at 6 pm.

Other buses also cover these destinations and a few others besides, including Tetouan for Dr20 and Fnideq (for the Ceuta frontier) for Dr20. There is a left-luggage counter at the station.

Taxi Grands taxis run from just outside the bus station on Ave de la Résistance. The standard run is to Ksar el-Kebir, which will be of little interest to most travellers. Anywhere else will probably be to be negotiated as a special *corsa* (ride).

If you get there early enough in the day, you might be able to get to Asilah (Dr10). In general, it's easier to do what the locals do, and use the frequent bus services out of town.

Getting Around

The main local bus stop is just outside the Casbah de la Cicogne. Bus Nos 4 and 5 go to Lixus and, during the summer (June to August), bus No 4 goes on to the beaches north of Larache. Many buses are unnumbered, so it is as well to ask.

For the beach try *ash-shaata'* (Arabic), *la plage* (French) or *la playa* (Spanish). The average ride costs Dr2.50.

AROUND LARACHE
Lixus

Four to 5km north of Larache, on a hillock overlooking the Loukkos estuary and the Tangier-Larache highway, are the Roman ruins of Lixus.

Although not as substantial or as well excavated as those at Volubilis, they are definitely worth a visit. An hour or so is sufficient for most people to explore these ruins. To get there, take bus No 4 or 5 (or simply ask for Lixus, as many of the local red and blue buses have no number at all) and ask to be dropped at the turn-off.

There's no entry fee and the site is not enclosed, so you're at liberty to wander around on your own. Inevitably, some local unemployed youth will offer his services as a guide.

The site was originally occupied by a prehistoric, sun-worshipping people about whom little is known, except that they left a number of stones in the vicinity of the citadel. The positioning of the stones suggests these people were in touch with developments in astronomy and mathematics that led to the building of stone circles in places as far apart as The Gambia and Scotland during the megalithic period.

The Phoenicians set up a colony here, known as Liks, in about 1000 BC – about the same time they settled Cádiz (Gades or Gadera, as it was known to them) in Spain. Trade in Lixus – as well as the later-established colonies of Tingis (Tangier), Tamuda (Tetouan), Russadir (Melilla) and Chella (Rabat) – was principally in gold, ivory and slaves.

Nevertheless, the Atlantic colonies were never very important to the Phoenicians until the destruction of the mother city of Tyre by Nebuchadnezzar in the 6th century BC and the subsequent rise of the city-state of Carthage.

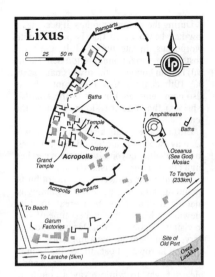

Lixus

0   25   50 m

Ramparts

Baths

Temple

Amphitheatre

Baths

Oratory

Grand
Temple

Acropolis

Oceanus
(Sea God)
Mosiac

To Tangier
(233km)

Acropolis Ramparts

To Beach

Garum
Factories

Site of
Old Port

Oued
Loukkos

To Larache (5km)

As a result of explorations as far south as the mouth of the Niger River by the Carthaginian Hanno, Carthage is said to have been able to monopolise the trade in gold from West Africa and to keep its source a secret.

There is some dispute as to whether or not Hanno or any other Carthaginians really did find gold. Liks was, at any rate, a key trading base and, even when Carthage fell to the Romans in 146 BC, it continued to exert a civilising influence on this area until the establishment in 25 BC of the Roman vassal state of the Berber king Juba II.

Direct Roman rule over this part of the world came in AD 42 under Emperor Claudius, and Lixus now entered its second period of importance. Its main exports during Roman times were salt, olives, *garum* (an aromatic anchovy paste) and wild animals for the various amphitheatres of the empire.

Lixus rapidly declined following the Roman withdrawal north under Diocletian, but was not finally abandoned until some time in the 5th century AD, when the Roman Empire fell apart.

Most of the ruins at Lixus date from the Roman period and include the garum factories alongside the highway. Just beyond these (at the end of a line of green-painted railings), a gravel track leads up the hillside past a number of minor ruins to the public baths and amphitheatre. Restoration has been done on these and they're undoubtedly the most impressive of the ruins here.

Also to be found is a mosaic of Oceanus (the Greek Sea God) – the only such mosaic to be seen at Lixus. Unfortunately, as it's been exposed both to the elements and to local vandalism, very little remains of the Sea God's face.

Carrying on to the top of the hill, you come to the citadel where most of the civic buildings were located, including the main temple and associated sanctuaries, an oratory, more public baths and what remains of the city walls. The view over the estuary of the Loukkos is excellent from here, but most of the antiquities are in an advanced state of decay and there's been some woefully amateurish restoration done on them.

It's a pity Lixus has been allowed to decay to the degree that it has. Were it in Europe, it would no doubt be regarded as an important national monument. On the other hand, there is something exhilarating about finding this place in its overgrown state, largely unprettified by human hands. In winter, your only companions will be the wind and the odd goat. Sole women travellers may find this a bit disconcerting and are advised to avoid coming here alone during the low season.

To get back to Larache, you could walk (one hour), try to hitch or wait for one of the infrequent buses. If you have your own transport, you may want to explore the surrounding area for the excellent **birdlife**.

One of the best spots is the marshes surrounding the Oued Loukkos dam (follow the sign just after the bridge over the Loukkos estuary, around 2km north of Larache on the main road south). The area attracts a very good selection of ducks and waders. Keep an eye out also for the spoonbills, glossy ibis and little bustards.

Ksar el-Kebir

In Almoravid and Almohad times, the 'Great Castle', 36km south-east of Larache on the main road to Rabat, was a comparatively important base. It was near here, too, that the Battle of the Three Kings was fought in 1578, costing the lives of the king of Portugal and two Moroccan sultans.

Today, nothing much remains as a reminder of its past, but the town does boast one of the largest weekly souqs of the region every Sunday. If you're in the area, it's definitely worth a visit – just head for the bus station.

If you want to stay here, one of the most agreeable places is *Hôtel Ksar al-Yamama* (☎ 907960) at 8 Ave Hassan II. Spotless and very comfortable singles/doubles without shower cost Dr89/116 and with shower Dr116/133. The hotel has a lovely terrace overlooking the town.

Moulay Bousselham

West of Ksar el-Kebir, and around 40km due south of Larache, is the little fishing village of Moulay Bousselham.

During the summer months, it becomes a low-key beach resort that is popular with Moroccans. In late June or July, the town hosts an important annual *moussem* (festival) held in honour of the town's namesake, the 10th century Egyptian saint who is also commemorated in one of the *koubbas* (shrines) that line the slope down to the sea.

Little more that a one-street town, Moulay Bousselham offers little of interest to the traveller, beyond its situation perched high above a large coastal lagoon.

In winter this attracts thousands of birds, including wildfowl, waders and flamingos, making it one of the best areas for bird viewing in Morocco. The best time of year to visit the lagoon is from December to January, when there are most migrants.

Trips in rowing boats to see the flamingos in the lagoon are easily arranged and a pleasant way to while away a couple of hours in the morning or afternoon.

If you're keen to see rarer species, however, you should head straight for the Café Milano on the main street and ask for Has-

---

The Battle of Three Kings

Dynasties wouldn't be true to their nature without dynastic quarrels, but one that began in 1574 in Morocco was destined for quite a Shakespearian end.

When Mohammed al-Mutawwakil took the reins of Saadian power in 1574, on the death of his father, he contravened the family rule that the eldest *male* in the family should succeed, not the eldest *son*. Al-Mutawwakil's uncle, Abdel Malik, then in Algiers and an ally of the Ottoman Turks, decided to rectify the situation and, after two victories with the help of Turkish troops in 1576, he succeeded in evicting his nephew.

Al-Mutawwakil fled and asked Philip II of Spain to help him regain power. Philip declined in what turned out to be a very astute move, and sent Al-Mutawwakil to King Dom Sebastian of Portugal.

Promised a virtual protectorate over Morocco in exchange for his help, Dom Sebastian could not resist. Abdel Malik went to considerable lengths to dissuade Dom Sebastian, offering Portugal a Moroccan port of its choice, but to no avail.

When, in 1578, the Portuguese army of some 20,000 landed in northern Morocco, Abdel Malik gathered a force of 50,000 to meet it. On 4 August, caught in marshy territory near Ksar el-Kebir, Dom Sebastian was routed. He and Al-Mutawwakil drowned trying to flee across the Oued Makhazin (hence the Arab name of the battle) and Abdel Malik died of an illness that had long plagued him, although some say it was a heart attack.

Ahmed al-Mansour succeeded in Morocco, but in Portugal there was no heir. Philip II of Spain became the biggest winner of all, swallowing Portugal into his empire. ■

san Dalil. You can also contact him at home on ☎ 432603.

Hassan has been guiding since childhood and can generally locate the species you're interested in seeing. He speaks French and adequate English, as well as a little German and Spanish, and charges Dr200/300 for a half/whole day (Dr100/200 if you're on your own).

A rowing boat will cost another Dr100 and a motor boat around Dr50 per hour. Boats generally accommodate a maximum of five people and trips are arranged in two sessions: from around dawn until noon and from 3 pm to dusk. The best time for bird activity in the lagoon is the morning.

Birds commonly seen in the lagoon include shelduck, teal, shovelers and godwits. More unusual are the numerous gulls (including Audouin's gull), terns and out at sea, gannets. The lagoon is also considered one of the best places in Morocco to see the African marsh owl.

The greatest drawcard, and attracting birders from around the world was the slender-billed curlew. Unfortunately, and possibly as a result of the severe drought in 1995, the last sighting was on the 25th March 1995 and the species is now considered extinct in Morocco.

The hard-core bird spotter may also want to explore the attractive lake of Merdja Khaloufa, about 8km east of Moulay Bousselham, which offers good views of a variety of wintering wildfowl. You may want to consult the detailed log book available at the Café Milano which is updated by birders from all over the world.

Places to Stay & Eat About 500m before the entrance to the town, you'll find the Camping on the left. It's not that well maintained and in summer the mosquitoes are a problem.

It charges Dr12 per person, Dr7/20 per car/caravan and Dr15 for electricity.

The Hostal Flora (☎ 912250) is the best lower-range deal in town, although it doesn't rent singles. Clean, quite attractive doubles cost Dr100.

The Hôtel Le Lagon (☎ 432603), close to the entrance to the town, charges Dr150/200 for doubles/triples with private shower (no singles). An extra bed costs Dr60. The rooms are fairly run-down, but they have good terraces overlooking the lagoon and it's the only place in town where you can get a drink (Dr13/25 for a beer/aperitif). The hotel also has a pool.

The most comfortable place in town is the Hôtel Villanora (☎ 432071) on the seafront at the far end of town. It's run like a bed-and-breakfast by a British brother and sister. Rooms are homely and comfortable and meals are eaten en famille. Singles/doubles with shared bathroom start from Dr200/400, including breakfast. There are just five rooms, so it's a good idea to make a reservation.

If you plan to hang around here for a few days, there are plenty of apartments to be rented, particularly outside the high season. Two very good ones can be arranged through Said Ezouaki at the Restaurant Ocean (see below) or by phoning him on ☎ 432412.

The apartments are newly furnished, modern and well equipped. The first apartment (for a maximum of four) costs Dr150 per day and the second (for up to eight people) costs Dr250. Both are excellent value.

The Restaurant Ocean on the main street, is the best place in town for a generous portion of good value fare. Fresh and tasty fish dishes cost Dr35 and more traditional Moroccan dishes, such as tajine and couscous, are also available for the same price. It's also a good place for breakfast where toast/omelette with coffee cost Dr10/13.

Getting There & Away There are regular buses and grands taxis to Moulay Bousselham from the little town of Souk el-Arba du Rharb, around 45km to the south-west. If you have your own vehicle, take the S216 from Souk el-Arba and, after about 35km, turn left on to the 2301.

If you're coming from the north, the town is well signposted from Larache.

KENITRA

About 40km north of Rabat lies the French-built town of Kenitra (population about 100,000). The country's sixth largest port, it was known until 1958 as Port Lyautey.

There is nothing in the town of particular interest, but the nearby Plage Mehdiya and nature reserve of Lac de Sidi Bourhaba are worth a stop, for those with time.

Information

The post office and a couple of banks, including the BMCE, are at the junction of Blvd Mohammed V and Ave Hassan II.

Places to Stay

There are a couple of basic hotels around. The *Hôtel Marignan* (☎ 363424) near the train station is the best value. It has simple but clean and decent rooms without shower for Dr40/60 and with shower (cold) for Dr50/70.

A bit more expensive is the *Hôtel du Commerce* (☎ 371503) at 12 Rue Amira Aïcha, near the town hall. It charges Dr70/100 for clean, reasonably furnished rooms, including some with balconies. There is also hot water.

In the middle range, the best value by far is the excellent *Hôtel Ambassy* (☎ 379978) at 20 Ave Hassan II. It charges Dr156/211 for spotless and comfortable singles/doubles with shower and a miniature kitchen. A good breakfast is also included in the price; ask to have it in the peaceful garden.

Back near the town hall is the fancier *Hôtel Mamora* (☎ 371775; fax 371446) with rooms for Dr276/364. Top of the tree is the four-star *Hôtel Safir* (☎ 312211/311937), near the town hall on Place Administrative, which charges Dr407/524. The swimming pool is open to hotel guests only.

An alternative is the three-star *Hôtel Atlantique* (☎ 388116) on Mehdiya beach which has doubles only for Dr190/229 with/without shower.

Places to Eat

You'll find a few simple eateries and cafes in the town centre, especially along Ave

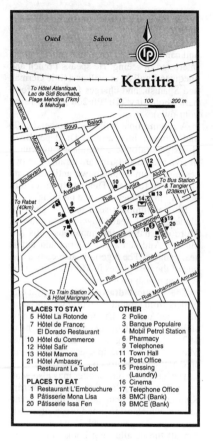

PLACES TO STAY
5 Hôtel La Rotonde
7 Hôtel de France;
   El Dorado Restaurant
10 Hôtel du Commerce
12 Hôtel Safir
13 Hôtel Mamora
21 Hôtel Ambassy;
   Restaurant Le Turbot

PLACES TO EAT
1 Restaurant L'Embouchure
8 Pâtisserie Mona Lisa
20 Pâtisserie Issa Fen

OTHER
2 Police
3 Banque Populaire
4 Mobil Petrol Station
6 Pharmacy
9 Telephones
11 Town Hall
14 Post Office
15 Pressing
   (Laundry)
16 Cinema
17 Telephone Office
18 BMCI (Bank)
19 BMCE (Bank)

Mohammed Diouri. The *Restaurant L'Embouchure*, on the corner of Ave Mohammed Diouri and Rue Souq Baladi, has respectable pizza imitations for around Dr45, plus ice cream for dessert.

For something a bit more upmarket, you could try the restaurant *Le Turbot* at the Hôtel Ambassy. It specialises in fish dishes (Dr70 to Dr90) and has a good fixed menu for Dr85. It's a reasonable choice for vegetarians; beer is also available for Dr14. The restaurant is open from noon to 3 pm and from 6 to 11 pm.

For a splurge, try the restaurant at the Hôtel Safir which has a set menu for Dr154.

If you're pining for a western breakfast, head for the *El Dorado* at 64 Ave Mohammed Diouri, close to the Hôtel de France.

It's a cheap but clean place and serves toast, omelettes and other egg dishes. It also does decent hamburgers which are popular with the locals.

Patisseries The *Pâtisserie Mona Lisa* at 80 Ave Mohammed Diouri is the best patisserie in town. It's a cool (air-conditioned in summer), calm and relaxed place and is great for breakfast. It's open every day from 6 am to 8.30 pm.

The *Pâtisserie Issa Fen*, opposite the Hôtel Ambassy, has a reasonable selection of French and Moroccan-style goodies to take away.

Entertainment
The bar and nightclub at the *Hôtel Safir* are about the best bet for a drink or night out. The nightclub is open from 11 pm to 3 am and charges Dr50/30 for entry/drinks.

Getting There & Away
There are regular trains and buses to Rabat, 40km to the south. Going by train is probably the easiest bet.

The one way, 2nd class fare costs Dr13. There are also trains to Asilah (Dr60) and to Tangier (Dr76).

AROUND KENITRA
Mehdiya
Apart from the beach (Plage Mehdiya), which is popular with locals – though hardly Morocco's best – there are also the ruins of a **kasbah** built by Moulay Ismail. You pass them on the way in from Kenitra. For many, the best reason for coming here is to visit the excellent bird sanctuary at the Lac de Sidi Bourhaba.

Places to Stay & Eat If you want to stay the night, the only hotel in town is the *Hôtel Atlantique* (☎ 388116), where prices seem to vary according to the season and how wealthy you look.

Even after hard bargaining, you're probably looking at around Dr190/229 for dark, lugubrious rooms (doubles only) with/without a basic shower. The best reason for staying here is to hear the local *chanteuses* (singers) who perform exuberantly in the local bar until the wee hours of the morning.

If you plan to hang around a few days and want to hire a basic apartment (Dr150 per day), you should contact Driss at the Restaurant Le Dauphin (see below).

A great place for a coffee or a full lunch is the *Café Restaurant Belle Vue* next to the steps leading up to the ruins of the kasbah. There is a very pleasant, shady terrace overlooking the port. Salads cost from Dr12 and main courses, including fish, from Dr65 to Dr85.

Closer to the beach, and a cheaper option, is the simpler *Restaurant Le Dauphin* run by the indefatigable Driss, who often does the cooking, too. Main courses cost around Dr35 and there are good fruit juices for Dr5.

Getting There & Away Local bus No 15 and the orange grands taxis leave fairly regularly from Ave Mohammed Diouri to make the 7km run to Mehdiya from Kenitra. The fare should be a couple of dirhams.

Lac de Sidi Bourhaba
Situated a couple of kilometres inland from Mehdiya beach is the large, freshwater lake of Sidi Bourhaba. It's a peaceful place and a very pretty spot for a picnic, but for those into birds it provides some of the best viewing in the country.

Covering an area of more than 200 hectares, the lakes serves as a refuelling stop for many thousands of birds migrating between Europe and sub-Saharan Africa. Many species choose to winter or nest here – among them a number of rare or endangered species. This has earned the lake international recognition and it's now one of Morocco's very few protected areas.

More than 200 species of birds have been seen here – almost half of Morocco's total complement. Considered the *bijou* (jewel) of the reserve is the marbled duck and this is one of the last places on earth where it can still be seen in large numbers. You can recognise it by the dark patch around its eyes.

Other birds to look out for include the beautiful marsh owl (seen most often at dusk), the crested coot and the black-shouldered kite.

The information centre (☎ 747209) on the east side of the reserve reopened in March 1996 and has good educational exhibits, videos, and interactive displays for children. At the weekend, there are interesting guided tours of the sanctuary every hour from noon to 4 pm, although there is a limit of 10 people to each tour.

If you want to make your own way around, there are three marked trails which take from 30 minutes (specially designed for people in wheelchairs or other mobility difficulties) to 90 minutes.

A hide has been set up overlooking the lake and provides great viewing of the birds. Around a dozen telescopes and pairs of binoculars can be hired at the centre. If the hide is too crowded, you may be allowed onto the centre's roof terrace, which also has good views.

The centre is open Monday to Friday from 10 am to noon and from 2.30 to 4 pm, and on weekends from 10 am to 4 pm. You are free to visit the lake every day from dawn to dusk. The best time to visit the sanctuary is between the months of October and March.

To get there with your own transport, follow the signs from Mehdiya. Otherwise take a grand taxi from Kenitra. It may be possible to hitch back to Kenitra or on to Rabat.

Rabat

The modern capital of Morocco has had something of a roller coaster history, climb-ing at one point to imperial capital only to descend later to the level of a backwater village, before finding favour again. The great walls enclose a largely modern city, but there remain several quarters to remind you of Rabat's rich past, including Salé – home to the corsairs – across the river Bou Regreg.

There is enough to keep the sightseer occupied for a few days and the atmosphere is relaxed enough to encourage some to stay a little longer. In contrast to the great tourist attractions of the interior, such as Fès and Marrakesh, there is virtually no sign of hustle and hassle here, not even in the souqs.

The new city is comparatively quiet and, although its people appear as cosmopolitan as their counterparts down the coast in Casablanca, Rabat lacks the gritty, big-city edge of its economic big brother.

History

Apart from two brief spells as imperial capital, Rabat has been the capital of Morocco only since the days of the French protectorate. However, as far back as the 8th century BC, indigenous people had a settlement in the area of the necropolis of Chellah. They were followed by the Phoenicians and the Romans, who successively patrolled the coast and set up outposts of the empire.

The Roman settlement, known as Sala Colonia, was built along the river of the same name (today's Bou Regreg, which has since altered its course). Like Volubilis, it lasted long beyond the fall of the Roman Empire and eventually became the seat of an independent Berber kingdom.

The settlement's fate is obscure enough to have given rise to varying stories about what happened next. It appears the people of Sala Colonia embraced Islam on the arrival of the Arabs in the late 7th century, but with unorthodox modifications.

The first Moroccan dynasties, the Idrissids and Almoravids, largely neglected Sala Colonia and, as its river port silted up, the town declined.

By the 10th century, the new town of

Salé had sprung up on the north bank of the river. Its inhabitants, of the Zenata tribe (although some sources attribute the rise of the new town to the people of the old), built a *ribat* (fortress-monastery) on the present site of Rabat's kasbah, as a base for fighting a rival and heretic tribe south of the river.

Whether Sala Colonia had already been emptied of its population by then, or whether the process was accelerated by the fighting, is unclear.

Things changed with the arrival of the Almohads in the 12th century. They put an end to the fighting and built the kasbah on the site of the ribat. Their intention was to make it the jumping-off point for campaigns against the Christian Reconquista in Spain.

It was under Yacoub al-Mansour ('the Victorious') that Rabat enjoyed a brief peak of glory. After successful campaigns in Spain, Ribat al-Fatah ('Victory Fortress') was to become a great capital. Al-Mansour had extensive walls built, added the Oudaia gate to the kasbah and began work on what was intended to be the greatest mosque in all of the Muslim west, if not in all Islam.

His death, in 1199, brought an end to these grandiose schemes. The great Hassan Mosque, overlooking the bridge across the Oued Bou Regreg, was never completed – all that remain today are the impressive, squat (and incomplete) minaret (the Tour Hassan) and some columns that have since been re-erected on the site. The city lost all significance quickly thereafter.

Rabat's fortunes began to change in the 17th century with the arrival of Muslim refugees from Christian Spain. At the same time, the population of the sister cities of Rabat and Salé received a colourful injection of Christian renegades, Moorish pirates, freebooters and adventurers of many nationalities.

The two cities flourished as those whom English chroniclers called the Sallee Rovers (or corsairs) set about intercepting merchant ships and men-of-war, especially those returning to Spain and Portugal from the Americas. They brought such a rich booty in gold, Christian slave labour and other goods that the cities briefly formed the independent Republic of Bou Regreg, in the first half of the 17th century.

Although the first Alawite sultans curtailed their activities, no sultan ever really exercised control over the corsairs, who continued plundering European shipping until well into the 19th century, by which time Europe's wishes were becoming writ in Morocco.

Sultan Mohammed ben Abdallah briefly made Rabat his capital at the end of the 18th century, but with little appreciable effect on its destiny.

France decided to shift the capital of its protectorate, established in 1912, from Fès to Rabat. The new capital was on the coast and therefore easily supplied and defended. It was also far from the hornet's nest of political intrigue and potential unrest of Fès or Marrakesh – long the traditional choices for capital. Since independence (in 1956), it has remained the seat of government and home to the king.

Orientation

Rabat is best approached by rail, since the central train station lies on the city's main thoroughfare – the wide, tree-lined Ave Mohammed V.

Arrival by bus is inconvenient, as the bus station lies a good 4 to 5km outside the centre and you will need to take a local bus (No 30) or taxi into the centre – not always an easy task because of the competition.

If you do arrive by bus from northern destinations, it is easier to get off at Salé and take a local bus or grand taxi into central Rabat. That way you'll be looking for a hotel before the bus you were on has even made it to Rabat's main bus terminal.

All the main administrative buildings and many of the hotels lie on, or just off, Ave Mohammed V, although there are others further afield. Most of the embassies are scattered around the streets to the east, between Ave Mohammed V and Place Abraham Lincoln.

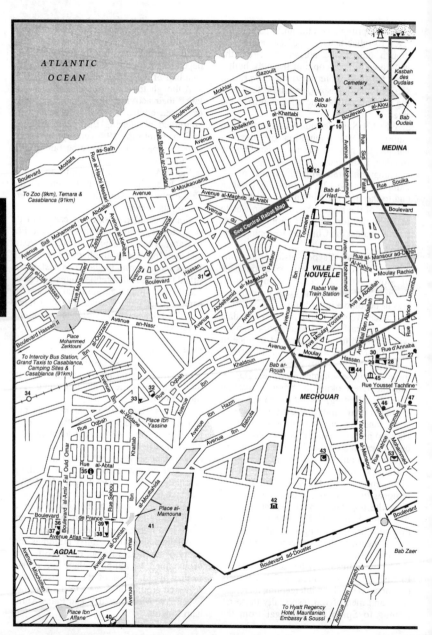

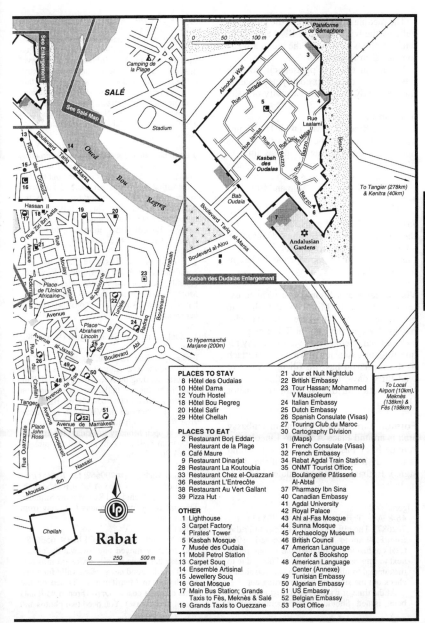

PLACES TO STAY
8 Hôtel des Oudaias
10 Hôtel Darna
12 Youth Hostel
18 Hôtel Bou Regreg
20 Hôtel Safir
29 Hôtel Chellah

PLACES TO EAT
2 Restaurant Borj Eddar;
  Restaurant de la Plage
6 Café Maure
9 Restaurant Dinarjat
28 Restaurant La Koutoubia
33 Restaurant Chez el-Ouazzani
36 Restaurant L'Entrecôte
38 Restaurant Au Vert Gallant
39 Pizza Hut

OTHER
1 Lighthouse
3 Carpet Factory
4 Pirates' Tower
5 Kasbah Mosque
7 Musée des Oudaia
11 Mobil Petrol Station
13 Carpet Souq
14 Ensemble Artisinal
15 Jewellery Souq
16 Great Mosque
17 Main Bus Station; Grands
   Taxis to Fès, Meknès & Salé
19 Grands Taxis to Ouezzane

21 Jour et Nuit Nightclub
22 British Embassy
23 Tour Hassan; Mohammed
   V Mausoleum
24 Italian Embassy
25 Dutch Embassy
26 Spanish Consulate (Visas)
27 Touring Club du Maroc
30 Cartography Division
   (Maps)
31 French Consulate (Visas)
32 French Embassy
34 Rabat Agdal Train Station
35 ONMT Tourist Office;
   Boulangerie Pâtisserie
   Al-Abtal
37 Pharmacy Ibn Sina
40 Canadian Embassy
41 Agdal University
42 Royal Palace
43 Ahl al-Fas Mosque
44 Sunna Mosque
45 Archaeology Museum
46 British Council
47 American Language
   Center & Bookshop
48 American Language
   Center (Annexe)
49 Tunisian Embassy
50 Algerian Embassy
51 US Embassy
52 Belgian Embassy
53 Post Office

The medina is divided from the ville nouvelle by the wide and busy Blvd Hassan II, which follows the line of the medina walls to Oued Bou Regreg.

Rabat is an easy and pleasant city to walk around, and you will probably need public transport only to visit its twin city of Salé.

Information

Tourist Offices ONMT (☎ 681531), just off Rue al-Abtal in the west of the city, is not conveniently located and has little to offer anyway beyond the usual brochures and a small town map. It's open Monday to Friday from 8.30 to 11.30 am and from 3 to 6.30 pm.

There is a tourist office at 22 Ave al-Jazaïr, but it's an administrative centre for the ministry only. The Syndicat d'Initiative, south of the city centre on Rue Patrice Lumumba, is supposed to reopen at the beginning of 1998.

Visa Extensions Should you want to extend your visa in Morocco, the place to go is the Sûreté Nationale, off Ave Mohammed V (see the Central Rabat map).

You need a letter from your embassy requesting the extension and a photo to attach to the form you have to fill in. Expect to wait three days. For more on this, see the Visas Section in the Facts for the Visitor chapter.

Foreign Embassies The main embassy area is around Place Abraham Lincoln and Ave de Fas ('Fas' is the same as 'Fès' and is the way it appears on some of the street signs). Embassies and consulates in Rabat include:

Algeria
46-8 Ave Tariq ibn Zayid (☎ 765474; fax 762687). The office is open Monday to Friday from 8.30 am to 3 pm, but since early 1994 total confusion has reigned and it may prove next to impossible to get a visa. This is due to the internal troubles in Algeria and you should check out the situation before setting out.

At the time of writing, no tourist visas were being issued. Should normal operations ever resume, you will need four photos and a photocopy of your passport details to apply for a visa. You will also have to provide documentation for your car if you intend to drive. If issued, the visa will be valid for a month's travel in Algeria, and is renewable inside the country. Costs at the time of writing were as uncertain as everything else. In late 1993, Australians paid nothing, US citizens about Dr150 and Britons about Dr350. Note that Britons must apply in person in Rabat, and not at the Oujda consulate.

All applications are sent to Algiers. Visas used to take an average of 10 days to process, but often the wait turned into one of weeks or even months. All you can do is find out the latest position when you get there. Some travellers have found it easier to pick up the Algerian visa before leaving their home country and, at the time of writing, the Algerian embassy in London was issuing visas to tourists flying between the two countries.

Australia
The Australian embassy in Paris has full consular responsibility for Morocco. However, consular services to Australian citizens in Morocco are provided by the Canadian embassy (under Australia's consular sharing agreement).

Canada
13 Zankat Jaafar as-Sadiq, Agdal (☎ 672880)

France
Embassy: 3 Rue Sahnoun, Agdal (☎ 777822) Consulate (visas): Although there is a large consular building on Ave Allal ben Abdallah, you will be directed to the Service de Visas on Rue Ibn al-Khattib (☎ 702404), off Blvd Hassan II. The Service de Visas can also issue visas for Togo, Djibouti and Burkina Faso. The office is open Monday to Friday, for applications from 8.30 to 11.30 am and for pick-up from 1.30 to 3 pm.

Germany
7 Zankat Madnine (☎ 709662; fax 706851), on the intersection of Rue Allal ben Abdallah, Rue Moulay Rachid and Rue Moulay Slimane. The embassy is open Monday to Friday from 9 am to noon.

Mauritania
Villa No 266, Souissi II, OLM (☎ 656678). This recently moved and awkwardly placed embassy has some equally awkward information. First the good news. Visas valid for a one month stay in Mauritania are issued on the same day at a cost of Dr70 (French nationals do not need a visa). You need two photos and

a letter of recommendation from your embassy; some embassies charge for this service.

Now the bad news. No visa will be issued for overland travel, and to get any visa at all you must present a *return* air ticket with Air Mauritanie, which has an office in Casablanca. To get there, take a petit taxi or bus No 1, 2, 4 or 8 from the main city bus terminal. Ask the driver to let you off at Ave John Kennedy. The embassy is in a small street parallel to the avenue (to your right as you head out of the city centre). The nearest landmark on the avenue itself is the Pharmacie al-Andalous, on the left – if you pass a Shell and then a Mobil service station (also on the left), you've gone too far.

The embassy is open from 8.30 am to 3 pm Monday to Thursday and until noon on Friday.

New Zealand
New Zealand's affairs in Morocco are handled by the embassy in Madrid, Spain.

Netherlands
40 Rue de Tunis (☎ 733512; fax 733333). Opening hours are from Monday to Friday from 8 am to 3 pm.

Spain
Embassy: 3-5 Zankat Madnine (☎ 768989) Consulate: 57 Rue du Chellah (☎ 704147/8; fax 704694). Nationals of various countries require visas to enter Spain (this means Ceuta and Melilla, too), including Australians, South Africans, Israelis and Malaysians.

From 1995, the Schengen agreement took effect. The new visa covers all member countries of the EU (except the UK, Ireland and Denmark) and replaces those previously issued by individual countries. In addition to supplying three photos, you may also be asked for photocopies of passport details, credit cards and/or bank statements.

The Spaniards prefer you to apply for a visa in your country of residence – an awkward requirement, so be prepared for some diplomatic haggling. If they go along with your request, it takes at least 24 hours to issue. Apply between 9 am and noon and pick up the following day (1 to 2 pm). The consulate is open Monday to Friday.

Tunisia
6 Ave de Fès (☎ 730636/7; fax 727866). EU, US and Japanese citizens are among those who do not require a visa for Tunisia. Australians are among those who do (although for a one-month stay, you technically shouldn't).

A visa costs Dr50, is valid for one to three months (seemingly depending on your luck) and could take as long as a week to issue. You need three photos and three photocopies of your passport. The office is open Monday to Friday from 9 am to 2 pm.

UK
17 Blvd de la Tour Hassan (☎ 720905; fax 720906). The embassy is open Monday to Friday from 8.30 am to 12.30 pm and 2 to 5 pm.

USA
2 Ave de Marrakesh (☎ 762265; fax 765661). The embassy is open Monday to Friday from 8.30 am to 12.30 pm and 2.30 to 6.30 pm.

Money The banks are concentrated along Ave Mohammed V. The BMCE is open from 8 am to 8 pm Monday to Friday; on weekends it's open from 10 am to 2 pm and 4 to 8 pm.

There are plenty of banks dotted around the ville nouvelle; some are marked on the map.

Post & Communications The post office, on the corner of Rue Soekarno and Ave Mohammed V, is open from 8.30 am to 6.30 pm Monday to Friday.

The phone office across the road is open 24 hours a day, seven days a week. Poste restante is not in the main post office building, but in the telephone office across the road. Enter via the door marked 'Permanence Télégraphique et Téléphonique'.

To collect mail you need to show your passport as proof of identity and there's a small charge for each letter collected. Parcel post ('Colis postaux') and EMS ('Poste Rapide') are in a separate office, to the right of the main entrance.

Travel Agencies At 28 Ave Allal ben Abdallah, Africa Voyages (☎ 709646) is an agent for several airlines, including British Airways, Air France, Swiss Air and Lufthansa. It also handles ferry reservations. Opening hours are from 8.30 am to noon and from 2.30 to 7 pm (on Saturday to noon only).

Carlson Wagonlits (☎ 709625) is nearby at on Ave Moulay Abdallah.

Bookshops & Newsstands The English Bookshop (☎ 706593) is at 7 Zankat Alyamama and is run by Mohammed Belhaj.

He's a friendly person and stocks a good selection of mainly second-hand English and American novels, some guides, language books, dictionaries, etc. Books taken back in under two weeks will entitle you to another for half the price.

Mohammed will also buy books from you (though prices paid will depend on how easy they are to resell). He generally pays around Dr50 for a 'best seller' and Dr30 for a lesser known author.

The American Bookstore, part of the American Language Center (☎ 767103; fax 766255) at 4 Rue Tanger, has a smaller collection of new books, including English novels, guidebooks, travel books and English-Arabic dictionaries.

It also has a modest, but very interesting, stand on Morocco, which includes (largely American) writing on social, anthropological, historical and religious issues. There's also some feminist writing by Moroccan authors.

The shop is the best source of books of this kind in Morocco, and probably in Europe too. It's open Monday to Friday from 9.30 am to 12.30 pm and from 2.30 to 6.30 pm.

Rabat has the best bookshops in Morocco for Francophone readers. There are several along Ave Mohammed V and Ave Allal ben Abdallah. The best in town is the Librairie Libre Service (☎ 724495), at 46 Ave Allal ben Abdallah. Its main market is students, but it also stocks a reasonable selection of guidebooks on Morocco, some coffee-table books and a few more academic works. They also have a large selection of French novels.

All of the French press is available at newsstands scattered around the ville nouvelle. For other foreign press, there is a few places – the shop inside the Rabat Ville train station is as good as any.

Maps The Cartography Division of the Conservation & Topography Department (☎ 705311; fax 705885) is at 31 Ave Moulay Hassan. It stocks a range of maps of Morocco, including topographical maps (useful for hiking) and city and town plans. Unfor-

tunately, due to increased state security, it's no longer as easy to obtain them as it once was.

If it's just one or two maps you want, you might be in luck, but you'll still have to go through the official procedure. This involves making a formal demand (in French) for the maps you want, explaining who you are and why you want them.

A panel will then meet the following Friday and you will be notified of their decision – positive or, as is more often the case, negative – on the Monday. Maps cost Dr40 a sheet. The office is open on weekdays from 8.30 to 11 am and 2.30 to 5.30 pm.

Film & Photography There are plenty of places along Ave Mohammed V that sell photographic supplies and develop film.

One that's recommended is the Photolab Photomagic, on the corner with Rue Ghazzah.

Cultural Centres Apart from those listed below as language schools, the Institut Français (☎ 701138) has a branch at 2 Zankat al-Yanboua. They put on films, theatrical performances and lectures, and have a library open Tuesday to Saturday from 10 am to noon and 2.30 to 7 pm.

The German Goethe Institut (☎ 706544) is at 10 Rue Djebli.

Spain maintains a Centro Cultural Español (☎ 708738) by its embassy, at 5 Zankat Madnine. The Istituto Italiano di Cultura (☎ 720852) is at 2 Zankat al-Aghouat, near Place de l'Union Africaine, south-east of the city centre. Its library is open Monday, Wednesday and Friday from 9 am to noon.

Language Schools The British Council (☎ 760836) is at 34 Rue Tanger (or Zankat Tanja). As well as a library, which holds a stock of some 14,000 books and periodicals, they have a programme of feature films and occasional lectures. The library is open from 9.30 am to 7 pm Tuesday to Friday and 9.30 am to 1.45 pm on Saturday. It is closed on Monday.

You could try to wangle some part-time work as an English teacher here, but you need to be British by nationality and qualified. The chances of full-time work are low, as teachers are usually recruited in London.

Another possible source of work as an English teacher is the American Language Center (☎ 767103; fax 766255), at 4 Rue Tanger. Contact the director Gary Butzbach or, if in town, pick up an application form; they prefer people with experience. Teachers here get the opportunity to learn Arabic at free language classes.

You could also try your luck at the International Language Centre (☎ 709718) at 2 Rue Tihama.

Laundry The Gentleman Pressing is at 2 Rue Jeddah in the ville nouvelle, and is open from 8.30 am to 12.30 pm and from 2.30 to 7.30 pm.

Medical Services & Emergencies As throughout Morocco, the emergency police phone number is ☎ 19. For the fire brigade or ambulance call ☎ 15. To keep up to date on where there are late-night chemists, pick up one of the local French-language papers, such as *Le Riverain*. They usually have a listings page with the day's rostered 'pharmacies de garde' on it.

Medina
The walled medina is far less interesting than those in Fès, Meknès and Marrakesh, and dates only from the 17th century. It's still worth a stroll, and there is no hustling to worry about.

About the most interesting medina street is Rue Souika. Starting out from the corner of Rue Sidi Fatah and heading east, you will find mainly food, spice and general stores until you reach the area around the Great Mosque.

From here to the Rue des Consuls, you are in the Souq as-Sebbat, where jewellery is the main item for sale.

If you continue past the Rue des Consuls (so called because foreign diplomats lived here until 1912), you end up in a flea market

before emerging at the river. Most of the stuff is junk, but you never know what a rummage might turn up.

If you head north along the Rue des Consuls on the way to the kasbah, you will find yourself surrounded on all sides by carpet and rug shops, along with the occasional leatherwork, *babouche* (leather slipper) or copperwork place. The street ends in a fairly broad, open area that leads up the hill to the kasbah. In the days of the Sallee Rovers, this was the site of the slave auctions.

Kasbah des Oudaias
The Kasbah des Oudaias, built on the bluff overlooking the estuary and the Atlantic Ocean, dominates the surrounding area and can be seen from some distance. It is unfortunate that a much-used city circular road runs right past the entrance. You can only

---

The Evil Eye

The power of the evil eye is a potent force in the minds of many Moroccans. A common symbolic means of warding it off is to the show the open palm of the hand, fingers pointing upwards. This 'hand of Fatima' (the prophet's daughter) frequently can be spotted painted on doors, as jewellery, or engraved on some object.

There are more powerful methods of dealing with the evil eye, and you may come across one of them in the herb and spice markets – the chameleon (*al-boua*). This highly adaptable little creature is valued in the home as it eats flies and mosquitoes.

However, if Moroccans feel they've been struck by misfortune from a spiritual source beyond their control, one option is to throw the chameleon into a small, wood-fired oven and walk around it three times. If the chameleon explodes, then the evil has been averted, but if it just melts down to goo, then they're still in trouble. Not that either outcome is any consolation to the hapless chameleon. ■

guess at the long-term damage done to the buildings by the passing traffic.

The main entry point is the enormous Almohad gate of **Bab Oudaia**, built in 1195. This is one of the few places in Rabat where you will encounter 'guides'. It's completely unnecessary to take one. Once through the gate, there's only one main street, Rue Jamaa, so you can't get lost.

Most of the houses here were built by Muslim refugees from Spain. There are great views over the estuary and across to Salé from what is known as the *'plateforme du sémaphore'*, at the end of Rue Jamaa. On your left as you head towards the viewpoint is the oldest **mosque** in Rabat, built in the 12th century and restored in the 18th.

From just inside Bab Oudaia you can turn to your right (south) and walk down to a passage running more or less parallel to Rue Jamaa. Turn into this and on your right is a 17th century palace built by Moulay Ismail. It now serves as part of the **Musée des Oudaia** (Museum of Moroccan Arts). To get tickets, however, you have to proceed a little further south into the Andalusian Gardens (actually laid out by the French during the colonial period).

Built into the walls of the kasbah are two small galleries that form part of the museum. The northernmost of these contains a small display of traditional musical instruments and the ticket desk for the whole museum, while the second gallery houses a display of traditional costumes.

Back up in Moulay Ismail's palace (which later became a medersa), two of the four galleries are devoted to Fès ceramics and one to jewellery. The last has been decked out as a traditional, high-class Moroccan dining and reception room. Tickets cost Dr10, and the rooms are open from 9 am to noon and 3 to 5 pm (6 pm in summer). The gardens stay open later.

Tour Hassan

Rabat's most famous landmark is the Tour Hassan, which overlooks the bridge across the Oued Bou Regreg to Salé. Construction of this enormous minaret – intended to be the largest and highest in the Muslim world – was begun by the Almohad sultan Yacoub al-Mansour in 1195, but abandoned on his death some four years later.

Meant to reach a height of more than 60m, it only made it to 44m. The tower still stands, but little remains of the adjacent mosque, which was all but destroyed by an earthquake in 1755. Only the re-erected, shattered pillars testify to the grand plans of al-Mansour.

On the same site is the **Mausoleum of Mohammed V**, the present king's father. Built in the traditional Moroccan style and richly decorated, the tomb of the king is located below ground in an open chamber. Above, visitors enter a gallery from which they can see the tomb below. Entry is free, but you must be dressed in a respectful manner.

FRANCES LINZEE GORDON

On guard outside the Mausoleum of Mohammed V, Rabat.

FRANCES LINZEE GORDON

A worshipper wanders between the columns of the
unfinished and ruined Hassan mosque. Begun in 1195, the mosque,
dominated by the 44m Tour Hassan, was to be the second largest in the Muslim world.

Women travelling alone should beware some members of the Royal Guards; under the pretence of pointing something out to you, they may well try and snatch a kiss instead!

Chellah

Beyond the city walls, in the south of the city at the end of Ave Yacoub el-Mansour at the junction with Blvd ad-Douster, are the remains of the ancient Roman city of Sala Colonia. It's enclosed by the walls of the necropolis of Chellah, built here by the Merenids in the 13th century. The city of Rabat had by this time fallen on hard times, and this pretty spot south of the city gates was as close as the Merenids came to taking an interest in it.

The construction has a defensive air about it, which is no coincidence. The sultan who completed it, Abu al-Hassan Ali, was intent on protecting his dynasty from possible attack or interference.

After entering through the main gate, you are pretty much obliged to follow a path heading diagonally away from the gate. You can see what little remains of the Roman city, but it is all fenced off. Around you, fig, olive, orange and banana trees, as well as all sorts of other vegetation, prosper amid the tombs and *koubbas* (shrines). You'll notice abundant birds and butterflies flitting around, too.

At the bottom of this short walk are the remains of a mosque. A couple of fairly half-hearted would-be guides hang about here – you're in no way obliged to take up their offers. Penetrate into the mosque: behind it a chunk of wall is still standing and in front of it are a couple of tombs. Here lie Abu al-Hassan Ali and his wife.

As you enter the site, on the far right are the tombs of local venerated saints, and a walled pool. Infertile women come here with peeled boiled eggs to feed the eels that dwell in the murky waters of the pool.

You will have already noticed a minaret topped by a stork's nest (hardly anything here *isn't* topped by a stork's nest). At one point this was a small medersa that functioned as an endowment of Abu al-Hassan Ali. You can make out where the students' cells were on either side of the building, as well as the *mihrab* (prayer niche) at the end opposite the minaret.

This peaceful, half-overgrown monument is open daily from 8.30 am until 6 pm (5 pm in winter). Entry costs Dr10.

Archaeology Museum
The best museum in Morocco, at least among those dealing with the country's ancient past, is Rabat's modern Archaeology Museum. It's almost close to the Hôtel Chellah at 23 Rue al-Brihi, off Ave Moulay Hassan.

The ground floor is given over to displays of implements and other finds from the oldest known civilisations in Morocco. Some of the material dates back 350,000 years to the Pebble Culture period.

In a courtyard to the right are some prehistoric rock carvings. On the 2nd floor you can see finds from Morocco's history, from the Roman era to the Middle Ages. There are indepth studies of several towns, but the explanations are in French.

In a separate building is the highlight of the collection, the Salle des Bronzes. Most of the ceramics, statuary and implements in bronze and other metals date from the period of Roman occupation and were found at Volubilis, Lixus and Chellah.

Don't miss the beautiful head of Juba II. It's in complete contrast to the unforgiving realism of Cato the Younger's bust, complete with good Roman nose, stubborn brow and sticky-out ears.

Look out also for the much smaller, but charming *Vieux Pecheur* (old fisherman) with his weather-beaten face and bandy legs. If you look closely, you'll see the mark of a slave branded on his chest. There are various bronze plates with Latin texts, including a 'military diploma' awarded by the emperor to a local worthy.

The museum is open daily (except Tuesday) from 9 to 11.30 am and from 2.30 to 6 pm (to 5.30 pm in winter). Entry costs Dr10.

Royal Palace
Of the four remaining Almohad gates in Rabat's city walls, by far the most impressive is Bab ar-Rouah (Gate of the Winds), which forms the north-west corner of the walls around the Royal Palace complex.

You can get into the palace grounds through several entrances. The main one is off Ave Moulay Hassan, a little way inside Bab ar-Rouah. It takes you south towards the *mechouar* (parade ground), on the east side of which is the Ahl al-Fas (People of Fès) Mosque. If you're lucky, you might catch the king making a grand entry for the Friday prayers around noon.

All the palace buildings, which were built in the last century, are off-limits, so you're not likely to be tempted to hang around here for long. It makes a pleasant enough walk on the way from the centre of town out towards Chellah.

Musée Nationale des PTT
There is a small and much-ignored postal museum on Ave Mohammed V which has a collection of stamps and first-day covers going back to pre-protectorate days. Entry is free, and the museum is open during office hours.

Places to Stay – bottom end
Camping The nearest camp site is *Camping de la Plage* (☎ 782368), back in from the beach at Salé; it's well signposted from the Salé end of the bridge over the Oued Bou Regreg. It's open all year and costs Dr10 per person, Dr10 per car, caravan or camping van and Dr10 for a power line. They charge Dr5 per child (under 12) and for water (for two people).

There's very little shade – just a few small trees, but you can get refreshments. Tea or coffee costs Dr4, breakfast Dr12 and, for lunch and dinner, you can order traditional Moroccan dishes such as tajine for

Dr50. Facilities include showers and toilets, and there's a supermarket nearby where you can buy alcohol.

There are several more camp sites on the road south towards Casablanca. The first of them is the *Palmeraie*, about 15km south of Rabat, on the beach at Temara. Another 10km south, near Ech-Chiahna beach, are two others: *Camping Gambusias* (☎ 749142) and *Camping Rose Marie* (☎ 749251). Both are OK and the location is pleasant enough.

Hostel The *youth hostel* (☎ 725769) is at 43 Rue Marassa, opposite the walls of the medina (see the Rabat map). It's a pleasant place with an attractive and verdant courtyard, and costs Dr26 per night (Dr31 without a card) in dormitory accommodation. There are cold showers, but no cooking facilities. The hostel is open from 8 to 10 am, noon to 3 pm and 6 to 10.30 pm.

Hotels – Medina There are several basic budget hotels on or just off the continuation of Ave Mohammed V as it enters the medina.

Few make any concessions to creature comforts and some don't even have showers – cold or otherwise. An extra dollar or two will buy you better accommodation outside the medina. Except where indicated, all of these hotels are on the Central Rabat map.

One of the cheapest is the *Hôtel Chaab* (☎ 731351), in the first lane inside the medina wall between Ave Mohammed V and Rue Sidi Fatah. Basic singles/doubles cost (Dr30/50).

Close by, the *Hôtel du Centre* charges about Dr35/70. Rooms are clean, with table, chair and washbasin, but there are no showers.

The *Hôtel France* (☎ 723457) at 46 Rue Souk Semara is a basic but adequate place and some rooms look on to a courtyard with enormous banana trees. Singles cost Dr30 to Dr35 and doubles/triples cost Dr50/60. The nearby *Hôtel Assaada* has very adequate, clean rooms for Dr35/70, but you'll probably have to use the Arabic language crib at the beginning of the book to get one!

The *Hôtel d'Alger* (☎ 724829), at No 34 Rue Souk Semara, is about the best deal in the lower half of this category. Rooms are quite large, clean and quiet and look on to a pleasant courtyard, but there are no showers. Singles, doubles, triples and quads cost respectively Dr35, Dr70, Dr90 and Dr110.

A little more expensive, but one of the best bets in this area, is the recently renovated *Hôtel Magreb*. The new tiles, sinks and showers positively gleam. Simple, spotless singles/doubles cost Dr50/80.

Right up at the kasbah end of the medina is a quiet little place, the *Hôtel des Oudaias* (☎ 732371), at 132 Blvd al-Alou (see the Rabat map). It's in a bit of a laneway just parallel to the main street). It's not top value for money, at Dr60/100 for basic rooms and Dr12 for hot showers, but it is in a pleasant location. They have a nice little tearoom downstairs.

A little more expensive is the *Hôtel Darna* (☎ 736787), at 24 Blvd al-Alou (see the Rabat map). It's a bit rundown, and could be cleaner, but rooms come with shower or, if you're lucky, full bathroom. They cost Dr80/120. Reception is in the busy cafe downstairs.

The best by a mile at the higher end of this category is the friendly and immaculate *Hôtel Dorhmi* (☎ 723898) at 313 Ave Mohammed V, next door to the Banque Populaire. The hotel, which has been completely renovated, is in a good location and has rooms for Dr80/100. Hot showers are Dr7 more. There is a good view of the medina from the roof terrace.

Hotels – Ville Nouvelle West of Bab al-Had, there is a small clutch of hotels on and around Blvd Hassan II. The area is nothing special, but it's close enough to the action if you're having trouble elsewhere.

The best of the cheapies is the *Hôtel d'Alsace* (☎ 722611), although the toilets can get a bit pongy. It's a quiet place in a back lane just off Blvd Hassan II. Most of the rooms, which cost Dr45/80, look onto a cool internal courtyard. Hot showers cost Dr8.

Back inside the city walls, a couple of places along Blvd Hassan are worth considering. The *Hôtel Petit Vatel* (☎ 723095) looks very basic, but has adequate rooms for Dr50/90 and showers are Dr5.

Virtually next door is the *Hôtel Majestic* (☎ 722997) at 121 Blvd Hassan II. Through the dust, you can almost see that it might once have been majestic, but it's still not a bad deal at Dr80/120 for rooms with private shower or Dr60/90 without. Most rooms are quite large, reasonably furnished and have a balcony. Try for one at the front.

A block south is the *Hôtel Mamounia* (☎ 724479), at 10 Rue de la Mamounia. Despite the uninviting entrance, and the climb up to the 3rd floor, it's a peaceful, bright and clean place. Simple singles go for Dr50/60 (depending on the size) and doubles for Dr90. Some rooms have balconies; hot showers are available for Dr5 extra.

Long a popular place and still one of the best budget deals, the *Hôtel Central* (☎ 707356), at 2 Zankat al-Basra, has spacious, well maintained and very clean rooms with basin, bidet, wardrobe, table

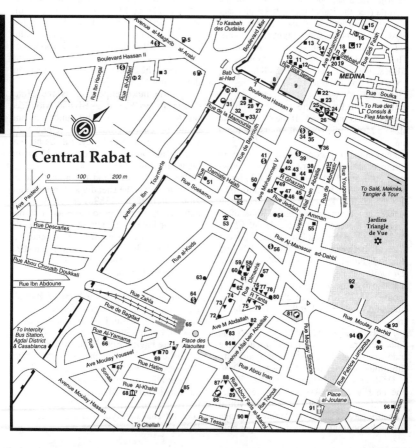

Central Rabat

and chairs. Rates are Dr80/99 without shower and Dr125/146 with shower. The (shared) showers are not cheap at Dr9, but they are steaming hot (mornings only).

A little more expensive for single rooms, but a definite rival for value in doubles, is the *Hôtel Velleda* (☎ 769531) at 106 Ave Allal ben Abdallah. Fairly spacious rooms without private shower cost Dr83/99 and rooms with shower and toilet cost Dr125/146. Hot water is available from 8 pm to 8 am, but it's more warm than hot in the morning. For disabled travellers, there is a lift.

PLACES TO STAY
3   Hôtel d'Alsace
10 Hôtel France
11 Hôtel d'Alger
12 Hôtel Assaada
13 Hôtel National; Douche (Public Shower - Men Only)
15 Hôtel Renaissance
19 Hôtel Maghreb
22 Hôtel Dorhmi; Banque Populaire
23 Hôtel du Centre
24 Hôtel Chaab
28 Hôtel Petit Vatel
29 Hôtel Majestic
32 Hôtel Mamounia
38 Hôtel Capitol
43 Hôtel Splendid; Chez Thami Music Store
44 Hôtel de la Paix
55 Hôtel Royal
61 Hôtel Central
62 Hôtel Balima
67 Hôtel Bélère
70 Hôtel d'Orsay
71 Hôtel Terminus
84 Hôtel Velleda
90 Hôtel Les Oudayas
93 Grand Hôtel
96 Hôtel La Tour Hassan

PLACES TO EAT
7   Cheap Fish Restaurants
8   Pâtisserie Salon de Thé Bami
14 Restaurant de la Libération
18 Restaurant Taghazout
20 Pâtisserie Traiteur Lailati
21 Café de la Jeunesse
25 Restaurant El Bahia
27 Fax Food
33 Friterie (Chip Shop); Sandwich Store
36 Pizzeria Le Passage
40 Pâtisserie 4 Saisons; Restaurant Hong Kong
47 Pâtisserie Palais Gourmand
48 Restaurant La Comédie
49 Tagardit Restaurant
59 Taki Fried Chicken
69 Boulangerie Pâtisserie L'Epi d'Or; Restaurant La Clef
73 Restaurant Le Fouquet's
75 Café
76 La Bidoche
77 La Dolche Vita (Ice-Cream)
78 La Mamma; Restaurant Equinox
79 La Bamba
82 Patisserie la Petite Duchesse; Carlson Wagonlits (Travel Agency)
83 McDonald's
87 City VIPS
88 Pâtisserie Lina

OTHER
1   BMCI Bank (ATM)
2   Bains Douches (Hammam)
4   Crédit Agricole (Bank)
5   Total Petrol Station
6   Shell Petrol Station
9   Municipal Market
16 Douches Modernes (Public Showers)
17 Mosque
26 Petit Taxi Stand
30 Douche al-Mamouniya (Public Showers)
31 Bus Nos 30 (to Bus Station) & 17 (to Temara via Zoo)
34 Wafabank
35 Total Petrol Station
37 Amnesia Nightclub
39 BMCE Bank (ATMs)
41 BMCE Bank (ATM)
42 Photolab Photomagic
45 Librairie Libre Service (Bookshop)
46 Gentleman Pressing (Laundry)
50 Cinéma Renaissance
51 Sûreté Nationale (Immigration Office)
52 Post Office
53 Telephone Office
54 Ministry of Information
56 Banque du Maroc
57 Mini Marché du Centre (Supermarket & Liquor Store)
58 Arc-en-Ciel Nightclub
60 Air France
63 Chambres des Représentants (Parliament)
64 BMCI Bank (ATM)
65 Rabat Ville Train Station
66 English Bookshop
68 Musée Nationale des PTT
72 Royal Air Maroc
74 International Language Centre
80 Africa Voyages (Travel Agency)
81 German & Spanish Embassies; Centro Cultural Español
85 Hertz (Car Rental)
86 French Consulate
89 Avis (Car Rental)
91 St Pierre Cathedral
92 Théâtre Mohammed V
94 Syndicat d'Initiative
95 Europcar (Car Rental)

NTH ATLANTIC COAST

The one-star *Hôtel Capitol* (☎ 731236), at 34 Ave Allal ben Abdallah, has singles/doubles with shared shower for Dr80/99. Rooms with attached shower are Dr89/110 and with shower and bathroom are Dr125/146. Most rooms are large, clean and light and have a balcony. There is also a lift. The restaurant is simple, but clean and restful place which does a good set menu (harira and tajine) for Dr35.

The *Hôtel Splendid* (☎ 723283), at 8 Rue Ghazza, charges Dr90/130 for rather tatty but clean rooms without shower, and Dr160/202 with private shower and toilet. Showers cost Dr5. The hotel boasts a pleasant internal courtyard.

One of the best places in town is the *Hôtel de la Paix* (☎ 722926), 2 Rue Ghazza. It offers recently renovated and attractively furnished rooms without shower for Dr86/100. Heading into the middle-range category, they also have rooms with private toilet and shower for Dr126/156.

Places to Stay – middle

For those in search of a tad more comfort, there are a few decent two-star possibilities. Except where indicated, all of these hotels are on the Central Rabat map.

The *Hôtel Royal* (☎ 721171; fax 725491), at 1 Rue Jeddah Amman, has 67 comfortable and reasonably furnished rooms with telephone and bathroom. Singles/doubles cost Dr131/154 with private shower, or Dr164/194 with shower and toilet. There is piping hot water all day. Try to get a room with views over the park.

Going up in price, there are two three-star hotels near the train station at the junction of Ave Mohammed V and Ave Moulay Youssef. The cheaper of the two is the *Hôtel d'Orsay* (☎ 202277; fax 701926) at 11 Ave Moulay Youssef. It's quite an attractive place and is good value. It has just 31 rooms, of which five are without private shower (Dr102/143). The others come with shower, toilet and satellite TV (Dr211/264). A shower in the communal bathrooms costs Dr12.

Around the corner, the *Hôtel Terminus* (☎ 700616; fax 701926), at 384 Ave Mo-

hammed V, has singles and doubles with private shower and toilet for Dr256 and Dr313 respectively.

Further north, along Ave Mohammed V, is the huge *Hôtel Balima* (☎ 707755; fax 707450) which has comfortable and self-contained singles and doubles for Dr256 and Dr313 respectively. Some rooms are very spacious.

Better value, but further afield and not really offering anything more than the better two-star hotels, is the *Grand Hôtel* (☎ 727285), at 19 Rue Patrice Lumumba. It has self-contained singles/doubles for Dr155/210 (including breakfast), a restaurant and the somewhat seedy Bar Manhattan.

Better still is the *Hôtel Bou Regreg* (☎ 724110). It's near the main city bus terminal, on the corner of Rue an-Nador and Blvd Hassan II (see the Rabat map). The location is a little noisy, but it's handy for the medina and buses to Salé. It has very clean, self-contained rooms with phone. Unfortunately, it was closed for renovation at the time of writing, but should be open again by now, charging in the region of Dr160/190. The hotel has a restaurant and a cafe.

Heading off into four-star territory is the *Hôtel Les Oudayas* (☎ 707820; fax 708235) at 4 Rue Tobrouk. Self-contained singles/doubles cost Dr256/313.

Places to Stay – top end

The two four-star hotels in Rabat are the *Hôtel Bélère* (☎ 709801; fax 203302), at 33 Ave Moulay Youssef, and the *Hôtel Chellah* (☎ 701051; fax 706354), at 2 Rue d'Ifni, near the Archaeological Museum (see the Rabat map). The Bélère is a little more expensive, at Dr432/588 including breakfast. The Chellah charges Dr408/526.

There are three five-star hotels. The *Hyatt Regency* (☎ 771234; fax 772492) is out in the swish Rabat suburb of Souissi, south of the city centre. The *Hôtel La Tour Hassan* (☎ 721491; fax 725408), at 26 Ave Abderrahman Annegai, has more character and charges from Dr914/1064 for singles/doubles.

Finally, the best placed of them is the *Hôtel Safir* (☎ 726431; fax 722155), on Place Sidi Makhlouf (see Rabat map). It offers all you would expect from such places and charges Dr1100/1250 a night, plus taxes.

Hammams

The Bains Douches on Rue al-Abdari, west of the city walls, are open every day from 6 am to 10 pm. A little more central is the *Douche al-Mamouniya* which is just off Blvd Hassan II, close to the Majestic Hôtel.

In the medina, there is a douche (unmarked) for men only next door to the Hôtel National, and a couple more hammams (for men and women) in the lane one block north of Rue Sebbahi. There are various other hammams marked on the map.

Places to Eat

Medina Except where indicated otherwise, all of these places are on the Central Rabat map. Perhaps cheapest of all is the collection of small restaurants under a common roofed area directly opposite the Hôtel Majestic, on the medina side of Blvd Hassan II. In some of them you can get fried fish along with the usual chips and salad, although you will probably be offered more standard, red meat dishes. For a full meal, you are looking at around Dr25.

Equally cheap are the restaurants close to the market on Ave Mohammed V. One that has been popular with travellers for years is the *Café de la Jeunesse* at 305 Ave Mohammed V, where you can get a more-than-sufficient meal of meat, chips, rice and olives, plus a soft drink, for Dr21. It gets quite packed with locals in the early evening. You can eat upstairs in the large seating area or get takeaway food downstairs.

Virtually across the road at No 256 is the *Restaurant de la Libération*, where a decent tajine costs Dr26 and a sandwich Dr15. On Rue Sebbahi, opposite the Hôtel al-Alam, is one of the best bets in the area.

The *Restaurant Taghazout* is a clean and very good value place which does decent

main courses, including couscous for Dr22. A good bowl of harira soup costs just Dr3 and an omelette Dr5.

Built into the medina walls on Blvd Hassan II is the pleasant *Restaurant El Bahia*. You can sit in the Moroccan-style interior section upstairs, in a shaded courtyard or outdoors on the terrace. It's also quite good value: a tajine with a drink costs about Dr35.

For a splurge in one of the traditional Moroccan palace-restaurants, you could try the *Restaurant Dinarjat* (☎ 704239), at 6 Rue Belgnaoui in the heart of the medina, opposite the cemetery (see the Rabat map). It was built as a private house at the end of the 17th century and is done out in the Andalusian palace style.

Main courses, including couscous and tajine, cost a fairly reasonable Dr125, but with the cover charge (Dr10), 10% service charge and the 19% tax, it soon adds up. The restaurant is licensed (a bottle of wine costs Dr70) and there are *spectacles* (traditional entertainment) in the evening.

It's open every day for lunch and dinner, but it's best to reserve in advance. A lantern-bearing guide will be sent to pick you up from the medina entrance, just south of the Hôtel des Oudaias on Blvd al-Alou, and lead you for the last bit of the journey.

Ville Nouvelle The *Pizzeria Le Passage*, at 1 Ave Allal ben Abdallah, is a good place for rock-bottom pizza (Dr20 to Dr37). They also do hamburgers and chips for Dr18 and harira soup for Dr5. It's a popular place with the locals.

A couple of *Pizza Huts* have recently opened in town, although they're very expensive at Dr69 for a small pizza. One is at 107 Ave Fal Ould Oumeir in the Agdal district.

Next door to the Hôtel Mamounia, there is a *Friterie* (chip shop) where a good bag of chips and mayonnaise or ketchup will cost you Dr5. If you want a hamburger as well, it will come to Dr10. A few doors down there is also a sandwich store.

The *Restaurant La Comédie*, on the

NTH ATLANTIC COAST

corners of Ave Mohammed V and Rue Jeddah, is a popular place with the locals. It has a lively cafe downstairs, while the restaurant upstairs offers solid set menus for around Dr40.

The *Restaurant La Koutoubia*, at 10 Rue Pierre Parent (see the Rabat map), is a colourful place with a fragile-looking, mock Andalusian extrusion at the entrance. The house speciality is tajine and they have a good selection, although it's a bit on the pricey side (Dr60). They also have brochettes for Dr30. Beer/wine is also available here for Dr14/70 per bottle.

A block behind the Hôtel Balima is a cluster of good, but a little more expensive, restaurants. For a romantic night out, you could try the candlelit *La Bamba* which specialises in fish dishes, both French and Moroccan, from Dr60 to Dr90. It also does good, three course menus for Dr65/95. You can also get beer here (from Dr17) and wine (from Dr72 a bottle).

Across the road is one of the best restaurants, and certainly the best pizzeria in Rabat. *La Mamma* (☎ 707329) has been run by the same Italian-French family since 1964 and is a very popular place with expats. It's an atmospheric restaurant decorated *á l'Italien* with wooden beams, old candlelit tables and an open pizza oven. You can sit at the central bar for a pre-dinner drink (prices are the same as at La Bamba). Pizzas (all for Dr50) are excellent, but they also serve fresh pasta (Dr45) and some meat dishes (Dr60 to Dr90). It's open every day from 11.30 am to 3 pm and from 7 pm to 1 am, and they also deliver.

Close by is the new and trendy *Equinox* restaurant at 2 Rue Tanta. It's decorated in an Art Nouveau style and is a mellow, relaxed place for women travellers. Main courses cost from Dr50 to Dr70 and salads from Dr27 to Dr35. They also have a selection of eight set menus (of up to three courses) which are good value.

For Chinese and Vietnamese food, try the *Hong Kong* (☎ 723594) at 261 Ave Mohammed V, below the Hôtel Berlin. Main courses cost from Dr55 to Dr60 and are

quite respectable. It's open every day except Monday.

For Moroccan food in a more traditional setting, but with prices about a third those of the Dinarjat in the medina, try the *Restaurant Chez el-Ouazzani* (☎ 779297) at Sahat Ibn Yasine in the Agdal district (see the Rabat map). The lovely *zellij* tile work and cedar ceilings are genuine, and the place is filled not with tourists, but local civil servants who swear by it. The house speciality is brochettes (usually about the only thing on offer) which cost Dr50 for a big plate with a salad, drink and as many chips as you can eat. It's a lively place and is open every day for lunch and dinner (until 10.30 pm).

The best place for an excellent selection of traditional Moroccan fare is the *Restaurant La Clef* (☎ 701972), a couple of doors down from the Hôtel D'Orsay on Ave Moulay Yossef. It makes a half-hearted effort to look traditional with mock zellij tile work and plaster mouldings, but is a pleasant, relaxing little place.

It does an excellent value, three course dinner for Dr55. Main courses, if ordered separately, cost around Dr45. There's also salads for Dr11 to Dr20 and omelettes from Dr11.

If you fancy an apéritif before dinner, there's a local bar downstairs, or you can have wine/beer with your meal for Dr14/71 per bottle. In summer, you can sit outside on the little terrace. It might be a good idea to make a reservation during this period, as the restaurant is popular.

There is a number of chic, French-style restaurants in Rabat with good reputations, although you're talking around Dr250 per head.

L'Entrecôte (☎ 671108) at 74 Blvd al-Amir Fal Ould Omar (see Rabat map), is a good place where main dishes cost around Dr95.

Not far away on the corner of Ave Atlas and Rue Sebou is the *Au Vert Gallant* (☎ 674247). It has an excellent reputation and you'll be looking about Dr350 per person. Both restaurants are in the wealthy

Agdal district, some way from the centre of town; you'll need to get a petit taxi there.

The *Restaurant de la Plage* (☎ 723148) and the *Borj Eddar* (☎ 701501) serve fish and seafood down by the Rabat beach, catering to well-heeled Rabatis and tour groups. Main courses cost from Dr90 to Dr180. To get to them, just follow Blvd Tariq al-Marsa past the kasbah (see the Rabat map). The restaurants are generally closed in winter, although the former keeps a cafe open all year.

Cafes & Bars Rabat is crawling with largely European-style cafes, which are great places for a morning croissant and coffee. Some of them double as bars (alcohol can be consumed inside only), and there are a few simple drinking holes around, too. Not many cafes or bars are open after about 9.30 pm.

The most fashionable place for a drink, particularly around pre-dinner time, is the pleasant (but not cheap) terrace of the *Hôtel Balima* on Ave Mohammed V. You can also eat there; sandwiches cost from Dr30 and a three-course, set menu Dr118.

In the old part of town, the most pleasant cafe by far is the *Café Maure* in the Kasbah des Oudaias on the far side of the Andalusian Gardens (see the Kasbah enlargement on the Rabat map).

It's a very pleasant, calm and shady spot looking out over the estuary to Salé, and is a favourite with young Moroccan courting couples. They serve coffee and mint tea (Dr4), soft drinks (Dr5) and a small selection of excellent, although comparatively expensive, Moroccan pastries (Dr6). They're worth it: try the doigts de jeunes filles (little girls' fingers) or the bracelets aux amandes (almond bracelets).

Keep a careful account of the tally; waiters can be a bit 'absent-minded'; don't let them bully you into paying a high 'service charge' (leave a tip if earned) or a 'special tourist price'. All prices are posted up on a board. The cafe is open every day from 9 am to 5.30 pm – often longer hours in summer.

Fast Food A *McDonald's* has opened in the last two years on Ave Mohammed Abdallah. Though popular with middle-class Moroccans, it's hardly good value compared with local fare. A Big Mac, chicken or fish burger costs Dr36.

Nearby, with much more character, is *La Bidoche* where decent burgers cost from Dr14. They also do brochettes for Dr15. Another recommended place, where you can get a filling meal for Dr20 to Dr30, is *Fax Food* on Blvd Hassan II. It is very popular with locals and has a large seating area. Hamburgers cost Dr16 and brochettes Dr22.

The *City VIPS*, at 47 Ave Allal ben Abdallah, is another good place that's very popular with the young. Hamburgers cost Dr26.

Taki Fried Chicken at 281 Ave Mohammed V, is a wonderful rip-off of the real thing, complete with servers in red uniforms, and, more bizarrely, an entire family of stuffed chickens on display on the counter. The chicken burgers aren't bad and cost Dr35 to Dr39 (with chips).

Patisseries & Ice Cream If you haven't had much joy with the tourist office in Agdal (see the Rabat map), the *Boulangerie Pâtisserie Al-Abtal*, just round the corner, should make up for it. It does good ice cream and outstanding fruit tarts including a tarte au citron to die for.

The *Pâtisserie Palais Gourmand* at 2 Rue Jeddah, has a good selection of cakes to take away and some delicious mini-pizzas. The *Pâtisserie 4 Saisons*, next door to the Hôtel Berlin on Ave Mohammed V, is a popular meeting place with the younger crowd and has good cakes and pizzas, as well as a large upstairs seating area.

The *Pâtisserie Lina*, at 45 Allal ben Abdallah, is a fashionable place around tea time and is also the best place in town for breakfast. It has a great selection of sweets, including more unusual French-style treats, such as a very rich chocolate cake. It's a tranquil place for women travellers, and is one of the very few places in Morocco which is non-smoking. The patisserie is open every day from 6.30 am to 9.25 pm.

If you have a long train journey ahead of you, the *Boulangerie Pâtisserie l'Épi d'Or*, just across from the train station, is a great place to stock up for a picnic. It has an excellent selection of French and Moroccan sweets and savouries, including delicious mini-pizzas and quiches.

They also do good, freshly baked bread and you can ask them to prepare you a simple sandwich. It's open every day from 6.15 am to 9.30 pm.

Just inside the medina, beside the municipal market, is the *Pâtisserie Salon de Thé Bami*. It has a very good selection of French and Moroccan sticky cakes, including some heavenly strawberry-banana tarts. You can have them on the busy terrace outside or in the large and peaceful seating area upstairs.

Also in the medina, opposite the Restaurant de la Libération, is the *Pâtisserie Traiteur Lailati* at 271 Mohammed V.

The *Pâtisserie La Petite Duchesse* at 1 Ave Moulay Abdallah, is considered by some to be the aristocrat of patisseries in Rabat. It makes high-quality sweet and savoury eats to take away, and also does chocolates. Try the speciality of the house – dates or walnuts wrapped in marzipan. It's open every day from 6 am to 1 pm and from 4.15 to 8 pm.

For ice cream, head straight for the excellent *La Dolche Vita* on Rue Tanta. It's owned by the Benenatis, the same family who have the Pizzeria La Mamma next door. The 43 or so flavours are home-made in the traditional Italian style and are delicious. Cones cost Dr7 and a tub Dr12. It's open every day from 7.30 to 1 am, and makes a great late stop on a warm night.

Self-Catering The *Mini Marché du Centre*, on Rue Dimachk in the ville nouvelle, stocks a small selection of groceries and a rather better selection of alcoholic beverages. It's open from 8.30 am to 1 pm and from 3 to 7.30 pm.

The *Hypermarché Marjane* is on the road towards Salé and the airport.

Entertainment

Nightclubs There's a good choice of nightclubs in Rabat, some of which are attached to the more expensive hotels, and they're all popular with well-heeled young people. The music is standard international disco fare. They normally charge Dr60 for entry (which includes the first drink) and the same amount for subsequent drinks.

Some of the better nightclubs include the disco at the *Hôtel Balima*, the *Arc-en-Ciel* on Rue Dimachk, *5th Avenue* in the Agdal area (see the Rabat map) and the fashionable *Amnesia*, not far from the Hôtel Royal.

The latter is a popular place with expats and can be fun. It's done out like an American bar complete with American trains, trucks and even an aeroplane suspended from the roof. There's also a pool table and, for the nostalgic, a Brit telephone box. It plays a European mix of music. Entry is Dr60 during the week (free to women) and Dr100 during the weekend.

Gay places are, as usual, rather limited, but you could try the nightclub *Jour et Nuit* (see the Rabat map), the terrace of the *Hôtel Balima* in the early evening, or *Amnesia* which seems to attract a bit of everybody.

Most clubs are open from around 10.30/11 pm (though at weekends they don't get going until around midnight) and go on until 2, 3 or 4 am. You'll need to be suitably dressed to get in.

Cinemas Rabat has a wide choice of cinemas, although only a few are of any serious interest. The best in town is the *Cinéma Renaissance* on Ave Mohammed V. There are four showings a day at 2.30, 5, 7.30 and 10 pm, and tickets cost Dr15/20 depending on the seats. Avoid the Royal, near the hotel of the same name, which is reputed to be a hashish den.

The French-language newspapers advertise what's on around town. Films, if they are not French, tend to be dubbed into that language.

Theatre The *Théâtre Mohammed V* puts on a wide variety of performances, ranging from classical music recitals to dance or the occasional play. The theatre is centrally located on Rue Moulay Rachid.

Things to Buy

Rabat is known for its carpets (see the Arts & Crafts section earlier in this book). If you're interested in buying one, first try the Ensemble Artisinal on Tariq al-Marsa by the Oued Bou Regreg. There you can get an idea of the range of quality and maximum prices to pay in the medina. There is also a carpet factory in the kasbah.

Rue des Consuls, not far from the kasbah, is one of the best places for purchases, particularly around the upper end. On Tuesday and Thursday mornings, the whole place becomes a kind of carpet souq, with locals bringing in their wares to sell. Try to get there early.

For traditional Moroccan and Arabic music, try the music store Chez Thami, next door to Hôtel Splendid at 22 Rue Ghazza. It also has a small western selection. They sell mainly cassettes, though there are a few CDs.

Getting There & Away

Air Royal Air Maroc (☎ 709766 for inquiries or 769710 for bookings) and Air France (☎ 707066) are both on Ave Mohammed V. It's unlikely that you'll fly into Rabat's local airport, which is near Salé, 10km north-east of town. RAM does have a few direct international flights from here, as well as daily flights to Casablanca (Mohammed V international airport).

Most of the internal flights from Rabat-Salé go via Mohammed V, so it makes more sense to go there directly, by express train.

Bus The intercity bus station (*Gare Routière*) is inconveniently situated about 5km south-west of the city centre on the road to Casablanca. Fortunately, there are local buses (No 30 is the most convenient) and petits taxis (about Dr15) into the centre. There is a left-luggage service at the station which charges Dr3 per item per day. It's open from 6 am to 9 pm.

All the various bus companies have their offices in this cylindrical building.

There are 13 ticket windows, stretching around to the left of the main entrance to the CTM window (interrupted by a cafe on the way). You may notice the whiteboards above the windows, with destinations in Arabic – the number written on each indicates the window number.

Window Nos 1 to 6 deal mainly with destinations north and east of Rabat, while Nos 7 to 13 are for southern destinations. Next to Window 13 is the CTM booth. Tickets for various destinations can be bought at the following ticket windows.

Window No 1
  Tangier, Tetouan and Ouezzane
Window No 2
  Fès, Meknès, Er-Rachidia, Kenitra, Kacem, Sidi and Moulay Idriss
Window No 3
  Fès, Meknès, Er-Rachidia, Khenifra, Sefrou, Al-Hoceima, Nador and Oujda
Window No 4
  Tangier, Tetouan, Chefchaouen, Sefrou, Er-Rachidia, Nador and Oujda
Windows No 5 & 6
  Minor destinations
Window No 7
  Mohammedia and El-Jadida
Window No 8
  El-Jadida, Safi and Essaouira
Window No 9
  Not in use
Window No 10
  Agadir (eight departures a day), Taroudannt and Ouarzazate
Window No 11
  Marrakesh (departures every hour or so) and Casablanca
Windows No 12 & 13
  Casablanca

CTM has buses to Casablanca (Dr26; six times daily), Fès (Dr54; 3½ hours; seven times daily), Tangier (Dr78; 5½ hours; six times daily), Er-Rachidia (Dr133), Oujda (Dr139), Tetouan (Dr79), Tiznit (Dr184) (via Agadir Dr162), Marrakesh (Dr90; 5½ hours), Essaouira (Dr118; about eight hours), Agadir (Dr162), Taroudannt (Dr178), Ouarzazate (Dr146; ten hours),

Safi (Dr89; 5½ hours), and El-Jadida (Dr51; 3½ hours). Non CTM buses are, as usual, between 15% and 30% cheaper.

If you arrive from the north, you're better off alighting at Salé and catching a local bus or grand taxi from there into central Rabat.

Train This is the best way to arrive in Rabat, as the Rabat Ville station is in the centre of town, on Ave Mohammed V at Place des Alaouites. (Don't get off at Rabat Agdal to the west of the city.)

There are more than 20 shuttle trains (Trains Navettes Rapides – TNR) from Rabat Ville to Casablanca. The first leaves at 6.28 am and the last at 9.34 pm, and they take 50 minutes.

Most go to the more convenient Casa-Port station and the rest to Casa-Voyageurs. This is in addition to other, slower trains passing through Rabat on the way to Casablanca and making intermediate stops.

For Fès and Meknès, there are eight departures a day from 7.12 am to 11.42 pm. They take about three hours and 40 minutes to Fès.

There are three daily trains to Tangier, leaving at 7.52 am, 6.57 pm and 12.57 am. The trip takes about 5½ hours.

To Marrakesh, there are six trains a day via Casablanca – the first at 4.05 am and the last at 11.14 pm. The trip takes a little less than six hours.

Some 2nd class ordinary/rapide fares are: Casablanca (Dr20/25.50), Fès (Dr55/67), Marrakesh (Dr76/95.50) and Tangier (Dr67.50/84).

For information on trains you can ring ☎ 701469, or go to the helpful information counter in the station. It's open from 7.15 am to 11 pm every day. There is also a BMCE exchange counter in the station, (open from 9 am to noon and from 3.30 to 7 pm), a Budget office for car rental and a left-luggage counter which charges Dr2.50 per item per day, but everything must be locked.

Taxi Grands taxis leave for Casablanca from just outside the intercity bus station. They cost Dr25. There are other grands taxis from a lot between the main city bus station and the Hôtel Bou Regreg on Blvd Hassan II (see the Rabat map). They leave for Fès (Dr55), Meknès (Dr40) and Salé.

You can't take petits taxis between Rabat and Salé, because they come under separate city jurisdictions.

Car The following are among the car rental agencies located in Rabat:

Avis
    7 Rue Abou Faris al-Marini (☎ 769759)
Budget
    Train station, Ave Mohammed V (767689)
Europcar
    25 Rue Patrice Lumumba (☎ 722328, 724141)
Hertz
    46 Ave Mohammed V (☎ 709227)

There is a good parking spot behind the petit taxi stand and in front of the Restaurant El Bahia on Blvd Hassan II. You pay the guardian around Dr5 per day to keep an eye on the car.

Getting Around
The Airport Buses no longer run between Rabat and Mohammed V international airport.

There are at least ten shuttle trains a day between 4.46 am and 7.30 pm. All go via Casablanca and some involve a change, so check carefully before departing. They leave from Rabat Ville station, take 1¼ hours and cost Dr67.50/45 in 1st/2nd class.

The local Rabat/Salé airport is 10km north-east of town, but it's unlikely that you'll need to use it unless you catch an internal flight to Rabat.

Bus The main city bus station is on Blvd Hassan II (see the Rabat map). From here, bus No 16 goes to Salé (get off at the Salé intercity bus station). Bus Nos 2 and 4 go to Bab Zaer for Chellah.

Bus Nos 30 and 17 run past Rabat's intercity bus station; they leave from a bus stop around the corner from the Hôtel

Majestic, just off Blvd Hassan II, inside Bab al-Had (see the Central Rabat map). No 17 goes on past the zoo to Temara. Bus Nos 37 and 52 also go from the intercity bus station into central Rabat. Tickets cost around Dr3 (hold on to them for inspection).

Taxi Grands taxis to Salé leave when full from just near the Hôtel Bou Regreg on Blvd Hassan II (see the Rabat map) and cost Dr2.50 a head.

A ride around town in the blue petits taxis will cost around Dr10, depending on where you want to go. It's about Dr15 to the intercity bus station.

There is a petit taxi stand close to the entrance of the medina on Blvd Hassan II.

SALÉ

Although just across the estuary from Rabat, the white city of Salé has a distinct character. Little within the city walls seems to have changed over the centuries and it is difficult to escape the feeling that Salé has been left by the wayside while Rabat forges ahead.

With a long history of action independent from central authorities, Salé is also a strongly traditional enclave amid the comparative liberalism of its sister city.

The two elements are best symbolised by the presence here of Abdessalam Yassine, who heads the Al-Adl wal-Ihsan (Justice & Charity) religious movement. He is here under house arrest and has long been considered a threat to the king and the central government – never more so than today with the fundamentalist ferment gripping, to some extent, the rest of North Africa.

Salé is not the most interesting of towns and can seem pretty grubby and worn out. It's also a bit difficult to find your way around, but it's worth persevering for the beautiful medersa in the medina.

History

The origins of the town are little known, but Salé rose as Sala Colonia, south of the Oued Bou Regreg, sank into obscurity. The Al-

mohads took control of the area in the 12th century, putting an end to local warring and establishing neighbouring Rabat as a base for expeditions to Spain.

Salé's walls were not built until the following century. The Merenids, who otherwise took little interest in either Salé or Rabat, built them after a raid in 1260 by Spanish freebooters. A canal was dug from the river to Bab Mrisa to allow safe access for shipping.

Salé subsequently entered its most prosperous period, establishing trade links with Venice, Genoa, England and the Netherlands. It was this position as a trading city on the coast that led to Salé and Rabat becoming home to the Sallee Rovers (see the Rabat History section) in the 16th century. Both cities prospered from the pirates' activities, and an influx of Muslim refugees from Spain in the 17th century only improved matters.

The end of pirating in the 19th century, in conjunction with Rabat's promotion to capital under the French, left Salé to turn in on itself.

Orientation

The town's sights can be seen in half a day. The city's main point of access is Bab Bou Haja, on the south-western wall, which opens onto Place Bab Khebaz. From here it's a short walk to the souqs, although getting from these to the Great Mosque through the somewhat complicated system of narrow alleyways and arches can be tricky. You may need to ask the local people for directions.

Alternatively, you can approach the Great Mosque via the road that follows the line of the city walls past Bab el-Jedid and Bab Malka.

Information

Various banks and the post office can be found in the south-eastern corner of the city.

Great Mosque & Medersa

These are two of the most interesting buildings in Salé. The Great Mosque, built during

NTH ATLANTIC COAST

Almohad times, is out of bounds to non-Muslims. The medersa, on the other hand, no longer functions as such and is open to visitors.

Constructed in 1333 by sultan Abu al-Hassan Ali, the mosque is a superb example of Merenid artistry and, although smaller, is certainly the equal of the Medersa Bou Inania in Fès. It follows a formula that will be familiar to those who have already seen Merenid medersas: all the walls display a zellij-tile base, topped by intricately carved stucco and elegant cedarwood

work (for more information see the special section on Architecture in the Facts About the Country chapter).

Students once occupied the small cells around the gallery. A narrow flight of stairs leads onto a flat roof above the cells, from which there are excellent views of Salé and across to Rabat. Entry to the medersa costs Dr10 and the guardian who shows you around will expect a small tip (they don't get many visitors, so their income is limited).

There is also a notorious faux guide who

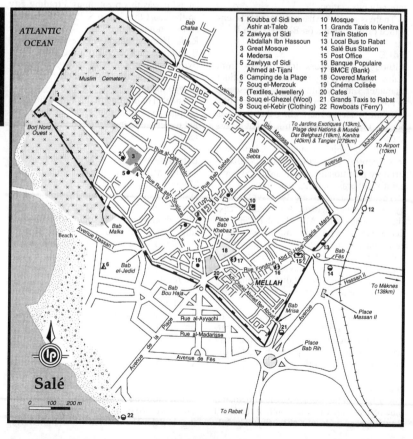

1 Koubba of Sidi ben Ashir at-Taleb	10 Mosque
2 Zawiyya of Sidi Abdallah Ibn Hassoun	11 Grands Taxis to Kenitra
3 Great Mosque	12 Train Station
4 Medersa	13 Local Bus to Rabat
5 Zawiyya of Sidi Ahmed at-Tijani	14 Salé Bus Station
6 Camping de la Plage	15 Post Office
7 Souq el-Merzouk (Textiles, Jewellery)	16 Banque Populaire
8 Souq el-Ghezel (Wool)	17 BMCE (Bank)
9 Souq el-Kebir (Clothing)	18 Covered Market
	19 Cinéma Colisée
	20 Cafes
	21 Grands Taxis to Rabat
	22 Rowboats ('Ferry')

hangs around here. He may well pretend that he has just seen off a potential assailant on your behalf, and will expect you to allow him to guide you around the medersa (and show your gratitude with a large tip afterwards).

Photography is allowed inside the medersa and from the roof. It's open every day from 9 am to noon and from 2.30 to 6 pm.

At the back of the Great Mosque is the Zawiyya of Sidi Abdallah ibn Hassoun, the patron saint of Salé. Revered by many Moroccan travellers (in much the same way as St Christopher is among Christians), this respected Sufi died in 1604.

He is the object of an annual pilgrimage and procession through the streets of Salé on the eve of Mouloud, the Prophet's birthday. On this day, local fishers dress in period costume, while others carry decorated candles and parade through the streets, ending up at the marabout's shrine.

It's one of three shrines in Salé – the other two are the Zawiyya Sidi Ahmed at-Tijani, in the lane between the mosque and medersa, and the white koubba of Sidi ben Ashir at-Taleb ('the doctor'), in the cemetery north-west of the mosque.

Souqs

The souqs are connected to the Great Mosque via Rue Ras ash-Shajara (also known as Rue de la Grande Mosquée), along which rich merchants in previous times constructed their houses.

There are three souqs in all, but perhaps the most interesting of them is the Souq el-Ghezel, the wool market. Here under the shade of trees you can watch wool being bought and sold with the aid of scales suspended from a large tripod, as it has been for centuries.

Close by is the Souq el-Merzouk, where textiles, basketwork and jewellery are made and sold. A little further out is the Souq el-Kebir, featuring second-hand clothing and household items.

Places to Stay & Eat

Hotel options are limited in Salé, and those that are available tend to be basic. Unless you want to stay at *Camping de la Plage* (see Places to Stay in Rabat), there seems little point in staying here. There's a much better choice of accommodation in Rabat.

There are plenty of hole-in-the-wall cafes in the souqs and surrounding streets, as well as the area just south of Place Bab Khebaz, where refreshments and good, cheap meals can be found. It's worth calling into one or more of them to soak up the unhurried atmosphere of this timeless place.

Getting There & Away

Bus Bus No 16 passes the intercity bus station near Bab Fès on its way to Rabat's main bus station.

Bus No 28 stops at the same bus station on its way north towards the town of Bouknadel and the Plages des Nations. Fares cost around Dr3.

Train It's possible also to take the train to Rabat, but buses or grands taxis are probably the simplest options.

Taxi There are grands taxis to Blvd Hassan II in Rabat from Bab Mrisa (Dr3). Note that Salé's beige petits taxis are not permitted to cross into Rabat. Grands taxis for Kenitra leave from a lot just north of the train station.

Boat Small boats run across the Oued Bou Regreg from just below the mellah in Rabat to Salé and back. They operate all day, leaving when full.

On the far side, simply follow the rest of the people up the rise to Bab Bou Haja. It costs locals half a dirham, but you'll probably find yourself paying more.

AROUND RABAT-SALÉ
Jardins Exotiques

About 13km north of Rabat on the road to Kenitra, the Jardins Exotiques are as much a monument to one man's persistent eccentricity as anything else.

Created in 1951 by one M François, a horticulturist, the gardens contain a sampling of flora from all over the world.

Although they appear a little disappointing when you first enter, they are quite interesting once you are further inside. François spent a lot of time roaming the forests of Africa. His conclusion on his own efforts was that, 'it is poetry that recreates lost paradises; science and technology alone are not enough'.

The gardens are open from 9 am to 5.30 pm and entry costs Dr5 (children Dr3). The best time to visit them is between March and April. Have the exact change ready, as the fellow in the ticket booth does not have any.

You can get there on the No 28 bus from the bus station in Salé – ask to be let off; there's a sign to the gardens on the left-hand side of the road.

Musée Dar Belghazi & Plage des Nations

The same bus will take you part of the way further on to the Plage des Nations, which is 6km north of the gardens. A track leading from the end of the bus line will get you to the beach, which is also known as Sidi Bouknadel (not to be confused with the nearby town of Bouknadel).

There are a few cafes and a hotel here, and it's a much more pleasant place to swim than the city beaches in Rabat or Salé.

On your way to the Plage, and almost exactly halfway between Rabat and Kenitra, is the Musée Dar Belghazi (☎ 822178). Look out for the large sign just off the road when travelling towards Kenitra. It's a new museum and the only one in Morocco under private ownership.

Entry is expensive (Dr40), but if you're keen on traditional Moroccan art, it's not to be missed.

The museum's collection, housed in an old *riad* (large villa), has been amassed by the Belghazi family over three generations and contains some stunning examples of Andalusian and Islamic art. With some 6000 items, the museum claims to be the largest in Africa, and pieces are sent to international exhibitions all over the world.

Objects on display include carpets from the 17th century; exquisitely carved wooden pieces, such as minbars, doors, cupolas and ceilings dating from as early as the 10th century; and exceptional pottery and embroidery from Fès. Look out for the tiny antique kaftans made for brides as young as 12 years old. Captions are in English and French.

If you're really fired up by the exhibits, you can ask to see the reserve collection for another Dr60.

If you're lucky you may get a guided tour from Mr Belghazi himself, a master craftsman in his own right and an impassioned connoisseur. The museum is open every day from 8 am to 5 pm.

National Zoo

The Parc Zoologique National, 9km south of Rabat on the road to Temara, is a surprisingly clean, well kept place. Most of the animals – and there's a wide range – have more space to move around than those in many European zoos.

The impressive collection of cats (including tigers, pumas, jaguars and a black panther) are less fortunate and are housed in rather cramped cages. There's also a good collection of African birds. Look out for the storks nesting rather spitefully on top of the macaws' cage!

There are snack stands and games for the kids. It's open Monday to Saturday from 10 am to 6 pm and on Sunday and holidays from 9 am to 6 pm; entry is Dr7/3 for adults/children. Parking costs Dr2. If you need to visit the toilet, ask the girl at the ice cream stand at the entrance to the zoo and she will show you the staff one.

There are several buses on this route, including Nos 17, 41 and 45. No 17 leaves from a side street off Blvd Hassan II, just inside Bab al-Had. Ask to be let off at the zoo.

From the main road, you have to walk a few hundred metres off to the left (east), as the entrance is at the back. You'll notice a shantytown spilling over opposite the zoo entrance.

Forests of Mamora & Zaër

For those travellers with their own vehicle, the enormous cork and eucalyptus forests of Mamora – which dominate the area north-east of Rabat – provide an excellent escape from the city and a cool spot for a picnic.

There is abundant wildlife in the region including wild boar, although much of the area forms part of a protected royal hunting reserve.

South of Rabat is the picturesque area known at the Forest of Zaër which is a good place to explore with a car. One particularly scenic route follows the P22 around 30km south of Rabat to the little village of Aïn el-Aouda.

If you want to make a circuit of it, you could continue on for another 10km until you reach the tiny S216 road to Merchouch, signposted to the right.

At Merchouch, you should bear right again onto the S106 towards Sidi Bettache and Ben Slimane, which takes you through green valleys and impressive gorges. There are also some good views to be had before starting the descent to the main road for Rabat or Casablanca.

If you're keen on **birds**, you may prefer to take the S208 back towards Rabat. The road begins at Sidi Bettache and heads northwards through a region that has become well known in ornithological circles for its rich birdlife.

The area considered most favoured is around the hunting lodge about 15km south of the village of **Sidi-Yahya**.

Sightings include numerous larks, bush-shrikes, black-shouldered kites and double-spurred francolins. More commonly seen are spotted flycatchers and white storks.

There are plenty of other possibilities for motor excursions, particularly around the town of Ben Slimane.

Some roads are little more than tracks, but are perfectly negotiable in dry weather and penetrate right into the heart of the forests.

Keep a look out for wild boar crossing the path in front of you.

Casablanca

With a population of 3 million, Casablanca is by far Morocco's largest city, industrial centre and port. This growth is a fairly recent phenomenon, dating from the early days of the French protectorate, when Casa was chosen to become the economic heart of the country.

The dimensions of the modest medina give some idea of just how small the place was when the French embarked on a massive building programme, laying out a new city in grand style with wide boulevards, public parks and fountains, as well as imposing Hispano-Moorish civic buildings.

The port handles almost 60% of Morocco's total sea traffic – the lion's share being phosphate exports. Some 20 million tonnes of goods are processed here each year. As this is not a natural haven, ships docked here are protected from the Atlantic by a 3180m-long jetty.

With all this economic activity, Casa became, and to some extent remains, the place to which Moroccans aspiring to fame, fortune or simply a better standard of living tend to gravitate.

The influx of hopefuls from the countryside in search of a job has fuelled the creation of *bidonvilles* (slums), as in any other conurbation, although the problem has been brought under control in the past 20 years. Many of those who arrived hopeful have ended up broken – the parade of well-heeled Casablancans who have made it stands in stark contrast to the beggars, prostitutes and other less fortunate residents.

Amid the striking white medium-rise 1930s architecture – and there are many jewels (Art Deco and otherwise) of this period to be found – it is the people who make the greatest impression. You hardly ever see the veil and it is hard to imagine the mini-skirt anywhere else in the Muslim world.

Men and women mix more easily here than in other Moroccan cities, especially

NTH ATLANTIC COAST

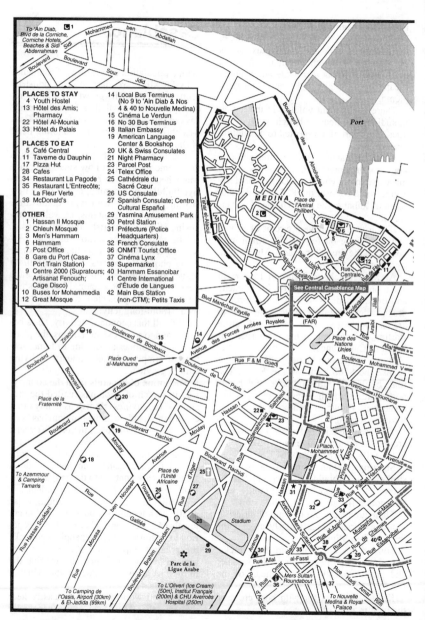

PLACES TO STAY
4   Youth Hostel
13 Hôtel des Amis;
    Pharmacy
22 Hôtel Al-Mounia
33 Hôtel du Palais

PLACES TO EAT
5   Café Central
11 Taverne du Dauphin
17 Pizza Hut
28 Cafes
34 Restaurant La Pagode
35 Restaurant L'Entrecôte;
    La Fleur Verte
38 McDonald's

OTHER
1   Hassan II Mosque
2   Chleuh Mosque
3   Men's Hammam
6   Hammam
7   Post Office
8   Gare du Port (Casa-
    Port Train Station)
9   Centre 2000 (Supratours;
    Artisanat Fenouch;
    Cage Disco)
10 Buses for Mohammedia
12 Great Mosque

14 Local Bus Terminus
    (No 9 to 'Ain Diab & Nos
    4 & 40 to Nouvelle Medina)
15 Cinéma Le Verdun
16 No 30 Bus Terminus
18 Italian Embassy
19 American Language
    Center & Bookshop
20 UK & Swiss Consulates
21 Night Pharmacy
23 Parcel Post
24 Telex Office
25 Cathédrale du
    Sacré Cœur
26 US Consulate
27 Spanish Consulate; Centro
    Cultural Español
29 Yasmina Amusement Park
30 Petrol Station
31 Préfecture (Police
    Headquarters)
32 French Consulate
36 ONMT Tourist Office
37 Cinéma Lynx
39 Supermarket
40 Hammam Essanoibar
41 Centre International
    d'Étude de Langues
42 Main Bus Station
    (non-CTM); Petits Taxis

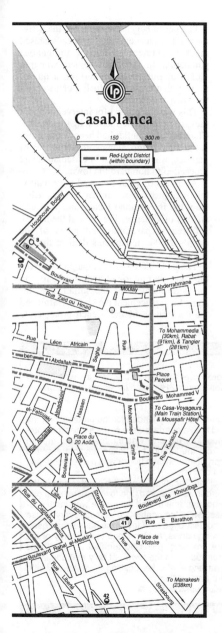

those of the interior. On the ocean beaches and in the clubs, the bright young things strut their stuff much like the beautiful youth of many western countries.

Casablanca has all the hallmarks of a brash western metropolis, with a hint of the decadent languor that marks many of the southern European cities it so closely resembles. But alongside the natty suits, designer sunglasses and high heels are the flowing robes of the old *jellabas* and *burnouses* of traditional Morocco.

True, the latter almost seems out of place here, but the mix of the population serves to remind you of where you are. And if you were in any doubt, laying eyes upon one of the marvels of modern religious architecture – the enormous Hassan II Mosque – should set you straight.

The mosque itself is just one element of an ambitious urban redevelopment plan that will ultimately result in a lot of changes to road layout and the construction of a huge US$100 million marina.

Despite the pressures of urban living, it's relatively easy to strike up conversations with Casablancans, which is another reminder that you're not in one of the frenzied financial powerhouses of the west.

History
Settlement of the Casablanca area has a long history. Prior to the Arab conquest, what is the now western suburb of Anfa was the capital of a Berber state set up by the Barghawata tribe. The Almoravids failed to bring this state into their orbit and it was not until 1188, during the time of the Almohads, that it was finally conquered.

Some 70 years later, Anfa was taken by the Merenids, but when that dynasty became weak, the inhabitants of the area reasserted their independence, taking to piracy and trading directly with England and Portugal.

By the second half of the 15th century, the Anfa pirates had become a serious threat to the Portuguese. A military expedition, consisting of some 10,000 men and 50 ships, was launched from Lisbon. Anfa was sacked and left in ruins. It wasn't long before the pirates were active again, however, and in 1515 the Portuguese were forced to repeat the operation. Sixty years later they arrived to stay, renaming the port Casa Branca and erecting fortifications.

Although harried by the tribes of the interior, the Portuguese stayed until 1755, when the colony was abandoned following a devastating earthquake (which also destroyed Lisbon). Sultan Sidi Mohammed ben Abdallah subsequently had the area resettled and fortified, but its importance declined rapidly and by 1830 it was little more than a village, with some 600 inhabitants.

It was about this time that the industrialised nations of Europe began casting their nets abroad for ever-increasing quantities of grain and wool – two of the main products of the Chaouia hinterland (the fertile area surrounding Casablanca). To secure these commodities, European agents established themselves in the city, renamed Casablanca (*Dar el-Baïda* in Arabic) by Spanish merchants.

Prosperity began to return, but the activities and influence of the Europeans caused much resentment among the indigenous population. In 1907, this spilled over into violence; European workers on a quarry railway that crossed a Muslim cemetery in the town were killed.

This was the pretext for intervention that the pro-colonialist faction in the French Chamber of Deputies had been waiting for. A French warship, along with a company of marines, was dispatched to Casablanca and proceeded to bombard the town.

Accounts of what followed vary wildly, but it appears that French troops, tribes from the interior and locals collapsed into an orgy of violence. The Jews of the mellah suffered in particular and many of the town's 20,000 inhabitants died in the upheaval.

The incident led to a campaign to subdue the Chaouia hinterland and, eventually, to the dethronement of the sultan, Abd al-Aziz; his replacement by Abd al-Hafid; and the declaration of the French protectorate

---

The Bombing of Casablanca

Walter Harris, the London *Times'* man in Morocco at the turn of the century, was quickly on the spot after the French bombarded Casablanca. His account appears in *Morocco that Was*:

A French warship arrived on the scene, and an armed party landed for the protection of the European population of the town. The forts and native quarters were at the same time bombarded. Scenes of the wildest confusion ensued, for not only was the town under the fire of the cannon of the warship, but the tribes from the interior had taken advantage of the panic to invade and pillage the place. Every sort of atrocity and horror was perpetrated, and Casablanca was a prey to loot and every kind of crime.

The European force was sufficient to protect the Consulates, and the greater part of the Christian population escaped murder. When order was restored, the town presented a pitiful aspect. I saw it a very few days after the bombardment, and the scene was indescribable – a confusion of dead people and horses, while the contents of almost every house seemed to have been hurled into the streets and destroyed ... Many of the houses had been burned and gutted. Out of dark cellars, Moors and Jews, hidden since the first day of the bombardment, many of them wounded, were creeping, pale and terrified ... Blood was everywhere. In what had once been the poorer quarter of the town ... I only met one living soul, a mad woman – dishevelled, dirty but smiling – who kept calling, 'Ayesha, my little daughter; my little son Ahmed, where are you: I am calling you'.

It was the beginning of the French occupation of Morocco. ∎

in 1912. General Lyautey, previously the French commander of Oran, was appointed the first French resident-general.

He pursued a programme aimed at expanding Casablanca as the main port and economic centre of the new protectorate.

It was largely his ideas on public works and the layout of the new city that made Casablanca what it is today.

Orientation

Casablanca is a huge, modern metropolis. However, with few of the complications posed by the arcane medinas of the cities of the interior, it is easy enough to find your way around.

The heart of the city is Place des Nations Unies (formerly Place Mohammed V).

From this large traffic roundabout at the southern end of the medina, the city's main streets branch out – Ave des Forces Armées Royales (FAR), Ave Moulay Hassan I, Ave Hassan II, Blvd Houphouet Boigny and Blvd Mohammed V.

Casa-Port train station lies about 600m north of this main square, at the end of Blvd Houphouet Boigny. The CTM bus station is about 600m east of the square on Rue Léon L'Africain.

The city's main administrative buildings are clustered around Place Mohammed V. Just to the south-west are the carefully maintained lungs of the city centre – the Parc de la Ligue Arabe.

West of the gardens lies the exclusive suburb of Anfa, the site of the original medieval Berber town.

The main bus station (non-CTM) is a few kilometres south-east of Place des Nations Unies, just off Rue Liberté, while the principal train station, Casa-Voyageurs, is about 4km east of the town centre off Blvd Mohammed V.

Most of Casablanca's budget and mid-range hotels are in the area bounded by Ave des FAR, Ave Hassan II, Ave Lalla Yacout (named after the mother of King Mohammed V, Hassan II's predecessor) and Blvd Hassan Seghir.

Visible, street prostitution is an unaccustomed sight in Muslim countries, but Casablanca offers this dubious attraction in abundance. The 'red light' district extends over a surprisingly large part of the central area and for every *fille de joie*, there seems to be a pimp.

The atmosphere at night is decidedly seedy and travellers (particularly women) should take care walking in these areas after dark. Occasional attempts by the police to clear the area appear to have made little impression.

Street Names Casablanca is undergoing a name-change nightmare, and it is not uncommon to strike three versions for the one street. It is largely a matter of Arabisation, but there are a few other spanners in the works.

The two main squares – Place des Nations Unies and Place Mohammed V (on Ave Hassan II) – have had their names swapped around by royal decree.

Worse, what is now known as Place des Nations Unies sometimes seems to take the name of the street linking it to Casa-Port train station (Houphouet Boigny) – itself a recent change.

Where possible, the latest names (or what seem to be the latest names) appear on the maps, but be aware of the problem if you buy local street directories.

Information

Tourist Offices The Délégation Régionale du Tourisme or ONMT (☎ 271177) is at 55 Rue Omar Slaoui, off Ave Hassan II south of the city centre.

The Syndicat d'Initiative is at 98 Blvd Mohammed V, on the corner of Rue Chaoui. Neither will overwhelm you with useful information, but the Syndicat has the advantage of being open on weekends.

The ONMT is open from 8.30 am to noon and 2.30 to 6.30 pm Monday to Thursday, and on Friday from 8.30 to 11.30 am and from 3 to 6.30 pm.

The Syndicat has the same hours Monday to Friday, and is also open from 9 am to noon on Saturday.

NTH ATLANTIC COAST

Foreign Consulates The main consulates are in the area to the south-west of Place Mohammed V:

Belgium
13 Blvd Rachidi (☎ 223049). It's open Monday to Friday from 9 am to noon.
France
Rue Prince Moulay Abdallah (☎ 265355). Hours are Monday to Friday from 8.45 to 11.45 am and 2.45 to 4.45 pm.
Germany
42 Ave des FAR (☎ 314872). It's open Monday to Friday from 8 to 11.30 am.
Italy
21 Ave Hassan Souktani (☎ 277558). The office is open Monday to Friday from 9.30 am to noon.
Spain
31 Rue d'Alger (☎ 220752, 276379; fax 205048). The office is open Monday to Friday from 8 am to 1 pm.
Switzerland
43 Blvd d'Anfar (☎ 205856; fax 205855). It's open Monday to Friday from 8 to 10 am.
UK
60 Blvd d'Anfa (☎ 221653; fax 265779). The office is open Monday to Friday from 8 to 11.20 am.
USA
8 Blvd Moulay Youssef (☎ 264550; fax 204127). It's open Monday to Friday from 8.20am to 1.30 pm.

Money There are plenty of banks in Casablanca, so changing money should pose no problems. A few are marked on the maps, including BMCE branches on Ave Lalla Yacout and Ave des FAR. They have ATMs.

There are also branches of the BMCE and Banque Populaire (with ATMs) at the Mohammed V international airport. Opening hours coordinate with flight arrivals (between 5 to 7 am until midnight).

American Express is represented by Voyages Schwarz (☎ 222946/7) at 112 Rue Prince Moulay Abdallah.

If you're stuck for money outside regular banking hours, try one of the big hotels, such as the Hôtel Safir on Ave des FAR or the Hyatt Regency on Place des Nations Unies.

Post & Communications The main post office is at the junction of Blvd de Paris and Hassan II. The front of the building is closed off, so entrance is through a side-door. It's open from 8 am to 6.30 pm Monday to Friday and until noon on Saturday.

The poste restante counter shares the same section as the international telephones. The entrance to this part of the building is the third door along Blvd de Paris. The telephone service is open 24 hours a day and sells phonecards. They don't have phone books, but you can call ☎ 16 for information.

The parcel post office is further west along Blvd de Paris, opposite the music conservatory. The telex office is around the corner to the left.

The main post office building, erected in 1918, merits a look as part of the impressive array of Moorish administrative edifices that face onto the Mohammed V square. Marshal Lyautey opened the post office in June 1919 – the commemorative plaque is inside, to the right of the entrance. Another post office can be found near the Youth Hostel in the medina.

The Hôtel Sheraton (☎ 317878) at 100 Ave des FAR, has recently opened the city's first Cyber Café. An hour on the Web will cost you Dr50. The cafe is open every day from 9 am to 10 pm (until 7 pm on Sunday), but it's a good idea to come outside weekends as it can get very busy.

Travel Agencies There are innumerable travel agencies squeezed into the same area as the bulk of the hotels. The Carlson Wagonlits representative (☎ 203051) is at 60-62 Rue El Araibi Jilali (Ex Rue de Foucould). Transmediterranea and Intercona (☎ 221737) have a representative on Place 16 du Novembre.

Wasteels (☎ 314060) at 26 Rue Léon L'Africain, by the CTM bus station, is a good place for cheap intercontinental rail tickets. Comanav (☎ 312050) takes bookings for boats from Tangier to France and is at 43 Ave des FAR. Supratours (☎ 277160), the bus service of the ONCF railway company, is in the Centre 2000 next to the Casa-Port train station.

Bookshops & Newsstands Casablanca is a little disappointing for the bibliophile. For books in English, the best bet is the American Language Center bookshop (☎ 277765, 275270) at 1 Place de la Fraternité, just down from the US consulate. The English Forum (☎ 269846), at 27 Rue Mouftaker Abdelkader, is aimed mainly at students of English, but has a reasonable selection of novels (mainly classics). Otherwise, try the Librairie Farairre, on the corner of Blvd Mohammed V and Rue Araibi Jilali.

There are several reasonable newsstands around Place des Nations Unies, Casa-Port and Casa-Voyageurs train stations, and in the big hotels. The one across the road from the Hôtel Excelsior is as good as any.

A free weekly publication worth picking up is 7 Jours à Casa. It's a small magazine, but has some useful local listings of restaurants, cinemas, shows and events, as well as the odd interesting article (providing you read French). The tourist offices should have copies and it is often lying around in hotels and more expensive restaurants.

Casablanca is also the easiest place to encounter La Quinzaine du Maroc, a more comprehensive listings booklet covering the main cities throughout Morocco.

Film & Photography There are quite a few places where you can buy film or have it developed, including in the Centre 2000, by Casa-Port train station and along Blvd Mohammed V.

Cultural Centres Several countries maintain cultural centres in Casablanca. The Institut Français (☎ 259078) is at 121 Blvd Mohammed Zerktouni, south of the city centre. It runs films, lectures and other events, and have a library. It's open from Tuesday to Saturday from 9 am to 2.30 pm.

The German version, the Goethe Institut (☎ 200445), right on Place du 16 Novembre, is a more modest affair. They conduct German classes and also put on the occasional film.

The Centro Cultural Español (☎ 267337) is next door to the Spanish consulate at 31 Rue d'Alger. Its library is open on weekdays from 10 am to 1 pm and 4 to 6 pm.

Language Schools The American Language Center (☎ 277765, 275270), at 1 Place de la Fraternité, might be your best hope for finding work teaching English in Casablanca. Failing this, you could try the Centre International d'Étude de Langues (☎ 441989; fax 441960) on the 4th floor, Dar Mabrouka, Place de la Victoire.

Hairdresser If you're in need of a haircut, you can try the Coiffure Dali (☎ 313871) near the Majestic Hôtel at 55-58 Ave Lalla Yacout. Mr Dali is French-trained and charges Dr50/20 for women/men.

Medical Services & Emergencies There are several decent hospitals in Casablanca. Among them is the CHU Averroès (Ibn Rochd; ☎ 224109), on Ave du Médecin Général Braun, south of the city centre.

For medical emergencies, ring SOS Médecins Maroc (☎ 444444). The doctors operate around the clock and can come to your hotel.

There's a night pharmacy on the corner of Place Oued al-Makhazine and Blvd d'Anfa. The local French-language newspapers list other pharmacies. The police can be contacted on ☎ 19.

Medina

The medina, although comparatively small, is definitely worth a little time and is a pleasant, bright place to stroll around.

If you want to get to the Chleuh Mosque, the old city's main Friday mosque, just follow Rue Chakab Arsalane and its continuation.

For shopping in the medina, see the Things to Buy entry later in this section.

A pleasant spot for a cup of coffee is down on Place de l'Amiral Philibert, where the youth hostel is located.

Hassan II Mosque

North of the medina and rising up on a point above the Atlantic ocean, the Hassan II Mosque is the biggest religious monument in the world after Mecca. It was finished in August 1993 (in time for Hassan II's 60th birthday) after 6000 Moroccan craftsmen worked on it day and night for five years.

Designed by the French architect, Michel Pinseau, the mosque itself can hold 25,000 worshippers. Up to 80,000 more can be held in the esplanades around it. Hassan wanted the highest minaret in the world and, at 210m, it is visible from miles around. At night, the powerful laser beams projected from the top of the minaret in the direction of Mecca form quite a spectacle.

No less high-tech is the interior of the mosque, fitted out with a centrally heated floor, electric doors and a sliding roof.

Box: Tracery with repeated lozenge motif.

Below: The intricate ornamentation of the facade and minaret.

The vast prayer hall is said to be large enough to house Notre-Dame or St Peter's comfortably and, if the exterior is French-inspired, the interior is all Moroccan. Cedarwood was brought in from the Middle Atlas, marble from Agadir and granite from Tafraoute. The best master craftsmen in the country were assembled and put to work on it, producing astonishing wood carving, zellij work and stucco moulding.

FRANCES LINZEE GORDON

The mosque is said to have cost nearly US$800 million and, remarkably, was paid for largely by public subscription. Although you will occasionally hear mutterings about how this vast sum might have been better spent, most Moroccans, particularly from Casablanca, are very proud of their modern monument. For many it's living proof that the world-famous Moroccan craftsmen have lost none of their ancient mastery. In many homes and shops, you will see little certificates displayed as a testimony to their personal contribution.

The mosque is well worth a visit and has the added attraction of being one of the very few religious buildings open to non-Muslims. It also provides a welcome breath of fresh, sea air away from the noise and pollution of the city.

Guided Tours It's only possible to see the mosque by taking a guided tour and visitors must be 'decently and respectfully dressed'. Don't forget to remove your shoes – you'll be handed a plastic bag in which to carry them.

There are four tours each day (except Friday) at 9, 10 and 11 am and 2 pm (2.30 pm during summer). Tours are in French, Spanish and English, but French is the most common. If you want to be sure of a tour in your language, arrive early. The circuit takes in the prayer hall, ablution rooms, the hammam and the Turkish baths (not yet open) and lasts about an hour. Prices are Dr100 (Dr50 for school and university students with a card). For details, contact Mme Widad on ☎ 222563.

The easiest way to the mosque is along Blvd des Almohades (which turns into Blvd Sidi Mohammed ben Abdallah) from near Casa-Port train station. It's about a 20 minute walk.

You may run into the occasional kid asking for pens. Try to resist the temptation to oblige them. Also keep a keen eye on your belongings, as things have a habit of disappearing. A petit taxi from the centre should cost around Dr10.

Left : Detail of carved, painted cedar door.

Below: Horseshoe arch and ablution fountain.

FRANCES LINZEE GORDON

FRANCES LINZEE GORDON

Nouvelle Medina & Royal Palace

A kilometre south-east of town is the nouvelle medina, also known as the Quartier Habous. It was built by the French in the 1930s in an attempt to sort out the housing crisis.

The French architects tried to marry the best features of traditional Moroccan architecture with modern techniques and facilities. The result is a kind of idealised French version of a Moroccan medina and, while a bit twee, is nevertheless attractive.

For the souvenir hunter, the nouvelle medina houses a large collection of bazaars and craft shops. Although it lacks the vitality of the old medina, the nouvelle medina does have a good selection of wares.

Bordering the boulevard to the north is the Royal Palace (closed to the public).

To get to the nouvelle medina, take bus No 4 or 40 from the local bus terminus (see the Casablanca map).

Ville Nouvelle

Place Mohammed V Formerly known as Place des Nations Unies, this animated square is flanked by what are probably the country's most impressive examples of Hispano-Moorish architecture. This French approximation of Arabo-Andalusian design has produced a not unhappy result.

The main buildings of interest are the post office (on the western side), the law courts (on the eastern side and a little further south) and the préfecture (police headquarters), closing off the southern side of the square.

What is now the fenced-off rear of the French consulate lies between the last two buildings and contains a statue of General Lyautey.

Parc de la Ligue Arabe The biggest park in the city, the Parc de la Ligue Arabe has an essentially French layout, although the flora is more faithful to its location in Africa. It is an extremely pleasant place to walk, take a leisurely coffee or enjoy the diversions of the Yasmina amusement park. Entry is Dr1.50.

Cathédrale du Sacré Cœur Built in 1930, the somewhat neglected former cathedral is an unexpected sight in the heart of a Muslim city and symbolic of modern Casablanca's essentially European genesis.

Sitting on the edge of the Parc de la Ligue Arabe, it reflects the best of the more adventurous architectural products of the Art Deco era. Deconsecrated some time ago, it has been converted into a school.

Beaches

Casablanca's beaches are west of town along Blvd de la Corniche, at the end of which (where it becomes Blvd de Biarritz) begins the affluent beachside suburb of 'Ain Diab. It's a trendy area, lined with four-star hotels, upmarket restaurants, bars, coffee shops and nightclubs, and you may feel a little out of place unless you dress accordingly and have a wallet to match.

In high summer the beaches are generally covered wall-to-wall with chic Casablancans, but for the rest of the year you can usually find some space pretty much to yourself at the southern end of 'Ain Diab. When it's not crowded, the beaches are perfectly all right, although they are better suited to a lazy afternoon than a 'beach holiday'. For the latter, you are better off heading further south-west towards Essaouira.

Bus No 9 takes you along the southern end of the beaches at 'Ain Diab from the local bus terminal at Place Oued al-Makhazine, just to the west of Place des Nations Unies.

Sidi Abderrahman

A few kilometres south of the 'Ain Diab beaches, atop a tiny rocky outcrop jutting into the Atlantic, is the small marabout and settlement of Sidi Abderrahman. At high tide, it's cut off from the mainland, but otherwise you can stumble across the rocks.

Non-Muslims are not allowed into the shrine itself, but you can walk past the handful of houses and sit down to look out over the ocean. It's about a half-hour walk along the beach south of the No 9 bus terminal at 'Ain Diab.

Language Courses

If you want to learn Arabic, there are a number of private schools in the city.

One with a good reputation is École Assimil (☎ 312567), close to the Hôtel Touring on Rue Allal ben Abdallah. They have regular day and evening classes, and also offer private tuition.

Places to Stay – bottom end

Camping Campers should head for *Camping de l'Oasis* (☎ 253367) on Ave Mermoz. It's a long way from the centre (9km out on the P8 road to El-Jadida) so unless you have your own transport, it's hardly worth it, although bus No 31 runs past it. It charges around Dr10 per person, per car and per tent.

About 18km along the road to Azemmour, south-west of Casablanca, is *Camping Tamaris* (☎ 330060) which charges Dr8.25 per person per night. It has a pool, bar, restaurant, grocery store and laundry facilities.

Hostel The *youth hostel* (☎ 220551 fax 227677), at 6 Place de l'Amiral Philibert, faces a small, leafy square just inside the medina, off Blvd des Almohades.

It's quite a large place, with 58 dormitory beds, and is comfortable and clean. The director, Hariss, manages the place like a school master – efficiently and with great pride.

It costs Dr40/42 per person with/without a membership card, including breakfast. They also have six 'family rooms' (large double rooms with space for extra beds) which are good value for Dr100. Guests can use the kitchen facilities and there are hot showers.

It's open from 8 to 10 am and from noon until curfew time at 11 pm (midnight in summer).

From Casa-Port train station, walk out to the first major intersection and then turn right along Blvd des Almohades. Turn left when you get to the second opening in the medina wall. Go through it and you'll see the hostel on the right.

Hotels – Medina All the hotels in the medina are unclassified.

The majority are cheap (around Dr40), very basic and uninviting. For a little more money, you can find something better in the centre of town.

For the medina die-hards, there are a number of hotels clustered around the little square between Rue Centrale (or Rue al-Markiziya) and Rue de Fès (or Rue Mohammed al-Hansaly) in an interesting part of the medina. They are very basic and usually pretty grubby and noisy.

About the best of these is the *Hôtel Des Amis* (☎ 475899). Rooms are at least clean, but as is usual in these places, there is just one cold shower. Singles/doubles cost Dr40/60.

Hotels – Central Casablanca During the months June, July and particularly August, a lot of the lower-end hotels are full, so it is best to make reservations in advance or arrive in the morning, between 8 am and noon.

Many of the lower-end hotels have just one shower (usually cold) shared between up to 25 rooms. Many of the hotels are located in the red-light district, so women should be careful when returning to the hotel at night.

The *Hôtel du Palais* (☎ 276191) at 68 Rue Farhat Hachad, near the French Consulate, offers about the best value for money you'll find.

It has clean and spacious rooms, some with balconies, for Dr62, Dr76 and Dr111 for singles, doubles and triples respectively. The showers are communal and cold. The place is popular and often full.

If price is the main concern, you could try the *Hôtel Volubilis* (☎ 207789) at 20-2 Rue Abdel Karim Diouri. Rooms come with a table, washbasin and bidet. They're OK, if a little on the musty side, and cost Dr60/90.

There's a cluster of cheapies on and around Rue Allal ben Abdallah. Virtually across the road from one another are the *Hôtel Kon Tiki* (☎ 314927) and the *Hôtel*

NTH ATLANTIC COAST

Touring (☎ 310216) at No 87. The former is pretty ordinary, with rooms at Dr62/76 (Dr6 extra for a hot shower). The latter is adequate with clean rooms and big beds. Singles/doubles cost Dr63/78 (Dr7 for a hot shower).

South of Rue Allal ben Abdallah, at No 38 Rue Chaoui, is the pleasant and clean *Hôtel Colbert* (☎ 314241). It's an excellent choice and offers singles, doubles and triples, without shower or toilet, for Dr63, Dr78 and Dr114 respectively. With bathroom it's Dr84, Dr100 and Dr130. It may not look like much from the outside, but as one of the best value places around, it is often booked out.

Two hotels that have long been popular with travellers are the unclassified *Hôtel du Périgord* (☎ 221085), at 56 Rue Araibi Jilali (ex-Rue Foucauld) and, virtually next door, the *Hôtel de Foucauld* (☎ 222666), at No 52. The former has rooms for Dr62, Dr82

and Dr127. The singles are pretty cramped, and the place has cold showers only, but it's OK for the money.

The Foucauld has singles/doubles without shower for Dr75/100, with shower for Dr110/140, and with shower and toilet for Dr125/155. It has a nice entrance hall and is very clean.

Further south, at 36 Rue Nationale, the *Hôtel du Louvre* (☎ 273747) is not a bad place, although some rooms are definitely better than others. Singles/doubles start at Dr50/70, rooms with shower cost Dr65/78, and those with private shower and toilet cost Dr80/110. Add Dr16 for taxes and a compulsory breakfast.

The best value of all in this category is the *Hôtel Rialto* (☎ 275122) at 9 Rue Salah Ben Bouchaib (just south of Blvd Mohammed V) which has doubles/singles with a basic shower for Dr84/112. The place, though simple, is well run and spotless. It's

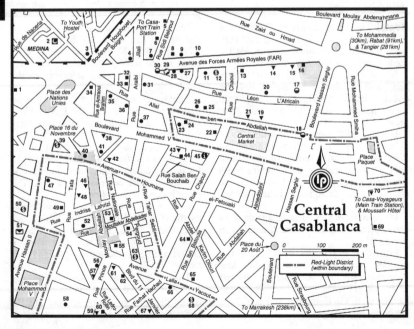

usually full, so you'll need to make a reservation here.

Places to Stay – middle

The jump in quality from one-star to two-star is quite startling. If you're prepared to pay about Dr170/220, you can choose from a number of places and end up with a very comfortable deal.

Possibly one of the first hotels you'll notice if you're walking up from Casa-Port train station is *Hôtel Excelsior* (☎ 200263), just off Place des Nations Unies at 2 Rue el-Amraoui Brahim (ex-Nolly). It's OK, but is cashing in on its fast-fading status as one of Casablanca's former premier hotels. The common parts are very nice, but the rooms are a bit faded. Rooms come with a phone, and breakfast is included, but for the price you can find better. Singles/doubles with shower cost Dr169/215. Those with a bathroom go for Dr205/264.

The *Hôtel du Centre* (☎ 446180; fax 446178), just off Ave des FAR, offers better value than the Excelsior. It smells a little damp, but has clean, modern rooms with bathroom and phone for Dr176/206.

If you prefer a bit more atmosphere, you could take a look at the *Hôtel Majestic* (☎ 446285; fax 446285), at 55 Ave Lalla Yacout, whose foyer is decorated after the fashion of the Merenid era.

The rooms are a little faded and include a shower and toilet, plus a (usually) non-functioning lamp and phone. They cost Dr160/180 plus taxes and breakfast. Ask to

NTH ATLANTIC COAST

PLACES TO STAY		
1 Hyatt Regency Hotel	19 Brasserie La Bavaroise	29 German Consulate
5 Hôtel Toubkal	21 Restaurant de	30 Petit Taxi Rank
6 Hôtel du Centre	l'Étoile Marocaine	31 Hertz (Car Rental)
8 Hôtel Royal Mansour	38 McDonald's	35 Air Algerie
13 Hôtel Sheraton;	42 Pâtisserie Le Viennois	36 Carlson Wagonlits
Cyber Café (Internet)	43 Restaurant Au Petit	(Travel Agency)
16 Hôtel Safir	Poucet	37 Librairie Farairre
22 Hôtel Colbert; Rôtisseries	46 Restaurant Le Tonkin	(Bookshop)
24 Hôtel Kon Tiki; Bar Ben	48 Restaurant Snack	39 Wafabank
Omar (Fruit Juice Bar)	Bar California	40 Transmediterranea
25 Hôtel Touring;	57 Igloo Pâtisserie	& Interconal (Travel
Restaurant Point Central	59 Restaurant Al-Mounia	Agencies)
32 Hôtel de Foucauld	61 Café National	41 Goethe Institut
33 Hôtel du Périgord	67 Pâtisserie de l'Opéra	45 Tourist Office; Post Office
34 Hôtel Excelsior	70 Restaurant Le Marignan	47 Exposition Nationale
44 Hôtel Rialto		d'Artisinat
49 Hôtel de Lausanne	**OTHER**	50 Citibank
53 Hôtel du Louvre	2 Al-Djemma Mosque	51 Main Post Office
54 Hôtel Guynemer	3 Clock Tower	52 English Forum Bookshop
55 Hôtel de Paris; Swiss	4 Air France	56 Voyages Schwarz
Ice Cream Factory	7 Iberia Airlines	(American Express);
60 Hôtel Astrid	9 Avis (Car Rental)	Pâtisserie Triomphe
62 Hôtel de Noailles	10 Comanav (Travel	58 Law Courts
64 Hôtel Volubilis	Agency)	63 BMCE Bank (ATMs)
65 Hôtel Majestic; Cinéma	11 Budget (Car Rental)	66 Le Comptoire Marocain
Lux; Coiffure Dali	12 BMCE Bank (ATMs)	de Distribution de
Hairdresser	17 CTM Bus Station	Disques (Music Shop)
69 Hôtel Métropole	18 Grands Taxis for Rabat	68 BMCI Bank
	20 Wasteels (Travel Agency)	
PLACES TO EAT	23 Car Rental Companies	
14 Cafe	26 École Assimil	
15 Bar Nueva	27 Royal Air Maroc	
	28 Europcar (Car Rental)	

see several rooms, as some are definitely better than others. This hotel is in the very heart of the red-light district and at night its bar gets fairly rowdy (until it shuts down at around 1 am).

A very good place, along much the same lines as the Hôtel du Centre, is the *Hôtel de Lausanne* (☎ 268690) at 24 Rue Tata (ex-Rue Poincaré). Its 31 spotless rooms, each with full bathroom, carpeting and phone, cost Dr181/216 for a single/double. There is a more luxurious double room (No 19) available for Dr300. The sign outside the hotel is written in Arabic on one side and English on the other.

There are a couple of surprise packets away from the city centre. The *Hôtel Astrid* (☎ 277803; fax 293372), at 12 Rue Ledru-Rollin off Rue Prince Moulay Abdallah, has good, clean and quiet rooms with en suite bathroom, and some with balconies for Dr181, Dr216 and Dr282. The paint job on the doors is a little on the garish side, though.

Moving into the three-star bracket, there is the excellent and well situated *Hôtel de Paris* (☎ 273871; fax 29 8069), on Rue Ech-Cherie Amziane (Ex Rue Branly) in the pedestrian zone off Rue Prince Moulay Abdallah. The hotel is decorated in the traditional style and the spotless rooms have heating, phones, TV and plenty of hot water. They cost Dr274/331.

At 22 Blvd du 11 Janvier, is the somewhat more expensive *Hôtel de Noailles* (☎ 260583; fax 220589). It has very clean, elegant rooms for Dr228/276 and the tearoom (open until 9.30 pm) on the 1st floor is a very civilised affair indeed.

The *Hôtel Métropole* (☎ 301213; fax 305801), at 89 Rue Mohammed Smiha (see the Casablanca map), is a reasonable alternative to the above if you are having problems finding a room. It costs Dr274/286 with bathroom and TV.

As usual, the *Moussafir Hôtel* (☎ 401984; fax 400799) chain is represented, just outside Casa-Voyageurs train station. Its modern, comfortable rooms go for Dr272/327.

The *Hôtel Guynemer* (☎ 275764; fax 473999), at 2 Rue Mohammed Belloul (Ex Rue Pegoud), has been recently refurbished and upgraded to a three-star rating. It has comfortable singles/doubles with bathroom and satellite TV for Dr274/330. Breakfast is an extra Dr31.

The best value of all at the top-end of this category is the four-star *Hôtel al-Mounia* (☎ 203211; fax 203323) at 24 Blvd de Paris, opposite the main post office (see the Casablanca map). It has excellent singles/doubles for Dr274/331.

Places to Stay – top end

Most of Casablanca's top-end hotels are on Ave des FAR. Just off the avenue, at 9 Rue Sidi Belyout, is the four-star *Hôtel Toubkal* (☎ 311414; fax 311146). It has singles/doubles from Dr617/749 which are quite good value in this category, although some travellers have complained of the service.

Of the five-star hotels are the traditional-style *Hôtel Royal Mansour* (☎ 313011; fax 314818) at 27 Ave des FAR, which has singles/doubles from Dr1700/2200; and the *Hôtel Sheraton* (☎ 317878; fax 315136) at No 100 with singles/doubles for Dr2200/2400.

Right on Place des Nations Unies is the five-star *Hyatt Regency Hôtel* (☎ 261234; fax 220180) with rooms for the same price.

Most other top-end hotels overlook the beaches along Blvd de la Corniche.

They include *Hôtel Tarik* (☎ 391373; fax 367593) at no 41, the *Hôtel de la Corniche* (☎ 363011; fax 391110) and *Hôtel Suisse* (☎ 360202). All of them charge 423/568 for rooms.

More expensive, and the best of the lot by the beach, is the five-star *Hôtel Riad Salam* (☎ 391313; fax 391345) which charges Dr1364/1528. Facilities include a pool, health club and thalassotherapy (seawater bathing) centre.

Swimming Pools

The Hyatt Regency Hôtel has a pool which is open to non-guests for a steep Dr150 per day. It's open every day from May until September from 7 am to 7 pm.

NTH ATLANTIC COAST

Hammams

There is no shortage of hammams in Casa, with at least one in every *quartier* (neighbourhood) of the city. In the medina, there are a couple of hammams and public showers (douches) for men and women around Place de l'Amiral Philibert.

In the ville nouvelle, one that is reasonably central and clean is the Hammam Essanoibar at 70 Rue Essanoibar. One half is for men and the other for women, and each has its own door. The baths cost Dr6 and a complete head-to-toe, plus massage, costs Dr20. The door attendant speaks only Arabic, but if you hand him the right amount, he should let you in. It's open every day from 6 am to 11pm.

If you prefer something a bit grander or fancy a bit of pampering, you could try one of the big hotels, some of which have hammams open to non-guests. The most luxurious of these is the hammam at the Hôtel Riad Salam on the Corniche.

Places to Eat

Casablanca has the greatest variety of places to eat in Morocco. Restaurants range from cheap and cheerful seafood places to gastronomique French tables, with a whole host of African, Middle-Eastern and Oriental places in between.

Prices, even at the more expensive tables, are reasonable by western standards and even on the tightest budget you shouldn't go hungry.

Central Casablanca The best place for cheap restaurants, particularly rôtisseries (roast chicken places), is the area opposite the Central Market on Rue Chaoui.

Restaurants are cheek-by-jowl and the best thing is to peruse them until one takes your fancy. The number of people seated outside a place is the most obvious indication of its quality. Most restaurants stay open until 2 am and, for around Dr15 to Dr25, you can get a generous sandwich with meat, chips and salad to take away. A sit-down meal will cost you around Dr40.

A more upmarket snackbar serving delicious Lebanese snacks, including sandwiches for Dr22 and shwarma kebabs for Dr45, is the literally 'new' *Bar Nueva* between the Sheraton and Safir hotels.

Close by, next door to the Hôtel Touring, is the *Restaurant Point Central* which does a popular midday tajine for Dr15. It also serves thick harira soup for just Dr3, salads for Dr4 and quarters of chicken plus chips for Dr18. On Friday, it usually runs up a decent couscous too.

The Restaurant *Au Petit Poucet*, next to Le Matin newspaper on Blvd Mohammed V, is a die-hard relic of 1920s France and has become a bit of an institution. Look out for the letters posted on the wall from Saint-Exupéry, the French author and aviator, thanking the patron for his delicious food. He used to spend time here between mail-flights south across the Sahara on the Toulouse to Chile service.

Some travellers have highly recommended the snack bar *La Fleur Verte* at 88 Ave Mers Sultan, just down from the restaurant L'Entrecôte (see the Casablanca map). They do couscous on Friday and have sandwiches for Dr14 and brochettes for Dr34.

One of the best places for cheap, tasty grub is the *Restaurant Snack Bar California* at 19 Rue Tata (ex Poincaré). It's a clean, bright and pleasant place, recently redecorated in the traditional style. Harira costs Dr6, tajine from Dr30 and delicious brochettes served with two types of vegetables plus chips costs Dr30. They also do vegetarian dishes such as vegetable couscous or tajine (Dr30). It's a peaceful and relaxing place for women travellers.

If you're after traditional Moroccan food in traditional surroundings, the *Restaurant Al-Mounia* (☎ 222669) at 95 Rue du Prince Moulay Abdallah is the best place in town for a splurge. There is a lovely, cool garden at the front where you can dine under the shade of an ancient faux-poire (false pear) tree. The interior of the restaurant is air-conditioned in summer. Main courses cost from Dr80 to Dr130 and vegetable dishes are available. The food is excellent.

For those on a tighter budget, the unlicensed *Restaurant de l'Étoile Marocaine* (☎ 314100), at 107 Rue Allal Ben Abdallah not far from the Hôtel Touring, is an excellent alternative to the Al-Mounia.

It serves decent Moroccan food in traditional surroundings and is a very friendly little place. A good variety of dishes is on offer, including occasionally a delicious pastilla (pigeon pie) for Dr48. If you've yet to try this dish, don't miss it here. The restaurant is open in the evening until 11 pm and the waiters will walk lone women travellers back to their hotel.

If you're hankering after south-east Asian food, you could head for *Restaurant Le Tonkin* at 34 Rue Prince Moulay Abdallah (☎ 291913), on the pedestrian mall.

Another is *La Pagode* (☎ 277185) at 98 Rue Farhat Hachad, which is close to the Hôtel du Palais (see the Casablanca map). A main course at either will cost you around Dr70.

On the other hand, you could try the Korean/Vietnamese restaurant, *Le Marignan* (☎ 316199), at 69 Rue Mohammed Smiha, on the corner of Blvd Mohammed V (see the Casablanca map).

It has main courses for around Dr60 and the house speciality is food cooked sur plaques (Japanese style) in front of guests. It's open until midnight every day and is air-conditioned.

For a little more money, you could have an excellent French meal at the *Brasserie La Bavaroise* (☎ 311760) at 129 Rue Allal Ben Abdallah. Manu, the French chef, prides himself on his daily *plat de jour* which ranges from pheasant pâté to duck conserve and wild boar stew (all around Dr70 to Dr100). Desserts include profiteroles and chocolate mousse – heavenly if you haven't seen them for a while.

For seafood, head straight for the *Taverne du Dauphin* (☎ 221200) at 115 Blvd Houphouet Boigny (see the Casablanca map). It was founded in 1958 by a French lady from Marseilles and is now run by her grandson, the charming Jean-Claude and his wife.

It may not look much, and you'll have to push through to the tables at the back of the restaurant (which are much more pleasant), but the food is fresh, beautifully cooked and not overly expensive.

A fish fillet will cost around Dr65, calamares Dr45 and unbelievably delicious grilled Dublin prawns Dr46 per 100g (enough for a starter). They also have a good selection of beer, spirits and wine. If you don't fancy a full meal, you can pop in for a snack at the bar at the front of the restaurant.

'Ain Diab For seafood in a totally different atmosphere, you could head out to the beaches and 'Ain Diab. *Le Cabestan, La Mer* and *La Petite Roche* are three of the more upmarket restaurants gathered around the El-Hank lighthouse. A meal will cost around Dr250.

The splurge of the city would have to be *A Ma Bretagne* (☎ 362111), a few hundred metres south of Sidi Abderrahman along the coastal road.

It is run by a French *maître cuisinier* (master chef), André Halbert, who concentrates on seafood specialities. It also has an excellent wine cellar.

Cafes There are a few cafes in the medina; perhaps the most pleasantly located is the *Central* on Place de l'Amiral Philibert (see the Casablanca map).

The city centre is filled with French-style cafes – some of them interesting examples of the Art Deco style.

Cafes are still largely the preserve of men, although the sight of a western woman sitting down for a coffee, especially at outdoor tables, shouldn't arouse too much attention.

Some women may still prefer the patisseries which are quieter and which attract a few local (accompanied) women.

A very pleasant spot for a coffee is at one of the string of cafes in the northern part of the Parc de la Ligue Arabe (see the Casablanca map). It's also an excellent spot for a picnic.

Patisseries, Ice Cream & Fruit Juice Bars *L'Oliveri* at 132 Avenue Hassan II (south of the city centre) is considered the best *glacier* (ice cream parlour) in Casa.

There is not a huge selection of flavours – about 10 – but the quality is high. A *coupe* (small tub) costs Dr20. There's also a good selection of ice-cream cakes, milkshakes and fruit juices which you can enjoy in the genteel tea room. It also makes a good refuge from the heat and the traffic outside.

The Swiss Ice Cream Factory next to the Hôtel de Paris, is a new place popular with the young.

The ice cream is home-made and as good as, if not better than, L'Oliveri's. It's open every day from 7 am to 9.30 pm. Both places are very good for women travellers to unwind.

The *Pâtisserie Triomphe* next door to the Voyage Schwarz, has an excellent selection of sticky cakes to take away and is a favourite among the locals.

Better known, and still centrally located, are *Pâtisserie Le Viennois*, in the Passage Summica off Ave Houmane el-Fetouaki, and *Pâtisserie de l'Opéra*, at 50 Blvd 11 Janvier.

The latter is run by a German-gone-local and is a civilised, tranquil place, great for a quiet coffee or tea (from a real teacup!) Fresh bread is baked on the premises.

There is a good fruit juice bar in the Centre 2000. An even better one is the *Bar Ben Omar*, next to the Hôtel Kontiki, which serves a wide selection of juices from Dr5 to Dr8 and good, fresh cakes.

Fast Food If you can't do without a Big Mac (although it's poor value compared with local fare), then Casa-blanca's a good place to be. *McDonald's* is doing very well in Morocco among bourgeois families (who can't resist the gimmicky toys) and two more have sprung up in the last couple of years.

There are branches at 6 Blvd de la Corniche (the continuation of Blvd Sidi Mohammed ben Abdallah which runs past the Hassan II Mosque), off the roundabout at the end of Ave Mers Sultan (at No 53), and at No 8 Blvd Mohammed V.

For *Pizza Hut*, head for Place de la Fraternité, near the American Language Center.

Self-Catering There is a supermarket on Blvd Rahal el-Meskini, close to the Mers Sultan roundabout.

The Central Market, between Blvd Mohammed V and Ave Allal ben Abdallah, is well known for the variety, quality and freshness of its produce. It's a great place for a do-it-yourself lunch.

Entertainment
Cinemas There are about half a dozen cinemas around the city centre. The Cinema Lynx (☎ 220229) at 50 Ave Mers Sultan, although not the largest (with just one salon), is considered the best in town.

The salon is spacious and comfortable and has an excellent DTS sound system. Tickets cost Dr35/25/20 for seats in the *Club/Balcon/Orchestre*. You can quite often catch films only recently released in the west, although there are no guarantees about what is cut out. Those films that are not French are generally dubbed into that language.

Nightclubs Nightlife in Casablanca can seem rather disappointing. Basically, there are three alternatives. First you've got the seedy cabaret joints in downtown Casa. Second, there are the more upmarket places that are concentrated out in the 'Ain Diab, but they are expensive (at least Dr100 to get in, the same for a drink), less accessible and can be picky about dress code. The last option for a night out is at the hotel bars, but they're also on the expensive side and can be a bit predictable.

Prostitutes work all of these places, particularly the cabarets, and men will be expected (at least) to pay for the drinks of any woman who befriends them. Women travellers shouldn't expect hassle-free drinking anywhere, although of the three, the hotel bars are about the best bet.

Of these, about the best are the *Caesar* at the Sheraton and *Black House* at the Hyatt. They generally get swinging from about 11 pm until 3 pm. Entry costs Dr120/150 during the week/weekend and drinks are around the same price.

A new place, and less easy to categorise, is the *Cage* disco in the Centre 2000. It's a popular place with the young, and entry costs around Dr100 (though it varies according to the day of the week).

Gay travellers should head for *Le Village* in the Corniche, although don't expect anything too exciting. For a drink you could try *Armstrong's*, also in the Corniche.

Bars There is a popular misconception that Casablanca doesn't have many bars. Nothing could be further from the truth. The city centre is riddled with drinking establishments, usually under the guise of cafes, bars, brasseries or even pharmacies, and some have been marked on the maps.

Almost all are spit and sawdust places, and attract a male-only clientele (plus prostitutes) that can be a little rough around the edges (this is a port after all). Most close around 6.30 pm. The most pleasant best of the local bars is the one in the Au Petit Poucet restaurant on Blvd Mohammed V.

Somewhat more refined and, like the discos, a better option for women, are the bars in the larger hotels which also stay open later.

One of the best of these is the *Bar Casablanca*, in the Hyatt, which is open from 10 am to 1 am. It has a happy hour, officially from 6.30 to 7.30 pm, but unofficially from 6 to 8 pm. Spirits, beer and soft drinks cost Dr70, Dr40 and Dr25 respectively, and during happy hour the second drink comes free. The place is plastered with posters and other references to the Humphrey Bogart classic, *Casablanca.*

Considered the hottest bar in town among the affluent, trendy set, is the *Villa Fadango* (☎ 398508) on Rue Hubert-Giron, close to the Restaurant Croc Magnon in the Corniche. It's a very popular latino-type bar serving up shots of tequila and Mexican beer. You'll need to be snappily dressed to get past the bouncers.

Things to Buy
The Exposition Nationale d'Artisanat on No 3 Avenue Hassan II (☎ 267064) has three floors of crafts, including leather goods, pottery and carpets. Prices are fixed, quality is not bad and they can ship goods to customers, but it's really just a place for getting an idea of quality and maximum prices to pay in the medina. It's open 8.30 am to 12.30 pm and 2.30 to 8 pm every day.

The Artisanat Fenouch (☎ 277287) at the Centre 2000 has a much more interesting and unusual variety of goods. Many crafts are of high quality, but unfortunately so also are the prices. Other branches of the shop can be found in the Hyatt Regency and Sheraton hotels.

In the medina, the busiest shopping areas are along Rue Chakab Arsalane and Rue de Fès. Such craft stalls as there are, mostly can be found outside the city walls (along Blvd Houphouet Boigny) and, just inside, on Rue Mohammed al-Hansali (which quickly changes its name to Rue de Fès).

Otherwise you could try the Habous or the area around the Royal Palace. Quality can be variable in these places and hard bargaining is definitely the order of the day.

If you want a new watch, this is the place to get it. Along with dope, watches seem to be the main illegal product on offer, and you're bound to be offered a good many 'Rolexes' during even a cursory visit.

For anyone with more than a passing interest in Moroccan music, a good place to go for LPs, cassettes and CDs is Le Comptoire Marocain de Distribution de Disques (☎ 369153), at 26 Ave Lalla Yacout opposite the Cinema Lux and close to the Hôtel Majestic (see the Central Casablanca map). They have, or can get, a pretty substantial range of recordings of most types of traditional Arab and Berber music.

Getting There & Away
Air From Casablanca's Mohammed V airport (30km south-east of the city), there are

Tanneries

Tanneries provide perhaps the greatest illustration of how resolutely some parts of Morocco have clung to practices developed in medieval times. Moroccan leather, and more particularly the Fassi leather produced in Fès, has for centuries been highly prized as among the finest in the world. One type of leather, a soft goatskin used mainly in bookbinding, is itself known (naturally enough) as *morocco*.

At the tanneries of Marrakesh and Fès, little has changed in centuries. Skins are still carried by donkey to the tanner's souq, tanning and dyeing vats are still constructed from mud brick and tile, the (strictly male) tannery workers are still organized according to medieval guild principles, and their health and safety practices are also scarily old-fashioned.

Along with being one of Morocco's (and the world's) oldest arts, with a history that stretches back at least 7000 years, leathermaking is undoubtedly also one of its smelliest. Rank odours abound at the tanneries of Fès el-Bali, and the delicate tourist who comes to view the work here will be offered a sprig of mint to hold to the nose and take the edge off the pong.

Among the exotic ingredients that add to the heady brew are pigeon poo, cow urine, fish oils, animal fats and brains, chromium salts and sulphuric acids.

Many travellers find that not only do they find the smell almost unbearable, but they also feel uncomfortably voyeuristic about their experience of viewing from the roof terraces the tannery workers tending the skins in the souq down below.

Still, a visit to the tanneries on the outskirts of the medinas of Fès and Marrakesh is right up there on the must-see list.

Carolyn Papworth

Box: Skins laid out to dry, Fès tanneries (photograph by Frances Linzee Gordon).

Right: A feast for the eyes and an assault on the nose, tanneries are best viewed high up and from a distance.

RICHARD I'ANSON

FRANCES LINZEE GORDON

FRANCES LINZEE GORDON

FRANCES LINZEE GORDON

RICHARD I'ANSON

Top Left: Dehairing is the first stage of tanning. The hair and extraneous flesh are first loosened in a bath of lime and water, and then scraped off, by hand or by machine.

Top Right: Red is the colour traditionally associated with Fès. Marrakesh's colour is yellow, while green is the colour of the Saharan Taureg, for whom it is magically related to the earth, fertility and healing.

Middle: Following their few days soaking in the tannic acids, hides are hung up or spread on the ground to dry, in preparation for the last three steps – dressing (lubrication), skiving (scraping and polishing) and dyeing.

Bottom: The tannery vats, Fès.

regular connections to most countries in Western Europe, as well as to West Africa, Algeria, Tunisia, Egypt and the Middle East.

Internally, the vast majority of Royal Air Maroc's flights go via Casablanca, so you can get to any destination directly from Casablanca. For instance, there are three to five daily flights to Agadir (Dr736, one hour), five weekly flights to Fès (Dr526, 50 minutes), at least two daily flights to Marrakesh (Dr451, 50 minutes) and at least one flight a day to Tangier (Dr571, one hour).

For detailed information on airport services and transport, see the Getting There & Away chapter and the Getting Around entries in the Casablanca and Rabat sections of this chapter.

Airlines flying into and out of Mohammed V international airport include:

Aeroflot
    47 Blvd Moulay Youssef (☎ 206410)
Air Afrique
    Tour des Habous, Ave des FAR (☎ 318379)
Air Algérie
    1 Rue el-Amraoui Brahim (☎ 266995)
Air France
    15 Ave des FAR (☎ 294040)
Alitalia
    Tour des Habous, Ave des FAR (☎ 314181)
British Airways/GB Airways
    Place Zellaqa (☎ 307629)
Iberia
    17 Ave des FAR (☎ 279600)
KLM
    6 Blvd Houphouet Boigny (☎ 203222)
Lufthansa
    Tour des Habous, Ave des FAR (☎ 312371)
Royal Air Maroc
    44 Ave des FAR (☎ 311122)
Sabena
    41 Ave des FAR (☎ 313991)
Swissair
    Tour des Habous, Ave des FAR (☎ 313280)
Tunis Air
    10 Ave des FAR (☎ 293452)

Bus – CTM The bus station (☎ 449224 for information) is on Rue Léon L'Africain, at the back of the Hôtel Safir (on Ave des FAR). They have a left-luggage counter which is open every day from 5 am to midnight.

There are regular CTM departures to Agadir (five times daily from 5.30 am to midnight), Essaouira (daily at 5.30 am and 5 pm), Fès/Meknès (every half hour from 7 am to 7 pm), Marrakesh (five times daily from 7.30 am to 9 pm), Oujda (twice daily at 8 and 8.30 pm), Rabat (every hour from 7 am to midnight), Safi, via El-Jadida (eight times daily from 5.30 am to 7 pm), Tangier (six times daily from 6 am to 11.30 pm), Taza (at 3 pm) and Tetouan (three times, the first at 8.30 am, the last at 11.30 pm).

Fares are Dr136 to Agadir (8-9 hours), Dr78 to Fès (five hours), Dr63 to Marrakesh (4 hours), Dr25 to Rabat (1½ hours), Dr63 to Safi (four hours) and Dr105 to Tangier (six hours).

CTM also operates international buses to France, Belgium and Spain from Casablanca. See the Getting There & Away chapter for further details.

Bus – Other The station for the other lines is just off Rue Liberté, two blocks down from Place de la Victoire, some way from the centre of the city. Buses here are less comfortable than the CTM equivalents, but they're between 15% to 30% cheaper, and departures are often much more frequent.

There are a couple of urban buses to Place de la Victoire and down Rue Strasbourg (parallel to Rue Liberté). See the following Getting Around entry for details. Alternatively, you could get a taxi.

Rue Strasbourg must be one of the noisiest and most air-polluted streets in North Africa, and the chaos of buses and touts could just about put you off trying to leave Casablanca. In fact, the touts are good news – they'll find you long before you find the bus you want.

Nevertheless, it might be an idea to squirm your way to the ticket windows – a lot of them have prices posted, which will give you an idea of what you should pay. Some of these companies offer 1st and 2nd class fares. The difference is usually a matter of a few Dirham.

There are buses to Agadir (Dr90), Er-Rachidia (Dr120), Fès (Dr55), Marrakesh

(Dr42), Midelt (Dr100), Ouarzazate (Dr90), Oujda (Dr120), Rabat (Dr18), Sefrou (Dr60), Tangier (Dr65), Tinerhir (Dr113) and Tiznit (Dr110).

There's a petit taxi stand next to the station – the fare into central Casablanca should not be more than Dr12.

The No 900 bus to Mohammedia leaves regularly from a stop near Casa-Port train station. The ticket costs Dr5.50.

Train Casablanca has five train stations. The main one is Casa-Voyageurs, 4km east of the city centre. The Casa-Port station is a few hundred metres north of Places des Nations Unies, right where you want to be. The other stations, 'Ain Sebaa, Nouvelle Medina and Mers Sultan, are of little interest to travellers. You can get the very useful ONCF 'Horaire des Trains' timetable here. Ask at any ticket counter.

Most departures are from Casa-Voyageurs station, which is a Dr15 taxi ride from the centre. There are also plenty of buses between the station and the centre – it's about an hour's walk, which is silly if you're carrying luggage.

Both stations have left-luggage facilities. The one at Casa Port charges Dr2.50 a day per item, but you must have a padlock on the zipper or they won't accept it.

There is one train per day to Azemmour via El-Jadida (1½ hours), six trains a day to Fès from 6 am to 10.30 pm (about five hours), eight trains a day to Marrakesh from 1.30 am to 7.28 pm (nearly four hours), three trains to Oujda from 6 am to 8.45 pm (10-11 hours) and one train to Tangier at 11.55 pm.

Departures from the Gare du Port ('Casa-Port' on the platform signs) include Fès (8 am and 8.45 pm; 4½ hours), Oujda (8.45 pm, 10½ hours) and Tangier (6.45 am 5.50 pm; five hours).

All trains to Fès call at Meknès. Trains to Oujda call at Meknès and Fès.

All trains heading north call at Rabat. The trip takes about 1¼ hours. However, the shuttle trains between the two cities are faster. There is a train every hour from around 7 am to midnight. Trains leave from both Casa-Port and from Casa-Voyageurs. They take 50 minutes.

Some 2nd class fares include El-Jadida (Dr28 for normal only), Fès (Dr72.50/ 92), Marrakesh (Dr54/70), Oujda (Dr154/194), Rabat (Dr18/25) and Tangier (Dr80/109).

Taxi Grands taxis to Rabat leave from Blvd Hassan Seghir, near the CTM bus station. The fare is Dr27.

Car The following are among the 50 or so car rental agencies in Casablanca. Many of the smaller agencies are concentrated around Ave des Far and Blvd Mohammed V. They often employ runners to bring in business – follow some of them and you could end up with a much better deal.

The airport is a great place to rent a car. All the companies have offices cheek-by-jowl, and you can beat prices right down (by more than 50% in the low season) by playing one offer off another.

Avis
   19 Ave des FAR (☎ 312424, 311135); Mohammed V international airport (☎ 339072)
Budget
   Tour des Habous, Ave des FAR (☎ 313737); Mohammed V international airport (☎ 339-157)
Europcar
   Complexe des Habous, Ave des FAR (☎ 313737); 44 Ave des FAR (☎ 314069); Mohammed V international airport (☎/fax 339 161)
Hertz
   25 Rue de Foucauld (☎ 312223); Mohammed V international airport (☎ 339181)

If you do rent a car, you should be aware of Casablanca's horrendous parking problems. It is very difficult to find a space in the centre between 8 am and 6 pm.

Getting Around
The Airport You can get from Mohammed V international airport to Casablanca or Rabat direct by train (TNR), but not by bus.

The trains leave from below the ground

floor of the airport terminal building, with 12 services a day from 7.35 am to 10.30 pm to Casablanca. Not all go to the more convenient Casa-Port; check in advance. Trains take 23 minutes to Casa-Voyageurs and 35 minutes to Casa-Port and are comfortable and reliable. The 2nd class fare costs Dr25.

Travelling from Casablanca to the airport, there are 12 trains a day from both Casa-Voyageurs and Casa-Port from about 5 am to 8 pm. If none of this suits you, the fare for a taxi into central Casablanca is Dr150, or Dr200 after 8 pm.

Bus The local bus terminal for the city buses is on Place Oued al-Makhazine (see the Casablanca map). There is even a faded route map posted up here. Some useful city routes are:

No 9
  From the terminal to 'Ain Diab and the beaches
No 5
  From the terminal to Place de la Victoire
No 30
  From Blvd Ziraoui to Casa-Voyageurs train station via Ave des FAR and Blvd Mohammed V
No 4
  Along Rue Strasbourg and down Ave Lalla Yacout to Blvd de Paris
No 15
  To the Hassan II Mosque

In addition, bus No 2 regularly runs along Blvd Mohammed V to Casa-Voyageurs and beyond. Coming from the train station, you could walk up to Place al-Yassir, from where you have a greater choice of lines serving the city centre.

Taxi There's no shortage of petits taxis in Casablanca, but you'll usually find drivers unwilling to use the meters, so negotiate the fare before getting in, especially if you're going a long way. Expect to pay Dr10 for a ride in or around the city centre.

There are plenty of petit taxi stands around town. One that's conveniently located between the medina and the centre of town can be found at the junction of Ave des FAR and Rue Leon L'Africain.

AROUND CASABLANCA
Mohammedia
About 30km north of Casablanca lies the local resort town of Mohammedia, which also doubles as the centre of Morocco's petrol industry. The two might seem incompatible, but Mohammedia, which until the 1960s was little more than a decaying fishing village (then known as Fedala), manages to keep the two activities apart.

Site of the SAMIR oil refinery, it is one of the country's busiest ports with the traffic almost entirely devoted to petroleum products. At the height of summer, the place tends to fill to bursting point with Casablancans, but out of season it makes a pleasant place to stop off for a day or two. The walls of an old kasbah still stand, but there is nothing much to see.

It's an easy day trip from Casablanca and not hard to find your way around. When you arrive by train or bus, head down the street leading north-west directly away from the station and you arrive on Ave Abderrahmane Sarghini. Turn right and you can continue all the way to the beach. Ave des FAR runs off a roundabout (note the BMCI bank) about 100m down Ave Abderrahmane Sarghini and leads to the main restaurant area, the Hôtel Miramar and the western end of the beach.

Information The main post office is on Ave Mohammed Zerktouni, a couple of blocks in from the beach. Several banks have branches in Mohammedia. BMCI is closest to the train station, just opposite the kasbah on Ave des FAR. There are no ATMs.

If the banks are closed, you can change money in the Hôtel Miramar or Sabah Hôtel. There's even a small Institut Français, in an arcade off Rue de Fès.

Places to Stay There are just two cheapies, both without telephone. The better of the two is the *Hôtel Ennasr*, on Rue Abdarrahmane Sarghini, which charges Dr75 for a single and Dr110 to Dr150 for doubles. Rooms are small and cell-like, but very clean.

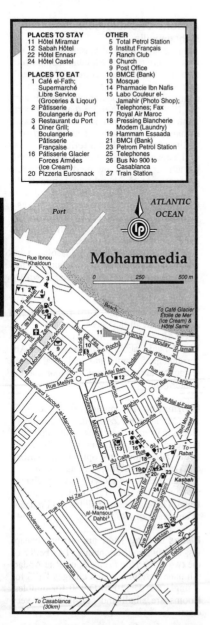

PLACES TO STAY	OTHER
11 Hôtel Miramar	5 Total Petrol Station
12 Sabah Hôtel	6 Institut Français
22 Hôtel Ennasr	7 Ranch Club
24 Hôtel Castel	8 Church
	9 Post Office
PLACES TO EAT	10 BMCE (Bank)
1 Café el-Fath;	13 Mosque
Supermarché	14 Pharmacie Ibn Nafis
Libre Service	15 Labo Couleur el-
(Groceries & Liqour)	Jamahir (Photo Shop);
2 Pâtisserie	Telephones; Fax
Boulangerie du Port	17 Royal Air Maroc
3 Restaurant du Port	18 Pressing Blancherie
4 Diner Grill;	Modern (Laundry)
Boulangerie	19 Hammam Essaada
Pâtisserie	21 BMCI (Bank)
Française	23 Petrom Petrol Station
16 Pâtisserie Glacier	25 Telephones
Forces Armées	26 Bus No 900 to
(Ice Cream)	Casablanca
20 Pizzeria Eurosnack	27 Train Station

Mohammedia

ATLANTIC OCEAN

Port

Rue Ibnou Khaldoun

0   250   500 m

Beach

To Café Glacier
Étoile de Mer
(Ice Cream) &
Hôtel Samir

Kasbah

To Casablanca
(30km)

The other option, the *Hôtel Castel* on Ave Abderrahmane Sarghini, is cheaper at Dr50/80, but is very grubby and run down.

Otherwise, there are just two four-star hotels. The *Hôtel Samir* (☎ 310 770; fax 323330), on Blvd Moulay Youssef, has singles/doubles for Dr369/458, while the new *Sabah Hôtel* (☎ 321451; fax 321456), at 42 Ave des FAR, charges Dr394/473.

The town's premier establishment is the *Hôtel Miramar* (☎ 322021; fax 324613). It was closed at the time of writing for complete renovation. It should reopen at the beginning of 1998.

Hammams The Hammam Essaada is conveniently located close to the cheaper hotels. It's through the unmarked door on the corner of Blvd Bir Anzarane and Rue al-Mansour ed-Dahbi, and is open from 6.30 am to 9 pm to both men and women (in separate parts). A bath costs Dr6. You may like to try the local shampoo and soap which you can buy here.

Places to Eat The waterfront is lined with cafes, and there are a few standard hole-in-the-wall places on Ave des FAR and in the area around the train station. There is also a collection of decent restaurants around Rue de Fès and its continuation, Rue Farhat Hachad, west of the Miramar Hôtel. Not surprisingly, fish is the theme.

The *Pizzeria Eurosnack* on Rue al-Mansour ed-Dahbi is a favourite with the locals and does good, cheap fare such as hot sandwiches for Dr12 to Dr22, hamburgers for Dr10 to Dr14 and pizzas for Dr35 to Dr85.

The *Diner Grill*, on Rue Farhai Hachad, is a simple, but peaceful and friendly place, which does a good value paella for Dr40 and fish dishes for Dr30 to Dr45.

The *Restaurant Bec Fin* on Rue Cheikh Chouaïb, not far from the Pâtisserie Boulangerie du Port, is a charming, tucked-away little place with whitewashed walls and fishing net hung from the rafters. It has just nine tables, but does excellent seafood paella for two people for Dr100 or, for a splurge, the Paella Royal (Dr150), made with Dublin prawns. Other mains cost from Dr50 to Dr80 and the restaurant is licensed. You'll need to ask directions to get there from the patisserie, as it's rather hidden away.

Another attractive place, which has a high reputation for the quality of its food, is the *Restaurant du Port* (☎ 322466) at 1 Rue du Port. It specialises in Spanish food and has excellent set menus for Dr150. Main courses cost from Dr65 to Dr90.

A good place for cakes is the *Pâtisserie Boulangerie du Port* on Rue Tafilalet. Try the delicious doughnuts for Dr2; you can take them around the corner to have with a coffee at the *Café el-Fath*. The patisserie is open every day from 6 am to 1 pm and from 3 to 8 pm.

For ice cream, head for the *Glacier Étoile de Mer* on the seafront, or the *Pâtisserie Glacier Forces Armées* on Ave des FAR.

For a little nightlife, try the *Ranch Club* on Ave Mohammed Zerktouni. It costs Dr70 (drinks Dr40 to Dr50), plays a kind of 'Europop' and is open from around 10 pm to 2.30 am.

Getting There & Away Bus No 900 is virtually a suburban bus and runs every eight minutes (every 15 minutes on Sunday) from around 6 am to 8.45 pm between a stop by Casa-Port train station and the square in front of Mohammedia's train station. It costs Dr6. The 2nd class (normal) train fare is Dr12.50.

Getting Around You're highly unlikely to need them, but there are lime-green petits taxis should you be in a hurry to get somewhere.

A couple of buses run down to the beach from the square in front of the train station.

Berber seed symbol
Associated with fertility.

NTH ATLANTIC COAST

The Atlantic – South of Casablanca

From Casablanca, the Atlantic coast stretches some 350km south-west to the former Portuguese port town of Essaouira, an excellent windsurfing spot and one time hippie mecca, before dropping south to Agadir. From there it sweeps south-west for 300km to the tiny coastal town of Tarfaya, just north of the Western Sahara desert.

Along the way, you're reminded of Europe's long history of interference on the Moroccan seaboard. Azemmour, El-Jadida, Safi, Essaouira and Agadir were all at one time European military and commercial bridgeheads, and all but Agadir retain architectural evidence of this. Agadir, the country's premier beach resort, is where modern Europeans, in the guise of package tourists, choose to invade the country today.

In between these towns are plenty of beaches and some stunning, wild coastal scenery. There are also some prime bird-watching opportunities along this stretch of coast, particularly around Oualidia, Essaouira and Agadir.

Stretching hundreds of kilometres south of Tarfaya to the Mauritanian border is the disputed territory of the Western Sahara. Occupied by Morocco when the Spaniards left in 1975, it's a vast, desolate and lightly populated tract of stony desert.

Its people are mainly fishermen, work-hungry northern Moroccans, and soldiers. The latter are here to keep an eye on the rebel group, Polisario, and also to maintain Morocco's claim on the area (which neighbouring Mauritania has never relinquished).

HIGHLIGHTS

Oualidia – a quiet seaside spot with oysters, waterbirds and lagoon swimming

Essaouira – good beaches and impressive Portuguese fortifications feature in this colourful port city

Taroudannt – an elegant Berber town and gateway to the Western High Atlas

Tafraoute – a relaxed Berber village in the heart of the Anti-Atlas mountains

Sidi Ifni – fading Art Deco architecture is a highlight of this quirky former Spanish Saharan town

Id Aïssa – a well-preserved dramatic hilltop agadir

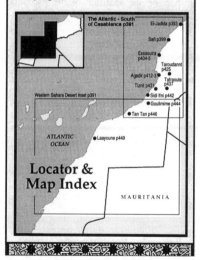

The Atlantic – South of Casablanca p391

El-Jadida p393
Safi p399
Essaouira p404-5
Taroudannt p425
Agadir p412-3
Tafraoute p437
Tiznit p431
Sidi Ifni p442
Goulimime p444
Tan Tan p446

Western Sahara Desert inset p391

ATLANTIC OCEAN

Laayoune p449

Locator & Map Index

MAURITANIA

Central Coast

EL-JADIDA

The historic centre of this quiet, relaxed town of 150,000 is one of the best preserved examples of Portuguese military architecture in the country. The rambling lanes, impressive ramparts and elegant old cistern of the Cité Portugaise (the old Portuguese fortress) are well worth a visit.

During the summer months, Moroccan city dwellers flock to El-Jadida for the beaches, so if you're thinking of visiting

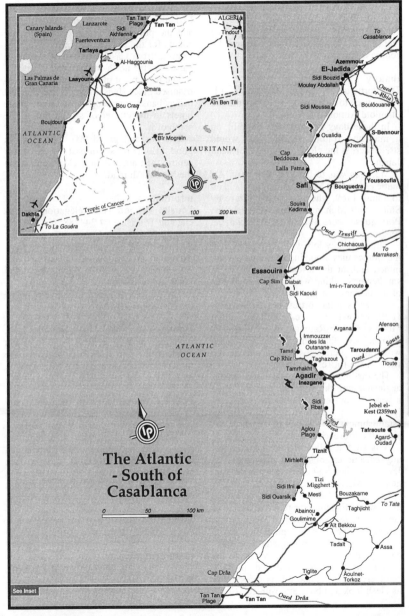

The Atlantic
- South of
Casablanca

in July or August it may be a good idea to book your accommodation ahead. In general the town has an open, hassle-free feel to it and is a pleasant place to spend a couple of days.

History
The Portuguese founded Mazagan, as El-Jadida used to be known, in 1513 on the site of an old Almohad fortress.

In those days Portugal was building up a maritime trading empire that would stretch across the globe, as far as China and Japan.

Mazagan was to become their main Atlantic entrepôt in Morocco and they held on to it until 1769, when, following a siege by Sultan Sidi Mohammed bin Abdallah, the Portuguese were forced to evacuate the fortress.

Although they left with little more than the clothes they stood in, the ramparts were mined and, at the last moment, blown to smithereens, taking with them a good part of the besieging army.

The walls of the fortress lay in ruins until 1820, when they were rebuilt by Sultan Moulay Abd ar-Rahman. The Moroccans who took over the town after the Portuguese withdrawal preferred to settle outside the walls of the fortress.

The medina inside the walls was largely neglected until the mid-19th century, when it was recolonised by European merchants (particularly the Portuguese) following the establishment of a series of 'open ports' along the Moroccan coast.

A large and influential Jewish community became established at this time. The Jews controlled trade with the interior, particularly Marrakesh.

Contrary to common Moroccan practice, the Jews of El-Jadida were not confined to the *mellah* (Jewish quarter of Medina), but mixed with the general population.

Tourism, sardine fishing and a prosperous agricultural hinterland have made the modern town an animated and growing commercial centre, and this is reflected in its clean look and busy atmosphere.

Orientation
El-Jadida faces north-east onto the Atlantic, and the protection this affords partly accounts for the town's suitability as a port. Coming from Casablanca, the Cité Portugaise is at the north-western end of town.

The focal point of the town is the pedestrianised Place Hansali; you'll find the post office, banks, tourist office and some of the hotels in the cluster of streets just to the south of it.

The bus and grand taxi stations are a good kilometre south-east of the town centre; the train station is 2km south along the Marrakesh road.

Information
Tourist Offices The Délégation Provinciale du Tourisme (☎ 344788; fax 344789) is in the Chambre de Commerce on Rue Ibn Khaldoun, and is open Monday to Friday from 8.30 am to noon and 2.30 to 6.30 pm. They have a few useful handouts, including hotel and restaurant lists.

There is a Syndicat d'Initiative opposite the Municipal Theatre.

Money Several banks have branches here, including the BMCE, BMCI and the Bank al-Maghrib. The BMCE is probably the most efficient bank, and is the only one with an ATM.

Post & Communications There are plenty of téléboutiques scattered about town where you can make phone calls or send faxes.

The post and phone offices are together, on the block bounded by Ave Mohammed V and Ave Jamia al-Arabia, and are open Monday to Friday from 8.30 am to noon and 2.30 to 6 pm. You'll find a few card phones outside the office, on Ave Jamia al-Arabia.

Medical Services There's a night pharmacy (☎ 355252) at 10 Ave Jamia al-Arabia.

Cité Portugaise
There are two entrance gates to the fortress; the southernmost one, which is more convenient, opens onto the main street through

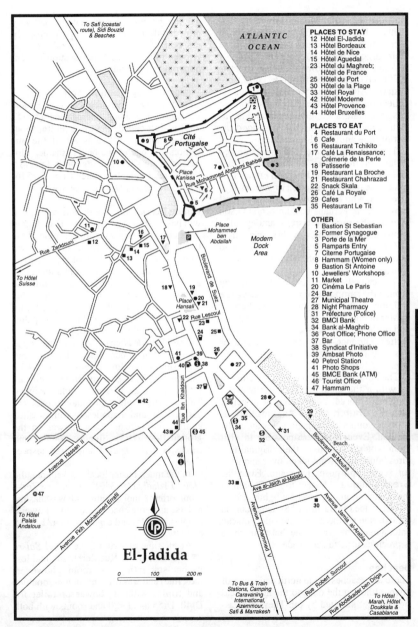

ATLANTIC OCEAN

PLACES TO STAY
12 Hôtel El-Jadida
13 Hôtel Bordeaux
14 Hôtel de Nice
15 Hôtel Aguedal
23 Hôtel du Maghreb;
   Hôtel de France
25 Hôtel du Port
30 Hôtel de la Plage
33 Hôtel Royal
42 Hôtel Moderne
43 Hôtel Provence
44 Hôtel Bruxelles

PLACES TO EAT
4 Restaurant du Port
6 Cafe
16 Restaurant Tchikito
17 Café La Renaissance;
   Crémerie de la Perle
18 Patisserie
19 Restaurant La Broche
21 Restaurant Chahrazad
22 Snack Skala
26 Café La Royale
29 Cafes
35 Restaurant Le Tit

OTHER
1 Bastion St Sebastian
2 Former Synagogue
3 Porte de la Mer
5 Ramparts Entry
7 Citerne Portugaise
8 Hammam (Women only)
9 Bastion St Antoine
10 Jewellers' Workshops
11 Market
20 Cinéma Le Paris
24 Bar
27 Municipal Theatre
28 Night Pharmacy
31 Préfecture (Police)
32 BMCI Bank
34 Bank al-Maghrib
36 Post Office; Phone Office
37 Bar
38 Syndicat d'Initiative
39 Ambsat Photo
40 Petrol Station
41 Photo Shops
45 BMCE Bank (ATM)
46 Tourist Office
47 Hammam

Cité Portugaise

Place Kanissa

Rue Mohammed Ahchemi Bahbai

To Safi (coastal route), Sidi Bouzid & Beaches

Rue Zerktouni

To Hôtel Suisse

Place Mohammed ben Abdallah

Modern Dock Area

Boulevard de Suez

Place Hansali

Rue Lescouf

Rue Ibn Khaldoun

Avenue Hassan II

To Hôtel Palais Andalous

Avenue Fkih Mohammed Errafli

El-Jadida

0   100   200 m

Beach

Boulevard al-Mouhit

Ave al-Jaich al-Malaki

Avenue Jamia al-Arabia

Avenue Mohammed V

Rue Robert Surcouf

Rue Abdelkader ben Driga

To Bus & Train Stations, Camping Caravaning International, Azemmour, Safi & Marrakesh

To Hôtel Marah, Hôtel Doukkala & Casablanca

STH OF CASABLANCA

the medina, Rue Mohammed Ahchemi Bahbai. The street ends at the Porte de la Mer, which is where ships used to discharge their cargo in the Portuguese era.

About halfway down the main street is the famed **Citerne Portugaise** (Portuguese Cistern). Although the Romans built water-collection and storage cisterns similar to this, it remains a remarkable piece of architecture and engineering that has stood the test of time and is still functional.

The reflection of the roof and 25 arched pillars in the water covering the floor creates a dramatic and beautiful effect. This hasn't escaped the attention of various film directors, who have shot scenes for several movies here. Perhaps best known is Orson Welles who used the cistern, among other Moroccan locations, in his acclaimed *Othello*. It's open daily from 8.30 am to noon and 2.30 to 6 pm (sometimes later). Entry costs Dr10.

You can take a pleasant stroll all the way around the **ramparts** of the Cité Portugaise – simply walk up onto them by the Porta de la Mer or enter through the large door at the end of the tiny cul-de-sac to the right of the fortress entrance. The man with the key for this is usually hanging around; if not, he won't be far away.

The Portuguese built a number of churches within the medina, but unfortunately, they're all closed. You can see the principal one, the **Church of the Assumption**, as soon as you enter the main gateway of the medina. Even if it were possible to visit them, you'd see little of their original features, since they were taken over and used for secular purposes long ago. Even the **Great Mosque**, adjacent to the Church of the Assumption, used to be a lighthouse.

Just inside the Bastion of St Sebastian, on the extreme northern seaward side, you can enter a one-time synagogue, but again there is precious little to see inside.

Beaches

There are beaches to the north and south of town, although the ones to the north occasionally get polluted by oil. They're pleas-
ant enough out of season, but can get very crowded during July and August. Possibly the best of them is Sidi Bouzid (see the Around following El-Jadida section), about 5km out of El-Jadida.

Places to Stay – bottom end

Camping On Ave des Nations Unies, *Camping Caravaning International* (☎ 342 755) is well outside the town centre, about a 15 minute walk south-east of the bus station. It's one of the better, shadier Moroccan camp sites. It costs Dr12 a person, Dr6.50 per car, Dr10 to pitch a tent, Dr5 for a hot shower and Dr11 for electricity.

Hotels Because this is a seaside resort, you will have to be prepared to pay much higher prices in the summer months in some of the hotels. The hotels also fill up quickly then, so it may be worthwhile booking ahead.

There is a trio of cheapies in some lanes a couple of hundred metres from the fortress. The cheapest of them is the *Hôtel Aguedal*, an extremely basic place offering beds in little rooms around a banana palm-filled courtyard for Dr15 a head.

The *Hôtel de Nice* (☎ 352272), nearby at 15 Rue Mohammed Smiha, has tidy but tiny, smoky-smelling rooms for Dr40/55. The best of the three is the *Hôtel Bordeaux* (☎ 354117), at 47 Rue Moulay Ahmed Tahiri, whose pleasant small rooms are gathered around a spotlessly whitewashed courtyard. There is a hot shower on the ground floor (Dr5). Singles, doubles and triples cost Dr40, Dr60 and Dr80 respectively.

In the much busier local market area, the *Hôtel El-Jadida* (☎ 340178), on Rue Zerktouni, offers simple rooms with washbasins, bidets and big beds, but no showers. Singles, doubles and triples cost Dr31, Dr45 and Dr78.

At the time of writing, the *Hôtel Suisse* (☎ 342816), at 147 Rue Zerktouni, had lost its one-star rating (the rooms, however, look fine) and was offering singles, doubles and triples without shower or toilet for Dr40, Dr55 and Dr80 and rooms with both for Dr50/80/100. Prices may well double if it manages to regain its rating. The hotel is about a 10 minute walk south-west of the Cité Portugaise fortress, well away from the bus station.

Two of the better budget deals are just off Place Hansali. The *Hôtel du Maghreb* and *Hôtel de France* (☎ 342181) are owned by the same guy. Some of the big rooms, with high wooden ceilings, look out to sea. They cost Dr40/55 and a hot shower is Dr4. Not so hot is the *Hôtel du Port* (☎ 342701), on Blvd de Suez, which has basic rooms for Dr31/47.

Quite adequate is the *Hôtel Moderne* (☎ 343133), at 21 Ave Hassan II. Rooms with basin and bidet cost Dr52/78, but some are rather small. Hot showers are free.

The one-star *Hôtel Bruxelles* (☎ 342072), at 40 Rue Ibn Khaldoun, offers clean if somewhat spartan rooms with private bathroom for Dr70/100.

The *Hôtel Royal* (☎ 341100), on Ave Mohammed V, is handy for the bus station. It has some big, bright rooms, and a bar and restaurant in a pleasant open courtyard. Singles/doubles without shower cost Dr62/80; rooms with shower cost Dr62/80.

On Ave Jamia al-Arabia, the friendly *Hôtel de la Plage* (☎ 342648), is also within reasonable distance of the bus station. It has clean, perfectly good rooms for Dr50/60/75. There is hot water in the bath on the corridor (Dr5).

Places to Stay – middle

El-Jadida's only two-star hotel, the *Hôtel Provence* (☎ 342347; fax 352115), at 42 Ave Fkih Mohammed Errafil, is still one of the most pleasant places in town. Rooms with private shower and toilet cost Dr121, Dr149, Dr204 or Dr269 (plus taxes) and there are a couple of rooms without shower for Dr99.

Some rooms are definitely better than others. The hot water is very hot, and there is access to covered parking for Dr10 a day.

The Provence also has a popular licensed restaurant and a decent bar. Visa cards are accepted and English is spoken.

Places to Stay – top end

If you fancy a little luxury, then the three-star *Hôtel Palais Andalous* (☎ 343745; fax 351690), on Blvd Docteur de la Lanouy, is a lovely place to stay.

Once the palace of a local pasha, the place was converted into a spacious hotel in 1980. Full of exquisite Moroccan tiles and hectares of intricate plasterwork, the hotel has a pleasant courtyard, comfortable salons and a very good bar and restaurant. Rooms with everything (one even has a pasha-sized bed) cost Dr266/315 plus tax. In the low season, double rooms cost as little as Dr250. A garage is available for those with their own transport.

The hotel is a little out of the way; follow the orange 'hotel' signs up Ave Hassan II from the city centre.

Going up in price, the most expensive hotel in El-Jadida is the *Hôtel Doukkala* (☎ 343737) on Ave Jamia al-Arabia.

This rather grim concrete bunker of a hotel has all the amenities you would expect of a four-star establishment, including some tennis courts. Singles/doubles cost Dr375/472.

Nearby is the *Marah Hôtel* (☎ 344170), a rather seedy looking Art Deco place which has seen better days. Singles/doubles with full bathroom cost Dr266/315. The hotel has a bar.

Swimming Pools

The Doukkala and Marah hotels both have swimming pools.

Hammams

There's a small hammam for women just near the Bastion St Antoine in the north-west corner of the Cité Portugaise.

West along Ave Hassan II is a larger hammam which caters for both men and women.

Places to Eat

Restaurant La Broche, on Place Hansali, is a homely, family-run place which offers a range of Moroccan dishes at reasonable prices. The brochettes are exceptionally good. A full meal will set you back about Dr50.

The nearby *Restaurant Chahrazad*, on the other side of the Cinéma Le Paris, has similar prices to La Broche and the food is just as good.

Fish enthusiasts should investigate the *Restaurant Tchikito*, in a side lane a short walk north-west of Place Hansali. A filling meal of fresh fried fish (eaten with the fingers and accompanied by a plate of ear-busting chillies) can cost as little as Dr20.

The *Restaurant du Port* (☎ 342579), at the northern end of the dock area overlooking the ramparts of the fortress, offers excellent seafood in a great location. A three-course meal will cost between Dr80 and Dr100.

The restaurant at the *Hôtel Provence* serves very good Moroccan, French and seafood specialities in a similar price range. A bit more expensive, but well worth sampling, is the *Restaurant Le Tit*, just behind the post office.

Outside the bus station, *Snack Youm Youm* is a simple food stall which does a brisk trade in brochettes and chips for Dr13.

The tourist office has a complete list of the more up-market restaurants in town.

Cafes & Patisseries *Café La Royale*, across the road from the Municipal Theatre, is a comfortable spot for morning coffee and pastries.

In summer, along the seafront on Blvd al-Mouhit, there's a whole string of cafes from which to choose.

The *Café La Renaissance* and *Crémerie de la Perle*, both at the top of Place Hansali, are great people-watching places.

Nearby is a busy little patisserie where you can replenish your stash of Moroccan cookies.

There are a few cafes around the market area, on Rue Zerktouni.

Self-Catering For putting together picnic supplies, the best place to head for is probably the market area around Rue Zerktouni

where there are plenty of fruit and vegetable stalls and small grocery shops.

Entertainment

Bars The *Royal, Provence* and *Palais Andalous* hotels all have bars – the most comfortable is the one in the Provence. There is a rough sort of bar next door to the *Hôtel de la Plage* and a few unmarked, den-like watering holes scattered about town.

Getting There & Away

Bus The bus terminal (Gare Routière) is south-east of town on Rue Abdelmoumen el-Mouahidi, close to the junction with Ave Mohammed V. It's a 15 minute walk along Ave Mohammed V from the fortress.

There are buses to Casablanca, Rabat and Kenitra (window No 2), Azemmour (window No 5), Oualidia, Safi and Essaouira (window No 7) and Marrakesh (window No 8).

CTM has three runs to Casablanca: at 11 am (Dr25; 1st class), 3.45 pm (Dr17; 2nd class) and 5 pm (1st class). There are at least 11 local runs to Marrakesh (Dr35; about 3½ to four hours). In summer, buses to Casablanca and Marrakesh should be booked one day ahead. The fare to Azemmour is Dr3. There are two or three buses a day to Safi (Dr25) and Essaouira (Dr44).

Train The train station (☎ 342486, 352825) is 2km out of town along the Marrakesh road. There is one departure daily at 7.30 am to Casablanca (Dr26) and Rabat (Dr52). In summer there may be an extra evening train to Casablanca – check with the train station or the tourist office. There is a free bus service from the train station to the town centre; otherwise take a petit taxi.

Taxi Grands taxis gather along the side street next to the bus station. A place in a taxi to Azemmour costs Dr5.

'There is no blessing in a woman who travels, and there is no blessing in a man who does not travel.'
Moroccan Proverb

AROUND EL-JADIDA
Azemmour

While in El-Jadida, it's worth making a half-day excursion to this little-visited fortress town 15km to the north.

Here you'll find another monument to those energetic seafaring people, the Portuguese. Although they only stayed in Azemmour for a short while, from 1513 to 1541, it was sufficient time for them to build this fortress alongside the banks of the wide Oued Oum er-Rbia. One of Morocco's largest rivers, the Oum er-Rbia rises in the Middle Atlas and empties into the sea about 1km downriver from Azemmour. The best views of this fortress and its crumbling, whitewashed medina are from the bridge across the river.

Azemmour once had a thriving Jewish community, but since its exodus to Israel, the houses have fallen into ruin, with only the facades remaining in many cases. However, there is still a synagogue here, in reasonable shape, with lettering in Hebrew and English above the door saying 'Rabbi Abraham Moul Niss'.

The ramparts are open to visitors – the main entry is on the inside to the left after you enter the fortress town from Place du Souq. You could also enter by a door on the open square at the extreme north-eastern tip of the fort, but you might have to wait for the guardian to arrive with the keys.

In all probability you'll have been waylaid by kids before he gets to you, and they will take over as your guides. Whoever your guide may be, they'll expect a reasonable tip.

There's nothing much of interest in the new part of town outside the ramparts, but if you get here early in the day and aren't in a hurry to get back to El-Jadida, you might like to visit the **beach** (Haouzia), which is about half an hour's walk from Place du Souq (signposted). When the wind's not howling, it's not a bad spot. Bird-watchers should head for the dunes at the mouth of the river.

Information The Syndicat d'Initiative, post office, a branch of the BMCE bank, a hotel and some cafes are located on Ave Mohammed V, the main road in from El-Jadida. The fortress is immediately to the east of Ave Mohammed V. Azemmour's market day is Thursday.

Places to Stay & Eat There are at least two basic hotels in town. The *Hôtel de la Victoire* (☎ 347157), at 308 Ave Mohammed V (where a single room without shower costs Dr31), and the *Hôtel Moulay Bouchaib*.

The *Café El Manzeh*, on Place du Souq, is the most pleasant of a series of cafes along the main road. There are a few cafes down by the beach and the moderately priced *La Perle* restaurant, which is open in the summer.

Getting There & Away Local buses connect Azemmour with El-Jadida (Dr3), but grands taxis (Dr5 a head) are probably an easier bet as there are plenty of them.

The bus station is located east of Ave Mohammed V, near the town centre. Some of the trains that run from Casablanca to El-Jadida also stop at Azemmour.

Sidi Bouzid

About 5km south of El-Jadida is one of the area's better beaches, Sidi Bouzid. You can get local bus No 2 there from Place Mohammed ben Abdallah, near the Portuguese fortress.

There is a *camp site* here in the summer, a couple of *restaurants* and the rather expensive *Motel Club Hacienda* (☎ 348311). The motel has a pool, a tennis court and its own restaurant. Doubles cost Dr281.

OUALIDIA

The 76km drive (there are occasional buses) down the coast from El-Jadida to Oualidia is a pleasant one, at least once you get past the Jorf Lasfar phosphate port. Along the way, about 11km south of El-Jadida, you pass the fishing village of **Moulay Abdallah** and the ruins of a 12th century fortified monastery.

The coastal lagoons, creeks and saltpans which begin at **Sidi Moussa**, 36km south of El-Jadida, and continue beyond Oualidia to **Cap Beddouza** provide rich habitats for a variety of waterbirds. Bird-watchers may want to stop by the lagoon at Sidi Moussa to look for cormorants, ducks, gulls, terns and waders.

Oualidia is an attractive, relaxed seaside fishing village situated off the highway in between the sea and a picturesque lagoon. A growing cluster of holiday bungalows overlook the lagoon, which is famous for its oysters. The beach offers good swimming and windsurfing. In the summer you can hire windsurfing equipment here. Bird life on and around the lagoon includes flamingos, Mediterranean and Audouin's gulls, godwits, stilts and terns.

Places to Stay & Eat

The *Villa La Brise* (☎ 346917) at Sidi Moussa, is a well-located unclassified hotel looking out over the Atlantic. Singles/doubles without shower cost Dr49/64; rooms with shower cost Dr67/95.

The hotel has a restaurant, bar and swimming pool.

In Oualidia, the cheapest place to stay is *Camping Oualidia*, tucked behind the sand dunes not far from the lagoon. Two people with a campervan pay Dr36, slightly less with a tent. Hot showers cost Dr6.

Up on the main road is the *Hôtel La Lagune* (☎ 366477) which offers double rooms with half-board for Dr350. The *Complexe Touristique Chems* (☎ 366536), right on the edge of the lagoon, has small bungalows (for four people with fully equipped kitchen) for Dr500 in the high season and double rooms with shower for Dr200. In the low season bungalows/double rooms cost Dr350/180. There's a restaurant here also.

The restaurants *L'Araignée Gourmande* and *Les Roches* both offer excellent seafood menus. An alternative is to buy some from one of the fishers getting around town with the day's catch, and cook it up yourself.

SAFI (ASFI)

Largely a modern fishing port and industrial centre, Safi sits on the Atlantic coast in a steep crevasse formed by the Oued Chabah. Its industrial side is pretty obvious if you arrive from the north.

A lot of Morocco's raw phosphate rock and fertilisers pass through here, the latter produced in chemical plants south of the town.

The sardine fleet is one of the world's biggest, although the canning industry has declined from the peaks it reached under the French protectorate.

The city centre has a lively and charming walled medina and souq, with battlements dating from the brief Portuguese period of occupation. Safi is also well known for its traditional potteries, and even if you are not interested in buying any souvenirs, it is worth walking around the potteries to see how they work.

History

Safi's natural harbour was known to the Phoenicians, and was probably used by the Romans later on. The city was founded in the 12th century by the Almohads who established an important religious and cultural centre here.

Involvement with Europeans didn't really begin until the Portuguese arrived on the scene in 1508. The Portuguese built a fortress, using Essaouira as their base, but despite its monumental proportions (as with all Portuguese military installations), they didn't stay at Safi long, abandoning it in 1541.

In the late 17th century the French established a consulate at the port and were responsible for signing trading treaties with the indigenous rulers. By the 19th century, however, the port had faded into insignificance.

Its revival came in the 20th century, with the expansion of the sardine fishing fleet and the construction of a huge industrial complex for the manufacture of fertilisers and sulphuric and phosphoric acids using local pyrites and phosphate ores.

Orientation

The bus and train stations are a couple of kilometres to the south of the town centre. To get there it's a long walk, or a bus or taxi ride.

The post office and the bulk of the cheaper hotels, restaurants and banks are on or near Place de l'Indépendance and just inside the medina walls.

More expensive hotels, cafes, the main post office and the Syndicat d'Initiative are up the hill to the east and around Place Mohammed V.

Information

Tourist Offices The Délégation Provinciale du Tourisme (☎ 622496; fax 624553) is on Rue Imam Malek, a short walk south of the bus station. It's open Monday to Friday from 8.30 am to noon and 2.30 to 6.30 pm. The Syndicat d'Initiative (☎ 464553), on a lane just south of Place Mohammed V, is open Monday to Friday from 9 am to noon and 3 to 6.30 pm.

Money The BMCE and BMCI banks have branches on Place de l'Indépendance. The

STH OF CASABLANCA

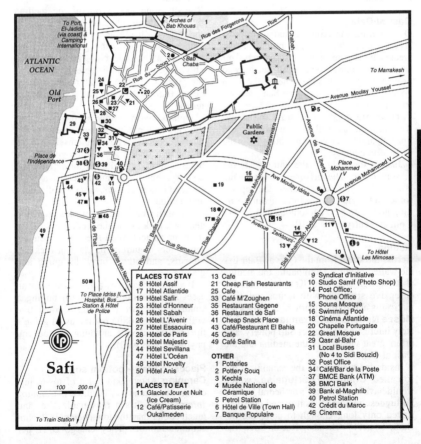

Safi

0   100   200 m

PLACES TO STAY
8 Hôtel Assif
17 Hôtel Atlantide
19 Hôtel Safir
23 Hôtel d'Honneur
24 Hôtel Sabah
26 Hôtel L'Avenir
27 Hôtel Essaouira
28 Hôtel de Paris
30 Hôtel Majestic
44 Hôtel Sevillana
47 Hôtel L'Océan
48 Hôtel Novelty
50 Hôtel Anis

PLACES TO EAT
11 Glacier Jour et Nuit
   (Ice Cream)
12 Café/Patisserie
   Oukaïmeden

13 Cafe
21 Cheap Fish Restaurants
25 Cafe
33 Café M'Zoughen
35 Restaurant Gegene
36 Restaurant de Safi
41 Cheap Snack Place
43 Café/Restaurant El Bahia
45 Cafe
49 Café Safina

OTHER
1 Potteries
2 Pottery Souq
3 Kechla
4 Musée National de
   Céramique
5 Petrol Station
6 Hôtel de Ville (Town Hall)
7 Banque Populaire

9 Syndicat d'Initiative
10 Studio Samif (Photo Shop)
14 Post Office;
   Phone Office
15 Souna Mosque
16 Swimming Pool
18 Cinéma Atlantide
20 Chapelle Portugaise
22 Great Mosque
29 Qasr al-Bahr
31 Local Buses
   (No 4 to Sidi Bouzid)
32 Post Office
34 Café/Bar de la Poste
37 BMCE Bank (ATM)
38 BMCI Bank
39 Bank al-Maghrib
40 Petrol Station
42 Crédit du Maroc
46 Cinema

Banque Populaire is on Place Mohammed V. There's an ATM outside the BMCE.

Post & Communications The phone section of the main post office, near Place Mohammed V, is open seven days a week from 8 am to 9.45 pm. There are téléboutiques dotted about and card phones outside the small post office just south of the walled medina.

Film & Photography There is a Kodak processing shop called Studio Samif on Ave Zerktouni.

Qasr al-Bahr

Overlooking the Atlantic and in impressively good shape is the main fortress erected by the Portuguese to enforce their short-lived control here. Built not only to protect the port, but also to house the town governor, the 'Castle on the Sea' was restored in 1963.

There are good views from the southwest bastion, as well as a number of old Spanish and Dutch cannons dating from the early 17th century.

Just to the right of the entrance is the prison tower. The prisoners went to the bottom, but you can climb to the top for some pretty views across the medina. Visiting hours are 8.30 am to noon and 2.30 to 6 pm and entry costs Dr10.

Medina

Across the street from the Qasr al-Bahr lies the walled medina. Dominating the medina at its eastern end is the **Kechla**, a massive defensive structure with ramps, gunnery platforms and living quarters. It houses the **Musée National de Céramique**, a moderately interesting display of Safi pottery, and offers great views over the medina and the Qasr al-Bahr.

Inside the medina are the remains of the so-called **Chapelle Portugaise**, which would have become Safi's cathedral had the Portuguese remained; as it turned out, they stayed only long enough to complete the choir. To get to it, head up Rue du Souq (the

main thoroughfare through the medina) and turn right just after the **Great Mosque**. It's about 100m down the alley.

Shortly before Rue du Souq leads out of the medina, you'll notice, off to your left, a colourful **pottery souq**. The shopkeepers in here are pretty low-key, and little inclined to bargain. If you are intent on buying a few pieces, take the time to look at the different shops and establish some prices – then head out to the potteries to see if you can't strike a better deal.

Potteries

Rue du Souq passes out of the medina by Bab Chabah. Outside this gate and to the left, you'll see an enormous series of arches; they look as though they were an aqueduct at one time, but in fact were probably associated with the defensive walls of the medina. Straight ahead, on the hill opposite Bab Chabah, are Safi's famous potteries.

Opinions vary wildly on the quality of the ceramics produced here. Some of the many cooperatives devote themselves to the production of the green tiles you see on many important buildings throughout the country, but many manufacture a wide range of bowls, platters, vases, candlesticks and the like.

It is well worth taking a walk around and getting a look inside the workshops. Apart from the ancient wood-fired kilns, you can see potters moulding the clay for tiles and utensils, and others busy designing and glazing.

If you're collared by a guide (possibly an asset here for the uninitiated), buying a small item or two from 'his' cooperative will save you forking out the usual guide's tip (not that there's anything to stop you paying a tip as well).

Places to Stay – bottom end

Camping About 2km north of town, just off the coast road to El-Jadida, is *Camping International*. It's a reasonable site, and much cooler than the town below in the hot summer months. They charge Dr12 per person, Dr9 per car, Dr9 to pitch a tent, Dr10 for a hot shower and Dr20 to use the pool. You'll need to get a petit taxi up here from the centre or the bus station.

Hotels There's a fair choice of budget hotels in Safi, most of them clustered around the port end of Rue du Souq and along Rue de R'bat. Many of the rooms are used by Moroccans from further afield who come to work in Safi during the week.

Inside the medina itself, the *Hôtel Essaouira* (☎ 464809) has comparatively small and gloomy rooms for Dr30/50/60. Warm showers are Dr5. It's adequate. Much the same is the *Hôtel de Paris*, where rooms cost Dr30 to Dr70. Warm showers are Dr5.

Further in is the *Hôtel d'Honneur*. It's cramped, but quite clean, and costs Dr30/50, including cold showers. Even cheaper is the *Hôtel Sabah*, a grim place with no shower at all.

The best value is the *Hôtel Majestic* (☎ 463131), right next to the medina wall, at the junction of Ave Moulay Youssef and Place de l'Indépendance. It offers very clean, pleasant rooms with washbasin for Dr30/60/90 (going up to Dr40/80/120 in the high season); shared showers with warm water are Dr5 extra. The best rooms look out onto the Qasr al-Bahr and the ocean. The staff are friendly, and one of the managers speaks French, Spanish and some English.

The *Hôtel L'Avenir* is another good place and charges the same as the Majestic. The rooms have toilets and some have cold showers.

The drawback is the cafe and small eatery inside, which can make it a bit noisy. There are good views from the roof.

On the south side of Place de l'Indépendance you can get yourself a tiny room for Dr25/50 in the *Hôtel Sevillana*, on Impasse Ben Hassan. The manager claims there are hot showers for Dr7.

Considerably better, but not up to the Majestic's standard, is the *Hôtel L'Océan* (☎ 464207), along Rue de R'bat. The rooms are quite OK, and there is a shower (Dr5 for a hot one) on each floor. Rooms cost Dr40/60. The *Hôtel Novelty* nearby, is unused to foreign guests. Its rooms (Dr20/40) are poky, but they are kept clean and the beds are fine. There are no showers, but there is a hammam nearby.

Places to Stay – middle

The only mid-range hotel close to the centre is the two-star *Hôtel Anis* (☎ 463078), on Rue de R'bat, where you can get a comfortable room with private shower and toilet for Dr122/150. They have limited parking.

The other mid-range hotels are higher up in the city, around Place Mohammed V. Rooms at the *Hôtel Assif* (☎ 622311; fax 621862), on Ave de la Liberté, are well decked-out, with heating, telephone and en suite bathrooms (Dr200/250). There is a restaurant in the hotel.

The *Hôtel Les Mimosas* (☎ 623208; fax 625955) consists of two block-like buildings either side of Rue Ibn Zeidoun. It can be a little confusing to find; follow Ave de la Liberté off the map, take the first right at Ave Allal Illane and a short way along turn left into Rue Ibn Zeidoun. Singles/doubles cost Dr157/187. The hotel has its own sauna, restaurant, bar and a nightclub called the *Golden Fish.*

Places to Stay – top end

There are two four-star hotels in Safi; the cheaper of the two is the *Hôtel Atlantide* (☎ 462160/1), on Rue Chaouki, at Dr249/300 for singles/doubles.

The Atlantide has a bar and restaurant and a little more character than its more expensive cousin up the road, the *Hôtel Safir* (☎ 464299), which sticks up on the hill on Ave Zerktouni. Rooms here cost Dr420/550 plus taxes. Amenities include a restaurant, bar and tennis courts.

Swimming Pools

The Hôtel Safir has a swimming pool and there's a small pool at the camp site north of town. Safi's municipal swimming pool is off Ave Mohammed V, by the public gardens.

STH OF CASABLANCA

Places to Eat

The real treat in Safi is sampling the seafood in the poky little *fish eateries* tucked away behind the Great Mosque. A meal of the freshest fish with chips, salads and soft drinks will cost about Dr20 per person. In the evening you'll find a few snack stalls set up at the port end of Rue du Souq. Offerings include tiny bowls of snails.

The *Café Restaurant El Bahia*, which takes up the whole top side of Place de l'Indépendance, has a cafe downstairs and a slightly fancier restaurant upstairs. A fairly ordinary meal will cost around Dr50. On the other side of Rue de R'bat, behind the Crédit du Maroc bank, is a small *snack place* open until late. A good-sized serving of chicken, rice, salad and bread costs Dr25.

The *Restaurant de Safi*, on Rue de la Maraine off Place de l'Indépendance, does reasonably priced brochettes. The *Restaurant Gegene*, on the same street, has a wider selection of dishes and is a little more expensive.

The only real alternatives to these places are the restaurants in the bigger hotels – the one in the *Hotel Assif*, up by Place Mohammed V in the swankier part of town, is said to be good.

Le Refuge (☎ 464354) is a very good fish restaurant a few kilometres north of Safi on the coast road to El-Jadida. It's closed on Mondays and is a little pricey, but is possibly *the* choice restaurant in the area. You'll need your own car or a petit taxi to get there.

Cafes & Patisseries There is no shortage of cafes along Place de l'Indépendance and Rue de R'bat. *Café M'Zoughen* is by far the nicest place for breakfast. A large coffee and a couple of fresh croissants will set you back Dr7. *Café Safina*, a short walk along the beach road south of the centre, looks out over the ocean.

You'll find plenty more cafes up around Place Mohammed V, though most of them are of the '500 men staring onto the footpath' variety. A selection of ice creams can be found at the *Glacier Jour et Nuit* and there's a good *patisserie* next door to the Café Oukaïmeden.

Entertainment

Bars & Nightclubs You can get a soothing ale in the *Café/Bar de la Poste*, on Place de l'Indépendance, and a couple of the other cafes here may serve alcohol inside. Otherwise, you're obliged to try the bars in the bigger hotels. Like many nightclubs in Morocco, the *Golden Fish*, in the Hotel Les Mimosas, has a bit of a dodgy reputation.

Getting There & Away

Bus Most of the CTM buses stopping in Safi originate elsewhere, so it might be a good idea to book in advance. Generally, though, you shouldn't have much trouble on the main runs. CTM has six buses a day to Casablanca, starting from 4.30 am (1st class Dr63; 2nd class Dr40). Its Marrakesh departure is at 7 am and costs Dr28.50. A bus to El-Jadida leaves at 8.30 am (Dr38; 1st class) and another at 1.30 pm (Dr24.50; 2nd class).

SATAS, the biggest bus company operating in southern Morocco, has a 7 am departure for Tan Tan, calling at Essaouira, Agadir and Tiznit on the way. It also has connections for Taroudannt and Tafraoute.

To the right of the CTM window is a booth advertising five runs a day to Essaouira and two early morning buses to El-Jadida.

Transport Chekkouri has several runs a day to Casablanca and to Marrakesh, as well as less frequent runs to Agadir and Rabat. There's also a 4 am departure to Taroudannt (Dr70).

Train A daily 5 am train connects with services to Marrakesh (Dr48), Casablanca (Dr53.50) and Rabat (Dr79) at Benguerir.

Getting Around

Both the bus terminal (Ave Président Kennedy) and the train station (Rue de R'bat) are quite some way from the centre of town, so it would be a good idea to either take a bus (No 7 from the bus station) or share a taxi (about Dr5) from these places to the centre (Place de l'Indépendance).

A bypass (Blvd Hassan II) circles the main part of town, which means buses don't go through the centre.

AROUND SAFI
Beaches
The beaches in the immediate vicinity of Safi are not much chop, so you need to go a little further afield. To the north you have the choice of **Lalla Fatna** (10km) and **Cap Beddouza** (20km). In summer there are local buses to both from Place de l'Indépendance. Otherwise, you'll have to take a grand taxi if you don't have your own transport. The coast road along the first 40km or so north of Safi is particularly breathtaking in parts.

About 30km to the south is **Souira Kedima**, populated by Moroccan summer holiday bungalows. This place is not special, whatever anyone in Safi may tell you. However, shortly before it, after you've cleared the Maroc Phosphore plant, there are a couple of wild and woolly Atlantic beaches that beg to be stopped at – if the wind dies down. ·

Essaouira

Essaouira (pronounced Esa-weera) is the most popular of the coastal towns with independent travellers, and only rarely do you see package tourists here. The town has a magnificent beach that curves for miles to the south, and its relaxed atmosphere is in complete contrast to the souq cities of Marrakesh, Fès, Meknès and Tangier.

It is also Morocco's best known windsurfing centre, and increasingly promotes itself as 'Windy City, Afrika'. Indeed, the Atlantic winds can be powerful, which is good news for windsurfers, but for much of the year bad news for sunbathers!

The fortifications of the old city are a mixture of Portuguese, French and Berber military architecture, and their massiveness lends a powerful mystique to the town. Inside them it's all light and charm. You'll find narrow lanes, whitewashed houses with blue painted doors, tranquil squares, pleasant cafes and artisans in tiny workshops beavering away at fragrant thuya wood.

The snug, fortified harbour, immediately south-west of the medina, is a hive of activity with nets laid out on the quayside, fishing boats unloading their catch, traditional wooden boats being built and fresh seafood sizzling on outdoor grills.

The **Île de Mogador**, south-west across the bay, is known for the Eleonara's falcons which come here to breed during summer.

Essaouira's reputation is spreading, and its tranquillity can be stretched to breaking point in summer. If you intend visiting during the high season, it's worth booking a room ahead.

It is a relatively laid-back place, but travellers should be prepared for a certain amount of hustling in Essaouira, mainly from out-of-towners who visit to try their luck during the summer season.

History
As far back as the 7th century BC, Phoenician sailors had discovered this part of the Moroccan coast, and it is believed the Romans followed in their footsteps. The main evidence for this comes from the little offshore islands, which were celebrated in ancient times for being the site for the manufacture of purple dyes (much used by the Romans). It is from this activity that the islets derived their name: the Purple Isles (Îles Purpuraires).

It was the Portuguese who established a commercial and military bridgehead here towards the end of the 15th century, which they named Mogador. They lost it in 1541, however, and the coastal town fell into decline.

Most of what stands today is the result of a curious experiment. In 1765, Sultan Sidi Mohammed bin Abdallah hired a French

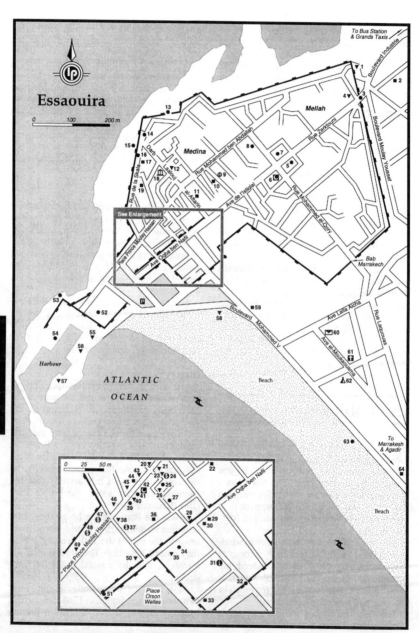

architect, Théodore Cornut, to design a city suitable for foreign traders. Renamed Essaouira, it became an open commercial link with Europe until the French protectorate was established in 1912, when it was rebaptised Mogador and lost much of its importance. With independence, in 1956, it again became Essaouira.

Orientation

Essaouira is a pretty compact place. Most of the cheaper hotels, restaurants, cafes, banks and shops are concentrated in or near the western third of the medina.

The bus station and grands taxis are about 1km to the north-east of the centre, in a fairly raggedy part of town.

Information

Tourist Office The Syndicat d'Initiative (☎ 473630) is within the town walls on Rue de Caire, just inside the main southern gate.

It's open Monday to Friday from 9 am to noon and 3 to 6.30 pm. It publishes four interesting booklets (in French) about the history and culture of Essaouira (Dr10 each) and can help out with brochures, maps and local information.

Money There are four banks around Place Prince Moulay Hassan. All are good for exchange and most can give credit-card cash advances. The Hôtel Beau Rivage will change money outside banking hours, but charges a commission of 10% to 15%.

Post & Communications The post office is a 10 minute walk south-east from Place Prince Moulay Hassan. The phone office, two doors down on the left, is open Monday to Saturday, but only during working hours. There are card phones outside and plenty of small téléboutiques around the medina.

Jack's Kiosk, on Place Prince Moulay Hassan, has a phone and fax service, operates a small travel agency and stocks a few English books and a good range of European newspapers and magazines.

STH OF CASABLANCA

PLACES TO STAY		
2	Hôtel Argana	
10	Hôtel Chakib	
11	Hôtel Riad Al Madina	
17	Hôtel Smara	
19	Hôtel des Remparts	
22	Hôtel Tafraout; Restaurant Dar Baba	
29	Hôtel Mechouar	
30	Hôtel Sahara	
33	Hôtel du Tourisme	
36	Hôtel Villa Maroc	
44	Hôtel Beau Rivage	
59	Hôtel des Îles	
62	Camping International	
64	Hôtel Tafoukt	

PLACES TO EAT		
1	Cafe	
4	Cheap Eats	
12	Restaurant El Khaima	
20	Snack Stand	
21	Café de la Place	
23	Driss Pâtisserie	
26	Chez Toufik	
28	Restaurant l'Horloge	
35	Restaurant El Minzah	
38	Restaurant Essalam	
40	Snack Stand	
43	Café/Pâtisserie L'Opéra	
45	Café de France	
46	Café Marrakesh	
49	Restaurant Bab Laachour	
50	Cafe	
55	Restaurant Le Coquillage	
56	Outdoor Fish Grills	
57	Chez Sam	
58	Restaurant Chalet de la Plage	

OTHER		
3	Bab Doukkala	
5	Jeweller's Souq	
6	Mosque	
7	Spice Souq	
8	Herbs & Cures Shop	
9	Hammam	
13	Bab al-Bahr	
14	Entry to Ramparts	
15	Skala de la Ville	
16	Wood Workshops	
18	Museum	
24	BMCE Bank	
25	Curio Shops	
27	Carpet Shops	
31	Syndicat d'Initiative	
32	Bab es-Sebaa	
34	Galerie d'Art	
37	Crédit du Maroc	
39	Afalkai Art	
41	Jack's Kiosk (Bookshop & Phone)	
42	Mosque	
47	Banque Populaire	
48	Banque Commercial du Maroc	
51	Bab al-Minzah	
52	Customs; Fish Market	
53	Skala du Port	
54	Shipyards	
60	Post & Phone Office	
61	Catholic Church	
63	Windsurfing Hire	

Ramparts

Heading north from Place Prince Moulay Hassan you can gain access to the ramparts and the **Skala de la Ville**, the impressive sea bastion built along the northern cliffs.

There's a collection of 18th and 19th century European brass cannon here and great views out to sea and across the medina. Down by the harbour, the **Skala du Port** offers picturesque views over the busy fishing port and of the Île de Mogador. Orson Welles filmed the dramatic opening shots of *Othello* on the ramparts of Essaouira.

Île de Mogador & Eleanora's Falcons

Just off the coast to the south-west is the Île de Mogador, where there's another massive fortification. It's actually two islands and several tiny islets – the famed Purple Isles of antiquity. There is a disused prison on the biggest of the islands.

These days, the islands are a sanctuary for Eleanora's falcons which come here to breed from April to October before making their incredible return journey south to Madagascar.

It is possible to arrange a boat trip across to the islands outside the breeding season, but you need to obtain permission from the local authorities (ask about this in the Syndicat d'Initiative or at Jack's Kiosk).

The falcons can easily be seen with binoculars from the town beach – the best time to spot them is in the early evening. Another viewing place is south of town, about 1km or so beyond the lighthouse, on the shore by the mouth of the river. The falcons sometimes come here for food. Other bird species you may see around this area include gulls, terns and Brown-throated Sand Martins.

Museum

The small museum on Darb Laalouj al-Attarin, opposite the Hôtel Majestic, was once the residence of Sultan Sidi Mohammed bin Abdallah's governor, and displays jewellery, costumes, weapons, musical instruments and tapestries.

There's a section explaining the signs and symbols used by local craftspeople and some interesting photographs of the town taken at the turn of the century. Admission is free.

Église Sainte Anne

The beautifully kept, light-filled Catholic church on Ave el-Moukaouama, just south of the post office, offers mass alternately in French, English, Dutch and German on Sunday at 10 am and every evening at 6.30 pm.

Beach & Watersports

The beach stretches some 10km down the coast to the sand dunes of Cap Sim. Free entertainment in the form of football matches often takes place at the top end of the beach. Further south you'll pass the ruins of an old fortress and pavilion partially covered in sand, as well as the wreck of a ship. The beach is safe for swimming and excellent for windsurfing.

Along the shore, just to the north of the Hôtel Tafoukt, you'll find a few places renting windsurfing equipment. Fanatic Fun Centre, a German-run place, charges Dr120 per hour for full gear. Next door is a more recently established Moroccan equivalent, the Royal Club, which charges a little less.

Both can organise horse-riding excursions along the beach towards Cap Sim (not cheap, and usually only possible in summer).

Fanatic Fun Centre can organise more ambitious horse-riding excursions further into the interior, lasting up to a couple of weeks.

Places to Stay – bottom end

Camping The best camp site is the one near Diabat (see Diabat in the Around Essaouira section below) about 5km out of town.

Camping International, along Blvd Mohammed V in Essaouira, is nothing but a patch of dirt with no shade. You'd have to be hard-up to stay here. (The toilets and showers leave something to be desired and one reader complained that the place was roamed by endless feral cats and dogs.) If you're willing to give the place a go, however, it costs Dr9 per person, Dr10 per car, Dr12 for electricity and up to Dr22 to pitch a tent. Hot showers are available.

Hotels Three of the most popular budget hotels are well situated near the ramparts and on Place Prince Moulay Hassan. If you arrive later in the day, don't be surprised to find them full.

The first (and probably the most attractive, because of the sea views) is the *Hôtel Smara* (☎ 472655) on Rue de la Skala. It is clean and friendly and offers singles, doubles and triples for Dr50, Dr70 and Dr90 respectively. Some of the rooms are rather small and claustrophobic.

The rooms with sea views are much sought after, so you may have to wait a day or so before you can get one. The same views can be had from the roof – which is not a bad place to catch some sun protected from the wind. Showers (warm rather than hot) cost an extra Dr2, and breakfast is available for Dr10.

The second place is the *Hôtel Beau Rivage* (☎/fax 472925), overlooking Place Prince Moulay Hassan. The staff are friendly, the rooms are clean and there are cafes and patisseries just outside the front door. Simple rooms with two beds cost Dr70. The same with private shower is Dr120. The reception desk downstairs sells film and other odds and ends and if the banks are closed you can change money here.

The third place is the *Hôtel des Remparts* (☎ 473166), on Rue Ibn Rochd, a big, slightly rundown building on three floors with a vast roof terrace. Unfortunately, few of the rooms have sea views (those that do cost Dr200 for a double). Singles/doubles cost Dr75/100, including use of a shared warm shower, and some rooms are equipped with a bath (cold water only).

On the other side of the main square, on Rue Mohammed ben Massaoud, the *Hôtel du Tourisme* (☎ 472075) is a decent place, though it could do with a bit of tarting up. It offers clean, quiet singles/doubles for

Dr36/47. Showers are available for Dr5. They also have bigger rooms that sleep up to four, and some rooms with views towards the port and beach. There's a roof terrace here, too.

Further afield, in towards the middle of the medina, is the fairly modern *Hôtel Chakib* (☎ 472291), which charges Dr40, Dr70 and Dr90 for singles, doubles and triples with shared bathroom (tepid if you're lucky). It's ordinary, but acceptable.

Outside the medina is the *Hôtel Argana*. Rooms here are OK for Dr40/60/90, but the dusty, shantytown location doesn't make it a hugely attractive option.

A little more expensive is the one-star *Hôtel Tafraout* (☎ 472120) at 7 Rue de Marrakesh (off Rue Mohammed ben Abdallah). It's clean, comfortable and very welcoming. Singles/doubles without private bathroom cost Dr60/80, while those with bathroom cost Dr75/90. The double rooms contain a double and a single bed. There's a terrace on the roof.

Places to Stay – middle
The two-star *Hôtel Sahara* (☎ 472292), on Ave Oqba ben Nafii, has a mixed bag of rooms, so if you can get a look at a few before deciding, so much the better.

Singles/ doubles without shower or toilet cost Dr81/110 plus tax. Those with shower and toilet are Dr157/187 plus taxes. Hot water is available all day.

Just next door is the *Hôtel Mechouar* (☎ 472828). Rooms here also vary a lot; the better ones are those at the front of the hotel. Singles/doubles with shower, toilet and washbasin cost Dr100/120. The plumbing can be unreliable. The hotel has a bar downstairs.

On the main road heading into the medina, practically right on the beach, is the three-star *Hôtel Tafoukt* (☎ 784504/5; fax 784416) at 58 Blvd Mohammed V. It has 40 self-contained singles/doubles for Dr288/ 300 including breakfast.

The rooms are clean, comfortable and have phones and the hotel has a restaurant and bar.

Places to Stay – top end

Hôtel Villa Maroc (☎ 473147; fax 472806), just inside the inner city walls at 10 Rue Abdallah ben Yassin, is one top-grade establishment well worth paying for.

Housed in two renovated 18th century houses, the villa has been exquisitely decorated – there are several intimate salons where you can sip mint tea and gaze at antiques and bowls brimming with rose petals. There are only a dozen or so rooms, so booking well ahead is essential – they can be booked up for months. Singles/doubles cost Dr435/555 plus taxes. The villa also has an excellent restaurant (about Dr150 per head), but you'll need to book.

The four-star *Hôtel des Îles* (☎ 784620; fax 472472), on Blvd Mohammed V, is closer to the medina than the Tafoukt, and is equipped with a bar, nightclub and all the conveniences you would expect from such a hotel (including mini bar, towelling robes and baskets of fruit). Its 70 rooms start at Dr485/610 for basic singles/doubles and rise to Dr2000 for the main suite. All prices are exclusive of taxes.

The *Hôtel Riad Al Madina* (☎ 472727; fax 472907), inside the medina at 9 Darb Laaouj al-Attarin, was scheduled to open in 1997. Originally a local pasha's villa, in the 60s and 70s it became the famed Hôtel du Pasha frequented by the likes of Jimi Hendrix, Frank Zappa, Leonard Cohen and Jefferson Airplane.

Painstakingly restored to its original 18th century splendour, it contains 27 rooms, four suites, a beautiful central courtyard, a restaurant and a sauna. Double rooms, all with bathroom, TV and telephone, cost around Dr300; the suites go from Dr400.

Swimming Pools

The Hôtel des Îles, on Blvd Mohammed V, has a pool.

Hammams

There are plenty of small hammams hidden about town; there's one for women across the road from the Hôtel Chakib, in the centre of the medina.

Places to Eat

For simple snacks and cheap hole-in-the-wall-type food, there are a few little places along Rue Mohammed ben Abdallah, Rue Zerktouni and in the old mellah just inside Bab Doukkala.

On Place Prince Moulay Hassan, there are two snack stands selling excellent baguettes stuffed with meat, salad and just about anything else you want for around Dr15. There's a reasonable food stall next to the Hôtel Chakib too.

The *Restaurant L'Horloge*, tucked away on a shady little square close to the inner walls of the medina, is a popular place with travellers, either for mint tea or a moderately priced Moroccan meal. Breakfast is Dr10 and there's a three course lunch or supper menu for Dr45.

Nearby is the more expensive *Chez Toufik*, which has been done up as a traditional Berber salon. A good range of Moroccan dishes are on offer and there's music most evenings.

Deservedly popular is the *Restaurant Essalam*, on Place Prince Moulay Hassan, where you can pick up an excellent meal for around Dr38. The tajine is exceptionally good. The restaurant is generally packed with foreigners, with good reason. They take credit cards here.

The *Restaurant Dar Baba*, just by the Hôtel Tafraout, offers a small range of Italian dishes at reasonable prices.

The *Restaurant El Minzah*, on Ave Oqba ben Nafii, has tasty set menus for about Dr70.

A step up in price, with a more formal atmosphere, the *Restaurant El Khaima* is set back on a small square off Darb Laalouj al-Attarin.

You can eat outdoors on the patio. Main courses generally cost about Dr60, and they offer two fixed menus: one for Dr80, and a seafood splashout at Dr180.

Chez Sam is a long-standing institution famous throughout Morocco for its excellent seafood. The restaurant overlooks the harbour at the far end of the port. You can either eat à la carte (reckon on about Dr100 a head, including wine) or take one of the two set menus (Dr70 or Dr170). Ask for recommendations on the best fish of the day. The restaurant is licensed (beer and wine), takes most major credit cards and is open daily for lunch and dinner.

The recently opened *Restaurant Le Co-quillage*, just on the left as you walk into the port, also specialises in seafood. Prices are on a par with Chez Sam.

In between Chez Sam and Le Coquillage you'll find several very cheap outdoor *fish grills* offering a fabulous selection of fresh seafood straight from the day's catch. Meals cost from Dr20. The grills are open from 11 am to 7 pm.

Back on Place Prince Moulay Hassan, the licensed *Restaurant Bab Laachour* also offers a range of seafood – the salads here are particularly good. You're looking at Dr70 or so for a full meal.

Also good for seafood is *Restaurant Chalet de la Plage*, which is on the beach, just outside the city walls. It offers four-course meals for Dr90 (extra for cheese, tea and coffee). Main courses a la carte range from Dr50 to Dr90.

Cafes & Patisseries The most popular and relaxing place for a slow breakfast is Place Prince Moulay Hassan. Some people spend the better part of a day here, slowly shifting from cafe to cafe with the moving sunlight.

The *Driss Pâtisserie* has a good range of croissants and other pastries to get the day going. Equally good is the *Café/Pâtisserie L'Opéra*, which spills out in front of the Hôtel Beau Rivage.

The *Café de France* is popular with locals right through the day, as is the *Café Marrakesh*.

The *Café de la Place* is not hot on pastries, but is a decent spot for coffee. The food is otherwise mediocre (about Dr30 for a main course and an outrageous Dr10 to Dr15 for soups).

Entertainment
Bars & Nightclubs Apart from enjoying a drink over dinner in the licensed restau-

rants, Essaouira doesn't have many night-time alternatives. Local drinkers gather in the bar under the *Hôtel Mechouar*. More upmarket tipplers can head to the rather kitsch *Orson Welles Bar* at the Hôtel des Îles – which also has a nightclub.

Things to Buy
Beneath the ramparts of the Skala de la Ville are dozens of wood-carving work-shops overflowing with exquisite mar-quetry work made from local thuya wood. The work is reputedly the best in Morocco.

The craftsmen, who toil away until the last fading light of dusk, are very accom-modating, so you can walk around and look at what they are doing without a great deal of pressure to buy (but because there's little hard sell, don't expect to be able to reduce their stated prices by much).

The woodcarvers of Essaouira work in thuya wood to produce everything from jewellery boxes to life-size statues.

STH OF CASABLANCA

A quality store where you can inspect a whole range of thuya wood products – from furniture to bizarre life-size statues – is Afalkai Art on Place Prince Moulay Hassan. Not the cheapest place around, it will nevertheless give you a good feel for what's available. The Galerie d'Art, on Ave Oqba ben Nafii, shows unusual woodwork by owner and designer Frederic Damgaard, as well as paintings by the many artists who live in Essaouira.

Carpet and rug shops, as well as bric-a-brac, jewellery and brassware shops, are clustered together in the narrow street, and on the small square between Place Prince Moulay Hassan and the ramparts that flank the Ave Oqba ben Nafii.

In the heart of the medina, up towards the mellah, you'll find a spice souq selling all sorts of medicinal herbs and spices, as well as perfumes and dyes. The nearby jewellery souq is worth a look. Jewish silversmiths, who traditionally made much of the jewellery of Morocco, moved to Essaouira and other southern towns when the mellahs of the big cities became overcrowded.

Getting There & Away

Bus The bus station is about 1km to the north-east of the medina centre. It's not signposted and is in a pretty shabby area.

CTM is at window No 7. There is a bus at 10.30 am to Safi for Dr21.50. Another at the same time goes to Casablanca (Dr56; 6½ hours) via El-Jadida (Dr40.50). The fast midnight bus to Casa costs Dr92 (five hours). The 12.30 pm bus to Agadir costs Dr37 (about three hours). This service goes on to Tiznit (Dr43).

SATAS has a more extensive network in the south than CTM. It runs a 10 am bus to Casablanca via El-Jadida, for about the same price. Buses to Agadir and on to Tiznit leave at 5.30, 9 and 11.30 am and 9.30 pm. There is a 9.30 am departure to Tan Tan, and buses to Safi, at 8 am, and 1 and 6 pm. The daily bus to Marrakesh leaves at 7 pm.

You can also get tickets on smaller lines to Safi (window No 3; up to seven services

a day) and Marrakesh (window No 9; up to 10 runs a day). The Marrakesh bus costs Dr30 and takes about 3½ hours.

Several other private-line buses also do the run to Casablanca, for about Dr60. Other destinations include Rabat, Taroudannt and Tafraoute.

Train Supratours, which has an office in the Hôtel des Îles, runs buses to connect with trains. The Supratours bus to Marrakesh train station leaves at 6.30 pm and takes 2½ hours; it's more expensive than a normal bus. You can buy a through ticket from here to any destination served by train.

Taxi The grand taxi lot is next to the bus station. The fare to Agadir (or nearby Inezgane) is around Dr50.

Getting Around

The blue petits taxis are a good idea for getting to and from the bus station (about Dr10). You can also take a ride around town in one of the horse-drawn calèches that gather just outside Bab Doukkala.

You can hire bicycles from a small place next to Chez Toufik, to the left off Place Prince Moulay Hassan, for Dr70 per day.

AROUND ESSAOUIRA
Diabat

Close to Cap Sim, and inland about 1km through sand dunes and scrub, is the Berber village of Diabat, which became a legend among hippies in the 60s after a visit by Jimi Hendrix.

It subsequently became a dope-smoking colony similar to those on the beaches of Goa (in India), but was cleared by the police in the mid-70s following the murder of several hippies by local junkies. These days it has returned to its own tranquil self, but there seems little reason to visit.

Several hundred metres further up the rocky track from Diabat is the long-established *Auberge Tangaro*. Once a basic and cheap place to stay, it has been done up by its Italian owner and costs Dr450 a double with half-board.

Driving from Essaouira, take the coast road for Agadir, and turn up the track just after the bridge about 5km out of town. There is a small camp site next door – though fairly basic, it's a much better alternative to the camping ground in Essaouira.

Sidi Kaouki

About 8km further south is a windsurfing spot that is fast growing in popularity. You need your own transport to get here or you could try negotiating a grand taxi from Essaouira.

There's a basic camp site here, too, and a small hotel, the expensive *La Residence Kaouki Beach* run by the owners of the Villa Maroc in Essaouira.

Agadir

Agadir is a modern city, which was completely rebuilt after a devastating earthquake in 1960. Sitting by a vast sweep of protected beach, the town has been specifically developed as a resort for short-stay package tourists from Europe, who arrive daily by the planeload in search of sun, sand and a sanitised version of the mysteries of the Barbary Coast.

Agadir's high tourist profile often leads people to forget its growing importance as a commercial and fishing port – a big chunk of Morocco's sardine catch now comes through Agadir, and the driver arriving in Agadir from the north can hardly fail to notice the sprawling port facilities.

The reek of Ambre Soleil and the rustle of *Paris Match*, *Der Spiegel* and the airmail *Sunday Times* fill the air. Not that it's unpleasant – it's just that it could be any resort town on the northern Mediterranean coast. Agadir is also one of the more expensive cities in Morocco (unless of course you are on a very cheap package tour).

The beach, however, is pleasant and Agadir is well placed for trips south-east into the Anti-Atlas and north-east into the High Atlas (a two hour drive from Agadir and you're into some pretty mountain country), as well as further south towards the Western Sahara.

Bird-watchers will find a rewarding estuarine area busy with bird life just a few kilometres south of Agadir.

History

Little is known of Agadir's distant past, but in 1505 an enterprising Portuguese mariner decided to build himself a fort, Santa Cruz de Cap de Gué, a few kilometres north of the modern city.

Sold to the Portuguese government eight years later, it became a busy centre of commerce, visited by Portuguese, Genoese and French merchants. Retaken by the Moroccans in 1541 and subsequently used as the main outlet for products (especially sugar cane) from the Souss region, it slowly began to decline, and was finally eclipsed by the rise of Essaouira in the late 18th century.

In 1911, shortly before Morocco became a French Protectorate, Germany took gunboat diplomacy to the limit with France by sending the warship *Panther* to make noises off the Agadir coast.

The Germans were miffed over French and British plans to keep North Africa to themselves. They managed to avoid going to war on this occasion, but only for three years.

On 29 February 1960, just four years after Morocco gained independence, Agadir was flattened by an earthquake, killing 15,000 people. Agadir has since been completely rebuilt, and continues to grow as Morocco's top beach resort.

Orientation

Agadir's bus station and most of the budget hotels are in a small area called Nouveau Talborjt in the north-east of the town. From here it's about a 20 minute walk down to the beach, lined with cafes, restaurants and expensive hotels. Most of the banks and the main post office are located between the beach and Ave du Prince Moulay Abdallah.

Information

Tourist Offices Délégation du Tourisme
(☎ 846377; fax 846378) is on the upper
level of the central market area, just off Ave
Sidi Mohammed. It's open Monday to
Thursday from 8.30 am to noon and 2.30 to
6.30 pm. On Friday it's open from 8.30 to
11.30 am and 3 to 6.30 pm.

The office also has an information desk
at the airport (☎ 839077) which is open
daily.

At the Syndicat d'Initiative (☎ 840307),
on Blvd Mohammed V at the junction with
Ave du Général Kettani, you can buy a
small *Guide d'Agadir*, which contains some
useful information (such as lists of car hire
companies, doctors and the like) for Dr10.
They also have a notice board with bus
timetables and details of market days in
surrounding towns. It's open Monday to
Friday from 9 am to noon and from 3 to 6
pm. During summer it's also open on the
weekend.

Money Most banks have branches here.
The BMCE and BMCI, both at the beach

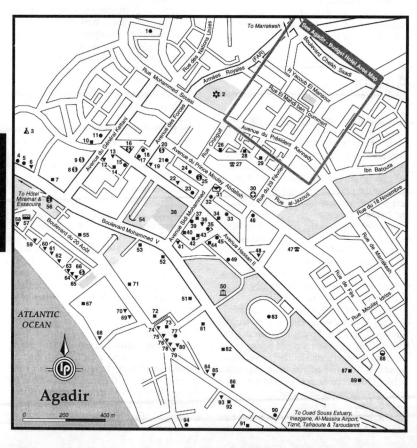

end of Ave du Général Kettani, also have ATMs.

The Banque Populaire, on Ave Hassan II opposite Restaurant La Tour de Paris, is good and doesn't charge commission on travellers cheques. It also has a bureau de change, further west on Ave Hassan II next to Hôtel Kamal, which is open on Saturday. The larger hotels can change cash and travellers cheques.

Credit du Maroc (☎ 840188), on Ave des Forces Armées Royales (FAR), represents American Express in Agadir.

Post & Communications The main post office, on Ave du Prince Moulay Abdallah, is open Monday to Friday from 8.30 am to 6.45 pm. There is another post office (La Poste), on Rue du 29 Février, in the budget hotel area.

The phone office is in the central post office. It's open seven days a week from 8 am to 9 pm.

There are plenty of téléboutiques around, including one about 50m up from the Hôtel Talborjt. They generally stay open until about 10 pm.

PLACES TO STAY
3 Camping Ground
7 Résidence Tilila
10 Hôtel Petite Suède
14 Hôtel Sud Bahia
26 Hôtel Talborjt
28 Hôtel Itrane
29 Hôtel Ayour
34 Atlantic Hôtel
37 Hôtel Kamal
40 Hôtel Les Palmiers
42 Hôtel Aladin
43 Résidence Sacha
44 Résidence Yasmina
51 Hôtel Salem
52 Hôtel Anezi
53 Hôtel Ali Baba
55 Sheraton Hôtel
67 Hôtel Tafoukt
71 Hôtel Europa Safir
72 Hôtel Al Medina Palace
73 Hôtel Tagadirt
81 Hôtel Transatlantique
82 Hôtel Adrar
86 Hôtel Mabrouk
87 Hôtel Solman
89 Hôtel Les Cinq Parties du Monde
91 Agadir Hôtel; Restaurant Complex
92 Résidence Club La Kasbah

PLACES TO EAT
6 Restaurant Marine Heim
12 Restaurant Darkoum
13 Restaurant La Tour de Paris
19 Cafes
22 Italian Restaurants
36 Restaurant Scampi
41 Restaurant La Tonkinoise
48 Café Tafarnout
58 Cafes
59 Restaurant Le Côte d'Or
60 Restaurant Don Vito
61 Café Le Kermesse
62 Restaurant Le Nil Bleu
63 Restaurant Le Vendôme
64 Hollywood Fast Food
65 The Palace Bar/Café
68 Restaurant La Perla del Mare
69 Pizzeria & Gelato
70 Restaurant Golden Gate
74 Café Le Central & Disco
75 Restaurant Imin
76 Restaurant Jockey
78 Restaurant Pizza Pino
79 Restaurant Le Petite Dôme
80 Restaurant La Mama
84 Restaurant El Marrakchi
85 Restaurant Grill du Soleil
93 Restaurant Jazz

OTHER
1 American Language Center
2 Jardin de Olhão
4 Budget (Car Rental)
5 Hertz (Car Rental)
8 BMCE (ATM)
9 BMCI (ATM)
11 Royal Air Maroc
15 Tour Agents
16 Banque Populaire
17 Newsstand
18 Supratours
20 Crédit du Maroc (American Express)
21 Cinéma Rialto
23 Uniprix Supermarket
24 Central Market
25 Tourist Office
27 Téléboutique (Phones)
30 Clinique Al Massira
31 Post Office
32 Hôtel de Ville (Town Hall); Pharmacie de Garde
33 Liquor Store
35 Car/Motorcycle Hire
38 Place de l'Espérance
39 Air France
45 Travel Agents (Local Excursions & Charter Flights)
46 New Labcolor (Kodak)
47 Téléboutique (Phones)
49 Royal Tennis Club of Agadir
50 Musée Municipal
54 Vallée des Oiseaux
56 Syndicat d'Initiative
57 Public Swimming Pool
66 Banque Populaire
77 Newsstand
83 Stadium
88 Place Taxis et Bus (Local Buses & Taghezout Grands Taxis)
90 Alhambra Cabaret
94 Newsstand

STH OF CASABLANCA

Foreign Consulates Foreign consulates in Agadir include:

Belgium
     Ave Hassan II (☎ 821700)
France
     Blvd Mohammed Saadi (☎ 840826)
Italy
     Rue du Souvenir (☎ 823013)
Spain
     42 Rue Ibn Batouta, Secteur Mixte (☎ 845681; fax 822126)
Sweden
     Rue de l'Entraide (☎ 823048)
UK
     Hôtel Sud Bahia, Rue des Administrations Publiques (☎ 827741)

Newsstands There are several newsstands with a fair selection of European and international press (usually a day or two late). There's a good one in front of Restaurant La Tonkinoise on Ave Sidi Mohammed, and another on the corner of Ave Hassan II and Ave des FAR.

Bookshops The Crown English Bookshop, a couple of doors down from the tourist office in the central market area, has reopened and once again offers a pretty good selection of English books.

Laundry There is a coin-operated laundry at the four-star Hôtel Al Medina Palace on Blvd du 20 Août. It's open Monday to Saturday from 9 am to 5 pm. A wash costs Dr30 and the dryer takes Dr10 coins. Most hotels will do laundry for you for around Dr20.

Film & Photography You can buy and develop film in several places. New Labcolor, on Ave du Prince Moulay Abdallah, is one of the nearest to the budget hotel area.

Language Schools The American Language Center (☎ 821589) has a branch at 6 Impasse de Baghdad.

The Moroccan Institute of Management (☎ 823356; fax 823335), on Ave Hassan II, operates as a representative for the International Language Centre.

Medical Services & Emergencies The Clinique Al-Massira (☎ 843238), on Ave du Prince Moulay Abdallah, is a large established clinic. The *Guide d'Agadir* contains lists of doctors, dentists, clinics and pharmacies. The main tourist office also posts a list of doctors.

There's an all-night chemist, Pharmacie de Garde (☎ 820349), near the Hôtel de Ville.

Musée Municipal

This modest museum contains very good displays of Saharan nomadic arts and crafts provided by Dutch art lecturer, and longtime resident of Marrakesh, Bert Flint (he has opened up the Maison Tiskiwin in Marrakesh with further displays). It's open Monday to Saturday from 9.30 am to 1 pm and 2.30 to 6 pm. Entry costs Dr10.

Vallée des Oiseaux

This pleasant strip of parkland running between Ave Hassan II and under Blvd Mohammed V to Blvd du 20 Août, contains a tiny aviary, a zoo and a children's playground. Admission is Dr5 for adults and Dr3 for children.

Kasbah

A few kilometres up the hill to the northeast of the town is what's left of the old kasbah. A Dutch inscription from 1746 still adorns the gateway, exhorting visitors to 'fear God and honour your king'.

The fort was built in 1540, overlooking the former Portuguese emplacement, and was restored and regarrisoned in 1752, in case Portugal decided to make a comeback.

The ramparts were partially restored after the 1960 earthquake, but nothing remains within. The grassy area below the kasbah, known as Ancienne Talborjt, covers the remains of Agadir's medina. Thousands of people lie here where they died when the quake hit.

Jardim de Olhão

These rather odd-looking gardens mark the twinning of Agadir with the Portuguese town of Olhão, and commemorate the 'historical ties' that have so often had Morocco and Portugal at loggerheads. The gardens are open from 2.30 to 6.30 pm only.

Oued Souss Estuary

A few kilometres south of Agadir (signposted off the main road to Inezgane) is an estuarine area busy with bird life. At the river mouth you're likely to see Oystercatchers, plovers, godwits, curlews, herons, Spoonbills, Flamingos, gulls and terns, to name but a few.

Just to the north of the river mouth is King Hassan's well-guarded Royal Palace. You can't visit the King, of course, but the floodlit perimeter of the palace is apparently a good place for watching Red-necked Nightjars!

Beach & Watersports

Agadir's main claim to fame is its fine crescent beach, which usually remains unruffled when the Atlantic winds are blustering elsewhere. It's very well kept and you can wander at will along the sands without being hassled. In front of the main beach hotels, you are supposed to pay a fee for use of the beach, deckchairs, umbrellas and the like. In practice you can generally plonk your towel down anywhere.

In the area down in front of the Hôtel Beach Club, towards the southern end of the beach, you can rent various implements to enhance your enjoyment of the water, including pedalos, jetskis, surfskis and surfboards (there is reported to be a good, though inconsistent, right-hand break at Anchor Point). Equipment hire isn't cheap. A surfboard will set you back Dr100 an hour and a wetsuit will be another Dr30. An hour on a surfski (which usually means paddling around) costs Dr150.

Further south along the beach you'll find people with horses, camels and dune trikes for hire. Prices, again, are high.

Most of the larger hotels organise all sorts of activities for their guests. Those interested in fishing may want to enquire about the possibilities. Otherwise, try Sports

Évasion Maroc (☎ 840122), next to the Hôtel Sud Bahia, which can organise ocean fishing trips, including shark fishing. They also offer horse-riding.

Organised Tours

Agadir is a thriving centre for locally organised tours, mostly aimed at charter flight tourists who are in Morocco for a week or two and are anxious to do more than lounge around on the sand. There is any number of agents, many of them branch offices of European package-tour companies.

You'll find a bunch of them clustered around the intersection of Ave Hassan II and Ave des FAR. There are a few more around Ave Sidi Mohammed.

Principal destinations include Marrakesh, Taroudannt, Tafraoute and Immouzzer des Ida Outanane. Of these, only the latter can be a little difficult to do under your own steam. This is by far the better way to approach them especially as none of the organised trips is cheap. They range from Dr200 for a day at Immouzzer to Dr1400 for a day trundling about in a 4WD.

Places to Stay – bottom end

Camping Agadir's camp site (☎ 846683), just off Blvd Mohammed V on the port side of town, is within walking distance of both the beach and town centre.

It's not the worst of Moroccan camping grounds, but the ground is pretty stony and campervans predominate. It costs Dr10 per person, Dr10 for a car, Dr10 to Dr15 to pitch a tent (depending on its size), Dr12 for electricity and Dr7.50 for a hot shower. There's a general grocery store.

Hotels Most of the budget hotels and a few of the mid-range hotels are concentrated near the bus area on Rue Yacoub El Mansour and around Rue Allal ben Abdallah (this is a slightly sleazy area with some prostitution taking place in the grubbier hotels – it's not unsafe, but women should be aware).

In the high seasons, you must get into

Agadir early in the day (or book ahead) if you want to be sure of a room. If you arrive late, you may have to pay through the nose at an expensive hotel. By standards elsewhere, you pay more for less in Agadir.

The two cheapest places are located just behind the SATAS office, on Place Lahcen Tamri (see the Agadir Budget Hotel Area map). The *Hôtel Canaria* (☎ 846727) has very basic rooms for Dr55/80/115 with shared shower, and the *Hôtel Massa* offers pretty much the same deal.

With a little more money, the choice widens somewhat. Although the rooms are little better, the *Hôtel Select*, down a lane off Rue Allal ben Abdallah, is a quieter, more pleasant place to stay than the above two. Rooms, without shower, cost Dr63/81.

The *Hôtel Aït Laayoune* (☎ 824375) and the *Hôtel Amenou* (☎ 845615), both on Rue Yacoub el-Mansour, charge Dr70/90 for singles/doubles and are a definite improvement on the above. The *Hôtel La Tour Eiffel* (☎ 823712), on Rue du 29 Février opposite the mosque, has rooms for the same price. Though the promised hot water may not materialise, these three places are all neat and clean, and fine for a night or two.

The *Hôtel Excelsior* (☎ 821028), across the road from the Hôtel Aït Laayoune, has reasonable rooms without shower for Dr68/87 (a warm communal shower costs Dr5) and with shower for Dr97/112.

The *Hôtel de la Baie* (☎ 823014), on the corner of Rue Allal ben Abdallah and Ave du Président Kennedy, is a mixed bag. The rooms without shower for Dr49/66 (a hot shower is Dr5) are adequate. The rooms with shower (Dr75/96) are not too bad, although for a dollar or two more you could

---

PLACES TO STAY
3	Hôtel Amenou
6	Hôtel Massa; Hôtel Canaria
8	Hôtel Sindibad
11	Hôtel Aït Laayoune
12	Hôtel Excelsior
13	Hôtel Moderne
15	Hôtel Diaf
16	Hôtel El Bahia
17	Hôtel La Tour Eiffel
20	Hôtel de Paris; Douche Étoile
25	Hôtel Select
27	Hôtel de la Baie

PLACES TO EAT
7	Restaurants Coq d'Or, Echabab & Mille et Une Nuits
9	Glacier (Ice Cream)
14	Café Pâtisserie Oufella
19	Café la Terrasse
22	Restaurant Tamouate
24	Restaurant Select
28	Café Les Arcades

OTHER
1	Post Office
2	Complexe Artisanal
4	Cinéma Sahara
5	SATAS (Buses)
10	CTM (Buses)
18	Mohammed V Mosque
21	Banque Populaire
23	BMCE Bank
26	Douche Select (Public Shower)

STH OF CASABLANCA

Agadir – Budget Hotel Area

The North Atlantic Coast
Top: Weathered ramparts, Asilah.
Middle: Walls of chellah, Rabat.
Bottom: Siesta in Casablanca Medina.

Atlantic – South of Casablanca
Top Left: Date palms fringe the Oued Assaka near Tafraoute.
Top Right: But is it art? Belgian artist Jean Veran's painted rocks, near Tafraoute.
Bottom: The massive Portuguese-built Qasr al-Bahr, Safi.

dramatically improve your quality of life elsewhere.

The *Hôtel Moderne* (☎ 823373), Rue El Mahdi ben Toummert, is in a quieter spot and offers parking space. Singles/doubles without shower cost Dr70/95 and rooms with shower are Dr106/134.

One of the better places in the area is the *Hôtel de Paris* (☎ 822694), on Ave du Président Kennedy. It has clean and very comfortable little rooms (with washbasin and wardrobe) for Dr88/108 without private bathroom, or Dr148/182 with. The rooms are gathered around peaceful courtyards dominated by two enormous rubber trees. You can sit up on the roof, too. The shared hot shower is generally steaming.

The *Hôtel Diaf* (☎ 825852), on Rue Allal ben Abdallah, also has decent rooms. You pay Dr106/134 for singles/doubles with private bathroom. Hot water is available only in the evening.

Places to Stay – middle

The *Hôtel Petite Suède* (☎ 840779; fax 840057) is a fairly tranquil, recently expanded place just off Ave du Général Kettani (see the Agadir map). For Dr133/154, the comfortable rooms with en suite bathroom are good value.

The hotel also offers one and two week deals which include double room and car hire. One week's accommodation plus hire of a Renault 4 costs from Dr3200.

There are three hotels on Rue de l'Entraide, just on the beach side of Ave du Président Kennedy. The cheapest is the *Hôtel Itrane* (☎ 822959), which charges Dr121/140 for reasonable singles/doubles, but is often full.

The two-star *Hôtel Ayour* (☎ 824976), at No 4, is a modern establishment that even boasts a solarium. It has decent-sized rooms with private bathroom and TV for Dr179/215.

More expensive still, but very good, the *Hôtel Talborjt* (☎ 841832) offers pleasant, carpeted rooms, some overlooking lush gardens. They cost Dr242/302 in the low season, Dr251/314 in the high season.

Back up in the heart of the budget hotel area are two slightly fancier hotels than the surrounding ones.

The *Hôtel Sindibad* (☎ 823477; fax 842474) has pleasant rooms with phone for Dr184/216. They also have a restaurant.

Another comfortable place, and one of the better hotels in this range, is the *Hôtel El Bahia* (☎ 822724; fax 824515). Again, rooms have a phone, and in winter are centrally heated. The cheapest rooms cost Dr110/130 (a hot shower is Dr6). Rooms with shower cost Dr150/180, while those with full bathroom are Dr188/220. The hotel has a roof terrace.

The well located *Hôtel/Restaurant Les Palmiers* (☎ 843719; fax 822580), on Ave Sidi Mohammed (see the Agadir map), is a friendly place close to several restaurants and not too far from the beach. Comfortable rooms with bathroom and TV cost Dr198/234.

A fine two-star place to stay is the *Atlantic Hôtel* (☎ 843661/2) on Ave Hassan II. It's clean and comfortable, and has boiling hot water 24 hours a day. Rooms cost Dr200/225. Breakfast is available in the pleasant, leafy courtyard. Better still is the *Hôtel Aladin* (☎ 843228; fax 846071), on Rue de la Jeunesse.

Rooms have balconies and cost Dr242/302 in the low season or Dr251/314 in the high season.

Centrally located on Ave Hassan II, the *Hôtel Kamal* (☎ 842817; fax 843940),has perfectly acceptable rooms with bathroom for Dr292/357.

The *Hôtel Les Cinq Parties du Monde* is a good, modern hotel on Ave Hassan II, out near the local bus and grand taxi lots. Under normal circumstances there'd be no reason to stay in this particularly ugly part of town, but if you're having trouble elsewhere, or arrive here late at night and can't be bothered going further afield, it's OK for a night.

Places to Stay – top end

You will find no shortage of expensive hotels in Agadir. The bulk of them are inhabited by block-booked charter groups, which generally get a considerable discount on the normal individual prices.

At the lower end of the scale, and not in the most appealing position compared to some of its beachside counterparts, the *Hôtel Sud Bahia* (☎ 840782; fax 846386), off Ave du Général Kettani, charges Dr205/290 in the low season. The rooms are modern and in reasonable shape, with bathroom and phone, and there are 246 of them, so the place is unlikely to be full.

If you want this kind of hotel, you'd be much better off hunting around the beachside places and seeing what kind of deal you can come up with.

The *Hôtel Miramar* (☎ 840770), at the western end of Blvd Mohammed V, is an older place – the only hotel in fact to survive the earthquake – offering just a few rooms for Dr222/282, including breakfast. The hotel has a bar and a good restaurant.

One of the newer, swankier hotels is the *Transatlantique* (☎ 842110; fax 842076). Their low-season rates start at Dr375/477. Places like the *Résidence Club La Kasbah* (☎ 823636) cost more like Dr850/1360.

There are numerous such places along Agadir's beachfront, particularly on Blvd Mohammed V and Blvd du 20 Août and on the beach itself (you can get a full list from the tourist offices and in the *Guide d'Agadir*). They tend to get more expensive the further south you go.

Swimming Pools
There's a public pool behind the Syndicat d'Initiative, at the top end of the beach. The mid-range Hôtel Aladin has its own small pool and almost all the top-end places, including the Hôtel Sud Bahia, have swimming pools.

Hammams
There are hammams to be found around the budget hotel area. The Hôtel Select, down a lane off Rue Allal ben Abdallah (see the Agadir Budget Hotel Area map), runs a public shower, Douche Select, next door for Dr5.

Hot showers are the same price at Douche Étoile, behind the Hôtel de Paris.

Places to Eat
Agadir is crawling with restaurants and cafes – many, but by no means all, are on the expensive side. In addition to the following, a few more are marked on the map. The best idea, especially if you do have a bit of money to throw around, is to wander about and see what takes your fancy.

The *Guide d'Agadir* also has a list of the more pricey places. Don't leave it too late – Moroccan foodies are no night owls, so a lot of places close their doors by 10 pm.

Budget Restaurants A number of cheap restaurants and sandwich bars are on the same street as the bus terminals, and they're reasonable value, serving almost anything from seafood to kebab sandwiches.

Just off Place Lahcen Tamri are three restaurants next to each other which are very popular with travellers and night strollers from the tourist district in search of a change. They are the *Restaurant Echabab*, the *Restaurant Mille et Une Nuits* and the *Café Restaurant Coq d'Or*. All offer you a choice of sitting inside or at tables in the open air. The food is very good and prices reasonable. Couscous or tajine costs about Dr25, a large salad is Dr20 and an omelette costs Dr15. You can order three course menus for Dr25.

The *Restaurant Select*, just by the hotel of the same name, does a solid range of old favourites, and you can eat well for about Dr20. Similar in style, but a little more expensive is the *Restaurant Tamouate*, next to the BMCE branch just off Ave du Président Kennedy.

A little flasher, and commensurately more expensive, *Restaurant Les Palmiers* is under the hotel of the same name. It does similar food to the others with little appreciable difference in quality. Main courses cost around Dr50.

Just where Ave Sidi Mohammed runs into Blvd Mohammed V, you'll find a Vietnamese restaurant, *La Tonkinoise*. Next door is a large, popular pizzeria. If you feel like trying some authentic Korean food, you could investigate *Restaurant Seoul*, upstairs in the central market a few doors down from the tourist office.

For cheap, ultra-fresh fish in less than salubrious surroundings, head to the entrance of the port where there are dozens of cheap *fish stalls* set up. Meals cost from Dr20. Tucked towards the back, near the fish market, is a popular place (full of locals rather than tourists) serving fish tajine. The stalls are open for lunch and dinner.

Expensive Restaurants The *Restaurant La Tour de Paris* is a fancy restaurant at the Ave du Général Kettani end of Ave Hassan II. The mainly French menu is tempting and the food of a reasonably high standard, but it costs a minimum of Dr170 per person.

No Moroccan tourist city would be complete without at least one 'Moroccan experience'-style restaurant, where you can eat in lavish Moorish surroundings, be entertained with traditional music and be served by waiters in impeccable white robes and red fezzes. In Agadir, the *Restaurant Darkoum* is that place. It's on Ave du Général Kettani, near the Hôtel Sud Bahia, and it will set you back about Dr170.

A particularly popular place with tourists and locals alike is the *Restaurant Scampi*, on Ave Hassan II opposite the Atlantic Hôtel. They have an excellent range of dishes and the food is very well prepared. A three-course meal for two, including wine, costs around Dr250.

The restaurant in the *Hôtel Miramar*, on Blvd Mohammed V overlooking the port, has an excellent reputation for seafood.

Set right on the beach, near the Hôtel Tafoukt, is the classy – and very pricey – *La Perla del Mare* (☎ 840065).

Along Blvd du 20 Août, in among some of the swish hotels and tourist boutiques, you'll find any number of upmarket restaurants to choose from. *Restaurant Pizza Pino* and *La Mamma*, predictably enough, do Italian food. The *Jazz* and *El Marrakchi*

serve Moroccan dishes – expect to pay in excess of Dr150 each for a full meal.

The Agadir Hôtel complex contains several restaurants, including *Le Cap*, *Pub L'Oasis* and the *Asmas Restaurant* which puts on evening performances of Moroccan music during meals.

Cafes & Patisseries There are plenty of cafes where you can relax from the rigours of Agadir beachlife or ease into the day with coffee and pastries.

The *Café/Patisserie Oufella*, just across the road from the Hôtel Diaf, on Rue Allal ben Abdallah in the budget hotel area, has a good range of patisseries. For ice cream, stop by the *Glacier* outside the Hôtel Sindibad.

Café Tafarnout is a busy patisserie and salon de thé on the corner of Ave Hassan II and Rue de la Foire.

On the beachfront by the swimming pool are a couple of pleasant cafes which serve drinks (including beer) as well as snacks. They're open 24 hours.

A little further south there is a string of cafes and restaurants leading up to a large open square.

Self-Catering The large Uniprix supermarket, on the corner of Ave Hassan II and Ave Sidi Mohammed sells everything from cheese and biscuits to beer, wine and spirits.

Saturday and Sunday are general market days in Agadir.

Entertainment
Bars & Nightclubs A lively little bar that's popular with the locals is located just by the southern entrance to the Vallée des Oiseaux.

You can also get a beer at quite a lot of the beachfront restaurants and cafes. Otherwise, there are countless bars to choose from in the bigger hotels.

If you want alcohol to take away, the Uniprix supermarket on Ave Hassan II has a reasonable choice. You could also try the liquor store in the street behind the post office.

STH OF CASABLANCA

Most of the bigger hotels have nightclubs. Two places recommended for women venturing out alone are the *Flamingo Club*, in the Hôtel Beach Club at the southern end of the beach, and *Jimmy's* at the Hôtel Al Medina Palace. For a comprehensive list of nightclubs, consult the *Guide d'Agadir*.

Remember that entry usually costs from Dr50 (a drink included), and subsequent drinks can cost as much again.

For glitzy tourist-orientated entertainment you could try the *Alhambra Cabaret*, near the Hôtel Sahara on Blvd du 20 Août.

Theatre & Cinemas The *Alliance Franco-Marocaine* (☎ 841313), at 5 Rue Yahchech, puts on films, theatre and lectures. You can usually pick up their programme in the Syndicat d'Initiative. Most performances are in French.

There are also a few cinemas scattered about town, including *Cinema Sahara* on Place Lahcen Tamri in the budget hotel area, and *Cinema Rialto* just off Ave Moulay Abdallah near the central market area.

Things to Buy

Agadir is not a great place to pick up souvenirs. Most of what's on offer is trucked in from other parts of the country, and the steady stream of package tourists, unaware of what's on offer elsewhere in the country, keep prices up on low-quality goods.

The Complexe Artisanal, on Rue du 29 Février, and the Uniprix supermarket both sell handicrafts at fixed prices. There are plenty of souvenir shops in the Central Market.

Getting There & Away

Air The new Al-Massira airport lies 28km south of Agadir. Take the Tafraoute road if you're driving out there. The airport bank (cash and travellers cheques only) and car hire offices are open during normal business hours. There are a couple of restaurants and a tourist information counter which is open seven days a week. The bulk of the traffic through here consists of European charter flights.

Royal Air Maroc (☎ 840795) has an office on Ave du Général Kettani. Most of its flights, internal and abroad, go via Casablanca. There are several flights a day to Casablanca (Dr722 one way; 50 minutes) and two a week to Marrakesh (35 minutes). In addition, there are flights to Laayoune twice a week (Dr817 one way; 11/2 hours direct). A weekly flight connects Agadir with Dakhla, too. RAM has a few direct international flights, including two a week to Paris (Dr5366 return) and two to Las Palmas in the Canary Islands (Dr2766 one way).

Bus Although a good number of buses and grands taxis serve Agadir (and they should be adequate for the purposes of leaving), there is a huge bus and taxi station in the nearby town of Inezgane. It is quite possible that you'll be dropped here when you arrive. There are grands taxis and local buses between Agadir and Inezgane (see the Taxi section below, and Getting There & Away under Inezgane).

In Agadir, all the bus companies have their terminals along Rue Yacoub el-Mansour in the budget hotel area.

CTM has buses to Casablanca at 7.30 am and 9.30, 10 and 10.30 pm (Dr136; 10 hours). The 9.30 pm bus goes on to Rabat (Dr162) and the 10.30 pm service goes on to Tangier (Dr233; 14 hours).

Buses for Marrakesh leave at 10 am, 3 and 7.30 pm (Dr67; four hours). A bus for Essaouira (Dr36.50) leaves at 11.30 am and goes on to Safi and El-Jadida.

There are buses for Tiznit at 6.30 am (Dr26; 1st class) and 4 pm (Dr15.50; 2nd class). A bus for Tafraout leaves at 5 am (Dr52).

At 11.30 pm there's a bus to Laayoune (Dr204) which continues to Smara. The Dakhla bus leaves at 8 pm (Dr325.50), and a bus for Taroudannt at 9.30 am (Dr19).

You can also get on to buses bound for France and Belgium here. You need to book a week in advance. See the Getting There & Away chapter for more details.

SATAS is the other main company operating out of Agadir. It has several buses to

Casablanca (Dr115 via Marrakesh; Dr95 via Essaouira); Tiznit (Dr18); Marrakesh (Dr60); Essaouira (Dr38); Taroudannt, Goulimime and Tan Tan (6 am and 1 pm); Safi; and El-Jadida.

About 10 other smaller companies have buses to most of these destinations as well.

Train Supratours (☎ 841207), which runs buses in connection with the train network, has an office at 10 Rue des Orangiers, just off Ave des FAR. Services to Marrakesh (Dr67; four hours) leave at 4.45 and 9.30 am and 1.45 pm, and you are dropped at the train station.

You can get a through ticket from Agadir to any rail destination.

Taxi Grands taxis to Tiznit (Dr23) leave from a lot about 1km south-east of the centre of town. Grands taxis also go to Inezgane (Dr5) from here.

Grands taxis for Taghazout (Dr10) leave from near the local bus station at Place Taxis et Bus.

Car & Motorcycle Some very good deals on car and motorcycle hire are to be found in Agadir, but you will have to hunt around and be prepared to bargain. It is well worth checking out local agencies: there's usually a good deal of room for haggling, especially in the low season.

Near the big hotels you'll find a series of booths that rent out motorbikes and scooters (the average charge for a motorcycle is about Dr200 per day). There are at least 40 car rental outlets to choose from, many of them on Ave Hassan II. Some of the main agencies are:

Avis
    Ave Hassan II (☎ 841755); Airport (☎ 839244)
Budget
    Bungalow Marhaba, Boulevard Mohammed V (☎ 844600)
Europcar
    Bungalow Marhaba, Boulevard Mohammed V (☎ 840203)
Hertz
    Bungalow Marhaba, Boulevard Mohammed V (☎ 840939); Airport (☎ 839071)

Getting Around

The Airport Airport transport is just a little complicated. Local bus No 22 runs from the airport car park to Inezgane every 40 minutes or so (Dr3) until about 9 pm. From Inezgane you can change to bus Nos 5 and 6 for Agadir, or take a taxi (Dr5).

Grands taxis between the airport and Agadir should not cost more than Dr100.

Otherwise, many travellers have stories of simply walking onto tour and hotel buses with other passengers – since most of them are generally on package tours, it's unlikely any questions will be asked.

Bus The main local bus station is a block in from Ave Hassan II, at Place Taxis et Bus, in the southern end of town. Bus Nos 5 and 6 go to Inezgane. The green-and-white No 12 goes to Taghazout.

Taxi The orange petits taxis run around town and prices are worked out by meter.

Bicycle There are several stands set up around the big hotels near the beach renting out bicycles for Dr20 an hour.

AROUND AGADIR
Immouzzer des Ida Outanane
This thoroughly recommended side trip, through a pretty river valley lined with palm trees, takes you about 60km north-east of Agadir to the village of Immouzzer des Ida Outanane in the foothills of the High Atlas.

The waterfalls (cascades), for which the village is best known, flow most strongly between February and August – at other times irrigation control reduces them to little more than a trickle.

From March to April the area is filled with white almond blossom and around late November you may be lucky enough to witness the olive harvest. At this time the groves are alive with villagers who climb up into the trees to shake the olives from the branches.

Places to Stay & Eat About halfway along the road to Immouzzer is the family-run

Ode to The Olive

In Islam the olive tree is associated with virility and with light, the symbol of the Prophet. The gnarled, silvery-green leafed olive trees growing on the rocky hillsides of Morocco have been there since Palaeolithic times. And the oil they produce is indisputably the best in the world. A feast in Morocco can simply be a round of fresh bread, a bowl of virgin olive oil and a big blue sky.

Nothing of the olive is wasted. The first 'virgin' pressing is used for marinades and dressings; the second and third are used for cooking; the fourth pressing is used in the manufacture of soaps, shampoos and beauty products; the pulp is used for fertiliser; the stones provide a lubricating oil and the wood is carved into bowls.

For oil the olives are allowed to ripen fully on the trees. The olives you can buy – green violet, deep red and black – are picked earlier. They are conserved in marinades flavoured with preserved lemons and herbs, bitter oranges or fiery hot red peppers. You'll often find them in tajines, where the added delight is fishing them out from the rich sauce with your fingers. ∎

Hôtel Tifrit set right by the river. Very clean rooms with separate shower and half-board (breakfast and dinner) cost Dr213/316. The hotel has a pleasant terrace and a small swimming pool.

In Immouzzer itself the only accommodation is the *Hôtel des Cascades* (☎ 826016) which has large well appointed rooms from Dr382 for a single. The hotel has an equally expensive restaurant, a terrace overlooking the valley, tennis courts and a swimming pool. From here there's a path leading down through the olive groves to the cascades.

There's a *restaurant/cafe* near the cascades which has a couple of basic rooms for Dr50/70. You can also camp nearby. There's some excellent walking to be had around here – the owner of the cafe, Aneflous Barek, can help plan treks of up to a week.

Getting There & Away One local bus a day leaves for Immouzzer from near the Agadir bus terminals at around 2 pm (departure times vary so ask around the day before).

You may have to wait until the following day for the bus back, although hitching isn't too difficult. The best time to get up here is Thursday, which is market day.

Northern Beaches

If you're looking for less-crowded beaches than those at Agadir, and for fellow independent travellers (most with their own transport), then head north of Agadir. There are beautiful sandy coves every few kilometres.

Most of the beaches closer to Agadir have been colonised by Europeans who have built their winter villas here. Further north, this gives way to a sea of campervans, but by the time you are 20 to 30km north of Agadir, you might find something resembling space and even peace and quiet.

The first village of any size you pass is **Tamrhakht**, about 12km north of Agadir, which has several cheap roadside cafes and dozens of banana stalls.

About 6km further on is **Taghazout**, which hosts a large and fairly ugly camping ground at the southern end of the village. It's usually crammed with campervans. You can rent basic private rooms in the village and there are a couple of eateries and cafes here too. The beaches nearby are OK, but it's really not a very appealing place to stay.

To get to peaceful and largely unspoilt beaches, you need to continue northwards. Those around 27km north of Agadir are more like it. You can find a few other attractive spots just south and north of **Cap Rhir** (easily identified by its shipwreck).

About 12km beyond Cap Rhir the road turns inland to **Tamri**. The lagoon here is reported to be the most reliable site in Morocco for spotting the very rare bald ibis. Other birds you may see here include Audouin's Gulls, Barbary Falcons, Lanner Falcons and passerines.

There are local buses from Agadir (Place Taxis et Bus) to Taghazout, but beyond that you'll have to rely on your thumb.

Inezgane

Situated 13km south of Agadir, Inezgane is one of the biggest transport hubs for the whole region.

It's not a tourist destination at all, but some travellers enjoy stopping off here rather than in Agadir for that very reason. A big market is held in the town on Tuesdays.

Places to Stay & Eat There are plenty of cheap hotels about. The *Hôtel El Marjane*, on the main square, has basic rooms with shared shower for Dr40/75.

The *Hôtel Issafen*, on Blvd Moulay Abdallah, has clean rooms with private shower for Dr100/130. A bit more expensive is the new *Hôtel Aday*, on Blvd Mohammed V, which has rooms with shower for Dr165/196.

You'll find dozens of cheap cafe/restaurants around the main square. Even cheaper are the *restaurants familiers* (small, family-run restaurants) in the side streets between Blvd Mohammed V and Blvd Moulay Abdallah.

The *Café/Restaurant Saâda*, on Blvd Moulay Abdallah, opposite the stadium, is particularly pleasant and well located.

Getting There & Away There are plenty of buses going in all possible directions from here. The bus station (Gare Routière) is just off the Agadir-Tiznit road. Even at 6 pm, you'll find touts trying to fill places on buses to Marrakesh, Casablanca, Essaouira and other cities.

There are daily services to Tafraoute (via Tiznit) and to Goulimime and a few weekly runs to Taroudannt. There are also loads of grands taxis to Essaouira (Dr50), Tiznit (Dr23) and Taroudannt.

Less regular taxis leave for Goulimime (Dr60) and Tan Tan. There are regular local buses and taxis running to Agadir and the airport.

The Massa Lagoon

About 60km south of Agadir, off a side track from the main P30 highway, is an important bird reserve around the Oued Massa, a tidal creek that attracts a phenomenal variety of birds.

Some of the species to be seen in the area include black-bellied sandgrouse, bald ibis, marbled duck, glossy ibis, cranes, little crake, warblers, black-headed bush shrike, brown-throated sand martin, flamingos, herons and even Bonelli's eagles.

There's a small hotel in the village of **Massa** a couple of kilometres south of the reserve. Just outside the reserve is the tiny village of Sidi R'bat. There's nothing much here, but the village makes two interesting claims.

According to one story, this is where the biblical Jonah is supposed to have been spewed up by the whale. And Uqba bin Nafi, the first Arab commander to penetrate Morocco, in the 7th century, supposedly rode his horse triumphantly into the sea here. Believe it or not.

At the time of writing, the small camp site at Sidi R'bat was closed; if you're thinking of heading down here, however, it's worth checking to see if it has reopened.

Taroudannt

Surrounded by magnificent, crenellated red mud walls and with the snow-capped peaks of the High Atlas beckoning beyond, Taroudannt looks every inch a traditional Berber market town. The French never tacked on a ville nouvelle here, which gives the impression of things having changed little in the past hundred or so years.

The town souqs are well worth a browse (though, as everywhere, you'll need to be prepared for a certain amount of hustling) and the small tanneries outside the walls make an interesting stop.

Taroudannt is a fairly easy day trip from Agadir (85km) and also makes a good base for travellers interested in trekking up into the little-explored Western High Atlas.

History

As far back as 1056, Taroudannt was overrun by the Almoravids at the beginning of their conquest of Morocco. It played only a peripheral role in the following years until, in the 16th century, the newly emerging Saadians made it their capital for about 20 years. This dynasty was responsible for the construction of the old part of town and the kasbah; most of the rest dates from the 18th century.

The Saadians eventually moved on to Marrakesh, but not before the fertile Souss valley, in which the city stands, had been developed into the country's most important producer of sugar cane, cotton, rice and indigo – valuable items of trade along the trans-Saharan caravan routes.

The city narrowly escaped destruction in 1687 at the hands of Moulay Ismail after it became the centre of a rebellion opposing his rule. Instead, Moulay Ismail contented himself with the massacre of its inhabitants.

It regained some of its former prominence when one of Moulay Abdallah's sons was proclaimed sultan here at the end of the following century, but his reign during this, one of the more turbulent periods in Moroccan history, was brief.

Taroudannt was to remain a centre of intrigue and sedition against the central government well into the 20th century, and indeed played host to the Idrissid El-Hiba, a southern chief who attempted to rebel after the Treaty of Fès (introducing French protectorate rule) was signed in 1912.

Orientation

Unlike many Moroccan towns of the same size and importance, Taroudannt was never chosen as a French administrative or military centre. Consequently, there is no 'European' quarter of wide boulevards and modern buildings.

On first arriving, you could be forgiven for thinking you'll never find your way around. The road layout seems chaotic, and few street signs are in French, so you just plunge into the heart of the medina.

In fact, you'll soon sort yourself out. The cheaper hotels are all located on or near the two central squares: Place al-Alaouyine (often called by its former Berber name, Place Assarag) and Place an-Nasr (formerly Talmoqlate). You'll find banks, restaurants and a small post office clustered in this area.

Most of the buses terminate at Place al-Alaouyine, while grands taxis and some smaller private bus companies are based just outside the southern gate of the medina, Bab Zougan.

Information

Money The BMCE and Banque Populaire have branches on Place al-Alaouyine, and there is a BMCI on Sharia Ibrahim ar-Roudani. All are good for changing cash and travellers cheques. The BMCE also does cash advances.

Post & Communications The main post and phone office is on Ave Hassan II, to the east of the kasbah and south of the Agadir-Marrakesh highway. There is a smaller post office on Rue du 20 Août, north-west of Place al-Alaouyine.

You'll find téléboutiques around the main squares.

Film & Photography You can buy films and have them developed at Photo Bourar on Ave Mohammed V, near Place an-Nasr.

Ramparts

Taroudannt's ramparts can be explored on foot, but it's better to hire a bicycle, or go by calèche. One nice idea advertised in the tourist literature is to take a moonlit ride around the walls.

The carriages gather just inside Bab el-Kasbah and a one and a half hour tour will cost from around Dr35.

Souqs

The Arab souq, to the east of Place al-Alaouyine, is relatively small, but some of

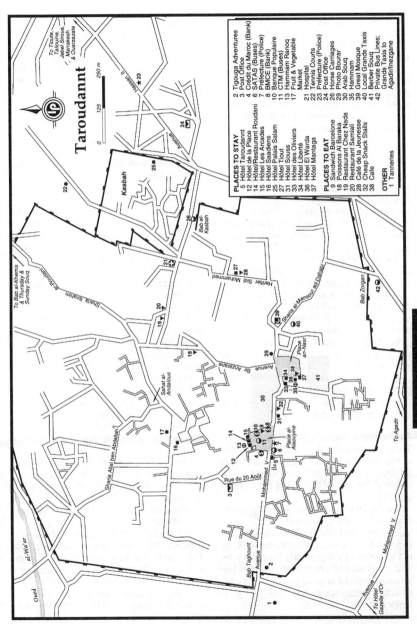

Taroudannt

0   125   250 m

To Troute,
Talioune,
Jebel Siroua,
Marrakesh
& Ouarzazate

Kasbah

Bab el-
Kasbah

To Bab al-Khemis
& Thursday &
Sunday Souq

Sahat al-
Andalous

Place al-
Alaouyine

Rue du 20 Août

Bab Taghount

To Hôtel
Gazelle d'Or

Oued

al-Wa'ar

PLACES TO STAY
2 Tigouga Adventures
5 Hôtel Taroudannt
12 Hôtel de la Place
14 Hôtel/Restaurant Roudani
15 Hôtel Les Arcades
16 Hôtel Saadiens
25 Hôtel Palais Salam
27 Hôtel Tiout
31 Hôtel Souss
33 Hôtel des Oliviers
34 Hôtel Liberté
36 Hôtel El Warda
37 Hôtel Mantaga

PLACES TO EAT
9 Sandwich Barcelone
18 Poissons Al Baraka
19 Restaurant Chez Nada
20 Restaurant Samlali
28 Café de la Jeunesse
32 Cheap Snack Stalls
38 Cafe

OTHER
1 Tanneries
3 Post Office
4 Crédit du Maroc (Bank)
6 SATAS (Buses)
7 Préfecture (Police)
8 BMCE (Bank)
10 Banque Populaire
11 CTM (Buses)
13 Hammam Ranoq
17 Fruit & Vegetable Market
21 Hospital
22 Tennis Courts
23 Préfecture (Police)
24 Post Office
26 Horse Carriages
29 Photo Bourar
30 Arab Souq
35 Hammam
39 Great Mosque
40 Local Grands Taxis
41 Berber Souq
42 Private Bus Lines;
     Grands Taxis to
     Agadir/Inezgane

STH OF CASABLANCA

the items for sale are of high quality; limestone carvings and traditional Berber jewellery are featured (the town is populated
mainly by Chleuh Berbers).

This jewellery has been influenced by the
tribes of the Sahara, as well as by the Jews;
the latter were a significant part of the community until the late 1960s. Only the core of
the market is devoted to crafts and souvenirs – the rest serves as the Roudanis'
(people of Taroudannt) shopping centre.

One shop worth visiting is that of Lichir
el Houcine (☎ 852145), at 36 Souq Semata,
which has an extensive array of items
ranging from carpets and fabulous jewellery
to antique couscous platters. Lichir consid-
ers himself a serious antiques dealer, and as
a result may be a tougher bargainer than
others. As always, the best advice is to take
your time to look around for what you want.

Taroudannt's Berber souq extends south
of Place an-Nasr and you'll no doubt have
a few guides wanting to usher you this way.

Although there are a few stalls selling
carpets and jewellery, this market deals
mainly in fruit, vegetables, spices and ordinary household goods.

On Thursday and Sunday, a large market
for people in the surrounding countryside
spreads out just outside Bab al-Khemis
(which means Thursday Gate) at the north-
east corner of town. It is interesting for the
spectacle rather than for the goods, but you
need to get there early.

Tanneries
There are tanneries here similar to the ones
at Fès, but much smaller. Head out of Bab
Targhount and turn left, then continue for
about 100m and take the first right (signposted).

You'll find lamb, sheep and goatskin
rugs (prices start at about Dr100), soft
leather bags and traditional red and yellow
slippers for sale here. The people working
in the tanneries are generally happy to give
visitors a tour and a brief explanation of the
process involved in getting to the rug stage,
which is interesting, and less likely to
happen in Fès.

Kasbah
The walls around the kasbah date mainly
from the time of Saadian rule in Taroudannt, and the area is worth a little stroll, though
there are no sights as such inside its walls.

Walled off as it is from the rest of the
city, it seems almost like a separate little
town.

Trekking
Taroudannt is the only sizeable town within
striking distance of the relatively little-
visited Western High Atlas region. The
walking here is less demanding than in the
Toubkal region, the climate is wetter and
the vegetation more lush.

It is, however, well off the beaten track.
There are no official refuges in this area, let
alone hotels or even towns. Though there
are plenty of Berber villages up in the
mountains, anyone thinking of trekking up
here should be prepared to camp and will
have to carry all necessary supplies, including detailed maps, food and water purification tablets.

You can get to the village of **Afensou**,
about 30km north of Taroudannt, fairly
easily by local *camionette* (Berber truck).
Jebel Aoulime (3555m), one of the notable
peaks in the Western High Atlas, is about
18km north-west of Afensou. Jebel Igdet
(3616m), the highest peak of the Western
High Atlas is more easily accessible from
the top of the **Tizi n'Test** pass. You could
also approach the region from the town of
Argana on the main Agadir-Marrakesh
road.

There is very little in the way of organised trips up into this neck of the woods
and, again unlike Toubkal, few official
mountain guides. There are, however, a
couple of much sought-after guides based in
Taroudannt.

Tali Abd al-Aziz, who runs Tigouga Adventures (☎ 853501) located just inside Bab
Targhount, is a very experienced English
speaking guide specialising in trekking expeditions in the Western High Atlas. Tali
can organise short local walks, multi-day
treks (including a 13 day trek all the way

across to Toubkal) or ski treks on the Tichka Plateau.

Prices are around Dr300 per person for a two or three day trek. If you're interested, it's worth contacting Tali well ahead of when you'd like to go. For more information, write to BP 132, Taroudannt Ville, Morocco.

El Aouad Ali is another English speaking mountain guide based in Taroudannt who knows the mountains very well. He can be contacted through the Hôtel Taroudannt or the Hôtel Saadiens.

Places to Stay – bottom end

Most travellers like to stay as close to the centre of activity as they can. In Taroudannt you can do this without spending a lot of money. There are many hotels around or close to Place al-Alaouyine, and there's not a huge difference in quality or price.

There are four budget places right on the square. One of the cheapest is the Hôtel de la Place which is pleasant enough and has a variety of rooms. Tiny singles cost Dr30 and more roomy doubles with views over the square can be had for Dr40. The shared shower is bracingly cold.

On the other side of the lane is the Hôtel/Restaurant Roudani (☎ 852219). There's good views from the upper terrace, but unlike the rooms on the lower floor, the rooms up here don't have private showers. This hotel is clean and the staff friendly. Singles/doubles, regardless of whether they have a private shower, cost Dr40/80. The Hôtel Les Arcades, virtually next door, costs the same and is on a par with the Hôtel de la Place.

Just off the square, heading towards Place an-Nasr, you'll find the Hôtel Souss. It's dirt cheap (Dr20 a bed), but not terribly inviting.

Closer to Place an-Nasr is the Hôtel des Oliviers (☎ 852021). It's not bad, and has clean beds for Dr50/60. The showers are cold. The Hôtel Mantaga, on a little lane off Place an-Nasr, has clean rooms with big beds for Dr35/45.

On the square itself, the Hôtel Liberté has beds for the same prices. The Hôtel El Warda, on the same lane as the Mantaga, has basic, clean rooms for Dr30/50.

There are two alternatives for people on tight budgets seeking a little more comfort.

The Hôtel Tiout (☎ 850341), on Ave al-Jama' al-Kabir, is a modern sort of place with decent, clean rooms and comfortable beds. Rooms, all with private bathroom, cost Dr100/150. The rooms upstairs have balconies.

While quite acceptable, the Tiout has none of the charm of one of the city's institutions, the Hôtel Taroudannt (☎ 852416).

Although fading, this hotel has a unique flavour to it, from the tree-filled courtyard to the creaky old dining room, where you can get good French and Moroccan food.

Singles, doubles and triples cost Dr45, Dr60 and Dr100 without bathroom, Dr60, Dr85 and Dr120 with private shower, and Dr80, Dr100 and Dr137 with shower and toilet.

The water is boiling hot, the hotel has one of the few bars in town and the food in the restaurant is moderately priced. This is easily the best deal in Taroudannt.

Places to Stay – middle

The only mid-range hotel in Taroudannt is the two-star Hôtel Saadiens (☎ 852589; fax 852118), on Borj Oumansour, which offers B&B for Dr155/199.

Used by some adventure travel groups, the hotel is clean, comfortable and functional, but unremarkable. They have a licensed rooftop restaurant, a pleasant salon de thé and access to locked parking.

Places to Stay – top end

The four-star Hôtel Palais Salam (☎ 852 312; fax 852654) is right inside the ramparts, in the kasbah, by the town's main roundabout and Agadir-Marrakesh road. Access is from outside the walls, not through the kasbah.

One of the best of the Salam chain, the building started life as a pasha's residence in the 19th century.

Set in luxuriant gardens, with bar and

restaurant, parking and tennis courts, it offers singles/doubles for Dr420/545.

A couple of kilometres south-west of town is the exclusive *Hôtel Gazelle d'Or* (☎ 852039; fax 852537). Built in 1961 by a French baron, it has 40 bungalows set in extensive gardens.

It has all the amenities you would expect of a five-star hotel, including tennis courts, horse-riding and even croquet. A bungalow for one costs Dr2445. Advance booking is compulsory.

Swimming Pools

Summer can be extremely hot in Taroudannt. The two top-end hotels both have pools; you can use the Hôtel Palais Salam's one for Dr30 a day, if the hotel isn't full. The Hôtel Saadiens also has a swimming pool.

Hammams

Those dying for a hot shower or bath can try the Hammam Ranoq, just behind Place al-Alaouyin near the Hôtel Roudani, or the public douche next to the Hôtel El Warda, off Place an-Nasr.

There's also a hammam tucked away behind the Hôtel Taroudannt.

Places to Eat

There are quite a few small cheap eateries along Ave Mohammed V, near the Hôtel Souss, where you can get traditional food such as tajines, harira and salads.

The restaurants on the ground floors of the hotels on Place al-Alaouyine offer good value set menus.

The *Hôtel/Restaurant Roudani* does the usual favourites – you can get generous helpings of brochettes, chips and salad for Dr30.

At *Sandwich Barcelone*, also on Place al-Alaouyine, you can buy yourself a very good, fat baguette stuffed with kefta, chips and salad for Dr15.

If you want a break from the centre of town, two popular places with locals, and just a little nattier than your run-of-the-mill hole in the wall, are the *Restaurant Samlali* and *Restaurant Chez Nada*, both on the main street that leads towards Bab el-Kasbah.

Poissons Al Baraka, further south on Ave Bir Anzarane, is just a small eat-with-your-fingers place, but offers very good fish (fresh from Agadir) along with the usual accompaniments.

In the evening, head for the restaurant and bar at the *Hôtel Taroudannt*. The menu here includes the old Moroccan reliables, but people looking for a change may want to opt for one of the various French dishes – they do a pretty good steak.

The restaurant also has a decent selection of local wines. Most main courses cost about Dr40 to Dr50, and a beer Dr13 to Dr15. They also have two set menus (Dr65 and Dr85).

A fair bit pricier, but very good, are the French and Moroccan restaurants at the *Hôtel Palais Salam.*

The *Hôtel Saadiens* has a moderately priced restaurant where you can dine within view of the alluring Atlas mountains.

If you have suitable attire (not to mention bank balance), you might like to dine at the exclusive *Hôtel Gazelle d'Or* and get to see how the other half holiday.

Cafes & Patisseries There's no end to the cafes scattered about Taroudannt's winding streets. The terrace of the *Hôtel/Restaurant Roudani*, on Place al-Alaouyine, is the best spot for breakfast and is well placed for a pleasant morning's people watching.

There are a couple of upstairs terraces on Place an-Nasr for mint tea and mountain views.

There's also a patisserie near the entrance to the Arab souq which has a wide selection of Moroccan cookies.

Self-Catering Travellers wanting to put together their own picnic foods won't have any problems in Taroudannt – the markets are brimming with fresh produce from the fertile Sous Valley.

In addition to the twice weekly souq and the Berber market, there's also a *fruit and vegetable market* near the Hôtel Saadiens.

For bread, bottled water, tins of sardines and French biscuits, you'll find plenty of *grocery shops* around the main squares.

Getting There & Away
Bus The main bus companies have terminals on Place al-Alaouyine. CTM, next door to the Hôtel Les Arcades, has a 9 pm bus to Casablanca (Dr150) via Agadir (Dr29). This bus goes via Marrakesh (Dr88) as well, avoiding the Tizi n'Test. Another bus goes to Ouarzazate (Dr68) en route from Agadir, passing through at about noon.

Across the square is the SATAS station, more useful in this part of Morocco. There is a daily 5 am bus to Marrakesh (Dr70) via Agadir. There are another two services to Agadir at 5.30 and 10.30 am. A bus to Igherm and Tata (Dr40) leaves at 8 am.

Several other small companies operate services from outside Bab Zorgan, the southern gate. Local buses going to Marrakesh, via the Tizi n'Test, leave from here at around 5 am.

Taxi The grands taxis also gather by Bab Zorgan. Apart from small towns in the area around Taroudannt, the main regular destination is Inezgane (for Agadir), and sometimes Agadir itself. Either way, the fare is Dr23.

A place in a grand taxi to Tata costs Dr60 and to Marrakesh the fare is Dr100. The pea-green taxis go to local villages, the Saharan blue ones go further afield. Camionettes for outlying Berber villages leave from a lot near the Great Mosque.

Getting Around
Car hire is available from Tansift Cars (☎ 843581 in Agadir) in the Taroudannt Tours travel agency on Place al-Alaouyine.

It's highly unlikely that you'll need one of the brown petits taxis, but if you do, they gather at Place an-Nasr.

You can hire bicycles (Dr5 an hour or Dr40 a day) from a workshop on Place al-Alaouyine.

Another possibility is touring around town in a calèche. They gather just inside

Bab el-Kasbah or can be found trotting around town. A one and a half hour tour will cost around Dr35.

AROUND TAROUDANNT
Tioute
Some 37km to the south-east of Taroudannt lie the impressive ruins of the kasbah of Tioute. Part of the kasbah has been turned into an expensive restaurant, but there's nothing to stop you simply enjoying the views over the palmeraies and village below. Scenes for *Ali Baba & The Forty Thieves*, starring Yul Brynner, were shot here in 1952.

Without your own transport, you'll have to organise a taxi to take you out there from Taroudannt.

If driving, take the main road towards Marrakesh for about 8km, turn right and cross the oued just before the village and ruined kasbah of **Freija**. From here it's another 21km down the S7025 towards Igherm before you hit a turn-off to the right. After 5km, this reverts to a 2km stretch of piste.

At the point where the bitumen ends, you're bound to be befriended by someone wanting to guide you up to the kasbah and restaurant.

Taliouine & Jebel Siroua
If you intend heading on to the southern oasis valleys from Taroudannt and don't want to go over the High Atlas to Marrakesh, you can continue eastwards along the P32 via the villages of Taliouine and Tazenakht. From there the road heads north to join the main Marrakesh-Ouarzazate road not far from the turnoff to Aït Benhaddou. This route may be particularly worthwhile for travellers interested in trekking up Jebel Siroua (3304m), an isolated volcanic peak of the Anti-Atlas.

Taliouine is a pretty village (saffron is grown here and there is a cooperative you can visit) with a couple of accommodation options. The *Grand Hôtel Ibn Toumert*, in the shadow of the ruins of a Glaoui kasbah, has comfortable, but expensive rooms. The

Auberge Souktana, a couple of kilometres east of the village on the main road, is very popular with travellers. The auberge has four attractive double rooms with private bathroom for Dr120. In summer it's possible to sleep on the roof terrace or camp in the grounds. Meals here are very good, with menus starting at Dr45.

The auberge is run by Ahmed Jadid and his French wife Michelle. Ahmed is also an experienced mountain guide and can help organise treks to Jebel Siroua.

There are buses passing through Taliouine from both Taroudannt and Ouarzazate, but they may not always have seats available. There is a daily morning bus service to Marrakesh. Grands Taxis head west to Oulad Behril, where you can change for Taroudannt, and east to Tazenakht. Taliouine's market day is Monday.

South Coast & Anti-Atlas

From Agadir, the main route south heads inland, maintaining a respectful distance from the coast until it hits Tan Tan Plage, 240km to the south-west.

At the 19th century fortress town of Tiznit, 95km south of Agadir, a minor road cuts across to the coast, taking you past pleasant beaches and down to the quirky former Spanish town of Sidi Ifni. From here the terrain rapidly becomes harsher, and by the time you leave Goulimime – the last town on anything approaching the 'tourist circuit' – the stony desert takes over.

Few travellers get beyond this point, and it has to be said that there is not an awful lot to see or do down here. It *is* refreshing to get away from the tourist buses, however, and the journey is potentially useful now that convoys are getting through from Dakhla (in the Western Sahara) to Mauritania.

Sitting calmly in the heart of the Anti-Atlas, 107km inland from Tiznit, is the Berber village of Tafraoute. There isn't a lot to do in the village itself, but the surrounding area of sparkling pink mountains, tranquil valleys and rich palmeries make it one of the prettiest and most relaxing stretches of walking country in Morocco.

TIZNIT

In an arid corner of the Souss Valley at the very end of the Anti-Atlas range, Tiznit has the appearance of an old town, with its 6km of encircling red mud walls. In fact, the town is a fairly recent creation, but still worth a short stay if you've come this far south.

It's also not a bad staging point for a couple of other destinations – Sidi Ifni, on the coast, and Tafraoute, to the east.

The best time to be in Tiznit is when the package-tour buses from Agadir have left (mid to late afternoon). It then reverts to normality and is a pleasant place to hang around and explore. This is also the best time to have a look at the silver jewellery, reputedly some of the best in the south, if not in all of Morocco.

Jewellery is not only made here, but is bought to be traded for tribal jewellery in the Saharan regions further south. You may be lucky enough to see some of these pieces before they're sold on to merchants in the big northern cities.

History

Although there was a settlement of sorts here previously, the town dates substantially from 1881. In that year it was chosen by Sultan Moulay al-Hassan as a base from which to assert his authority over the rebellious Berber tribes of the Souss and Anti-Atlas.

He was only partly successful in this quest; it wasn't until the 1930s – 20 years after Spain and France had divided Morocco between themselves – that the tribes were finally 'pacified'.

In the first decade of the 20th century, Tiznit became a focal point of the resistance against the 1912 treaty that turned Morocco into a French and Spanish protectorate.

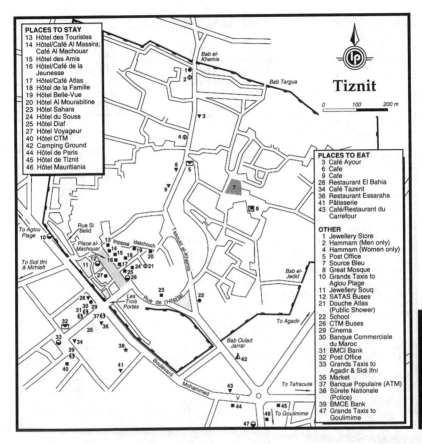

PLACES TO STAY
13 Hôtel des Touristes
14 Hôtel/Café Al Massira;
   Café Al Machouar
15 Hôtel des Amis
16 Hôtel/Café de la
   Jeunesse
17 Hôtel/Café Atlas
18 Hôtel de la Famille
19 Hôtel Belle-Vue
20 Hôtel Al Mourabitine
23 Hôtel Sahara
24 Hôtel du Souss
25 Hôtel Diaf
27 Hôtel Voyageur
40 Hôtel CTM
42 Camping Ground
44 Hôtel de Paris
45 Hôtel de Tiznit
46 Hôtel Mauritiania

PLACES TO EAT
3 Café Ayour
6 Cafe
9 Cafe
28 Restaurant El Bahia
34 Café Tazerit
36 Restaurant Essaraha
41 Pâtisserie
43 Café/Restaurant du
   Carrefour

OTHER
1 Jewellery Store
2 Hammam (Men only)
4 Hammam (Women only)
5 Post Office
7 Source Bleu
8 Great Mosque
10 Grands Taxis to
   Aglou Plage
11 Jewellery Souq
12 SATAS Buses
21 Douche Atlas
   (Public Shower)
22 School
26 CTM Buses
29 Cinema
30 Banque Commerciale
   du Maroc
31 BMCI Bank
32 Post Office
33 Grands Taxis to
   Agadir & Sidi Ifni
35 Market
37 Banque Populaire (ATM)
38 Sûrete Nationale
   (Police)
39 BMCE Bank
47 Grands Taxis to
   Goulimime

Tiznit

STH OF CASABLANCA

The resistance was led by El-Hiba, an Idrissid chief from Mauritania who was regarded as a saint and credited with performing miracles.

He had himself proclaimed sultan at Tiznit's mosque in 1912, and he succeeded in uniting the tribes of the Anti-Atlas and the Tuareg in what proved to be a vain effort to dislodge the French.

Ejected from Tiznit – and at one point forced to move to Taroudannt – he pursued the campaign of resistance until his death in 1919.

Orientation

The main drag, Blvd Mohammed V, runs just outside the south-west wall of the city.

At the main set of gates, known as Les Trois Portes, a road leads away from Blvd Mohammed V to the main grand taxi lot. The post office, a couple of banks, some restaurants and a food market are on this street.

Entering the town through the gates, you end up on Place al-Machouar, where you'll find the jewellery souq and most of the buses and cheap hotels.

Berber Jewellery

The tribal jewellery of Morocco is among the most beautiful in Africa. The traditional assemblage necklaces made in the southern oasis valleys are particularly striking, with some of the more exquisite featuring talismans of silver, pink coral, amazonite, amber, Czech glass and West African ebony beads.

The urban tradition of jewellery making in Morocco has been heavily influenced by Arab culture and uses gold or gilded silver. Rural jewellery has been influenced by Moorish Spain, but still essentially reflects the Berber animistic beliefs that pre-date Islam.

Berber jewellery is always made of silver (gold was considered to be evil) in combination with other materials, in the case of necklaces, and serves a much wider purpose than simple adornment. It identifies clan, symbolises wealth, reflects cultural traditions and is a source of supernatural and religious power for the wearer.

A woman will receive jewellery from her mother until she marries. Her future husband will commission pieces made by his mother or sister and these will be kept by her as dowry and added to throughout her life. Necklaces are important, but she will also have bracelets, fibulas (elaborate brooches, often triangular-shaped, used for fastening garments), anklets, earrings and headdresses. Some pieces will be worn

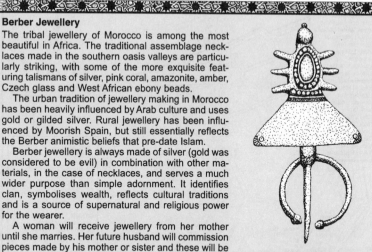

A fibula in the traditional style, used to fasten garments.

every day, but the finest will be worn for festivals, pilgrimages, funerals and so on.

The protective, medicinal and magical properties of jewellery are extremely important. The assemblage necklaces will contain charms bought from magicians or holy men, for all sorts of purposes including protection from the evil eye, warding off disease and accidents, and easing childbirth.

Silver is believed to cure rheumatism; coral symbolises fertility and is thought to have curative powers; amber is worn as a symbol of wealth and to protect against sorcery (it's also considered an aphrodisiac and a cure for colds); amazonite and carnelian stones are used in divining fortunes; and shells traded from East Africa symbolise fertility.

Talismans will feature stylised motifs of animals, suns, moon and stars, which all have various supernatural powers. A common symbol to ward off the evil eye is the hand of Fatima, the daughter of the prophet Mohammed. Any depiction of the hand (which represents human creative power and dominance), or of the number five is believed to have the same effect as poking the fingers into the evil eye with the words *khamsa fi ainek* (five in your eye).

Jewellery will feature numerous representations of the number five – as dots, lines, stars, crosses and as groups of five elements placed together. ∎

Five in your eye – the hand of Fatima.

Information

The banks in Tiznit include the BMCE, BMCI and Banque Populaire. The latter has an ATM.

The post office is open during normal office hours.

Things to See & Do

Apart from wandering around the sleepy interior of the town or hunting for bargains in the just-as-sleepy **jewellery souq**, there's little to see. Of note is the minaret of the **Great Mosque**, reminiscent of those found in Mali. Souls of the dearly departed supposedly use the perches sticking out of its mud walls to help them in their climb to paradise.

Nearby is a pretty mucky spring which is a popular bathing spot with local kids. Known as the **Source Bleue**, legend has it that a certain Lalla Zninia, a woman of ill repute, turned up at this spot, repented her wicked ways and gave her name to the village that preceded Moulay al-Hassan's 19th-century fortress town.

It's possible to climb onto sections of the city walls, at Bab Targua for instance. Things liven up a little on Tuesday and Thursday, which are market days.

Places to Stay – bottom end

Camping You'll find a fairly uninspiring camp site about halfway between the main roundabout and Bab Oulad Jarrar. Devoid of shade, it's really only of use to people with campervans. It costs Dr5 per person and the same per car (Dr10 per caravan). Water costs Dr2 and electricity Dr15.

Hotels Travellers generally prefer to stay at the hotels right on Place al-Machouar, the main square within the city walls. Many have rooftop terraces where you can escape the tourist hordes during the middle of the day. They're all much the same price and offer similar facilities, so where you stay will largely depend on what you take a fancy to and which hotel has a room.

One of the best is off the square, on Impasse Idakchouch. The *Hôtel Belle-Vue*

(☎ 862109) is a cheerfully done-up place with large, sunny rooms. Singles, doubles and triples cost Dr40, Dr60 and Dr80, and a hot shower is Dr5.

Many travellers stay at the *Hôtel/Café Atlas*, which has a lively restaurant. Singles/doubles cost Dr30/70, but frankly it's no better than the others. Some of the front rooms have good views of the square, but that's about it. There are warm communal showers.

The *Hôtel des Amis* has large rooms which cost Dr50 for one or two people. There's a shared warm shower.

The *Hôtel de la Jeunesse* has cheap, somewhat cramped rooms for Dr25/50 and the *Hôtel/Café Al Massira* has clean, basic rooms for Dr30/60.

The *Hôtel des Touristes* (☎ 862186), at the northern end of the square, has decent-sized, spotlessly clean rooms for Dr60/90. The communal shower is hot.

In addition to the Belle-Vue, there are half a dozen or so other cheapies along Impasse Idakchouch. The *Hôtel Al Mourabitine* (☎ 862755), at the end of the street, is not bad. Smaller rooms cost Dr20/40, but they have a bigger and more pleasant room at the front for Dr50/70. The hotel is up on the first floor with a little cafe. There is a warm shower.

A bit closer to the square, the *Hôtel de la Famille* has acceptable rooms for Dr25/50, but no shower. Across the road are two more hotels. Rooms in the *Hôtel du Souss* cost Dr25/50. The rooms are basic, but some are quite big. There's no shower. Next door, the *Hôtel Diaf* offers OK rooms for Dr30/45.

Further away from Place al-Machouar is the poky *Hôtel Sahara* (☎ 862498), which charges Dr25 per person. The rooms have clean double beds and little else.

There's a cheapie near the grand taxi lot, the *Hôtel CTM* (☎ 862211) – CTM used to have its office here. Small rooms cost Dr30/60, but they're clean enough. Hot showers are Dr5.

The *Hôtel Mauritania* (☎ 863632), which is on the road to Goulimime, has very good value rooms with private shower and toilet for Dr60/80/100. The hotel also has a bar and restaurant.

Places to Stay – middle
The only mid-range hotel in town is the two-star *Hôtel de Paris* (☎ 862865), on Blvd Mohammed V by the roundabout. Rooms here are comfortable and clean. Singles, doubles and triples with showers and toilets cost Dr108, Dr125 and Dr185. There is hot water and the hotel has its own restaurant.

Places to Stay – top end
Tiznit's top-range hotel is the three-star *Hôtel de Tiznit* (☎ 862411/21), on Rue Bir Inzaran, also close to the main roundabout. Self-contained singles/doubles with hot water cost Dr310/402. The hotel has a bar, restaurant and guarded parking.

Swimming Pools
The Hôtel de Tiznit has a small swimming pool.

Hammams
The *Douche Atlas*, down a side alley off Impasse Idakchouch, has separate showers for men and women (Dr5).

There's a hammam for men just inside Bab el-Khemis and one for women 200m further down the road.

Places to Eat
The *Restaurant Essaraha*, on the corner just across Blvd Mohammed V from Les Trois Portes, is a good basic place for cheap Moroccan meals – Dr25 will get you a 'petit tajine', which is quite enough for most appetites.

The *Restaurant El Bahia*, next to the cinema on Blvd Mohammed V, does excellent sandwiches and french fries.

You can bring your own fresh ingredients to the *Café Tazerzit*, near the market, and have a very cheap meal cooked up for you.

The restaurants in the *Hôtel Mauitiania*, *Hôtel de Paris* and the *Hôtel de Tiznit* are worth trying in the evening if you want a more comfortable option.

The first two are reasonably priced. The restaurant at the Hôtel de Paris is reportedly good for fish.

The new *Café/Restaurant du Carrefour*, opposite the Hôtel de Paris, offers well prepared Moroccan dishes and is a great place for breakfast – fresh bread served with little dishes of almond oil, spicy agane oil and olive oil.

Quite a few of the hotels on the main square have cafes offering food. One of the most popular is the one at the *Hôtel Atlas*.

Cafes & Patisseries
The best place for coffee and patisseries on the square is the *Café Al Machouar,* close to the Hôtel Al Massira.

There are quite a few cafes dotted about the town, some of them marked on the map. There's a good patisserie in a street off Blvd Mohammed V, just around from the Sûreté Nationale.

Self-Catering
Those who want to prepare their own meals should go to the covered market, just over Blvd Mohammed V from Les Trois Portes, which offers an excellent selection of meat, vegetables, fruit (fresh and dried) and many other foodstuffs.

Getting There & Away
Bus The CTM terminal is on Place al-Machouar. There's a 5.30 am service to Casablanca (Dr98.50) via Agadir (Dr15.50), Essaouira (Dr43), Safi (Dr64.50) and El-Jadida (Dr83.50).

At 9 pm a 1st class bus leaves for Tangier (Dr260, 16 hours) via Agadir (Dr27, 1¼ hours), Marrakesh (Dr95, 5¾ hours), Rabat (Dr184, 10½ hours) and Casablanca (Dr154, nine hours).

CTM also runs a 5 am service to Goulimime and a 7 am service to Tafraoute (Dr30).

SATAS, whose office is on the same square, has a 6 pm service to Casablanca via Marrakesh and buses to Agadir at 9.30, 10 and 11 am and 7.30 pm.

Buses go to Goulimime (Dr23) at 8 and 11 am and 4 pm; the 8 am and 4 pm services go on to Tan Tan. There's one service to

Ouarzazate at 6.30 pm. A bus to Akka and Tata departs at 9.30 am.

Several smaller companies run services from here, too; there's at least one daily bus to Tafraoute and two services to Sidi Ifni at 5 and 7.30 pm.

Taxi Grands taxis to Sidi Ifni (Dr25, about two hours) and Agadir (Dr23) leave from the main grand taxi lot, opposite the post office. Occasionally taxis go to Tafraoute (Dr35), but this depends on demand.

For Goulimime, there are grands taxis from a rank opposite the Hôtel Mauritania (Dr35 per person). You may also be able to get one through to Tan Tan.

Taxis to Aglou Plage leave from another rank, on Blvd Mohammed V by the city walls. A place costs Dr5.

AROUND TIZNIT
Aglou Plage
About 15km from Tiznit lies Aglou Plage, which has a reasonable beach and good surf, though you'll come across the occasional glass and plastic bottle, as well as other rubbish.

Most of the time it's deserted and, when Atlantic winds start blustering, it's a wild and woolly sort of place.

Places to Stay There's a walled camp site at the entrance to the village, but it's stony and has no shade whatsoever. Camping at the site (open only in summer) costs next to nothing.

At the time of writing, the basic *Motel Aglou* had closed down. Check with the locals in Tiznit for any new developments.

Mirhleft
Around 50km south of Tiznit, on the coastal road to Sidi Ifni, is the seaside village of Mirhleft.

Now with electricity and a decent water supply, it's becoming an increasingly popular spot with travellers looking for a good beach and some peace and quiet. There's a road leading to the beach just before you get to the village.

Places to Stay & Eat There are five basic hotels here, including the *Hôtel du Sud*, on the main street heading west off the highway, which has bright, clean rooms for Dr20/35 (and a reputedly good cafe/restaurant downstairs).

The *Hôtel Tafkout*, on the same street, has similar rooms for Dr50/60. In the low season, it's possible to rent houses for as little as Dr600 a month. There are a few quite basic cafes around and tonnes of fresh fish.

TATA
The small town of Tata makes a good stopover point on an excellent and little-travelled route which takes you 300km south-east of Tiznit through a series of desert oases then up over the Anti-Atlas another 200km to Taroudannt. Buses run to Tata from Tiznit and Bouzakarne (67km south of Tiznit) and also from Taroudannt.

A worthwhile side excursion along the way is to the magnificent agadir (fortified granary) at **Id-Aïssa**, north-east of the village of **Taghjicht** which is 35km from Bouzakarne. The well-preserved agadir sits high above the village, seemingly growing straight from the rocky mountain.

Ali, the friendly local gardien, will take you up on foot, or by donkey if you prefer. The main door to the agadir remains locked and must be opened with a massive wooden Berber key.

There are no facilities in the village, but you can camp by the river nearby. Back in Taghjicht, the *Hôtel Taghjicht* has clean, pleasant rooms with bathroom for Dr100/150.

There is a restaurant in the hotel. If you don't have your own transport, it is possible to negotiate a grand taxi from Taghjicht to Id-Aïssa.

Tata itself is a sleepy place with one colonnaded main street and everything painted in pastel shades of blue, pink and yellow. There's a Petrom petrol station as you come in from the west. The post office and a Banque Populaire are centrally located just off Ave Mohammed V.

Places to Stay & Eat

The *Hôtel Essalam* and the *Hôtel Sahara*, both on Ave Mohammed V, are basic hotels offering beds for Dr15 per person. Both have cafe/restaurants downstairs. There's another basic hotel and several cafes by the bus station.

The *Hôtel de la Renaissance* (☎ 802042), on Ave des FAR which runs into Ave Mohammed V, has clean, plain rooms with bathroom for Dr100/150. There's a pleasant restaurant downstairs.

Just before the town, coming in from the west, is the *Hôtel les Relais des Sables* (☎ 802301) which has comfortable, but quite small rooms with bathroom for Dr230/280. The hotel has a small swimming pool, flower-filled courtyards, a bar and a restaurant.

There are several cafe/restaurants offering simple Moroccan dishes along Ave Mohammed V. The *Café/Restaurant Snak Ourika* serves cheap but very good soup and tajines, as well as the ubiquitous chicken and chips.

Getting There & Away

You'll find buses and taxis towards the end of the town in a small square off Ave Mohammed V. SATAS has regular departures to Tiznit at 3 am (Dr69) and Taroudannt at 6 pm (Dr40). There's no shortage of brilliant blue grands taxis.

TAFRAOUTE

Nestled in behind the enchanting Ameln Valley is the village of Tafraoute, itself unspectacular, but extremely relaxed – the perfect base for days of hiking in the hills and Berber villages around it.

The more ambitious might consider scaling Jebel al-Kest or taking on guides to follow palm-filled gorges leading towards the bald expanses of the southern Anti-Atlas. Stay here a few days, go on some hikes around the countryside and you'll find it hard to leave.

The village can be reached on roads from Tiznit (107km) or Agadir (198km); ideally, a circuit taking in both would be the most

satisfying way of doing the trip. It is one where you'd definitely appreciate having your own transport.

From Tiznit, the road starts off ordinarily enough across gentle farming country, until it reaches Oued Assaka. From here it winds up into the mountains, which in the late afternoon light take on every hue imaginable – from soft pinks and mauves to golden browns.

Sprinkled about the hills are precarious Berber pisé (mud brick) villages (most of the Berbers in this region are Souss Chleuh), surrounded by the cultivated terraces that are worked all through the day – mostly by the women.

At 1100m you cross the stunning Col de Kerdous (there is a four-star hotel up here; see Places to Stay in Tafraoute), and from here you hardly lose altitude for the remainder of the run into Tafraoute.

The route to Agadir is just as fascinating. Leaving Tafraoute, the road passes through the eastern half of the Ameln Valley and over the Tizi Mlil pass before doubling back on itself for the trip north-west to Agadir. The land is generally much gentler and more heavily cultivated on this run, but the road passes through plenty of villages – often little agglomerations of houses, sometimes in the most unlikely places.

The most remarkable spot along the way is **Ida-ou-Gnidif**, perched on a solitary hilltop back from the highway, about 40km south of Aït Baha. From Aït Baha the road flattens out, and the final stretch up to Agadir is of little interest.

Tourism is on the increase in Tafraoute, which may well be good news for many locals. The region has a long history of emigration. A large percentage of the men leave their families in Tafraoute to spend their working lives in the big Moroccan cities or in France.

Apart from almond, argan and palm trees (it is said that where there's a palmeraie, there's a natural spring, and where there are almond or argan trees is a mere well), along with limited wheat and barley cultivation, there's not much to the local economy. For

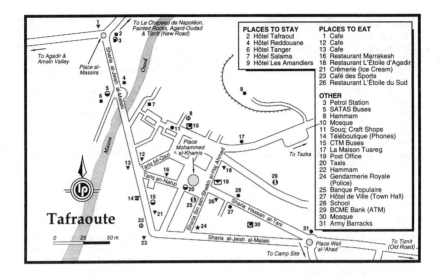

PLACES TO STAY
2 Hôtel Tafraout
4 Hôtel Reddouane
6 Hôtel Tanger
7 Hôtel Salama
9 Hôtel Les Amandiers

PLACES TO EAT
1 Cafe
12 Cafe
13 Cafe
16 Restaurant Marrakesh
18 Restaurant L'Étoile d'Agadir
21 Crêmerie (Ice Cream)
23 Café des Sports
26 Restaurant L'Étoile du Sud

OTHER
3 Petrol Station
5 SATAS Buses
8 Hammam
10 Mosque
11 Souq; Craft Shops
14 Téléboutique (Phones)
15 CTM Buses
17 La Maison Tuareg
19 Post Office
20 Taxis
22 Hammam
24 Gendarmerie Royale (Police)
25 Banque Populaire
27 Hôtel de Ville (Town Hall)
28 School
29 BCME Bank (ATM)
30 Mosque
31 Army Barracks

centuries, this strikingly beautiful area has allowed its inhabitants to eke out only the barest of livings.

Information

There are two banks in Tafraoute, the BMCE and the Banque Populaire. The post office is on the main square, Place Mohammed al-Khamis. There's a téléboutique opposite the CTM office.

A lively souq takes place just by the Hôtel Salam on Wednesday morning.

The Painted Rocks & Le Chapeau de Napoléon

Tafraoute is famous for its painted rocks – the work of Belgian artist Jean Veran. (He has done similar things in places like the Sinai in Egypt.)

In this case he had a collection of the smooth, rounded boulders, peculiar to this patch of the mountains, spray-painted in shades of blue in 1984.

To walk out to the rocks, take the road heading north-east to the village of Agard-Oudad (the opposite way to the Agadir exit). It's about 3km out. On the way you'll

notice a distinctive rock formation on the right, known as **Le Chapeau de Napoléon** (Napoleon's Hat).

At the sign indicating a fork in the road (about 2km), take the right branch and go through the village to the square, where there's a mosque. From here, turn right and then left to get around the mosque, and head out into the countryside for a couple more kilometres. You'll come to some pale-blue rocks on the left-hand side, but keep going and follow the track bearing left to another set, which includes a large blue boulder with a purple rock atop. Beyond is an even larger display of painted rocks.

If you're driving, head past Oulad Argad and follow the signs to a turn-off about 5km beyond the village. Follow the couple of kilometres of piste and leave the car where the track peters out. About 100m on you arrive at a good viewpoint over the rocks.

The Carved Gazelle

To get to this beautiful and apparently ancient carving, take the road for Tazka past the Hôtel Les Amandiers and head for the village on your right. The road climbs up a

STH OF CASABLANCA

STH OF CASABLANCA

Berber Houses

Traditional building methods throughout the Atlas Mountain villages had, until recently, changed little over the centuries. Prosperous mountain Berbers now use more modern techniques, but many subsistence farmers and their families continue to employ age-old methods.

The typical house is flat-roofed and made of pisé, a French term referring to the combination of clay, stone and sun or kiln-dried brick. A decent house has three or four floors; argan-wood beams and palm fronds are typically used for the ceilings between each floor.

The bottom floor is basically for the animals. Cows and the like are kept in a dark area, to reduce the number of flies. Scraps are dropped through a hole in the ceiling, from the kitchen above – a natural form of waste disposal. Farming tools are also kept on this floor, along with utensils for making flour and for grinding coffee and argan nuts for oil. If there is a toilet, it's down here.

A better house has a stairway or ladder up to the next floor, both inside and out. Visitors thus have no reason to see the bottom floor. The kitchen might occupy the main floor-space on this level. Gathered around it are what amount to corridors. One (the biggest) is the family dining room, while the rest serve as bedrooms. Occasionally, these rooms host women on festive occasions (there is traditionally, although not always, strict segregation of the sexes if men from outside the immediate family are visiting, whatever the reason).

A ramp leads up to the next floor, most of which is occupied by the most sumptuous room in the house, where the men usually eat with guests or take tea. Here you take your shoes off before walking on the mats, and all the silver teaware is brought out. On the same floor or above is the inevitable open terrace – especially important in the summer, when it can be far too hot to sleep inside.

The models vary (sometimes the 2nd and top floors are reversed), but the basic formula remains pretty much the same.

Some of these houses have been standing for hundreds of years, but only in a very loose sense. Habitation of villages has historically been cyclic. Berber villages were, until early this century, regularly exposed to epidemics and subject to raids by enemy tribes, and as a result were often abandoned, sometimes for generations.

Where the population was severely reduced, the excess houses stood empty and slowly began to crumble. In better days, these same old houses would be reoccupied, the top floors rebuilt and so the cycle begun again. ■

---

hill from here; you need to get in behind this hill and leave it to your left. You'll see a simple drawing of an animal on a rock on the hill. Walk up to it. The carving is on the top side of a fallen rock right in front of this one. The walk from Tafraoute should take about 20 minutes.

Trekking

Several local people have set themselves up as guides to the area around Tafraoute. Mohammed Sahnoun Ouhammou (☎ 800547) specialises in hikes and mountain bike trips in and around the Afella-Ighir oasis south of Tafraoute. He speaks English and French.

When you have negotiated a price, he will generally put you up in his home, where you can dump your heavier luggage before setting off.

Abid Ahdaj, from the village of Taska (contact him through the Maison Touareg on ☎ 800210), will also act as a guide for people wanting to explore the same area. Abdoulah Brahim, of the Maison Touareg, is based in Tafraoute from October to April and can help organise treks. If you want to be based in one of the more remote Berber villages, he can arrange to have food supplies delivered.

There's nothing to stop you setting off on

your own to explore the surrounding area, but you'll have to be prepared to carry all necessary supplies (mules are not used for trekking in these parts).

Most of the outlying villages don't have running water or electricity and you won't find many stores around.

Spring and autumn are the best seasons for walking – summer is roastingly hot.

Climbing
There are quite a few climbing opportunities around Tafraoute. Houssine Laarousi, who runs a small craft shop called Meeting Place of Nomads in the centre of town, has copies of routes and maps put together by climbers who have passed this way.

Places to Stay – bottom end
Camping *Camping Les Trois Palmiers* is set in a small stony compound – all the palm trees are outside the walls – but it's still not a bad little place. It costs Dr10 per person, the same to pitch a tent, Dr7.50 for a car and Dr7 for a hot shower. There are also two basic double rooms, which cost Dr50, and one room for four people, which costs Dr100.

Hotels Since there are only five hotels in town, it may be worthwhile booking ahead. The two cheapest places in Tafraoute are just opposite each other towards the Agadir exit end of town. Of these, the *Hôtel Tanger* (☎ 800033) is the more basic, offering singles/doubles for Dr25/45 – and a possibly hot shared shower (Dr7).

A better option is the *Hôtel Reddouane* (☎ 800066), where rooms cost Dr35/50, with hot shower included. There is a sun terrace, and the restaurant downstairs is a popular hang-out.

For a little more money you could make the leap to the *Hôtel Tafraout* (☎ 800060), Place Al-Missira Moulay Rachid. The guy in the fez is the manager, Ibrahim Arkarkour, and he's an affable chap.

The rooms are simple, but modern and clean (Dr40/100). Some of them overlook the square below and all are comfortable.

The shared showers are included in the price and are steaming hot. There's a terrace upstairs.

Places to Stay – middle
The *Hôtel Salama* (☎ 800026; fax 800448) has been rebuilt after 'blowing up' some years ago.

Large, comfortable singles/doubles with shower cost 105/133. There are a few basic rooms for Dr50, but there's no shared shower. The hotel has a pleasant terrace and a salon de thé.

Places to Stay – top end
The only remaining option in Tafraoute is the *Hôtel Les Amandiers* (☎ 800088; fax 800343), which sits on the crest of the hill overlooking the town. Self-contained singles/doubles with TV and phone cost Dr362/460 plus taxes. The hotel has a bar, restaurant and guarded parking. They also put on the occasional folkloric shows.

For those with their own transport, there is an infinitely better choice 47km west of Tafraoute on the road to Tiznit.

The *Hôtel Kerdous* (☎ 862063; fax 862835), open since 1992, is perched in a former kasbah right on the pass of the same name. There are extraordinary views on all sides, but especially towards Tiznit. The hotel has 39 rooms, two restaurants and a bar.

Rooms cost Dr312/377 plus taxes. It's worth stopping here for a drink en route to or from Tafraoute, just for the outlook.

Swimming Pools
The Hôtel Les Amandiers and the Hôtel Kerdous, on the way to Tafraoute, have swimming pools.

Hammams
There's a hammam behind the old mosque and another one near the Café des Sports.

Places to Eat
Both the cheap hotels have their own reasonably priced restaurants, and it's really a toss-up between the two. You can eat your

fill for about Dr25. Another option along similar lines is the recently renovated *Restaurant Marrakesh*, off the main square.

The *Restaurant L'Étoile d'Agadir*, just up from the post office, has undergone several name changes. They offer a filling breakfast of orange juice, bread, butter, cheese and jam, finished off with tea or coffee, for Dr15.

The best restaurant, if you have a bit of money to spare, is the *Restaurant L'Étoile du Sud*, opposite the post office on Sharia Hassan at-Tani. The Dr70 menu, although not offering much of a choice of main courses, is tasty. The interior is done up as a traditional Moroccan salon, and the atmosphere is laid back. You can also eat under the tent outside. For an ice cream you could try the *crémerie* near the CTM office.

Things to Buy
La Maison Touareg (☎ 800210), on the road up to the Hôtel Les Amandiers, has a large selection of carpets, and little hard sell.

If you fancy a pair of traditional leather slippers (yellow for men, red for women) Tafraoute is the place to buy them. You'll find dozens of slipper shops around the market area in the centre of town.

Getting There & Away
Bus The CTM office is on Sharia al-Jeish al-Malaki. Local buses gather along this street, too.

There's a CTM service to Tiznit (Dr30) and Agadir (Dr52) at 7 pm. This bus goes on to Marrakesh and Casablanca. Two local buses leave for Tiznit at 4 and 7 am. There's also a local service to Rabat.

Taxi The occasional grand taxi goes to Tiznit in the morning (Dr35). Otherwise, 4WD taxis do the rounds of various villages in the area around Tafraoute.

There is no rhyme or reason to their movements, except demand – which mostly means doing business on market days. If there are any to be had, they hang around Place Mohammed al-Khamis or on Sharia al-Jeish al-Malaki.

Getting Around
You can hire mountain bikes for Dr35 per day from La Maison Touareg.

AROUND TAFRAOUTE
Ameln Valley Tafraoute lies in a basin, largely surrounded by craggy gold-pink rocks and cliffs. To the north-west lies one such ridge, on the other side of which runs the Ameln Valley (Ameln is the name given to the local tribe of Chleuh Berbers). North again of this valley is a mountain range dominated by Jebel al-Kest.

The Agadir road takes you to the valley, which is lined by picturesque Berber villages, some of them only partly inhabited. Four km out of Tafraoute, the road forks; the right branch turning off to take you eastwards out of the valley and on to Agadir. The other proceeds west down the valley. You could take either way and then head off down to any of the villages. It is possible to hike for days, going directly from village to village through barley fields or following narrow goat tracks and irrigation channels.

One of the most visited of the villages is **Oumesnat**, a few kilometres further down the Agadir road after the fork and off to the left along a short piste. The main attraction here is the **Maison Traditionelle**.

Si Abdessalam decided to open up his three storey house (originally built some 400 years ago) to visitors as a way of drumming up a bit of income. Blinded as a young man in Tangier, he is a gentle host and gives you a tour of every nook and cranny of his home. He expects a small consideration for his efforts, and it's worth every dirham. A guide may well be useful, as Si Abdessalam speaks only Arabic and French.

Another village popular with foreigners is **Anameur**, although the only thing that sets it apart from the others is a natural spring. It's about 10km west of Oumesnat.

Taghdichte, between Oumesnat and Anameur, is used by several adventure-travel groups (mainly English and German) as a base for ascents of Jebel al-Kest (it's an all-day walk/scramble, but not a difficult climb).

Further west, before the village of Aït Omar, there's an unmarked piste, opposite a well, which leads to the village of **Tirn-matmat**. Small adventure groups sometimes base themselves here, too, and with good reason. The village sits in a lovely spot – there are some rock carvings along the river bed (the local kids will lead you there) and good walking in all directions. You can hire taxis to get you to some of the villages in the valley.

Afella-Ighir

From Tafraoute there are a couple of routes which take you south to the pretty oasis of Afella-Ighir. You could cover most of it in a 4WD (a Renault 4 will do it, too), but it's preferable to drive part of the way, then leave the car and do a circuit on foot or mountain bike.

The road south of Agard-Oudad takes you roughly 15km over a mountain pass (sometimes snowed over in winter) to Tlata Tasrite. From here it is possible to take several pistes that drop into lush palm-filled valleys, and do a loop of about 30 to 40km through to the Afella-Ighir oasis and back up to Tlata Tasrite.

At Oussaka, about 9km south of Souq al-Had, there are ancient animal carvings. More can be seen 8km further on at Tasselbte. It would be best to talk to a guide (see Trekking under Tafraoute) about the latter part of this hike. 4WD taxis will sometimes do the run to various villages of this area on market days (Wednesday in Tafraoute itself).

SIDI IFNI

Known to some simply as Ifni, this town is at the heart of the former Spanish Sahara. Shrouded for much of the year in an Atlantic mist, this haunting and short-lived coastal outpost of Spanish imperial ambitions (the Spanish originally christened it Santa Cruz del Mar pe quiñã) has a faded, but fascinating air about it.

The town dates largely from the 1930s and features an eclectic mix of Spanish Art Deco and traditional Moroccan styles.

Don't miss the church just off the main plaza, the old consulate, the lighthouse, and the house in the form of a ship on the edge of the cliff next to the Hotel Suerte Loca.

The fabulous balustraded esplanade is crumbling, the *calles* (streets) are half-empty, but even so the sleepy town attracts a surprising number of visitors who return year after year to soak up the atmosphere and enjoy the unhurried pace of life here.

The population of 15,000 lives mainly from small-scale fishing; most of the catch is sold in Agadir.

History

After the Spanish-Moroccan war of 1859, which Morocco lost (just 14 years after a defeat at the hands of a French army from Algeria), Spain obtained the enclave of Ifni by treaty.

Quite what they were going to do with it seems to have been a question in a lot of Spanish minds, because they didn't take full possession until 1934.

By the 1950s, some 60% of the town's population was Spanish, but under pressure from the UN, Spain agreed to cede the enclave back to Morocco in 1969. Morocco had sealed off its land borders three years before. Only three Spanish families now remain.

Information

There's just one bank in town, the Banque Populaire on Ave Mohammed V (away from the heart of the old Spanish town), where you can change cash and cheques. The post office is also on Ave Mohammed V (the letter box outside is still marked 'Correos').

Things to See & Do

Apart from wandering round the old Spanish part of town, the heart of which is Place Hassan II (formerly Plaza de España), there's precious little to do in the town. The beaches are largely deserted, though a little littered. If the whim takes you it's possible to go out fishing with the locals.

Walking south along the beach you'll come to the old Spanish port; just offshore

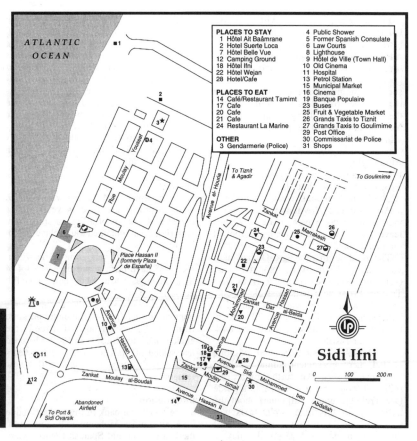

PLACES TO STAY
1 Hôtel Ait Baâmrane
2 Hotel Suerte Loca
7 Hôtel Belle Vue
12 Camping Ground
18 Hôtel Ifni
22 Hôtel Wejan
28 Hotel/Cafe

PLACES TO EAT
14 Café/Restaurant Tamimt
17 Cafe
20 Cafe
21 Cafe
24 Restaurant La Marine

OTHER
3 Gendarmerie (Police)

4 Public Shower
5 Former Spanish Consulate
6 Law Courts
8 Lighthouse
9 Hôtel de Ville (Town Hall)
10 Old Cinema
11 Hospital
13 Petrol Station
15 Municipal Market
16 Cinema
19 Banque Populaire
23 Buses
25 Fruit & Vegetable Market
26 Grands Taxis to Tiznit
27 Grands Taxis to Goulimime
29 Post Office
30 Commissariat de Police
31 Shops

ATLANTIC OCEAN

Place Hassan II (formerly Plaza de España)

To Tiznit & Agadir

To Goulimime

Sidi Ifni

0   100   200 m

Abandoned Airfield

To Port & Sidi Ovarsik

STH OF CASABLANCA

is an old land-sea conveyer which was used to take cargo from ships to the port. The new port is further south.

On Sunday a large, animated souq takes place in front of the abandoned airfield south of town.

For a glimpse into the past, you might visit Hassan Aznag, the second barber on Ave Mohammed V heading south, who has a collection of Spanish magazines and photos from the 1930s to the 1960s.

You can make several excursions into the countryside from Sidi Ifni (the drive from Tiznit, particularly where the road runs through the hills just in from the coast, is itself worthwhile, as is the 58km run to Goulimime).

One possibility would be to hike along the coastal piste to **Sidi Ouarsik**, a fishing village with a good beach 18km south of Sidi Ifni.

The trip to **Mesti**, a Berber village 25km out of Sidi Ifni, off the road to Goulimime, is another possibility.

The family who run the Hotel Suerte Loca can organise 4WD trips, incorporating some walking, to Mesti and other nearby areas.

Places to Stay – bottom end
Camping Just south of the hospital, a cheap but basic patch of ground has been set aside for campers, but it's really only any good for people with campervans.

Hotels The most popular hotel is the *Hotel Suerte Loca* (☎ 875350; fax 870003), at the end of Ave Moulay Youssef.

It's run by the very friendly Essaidi family, who all speak Spanish, French and English. The hotel is divided into two wings, one of them considerably newer than the other. The older rooms are perfectly comfortable, and some have balconies. They cost Dr50/80 (hot showers are Dr5 extra). The clean, cosy rooms in the new wing (Dr112/145) have en suite bathrooms and balconies overlooking the beach.

The hotel has a small collection of novels and the like to lend to guests, a good restaurant (excellent breakfast and crepes), live music three evenings a week, a terrace for sunbathing and mountain bikes for hire (Dr70 per day). Malika Essaidi runs a shop next to the hotel selling a variety of crafts at very reasonable fixed prices.

If the Hotel Suerte Loca is full (which is quite possible, particularly at Christmas), there are a few standard Moroccan cheapies scattered around Ave Mohammed V.

The *Hôtel Ifni*, near the bank, is as good as any, with very basic rooms for Dr20 a head. They have cold showers. The *Hôtel Wejan*, further up Mohammed V, has basic rooms for the same price. The nameless place on Ave Sidi Mohammed ben Abdallah has rooms with no frills for Dr25/50.

The *Hôtel Beau Rivage* was still closed at the time of writing.

Places to Stay – middle
The two-star *Hôtel Belle Vue* (☎ 875072), at 9 Place Hassan II, has comfortable singles/doubles with bathroom for Dr136/156. Some rooms have sea views while others look onto the plaza. The hotel has a

bar and restaurant, and a great candy coloured terrace with views of the beach.

Down on the beach itself, the *Hôtel Ait Baâmrane* (☎ 875267), has tattier rooms with private shower for Dr100/127. There is a restaurant, an unsalubrious bar and a ruined swimming pool.

Hammams
If you want a hot shower, there is a public douche just up the road from the Hotel Suerte Loca. There are separate times for men and women.

Places to Eat
Apart from a few small cafe/restaurants on Ave Hassan II and dotted about the town, the only choices are really the hotel restaurants. The one at the *Hotel Suerte Loca* is particularly good value – they'll cook up whatever you feel like eating, including freshly caught fish and any number of Spanish and Moroccan specialities.

The *Restaurant La Marine*, off Ave Mohammed V, serves cheap fish and standard Moroccan dishes.

The *Café/Restaurant Tamimt*, down by the airfield, does a pretty good chicken and chips. There are also roadside snack stands along Ave Mohammed V in the evenings.

Self-Catering There's a busy *fish market* open from 5 until 8 pm at the Municipal Market and a fruit and vegetable market tucked in behind Zankat Marrakesh.

There are grocery shops along Ave Mohammed V.

Getting There & Away
Bus Buses depart Sidi Ifni from along Ave Mohammed V early in the morning. There is a 5 am bus to Marrakesh (Dr85) via Tiznit (Dr18) and Agadir (Dr36). There's also a 6 am service to Goulimime (Dr18) and another bus to Agadir at 7 am.

Taxi By far the easiest way to get to and from Sidi Ifni is by grand taxi. Taxis leave from a couple of dirt lots around the corner from the northern end of Ave Hassan I and cost Dr20 a head to either Tiznit (about 1½ hours) or Goulimime (one hour). A place in a taxi to Agadir costs Dr40.

GOULIMIME

The most striking thing about Goulimime (pronounced Gooly-meem), the dusty little town that proclaims itself the Gateway to the Sahara, is the bold crimson colour of almost all the buildings. Apart from that, and the chance to see a variety of desert bird life in the surrounding area, Goulimime doesn't have a great deal to offer the traveller.

Once upon a time, 'blue men' came in from the desert every week to buy and sell camels at a souq just outside town. In the evenings, the women would perform the mesmerising *guedra* dance to the beat of drums of the same name.

This is what the package tourists pile into Goulimime for on Friday night and Saturday, but they must leave sorely disappointed. Economic considerations have long since rendered the camel market obsolete. There is a large souq held every Saturday a couple of kilometres outside town, along the route to Tan Tan. You'll see plenty of fruit here and quite a lot of over-priced souvenirs, but very few camels. Be prepared for some insistent hustlers and touts around Goulimime.

Bird-watchers may like to look out for a variety of desert bird species off the main road heading south of Goulimime. Birds that have been seen around here include warblers, wheateaters, sandgrouse and larks, as well as eagles, buzzards and falcons.

Information

The tourist office (☎ 872911) is at 3 Résidence Sahara, Blvd d'Agadir. Should you find yourself stuck here for any reason, four banks have branches in Goulimime, so changing money should be no problem. The post office is near the mosque between the two main roundabouts.

Places to Stay – bottom end

Refer to the following Around Goulimime section for camping options. There are five cheap hotels to choose from in town, the best of which is the new *Hôtel Tinghir* (☎ 871638), next to the CTM office on the road to Agadir. Clean singles/doubles cost Dr35/70. A hot shower costs Dr6. There's a decent cafe/restaurant downstairs.

The *Hôtel Bir Anazarane* and the *Hôtel Oued Dahab*, both on the roundabout opposite the Banque Populaire, have very basic rooms for around Dr20/35. There is no shower in the Bir Anazarane and a cold one in the Dahab.

Further down Blvd Mohammed V you'll find the similarly priced *Hôtel La Jeunesse* and the *Hôtel L'Ere Nouvelle*. The latter has a warm communal shower.

Places to Stay – middle

The only hotel in this range is the one-star *Hôtel Salam* (☎ 872057), which has its own bar and restaurant and costs Dr88, Dr116 and Dr161 for singles, doubles and triples

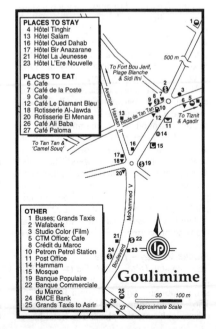

PLACES TO STAY
4   Hôtel Tinghir
13   Hôtel Salam
16   Hôtel Oued Dahab
17   Hôtel Bir Anazarane
21   Hôtel La Jeunesse
23   Hôtel L'Ere Nouvelle

PLACES TO EAT
6   Cafe
7   Café de la Poste
9   Cafe
12   Café Le Diamant Bleu
18   Rotisserie Al-Jawda
20   Rotisserie El Menara
26   Café Ali Baba
27   Café Paloma

OTHER
1   Buses; Grands Taxis
2   Wafabank
3   Studio Color (Film)
5   CTM Office; Cafe
8   Crédit du Maroc
10   Petrom Petrol Station
11   Post Office
14   Hammam
15   Mosque
19   Banque Populaire
22   Banque Commerciale du Maroc
24   BMCE Bank
25   Grands Taxis to Asrir

500 m

To Fort Bou Jerif, Plage Blanche & Sidi Ifni

To Tiznit & Agadir

To Tan Tan & 'Camel Souq'

Avenue Hassan

Route de Tan Tan

Boulevard Mohammed V

Goulimime

0   50   100 m
Approximate Scale

with private shower and toilet. They also have cheaper rooms without toilet. It is advisable to book ahead here if you want to turn up for the camel charade.

Hammams
There's a hammam next to the mosque.

Places to Eat
There are a couple of good little rotisseries near the Hôtel Bir Anzarane – it's a toss-up between *Al-Jawda* and *El Menara*. You can get a filling meal of chicken, chips and salad for around Dr30.

Something more like a restaurant, with the usual Moroccan fare, is the *Café de la Poste*, on the Wafabank end of the Route de Tan Tan. A full meal here costs about Dr50.

Similar food is on offer at the *Café Le Diamant Bleu* and in the cafe below the *Hôtel Tinghir*. There's a reasonably priced restaurant, and the town's only bar, at the *Hôtel Salam*.

The most pleasant cafes are the *Café Ali Baba* and the *Café Paloma*, about half a kilometre south of the main roundabout, opposite the Asrir grand taxi lot.

Getting There & Away
Bus The main bus and grand taxi terminals are about 1km north of the town centre, although CTM also has a small office on the Agadir road.

CTM has several daily buses to Agadir (Dr45) and one bus to Casablanca (Dr178) via Marrakesh (Dr118) at 8 pm. There's also a 12.30 am run to Dakhla (Dr266) via Laayoune (Dr140) and a 6.30 am service to Tan Tan (Dr34).

SATAS also operates out of this station, along with several smaller local companies, so you have a reasonable choice.

Taxi If bus departure times look inconvenient, you're probably better off with a grand taxi. They leave from behind the bus station. You can get a taxi to Sidi Ifni (Dr20), Tiznit (Dr30), Tan Tan (Dr36), Inezgane (for Agadir; Dr52) and Laayoune (Dr130).

AROUND GOULIMIME
Fort Bou Jerif
Well worth getting to if you have your own transport is Fort Beau Jerif (fax 873039), a wonderful oasis of civilisation in the desert about 40km north-west of Goulimime (the last 18km is rough piste).

Built near a ruined military fort and run by a very welcoming French couple, Guy and Evy Dreumont, Fort Beau Jerif has simple rooms (Dr120/150), hot communal showers, plenty of camping space (Dr20), beds in comfortable nomad tents (Dr30), a superb restaurant (Dr130 for a full meal) and good French wine.

The Dreumont's offer 4WD trips to **Plage Blanche**, a little-visited and unspoilt stretch of Atlantic beach further south of the fort, as well as donkey treks around the area.

Abainou
On the road down from Sidi Ifni, about 15km north of Goulimime, is the tiny oasis village of Abainou where you can bathe in hot springs. There are separate round bathing pools for men and women. Entry costs Dr5. The water is said to be very beneficial, especially for the skin. There's a basic camp site here which costs Dr5 per person, Dr5 for a car and Dr3 for a tent.

The *Hôtel Abainou* is a fairly comfortable place with double rooms (and cold communal showers) for Dr100 including breakfast. The hotel has a restaurant and bar. There are a couple of simple cafes in the village, too.

Aït Bekkou
About 17km south-east of Goulimime, Aït Bekkou is a pleasant oasis village – you'll probably see more camels here than in Goulimime on a Saturday, but don't fall for the old 'Berber market, today only' story.

You can get grands taxis as far as Asrir, but you may well have to hitch the remaining 7km of piste to Aït Bekkou. Alternatively, you could hire a taxi for the day.

If you want to stay overnight, the *Hôtel Tighmert* has clean, comfortable rooms for Dr100/150.

TAN TAN

Taking the road south from Goulimime, you soon get the feeling you're heading well into the unknown – few travellers get this far.

The 125km of desert highway is impressive in parts, but is harsh *hammada* (stony desert) rather than the soft, sandy dune variety. Breaking up the monotony, the road also crosses several oueds, including the Oued Drâa, which is usually dry this far away from its sources.

Police roadblocks become more frequent as you head south. Passing through them is usually straightforward; you will be asked your destination, nationality and profession and then waved on with the usual 'Welcome to Morocco'.

You could drive through the main street of Tan Tan (population 50,000) and not realise you had missed most of the town, which spreads south of the highway (known as Ave Hassan II within the town boundaries).

If you're on a bus or grand taxi, however, there's no danger of this. Tan Tan is situated in what was once part of Spanish-occupied Morocco, an area known under the Spaniards as Tarfaya which stretched south to the border of the former Spanish Sahara, a colony Spain abandoned only in 1975 (for details, see the following Western Sahara Desert section).

The Tarfaya zone was handed over in 1958, two years after independence.

There's nothing much to do in Tan Tan, although it has quite a busy air about it. There's a fairly high army and police presence due to the proximity of the long-disputed Western Sahara region. If you are heading south, it makes a more interesting overnight stop than Tarfaya (to the south).

Information

There's a BMCE bank next to the Shell petrol station, where Ave Mohammed V runs into Ave Hassan II, and a Banque Populaire on the first square heading down Ave Mohammed V away from Ave Hassan II.

The post office is east along Ave Hassan

II. There's a telephone office on the main square and several téléboutiques scattered around town. Tan Tan's weekly souq takes place on Sunday.

Places to Stay & Eat

There are plenty of cheap hotels in Tan Tan, so you should have no trouble finding a bed. The best hotel around the bus station square is the *Hôtel/Café Dakar*, although it's hardly palatial. Rooms with a double bed cost Dr60 or Dr80 with private shower.

The others here, and in the side lanes heading north along Ave Mohammed V, are basic places costing about Dr30 to Dr40 per person. Most offer cold showers at best, but can direct you to a hammam (there's one near the bus station).

There are several more such hotels on the main square. Here you can try the *Hôtel/Restaurant du Sud*, *Hôtel/Café Chahrazad*, *Hôtel/Café Sahara* or *Hôtel/Café Essaada*.

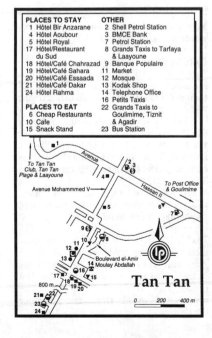

PLACES TO STAY	OTHER
1 Hôtel Bir Anzarane	2 Shell Petrol Station
4 Hôtel Aoubour	3 BMCE Bank
5 Hôtel Royal	7 Petrol Station
17 Hôtel/Restaurant du Sud	8 Grands Taxis to Tarfaya & Laayoune
18 Hôtel/Café Chahrazad	9 Banque Populaire
19 Hôtel/Café Sahara	11 Market
20 Hôtel/Café Essaada	12 Mosque
21 Hôtel/Café Dakar	13 Kodak Shop
24 Hôtel Rahma	14 Telephone Office
	16 Petits Taxis
PLACES TO EAT	22 Grands Taxis to Goulimime, Tiznit
6 Cheap Restaurants	& Agadir
10 Cafe	23 Bus Station
15 Snack Stand	

They all have cafes or restaurants downstairs. The *Hôtel Aoubour*, on Ave Hassan II, is more convenient for people with their own transport, but it's no great shakes.

The *Hôtel Bir Anzarane* (☎ 877834), west along Ave Hassan II, has rooms for Dr50 per person (shared hot showers), but is well overpriced.

The best hotel in town by a long chalk is the new *Tan Tan Club* (☎ 878895) on the road to Laayoune. Large, clean rooms with hot shower and toilet cost Dr80/130. There's a reasonable restaurant here (though the same food in town will cost a lot less) and a popular cafe.

Getting There & Away

Bus All the buses leave from the bus station (Gare Routière), about 1km south of the main central square.

CTM and SATAS are the best companies operating buses from here, although a lot of the services are through runs from other towns. There are plenty of local buses. Services include Laayoune (Dr60), Casablanca (Dr180), Agadir (Dr60) and Marrakesh (Dr120).

Taxi Grands taxis to Laayoune and, occasionally, Tarfaya leave from a small square off Blvd el-Amir Moulay Abdallah. Others, for Goulimime (Dr36), Tiznit, Inezgane and Agadir (Dr70), leave from a lot by the bus station.

Car Much cheaper petrol is available in the Western Sahara, which begins just south of Tarfaya. The first of the Atlas Sahara petrol stations is just outside Tarfaya and about 240km south of Tan Tan.

AROUND TAN TAN
Tan Tan Plage

About 27km west of Tan Tan is the beach of the same name. It's a rather uninspiring little spot, with a few cafes in among the scruffy housing and public buildings. With the main business being fish exports, the port area does nothing to improve the atmosphere on the beach.

Western Sahara Desert

What the Moroccan tourist brochures refer to as the Saharan provinces largely comprise the still-disputed territory of the Western Sahara (see the main map at the beginning of this chapter).

Evacuated by Spain in 1975, Morocco and Mauritania both raised claims to the sparsely populated desert territory, but the latter soon bailed out. This left Rabat to fight the rebel group, Polisario, which had contributed to Madrid's decision to abandon the phosphate-rich region in the first place.

In November 1975, King Hassan II orchestrated the Green March – 350,000 Moroccans, largely unarmed civilians, marched in to stake Morocco's historical claims to the Western Sahara. The border of what had been Spanish Sahara ran just south of Tarfaya.

In the following years, as many as 100,000 troops were poured in to stamp out resistance. As Polisario lost Algerian and Libyan backing, and the Moroccans erected a 1600km-long sand wall to hamper the rebels' movements, it became increasingly clear that Rabat had the upper hand. The UN organised a ceasefire in 1991, which raised the prospect of a referendum to settle the issue of the Western Sahara region's status. The ceasefire has largely held, but the referendum is yet to materialise.

In late 1996, the UN, after spending some US$250 million on peace-keeping operations in the area, pushed for a series of meetings between parties in a bid to reach a compromise (for more information see the History section in the Facts about the Country chapter).

Since the ceasefire, Morocco has strengthened its hold on the territory, pouring money into infrastructure projects and expanding the city of Laayoune. Moroccans from the north have been enticed to move down by the prospect of employment and tax-free living (hence the cheap petrol).

To all intents and purposes, Morocco appears to have succeeded, with the world community too preoccupied by crises elsewhere and foreign diplomats questioning the legitimacy and practicality of Polisario's independence demands.

Apart from the endless police roadblocks and checks, going south to Dakhla is now a routine affair, and it has been possible to cross into Mauritania in convoy since the running of the 1994 Paris-Dakar rally.

Information
As part of a drive to attract Moroccans into Western Sahara, many items are tax free. This includes petrol, which costs a couple of dirham less per litre than elsewhere.

There is an Atlas Sahara service station just outside Tarfaya on the road to Laayoune (and the only one until you reach that city) where you can stock up on cheap petrol.

TARFAYA
The 235km drive from Tan Tan to Tarfaya takes you across a relatively monotonous stretch of desert highway. The road, however, is reasonably good and traffic is relatively light – just the occasional lorry and pale yellow or Saharan blue taxis stuffed with turbaned passengers.

Along the route you'll see fishermen's huts perched on the clifftops (many sell fish by the roadside) and further south herds of camels wandering slowly through the hammada.

Around 150km south of Tan Tan is the tiny roadside village of **Sidi Akhfennir** which has a string of mechanics workshops and several cafes serving fish straight from the sea. The area just north of Tarfaya is the most scenic, with wild, untouched beaches and a series of shipwrecks clearly visible from the road.

The raggedy little coastal town of Tarfaya is itself unlikely to hold anyone's attention for long. Located near Cap Juby,

it was the second-largest town in the Spanish-controlled zone of the same name, but in fact started life late in the 19th century as a minor British trading post.

The population of the surrounding area is largely nomadic, and the town itself boasts a small fishing industry.

Things to See
Possibly the most interesting thing about the town is the unusual building stuck well out from the beach amid the Atlantic breakers. Known as **Casamar** (from 'casa del mar', or house in the sea), it was once a British trading house.

Otherwise, there is a monument to the French pilot and writer Antoine de Saint-Exupéry (perhaps best known for his children's story *The Little Prince*), one of several aviators who, in the interwar years, used the town as a stopover on the French airmail service between Toulouse and Dakar.

Places to Stay & Eat
At the time of writing, Tarfaya's only hotel was closed. There are a few simple cafes around where you can get standard Moroccan meals.

Getting There & Away
There are occasional buses and grands taxis linking Tarfaya to Tan Tan and Laayoune, but they are infrequent.

LAAYOUNE (AL-'UYUN)
Laayoune, once a neglected Spanish administrative town, has been transformed out of all recognition since the Moroccans took it back in 1975. Although you'll still see the odd street name posted as a 'calle', little evidence of the Spanish presence remains. With a population of 120,000 – mostly outsiders – it is Rabat's showpiece in the Western Sahara.

The 115km road south from Tarfaya is unexciting, cut by the occasional dry riverbed and occasionally awash with sand. There are few beaches to speak of, with the desert simply dropping away in sheer cliffs into the ocean below. Sixty-five km north of Laayoune, in the Tah depression (55m below sea level), there is a monument commemorating a visit this far south by Sultan Moulay al-Hassan I back in 1885 (probably on an expedition to punish unruly tribes and extract taxes) and Hassan II's 'return' on a visit 100 years later.

There is not an awful lot to see in Laayoune itself, although the atmosphere is odd enough to make a stay of a day or two worthwhile. In any case, whether you're heading north or south, the distances involved are such that you'll almost have no choice but to sleep over for at least a night.

Orientation

Although the showpiece town focus is the shiny new Place du Mechouar (where bored Moroccan youths hang about at night), there is no really obvious centre. Most of the practical considerations, such as post and phone offices, banks and some of the hotels, are somewhere along or near Ave Hassan II.

There is a collection of budget hotels at the north-west end of town in a lively market area. SATAS buses also gather there, but CTM has its office and bus departure area on Ave de Mecca.

Grands taxis north are on a square at the north-west end of Ave Hassan II, but there are several other stations scattered about town.

Information

Tourist Office The Délégation Régionale du Tourisme (☎ 891694; fax 891695) is just back from Ave de l'Islam, virtually across the road from the Hôtel Parador. It's open Monday to Friday from 8.30 to 11.30 am and 2 to 6 pm. Apart from a couple of brochures, they have little to offer, but they are anxious to please and can tell you how to get to bus stations and the like.

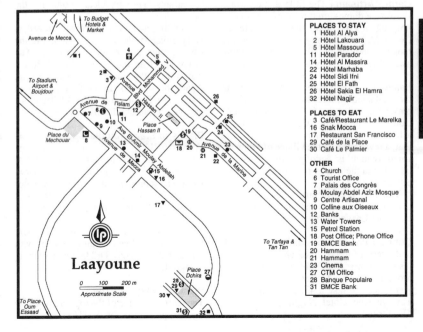

PLACES TO STAY
1 Hôtel Al Alya
2 Hôtel Lakouara
5 Hôtel Massoud
11 Hôtel Parador
14 Hôtel Al Massira
22 Hôtel Marhaba
24 Hôtel Sidi Ifni
25 Hôtel El Fath
26 Hôtel Sakia El Hamra
32 Hôtel Nagjir

PLACES TO EAT
3 Café/Restaurant Le Marelka
16 Snak Mocca
17 Restaurant San Francisco
29 Café de la Place
30 Café Le Palmier

OTHER
4 Church
6 Tourist Office
7 Palais des Congrès
8 Moulay Abdel Aziz Mosque
9 Centre Artisanal
10 Colline aux Oiseaux
12 Banks
13 Water Towers
15 Petrol Station
18 Post Office; Phone Office
19 BMCE Bank
20 Hammam
21 Hammam
23 Cinema
27 CTM Office
28 Banque Populaire
31 BMCE Bank

Laayoune

0   100   200 m
Approximate Scale

STH OF CASABLANCA

Money The BMCE has a branch on Place Hassan II, next to the post office. There is a Banque Populaire and a couple of other banks up from the intersection of Ave Hassan II and Blvd Mohammed V. There is another Banque Populaire on Place Dchira.

Post & Communications The post and phone offices are lumped together at the south-eastern end of Ave Hassan II, and are open Monday to Friday from 8.30 am to noon and 2 to 6 pm. There are numerous téléboutiques around.

Things to See

Colline aux Oiseaux On the hill between the tourist office and Ave de Mecca, this small aviary features a number of quite spectacular parrots and other birds. Enter through the Centre Artisanal on Ave de Mecca. It's free.

Centre Artisanal The little domed workshops (the domes are typical of the simpler housing in Laayoune) that constitute the Centre Artisanal on Ave de Mecca are mostly inhabited by silversmiths tinkering away. Pressure to buy is at a minimum.

Laayoune Plage About 25km out along the road south to Boujdour and Dakhla is a reasonable little beach. There is a simple camp site and Club Med has organised a few rooms here for anglers. Apart from that, a few houses in the village of Foum el-Oued (which is a couple of kilometres inland) and the nearby port, there's nothing else to it.

You may need to hire a taxi to get out here, or join the hitchers at the Boujdour exit from Laayoune, near the new stadium.

Dunes Kilometres of dunes spread north and west of Laayoune, and are clearly visible from several vantage points in and around the city. To get in among them, you'd need to take a 4WD off the road to Tarfaya (the Hôtel Nagjir can organise 4WD trips).

Places to Stay – bottom end

Camping There is a simple *camping ground* with minimal facilities at Laayoune Plage (Foum el-Oued).

Hotels You will probably find most of the hotel guests at the budget end are soldiers – there are a lot of them about.

There is a collection of cheapie hotels on Ave Maître Salem Bida, out near the market in the north-west end of town. These include the *Hôtel La Victoire*, *Hôtel Atlas*, *Hôtel Tafilalet*, *Hôtel Inezgane* and the *Hôtel Errimal Eddahabia*. Singles/doubles in all these places cost Dr31/42. They are quite basic and the best cleaning material you can hope for is a cold, salty bore-water shower.

A number of similar places (with similar prices) back near Place Hassan II include the *Hôtel Sakia El Hamra*, *Hôtel El Fath* and *Hôtel Sidi Ifni*. The *Hôtel Massoud*, up near the church and close to a couple of restaurants, has very clean rooms for the same price.

Slightly better and popular with travellers is the *Hôtel Marhaba*, on Ave de la Marine (the continuation of Ave Hassan II). The rooms are clean and have a table, chair and wardrobe, but the mattresses are rather thin. Again the showers are cold and it's bore water only. Rooms cost Dr31/42. There's a cafe and restaurant downstairs.

Places to Stay – middle

From the Hôtel Marhaba there is a huge leap in prices. The cheapest is the *Hôtel Al Alya* (☎ 894144) at 1 Rue Kadi El Ghalaoui. The rooms are only marginally better than in the Marhaba and hot water isn't guaranteed. Rooms with bath and toilet cost Dr120/150.

Much better is the *Hôtel Lakouara* (☎ 893378) on Ave Hassan II. Rooms with private bathroom cost Dr235/320, including breakfast.

Places to Stay – top end

The least expensive of the top-end places is the *Hôtel Nagjir* (☎ 894168) on Place

Dchira. Comfortable singles/doubles cost Dr385/496, but the rooms are often occupied by UN staff. The hotel has a restaurant, bar and disco.

The two top hotels are the *Hôtel Al Massira* (☎ 894225; fax 890962) and the *Hôtel Parador* (☎ 894500). Both have all the facilities of expensive hotels, but for years now have been block-booked by the UN. The bar and restaurant of the Hôtel Al Massira are open to non-UN people.

Hammams
There are hammams on Ave de la Marine, just east of the BMCE bank.

Places to Eat
The cheapest (and probably best) place to hunt for food is around the budget hotel and market area. There are plenty of small stalls and simple restaurants selling the usual meat dishes, salads and good local fish. Dr25 should get you a filling meal.

The *Restaurant San Francisco*, on Ave de Mecca, is a very popular place serving simple chicken and chips, salads, hamburgers and very good harira. A full meal costs around Dr30. *Snak Mokka* across the road does a pretty good plate of brochettes.

The *Café/Restaurant Le Marelka*, on Ave Hassan II near the Hôtel Lakouara, offers both French and Moroccan dishes and is licensed to sell beer.

There are a couple of pleasant cafes on Place Dchira, near the CTM office, and plenty of others scattered about town.

Getting There & Away
Air Royal Air Maroc (☎ 894071) has an office at 7 Place Bir Anzarane, next to the Hôtel Nagjir. It has five weekly flights to Casablanca for Dr1387 one way. There are twice weekly flights to Dakhla (Dr582) and to Las Palmas in the Canary Islands (Dr1436).

Bus The CTM office and terminal is on Ave de Mecca. A bus leaves for Dakhla at 8 am (Dr140.50). There are services to Agadir at 4, 6 and 8 pm (Dr204) via Tan

DORINDA TALBOT

More common than a stop sign: a 'camels crossing' sign in the Western Sahara.

Tan and Tiznit. A bus leaves for Casablanca (Dr325) via Marrakesh (Dr262) at 4 pm.

SATAS has slightly more runs, and its buses leave from a dirt lot in among the budget hotels and market area.

Train It is possible to book a bus-train ticket to anywhere on the Moroccan rail network. The Supratours/ONCF office is on Place Oum Essaad.

Taxi Grands taxis to Tan Tan, Goulimime and Inezgane (for Agadir) leave from a lot at the north-western end of Ave Hassan II. You might even be able to get one right through to Marrakesh.

Taxis to Boujdour, Smara and Dakhla leave from another lot (ask for the *station taxis Boujdour*) on the southern periphery of town. A red-and-white petit taxi there will cost you Dr5.

SMARA (AS-SMARA)
About 240km east of Laayoune (245km south of Tan Tan) lies what the ONMT brochure bluntly calls 'A Historic City'. The original town was established here on a Saharan caravan route a century ago. There's really very little left of the old town, except for the mosque.

There are banks and a post office and a few hotels largely full of Moroccan soldiers and UN observers. Buses and taxis run between Smara, Laayoune and Tan Tan.

STH OF CASABLANCA

DAKHLA (AD-DAKHLA)

Established by the Spanish in 1844 and formerly called Villa Cisneros, Dakhla is just north of the Tropic of Cancer on the end of a sandy peninsula stretching out 40km from the main coastline.

It's a very long, lonely 542km drive from Laayoune through endless hammada, and only worth the effort if you are making an attempt to get into Mauritania.

The place is crawling with soldiers, but with the threat posed by Polisario receding, there is little sense of danger.

Dakhla has a bit of a name for ocean fishing, so that may be an added incentive for those travellers who like to catch and cook their own fish. It's not a bad place to take a surfboard either.

Information

The tourist office (☎ 898388) is at 1 Rue Tiris. There is a branch of the BMCE bank on Blvd Mohammed V.

Places to Stay

There's a camping ground 7km north of Dakhla, which costs Dr10 per person plus charges for a car and tent. There are plenty of cheap hotels in town, but they can often be full of soldiers.

You'll find quite a few places near the market area, including the *Hôtel Sahara*, which has clean basic rooms for Dr50 per person. The town's top hotel is the three-star *Hôtel Doums* (☎ 898045/6), on Ave al-Waha, where rooms with shower and toilet cost Dr230/284. The hotel has a bar.

Getting There & Away

Air The airport is 5km out of town. Royal Air Maroc (☎ 897049), on Ave des PTT, has three flights a week to Casablanca, one of them stopping in Laayoune and the other two in Agadir.

Bus, Train & Taxi There's a daily CTM bus to Laayoune for Dr140.50. SATAS also has buses between Dakhla and Laayoune. One bus a day leaves for Agadir (18 hours). Tickets cost Dr325 and should be booked ahead.

There are grands taxis and it is also possible to organise a bus-train ticket from Dakhla with Supratours to any destination on the rail network.

Mauritania Since the beginning of 1994, the border with Mauritania has, as far as Rabat is concerned, been open.

There are no buses doing this run, so you need to arrange transport (which would have to be good to cope with travelling on the Mauritanian side of the frontier). Once this is done you have to get a permit from the military.

Finally, you have to wait until a convoy of at least half a dozen vehicles is assembled. It is then escorted (in case of an attack by Polisario) 363km to the frontier (across a minefield).

It is possible to have Mauritanian visa issued in Rabat, but you are strongly advised to get one before arriving in Africa. French citizens do not require visas to enter Mauritania.

Berber spider symbol
Associated with fertility and magic rites.

The High Atlas

The ochre-coloured city of Marrakesh is, alongside Agadir, Morocco's biggest drawcard. Founded almost 1000 years ago, it is one of the great cities of the Maghreb and is home to its most perfect Islamic monument, the Koutoubia Mosque.

Marrakesh is above all a city of drama. Its spectacular setting against the snow-capped High Atlas mountains lingers long in the mind of most travellers, and the famous Djemaa el-Fna square provides perhaps the greatest open-air spectacle in the world. There's plenty of entertainment to be found in the medina too, where travellers can drift with the smells and sounds of the souqs, haggle passionately for carpets, or dine in some of the best and most extravagant restaurants in the country.

The city is also blessed with an ideal location. Just one hour away from the heat and the crowds of the city, you can be strolling through the High Atlas foothills of the Ourika Valley, or striking off into the wilder territory around Mount Toubkal, barely visited except by the animals and their Berber shepherds.

Valleys cut through the range and spill out south and east towards the Sahara. Dotted with red-coloured kasbahs, riotous palm groves and largely unremarkable towns, the spectacular natural settings exemplify the maxim that 'it is better to travel than to arrive'. The best time to visit is undoubtedly early spring. If you can, avoid Marrakesh during the months of July and August.

Marrakesh

Basking in the clear African light of the south, Marrakesh has an entirely different feel from its sister cities further north. It is unmistakably more African than cosmopolitan Casablanca, more Moroccan

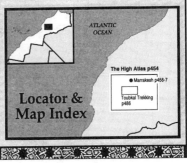

HIGHLIGHTS

Toubkal Region – remote Berber villages & the highest peaks of the High Atlas

Tin Mal Mosque – a beautiful memorial to the founder of the Berber Almohad dynasty

Tizi n'Test – breathtaking mountain pass linking Marrakesh with Agadir

Imilchil – remote central High Atlas village with a famous moussem each September

Marrakesh – an Imperial city more famous for its people than its monuments

ATLANTIC OCEAN

The High Atlas p454

Marrakesh p456-7

Toubkal Trekking p486

Locator & Map Index

than sanitised Rabat, and more Berber than the proud, aloof and intensely Arab city of Fès.

With a population of around 1.5 million, Marrakesh is Morocco's fourth-largest city. To a certain degree, it serves as a second Rabat, a kind of capital of the south, and attracts merchants and traders from all over the surrounding plains, the High Atlas and the Sahara.

It's positioned on an important crossroads linking the south to the north, and the west to the east. It's also the southernmost terminus of the train network.

Just as the colour blue is synonymous with the city of Fès, green with Meknès and white with Rabat, so red has become the

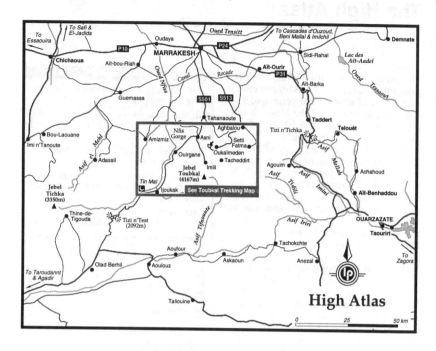

colour of Marrakesh. Red earth walls surround the medina of flat-roofed red houses.

A local Berber legend has it that when the Koutoubia was planted in the city's heart, it poured so much blood that all the walls, all the houses and all the roads turned this colour. At dusk, in the last rays of the setting sun, the walls of the city turn almost crimson. Don't miss it.

History
Once one of the most important artistic and cultural centres in the Islamic world, Marrakesh was founded in 1062 AD by the Almoravid sultan Youssef bin Tachfin. It experienced its heyday under Youssef's son, Ali, who was born to a Christian slave mother. It was Ali who had the extensive underground irrigation canals (*khettara*) built that still supply the city's gardens with water.

As the Almoravids proceeded with their conquest of Spain, much of the wealth that flowed to the kingdom was lavished on extending and beautifying the city. When Youssef bin Tachfin died in 1106, he could do so content in the knowledge that he had not only consolidated his dynasty's control of Morocco and Spain (in 1085 he had defeated the Christians after they had seized the city of Toledo), but he had also bequeathed an urban jewel to his successors.

Meanwhile, inside the city's red stone and earthen ramparts, artisans from Muslim Spain erected the first of the refined, Andalusian-style buildings that were to grace the city.

These buildings were largely razed by the Almohads in 1147, although the walls and the gateway to Ali's huge palace were spared. The city was rebuilt shortly afterwards and, again, it was artisans from Andalusia who were responsible for the greater part of its construction. Marrakesh remained the capital of the Almohad empire until its collapse in 1269, when the Merenids moved the capital north to Fès, which then became the focus of Moroccan brilliance in the arts.

With the rise to power of the Saadians in the 16th century, Marrakesh again became the capital, following a brief period when the city of Taroudannt enjoyed that particular honour. The city had experienced hard times prior to the Saadian takeover. Even the Portuguese had tried to capture Marrakesh in 1515, and in the following years famines had crippled activity in the city and surrounding countryside.

Saadian control brought prosperity once again. During the Saadian reign the Portuguese were forced to abandon the bulk of their coastal enclaves. The mellah, the huge Mouassine Mosque and the Ali ben Youssef Medersa were built in these times. The Saadians also set up a customs house for the Christian colony that had been established in Marrakesh.

Ahmed al-Mansour was one of the more outstanding of the Saadian sultans, and was known as 'the Golden One' because of his riches, largely accumulated in his 'conquest' of Timbuktu. His legacy included the exquisite Andalusian El-Badi Palace and the long-hidden necropolis of his dynasty, now known simply as the Saadian tombs.

As so often in Morocco's turbulent history, the golden days were soon followed by chaos and decadence. The Saadians' successors, the Alawites, moved the capital to Meknès.

Marrakesh could not be ignored, however. While Moulay Ismail was responsible for tearing apart the El-Badi Palace for its building materials, his successor, Sidi Mohammed bin Abdallah, poured resources into rebuilding or restoring the walls, kasbah, palaces, mosques and mechouars (royal assembly palaces) of the city, as well as creating new gardens (such as the Jardin Ménara).

By the 19th century, Marrakesh was again on the decline, although it did regain some of its former prestige when Moulay al-Hassan I was crowned there in 1873. Its most recent return to good fortune is largely the result of French activities during the protectorate period, when the ville nouvelle was built, the medina was revitalised and resettled, and the Place de Foucauld was created below the Djemaa el-Fna.

Increasing tourism in Marrakesh since then has ensured its continued prosperity. The importance attached to the city by Morocco itself was symbolised in April 1994, when it was chosen as the location for the final signing of the international GATT agreements on world trade.

Orientation

As in Fès and Meknès, the old city and the ville nouvelle of Marrakesh are about the same size. It takes about a half an hour to walk from the centre of activity in the ville nouvelle to the Djemaa el-Fna, the main square in the heart of the old city, so you may find it convenient to use public transport to get from one to the other.

The two main areas of the ville nouvelle are Gueliz and Hivernage. The latter contains little more of interest than some middle and top-range hotels, and it borders on the Jardin Ménara.

Gueliz forms the working centre of the ville nouvelle. The bulk of the city's offices, restaurants, cafes and shops, plus a collection of hotels, are all clustered on or near the city's main thoroughfare, Ave Mohammed V. The train station lies south-west of Place du 16 Novembre along Ave Hassan II. The main bus station is near Bab Doukkala, about a 10 minute walk northeast of the same square, and about 20 minutes on foot from the Djemaa el-Fna (see the Marrakesh Budget Hotel Area map).

The medina walls enclose a far more open area than that found behind the walls of Fès and Meknès. It is not until you have penetrated the heart of the old city, the Djemaa el-Fna, that you reach the familiar maze of souqs and twisting alleys.

The Djemaa el-Fna itself is a large, irregularly shaped square dominated from a distance by the city's most prominent

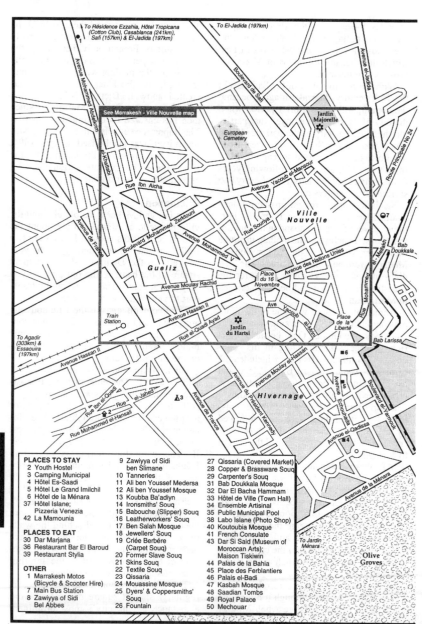

Map labels (top and edges):

To Résidence Ezzahia, Hôtel Tropicana
(Cotton Club), Casablanca (241km),
Safi (157km) & El-Jadida (197km)

To El-Jadida (197km)

Avenue el-Jadida

Avenue Mohammed Abdelkrim

Boulevard de Safi

Jardin
Majorelle

See Marrakesh - Ville Nouvelle map

European
Cemetery

Route Principale No 24

el-Khattabi

Rue Ibn Aicha

Avenue Yacoub el-Mansour

Avenue de France

Boulevard Mohammed Zerktouni

Avenue Mohammed V

Rue Souriya

Ville
Nouvelle

Bab
Doukkala

Gueliz

Avenue des Nations Unies

Rue Mohammed

Avenue Moulay Rachid

Place
du 16
Novembre

Train
Station

Avenue Hassan II

Rue el-Quadi Ayad

Ave Yacoub

Jardin
du Hartsi

Place
de la
Liberté

To Agadir
(303km) &
Essaouira
(197km)

Avenue Hassan II

Bab Larissa

Rue Ibn el-Quadi

Rue el-Jahed

Rue Mohammed el-Hansali

Avenue de France

Avenue du Président Kennedy

Avenue Moulay el-Hassan

Hivernage

Avenue Echouhada

Boulevard el-Yarmouk

Avenue el-Qadissa

Avenue de la Ménara

To Jardin
Ménara

Olive
Groves

PLACES TO STAY
2 Youth Hostel
3 Camping Municipal
4 Hôtel Es-Saadi
5 Hôtel Le Grand Imilchil
6 Hôtel de la Ménara
37 Hôtel Islane;
   Pizzeria Venezia
42 La Mamounia

PLACES TO EAT
30 Dar Marjana
36 Restaurant Bar El Baroud
39 Restaurant Stylia

OTHER
1 Marrakesh Motos
   (Bicycle & Scooter Hire)
7 Main Bus Station
8 Zawiyya of Sidi
   Bel Abbes
9 Zawiyya of Sidi
   ben Slimane
10 Tanneries
11 Ali ben Youssef Medersa
12 Ali ben Youssef Mosque
13 Koubba Ba'adiyn
14 Ironsmiths' Souq
15 Babouche (Slipper) Souq
16 Leatherworkers' Souq
17 Ben Salah Mosque
18 Jewellers' Souq
19 Criée Berbère
   (Carpet Souq)
20 Former Slave Souq
21 Skins Souq
22 Textile Souq
23 Qissaria
24 Mouassine Mosque
25 Dyers' & Coppersmiths'
   Souq
26 Fountain
27 Qissaria (Covered Market)
28 Copper & Brassware Souq
29 Carpenter's Souq
31 Bab Doukkala Mosque
32 Dar El Bacha Hammam
33 Hôtel de Ville (Town Hall)
34 Ensemble Artisinal
35 Public Municipal Pool
38 Labo Islane (Photo Shop)
40 Koutoubia Mosque
41 French Consulate
43 Dar Si Said (Museum of
   Moroccan Arts);
   Maison Tiskiwin
44 Palais de la Bahia
45 Place des Ferblantiers
46 Palais el-Badi
47 Kasbah Mosque
48 Saadian Tombs
49 Royal Palace
50 Mechouar

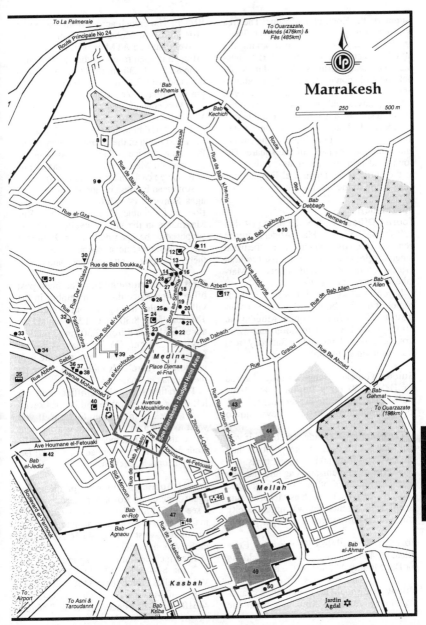

landmark, the Koutoubia Mosque. The area is in many ways rather nondescript. There are no grand monuments overlooking the jumble of people, food stalls, tourists, hustlers and snake charmers who lend it its life, but you will soon be beguiled by its atmosphere. For centuries, traders, farmers, thieves, slaves and just about every other possible species have milled around here.

Most of the budget hotels are clustered in the narrow streets branching off the eastern and south-eastern sides of the square. The souqs and principal religious buildings lie to the north of the Djemaa el-Fna, and the palaces are to the south.

Information

Tourist Office The ONMT office (☎ 448 889; fax 436057) is on Place Abdel Moumen ben Ali in the ville nouvelle. It has the usual range of glossy leaflets and a list (without prices) of the classified hotels in Marrakesh, but not much else.

If you're lucky, it will have a couple of copies of the free booklet *Welcome to Marrakesh*. The office is open Monday to Friday from 8.30 am to noon and again from 3.30 to 6.30 pm, and on Saturday from 9 am to noon and from 3 to 5 pm.

Guides You can arrange an official guide for Dr150/120 for a full/half day at the tourist office or in the bigger hotels. Entry to the monuments, taxi journeys and so forth are of course extra.

The benefits of a guide, especially if you don't have a lot of time, are twofold: they can save you from taking wrong turns, and they serve as immunisation against the persistent advances of other would-be guides. Many travel agencies such as Ménara Tours (see Travel Agents below), organise city tours which cost around Dr200 per person.

Foreign Consulates The French Consulate (☎ 444006), is on Rue Ibn Khaldoun (or Dar Moulay Ali, just by the Koutoubia).

Money You should have no trouble changing money. As usual, your best bet is the

BMCE. The branch across from the tourist office, on Ave Mohammed V in the ville nouvelle, has an ATM as well as a change office. It is open from Monday to Thursday from 8.15 to 11.30 am (to 11.15 am on Friday) and from 2.15 to 4.30 pm (2.45 to 4.45 pm on Friday). You can change cash and travellers cheques or get a cash advance on Visa or MasterCard.

The BMCE branch on Rue de Moulay Ismail, just south of the Djemaa el-Fna, offers the same services. The Bank al-Maghrib (Banque du Maroc) on the Djemaa el-Fna will change cash and travellers cheques.

American Express is represented by Voyages Schwarz (☎ 436600/3) on the first floor of Immeuble Moutaouakil, at 1 Rue Mauritania in the ville nouvelle. They are supposed to be open daily from 9 am to 1 pm, though there never seems to be anyone there. It's best to ring in advance and check.

Post & Communications The main post office is on Place du 16 Novembre in the ville nouvelle. It's open from Monday to Thursday from 8.30 am to 12.15 pm (11.30 am on Friday) and from 2.30 pm (3 pm Friday) to 6.30 pm. On Saturday, it's open from 8.30 to 11.30 am. Poste restante is at window 6. There's also a branch office on the Djemaa el-Fna.

The rather small phone office is to the left of the main entrance and is open seven days a week from 8.30 am to 9 pm. If you want to send a package, there is a separate office around the corner on Ave Hassan II. Your parcel can be wrapped for a small fee after customs inspection.

Travel Agencies The bulk of the travel agents (including Royal Air Maroc's office – see the Getting There & Away entry later in this chapter) are located around Ave Mohammed V, west of Place du 16 Novembre in the ville nouvelle.

They include Carlson Wagonlits (☎ 431 687; fax 624436) at 122 Ave Mohammed V, Nouvelles Frontières at 34 Rue de la Liberté, and Ménara Tours (☎ 446654; fax 446107) at 41 Rue de Yougoslavie. The latter represents GB Airways, which has a couple of flights a week linking the UK to Marrakesh via Gibraltar.

Bookshops & Newspapers For books in English, about the only option is the American Language Center bookshop (see Cultural Centres below), which has a range of English literature and a fair number of titles on Morocco. It's open from 3 to 7 pm.

The best bookshop in town for French speakers is the Librairie Chatr (☎ 447997) at 19 to 21 Avenue Mohammed V in the ville nouvelle.

Across the road at No 44 is the Gillot bookshop which has a rival selection. Both stores sell maps of Marrakesh.

English, American and French newspapers can be bought from the newspaper stand in front of the Avis office on Ave Mohammed V. The English papers are generally a day old.

Film & Photography There are several places along Ave Mohammed V where you can buy film and get it processed.

Two with good reputations are Labo Islane (☎ 444691), close to the Hôtel Islane at 279 Ave Mohammed V (see the Marrakesh map), and Felix Labo, at 133 Ave Mohammed V in the ville nouvelle. Both are open every day from 8.30 am to 8.30 pm.

Cultural Centres The Institut Français is located in the ville nouvelle, off Route de la Targa, close to the Victor Hugo school. It's an active, well-run place which, apart from French classes, organises a range of films, plays, lectures and the like which are open to all. The library houses a good collection of books on Islam and the Arab world.

The Institut is open every day except Monday, from 8.30 am to noon and from 2.30 to 6.30 pm (until 10 pm on Tuesday).

The American Language Center (☎ 447 259) has a branch in the ville nouvelle at 3 Impasse du Moulin.

The center's main activity is its English classes for Marrakshis – and if you're looking for work you might want to drop by on the off-chance there's a teaching vacancy.

Otherwise, they put on the occasional film and lecture, and have a small library. The center is open Monday to Friday from 9 am to noon and from 3 to 7 pm. The library is open from Monday to Friday from 2.30 to 6 pm, and on Saturday from 9 am to noon.

Medical Services & Emergencies There is an all-night pharmacy (☎ 430415) on Rue Khalid ben el-Oualid, just off Place de la Liberté in the ville nouvelle. A doctor is also permanently available there. Ambulances can be called on ☎ 443724.

Should you need a doctor, you can contact Dr Berrada Naïma on ☎ 308798, or through the Hôtel Ali. In emergencies, she can be contacted at her home on ☎ 434847.

In the event of dental trouble, you can visit Mr Abdelaziz Mekouar's ultra-modern surgery (☎ 446681) at 39 Rue de Loubnane (also in the ville nouvelle). Both are highly recommended and speak English and French.

Dangers & Annoyances Marrakesh has long been a magnet for travellers, and during the early 1960s and 70s formed one of the great hippie destinations of the Orient, along with Istanbul, Kabul and Kathmandu.

Next on the scene, and hard on their heels, came the hordes of package tourists armed with much more money, but far less time. In a city with little money and high unemployment, this onslaught gave birth to the rise and rise of Morocco's most unpleasant phenomenon, the *faux guide* (see the Touts, Guides & Hustlers entry in the Facts for the Visitor chapter).

In recent years, and following a national policy pursued in the principal cities across the country, a special *Brigade Touristique* (tourist police) has been set up to clamp down on these hustlers.

Any person suspected of trying to operate as an unofficial guide is liable for a prison sentence of between six months and three years and a fine of between Dr10,000

THE HIGH ATLAS

and Dr20,000. These days, tourist police cars (white Fiat Unos) patrol the streets.

The effect of all this has significantly reduced, but not yet eliminated, the problem of the faux guides. As long as unemployment remains at such high levels, they will probably never be entirely wiped out. The bulk of them hang about the main entrances to the souqs on Djemaa el-Fna. Once inside the souqs proper, you will largely be left alone – unless of course you strike some more persistent ones who follow you right in.

If you end up with one of these people (you really should not pay an unofficial guide more than about Dr25 for two or three hours), remember their main interest is in making a commission on articles sold to you in the souqs.

First-time visitors may find this part of Moroccan culture rather overwhelming. If you wish to purchase something in the souqs of Marrakesh, you should prepare yourself for some extremely heavy selling. Shop owners size up their potential clients early on, and it is claimed they have a sliding scale of prices, according to how much cash and how little sense they credit you with. Some of them can get quite nasty if you don't want to buy. Try and remain polite, calm and firm.

Never spend a lot of time in any one shop unless you are seriously interested in the merchandise, otherwise you may well be in for a wearing, some would even say traumatic, experience.

This combination of hustlers and heavy sell has had an adverse effect on the city's tourism. According to a government study, 94% of first-time visitors to Marrakesh never come back for seconds! This is one of the lowest rates for a city in the entire world.

Although an undoubted irritant, travellers should never let this normal part of Moroccan life colour their impressions of this vibrant and beautiful city.

The best approach is to do what the Moroccans do. Ignore unwanted attention entirely, and above all keep your sense of humour.

Gauche, Green and Gullible

Many Moroccans genuinely believe that 'westerners', though perhaps more sophisticated than themselves, are more naive, gullible and even plain stupid. Some, including the notorious *faux guides* (unofficial guides), may try and exploit this.

Very early on in your encounter with these guides, you will be sized up for what you're worth. Apart from the physical indications, such as your watch, shoes, haircut and clothes, you will be assessed from a series of questions: how long you've been in the country, whether it's your first visit, what your job is, whether you have a family (an indication of wealth) etc.

Considered to be the most lucrative nationalities, in descending order, are the Japanese, Americans, Canadians, Australians, northern Europeans, southern Europeans, and Middle-Eastern Arabs. Considered the least lucrative are sub-Saharan Africans and Arabs from other North African countries.

Always pretend that you know the city or country well. A few words of Arabic will convince them of this beyond doubt.

If you feel you're being categorised, you can always cause confusion by pretending you're from some very obscure land. Some times it's useful just to play plain stupid and control the situation that way. ■

Djemaa el-Fna

The focal point of Marrakesh is the Djemaa el-Fna, a huge square in the old part of town where many of the budget hotels are located. According to Paul Bowles, without it Marrakesh would be just another Moroccan city. Other than the souqs, this is where everything happens; visitors are destined to spend a lot of time here.

Although it's a lively place at any time of day (look out for the Berber acrobats around 4 pm), it comes into its own in the evening, reaching its peak between 7 and 9 pm. Then the curtain goes up on one of the world's most fascinating spectacles. Rows and rows of open-air food stalls are set up and mouth-watering aromas fill the square.

Jugglers, storytellers, snake charmers, magicians, acrobats and benign lunatics take over the rest of the space, each surrounded by jostling spectators who listen and watch intently, or fall about laughing and move on to another act starting up nearby. Before they can get away, assistants hassle them for contributions.

If you are feeling poorly, you might want to try some herbal cures, which the Marrakshis swear by.

The vendors of herbs and potions can prescribe something for the common cold or something a little stronger to administer to your worst enemy.

In between the groups of spectators, diners, shoppers and tourists, weave hustlers, thieves, knick-knack sellers and the occasional glue-sniffing kid. On the outer edges, kerosene lanterns ablaze, are the fruit and juice stalls.

It is a scene that, to one extent or another, was previously played out in the great squares of many Moroccan cities. Unfortunately, TV has killed off much of it. It is often claimed that the activity in the Djemaa el-Fna survives mostly because of the tourists. In the case of the water sellers and snake charmers this may well be the case, but how do you explain the crowds around the storytellers? Precious few outsiders know what marvels or lunacies they are recounting to the obvious delight of the locals.

Around the edge of the square you can take a balcony seat in one of a number of rooftop cafes and restaurants and take in the whole spectacle at a respectful and more relaxing distance. Down below, the medieval pageant presents its nightly cornucopia of delights; Bruegel would have had a field day here.

Those places offering the best views include the Hôtel CTM, with its large rooftop terrace. Unfortunately, it's usually only open only to hotel guests.

Next door, the rooftop Café Glacier has perhaps the best views of all, but refreshments (Dr5 per person) are obligatory. It's open every day from 9 am to 7.30 pm.

Traditional Tall Tales

Providing some of the liveliest daily entertainment on the Place Djemaa el-Fna are the *halqas*, or Moroccan entertainers. *Halqa*, meaning circle, derives its name from the audiences who cluster around to hear the principal character, the story-teller, recite his fabulous tales.

With mesmerising skill, very few props, and often to the dramatic accompaniment of music, the narrator will begin to recount some of the ancient and colourful tales of Morocco's vibrant oral tradition. With rising tones and extravagant gestures, he will recall the bravery of Antar, the misfortunes of Chehrazad, the craftiness of Myriam Zennaria or the wisdom of the prophet Loukman.

Sometimes myths and legends will be mixed up with the present, or current events with myths and legends. Each performance is quite original and improvised, and is inspired to a large extent by the audience who participate. Suddenly, and just at the most salacious or cliff-hanging moment, the narrator will interrupt his tale to pass around a hat. Only once it has been amply filled, will he conclude the saga.

Other halqas found on the square, but drawing more modest crowds, are those with conjurers, magicians, or magic potion doctors as their protagonists. Sometimes a geometrician can also be found, fascinating the crowds with brilliant, lengthy and unfathomable calculations. ∎

FRANCES LINZEE GORDON

Charming the cobra in the
Djemaa el-Fna, Marrakesh.

Souqs

Just as the Djemaa el-Fna is famous for its energy and life, the souqs of the Marrakesh medina are some of the best in Morocco, producing a wide variety of high-quality crafts, as well as a fair amount of rubbish.

The streets here are just as labyrinthine as in Fès and every bit as busy. On the other hand, the shops selling arts and crafts come to an abrupt end at the Ali ben Youssef Mosque, making the hard-sell part of the medina comparatively compact. Head north or east and you find yourself in more peaceful territory.

As in Fès, it is probably a sensible policy to engage a guide for your first excursion into the medina's souqs and monuments. This is not to say that you really need one. However tortuous the lanes become, the first rule of navigation applies – if you keep to the main streets, you will always emerge, eventually, at a landmark or city gate.

Most of the shops in the souqs have stickers displaying the fact that they accept American Express, Diners Club, Visa and MasterCard, as well as many other more obscure credit cards.

The main entrance to this part of the medina is along Rue Souq as-Smarrine, flanked mainly by **textiles** shops and various souvenir stalls. Tucked inside a group of buildings before the entrance is a **pottery souq**. Inside the main entrance, and to the left, is a **qissaria**, or covered market.

Just before Rue Souq as-Smarrine forks into Rue Souq al-Kebir and Rue Souq al-Attarine, a narrow lane to the right leads to the Place Rahba Qedima, a small square given over mainly to **carpet** and **sheep-skin** sales. The carpet souq is also known as the Criée Berbère, and it is situated near the former slave souq.

Back on the Rue Souq as-Smarrine, you could take either fork. Both more or less lead to the Ali ben Youssef mosque and medersa. If you take the left fork and veer off to the west, you will find yourself among **dyers**, **carpenters** and **coppersmiths**. Much of their work is not really aimed at tourists, and the atmosphere is a little more relaxed.

Remedies and Cures
Pre-Islamic folklore is still widespread in Morocco. A trip to a good spice market in any souq will bear that out. In cages, stuffed or dried, you'll find an extraordinary collection of amphibians, reptiles, bird and mammals. What to do with them?

For, 'syphilis of the throat and mouth, swallow the ashes of a crow which has been knocked down and stunned, then cremated in a new cooking pot'.

Syphilis used to be so widespread in Morocco, that there is a saying: 'He who doesn't have syphilis in this world will have it in the next. ■

Closer to the mosque, all gives way to the clamour of the iron forges that dominate here. With a little luck, you'll emerge at either the mosque or the Koubba Ba'adiyn. Along the right fork, you'll encounter **jewellers**, whose stores then give way to **leatherwork** and **babouche** shops.

Mosques & Medersas

Like their counterparts elsewhere in Morocco, the mosques and working medersas in Marrakesh are generally closed to non-Muslims, and those inside the medina are so hemmed in by other buildings that little can be seen from the outside.

Koutoubia Mosque The only mosque with a perspective you can really appreciate, and the one you are most likely to encounter first, is the Koutoubia, across the other side of Place de Foucauld, south-west of the Djemaa el-Fna (see the Marrakesh map). It is also the tallest (70m) and most famous landmark in Marrakesh, visible for miles in any direction.

Constructed by the Almohads in the late 12th century, it features the oldest and best preserved of their three most famous minarets – the others are the Tour Hassan in Rabat and the Giralda in Seville (Spain). The name (from *koutoub* or *kutub*, Arabic for books) comes from a booksellers' market that once existed around the mosque.

The Koutoubia minaret is a classic of Moroccan-Andalusian architecture; its features are mirrored in many other minarets throughout the country, but not one of these matches the Koutoubia's for sheer size.

When first built, the Koutoubia was covered with painted plaster and brilliantly coloured *zellij* tiles, but this decoration has all disappeared. What can still be seen, however, are the decorative panels, which are different on each face and practically constitute a textbook of Islamic design.

The views from the summit would be incredible, if non-Muslims were allowed to climb up there. Unfortunately, at the time of writing, the minaret was to some extent hidden by a thick web of sky-blue scaffolding.

Koubba Ba'adiyn After a stroll up through the souqs, the first monument open to non-Muslims that you'll probably come across is one of the smallest Marrakesh has to offer, but (restoration aside) about the oldest.

Although most of Almoravid Marrakesh was destroyed by the zealous Almohads who succeeded them, the Koubba is a rare exception. Built in the early 12th century, it is a small but elegant display of Muslim decorative invention.

Signposted on a small square in front of the Ali ben Youssef Mosque, entrance to the koubba is Dr10 and the guardian will want to show you around. He'll probably dig up a friend to 'guide' you to the Ali ben Youssef Medersa too, although it's just around the corner.

Ali ben Youssef Mosque The largest of the mosques inside the medina is the Ali ben Youssef Mosque, first built in the second half of the 12th century by the Almoravid sultan of the same name.

It's the oldest surviving mosque in Marrakesh, but the building itself is of fairly recent date, as it was almost completely rebuilt in the 19th century in the Merenid style in response to popular demand.

When first constructed it was about twice its present size, but it was severely damaged when the Almoravids were overthrown by the Almohads. It was later restored by both the Almohads and the Saadians. The mosque is closed to non-Muslims.

Ali ben Youssef Medersa Next to the Ali ben Youssef Mosque is the medersa of the same name, a beautiful and still peaceful and meditative place with some stunning examples of stucco decoration.

The medersa is the largest theological college in the Maghreb and was built by the Saadians in 1565 (and much restored in the 1960s). Heading east from the Koubba, simply follow the mosque walls around to the left, and you'll come to the entrance of the medersa on your right.

Although all Moroccan medersas at least loosely follow a similar ground plan (see

THE HIGH ATLAS

the special section on Moroccan Architecture in the Facts about the Country chapter), the Ali ben Youssef is not only bigger, but also quite different in layout.

You walk down a corridor and turn right onto the central courtyard, entering where you find yourself facing the *masjid* (mosque). Like virtually every other great medersa on view to non-Muslims, this was built under the Merenids and is typical of the style of those times, with intricate stucco decoration combined with a zellij tile base and crowned by carved cedar.

Go back to the corridor and take the entrance opposite the courtyard. Two sets of stairs lead up to students' cells. As usual, they are small and bare. It's hard to imagine how, as is claimed, they crammed as many as 900 people into these rooms!

The big difference between their arrangement here and that in other medersas is that many of them are clustered around seven small and charming 'mini-courtyards'. Moreover, a few look out on to the street – somewhat of an exception to the general rule of Moroccan and Andalusian architecture.

Mouassine Mosque The other big mosque in the medina is the Mouassine Mosque, built in the 16th century by the Saadians on land formerly occupied by the Jewish community.

Its most notable features are the three huge doorways and the intricately carved cedar ceilings. The fountain attached to this mosque still survives and is quite elaborate, with three sections – two for animals and one for humans. The mosque is closed to non-Muslims.

Ben Salah Mosque Of the other mosques in the medina, the Ben Salah Mosque (also known as the Ben Salah Zawiyya) is the most prominent; its brilliant green-tiled minaret can be seen from afar. It was built by the Merenid sultan Abu Said Uthman between 1318 and 1321. Again, it's closed to non-Muslims.

Zawiyyas In the north-western zone of the medina are two zawiyyas dedicated to two of the seven saints claimed by Marrakesh. Pilgrimage to the tombs of all seven is, in the popular mind at any rate, the equivalent of a pilgrimage to Mecca (a considerably more arduous undertaking for Moroccans).

North of the Sidi ben Slimane Zawiyya is that of Sidi Bel Abbes, the most important of the seven saints. Entry to the sanctuaries is forbidden to non-Muslims.

Palaces & Environs

Palais el-Badi The most famous of the palaces of Marrakesh is the Palais El-Badi, south of Place Djemaa el-Fna. Built by Ahmed al-Mansour between 1578 and 1602, at the time of its construction it was reputed to be one of the most beautiful in the world (and was known as 'the Incomparable'). It included marble from Italy and other precious building materials from as far away as India.

The enormous cost of building the palace was met largely from the ransom the Portuguese were forced to pay out following their disastrous defeat at the hands of the Saadians in 1578 in the Battle of the Three Kings.

Unfortunately, the palace is now largely a ruin, having been torn apart by Moulay Ismail in 1696 for its materials, which were used to build his new capital at Meknès.

What remains is essentially a huge square surrounded by devastated walls enclosing a sunken orange grove and a number of modern concrete pools. When you're inside by the orange grove, you'll notice a large structure to the west. This is the Koubba al-Khamsiniyya, which was used as a great reception hall on state occasions and was named after its 50 marble columns.

Proceed south towards the walls of the Royal Palace (which is closed to visitors) and you'll find yourself in a confusing maze of underground corridors, storerooms and dungeons. Which were which is a little hard to tell. For lovers of dark places, there's a bit of potential exploring to do – bring a torch (flashlight).

The Palais El-Badi is open to the public

daily, except on certain religious holidays, between 8.30 am and noon and 2.30 and 6 pm. Entry costs Dr10. You're free to wander around on your own, although guides will initially hassle you to engage their services. The palace is also the venue for the annual Folklore Festival, usually held in June.

The easiest way to get to the palace is to take Ave Houmane el-Fetouaki down from the Koutoubia mosque to Place des Ferblantiers, where the ramparts begin, and you'll see a large gate. Go through this and turn to the right. The entrance and ticket booth are straight ahead.

Palais de la Bahia The Palais de la Bahia was built towards the end of the 19th century, over a period of 14 years, as the residence of Si' Ahmed ben Musa (also

Water sellers wander the streets of Marrakesh, keeping thirsty shoppers on their feet.

known as Bou Ahmed), the Grand Vizier of Sultan Moulay al-Hassan I.

On Bou Ahmed's death it was ransacked, but much has since been restored.

It's a rambling structure with fountains, living quarters, pleasure gardens and numerous secluded, shady courtyards, but it lacks architectural cohesion. This in no way detracts from the visual pleasure of the place and there's a noticeable difference between the peace, quiet and coolness inside the palace and the heat, noise and chaos in the streets outside.

The Palais exemplifies the privacy-conscious priorities of Muslim architecture. You will often find that the multiple doorways linking various parts of the palace are so placed that you often can't see much past the open doorway, creating the impression of a series of separate and unconnected zones within the whole.

You can only visit part of the palace, as some of it is still used by the royal family and to house maintenance staff. You will be taken through a series of rooms, among them the vizier's sleeping quarters (he had separate ones for snoozing during the day and evening) and various courtyards set aside for his wives and concubines. The four wives each had a room arranged around a courtyard.

The sleeping quarters for the rather more numerous concubines were also gathered around a (separate) courtyard.

The palace is open daily from 8.30 am to 1 pm (11.45 am in winter) and 4 to 7 pm (2.30 to 6 pm in winter). Entry is free, but you must take and pay a guide.

To get there (orientation is easiest from the Palais el-Badi), go back to the Place des Ferblantiers, and keep following Ave Houmane el-Fetouaki away from the budget hotel area and around to the left (north). You'll soon come to the entrance, set in a garden, on your right.

Dar Si Said Further north of the Palais de la Bahia and again off to the right (it's signposted), the Dar Si Said, which now houses the **Museum of Moroccan Arts**, is well worth a visit.

Sidi Said, Bou Ahmed's brother, built what became his town house at about the same time as the grand vizier's palace was constructed. Today, the museum houses one of the finest collections in the country, including jewellery from the High Atlas, the Anti-Atlas and the extreme south; carpets from the Haouz and the High Atlas; oil lamps from Taroudannt; blue pottery from Safi and green pottery from Tamegroute; and leatherwork from Marrakesh.

As you enter, you will see a series of doors typical of the richer High Atlas and Anti-Atlas houses. At the end of this corridor is the oldest exhibit in the museum: an old marble basin dating back to about 1000 AD, brought to Marrakesh from Spain by Ali ben Youssef.

Next up are some delightful medieval precursors of the Ferris wheel for tiny tots.

The central garden and courtyard is flanked by rooms housing displays of heavy southern jewellery in silver, traditional women's garments, household goods, old muskets and daggers.

On the next floor is a magnificently decorated room; its characteristic stucco and zellij tiles capped by a stunning carved and painted cedar ceiling. From here, the signs lead you upstairs again and then down through various rooms dominated by rug and carpet displays. All the explanations are, unfortunately, in Arabic and French only.

It's open from 9 am to noon and 4 to 7 pm (2.30 to 6 pm in winter); closed Tuesday. On Friday it's closed from 11.30 am to 3 pm. Entry costs Dr10.

Maison Tiskiwin Virtually next door to the Dar Si Said is the house of Bert Flint, a Dutch art lecturer and long-time resident of Morocco.

It has been opened to the public as a small museum, and principally contains carpets and traditional textile work. The Maison Tiskiwin (☎ 443335) is only open in the morning.

Mellah The old Jewish quarter, established in the 16th century, is just south of the Palais de la Bahia. Much neglected and now populated mainly by Muslims, it still has quite a different look to it from the rest of the city.

The main entrance is off Place des Ferblantiers, and if you want to visit any of the small synagogues (one is still in use) you'll need a local guide.

Saadian Tombs Alongside the Kasbah Mosque is the necropolis, which was started by the Saadian sultan Ahmed al-Mansour in the late 1500s.

Unlike the Palais el-Badi, another of al-Mansour's projects, the tombs escaped Moulay Ismail's depredations – possibly because he was superstitious about plundering the dead. Instead he sealed the tombs and, as a result, they still convey some of the opulence and superb artistry that must also have been lavished on the palace.

Sixty-six of the Saadians, including al-Mansour, his successors and their closest family members, lie buried under the two main structures, and there are more than a hundred buried outside the buildings.

Although the mad sultan Moulay Yazid was laid to rest here in 1792, the tombs essentially remained sealed following Moulay Ismail's reign. They were not 'rediscovered' until 1917 when General Lyautey, his curiosity awakened by an aerial survey of the area, ordered the construction of a passageway down into the tombs. They have since been restored.

To get to the tombs from Place Djemaa el-Fna, take Rue de Bab Agnaou to Bab Agnaou itself (the only surviving Almohad gateway in Marrakesh), which is on the left and almost adjacent to Bab er-Rob. Go through Bab Agnaou and walk straight past a row of shops until you come to the Kasbah Mosque. Turn right down Rue de la Kasbah and, when you get to the end of the mosque, you'll see a narrow alleyway on the left. Go down it, and the entrance to the tombs is at the end.

After buying your ticket, you follow a

very narrow passage that opens onto the main mausoleum, which is divided into three small halls. Those at either end contain tombs of children. The central one, the Hall of the Twelve Columns, is held to be one of the finest examples of Moroccan-Andalusian decorative art.

Among the columns of Italian marble are the tombs of Ahmed al-Mansour, his son and grandson. The elegant little mausoleum set further in houses the tomb of al-Mansour's mother.

The tombs are open to the public every day, except Friday morning, from 8 am to noon and 2.30 to 7 pm (6 pm in winter). Entry costs Dr10 and you're allowed to wander around at will. If you prefer, a guardian will accompany you and explain what you are looking at. A tip will be expected at the end.

Tanneries

If you didn't see the tanneries in Fès, or feel you need another dose of them, you can give those at Marrakesh a whirl. They are out by Bab Debbagh, at the north-eastern end of the medina and a reasonably straightforward walk from the Ali ben Youssef Mosque.

If you have trouble finding them, just ask for the road to the gate or take up the offer of one of the young lads hanging around the entrance to the medersa to guide you there.

Gardens

A slightly more pleasant olfactory experience is provided by the several beautiful gardens which are laid out around the city.

Jardin Ménara About a 4km walk west of the Koutoubia, along Ave de la Menara, the Jardin Ménara is the most easily reached of Marrakesh's green spaces. Although it is quite popular with Marrakshis, it is generally a peaceful place to escape the summer heat and bustle of the city.

The centrepiece of what is basically a more organised continuation of the olive groves immediately to the east, is a large still pool backed by a pavilion built in 1866.

What is now open to the public was once the exclusive preserve of sultans and high ministers.

Jardin Agdal Stretching for several kilometres south from the Royal Palace, the vegetation is more varied here than in the Jardin Ménara and there are several pavilions.

To get there (a bicycle would be ideal), take the path that runs south from the southwestern corner of the mechouar (parade ground) in front of the Royal Palace. Unfortunately, the quarters are often closed. Check with the tourist office in advance.

Jardin Majorelle Now owned by Yves Saint-Laurent, these exquisite gardens were laid out by the French painter Jacques Majorelle, who lived here from 1922 to 1962. In among the floral smorgasbord is what was Majorelle's deep-blue villa, which now houses a modest museum of Islamic art.

The gardens are in the ville nouvelle, north of Ave Yacoub el-Mansour, and are open from 8 am to noon and 2 to 5 pm (3 to 7 pm in summer). Children and dogs are not allowed; they're a bit edgy about 'professional-looking' cameras. Look touristy and keep smiling. Entry costs Dr15.

Hôtel La Mamounia For the price of a very expensive coffee, you could get in to what in this century has become something of a monument itself.

La Mamounia (see Places to Stay in this section) was Winston Churchill's favourite hotel, and it is blessed with lush and sedate gardens that do as much good for the frazzled as any of the public gardens. There is a lovely walk through olive and orange trees.

Église des Saints-Martyrs

The Catholic church (built in 1926) is in the ville nouvelle, south of Ave Yacoub al-Mrinis. It's of mild interest, but was built in keeping with its environment and is a nice example of the European interpretation of Mauritanian architecture. Mass is celebrated every day.

THE HIGH ATLAS

Special Events

If you're in Marrakesh in June (the dates change), inquire about the Festival of Folklore which is held in the Palais el-Badi at that time. It's a folk-dancing and singing extravaganza, performed by some of the best troupes from throughout Morocco.

In July there's the famous *Fantasia*, a charge of Berber horsemen that takes place outside the ramparts. You often see pictures of it in the tourist literature.

It's not quite a festival, but if you enjoy watching athletics you might want to be around at the end of January for the annual Grand Prix de Hassan II Marathon.

Organised Tours

It is quite possible to organise tours down the Drâa Valley, into the Atlas mountains or to the Atlantic coast through agents in Marrakesh. Many organise a range of activities for groups (generally a minimum of four people), and although they cost more than they would doing it on your own, they are very useful if you've got limited time.

On the whole, they are well organised and can take you to places that are not easily accessible to the individual.

Ménara Tours offers day trips to the Ourika Valley (Dr200); Asni, Ouirgane and Tahanaoute (Dr200); Telouet in the High Atlas (Dr375); and the Cascades d'Ouzoud (waterfalls; Dr350). If you're keen to get off the beaten track, their 4WD vehicles can take you to more remote, far-flung areas (Dr600). Prices are per person and don't include meals.

Another agency with a good reputation is Pampa Voyage (☎ 431052; fax 446455) at 213 Blvd Mohammed V, near Royal Air Maroc. It specialises in tailor-made tours of a longer duration into the Atlas Mountains, and the Drâa Valley. Among other things, they can organise excursions into the desert with *meharis* (a kind of extra-speedy dromedary!) and bivouacs. A two day trip costs Dr1278 per person, with a minimum of four people. If it's mountains you're after, you can take a two day hike into the High Atlas for Dr1200.

For information on High Atlas trekking, the best source is the Hôtel Ali (see the Places to Stay below). They can suggest trekking routes from places such as Asni and Imlil, and help find you a guide (state approved). The National Association of Moroccan Mountain Guides (ANGAMM) can be contacted through them.

The Hôtel de Foucauld can help organise mountain-bike excursions, 4WD trips and cross-country skiing.

Places to Stay – bottom end

Camping *Camping Municipal* (☎ 431844) is just off the Ave de France, around five minutes south of the train station (see the Marrakesh map).

It's open the whole year round, but there's little shade and the ground is stony. Camping costs Dr12 per person/per tent, Dr10/8 for a car/motorbike and Dr16 for electricity.

Hostel The *youth hostel* (☎ 447713) on Rue el-Jahed, is also close to the train station (see the Marrakesh map).

It used to make a good first stop on arrival, but has become rather run down, shabby and gloomy. It's also a bit far from where things are going on, and can get extremely hot in summer and cold in winter. You'll need your membership card. Beds costs Dr20, hot showers Dr5, and it's open from 8 to 9 am, noon to 2 pm and 6 to 10 pm.

Hotels – Medina Most of the cheapest accommodation deals can be found in the area immediately south of the Djemaa el-Fna and east of Rue de Bab Agnaou, where there are scores of reasonably priced hotels. There's not much difference between them, other than whether they offer hot showers or not (not important in summer, but definitely so in winter), and how clean they are. Some places have no showers at all, in which case you could try one of the hammams.

Most of the cheapies will charge extra for hot showers (Dr5 to Dr10) and some even charge for cold showers (Dr2). Prices vary little and start at Dr30 a single, Dr50 a double and Dr70 to Dr75 a triple. Some of the better ones charge more, and in summer most of them hike up their prices according to demand, so you could end up paying more here than you would for a better room in a classified hotel.

One of the best rock-bottom places around is the *Hotel Afriquia* (☎ 442403) at 45 Sidi Bouloukat. It charges Dr30, Dr50 and Dr75 for pretty basic and cell-like singles, doubles and triples respectively, but has a very pleasant courtyard.

On the same street is another good value place, the *Hotel Medina* (☎ 442997) at 1 Sidi Bouloukat. It has clean singles/doubles for Dr30 to Dr35/60. A hot shower costs Dr5 and breakfast Dr8.

Also in this price-range, and in the centre of the budget hotel area, is the *Hôtel de la Paix* (☎ 445431) which has tiny but clean rooms for Dr30/50/75.

A short way down from the Djemaa el-Fna, between Rue Zitoune el-Qedim and Rue de Bab Agnaou is the *Hôtel El Atlal* (☎ 4278890), with bright and clean (if small) rooms upstairs for Dr35/70. Ask for a room off the street. A hot shower costs rather a pricey Dr10.

Adjacent to the El Atlal is the *Hôtel Souria* (☎ 445970). It's a little more expensive, but is one of the better cheapies and charges Dr60 for singles and Dr80/90 for doubles, depending on the room. There's also a room with two big beds which cost Dr120.

The *Hotel Chellah* (☎ 442977) just off Rue Zitoune el-Qedim is a very good deal and charges Dr40/60/90 for clean, bright rooms. Both these places charge Dr10 for a hot shower.

Not far away is the *Hôtel Essaouira* (☎ 443805). Its terrace, tiny cafe and clean rooms make it a cut above some of its neighbours, although most of the rooms are very small. You pay from Dr35/70 for a room, and a hot shower is Dr5. To reach it, the best approach is from the east from Rue Zitoune el-Qedim.

Three hotels that are a little more expensive, but can be recommended, are within a

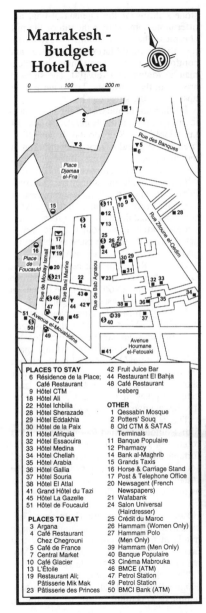

Marrakesh – Budget Hotel Area

0   100   200 m

PLACES TO STAY
6 Résidence de la Place;
   Café Restaurant
9 Hôtel CTM
18 Hôtel Ali
22 Hôtel Ichbilia
28 Hôtel Sherazade
29 Hôtel Eddakhla
30 Hôtel de la Paix
31 Hôtel Afriquia
32 Hôtel Essaouira
33 Hôtel Medina
34 Hôtel Chellah
35 Hôtel Arabia
36 Hôtel Gallia
37 Hôtel Souria
38 Hôtel El Atlal
41 Grand Hôtel du Tazi
45 Hôtel La Gazelle
51 Hôtel de Foucauld

PLACES TO EAT
3 Argana
4 Café Restaurant
   Chez Chegrouni
5 Café de France
7 Central Market
10 Café Glacier
13 L'Étoile
19 Restaurant Ali;
   Pâtisserie Mik Mak
23 Pâtisserie des Princes
42 Fruit Juice Bar
44 Restaurant El Bahja
48 Café Restaurant
   Iceberg

OTHER
1 Qessabin Mosque
2 Potters' Souq
8 Old CTM & SATAS
   Terminals
11 Banque Populaire
12 Pharmacy
14 Bank al-Maghrib
15 Grands Taxis
16 Horse & Carriage Stand
17 Post & Telephone Office
20 Newsagent (French
   Newspapers)
21 Wafabank
24 Salon Universal
   (Hairdresser)
25 Crédit du Maroc
26 Hammam (Women Only)
27 Hammam Polo
   (Men Only)
39 Hammam (Men Only)
40 Banque Populaire
43 Cinéma Mabrouka
46 BMCE (ATM)
47 Petrol Station
49 Petrol Station
50 BMCI Bank (ATM)

stone's throw of the Djemaa el-Fna, and offer more comfort than the run-of-the-mill cheapies. The *Hôtel Ichbilia* (☎ 390486) is just off Rue Bani Marine and has clean and comfortable (if you don't mind the colour mauve) rooms for Dr60/100. The showers are hot in the mornings. Try to get a room upstairs, as the street can be noisy.

Further north, and one of the best places in this category, is the *Hôtel Ali* (☎ 444979; fax 433609) on Rue Moulay Ismail. It's a friendly place and is very efficiently run by the charming manageress, Ilham. It's also excellent value with rooms for Dr70/90/125 with bath, toilet and sometimes balcony. For a night under the stars, you can sleep on the roof terrace for around Dr30. Breakfast costs Dr15 and there is a locker room where you can safely leave your luggage. Try to get a room around the back as the rooms giving onto the street can be a bit noisy.

Back on Rue Bani Marine, the *Hôtel La Gazelle* (☎ 441112) is a good place which offers rooms for Dr60/100 on the first night and Dr50/90 on subsequent nights.

On the Djemaa el-Fna itself you could try the *Hôtel CTM* (☎ 442325). The bus company of the same name used to be located here so there's plenty of parking space below. Singles/doubles without private shower cost Dr50/68, and with private shower and toilet Dr76/100. With its terrace cafe and great views of the Djemaa el-Fna, it's the location that really makes the place.

The *Hotel Eddakhla* (☎ 442359), at 43 Sidi Bouloukate Riad Zitoun Kedim, has rooms for Dr30/60/90. It's a clean, comfortable and pleasantly decorated place, and some rooms have windows overlooking the square. There is a pleasant room for six available here, complete with its own salon.

Hotels – Ville Nouvelle There are no unclassified pensions and not too many cheap hotels in the ville nouvelle. The few that there are can be found around Ave Mohammed V, west of Place du 16 Novembre.

The cheapest is the one-star *Hôtel Franco-Belge* (☎ 448472) at 62 Blvd Mohammed Zerktouni, close to the tourist office. It has a pleasant, peaceful courtyard and rooms cost Dr60/100 without shower (Dr5) and Dr100/130 with shower and toilet.

A few doors down is the one-star *Hôtel des Voyageurs* (☎ 447218), at 40 Blvd Mohammed Zerktouni, where singles/doubles without a shower or toilet cost Dr70/100. Those with shower and toilet cost Dr110/120. Both hotels are a bit frayed round the edges (cracked toilet seats and so forth), but are very clean.

Another good and very reasonable place is the *Hotel Toulousain* (☎ 430033) at 44 Rue Tariq Ibn Ziad. It has singles/doubles without shower for Dr67/85 and with shower for Dr85/105. It's a nice, calm and cool place with a wonderful old palm tree in the courtyard. There is hot water 24 hours a day and room for parking. Rooms on the first floor are better than those on the ground.

Slightly more expensive is the *Hôtel Oasis* (☎ 447179), at 50 Ave Mohammed V, which has rooms with private shower and shared toilet for Dr90/125.

Places to Stay – middle

Medina The *Hôtel Gallia* (☎ 445913; fax 444853), at 30 Rue de la Recette, is one of the most pleasant hotels in the medina area. Rooms with bidet cost Dr100/128, while those with a shower cost Dr149/184 (breakfast is Dr23). They have steaming hot showers, central heating in winter and the whole place is scrubbed from top to toe every day. It is often booked out, especially during holidays and on weekends, so make a reservation or arrive early.

The recently opened *Hotel Sherazade* (☎/fax 429305) at No 3 Derb Djama, provides an over-spill to the Hôtel Gallia and has been highly recommended by some travellers.

Housed in an old merchant's residence, the hotel is decorated in the traditional style and is a very pleasant, comfortable place to stay. You'll be well looked after by the friendly staff, including the Moroccan owner and his German wife.

Day trips, official guides and car hire can all be arranged through the hotel. Prices for the 14 rooms are from Dr110/150 for singles/doubles without shower and from Dr150/180 to Dr250/300 for singles/doubles with bathroom. Children under three stay free; children from four to 12 years are charged Dr50. There are also mini-apartments available from Dr300 for two people. Breakfast costs Dr25 and set meals from Dr70 to Dr90.

The *Grand Hôtel du Tazi* (☎ 442787; fax 442152), on the corner of Ave El-Mouahidine and Rue de Bab Agnaou, is a larger and more expensive hotel which charges Dr214/275 for rooms with shower, toilet, TV and phone. There is also a small pool, a bar and a restaurant. Guests are entitled to a 20% discount at the restaurant. Ask for a room away from the street. Room Nos 259 to 267 have balconies which overlook the pool; it's a good place for anxious parents with children. There is also a roof terrace and parking.

A little further away, on Ave El-Mouahidine, is the cavernous *Hôtel de Foucauld* (☎ 445499; fax 441344). Although some of the rooms can be noisy and a tad small, they are clean, nicely decorated and comfortable, and not bad value at Dr145/184. They come with shower, toilet and hot water 24 hours a day. Again, ask for a room away from the street. The hotel has a tiny pool and a traditional-style restaurant hung with carpets.

Along Ave Mohammed V, heading west towards Bab Larissa and the ville nouvelle (see the Marrakesh map), is a good two-star place, the *Hôtel Islane* (☎ 440081/3; fax 440085). The rooms are modern and comfortable, and some have balconies with views across to the Koutoubia mosque. This hotel boasts a pleasant rooftop restaurant and cafe, and the rooms have toilet, shower and phone.

During the high season (usually August to October) singles/doubles go for Dr214/ 275, which includes breakfast. The evening meal is also obligatory and costs Dr90. In the low season, rooms are Dr190/ 227 and breakfast/dinner are not obligatory. It has parking, and accepts credit cards – as do most Marrakshi hotels in this class up.

Ville Nouvelle The bulk of the mid-range hotels are located outside the medina, mostly in Gueliz, with a couple closer to the medina boundary in the Hivernage area. There are a lot of them, especially in the three and four-star category.

An older place with a bit of character and reasonable rooms is the *Hôtel des Ambassadeurs* (☎ 447159) on Rue Ibn Aicha. It has a restaurant and bar next door and, as it's in the more lively part of Gueliz, there is a good choice of eateries and cafes nearby. Rooms with bathroom cost Dr223/ 290/357.

Back on Ave Mohammed V is the three-star *Hôtel Amalay* (☎ 431367; fax 431554) and around the corner, past the former Hôtel de la Renaissance, is the *Hôtel Tachfine* (☎ 447188; fax 437862). Both charge Dr254/312 (Dr30 for breakfast) and have bars and restaurants with set menus for Dr80/110.

Heading back down Ave Mohammed V towards the medina is the *Hôtel Hasna* (☎ 449972; fax 449994) at No 247, which has spotless and new-looking rooms (with terrible paintings) for Dr280/342 (breakfast Dr36). All rooms come with satellite TV and telephone and there is a very small pool at the back. The hotel also has its own hammam open to guests only for Dr40, and quite a pleasant Moroccan restaurant complete with *poofah* seats and Dr130 set menus.

Closer to the medina and in a quiet setting are the *Hôtel de la Ménara* (☎ 436478; fax 447386), overlooking Place de la Liberté, and the three-star *Hôtel Le Grand Imilchil* (☎ 447653; fax 446165) on Ave Echouhada (see the Marrakesh map). Rooms at both hotels come with full bathroom, central heating in winter and air-con in summer. The former is probably preferable, as its rooms are generally more spacious and have balconies. It charges Dr231/312 including breakfast and all taxes, while Le Grand Imilchil charges

THE HIGH ATLAS

Marrakesh - Ville Nouvelle

0   100   200 m

PLACES TO STAY
2   Résidence Al Bahja
4   Hôtel des Ambassadeurs
5   Hôtel Oasis; Gillot (Bookshop)
10 Hôtel Amalay
11 Hôtel Oudaya; La Petite Auberge
18 Hôtel Tachfine; Mirador Bar (Hôtel & Café de la Renaissance)
26 Hôtel des Voyageurs
27 Hôtel Franco-Belge
41 Hôtel Toulousain
44 Hôtel Nassim
50 Hôtel Le Marrakesh; Disco Diamant Noir
54 Hôtel Hasna
59 Hôtel Moussafir

PLACES TO EAT
13 Oliveri (Ice Cream)
14 La Trattoria
16 Restaurant La Taverne
19 Restaurant Chez Jack'Line
20 Brasserie Le Petit Poucet
21 Fener Sarl Traiteur Charcuterie
22 Café Restaurant Agdal
24 Boulangerie Pâtisserie Hilton; Café Boule de Neige (Ice Cream)
25 Jacaranda
28 Dragon d'Or
39 Le Liberty's
42 Restaurant Le Catanzaro
43 Marché de Gueliz (Market)
45 Pâtisserie Al Jawda (Chez Mme Alami)
48 Café Snack Sindibad; Le Fouquet's
52 Pizza Hut; Bank
53 Restaurant Al-Fassia
58 Bagatelle

OTHER
1   Hospital
3   Somardis Supermarket
6   Supermarket
7   Shell Petrol Station
8   Librairie Chatr (Bookshop)
9   Artisinat Marocain
12 CTM Booking Office; Bus Stop
15 Ménara Tours (Travel Agency)
17 Cinéma Le Colisée
23 Shell Petrol Station
29 American Language Center; Bookshop
30 Europcar (Car Rental)
31 Petrol Station
32 BMCE Bank (ATM)
33 Tourist Office
34 Carlson Wagonlits (Travel Agency)
35 Felix Labo (Photo Shop)
36 Avis (Car Rental)
37 Hertz (Car Rental)
38 Nouvelles Frontières (Travel Agency)
40 Dentist
46 Voyages Schwarz (American Express)
47 Royal Air Maroc; Car Hire Companies; Pampa Voyage
49 All-Night Pharmacy
51 Le Star's House; Café Jet d'Eau
55 Église des Saints-Martyrs
56 Main Post Office
57 Panarea Pub Club
60 Train Station
61 Supratours Bureau

Dr243/302 without breakfast. Both have pleasant pools and gardens, beer is available, and laundry can be done for you, but it's expensive.

If you have the money and arrive on a late train, you might well want to spend a night at the three-star *Hôtel Moussafir* (☎ 435929; fax 435936); like other hotels in this chain, it is right by the station. It's a reliable, modern choice and has a small pool set in a peaceful garden full of willow trees and birds. Rooms cost Dr266/327/457.

This in no way exhausts the list of three-

star hotels, but should provide enough scope for choice. If you're in trouble, you could try the *Hôtel Oudaya* (☎ 448751; fax 435400) at 147 Rue Mohammed el-Beqal, which has singles/doubles for Dr266/327. Guests can use the hammam for Dr35.

Places to Stay – top end
There are at least 26 hotels in the four and five-star bracket. Among them is the *Hôtel Nassim* (☎ 446401; fax 447458) in the centre of the action in Gueliz on Ave Mohammed V. It's a good place for busi-

ness travellers, with conference facilities and fax machines available. There are plans to get access to the Internet in the future, too. Sound-proofed and comfortable rooms start at Dr500/650 for singles/doubles (Dr50 less per person in low season). There's also a small pool.

The *Hôtel Le Marrakesh* (☎ 434351; fax 434980) near Place de la Liberté charges Dr500/618 for rooms and Dr55 for breakfast.

Other hotels in the four and five-star categories are on the Ave de France and further out of town on the road to Casablanca and the Semlalia part of town (see the Marrakesh map). *Hotel Es Saadi* is a five-star hotel (☎ 448811; fax 447644) with singles/doubles for Dr1100/1300.

On Ave Houmane el-Fetouaki, just inside Bab el-Jedid, is the jewel in the crown of Marrakesh's hotels – the *La Mamounia* (☎ 448981; fax 444660), although at five-star 'luxe', you'd want to be on an expense account to stay there.

The hotel was built between 1925 and 1929 for the (French-controlled) Moroccan railways and it was the favoured destination of well-heeled Europeans, many of them taking a break from the decadence of Tangier. Guests as diverse as Winston Churchill (who came for the climate and to indulge in his hobby of painting) and Eric von Stroheim have passed through.

Renovated in 1986, it has lost some of its charm, but jet-setters still patronise it. Rooms start at Dr1700 for a single in the low season and finish in the vicinity of Dr30,000 for a suite of three rooms (and Dr170 for breakfast).

Another luxurious and more unusual place is the *Palais Rhoul* (☎ 45721300; fax 329496) in the affluent residential area of Marrakesh, La Palmeraie. It's an imposing neo-Classical palace, built as the private residence of a French countess. It has just five rooms and three suites. Prices range from Dr1750 for one person to Dr6000 for a suite for two in the high season.

Holiday Residences Apart from the Club

Med on the Djemaa el-Fna, there are a couple of residences offering long-term lets of self-contained flats. They are good for families or groups intending to spend some time in the area, and must usually be booked at least a month ahead. The tourist office has a complete list.

Right on the Djemaa el-Fna at No 47, is the *Résidence de la Place* (☎ 445174). It is the least good of the résidences, but the main attraction is, as usual, its position overlooking the square. Tatty and rather run-down apartments (for up to 6 people) cost Dr400 per day. Two of the apartments have wonderful balconies overlooking the square (although light sleepers may well prefer something on the courtyard out the back). For those who don't get the views from the apartments, there is a terrace cafe overlooking the Place.

An altogether more upmarket place is the *Résidence Al Bahja* (☎ 448119; fax 346063) in Gueliz. It offers 13 well maintained and well equipped apartments which sleep up to eight people for anything from a week up. If business is slow, you could stay for a day or two. The daily rates are Dr250, Dr350 and Dr600 (for one person, two people, or a family with up to three children), weekly rates are Dr1500, Dr4300 and Dr6000; and monthly rates are Dr5500, Dr8000 and Dr12,000.

The Résidence has well equipped kitchens, central heating, telephone, roof solarium, balconies and terrace. Evening meals can be ordered for about Dr90.

Another that can be recommended, but further out on Ave Mohammed Abdelkrim el-Khattabi on the road to Casablanca, is the *Résidence Ezzahia* (☎ 446244; fax 430028. It's bigger, with nearly 50 apartments on four floors and lift, pool, and restaurant, though it's location on the busy road can make some apartments a bit noisy. Credit cards are accepted.

Swimming Pools
If you fancy a dip while in Marrakesh, there are two options. The public municipal pool (see the Marrakesh map) is the cheaper

alternative, but it can get very overcrowded and women travellers should be warned that it is almost exclusively the reserve of adolescent male Moroccans. It is open from June to September only.

The second option is the hotels. The Moussafir hotel charges Dr50 per day to non-residents and the Palmerie Golf Palace Dr80.

Hammams

There are a couple of hammams a few minutes' walk south of Place Djemaa el-Fna for men and women. Both places are clean and popular with some tour groups. Entrance is Dr5 for a straight *bain* (bath) and Dr10 for a full scrub and massage.

The best hammam in town is the Dar El Bacha at 20 Rue Fatima Zohra (see the Marrakesh map). It will cost you Dr5 for a bath and Dr10 for a massage, and it's open for men from 7 pm until 12 pm and for women from 12 pm to 7 pm.

Places to Eat

Restaurants About the liveliest and cheapest place to eat in the evening is right on the Djemaa el-Fna.

By the time the sun sets, a good portion of the square is taken over by innumerable stalls, each specialising in certain types of food. At some you can pick up kebabs with salad, while at others it's fish and chips Moroccan style or even snails and sheep heads. You point to whatever takes your fancy, and before you know it, it's in front of you with chips, salad and whatever else might be on offer. At others, you can just sit down to munch on bread rolls stuffed with potato. It is easy to eat your fill for Dr25 or even less. Wash it down with a Dr5 orange juice from one of the many juice stands.

If you feel a bit iffy about eating here (the food is cooked quite publicly, so there's little to worry about), try the small restaurants on Rue Bani Marine and Rue de Bab Agnaou. *L'Etoile*, for example, offers a filling set menu for Dr40. Vegetarians should ask for the vegetable couscous.

If your purse strings are a little less tight,

a place that is deservedly popular with travellers is the buffet in the *Hôtel Ali* served from 6.30 to 10.30 pm. For Dr60 (or Dr50 for hotel residents), you can load up your plate from various pots of typical Moroccan fare, along with a selection of cooked vegetables and/or salad, fruit or dessert. There's usually a musician to provide that 'authentic' touch. It might sound a little touristy, and it is, but it has a lively atmosphere and the food is fresh and good.

Back on the Djemaa itself, most of the rooftop cafes have restaurants attached to them. Some are better than others. The *Argana* (you can't miss the bright neon sign at night) is directly opposite the Bank al-Maghrib. Its set menu is Dr61. The food is fine, but the crepes for dessert are better.

Café Restaurant Chez Chegrouni, on the Place at No 4-6, is a very popular place and is probably the best bet on the square. Salads cost from Dr3.50 and main courses such as couscous from Dr25.

Three doors down from the Hôtel La Gazelle is another excellent place, the *Restaurant El Bahja*. It has good set menus for Dr44 to Dr50 which include a salad and a main course such as couscous, tajine, or brochettes served with chips, yoghurt and tea. It's a simple but clean place and is very popular with the locals.

Further south, both the *Grand Hôtel du Tazi* and *Hôtel de Foucauld* have restaurants (the former on their roof terrace), with 'menu touristiques' for Dr85/100 (plus Dr105 tax). They're OK, but they lack the visual feast of the terrace restaurants on the Djemaa and the atmosphere of some of the others listed above. On the other hand, you can get a beer at these places.

For at least Dr100 a head, you could eat in the rooftop restaurant *Pizzeria Venezia* in the Hôtel Islane (see the Marrakesh map). It boasts a wonderful view of the Koutoubia though the traffic below can be a bit noisy during the day. It serves traditional Moroccan fare as well as Italian food. Pizzas cost between Dr40 and Dr50, and the other main courses between Dr60 and Dr65. A bottle of beer is from Dr15 to Dr20.

There are any number of places to eat in the ville nouvelle; a good collection of them is concentrated on or around Ave Mohammed V and Blvd Mohammed Zerktouni.

For bottom-rung local food, you'll find a group of hole-in-the-wall places on Rue Ibn Aicha, where a solid meal of brochettes, chips and salad will cost about Dr25.

Fener Sarl at 72 Ave Mohammed V is a French-style 'traiteur charcuterie' (delicatessen) which sells delicious pizzas, quiche, tartes and other savoury French delicacies for around Dr8. *La Petite Auberge*, next door to the Hôtel Oudaya, is a good place for women on their own. They do good pizzas from Dr20.

The *Hotel Oasis* has some good value set menus for Dr50 (4 courses) plus 10% service, and beer for Dr10.

Otherwise, meals start getting a little more expensive, and it'll be hard to find anything for under about Dr60 a head. If you're desperate to fill up on greens, you could try *Pizza Hut* (☎ 43 19 72) on No 6 Ave Mohammed V which has a good self-service salad bar for Dr31. Pizzas cost from Dr49 to Dr79.

Restaurant al-Fassia (☎ 434060), at 232 Ave Mohammed V across from the Hôtel Hasna, has a good reputation for its traditional Moroccan cuisine. It's a very attractive place with a cool, peaceful garden and two cushioned pavilions. There is a good set menu for Dr120 (plus tax) which is served just at lunch time; otherwise it's a la carte with main courses for between Dr75 and Dr95. It's open every day from noon to 2.30 pm and from 7.30 to 11 pm.

Across the road from the Hôtel Tachfine is the *Restaurant La Taverne* (☎ 446126), which offers a mix of Moroccan and French cuisine and has an excellent four-course set menu for Dr80. During the summer the garden at the back provides a very pleasant escape from the heat and traffic.

The restaurant *La Trattoria* (☎ 432641) at 179 Rue Mohammed el-Beqal, is run by an Italian, Giancarlo, who has owned the restaurant for 20 years. It's an extraordinary, palatial place behind a large gate

that's unlocked by a Quasimodo-type figure. The open log fire and the dachshund curled up beside it make the trattoria a very homely place in winter. Pasta/meat/fish dishes cost from Dr60/70/120.

The restaurant *Bagatelle* (☎ 430274), at 101 Rue Yougoslavie, serves good French food. There's not much atmosphere in the restaurant itself, but there's a lovely garden outside covered by a canopy of vines. Main courses are from Dr50 to Dr90. It's open every day except Wednesday.

At no 63 Ave Mohammed V ,across from the Hôtel Al Mouatamid, the *Restaurant Chez Jack'Line* (☎ 447547) is a place full of character which is done out like a French bistro. Look out for the 22-year-old parrot, who seems as much in charge of the place as Madame Jack'Line herself. It does very good three-course set menus for Dr68/80. A la carte, main courses are around Dr70. It serves Italian and French-style food and is open every day.

The restaurant *Le Catanzaro* (☎ 433731 is a good Franco-Italian place open Monday to Saturday. It's on Rue Tarik Ibn Ziad and has pizzas and pasta dishes from Dr35 to Dr45, and meat courses from Dr65 to Dr70.

The French restaurant *Jacaranda* (☎ 447 215), at No 32 Blvd Mohammed Zerktouni, serves very good French food such as frogs legs, calf brains and duck. It does good set lunch menus for Dr68/88 and an evening menu for Dr150. It has a good selection of fish, meat and desserts. It's run by the civil Philippe Coustal from Toulouse and boasts a wonderful seafood speciality, brochette Jacaranda.

If you feel like something Asian, head for the *Dragon d'Or* (☎ 430617), a Vietnamese restaurant at 10 Blvd Mohammed Zerktouni.

Virtually all the bigger hotels have at least one restaurant. *La Mamounia* has five rather expensive places. Meals are sometimes accompanied by a show of one sort or another. The *Dar Mounia* (☎ 431241) is a well established upper-end Moroccan restaurant, for which you must book tables in advance.

For a complete blow-out in lavish surroundings, you can try the restaurant-palace *Dar Marjana* (☎ 445773; fax 429152) open only upon reservation at 15 Derb Sidi Ali Tair (see the Marrakesh map). Considered one of the best restaurants in Marrakesh, it has hosted the likes of Dustin Hoffman and Isabelle Adjani.

Another similar place is the restaurant *Yacout* (☎ 382929; fax 382538) at 79 Sidi Ahmed Soussi in the medina. It was designed by the American architect Bill Willis and is an extraordinary place, complete with illuminated terrace, beautiful fountain and pool. Reservations are necessary here too and fixed menus go for a smooth Dr500 (including aperitifs and wine). It is open from 8.30 pm to midnight. Ask someone to guide you there.

The *Restaurant Bar El Baroud* (☎ 426009) is at 275 Ave Mohammed V along from the Hotel Islane (see the Marrakesh map). It's another place serving traditional food, but rather less expensively. Main courses cost from Dr85, couscous Dr120, and a bottle of wine Dr90. Credit cards are accepted.

The restaurant *Stylia* (☎ 443587/440505; fax 445837) at 34 Rue Ksour (see the Marrakesh map) is another lavish place serving the 'Haute Gastronomie Marocaine'. For many, it's the best place in Marrakesh. To get there, get a petit taxi to drop you off at Rue Sidi el-Yamani (the restaurant is signposted off Rue Fatima Zohra). A doorman will collect you and guide you through the dark winding streets to the palace which is hidden like a jewel in the medina.

Cafes & Bars As in any Moroccan city, Marrakesh is crawling with cafes and *salons thé*. The more interesting of them are gathered around the Djemaa el-Fna – but don't be surprised to be charged Dr5 for coffee or weak tea.

Ave Mohammed V in the ville nouvelle is the other part of town that usually attracts a people-watching crowd of tea-sippers.

The *Café Snack Sindibad* on Ave Mohammed V is a very popular place for breakfast. It looks rather like a Parisian cafe and has a nice terrace, but its appearance belies its prices which are very reasonable. Breakfast (toast, orange juice and tea/coffee) costs Dr14, salads from Dr8 to Dr14 and Moroccan main courses from Dr30 (including a vegetable couscous). It's open from 5 am to 11 pm.

A few doors down at No 200 is the cafe *Le Fouquet's* which does a good value continental breakfast including a boiled egg for Dr15.

The cafe *Boule de Neige*, at 30 Place Abdelmoumen (next to the Boulangerie Pâtisserie Hilton), is a good place for a peaceful coffee or ice cream.

Café Restaurant Agdal on Ave Mohammed V is one of the most pleasant and most reasonable cafes in the area. It has a three course set menu for Dr50 and does a very good value breakfast for Dr12 (Dr20 with omelette). It also has tasty salads from Dr14.

The best cafe/bar in town by far is the cafe/salon de thé *Le Liberty's* at 23 Rue de la Liberté (☎ 436416). It has a nice garden at the back (though overlooked by an horrendous tower block); it's open from 6.30 am to 12 pm. They also do a good Moroccan breakfast of crepes etc for Dr15, salads from Dr13 and sandwiches from Dr10. It has a very pleasant, colonial-style salon which is a good place for single women.

Possibly the most popular bar in town (and the most pick-uppy if you're a single woman) is at the top of the former Hôtel de la Renaissance, the *Mirador*. It also boasts the best view of Marrakesh in town, but a drink (Dr5) is compulsory. It's open from 9 am to 11 pm and you need to ring the bell by the lift in order to call the lift porter. The cafe on the ground floor of the same building is a great Art Deco relic and a good place for a beer (inside) or coffee (outside).

The *Brasserie Le Petit Poucet* on Ave Mohammed V is a pretty down-to-earth place to get a drink. Even more so is the bar next door to the Restaurant La Taverne. Some of the restaurants in Gueliz also have an alcohol licence.

Another place for a drink is the popular

Panarea Pub Club (☎ 436487) close to the main post office. It has cocktails for Dr40 and beer from Dr17. They have quite good pasta dishes for around Dr35 to Dr70 and are open until 12.30 am.

Patisseries & Glaceries *Pâtisserie Mik Mak*, next door to the Hotel Ali near Place Djemaa el-Fna, has a good selection of Moroccan and French-style cakes at reasonable prices; there's a restful seating section upstairs. It's open from 6 am to 10.30 pm every day.

Nearby is a new and smarter place, the *Pâtisserie des Princes* at 32 Bab Agnaou, which has a good selection of cakes and pastries and some ice cream. It's a cool, peaceful place for women travelling on their own. It's also good for breakfast. Try the delicious croissants aux amandes et chocolate for Dr5. It's open every day until 10 pm.

A very well known place in Marrakesh is the *Boulangerie Pâtisserie Hilton* opposite the Café de la Renaissance in the ville nouvelle. It is a veritable feast for your eyes, as well as your palate and nose, and sells a wide selection of traditional Moroccan sweet and savoury things including pastilla. It's open every day from 4 am to 11.30 pm.

The best ice cream parlour in town is *Oliveri* at 9 Blvd Mansour Eddahbi in the ville nouvelle. Its sister is in Casablanca, and both are well known for their homemade ice cream. They also sell good milk shakes (Dr16), fruit juices (Dr5.50) and ice cream cakes. You can also have breakfast here. It's open from 7 am.

With a smaller selection is the less ostentatious, but excellent, *Pâtisserie Al Jawda (Chez Mme Alami)* at 11 Rue de la Liberté. It's open every day from 8 am to 8.30 pm. Try the speciality of the maison, the melt-in-your-mouth Ficasse a la crème fraîche.

Self-Catering The *Somardis* supermarket on Rue Ibn Aicha in the ville nouvelle is a reasonable place to stock up on supplies you might find hard to get elsewhere – like Corn Flakes. It also sells alcohol. There is a liquor store next to the Hôtel Nassim.

Entertainment

Nightclubs If you want to party on, many of the hotels in the ville nouvelle have nightclubs. There are several others independent of hotels.

As elsewhere in Morocco, the usual entry fee varies between Dr50 and Dr100, which includes the first drink. Each drink thereafter costs at least Dr50. Most offer the predictable standard fare of western disco music.

One of them is a nightclub that caters to Moroccans in the street at the back of the Hôtel de la Renaissance. It kicks off around 11 pm with two hours of the best folk music you'll hear, after which it's contemporary Moroccan pop music mixed with normal disco music.

As far as regular discos go, one of the most popular is the *Diamant Noir* in the Hôtel Le Marrakesh, on Place de la Liberté. Another is the *Cotton Club*, in the Hôtel Tropicana on the road to Casablanca.

New Feeling is another popular place in La Palmaerie. *Le Star's House*, next door to the Café Jet d'Eau, is currently à la mode and is open until 4 or 5 am and costs Dr60.

You can also try the Hotel Mamounia *casino*, complete with fruit machines, blackjack tables and roulette wheels. It's open to all, but a jacket and tie are required for men, and smart skirts for women. Moroccan garb is out. It's open from 9 pm until late (usually until 3 or 4 am) depending on the clientele. Drinks are in the range of Dr100 to Dr200.

Gay Bars & Clubs You could try the *Café Renaissance* on the ground floor of the Hôtel de la Renaissance on Ave Mohammed V, which is a popular meeting place for the expat gay community. The bar in the *Grand Hôtel Tazi* is also worth a look.

As far as discos are concerned, *Sahara Inn* on the road to Casablanca attracts some gays as does occasionally *Le Star's House*.

THE HIGH ATLAS

Cinema The plushest cinema in Marrakesh is *Le Colisée* (☎ 448893) on Blvd Mohammed Zerktouni in the ville nouvelle. Seats are Dr20/30 (Dr5 less on Mondays) and the sound and comfort are excellent. Women customarily sit in the balcony.

There are three showings a day at 3, 7 and 9.30 pm; check the paper *L'Economie* for listings. Films are dubbed into French.

Folkloric Shows As already noted, there are several upmarket restaurants, some in the bigger hotels, that put on entertainment involving local tribal singing and dancing. Inquire at the tourist office or have a flip through the *Welcome to Marrakesh* booklet.

Things to Buy

As in most of the major Moroccan cities, the Ensemble Artisanal, on Ave Mohammed V in the ville nouvelle, is a sensible first stop to get an idea of the maximum prices to offer for souvenirs once you are rummaging around in the souqs.

It's better for sampling the quality of merchandise than for purchasing. It's also a good place to watch artisans at work.

If you can't face bargaining in the souqs, there are various other fixed price craft shops along the northern end of Ave Mohammed V. One with quite a large selection of goods at prices which aren't too extortionate is the Artisanat Marocain at No 27. It is run by a Berber family and is open from 8 am to 7.30 pm every day.

Many shops have notices posted in their windows listing a number to call if you feel you've been unfairly treated in a purchase, either on price or quality of the goods.

This is definitely worth doing, if you have a serious and fair cause for complaint. Believe it or not, any potential damage caused to the tourism industry is taken very seriously. The number to call is ☎ 308430 (ext 360).

Getting There & Away

Air Royal Air Maroc (RAM; ☎ 446444; fax 446002) has an office on Ave Mohammed V which is open from Monday to Friday 8.30 am to 12.15 pm and 2.30 to 7 pm.

There are three flights a day to and from Casablanca (Dr437, one way), and a flight every day to Agadir (Dr437) via Casablanca (except on Sunday, when two go direct). There are flights three times a week to Ouarzazate (Dr988), flights every Sunday to Fès (Dr692) and four each week to Tangier (Dr852). All of these flights go via Casablanca. The airport is 5km south-west of town.

Bus The main bus station from which all buses (regardless of the company) leave is just outside the city walls by Bab Doukkala (see the Marrakesh map). This is a 20 minute walk or a Dr8 taxi ride from the Djemaa el-Fna.

The main building is a big place with a good many booths covering all sorts of local and long-distance destinations.

Window No 10 is the CTM booking desk. CTM has two buses a day to Fès (Dr123; eight hours), one in the early morning, the other in the evening and two buses a day for Agadir (Dr67; 4½ hours), one in the morning and one in the early evening. CTM also has four daily buses for Casablanca from 4 am to 6 pm (Dr63; 3½ hours) and Ouarzazate (Dr55; five hours). There are also one to two buses a day for Safi, Er-Rachidia, M'Hamid (via Zagora), Laayoune and Tan Tan.

You can get tickets for other bus lines at the other windows. Tickets to Beni Mellal (Dr34.50) are sold at window No 1. Buses leave every hour from 4 am to 9 pm. At window No 2, tickets are sold for buses to Rabat (Dr77.40) via Casablanca (Dr55). There are 25 runs a day from 5 am to midnight.

You can buy tickets to Asni (for Jebel Toubkal) at window No 3 (Dr10.90). window No 4 is the Safi line, with 26 daily departures from 4.30 am to 6 pm. Tickets cost Dr26 (normal) and Dr27.50 (mumtaz). Next door at window No 5 is the El-Jadida line, with 10 buses a day from 5 am to 5 pm (Dr35.10). For buses to Ouarzazate, queue at window No 6 (Dr46.55). There are also 19 runs a day to Agadir (Dr53.50) from 5 am to 7.30 pm, and three runs a day to Taroudannt (Dr68).

For Essaouira, you want window 7 (Dr30). These buses go via Chichaoua (Dr14), which is famous for its rugs, but has little else of interest. There are three buses a day to Azilal. Tickets (Dr42) can be bought at window 18.

CTM also has a booking office on Blvd Mohammed Zerktouni, and some of the buses departing from Marrakesh stop outside it on their way out of the city.

Local buses to the villages on the north side of Jebel Toubkal, including Ourika and Asni, leave when full from a dirt patch on the southern side of the medina outside Bab er-Rob. The buses to Asni cost Dr8.

There is a left-luggage counter at the station which costs Dr4 per item per day. It's open 24 hours a day.

Train The train station is on Ave Hassan II, south-west of Place du 16 Novembre. Take a taxi or No 8 bus into the centre.

There are three direct trains from Marrakesh to Fès via Casablanca, Rabat and Meknès. They take 8¼ hours. You can also take a train to Casa-Voyageurs in Casablanca and pick up a train to Fès from there, but the journey takes a fair bit longer.

There are three trains a day to Tangier (via Casablanca and Rabat) including one overnight. The journey takes 10½ hours and should make it to Tangier in time for the first boat to Algeciras. You can book a couchette on this trip.

To get to Oujda, you have to take a train to Casablanca and then pick up one of two night trains from there.

All up, there are nine trains to Casablanca and eight on to Rabat. There are four trains to Safi (change at Ben Guerir).

Second class normal/rapide fares include: Casablanca (Dr56/71), Fès (Dr130/163), Oujda (Dr220/265), Rabat (Dr76/96) and Tangier (Dr153/180).

Supratours The ONCF organises buses through Supratours t... from Marrakesh to desti... such as Agadir (Dr63.50), ... Tiznit (Dr89.50), Tan Ta... Laayoune (Dr253.50), Smara ... Dakhla (Dr389). Ask if you ... one at the Supratours Kiosque out... train station. For general informatio... Supratours services, you can call ☎ 7765... (in Rabat).

Taxi Standard grands taxis to Ourika, Asni (Dr15; about one hour) and other nearby High Atlas destinations depart from outside Bab er-Rob near the Royal Palace.

Car There are at least 25 car-rental agencies in Marrakesh. For a more complete list, pick up the free booklet *Welcome to Marrakesh*. The addresses of the main companies are as follows:

Avis
  137 Avenue Mohammed V (☎ 433727; fax 449485)
Budget
  68 Blvd Mohammed Zerktouni (☎ 431187)
Europcar
  63 Blvd Mohammed Zerktouni (☎ 431228; fax 432769)
Goldcar
  Hôtel Semiramis Méridien, Route de Casablanca (☎ 431377)
Hertz
  154 Avenue Mohammed V (☎/fax 434680)
Zeit
  Apt 17, 129 Ave Mohammed al-Bakkal (☎ 431888; fax 431701)

Local car rental companies often offer more competitive deals, and you can try the cluster of them in the building next to Royal Air Maroc at 213 Ave Mohammed V.

Among them are Jawal Cars and AV Cars (☎ 439175; fax 419177) The competition is stiff and you should shop around ruthlessly before choosing.

Although you will be shown lists with official prices on them, you should be able to negotiate a 10% to 20% discount in the high season and a 30% to 40% discount in the low season (October to mid-December

...ably the best place to hire a car. Competition is stiff, and you should be able to play one company's quote off another's. Prices can drop dramatically by up to 60% or more in the low season. It's a good test of your haggling skills.

Bicycles & Scooters Marrakesh Motos (☎ 448359) at 31 Route de Casablanca next to the Goodyear garage, rents both mountain and ordinary bikes for Dr30/20 per whole/half day. Scooters cost Dr250/150 per whole/half day, and motorbikes (50cc plus) Dr350 per day. The store is open every day except Sunday afternoon from 8.30 am to 7 pm.

Various hotels rent out bicycles. Among them are the Hôtel Foucauld (Dr60/30 per half/full day), but you're not supposed to take them outside the Medina. The Hôtel Ali also rents bikes for Dr40/30 for a whole/half day.

Getting Around

The Airport A petit taxi from Marrakesh to the airport should be Dr60 but you'll rarely get it for that price. Bus No 11 runs irregularly to Djemaa el-Fna.

Bus & Taxi The creamy-beige petits taxis around town cost about Dr8 per journey, but insist that the meter is used. From the train station to the Djemaa el-Fna the official fare is Dr10 but you'll rarely get away with less than Dr15.

Local bus No 8 runs from the Djemaa el-Fna area, passing close by the Bab Doukkala bus station and then going on to the main post office and train station. Nos 1

and 20 run right up Ave Mohammed V from near the Djemaa el-Fna into Gueliz. No 11 runs between the airport and the Djemaa el-Fna. The No 3 bus goes to the Bab Doukkala bus station from the Djemaa el-Fna and then on to the main post office.

Horse-Drawn Carriages Horse-drawn carriages (calèches) are a feature of Marrakesh you won't find in many other Moroccan cities, and they can be a pleasant way to get around – if you establish the right price. Theoretically, this should present no difficulties. Posted up inside the carriage are the official fares: Dr9 for a straightforward trip from A to B 'intramuros' (within the medina walls) and Dr13 or the same 'extramuros' (outside the medina walls). Otherwise, it's Dr65 an hour for pottering around the sights. This may seem steep – it isn't cheap – but at least you know where you stand. If you're interested, they're based at the south-western side of the Djemaa el-Fna.

AROUND MARRAKESH – NORTH
Cascades d'Ouzoud

About 167km north-east of Marrakesh are the best waterfalls you'll see in Morocco; they're well worth the effort of getting there. If you have a car, it's an easy enough proposition as a day trip; otherwise, you might have to be prepared to stay overnight in the area – not a bad option.

The falls (ouzoud is Berber for olives and refers to the cultivation of olive trees in the area) drop about 100m into the river below, forming natural pools that are great for a swim.

It is possible to walk along the course of the river to the **Gorges of Oued el-Abid**, and indeed the whole area is good hiking territory.

An increasingly popular destination is the village of **Tanaghmelt**, on the wooded slopes of the hills a short hike beyond the waterfalls. Plenty of locals and foreign tourists come here, and the souvenir stalls are proof of its popularity, but as yet it is all on a modest scale.

DAMIEN SIMONIS

DAMIEN SIMONIS

FRANCES LINZEE GORDON

The High Atlas
Top Left: Across lush green valleys to the Toubkal massif.
Top Right: Hill houses the colour of the earth, Aït Souka, near Imlil.
Bottom: Herding in a High Atlas valley.

The High Atlas
Great for a swim – the Cascades d'Ouzoud (waterfalls of the olives) drop about 100m to natural pools below.

The Olive Oil Expedition

The opportunity to join an expedition across the High Atlas to collect an entire village's supply of oil straight from the press promised to be a bit more exciting than the average trip to the supermarket.

The owner of the olive oil 'factory', whose shiny black close-cropped hair, coppery olive Berber skin and deep brown-black eyes made him resemble an olive, rode in the back of the 4WD, directing us along ever-worsening pistes.

After two hours we arrived at a village so tucked away from any main roads that it would probably never see casual travellers. Once there, Hassan, the olive man, took us straight to his home where we were warmly greeted by his wife and the delighted giggles of countless children. Before any work began, a good hour was spent sipping hot mint tea and eating fresh walnuts.

Filling the empty drums with oil turned out to be a slow, often hilarious process featuring good-natured disputes over whether a drum was properly filled and the frequent failure of the hose-and-gravity method of decanting. While this was going on the women of the house were in the earthen-floored kitchen making rounds of bread in a pan over a brazier and stirring a simmering tajine. The drums were finally filled just as the sun was thinking about setting. But before we could leave, the tajine flew out of the kitchen, a low table and stools appeared in the courtyard and we were encouraged to eat.

Then there was a final treat. Walking down the village path to the truck, Hassan beckoned us through another village doorway. Crammed inside a very dark, low-ceilinged room was the olive oil press. How ancient it was would be anybody's guess. It consisted of a great stone three or four metres across attached to an enormous tree trunk which in turn was harnessed to a donkey. And all around the darkened room, beaming smiles and twinkling olive eyes. ■

The drive between Ouzoud and Afourer, which brings you to the main Marrakesh-Beni Mellal road, is a treat in itself, especially the views of the lake formed by the **Bin el-Ouidane Dam**.

Places to Stay & Eat Around the falls there are several shady camp sites, which are all much of a muchness. It is a beautiful place to pitch a tent, and generally you're looking at about Dr10 per person and Dr7 to pitch a tent. The *Hôtel Salam* has basic rooms for Dr30 per person. Meals are available in the hotel if you give them plenty of notice. There are several cafes on the way down to the falls serving good Moroccan standards.

In the nearby village of Azilal, at the Beni Mellal exit, is the pleasant two-star *Hôtel Tanoute* (☎ 488281). Singles/doubles with shower cost around Dr121/142, while those with full en suite bathroom are Dr153/179, plus taxes.

There are two other accommodation possibilities in this area. About 27km from Azilal, just north of Bin el-Ouidane Dam, is the *Hôtel du Lac*. It's well signposted and in an idyllic position. You can camp there, too. In the town of Afourer, 62 winding kilometres from Azilal, there is the four-star *Hôtel Tazarkount*.

Getting There & Away If you're coming from Marrakesh, it would be preferable to get transport direct to Azilal. Two buses a day run from the Bab Doukkala bus station and cost Dr40. From Azilal, there are daily morning and afternoon departures to Marrakesh. There's one daily bus service to Beni Mellal (Dr20).

A place in a grand taxi between Marrakesh and Azilal costs around Dr60.

Travelling between Azilal and Ouzoud is fairly straightforward, with local grands taxis doing the 38km run fairly regularly for Dr12 a head. When you arrive at Ouzoud, follow the dirt track lined with snack and souvenir stalls to get to the waterfalls.

Beni Mellal

Situated about 200km north-east of Marrakesh, the small but rapidly growing town of Beni Mellal makes a good stopover point en route to or from Marrakesh. Though not particularly attractive in itself, the town has a good range of accommodation and is well placed for those interested in treks into the Middle Atlas and (for the adventurous) the High Atlas.

The Bou Goumez Valley, to the south-west of Beni Mellal, beyond Azilal, provides access to Jebel M'Goun (4071m), the second highest peak in the country. Guides and mules can be found in Beni Mellal and it's also possible to arrange 4WD expeditions there.

The main street, Ave Mohammed V, runs off the P24 to Marrakesh through the centre of the town. The medina is south of Ave Mohammed V and the bus station north of the centre, about a 10 minute walk up Ave des FAR.

The tourist office (☎ 483981) is south of the medina on the first floor of Immeuble Chichaoui on Ave Hassan II. A large market is held on Tuesday.

Places to Stay & Eat There are a few cheap hotels scattered near the bus station. The *Hôtel El Amiria* (☎ 483531), south of the bus station on Ave des FAR, has decent clean singles/doubles without shower for Dr50/80. There are shared hot showers.

Closer to the centre of town, the *Hôtel Es-Saada* (☎ 482991), at 129 Rue Tarik Ibn Ziad off Ave Mohammed V, has similar rooms for the same price.

The *Hôtel des Voyagers* (☎ 482472), on Ave Mohammed V not far from the medina, has clean basic rooms for Dr40/60. There are shared cold showers and a roof terrace.

The *Hôtel Än Asserdoun* (☎ 483493), on Ave des Far, has modern rooms with bathroom for Dr100/150. The hotel has its own restaurant.

There are plenty of cheap cafe/restaurants

along Ave Mohammed V and food stalls around the medina. The restaurant at the *Auberge du Vieux Moulin*, on Ave Mohammed V, serves very good French and Moroccan meals. It also has a decent bar.

For coffee and pastries, try the *Salon de Thé Azouhour*, also on the main street.

Getting There & Away CTM runs frequent daily services to Marrakesh (Dr35) and three daily services to Fès. There's a daily bus to Azilal (Dr20).

Imilchil

Although it is stretching the idea to describe this remote High Atlas village as 'around Marrakesh', it is from Marrakesh that the bulk of the tours to Imilchil depart.

Some 363km distant, Imilchil has become known for its September moussem, a kind of tribal marriage market where the women do the choosing. Though somewhat less tribal than it once was, it remains a big event. There are two basic *hotels* in the village and several *cafe/restaurants*. There are several experienced mountain guides based in Imilchil.

You can get to Imilchil under your own steam, but it requires some patience. The easy bit is heading north-east by bus or a series of grands taxis to Kasba Tadla. From there you need to get another grand taxi to El-Ksiba. Here you may have to wait to get something for Aghbala. The turn-off for Imilchil is near Tizi n'Isly, about 10km before Aghbala. From there 61km of piste lead south to Imilchil. Around here you will have to rely on souq lorries – market days in Imilchil are Friday and Sunday. If you have plenty of time, it's also possible to get to Imilchil (160 breathtaking kilometres by souq lorries or 4WD) from Boumalne du Dadès or Tinerhir.

AROUND MARRAKESH – SOUTH

Several roads lead south from Marrakesh. The principal one, the P31, leads south to Ouarzazate over the **Tizi n'Tichka**. It's a popular route with tourists exhausted by Marrakesh and eager to experience the oasis valleys of the south. For more on this route see the Marrakesh to Ouarzazate section in the Central Morocco chapter.

Two other minor roads wind south of Marrakesh into the High Atlas. The S513 goes down the **Ourika Valley** to the ski resort of Oukaïmeden, and the S501 goes over the **Tizi n'Test** towards Taroudannt and on to Agadir. This latter road takes you to Asni, from where the bulk of trekkers take off into the High Atlas, usually with **Jebel Toubkal** as their goal. For more on Asni and trekking, see the High Atlas Trekking section later in this chapter.

Ourika Valley

Skiers and trekkers (spring/summer only) alike could skip the Asni-Imlil area (see the High Atlas section later in this chapter) and instead head down the Ourika Valley, to the east of Jebel Toubkal. The main options as bases are the ski resort of Oukaïmeden (virtually deserted outside the November-April snow season) or the village of **Setti Fatma** further east.

During spring Oukaïmeden is beautiful. In addition to long treks, you can explore the immediate vicinity of the resort in search of rock carvings (see *Gravures Rupestres du Haut Atlas* by Susan Searight & Danièle Hourbette). It is also a very good location for bird-watching.

The most reliable months for skiing are February, March and April. Lift passes cost about Dr80 a day and equipment hire (there are several outlets in the town) is about Dr100 a day. Oukaïmeden boasts the highest ski-lift in Africa (3273m). In August 1995 severe flooding of the valley resulted in the loss of several hundred lives.

Setti Fatma, 24km away along a poor road, is the site of an important moussem in August and another starting point for treks. For more details on trekking see the High Atlas section later in this chapter.

Places to Stay & Eat On the way to Oukaïmeden there are two fairly expensive hotels about 42km out of Marrakesh. The more expensive of the two is the *Hôtel*

Ourika (☎ 117531) which has singles and doubles at Dr262 and Dr327 respectively. Just beyond it is the more modest *Le Temps de Vivre*.

There is a good Club Alpin Français (CAF) refuge in Oukaïmeden with 80 dormitory beds, hot showers and a basic kitchen. Rates are Dr26 for CAF members, Dr39 for HI members and Dr52 for non-members. You'll need your own sleeping bag. For reservations, contact the CAF (☎ 270090; fax 297292) at BP 6178, Casablanca, or BP 888, Marrakesh.

The comfortable *Hôtel L'Angour – Chez Ju Ju* (☎ 319005; fax 319006) charges Dr250 per person for rooms with full board during the ski season. Cheaper dormitory accommodation is also available. The hotel has a bar and the restaurant has received rave reviews from several travellers.

There are several other hotels here which are only open during the winter. There are no shops in Oukaïmeden so bring any provisions you require with you.

In Setti Fatma, the best place to stay is the *Hôtel Tafoukt* which has rooms with shower and toilet for Dr90/127. There are a handful of basic cafe/restaurants which rent out rooms for about Dr40/60.

Getting There & Away Out of season there is little or no transport to Oukaïmeden from Marrakesh, although you should be able to arrange a grand taxi, for a price.

Otherwise you could take a bus or grand taxi as far as Aghbalou (there are basic rooms to rent here) and try hitching up the mountain. Buses to Setti Fatma from Bab er-Rob in Marrakesh cost Dr10.

To the Tizi n'Test

Ouirgane Ouirgane is a pretty spot about 15km south of Asni (see the High Atlas Trekking section below), and it makes an attractive place to stop for a night or two if you're in no particular hurry.

The cheapest place to stay is the French-run *Au Sanglier Qui Fume* (☎ 117447) where double rooms cost Dr226. It has a swimming pool and the rooms are heated in

THE HIGH ATLAS

winter. You can camp in the grounds for Dr20 a person.

A little further back along the road to Marrakesh is the beautiful and expensive *Résidence de la Roseraie* (☎ 432094; fax 432095 in Marrakesh), where you're looking at Dr500 a person. It has a pool and hammam, and can organise (expensive) horse rides. The hotel also organises a shuttle to and from Marrakesh for guests.

Tin Mal Mosque Heading south to Tin Mal, along the pretty Oued Nfiss and just past a couple of **kasbahs** (you can't miss the one on the left, perched up on a rocky outcrop), travellers with their own transport should take the time to stop at one of only two mosques in Morocco which non-Muslims can enter.

Built in 1156 by the Almohads in honour of Mohammed ibn Tumart, the dynasty's 'founding father' and spiritual inspiration, it is now in the process of restoration. Work is expected to continue until the end of the century.

The building, all a soft rose-coloured pink, contains some beautifully decorated archways. From the outside it looks inviolate, inside the immense doors it has a feeling of great tranquillity and openness.

On Friday the mosque is used for prayer, but on other days the guardian will be happy to show you around (a tip is expected). If you climb up to the minaret you may also be lucky enough to see the resident owl who sleeps in the rafters.

An excellent five or six day trek takes you through the Agoundis Valley from Imlil to Tin Mal (see the High Atlas Trekking section below).

Tizi n'Test Over the next 30km, the road winds its way rapidly up to the pass known as Tizi n'Test – at 2092m, one of the highest in the country.

The views are breathtaking from numerous points along the way, but if you are driving, note that heavy cloud and mist often cuts vision to near zero at the top of the pass and during the descent on the Taroudannt side. In winter it is quite possible that you'll find the road blocked by snow, so be prepared.

If you're going the other way, local buses leave Taroudannt to Marrakesh at 5 am. The road from Taroudannt heads straight on to Agadir on the coast.

High Atlas Trekking

The highest peaks of the High Atlas lie within the Jebel Toubkal (4167m) region, North Africa's highest mountain. Roughly bounded by the Tizi n'Test to the west and the Tizi n'Tichka to the east, this area is by far the most popular trekking destination in Morocco.

The High Atlas range is characterised by jagged peaks and steep-sided valleys, with flat-topped Berber villages and cultivated

This ceremonial headdress, the *serdal*, is a woollen band decorated with coral and coins.

green stepped terraces scattered throughout. The traditional culture of the Berbers remains little changed after centuries.

There are village *gîtes* and refuge huts established in this region and more than 60 official mountain guides who know the area extremely well. A large network of well maintained mule trails wend their way over high passes and dramatic valleys, linking village to village.

There are walks here to suit all abilities – you can set off with mules, porters and cooks for weeks at a time or base yourself in the one of the bigger villages and explore from there.

Many travellers return home warmed and heartened by the hospitality of the Berber people. As the number of visitors increases, so of course does the pressure on the inhabitants.

To maintain the goodwill that is so openly given, it is worth bearing in the mind that the mountain economy is one of basic subsistence farming.

In outlying villages there may be little in the way of surplus food – be generous when buying provisions for yourself, guides and so on.

Always obtain permission to camp if anywhere near a village. Dress modestly (see the Society & Conduct section in the Facts About the Country chapter) – this is extremely important; it may not be obvious, but locals can be terribly offended by what they perceive to be a lack of respect.

When staying in village accommodation be prepared to pay the same rates as in refuges and basic hotels. Take some time to learn a few basic Berber words. Above all, don't be in a hurry to do anything.

It is possible to trek in the Toubkal region year round, but the best time to visit is probably late spring, between April and May. The bulk of the snow will have melted (Jebel Toubkal itself is usually under snow from November until mid-June), spring flowers will be in bloom and the days will be pleasantly warm.

You'll still need a good sleeping bag and warm clothes as the nights will be chilly. In mid-summer, temperatures in the higher areas never become stifling, but it can be unbearably hot in the lower valleys.

By autumn, temperatures are substantially cooler with snow falling on the higher peaks by the end of September.

Late winter can be an excellent time to visit, if you don't mind night time temperatures dropping to well below freezing (-20°C on a bad night). The days are surprisingly warm, the skies generally clear and the valleys extremely quiet and peaceful at this time of year.

Jebel Toubkal is an easy two day trek and provided there's no snow around you don't need mountaineering skills to get to the top.

Winter conditions, however, can be treacherous (there have been several fatalities on the mountain) and at this time inexperienced climbers are advised to trek below the snow line.

Anyone attempting the ascent after snow has fallen should have some winter climbing experience. You won't get to the summit unless you have full alpine gear – and that means ice axes, crampons, wet weather clothing and a very warm sleeping bag.

Altitude sickness, caused by lack of oxygen, is a possibility at heights above 3000m. Symptoms can include headaches, nausea, dizziness, a dry cough and insomnia. Symptoms usually abate as you acclimatise, but if they persist or worsen you must descend immediately (see the Health section in the Facts for the Visitor chapter for more information).

The usual starting point for Jebel Toubkal and many of the other treks in the area is the village of Imlil in the Mizane Valley, 17km south of Asni.

Other possible starting points are the villages of Setti Fatma and Oukaïmeden in the Ourika Valley.

Information

Guides You don't need a guide if you just want to whiz up Toubkal and back, but if you're going further afield or for a longer

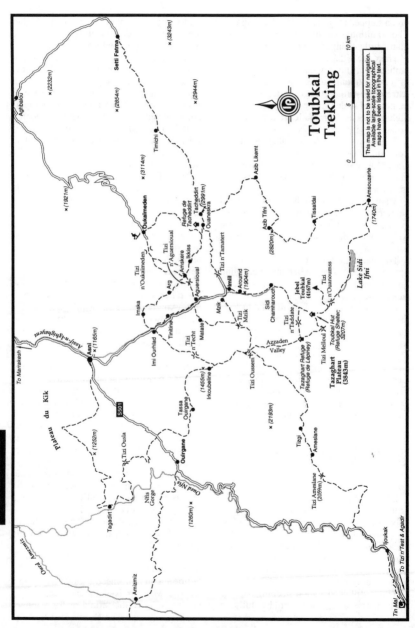

Toubkal Trekking

This map is not to be used for navigation. Available large-scale topographical maps have been listed in the text.

0   5   10 km

period, then you're going to want to engage one and possibly also a mule to cart your gear. Imlil is by far the best place to do this. There is a small Bureau des Guides et Accompagnateurs in the village which has a list of official guides and even mugshots for on the wall. Some of the official guides specialise in canyoning, climbing or ski-trekking. The latter, known to French trekkers as *ski-mulet*, involves a combination of walking with mules to carry your equipment and then skiing downhill or on cross-country runs. All guides speak French and a few speak a little English.

It is important, especially in times of uncertain weather, to have an official guide with you rather than any old local who can probably lead you up the path, but won't have a clue how to deal with any difficult situation, let alone an emergency.

More than 60 official guides are based in the Toubkal area and all carry cards to prove their training. Have a good look at the cards, and check any potential guide's credentials with the Bureau des Guides et Accompagnateurs.

Experienced guides based in Imlil include Brahim Toudaoui, who speaks English and French (contacted by post at BP 37, Asni, Région de Marrakesh); Mohammed Aït Idir (BP 26, Asni, Région de Marrakesh); Brahim Aït Talaoul (BP 38, Asni, Région de Marrakesh); Brahim Aziam, who runs the Café Soleil in Imlil; and Mohammed Bouredda, whose village home is a 15 minute walk west of Imlil, on the route to Tizi Oussem.

All these guides (and many others) can also be contacted through the Hôtel Ali in Marrakesh (☎ 444979; fax 433609). Those starting off from the Ourika Valley could ask for Lahcen Izahan at the Café Azagya, about 2km before the village of Setti Fatma, who also knows the Atlas like his pockets.

Costs Check the current rates for mountain escorts, porters and so on published in the Moroccan Tourist Office booklet described below. At the time of writing, the rate for official guides was Dr160 a day and Dr200

for specialist guides (skiing or rock-climbing, for example).

A mule (which can carry the loads of up to four people) and muleteer cost around Dr80 a day, and porters from Dr50 to Dr70 a day, depending on the season and the difficulty of the terrain. A cook would want Dr70 a day.

These rates apply to a normal working day and don't include food and accommodation expenses. You can hire crampons and ice-axes in Imlil for about Dr50 per day.

Guidebooks & Maps An extremely useful booklet *The Great Trek through the Moroccan Atlas* is published by the Moroccan Tourist Office every year.

Available in several languages, it includes a list of guides for various regions in the Atlas (including Toubkal); lists of *gîtes*, huts, refuges and the like and the names of their owners; a table of official prices for guides, mules, muleteers and porters; and a list of village market days. Recommended maximum fares on some of the public transport routes also appear.

This booklet is not easy to obtain in Imlil or elsewhere in the mountains. Ideally, you should grab a copy in Marrakesh or any main tourist office in Morocco or abroad.

Another useful tool to have, and equally scarce in Imlil, is a decent map. There is a mapping division in Rabat that publishes topographical maps on a scale of 1:100,000 and 1:50,000. The Jebel Toubkal area map, on a scale of 1:50,000, is useful; a set of four maps covering a wider area on a scale of 1:100,000 is also available. They can be purchased in Rabat for Dr80 a sheet (see the Rabat Information section in the North Atlantic Coast chapter for details). Toubkal maps are occasionally available in Imlil.

Those intending to do more than the two day Toubkal trek would be advised to buy the guide *Great Atlas Traverse – Morocco* by Michel Peyron. Volume one (Moussa Gorges to Aït ben Wgemmez) covers the Toubkal area as well as the Western High Atlas.

Karl Smith's *The Atlas Mountains – A Walker's Guide* contains good sections on the Toubkal region, Jebel M'Goun and Jebel Sarhro.

Another excellent guide, in French, is *Le Haut Atlas Central* by André Fougerolles. This is intended for serious alpinists, not trekkers, and is occasionally available in bookshops on Ave Mohammed V in Marrakesh, as well as in Rabat and Casablanca.

Organised Treks

If you'd prefer to join an organised trek into the High Atlas – for walking, biking or bird-watching – your best bet in Morocco is Marrakesh (see that section for a list of tour operators).

Outside the country, there are a surprising number of adventure travel companies offering some excellent trekking itineraries in the High Atlas (as well as the other mountain ranges and the sub-Sahara). Trips generally range from five to 15 days and are often very reasonably priced. See Organised Tours in the Getting There & Away chapter for suggested operators in Europe.

Getting to Asni & Imlil

There are frequent buses to Asni from Marrakesh which leave from the Bab er-Rob when full. They take two hours and cost Dr10. Alternatively, you can take a shared taxi to Asni from the same place. These cost Dr13 per person and take about one hour. From Asni there are fairly frequent trucks to Imlil and you can easily get a lift with them for around Dr15. The journey takes about an hour and the road is fairly rough for much of the way.

There are also taxis from Asni to Imlil, but you'll have to negotiate a price, as they could be stuck up there for hours waiting for a return fare.

ASNI

The roadside village of Asni is only really worth a stop if you're around for the large Saturday souq (don't miss the barbers with their fold-away salons) or in need of a hammam after a long dusty trek.

The large numbers of tourists and travellers of all types coming through here over the years have turned it into a minor den of iniquity.

Stay overnight if you must, but don't organise anything that even sounds like a trek. It may have been OK once, but there are now some very cheeky people ripping serious amounts of money off innocent travellers.

If you want to stay the night at Asni there is a *youth hostel* at the far end of the village, which has clean beds for Dr20 a night. You'll need your own sleeping bag.

The only other place to stay is the *Grand Hôtel du Toubkal* (☎/fax 319203), a pleasant three-star hotel with singles, doubles, and triples for Dr169, Dr208 and Dr282 respectively, plus taxes. The hotel has its own bar, restaurant, swimming pool and guarded parking.

There are several roadside *cafes* outside the entrance to the market, which serve cheap Moroccan dishes.

Buses and taxis leave here for Bab er-Rob in Marrakesh. You can also pick up the odd bus heading the other way to Ouirgane and Ijoukak.

IMLIL

Most trekkers give Asni a miss and stay in this fairly relaxed and attractive Berber village for the first night.

The area is best known for its walnut trees, but in recent times there has been some diversification, with apples, cherries and other trees being more systematically planted as well.

At the time of writing, the village was eagerly awaiting the arrival of electricity and telephone lines. There are no banks in Imlil or Asni.

The heavy rain that caused extensive damage and flooding in the Ourika Valley in August 1995, killing several hundred people, also affected Imlil – two people were killed and several cars and the Café Soleil were washed away when water came torrenting down into the Mizane River from the mountains.

Hollywood in the High Atlas

The acclaimed film director Martin Scorsese recently decided that the snow-capped peaks of the High Atlas looked sufficiently Himalayan to choose the tiny Berber village of Imlil as one of the locations for his movie about the Dalai Lama and his flight from Tibet (other scenes were filmed in Ouarzazate).

So, for a few days in 1996 the village of Imlil became a remote outpost in the Himalayas. The locals had never seen anything like it. The kasbah on the hill was transformed into a Tibetan temple and a border post (confusing trekkers no end) appeared along the road to Asni.

Dozens of trucks rumbled up the main street just after first light. Almost everyone in the village was to be employed in some way or another – even the village mules had jobs to do. By mid-morning the village square was crammed and mingling in the main street were locals in their pointy hooded jellabas, crimson-robed Tibetan monks, soldiers with rifles slung over their shoulders and jade earrings dangling from their ears, Italian wardrobe mistresses laden with great piles of heavy winter costumes, puzzled tourists, peak-capped American film crew mumbling into walkie-talkies, a dozen or more magnificent French horses and somewhere in among them all, Scorsese himself.

By the end of the day's filming it was difficult to distinguish who was who – actor-monks sat sipping mint tea with locals while villagers rode about with shaved heads, their robes flying. The Dalai Lama would have beamed with delight. ■

In 1996, Imlil was the scene of more positive excitement when Martin Scorcese turned up with a massive film crew to shoot scenes for his movie about the life of the Dalai Lama.

The snow-covered High Atlas doubled as Himalayan peaks and the kasbah on the hill north of the village was made to look like a Tibetan Buddhist temple. The India-Tibet border was halfway down the Imlil road.

Places to Stay

A good place to stay is the *Club Alpin Français (CAF) Refuge* right on the village square. It offers dormitory-style accommodation for Dr20 (members), Dr30 (HI members) and Dr40 (non-members). It also has a common room with an open fireplace, cooking facilities (Dr5 for use of gas), cutlery and crockery. It's possible to pitch a tent here, too.

Bookings for refuges (huts) further up can no longer be made from here, but instead must go through the CAF (☎ 270090; fax 297292), BP 6178, Casablanca 01, or through CAF, BP 888, Marrakesh. This could be awkward in summer without lots

of forward planning, so you might have to be prepared to sleep out. However, guides and local people are often more than willing to put you up for about what you would pay in the refuges.

The Oukaïmeden, Toubkal and Tazaghart (Lépiney) refuges cost Dr26 (CAF members), Dr39 (HI members) and Dr52 (non-members). Prices at the Tacheddirt refuge are the same as the Imlil refuge. You need your own bedding.

Back in Imlil, there are several other accommodation options. The best deal is the *Hôtel L'Aine*, which charges Dr30 per person in quite comfortable and bright rooms. It's the first place you pass on your right as you enter the village, and has a pleasant tearoom stacked with all sorts of ancient books. Some of the rooms are set around a small garden, and you can sit up on the roof for some private sunbathing. There is a hot shared shower and basic meals are available.

Near the Hôtel L'Aine, the *Café Tafraout* (☎ 390653 in Marrakesh) has rooms with shared hot shower for Dr30/60. They also have a small, basically equipped house to rent which costs Dr400 for up to 10 people. The *Café Aksoual*, on the main street virtually opposite the CAF, has fairly basic rooms for Dr25. The showers are cold.

On the little square is the *Café Soleil* (☎ 319209 in Asni), now rebuilt after being washed away in the floods of August 1995. Pleasant basic rooms with shower and small balcony cost Dr40/70. One room that sleeps four costs Dr25 per person. There's a terrace downstairs and a good restaurant where you can eat well for about Dr30.

A little further up the main street is the *Hôtel Étoile du Toubkal* (☎ 435663; fax 435682) which has clean but still fairly basic rooms for Dr110 to Dr300 (Dr20 less in the low season). There are hot showers. They can change money and have a restaurant offering a set menu for Dr70 and main courses of Moroccan fare for Dr40 to Dr50.

A 30 minute walk south of Imlil is the village of **Aroumd**, which is surrounded by extensive orchards and terraced fields. Accommodation options here include village rooms and the French-run *Atlas Gîte* (☎ 449105 in Marrakesh) where double rooms with bathroom cost around Dr60 per person. The French cooking here is said to be excellent.

Discovery Ltd, a small UK company which specialises in walking, biking, birdwatching and school field-studies trips, has restored the kasbah which overlooks Imlil and the valley. The kasbah has simple but comfortable rooms with shared hot shower starting at around Dr50 per person.

For information and bookings contact Thami at the Hôtel Foucauld in Marrakesh (☎ 445499; fax 441344). It may be possible to camp upstream from Aroumd, but you must ask permission first. Many local people in Imlil and the surrounding villages will be happy to put you up in their homes, but set prices in advance to avoid misunderstandings afterwards.

Places to Eat

Apart from the hotels and cafes already mentioned (they all do food and in the mountain air it all tastes fantastic) there are a couple of hole-in-the-wall places along the main street of the village where you can order tajines, salads, omelettes and so on. Wherever you go to eat, it's best to order your meals a couple of hours in advance.

There's also a bakery in the village and quite a few small grocery shops well stocked with basic goods such as dried fruit, nuts, olive oil, instant coffee, tins of sardines, processed cheese, powdered milk and biscuits. You can buy cigarettes in the village, but not alcohol.

You'll need to carry food with you when trekking, so you can either stock up here, or in Marrakesh where provisions will be cheaper and more plentiful. You may be able to buy bread, eggs and vegetables in villages further afield, but don't count on it. Water taken out of mountainside streams should be treated with purification tablets.

THE TOUBKAL TREK

Most people leave Imlil early in the morning for the five or six hour walk to the Toubkal (Neltner) Hut. Head up the main street of the village and then follow the mule track on the west side of the Mizane River to Aroumd. From here the trail follows the east side of the river, reaching the village of **Sidi Chamharouch** a couple of hours further on. Bottled drinks are usually available at both these villages.

The trail then climbs steeply and clearly up to the **Toubkal Hut** (3207m), which sits at the spring snow line. The stone cottage was built in 1938 and has beds for 29 people in two dormitories (you need your own sleeping bag). There's also a kitchen with a gas stove and a range of cooking utensils; hot water is available.

The charge is Dr52 per person for non-CAF members, plus an extra charge if you use the cooking facilities or need hot water. The resident warden will let you in. You must bring all your own food with you, as there's none for sale. The warden may, if you give him plenty of notice, prepare meals for you. Don't turn up at this hut without a booking in the high season or you may find it full (one reader also suggested bringing ear plugs). There are plans to build a second refuge near by.

The ascent from the Toubkal Hut to the summit (up a lot of exhausting scree slopes) should take between three and four hours and the descent about two hours. The South Cirque route is the most straightforward one and starts just behind the refuge. It's worth setting off as early as possible to gain the best chance of clear views from the top.

It's best to take water with you. Any water from mountain streams should be treated with purification tablets or there's a fair chance you'll pick up giardiasis. It can be bitterly cold on the summit, even in summer, so bring plenty of warm clothing.

OTHER TREKS

The following suggestions cover just some of the possibilities for longer treks in the area. You are advised to hire a guide and mules for all of them. Some routes have been suggested by an old hand in the High Atlas, Rick Crust, and others by guides based in the Imlil area. The first three routes are only really feasible in the spring.

Toubkal via Tazaghart

To do a longer circuit (four to five days) that gives you the option of taking in Toubkal, you could head south-west from Imlil over the **Tizi Mzik** to the village of **Tizi Oussem** (five hours) where there are two very welcoming village gîtes.

The following day, a harder trek takes you up the Azzaden Valley to the **Taza-ghart (Lépiney) Refuge**. There's good rock climbing (for the experienced only) around Tazaghart and climbers often base themselves at the refuge.

Options for the next day include scrambling up to **Tizi Melloul** (about four hours from the refuge) and then on to the vast and desolate **Tazaghart Plateau** (3843m). Be sure to leave early in the day so you can get back to the Tazaghart Refuge before dark. You will need a guide for this.

From the Tazaghart Refuge, you could also head east to the Toubkal refuge via the **Tizi n'Taddate** – this is hard going, but

worth it. Again, a guide is essential. The track is too steep for mules, but they can be sent back the long way round via Imlil and will probably arrive at about the same time. The following day you could climb Toubkal itself and return to Imlil via Sidi Chamharouch and Aroumd.

Oukaïmeden to Setti Fatma

This option (three or four days) starts from the ski resort of Oukaïmeden (see the Ourika Valley entry in the Around Marrakesh section). There are no mules to be hired here, but if you contact the CAF refuge or Hôtel L'Angour-Chez Ju Ju from Marrakesh a few days in advance you can arrange to have mules waiting for you.

You will need to bring all your own supplies with you from Marrakesh as there are no food shops at Oukaïmeden.

The first day is an easy walk (about four hours) down to **Tacheddirt**. There's a good CAF refuge here with panoramic views where you can stay for Dr40 plus Dr5 if you want to use the gas for cooking. The warden is helpful and can supply bread and eggs. It's a beautiful place and very relaxing (there are many other options from here, such as trekking down to Asni or Imlil and from there on to Toubkal).

The beautiful route from Tacheddirt to **Setti Fatma** follows a well-used mule track the entire way and offers some stunning views. The second day's walk takes you up to 3616m then down to the village of **Timichi** where there's a gîte. The third day involves a breathtaking descent down the **Ourika Valley** to Setti Fatma.

There are several accommodation options in the village and an important moussem takes place here in August. You can head back to Marrakesh from here by grand taxi (Dr15).

Eight Days from Imlil

Local guides can suggest several routes that could keep you going for eight days or more. You'll need plenty of provisions and camping gear.

One such route would take you in the

THE HIGH ATLAS

first two days to the Toubkal summit. On returning to the refuge you then push south-east over **Tizi n'Ouanoumss** to **Lake Sidi Ifni**, one of the largest lakes in the Atlas.

The third day would see you heading on eastwards to the village of **Amsouzerte**. There are village rooms and a camp site here. From Amsouzerte, a demanding two day hike northwards would get you to the Tacheddirt CAF refuge. You can camp the intervening night at **Azib Likemt**.

You have a few options from Tacheddirt. One of them is to head north to Oukaïmeden. A couple of tracks and passes lead you from there to the south-west. On this circuit you would go via the **Tizi n'Oukaïmeden** down as far as the village of **Amskere**. From there you could easily finish off the walk on the eighth day by heading to Imlil either via **Ikkiss** and the **Tizi n'Tamatert**, or south-west to the main Imlil-Asni road over the **Tizi n'Aguersioual**.

If you wanted to prolong the walk by a few days, you could either proceed from **Aguersioual** to **Matate** (there are village rooms here) and drop south to the Tizi Mzik and on to Tizi Oussem, or do the same from Imlil. From Tizi Oussem you could turn north for **Irkoubeline**. On the final day you could retrace your steps to Imlil, or proceed to **Tinitine** (Imlil-Asni road) via the **Tizi n'Techt** and then down to Imlil.

Winter Walks

The following three treks (ranging from three to six days, or longer if you have time) have been recommended by local guides as good winter possibilities. As with the other suggestions, you'll need a guide and a mule to carry supplies (and plenty of woollies). The first is a three day loop from Imlil.

On the first day you climb east for three or four hours, spending the night either in the pleasant Tacheddirt Refuge or in the nearby village of **Ouansekra**.

The following day is spent walking north-west along a river valley dotted with tiny villages. The night is spent in village homes in either **Arg** or **Imska**. The next day takes you on a long trek south-west to Tizi Oussem, where there's a comfortable gîte. In the morning you can head back to Imlil via the Tizi Mzik (about five hours).

The next option is a five or six day trek from Asni or Imlil to Tin Mal. If you plan continue to Taroudannt from here, it's ideal.

The starting place, **Imi Ourhlad**, is about halfway between Asni and Imlil, just to the west of the main road. The route takes you south-west through the pretty **Agoundis Valley** via the villages of **Tiziane**, **Tizgi** and **Ameslane**. Tizi Ameslane is probably the highest point of the walk at 2059m. From here you wend your way down the valley to **Ijoukak** on the Tizi n'Test road. You'll find some grocery shops, basic cafes, rooms to rent and a hammam here. Market day in Ijoukak is Wednesday.

From Ijoukak you're within striking distance (8km south-west) of the beautiful **Tin Mal Mosque**. Local buses stop at Ijoukak en route between Taroudannt and Marrakesh – check the times with the locals.

A third short winter walk, which covers a good range of terrain, takes you from Imlil to Tizi Oussem and then further west towards the **Ouigane Valley** and the **Nfis gorges**. Three or four days of fairly easy walking will take you to the seldom-visited **Plateau du Kik** via **Tassa Ouirgane**, Tizi Ousla and the village of **Tagadirt**. From the plateau, you can return to Asni.

Berber chessboard symbol
Believed to point the way to celestial existence.

Central Morocco

The central region of Morocco has to be one of the most exciting and romantic destinations in the entire country. Once over the High Atlas, you're into the sub-Sahara, a vast, open landscape shot through with the rich river valleys of the Drâa, Dadès and Ziz.

Crowded with palmeraies and overlooked by imposing red-earth kasbahs and immense desert skies, these valleys were the caravan routes which linked Morocco with the riches of the Sahara proper.

Apart from exploring the river valleys, there's good walking and climbing to be had in the stunning ochre-coloured Dadès and Todra gorges, and serious trekking possibilities among the jagged blue-black peaks of the Jebel Sarhro. In the far southeast, the alluring Saharan sand dunes of Merzouga are not to be missed.

If you had to choose one area in which to hire a car in Morocco, this may well be it, as much of the beauty of the region is on the road. Spring and autumn are the best times to explore the area. Midsummer will have you snapping off at the socks with the heat.

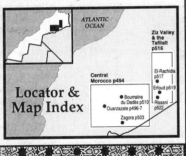

HIGHLIGHTS

Merzouga – a spectacular landscape of Saharan sand dunes

Dadès Gorge – stunning, ochre-coloured cliffs cutting into the High Atlas

Drâa Valley – 100 km of palm-filled oases and red earthen kasbahs

Jebel Sarhro – blue-black volcanic mountains for rugged trekking

The Tafilalt – oases, ruins and the historic head of the great caravan routes

ATLANTIC OCEAN

Ziz Valley & the Tafilalt p516

Central Morocco p494

El-Rachidia p517

Erfoud p519

Boumalne du Dadès p510

Rissani p522

Ouarzazate p496-7

Zagora p503

Locator & Map Index

Marrakesh to Ouarzazate

About 50km south-east of Marrakesh, the P31 to Ouarzazate crosses the Oued Zat (Le Coq Hardi, a hotel/restaurant of long standing, sits by the bridge) and soon after begins to climb towards the village of Taddert. Around here you'll see oak trees, walnut groves and oleander bushes.

After Taddert, the road quickly climbs and the landscape is stripped of its green mantle. The Tizi n'Tichka pass is higher than the Tizi n'Test to the west, but probably less spectacular. (Don't be surprised to be confronted by local boys urgently wav-

ing pieces of amethyst and other semi-precious minerals at you as you round the hairpin bends.) Once over the pass, however, a remarkable scene is unveiled: the lunar landscape of the Anti-Atlas and the desert beyond, obliterating memories of the dense woods and green fields behind you.

'Slowness comes from God and haste from the Devil'.
Moroccan Proverb

TELOUET
A recommended turn-off (if you have a car) is to the village of Telouet (you'll see the turn-off to the left a few kilometres after crossing the pass), 21km east off the highway. Watch out in winter, as the narrow road can be snowbound.

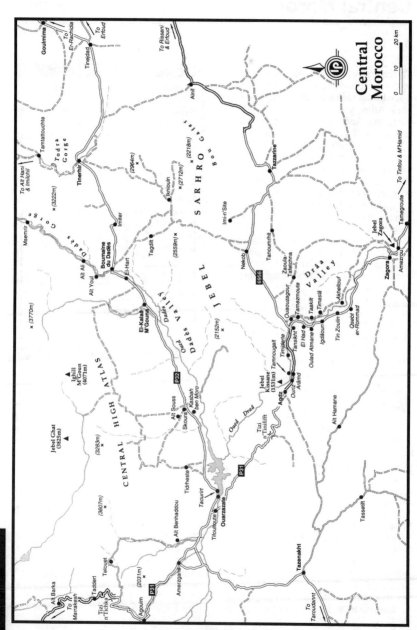

Central Morocco

The village is a lively little place and the drive itself is worth the effort. Telouet is dominated by a kasbah that once served as a palatial residence and headquarters of the powerful Glaoui tribe.

Until Morocco gained independence in 1956, the Glaouis were virtually given a free hand in central Morocco by the French administration, in return for support for the protectorate.

There is a small hotel here. Without your own transport, Telouet can be a little difficult to get to, as the closest major town is Ouarzazate.

Getting a bus or grand taxi to drop you at the turn-off is easy enough, after which you would have little choice but to stick out your thumb for the last 21km.

Those with a sturdy vehicle (or a couple of days to spare on foot or mountain bike) could follow the piste south from Telouet to Aït Benhaddou (see the Around Ouarzazate section later in this section) and back to the P31.

OUARZAZATE

Ouarzazate (pronounced War-zazat) was created by the French in 1928 as a garrison and regional administrative centre.

Before that, all there was around here was the Glaoui kasbah of Taourirt at the eastern end of the modern town on the road to Tinerhir.

It's something of a boom town and has a population of 30,000, but except for the kasbah it's a pretty quiet and nondescript place. Nevertheless, the Moroccans have been hard at work promoting Ouarzazate as a big destination, or at least as a launching pad for excursions along the Drâa and Dadès valleys.

Sparkling new luxury hotels continue to spring up, and regualr flights from Paris and Casablanca keep them at least half full.

Ouarzazate's biggest drawcards are outside the town, particularly the kasbah of Aït Benhaddou, off the Marrakesh road. It has long been a popular location for film-makers, and is well worth a visit.

Most travellers spend the night in Ouarzazate en route to or from Zagora in the Drâa Valley or the Todra and Dadès gorges.

If you're here in winter make sure you have plenty of warm clothes. Bitterly cold winds whip down off the snow-covered High Atlas Mountains, and can do so well into spring.

Information

Tourist Office The helpful Délégation Régionale du Tourisme (☎ 882485; fax 885290) is in the centre of town on Blvd Mohammed V, opposite the post office.

It's open Monday to Thursday from 8.15 to 11.30 am and 2.15 to 4.30 pm, and on Friday from 8.15 to 11.15 am and 2.45 to 4.45 pm. In summer and during Ramadan weekday hours are 8 am to 3 pm.

Money There are at least four banks in town. The main Banque Populaire on Blvd Mohammed V (just west of the post office) is open Monday to Friday during standard hours and on Saturday from 3 to 6 pm and on Sunday from 9 am to 1 pm.

For credit-card cash advances, go to the very efficient Crédit du Maroc at the western end of town on Blvd Mohammed V, on the corner of Ave Bir Anzaran. It's open during standard banking hours.

Post & Communications Both the post and phone offices, on Rue de la Poste, are open normal working hours.

There are a few card phones outside. There are plenty of téléboutiques around town with telephone and fax services.

Medical Services There is a hospital (☎ 882444) at the eastern end of Blvd Mohammed V.

Special Events

The *moussem* (pilgrimage) of Sidi Daoud is held in Ouarzazate in August.

Organised Tours

The big hotels organise pricey 4WD trips to destinations such as Telouet, Skoura, the Todra Gorge and Zagora.

Kasbah & Around

The only place worth visiting in Ouarzazate itself is the Taourirt Kasbah at the eastern end of town, off Blvd Mohammed V. During the 1930s, in the heyday of the Glaoui chiefs, this was one of the largest kasbahs in the area. It housed numerous members of the Glaoui dynasty, along with hundreds of their servants and workers. UNESCO has carefully restored sections of the building.

The 'palace' that the Glaouis occupied consists of courtyards, living quarters, reception rooms and the like, and is open from 8 am to noon and 3 to 6.30 pm seven days a week. Entry costs Dr10. You can take on a guide for extra if you want to know what each of the now empty rooms was used for.

There are some good views over the rest of the kasbah and the Oued Ouarzazate which, like the Oued Dadès, spills into the Al-Mansour ed-Dahabi dam to the immediate south, to become the Oued Drâa.

Opposite the entrance to the kasbah is another building in the same style, which houses the Ensemble Artisanal. Here you can find stone carvings, pottery and woollen carpets woven by the region's Ouzguita Berbers. It's open Monday to Friday from 8.30 am to noon and 1 to 6 pm, and on Saturday from 8.30 am to noon.

There are plenty of other craft shops around here too, but don't expect any bargains – Club Med is virtually next door and there are direct flights to Ouarzazate from Paris!

Places to Stay – bottom end

Camping You'll find a campground (signposted) next to the so-called Tourist Complex off the main road out of town towards Tinerhir, about 3km from the bus station.

There is some shade, and the camp site is right by Oued Ouarzazate. It also has a grocery store and restaurant. It costs Dr10 per person, Dr6 per car, Dr7 to pitch a tent and Dr10 for electricity.

Hotels There are effectively only half a dozen bottom-end hotels in Ouarzazate, so if you arrive late you may have to pay for something more expensive if they're all full (which does happen).

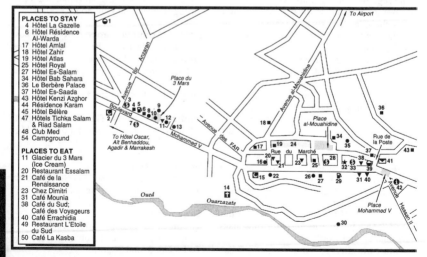

PLACES TO STAY
4   Hôtel La Gazelle
6   Hôtel Résidence
    Al-Warda
17 Hôtel Amlal
18 Hôtel Zahir
19 Hôtel Atlas
25 Hôtel Royal
27 Hôtel Es-Salam
34 Hôtel Bab Sahara
36 Le Berbère Palace
37 Hôtel Es-Saada
43 Hôtel Kenzi Azghor
44 Résidence Karam
45 Hôtel Bélère
47 Hôtels Tichka Salam
    & Riad Salam
48 Club Med
54 Campground

PLACES TO EAT
11 Glacier du 3 Mars
    (Ice Cream)
20 Restaurant Essalam
21 Café de la
    Renaissance
23 Chez Dimitri
31 Café Mounia
38 Café du Sud;
    Café des Voyageurs
40 Café Errachidia
49 Restaurant L'Etoile
    du Sud
50 Café La Kasba

To Airport
Place du 3 Mars
Place al-Mouahidine
Rue de la Poste
Rue du Marché
Place Mohammed V
To Hôtel Oscar, Aït Benhaddou, Agadir & Marrakesh
Oued Ouarzazate

CENTRAL MOROCCO

One of the cheapest places is the *Hôtel Royal* (☎ 882258) at 24 Blvd Mohammed V (entrance in the side street). Belkaziz, the owner, has all sorts of rooms for all sorts of prices. Small singles start at Dr36. Doubles without shower are Dr60 and those with private shower are Dr90. A quad made up of two adjoining rooms goes for Dr160. The beds are comfortable, the linen is super clean and the showers have hot water.

Across the road is the *Hôtel Es-Salam* (☎ 882512). The staff are friendly and the rooms fine. Singles without shower cost Dr40 and doubles are Dr70 (a shared shower costs Dr5). Those with shower cost Dr52/80. The hotel also offers basic cooking facilities.

Another decent cheapie is the *Hôtel Atlas* (☎ 882307) at 13 Rue du Marché. Clean singles cost Dr31, doubles Dr62 and triples Dr78 (all without shower), and Dr36/72/83 with private shower.

About 2km out of town on the Zagora road is an excellent deal – the *Hôtel La Vallée* (☎ 882668; fax 882810). It's right beside the road and is a friendly, buzzing place. There's a palmeraie just across the way.

Pleasant rooms with one big bed and a small bed (no singles) cost Dr120. There's even a TV in some rooms. The showers are shared and hot water is available. The hotel has a very good restaurant, too.

About 100m further on is the *Hôtel Saghro* on the right, but it's not as good or as well located as La Vallée.

There are three reasonably priced one-star hotels.

The *Hôtel Bab Sahara* (☎ 884722), on Place al-Mouahidine just near the water tower, has decent-sized, comfortable rooms. In the low season singles without shower cost Dr50, doubles Dr70 and triples Dr100. Rooms with shower cost Dr70/120/150.

The *Hôtel Amlal* (☎ 884030; fax 884600), a block in from Blvd Mohammed V, has clean, comfortable rooms with en suite bathroom (hot water in the evening) and wardrobe, and there is guarded parking out the front. Prices are Dr108, Dr128, Dr170 and Dr215.

The *Hôtel Es-Saada* (☎ 883231) at 12 Rue de la Poste, also has rooms for Dr108, Dr128 and Dr170, but they are gloomy and could do with a paint job.

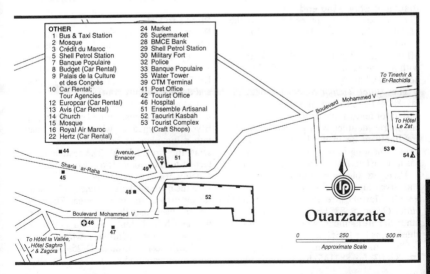

OTHER
1 Bus & Taxi Station
2 Mosque
3 Crédit du Maroc
5 Shell Petrol Station
7 Banque Populaire
8 Budget (Car Rental)
9 Palais de la Culture et des Congrès
10 Car Rental; Tour Agencies
12 Europcar (Car Rental)
13 Avis (Car Rental)
14 Church
15 Mosque
16 Royal Air Maroc
22 Hertz (Car Rental)
24 Market
26 Supermarket
28 BMCE Bank
29 Shell Petrol Station
30 Military Fort
32 Police
33 Banque Populaire
35 Water Tower
39 CTM Terminal
41 Post Office
42 Tourist Office
46 Hospital
51 Ensemble Artisanal
52 Taourirt Kasbah
53 Tourist Complex (Craft Shops)

To Tinerhir & Er-Rachidia

To Hôtel Le Zat

Ouarzazate

Boulevard Mohammed V

Avenue Ennacer

Sharia ar-Raha

Boulevard Mohammed V

To Hôtel la Vallée, Hôtel Saghro & Zagora

0   250   500 m
Approximate Scale

Places to Stay – middle

Before heading into the higher bracket of hotel options, there are three that cost moderately more than the one-star places.

Just by Place du 3 Mars on Blvd Mohammed V, the *Hôtel Résidence Al Warda* (☎ 882154) offers a potentially tempting deal. The rooms are basically mini-apartments with up to five beds, bathroom and kitchen. Hot water is promised, as are reductions on longer stays. The asking rates are Dr124.50/149 for singles/doubles.

The well-established *Hôtel La Gazelle* (☎ 882151; fax 884727), on Blvd Mohammed V, is very popular with tour groups, but seems to be living off a worn-out reputation. Singles with private bathroom cost Dr124 and doubles Dr152. The hotel has a restaurant and a basic bar, and cars can be parked safely in the front courtyard.

The *Hôtel Zahir* (☎ 885740), on Ave al-Mouahidine, north-west of the market, has spotlessly clean singles with private bathroom for Dr128 and doubles for Dr146. A suite for five people costs Dr50 per person. The hotel has a restaurant and there is a cafe/patisserie next door.

Places to Stay – top end

The cheapest of the top-end hotels is the *Hôtel Le Zat* (☎ 882521; fax 885394), a couple of kilometres out of the town centre off the road to Tinerhir. Comfortable rooms with private bathroom cost Dr225/275. The hotel has a kitsch 60s bar.

The *Hôtel Tichka Salam* (☎ 882206; fax 885680), on Blvd Mohammed V, was closed for renovation at the time of writing, but singles/doubles with private bathroom are likely to be in the Dr300/400 range. There's heating in the rooms and the hotel has its own bar, restaurant and tennis courts.

There are plenty of options in the four and five-star brackets. Just outside the town's Marrakesh exit is the fairly new *Hôtel Oscar* (☎ 882166; fax 882766), another Salam member, which has comfortable rooms for Dr360 a double.

Close to the kasbah, the *Hôtel Bélère* (☎ 882803; fax 883145) has similarly plush rooms for Dr424/545 plus taxes. The *Hôtel Kenzi Azghor* (☎ 886500), on Sharia ar-Raha, has singles/doubles for Dr450/550 plus taxes.

Heading up the line is the Salam chain's second representative here, the *Hôtel Riad* (☎ 883335; fax 882766), off Blvd Mohammed V.

The rooms are modern and the hotel boasts two restaurants (one of them is usually the stage for folkloric music performances and the like), a sauna and a tennis court. Singles cost Dr660, doubles Dr770 and triples Dr880, plus taxes.

Slightly more expensive again is the new *Le Berbère Palace* (☎ 883077; fax 883071), a rather sumptuous place with hammam, bar and boutiques. Singles/doubles are Dr700/850.

Apart from Club Med, that just leaves Pullman's *Résidence Karam* (☎ 882225; fax 882649), off Sharia ar-Raha, which offers apartments for four people from Dr500.

Swimming Pools

The Hôtel La Vallée and Hôtel La Gazelle have pools. All the top-end hotels have pools where a swim will cost around Dr50.

Places to Eat

Restaurants *Restaurant Essalam*, between Blvd Mohammed V and Rue du Marché, has a good selection of the old favourites. There are eight set-menu choices, all for Dr55. You get a salad, generous main meal and dessert (usually fruit).

Just as good, and cheaper, is the *Café de la Renaissance*, just around the corner on Blvd Mohammed V, where you can tuck into a big plate of brochettes, chips and salad for around Dr30. The restaurant attached to the *Hôtel Atlas* also serves reasonably priced basic meals.

In the evening there are cheap food stalls set up around the market area. There are several cheap and cheerful places to eat by the new bus station – a good one is the *Café/Restaurant Mimouza* where a full meal will cost as little as Dr25. There's a pool room here, too.

The restaurant at the *Hôtel La Vallée* is worth going to for well-prepared, moderately priced Moroccan dishes in pleasant surroundings. There's often music here as well. The restaurant at the *Hôtel Zahir* does a good homely couscous.

Chez Dimitri, on Blvd Mohammed next to the Hôtel Royal, once served as petrol station, general store, dance hall, telegraph office and just about everything else besides. The atmosphere is very relaxing and they have a good range of both Moroccan and French dishes. A full meal (with wine) will set you back about Dr170. The place is often packed to the hilt with tourists.

There are plenty of expensive restaurants to choose from in the bigger hotels.

Cafes & Patisseries There's a cluster of cafes around the middle of Ave Mohammed V. *Café La Kasba* is in a slightly better spot with a view of the Taourirt kasbah. You'll find a good patisserie next to the Hôtel Zahir, not far from the market, and an ice cream place on Place du 3 Mars.

Self-Catering You can pick up fresh local produce in the small *market* off Rue du Marché. The *supermarket* on Blvd Mohammed V carries an excellent range of goods including alcoholic drinks (beer and wine) and toiletries.

Getting There & Away

Air The airport is 1km north of town. Royal Air Maroc has an office (☎ 885102) on Blvd Mohammed V. There are flights to Casablanca (Dr557) at least five times weekly and direct flights to Paris (Dr3402) twice a week.

Bus The new bus terminal is about 1km north-west of the town centre. CTM has a terminal on Blvd Mohammed V, close to the post office. CTM has a bus to Zagora (Dr35; four hours) and on to M'Hamid (Dr52.50; seven hours) at 12.30 pm. A bus for Agadir (Dr86; seven hours) leaves at noon.

There are four departures for Marrakesh. Those at 8.30 am and 9 pm are 1st class services and cost Dr49. The others are 2nd class buses; they leave at 11 am and noon and cost Dr45. The trip takes about four hours. The 9 pm bus to Casablanca is a 1st class run and costs Dr120. At 10.30 am there's a bus to Er-Rachidia for Dr65.50. It goes via Boumalne du Dadès (Dr24.50) and Tinerhir and takes about nine hours.

SATAS and several other smaller bus lines all operate from the new bus terminal at Dour Ichams. SATAS has at least one departure a day to Marrakesh (Dr45) at 9 am, and to Agadir (Dr80), at 9 pm. The latter stops at Taroudannt on the way (Dr65). A bus leaves for Zagora and M'Hamid at about 6.30 am and another for Er-Rachidia at 8 pm.

The other lines between them have several runs to Agadir, Taroudannt and Zagora.

Taxi Grands taxis also leave from the bus terminal. A place in a taxi to Marrakesh costs Dr100. To Zagora the fare is Dr80. The fares to Agdz, Skoura and Tinerhir are Dr40, Dr25 and Dr60 respectively.

Car Since the Drâa Valley route down to Zagora and beyond to M'Hamid is such a spectacular and interesting journey, it's worth considering car rental before you leave Ouarzazate. With your own vehicle, you'll be able to stop wherever you like to explore the *ksour* (fortified strongholds) or take photographs.

In a bus or shared taxi you'll simply speed through all these places, catch only fleeting glimpses and probably arrive in Zagora feeling disappointed. It's far better to get a group together and hire a vehicle in Ouarzazate, as there are no car rental places in Zagora. Some of the agencies include:

Avis
  On the corner of Blvd Mohammed V and Rue A Sehraoui (☎ 884870)
Budget
  Résidence Al-Warda, Blvd Mohammed V (☎ 883565)
Europcar
  Bureau 4, Place du 3 Mars (☎ 882035)
Hertz
  33 Blvd Mohammed V (☎ 882084)

AROUND OUARZAZATE
Tifoultoute

About 7km north-west of Ouarzazate is another Glaoui kasbah, *Kasbah Tifoultoute* (☎ 884636), now converted into a hotel and restaurant, with evening performances of traditional dance and music.

The kasbah was first used as a hotel in the 1960s, when the cast of *Lawrence of Arabia* was put up here, and it has since become somewhat kitsch. Package-tour groups are ferried in here regularly for the dinner and show. Rooms cost around Dr150 for a double and the restaurant has set menus for Dr75 and Dr120.

To get there, take the road to Marrakesh and turn off at the sign for Tifoultoute. Without your own car, you'll need to negotiate for a taxi.

Aït Benhaddou

In the same direction, again off the road to Marrakesh and 32km from Ouarzazate, is the village of Aït Benhaddou. Here is one of the most exotic and best preserved kasbahs in the whole Atlas region. This is hardly surprising, since it has had money poured into it as a result of being used for scenes in as many as 20 films, notably *Lawrence of Arabia* and *Jesus of Nazareth*.

Much of the village was rebuilt for the filming of the latter. Its fame lives on, but the population has dwindled.

When you arrive, walk in off the road past the Auberge Al Baraka and you'll see the kasbah on the other side of the Ounila riverbed. Head down past the souvenir stalls and across the river, which is usually no more than a trickle with a ramp and stepping stones to cross, although it can flow more strongly in early spring. The main entrance to the kasbah complex is a little way upstream (you'll know you've found it when you see more souvenir stalls).

One of the locals may half-heartedly hassle you to engage him as a guide, but this is not really necessary. From the upper reaches of the kasbah there are magnificent views of the surrounding palmeraie and, beyond, the unforgiving *hammada* (stony desert).

Places to Stay & Eat There are three places to stay, and there is a lot to be said for doing so rather than bedding down in Ouarzazate.

The first you'll come across is the roadside *Auberge Al Baraka* (☎ 890305; fax 886273). It's the most basic of the three, but the rooms are clean and the staff very welcoming. Rooms cost Dr50/100. Only a couple of the rooms have showers.

The *Auberge El Ouidane* (☎ 890312) has better (but not spectacular) rooms for the same price. All the rooms have a shower. The views across to the kasbah from the adjoining restaurant and some of the rooms are wonderful.

Next door, the recently extended *Hôtel Restaurant La Kasbah* (☎ 890302; fax 883 787) has double rooms with demi-pension for Dr300. Meals are available in all three places.

Getting There & Away To get there, take the main road to Marrakesh and turn off after 22km when you see the signpost for the village; Aït Benhaddou is another 9km down a good bitumen road (stop at the signs for the hotels). Occasionally, local buses travel to Aït Benhaddou from Ouarzazate, but it's a lot easier to get there by sharing a taxi.

Otherwise, ask around among tourists in the restaurants or at Hôtel La Gazelle. Hitching is difficult.

Tamdaght

Five kilometres north-east of Aït Benhaddou, the road ends abruptly where it hits the river Ounila. On the other side it continues for awhile before turning into a poor piste leading north to Telouet (an increasingly popular 4WD, mountain-bike and hiking route).

About 1.5km north-east of where the river cuts the road stands yet another Glaoui kasbah, that of Tamdaght. It is not as spectacular as the Aït Benhaddou complex, but comparatively little visited. You can get sturdy vehicles with a high chassis over the stream, but don't try it if you are unsure;

leave your vehicle at the Café/Restaurant Defat La Kasbah and wade across.

If you're lucky, Larbi Embarak might be hanging around. He's quite a local character and will insist on giving you a piggyback across to keep your tootsies dry. He will also want to act as your guide and show you a tattered photo of himself as an extra for one of the several films which have been shot here. *The Man Who Would Be King*, with Sean Connery and Michael Caine, is one of them.

Drâa Valley

From Ouarzazate the P31 leads you southeast along the magical Drâa Valley, a long ribbon of technicoloured palmeraies, kasbahs and busy Berber villages. One of the longest rivers in Morocco, the Drâa originates in the High Atlas and wends its way through mountains and desert sands before finally reaching the Atlantic at Cap Drâa, just north of Tan Tan.

The fertile palmeraies that it feeds are crammed with date palms, olive and almond groves and citrus trees. The richest section of the valley lies between Agdz and Zagora, a stretch of about 95km. Beyond Zagora, a minor road takes you a further 96km south to the tiny village of M'Hamid, just 40km short of the Algerian border.

About 30km south of Agdz, a good, fully paved road now heads east all the way across to the oases of the Tafilalt (the last stop on the long caravan journeys which brought gold and slaves from West Africa) via the Jebel Sarhro mountain range and the small town of Tazzarine.

This means you can now do a loop from Ouarzazate south-east to the Tafilalt and then return west through the Dadès Valley (the 'road of a thousand kasbahs') and the Todra and Dadès gorges, or vice versa. To really do the trip justice (and take in the Drâa Valley), you'd need at least five days.

If you're travelling south from Ouarza-zate by car, beware of the false hitchhiker syndrome. A few less-than-honest Moroccans work the Ouarzazate-Zagora road looking for tourists to take home in 'gratitude' for the lift, only to start the hard-sell on carpets. Don't fall for the pretend car breakdown, either.

AGDZ

The road south from Ouarzazate only gets interesting as you cross the Tizi n'Tinififft pass, 20km north-west of the small administrative town of Agdz (pronounced Ag-a-dez).

There's not much to keep you here, although the palmeraie to the north and west of the town (hidden from view as you arrive), the nearby kasbahs and the weird-looking **Jebel Kissane** in the background warrant a wander. There are also several shops selling carpets, pottery and jewellery.

Ave Mohammed V, the main road, heads straight through the town to a square, Place de la Marche Verte, before heading off to the right and southwards towards Zagora.

Places to Stay & Eat

Camping Kasbah-Palmeraie (signposted) is located, as the name suggests, near a small kasbah.

There are two cheapies on Place de la Marche Verte. The *Hôtel Restaurant Draa* has big, simple rooms with double beds. Singles/doubles cost Dr35/70, and you may even get hot water in the shared showers. The *Hôtel des Palmeraies* is much the same.

The *Hôtel Kissane* (☎ 44 through the operator), at the Ouarzazate exit of town, offers more comfortable singles for Dr150, doubles for Dr230 and triples for Dr310 (a little less in the low season) plus taxes. The hotel has a cafe and restaurant.

There are a few simple *restaurants* on Place de la Marche Verte offering basic Moroccan dishes.

Getting There & Away

CTM, SATAS and several other buses stop here en route between Ouarzazate and Zagora. Sometimes you can get on, sometimes you can't. Otherwise, occasional grands taxis go to Ouarzazate and Zagora – Dr30 either way.

ZAGORA

Like Ouarzazate, Zagora is largely a fairly recent creation, dating from French colonial times, when it was set up as an administrative centre.

Nevertheless, the oasis has always been inhabited, and it was from this area that the Saadians began their conquest of Morocco in the 16th century. Moroccan rulers long before them passed through here too, and there are vestiges of an Almoravid fortress atop Jebel Zagora.

There are plenty of interesting places to explore in the vicinity and the town does have its moments, particularly when a dust storm blows up out of the desert in the late afternoon and the lighting becomes totally surreal. Zagora is also where you'll see that somewhat battered sign reading 'Tombouctou 52 jours' (by camel caravan).

Although little more than an oversized village (population about 15,000), Zagora has more than its fair share of expensive hotels and is a good place to rest up before heading onwards.

Information

There's a Banque Populaire about halfway along Blvd Mohammed V, the main street, which is open during normal banking hours. The post office is at the southern end of the street. There are phones here, too.

There's a twice weekly market, held on Wednesday and Sunday, where fruit (dates are the big commodity down here), vegetables, herbs, hardware, handicrafts, sheep, goats and donkeys are brought in to be sold.

Things to See & Do

The spectacular **Jebel Zagora**, which rises up across the other side of the river, is worth climbing for the views – if you have the stamina and you set off early in the morning.

FRANCES LINZEE GORDON

It's 52 days to Timbuktu by camel caravan from this famous sign just outside Zagora.

The beautiful, extensive **palmeraies** are within easy reach, and some close to the hotels and camp sites at the southern end of town.

If you are here over the period of Mouloud (check the Islamic calendar in the Facts for the Visitor chapter), you may well coincide with the moussem of Moulay Abdelkader, which brings the town to life.

It is possible to arrange **camel treks** of up to a week or so. Ask for Yassin Ali at the Hôtel La Fibule (☎ 847318). Prices start at about Dr200 per person per day.

PLACES TO STAY
1 Hôtel Riad Salam
10 Hôtel Tinsouline
11 Camping Sindibad
15 Hôtel des Amis
17 Hôtel Vallée du Drâa
27 Hôtel de la Palmeraie
30 Hôtel Club Reda
31 Hôtel Kasbah Asmaa
32 Hôtel La Fibule

PLACES TO EAT
2 Restaurant Toumour
4 Restaurant La Perle du Sahara
8 Café/Restaurant La Rose des Sables
14 Café Snak Ennahda
18 Bakery
20 Restaurant/Café Es Sahara
22 Restaurant Essaada
25 Restaurant Timbouctou

OTHER
3 Supermarket
5 Grands Taxis; Private Bus Lines
6 Newspaper Store; Films
7 Weekly Market
9 Maison Berbère
12 Petrol Station
13 Banque Populaire
16 Mosque
19 Bain En Nacer
21 Market
23 Barracks
24 Post Office
26 CTM Bus Terminal
28 Gendarmerie
29 Army Headquaters

Zagora

Approximate Scale
0   100   200 m

Places to Stay – bottom end
Camping Campers have a choice of three sites. About the most popular is *Camping d'Amezrou*, about 200m past the Hôtel La Fibule along the dirt track that runs alongside the irrigation channel. It costs Dr10 per person, Dr5 for a car, Dr5 to pitch a tent and Dr10 for electricity. Hot showers cost Dr5. The setting is attractive and close to the restaurants of Hôtel La Fibule and Hôtel Kasbah Asmaa.

Also over this side of town is *Camping de la Montagne*, at the foot of the mountain. You get to it by crossing the bridge over the irrigation channel immediately past La Fibule, and then following the signpost off to the left. It's about 1.5km down the dirt track from here. There are toilets and plenty of shade. Cold drinks are available, but you're advised to bring your own food. It costs Dr8 per person and the same for a car. Pitching a tent costs Dr4. Hot showers are free.

Camping Sindibad, off Ave Hassan II, is central and surrounded by palm trees. There are toilets, hot showers and a cafe. It costs Dr10 per person, Dr5 for a car, Dr10 to pitch a tent, Dr10 for electricity and Dr5 for a hot shower. There are also a couple of basic double rooms here for Dr50.

Hotels There are two unclassified hotels next to each other on Blvd Mohammed V. The better of the two, if you can get a front room, is *Hôtel Vallée du Drâa* (☎ 847210). Singles/doubles cost Dr46/65 with shared bathroom, Dr69/85 with private shower and Dr77/90 with private bathroom. It's clean and friendly and has its own restaurant.

Nearby, the *Hôtel des Amis* offers basic but adequate rooms for Dr20/50. There are shared showers.

Going up in price, there's the popular one-star *Hôtel de la Palmeraie* (☎ 847008; fax 847878), also on Blvd Mohammed V. The hotel has recently been extended and refurbished.

Singles/doubles without shower cost Dr35/70 and Dr85/120/165 with private bathroom. There's hot water in the showers.

If you have your own bedding they'll also let you sleep on the roof for Dr15.

The hotel has a lively if fly-blown bar, full of some very intriguing characters, and an excellent restaurant where you can get a three-course meal for about Dr70. Camel treks can also be arranged here.

Places to Stay – middle
It can be worth your while booking ahead in the high season for the following places, which are often full. On the other hand, you may well be able to get hefty reductions on room rates in the low season.

Two of the most relaxing places to stay in Zagora are both south of the town centre by the river and palmeraies. The *Hôtel Kasbah Asmaa* (☎ 847599; fax 847527) is a very pleasant, welcoming two-star hotel which has been built to resemble a Berber *ksar* (fortified stronghold). There is a lovely garden here, as well as an outdoor tea salon and a very good restaurant.

In the high season they don't distinguish between the price of single or double occupancy of the rooms, which cost Dr250. In the warmer months you can sleep in the nomad tents set up around the courtyard for Dr50.

Just 50m up the road is the very relaxing two-star *Hôtel La Fibule* (☎ 847318; fax 847271), which has its own shady garden, a bar and an excellent restaurant. The rooms have been built and furnished in the traditional Berber style, with the addition of showers (hot water in the morning and evening) and toilets. Doubles with shower cost Dr145 and with private shower Dr330. Both prices include breakfast.

Places to Stay – top end
The cheapest place to stay in this category is the *Hôtel Tinsouline* (☎ 847252) which has 90 rooms and its own bar and restaurant. Singles/doubles with private bathroom cost Dr250/300 plus taxes.

Next up is one of the more luxurious hotels in the Salam chain, the *Hôtel Riad* (☎ 847400; fax 847551). Rooms cost Dr485/545 plus taxes. The hotel has a pricey restaurant. The location by the Ouarzazate exit leaves a lot to be desired.

Top of the line is the cavernous *Hôtel Club Reda* (☎ 847079; fax 847012), set in the palmeraie next to the Oued Drâa. Singles/doubles with private bathroom cost a rather steep Dr660/770. The hotel has all the amenities you would expect, including bar, restaurant and tennis courts.

Swimming Pools
There are swimming pools in all the top-end hotels, as well as at the Hôtels de la Palmeraie, Kasbah Asmaa and La Fibule.

Hammams
There's a hammam, the *Bain En Nacer*, on Blvd Mohammed V, around the corner from the bakery.

Places to Eat
All the hotels have their own restaurants, and it's probably true to say that they all try hard to produce tasty Moroccan dishes. The *Hôtel des Amis* offers cheap meals from around Dr25. The *Hôtel Vallée du Drâa* has slightly more expensive fare. The *Hôtel de la Palmeraie* has a decent licensed restaurant with meals for around Dr70.

There are quite a few basic restaurants along Blvd Mohammed V, including the *Restaurant Essaada*, *Restaurant La Perle du Sahara* and the *Restaurant Timbouctou*. They're all popular places offering reasonably priced Moroccan meals.

The *Café Snak Ennahda*, across from the Hôtel des Amis, does excellent chicken and chips with a good fresh Moroccan salad. Another possibility is the *Café/Restaurant La Rose des Sables*, next to the Maison Berbère carpet and souvenir shop.

For excellent food in very pleasant surroundings, head to the restaurants at the *Hôtel Kasbah Asmaa* and *Hôtel La Fibule*. A three course meal with wine or beer will cost upwards of Dr100.

Cafes As usual there is no shortage of mint tea locations, but for atmosphere it has to be the hotels south of the river.

Getting There & Away

Buses and shared taxis will give you no chance to stop and take photographs of the many fascinating villages and ksour between Ouarzazate and Zagora, let alone give you time to explore them.

So, if there's any chance of car rental and the freedom this will give you, think seriously about it. You will have to organise this in Ouarzazate as there are no car rental agencies in Zagora.

Bus The CTM bus terminal is at the southwestern end of Blvd Mohammed V, and the main bus and grand taxi lot is at the northern end.

There's a CTM bus once daily to Ouarzazate at 7 am. This bus starts out at M'Hamid and comes past Hôtel La Fibule at about 6.30 am, so if you're staying there or at the nearby camp sites, you can flag it down right outside the door. The fare to Ouarzazate is Dr35, and the bus continues through to Marrakesh (Dr79).

The bus coming the other way leaves for M'Hamid at 4 pm (Dr18). There's also infrequent local buses to Rissani via Tazzarine.

Taxi If buses are scarce, a better bet might be a grand taxi. The best time to try is early in the morning. A place costs Dr80 to Ouarzazate, Dr30 to Agdz, Dr25 to M'Hamid, Dr40 to Tazzarine and Dr90 all the way across to Rissani.

SOUTH OF ZAGORA
Amezrou

Across the Oued Drâa, about 3km south of Zagora, is the village of Amezrou. It has an interesting old *mellah* (Jewish quarter of the medina), which still produces silver jewellery. Jews lived here for centuries and formerly controlled the silver trade, but they all took off for Israel after 1948, leaving the Berbers to carry on the tradition.

If you look like you might buy something, the locals will be willing to show you the whole process. Because the village is so close to Zagora, local children will leap on

you, offering to be guides, but it's fairly low-key hassle. Elsewhere in the palmeraie life goes on much as it always has. It's well worth spending a day wandering through the shady groves along the many tracks that dissect it.

The dates grown here are reputely the best in Morocco, but times have been getting harder because of Bayoud disease, a fungal disease that attacks and kills the palms.

Tamegroute

Further south, about 18km from Zagora, is Tamegroute. For many centuries, right up

---

Tattoos

Many Arab and Berber women (sometimes men, too) are tattooed. The simple stylised designs, usually tattooed during a ceremony, are found on the face, hands, ankles and elsewhere on the body. The tradition resulted from the belief that the body orifices were vulnerable to the evil eye.

Tattoos also indicate a woman's social group as well as its systems and values. Girls are often tattooed to mark their entry into adulthood; designs also communicate whether a woman is married or not.

Some tattoos are placed to enhance the sensuality of the female body, others are believed to have healing powers – special tattoos placed on a woman's back are thought to prevent infertility. ■

Keeping the evil eye at bay – tattoo design from the Middle Atlas mountains.

until recent times, the town was an important religious and educational centre whose influence was felt throughout the Drâa region and into the desert beyond.

Tamegroute consists of a series of interconnected ksour, at the centre of which is the *zawiyya* (religious sanctuary) and its famous library.

The **library** (signposted on the main road as 'Librairie Coranique') houses a magnificent collection of illustrated religious texts, dictionaries and astrological works, some of them on gazelle hides. The oldest texts date back to around the 13th century. Most of them are kept on shelves behind glass doors, but others are displayed in glass cases.

They're beautifully illustrated, but perhaps of limited interest to anyone other than an Arabic scholar. Visitors are allowed into the outer sanctuary and the library in the morning and late afternoon (it's generally closed from noon to 3 pm). You'll be expected to leave a donation for the upkeep of the place. The zawiyya remains a pilgrimage site for people needing charity and hoping to be cured of their ills.

There's also a small **pottery factory** in the village, which is worth a look, and a Saturday **souq**. There is no shortage of local people willing to act as guides, should you need one.

Places to Stay & Eat The town's only hotel and best restaurant is the *Hôtel Riad Nacir*, on the left-hand side as you enter town from Zagora. The hotel offers basic rooms for Dr30/60.

The owner of the hotel, Saaddine Naciri, is also an artist who produces prolific naive works commenting on modern Morocco.

Tinfou & the Dunes

About 5km south of Tamegroute you can get your first glimpse of the Sahara. Off the road to the left are a number of isolated sand dunes. If you've never seen sandy desert and do not intend to head to Merzouga, Tinfou is a pleasant spot to take a breather and enjoy a taste of the desert.

Places to Stay & Eat There's no village as such here, but there are a couple of attractive accommodation options. The *Auberge Repos du Sable* (☎/fax 848566) is a tumbledown kasbah-style building with simple rooms costing Dr50/80/120. There is hot water in the shared showers. The atmosphere is relaxed and the food very good (about Dr45). There is even a swimming pool, although it's not always in use.

The hotel is run by Majid el-Farouj, whose parents, Hassan and Fatima, are artists. Their work (which is for sale) covers the walls of the main courtyard, and the artists themselves occasionally grace the hotel with a visit. You can organise 4WD trips into the desert (Dr1500 to Dr2000 a day, up to eight people) and camel treks for a week or so.

A little further on, sitting back from the road, is the new and very comfortable three-star *Porte au Sahara* (☎ 848562; fax 847002), also built in kasbah style. The hotel offers spacious rooms, all with their own balcony and private bathroom, for Dr360 a double, including breakfast. There is also accommodation in nomad tents for Dr70 per person. The hotel has a fully licensed restaurant and a hammam.

M'Hamid

Most people who come to Zagora try to make it to the end of the road at M'Hamid, about 96km to the south. The attraction again is the journey itself. The road south of Tinfou soon crosses the Drâa and leaves it behind to cross a vast tract of implacable hammada. After crossing a low pass you hit the village of Tagounite, which has a couple of cafes, including the *Es-Saada* and *Sahara*.

A few more kilometres takes you over the dramatic Tizi Beni Selmane pass, from which the oases of the Drâa again come into view. The village and kasbah of Oulad Driss make a picturesque stop before the final run into M'Hamid.

With a population of about 2000, there's not an awful lot happening in M'Hamid. There's a section of dunes and sandy desert

10km to the south. The hotels can organise camel treks into the dunes and further afield (from Dr200 per person). If you have a sturdy vehicle, preferably a 4WD, you can drive out there.

There are a couple of small craft shops and a Monday market in M'Hamid. About 3km beyond M'Hamid are the remains of the old village.

Places to Stay & Eat About 6km back out along the road, tucked in among the palmeraies, is *Camping des Caravanes*, which costs Dr10 a person, Dr5 for a car and Dr10 for a tent. There are also a few basic rooms for Dr40 per person. You can have a meal cooked if you ask in advance.

Not far away is the *Camping Touareg*, which charges the same. There are six rooms here for Dr20 per person.

The *Hôtel Restaurant Sahara* (☎ 848009), run by Naamani M'Barek and his two brothers Habib and Hassan, has simple but adequate facilities, and charges Dr25 per person. There are shared cold showers. The hotel cafe is pleasant and serves decent meals. The three brothers are all very experienced camel guides and can organise treks for up to 15 days.

About 500m over the river, to the left of the Hotel Sahara, is the recently extended *Auberge Al Khaima* which offers simple, clean rooms for Dr15 per person. There are cold showers. There's space to pitch a tent here, too.

The new *Hôtel Restaurant Iriqui*, the first place on the right as you come into the village, has three basic, clean rooms for Dr50/60. There's a cold shared shower. Simple Moroccan dishes are available in the restaurant.

Getting There & Away There's a daily CTM bus from Zagora (originating in Marrakesh and passing through Ouarzazate) to M'Hamid around 4 pm; it returns the next day at 6 am in the summer and 5 am in the winter. The fare is Dr18. If you're lucky, you may be able to get a lift with other tourists or in one of the rare grands taxis.

If you don't have your own transport and just want to make a day trip from Zagora, it comes down to hiring a taxi. The usual charge is up to Dr400 for the day, although this is negotiable. Taxis take up to six people, so it's a good idea to get a group together to share the cost. This is the best way to see the area, as the driver will stop wherever you like.

The Jebel Sarhro

The starkly beautiful Jebel Sarhro range of mountains continues the line of the Anti-Atlas, rising up between the High Atlas and Dadès Valley to the north and the sub-Sahara which stretches away to the south.

Little visited and totally undeveloped (tourist-wise that is), it offers a landscape of flat-topped mesas, deep gorges and twisted volcanic pinnacles softened by date palms and almond groves. It's wild, isolated nomad country. The great warriors of the south were the Aït Atta people of this region and their last stand against the French took place here, on Jebel Bou Gafer, in 1933.

The best time to visit this area is spring or autumn (in the late autumn you'll see nomads moving their camps down from the higher mountains). Summer is scorchingly hot and in winter night-time temperatures drop to well below freezing. You can explore the area by car (4WD preferably), but it really is a landscape best appreciated on foot.

The paved 6956 heading east to Rissani from near Agdz skirts the southern edge of the range. Halfway along this route is the small town of **Tazzarine**, which has the simple, clean, reasonably priced *Hôtel Bougaffer* and a few basic cafes. Local buses run through Tazzarine from both Erfoud and Zagora.

Trekking

A good trek through the Jebel Sarhro could

Morocco's Travelling Acrobats

For hundreds of years, the remote region of Tazeroult in southern Morocco has been the traditional birthplace of Morocco's most famous acrobats, the sons of Sidi Hamed ou Moussa.

Taking their name from their patron saint, this Berber brotherhood of acrobats travels throughout the country, and is known for its spectacular and highly dangerous tumbling routines. At the beginning of this century, its reputation spread abroad, and they wandered as far as America. Soon there was hardly a circus in Europe which didn't lay claim to a Berber among its troupe.

The origin of the acrobats is believed to lie in a distant warrior tradition. Originally, this Berber clan were famous marksmen and agile warriors, greatly in demand above all for the accuracy of their aim. Acting as armed escorts or bodyguards for pilgrims or travellers, they were also recruited to fight in the tribal wars of the Anti-Atlas mountains.

Some have claimed that the immense human pyramids, now a major feature of the Berber repertoire, were devised in battle to scale the walls of fortified mountain kasbahs. The complicated tumbles may have formed part of a martial arts training, rather like karate or judo does for many soldiers today.

What is certain is that in times of peace these marksmen toured Morocco putting on demonstrations of their skills. This is the tradition that continues right up to the present day. Place Djemaa el-Fna in Marrakesh sees daily afternoon performances of the Berber acrobats, and remains the starting point for the majority of Europe's circus tumblers. ■

take anything from five to 15 days. All supplies should be carried, though you will come across eggs, dates, almonds, bread, chickens and goats for sale in the villages you pass.

Maps are hard to come by outside Morocco; you'll need to apply for one through the Department of Conservation & Topography in Rabat (see the Maps section in the Facts for the Visitor chapter).

You could set out from the towns of El-Kelaâ M'Gouna or Boumalne du Dadès, north of the range, but the ideal place to start from is the village of Nekob, 67km south-east of Agdz.

Market day in Nekob is Sunday – the day you'll find most local transport heading that way. You can hire mules in Nekob, but you will probably be better off organising guides, mules and so on through the Hôtel Ali or the Hôtel de Foucauld in Marrakesh. These two hotels are where the vast majority of the mountain guides of Morocco hang out.

One recommended route from Nekob would take you through the valley of Oued Hanedour, up Jebel Amlal, across the plateau of Tadaout n'Tablah, to the fabulous rock formation of Bab n'Ali and down to the village of Igli.

From the provincial town of Iknioulg you can get local transport to Boumalne, where a market is held on Wednesday.

Dadès Valley & the Gorges

Heading roughly east of Ouarzazate, the Dadès Valley threads its course between the mountains of the High Atlas to the north and the rugged Jebel Sarhro range to the south. The biggest oases on this route begin abruptly about 30km from Ouarzazate, just before the town of Skoura.

Further along the valley, the beautiful Dadès and Todra gorges cut back up into the High Atlas. From here rough pistes lead all the way over to the Middle Atlas.

SKOURA

Skoura lies about 42km east of Ouarzazate and makes an easy day excursion if you don't want to make a stop before heading further east. The oases here contain a collection of impressive kasbahs. One of the most easily accessible is the **Kasbah ben Moro**.

About 150 years old, it's just off the main road on the right, a couple of kilometres before you reach the town. The owners, who live next door, use it mainly for animals and storage space, but Mohammed will open it up for a small fee.

There's not an awful lot to see inside, but from the top there are great views of the palmeraie and another kasbah, **Amerdihl**, which is owned by a wealthy Casablanca family and cannot be visited.

Places to Stay & Eat

The *Hôtel Nakhil*, in the centre of town, is a basic place with rooms for Dr35. Apart from a few cafes and snack stands, there's not much in the line of restaurants here. Market day is Monday.

Getting There & Away

The odd bus passes through from Ouarzazate and Tinerhir (Dr10), but an easier bet is a grand taxi from Ouarzazate (Dr12).

If you want to get out on the same day, you'll have to be early, as there's not much happening in terms of transport from the late afternoon on.

EL-KELAÂ M'GOUNA

Another 50km north-east up the valley, the small town of El-Kelaâ M'Gouna is famous as a centre of rose-water production. You can visit the rose-water factory (and of course there's plenty of rose-water around to buy). In late spring the town celebrates the new year's crops with a colourful rose festival.

If you have decent transport, a meander through the **Vallée des Roses**, a 40km loop north of M'Gouna, makes a pleasant day's outing. In spring the entire area is awash with pink Persian roses.

If you want to stay, there are two accommodation options: the basic *Hôtel du Grand Atlas*, on the main street, and the four-star *Les Roses de Dadès* by the river.

BOUMALNE DU DADÈS

Another 24km north-east of M'Gouna brings you to a fork in the road. The left branch takes you up the stunning Dadès Gorge, while the main road veers off over the river to the hilltop town of Boumalne du Dadès.

Though you may want to press on up to the gorge, Boumalne itself is a pleasant, laid-back place and has a reasonable choice of accommodation. There is very little in the way of shops in the gorge, so if you need supplies it's best to stock up here.

Information

There's a Banque Populaire on Ave Mohammed V. The post office is over the hill on the way up to the Hôtel Salam. Market day is Wednesday.

Bird-watching

The hammada and grassy plains immediately to the south of Boumalne offer some rewarding bird-watching opportunities.

Take the piste leading off the main road beyond town south towards the village of Tagdilt (the Vallée des Oiseaux, or Valley of the Birds) to look for larks, wheat-ears, sandgrouse, buzzards and eagle owls.

Places to Stay – bottom end

About the first place you come across in the lower end of the town, the *Hôtel Adrar* (☎ 830355) is also about the best budget deal. It offers singles/doubles for Dr40/60. The hotel has a good restaurant and can organise treks into the Jebel Sarhro or shared taxis into the gorge.

A long walk up the hill from the bus station is the *Hôtel Salam* (☎ 830762). It's not too bad at Dr60 for a room (single or double occupancy) and the price includes hot showers. The hotel has its own restaurant and is unlikely to be full, even if other places are.

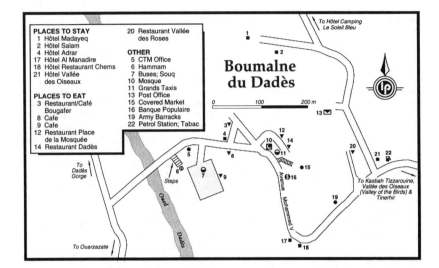

PLACES TO STAY
1 Hôtel Madayeq
2 Hôtel Salam
4 Hôtel Adrar
17 Hôtel Al Manadire
18 Hôtel Restaurant Chems
21 Hôtel Vallée
   des Oiseaux

PLACES TO EAT
3 Restaurant/Café
   Bougafer
8 Cafe
9 Cafe
12 Restaurant Place
   de la Mosquée
14 Restaurant Dadès

20 Restaurant Vallée
   des Roses

OTHER
5 CTM Office
6 Hammam
7 Buses; Souq
10 Mosque
11 Grands Taxis
13 Post Office
15 Covered Market
16 Banque Populaire
19 Army Barracks
22 Petrol Station; Tabac

Boumalne du Dadès

A little further on is the *Hôtel Camping Le Soleil Bleu* (☎ 830163). Popular with bird-watchers, it has clean rooms with hot shower for Dr60/100. You can pitch a tent for Dr15 per person, or sleep on the roof for Dr20.

You can also arrange treks and excursions to the Dadès Gorge or the bird-watching areas here.

Just off Ave Mohammed V on the way up to the Hôtel Salam, the *Hôtel Vallée des Oiseaux* (☎ 830764), has reasonable singles/doubles without shower for Dr80/110 and rooms with private shower and toilet for Dr95/120. The hotel has a restaurant.

The new *Hôtel Al Manadire* (☎ 830172), on Ave Mohammed V, is in a great spot overlooking the valley below. The hotel offers clean singles/doubles without shower for Dr30/50 and rooms with shower for Dr60/100.

Virtually next door, the well-established *Hôtel Restaurant Chems* (☎ 830089) is in an equally great location and has a pleasant restaurant. Doubles/triples with shower cost Dr110/180.

Places to Stay – middle
The new *Kasbah Tizzarouine* (☎ 830690; fax 830256), situated off Ave Mohammed V along a short stretch of piste, is built in traditional kasbah style and also offers wonderful views of the valley. Demi-pension, in comfortable rooms with private bathroom, costs Dr250 per person. You can also sleep in nomad-style tented accommodation for Dr120, including breakfast. Camping is also possible.

The hotel has an excellent restaurant (Dr80 for dinner) and is a good place to enjoy local Berber music.

The only other mid-range choice is the *Hôtel Madayeq* (☎ 830763), the weird-looking building sticking up on the hill beyond the Hôtel Salam. Rooms will set you back Dr288/360 plus taxes. The hotel has a swimming pool and an expensive restaurant and bar (the only place in town where you can buy alcohol).

Hammams
There's a hammam for men and women not far from the CTM office, down the stairs south off Ave Mohammed V.

Places to Eat

For cheap eats, the restaurant below the *Hôtel Adrar* serves a filling meal of tajine or brochettes with salad and a drink for about Dr35. Three other little restaurants compete for business nearby. The *Restaurant/Café Bougafer*, just up from the Adrar, has basic Moroccan dishes for about the same price.

The other two are next to each other near the mosque: the *Restaurant Place de la Mosquée* and the *Restaurant Dadès*. Up near the Hôtel Vallée des Oiseaux is the slightly more formal *Restaurant Vallée des Roses*, where a full meal will cost about Dr70.

The restaurant at the *Kasbah Tizzarouine* is particularly recommended for its excellent food (Dr80 for dinner) and service.

Getting There & Away

Bus The CTM office is at the bottom of Ave Mohammed V, just near the bus lot. CTM has two buses to Ouarzazate and on to Marrakesh at 9.30 am and noon. Going the other way, a bus passes through on its way to Tinerhir and Er-Rachidia at about 12.30 pm.

A couple of other buses pass through here, including one to Agadir (via Ouarzazate) at 6.15 pm and another to Rabat (via Ouarzazate) at 7.30 pm.

Taxi As is usual in smaller places like this, grands taxis are probably a better bet. The fare is Dr40 to Ouarzazate, about Dr13 to Tinerhir and about Dr10 to Aït Oudinar, at the top of the gorge.

THE DADÈS GORGE

The drive up to the gorge is a particularly pleasant one, taking you past almond and fig trees, some fabulous rock formations and impressive kasbahs and ksour.

The road snakes up in a leisurely fashion inside the wide walls of the gorge for about 25km to Aït Oudinar. Here the gorge narrows abruptly and the river flows right by the roadside.

A couple of kilometres further on, the bitumen gives way to piste as the trail winds up inside the main canyon in a series of hairpin bends. After a few kilometres of this, the road flattens out as you leave the best of the scenery behind you.

You can probably make it as far as **Msemrir** in an ordinary car, but beyond there you will definitely need a 4WD. Just north of Msemrir is a piste that leads east and then south down into the Todra Gorge.

There are some wild and largely untouched stretches of mountain scenery to be enjoyed throughout this area, but be aware that many of the pistes are impassable in winter or after wet weather. Whatever the weather, the pistes are extremely rough and the driving is very slow.

If you have plenty of time, you could easily spend several days pottering about in the gorge – watching nomads bring vast herds of goats down the cliffs to the river, fossicking for fossils and generally enjoying the natural splendour. There are some challenging walks up into some of the smaller mountain passes west and east of the Oued Dadès.

There's a particularly good trail heading north-west which begins just across the river from the cluster of hotels at Km27. For those wanting to trek further afield, a tempting journey would be to travel northwards from the gorge into the heart of the High Atlas and beyond to **Imilchil** (see the Around Marrakesh section for more on Imilchil).

It's a long way, but it's feasible if you combine days of walking with the occasional ride on local transport (there is a slow but regular and reliable market circuit).

Almost all the hotels in the gorge and in Boumalne du Dadès can put you in touch with guides who know the area well. Two recommended local guides are Ahmed Dinari and Mohammed Amgon. Both can be contacted through the Hôtel La Kasbah de la Vallée (see Places to Stay & Eat).

Places to Stay & Eat

The choice of places to stay in the gorge is growing rapidly, and most of what's on offer is good value. At Km14 is the *Café*

Mirguirne. Another kilometre on, the *Hôtel Restaurant Kasba* overlooks the fantastic rock formations on the other side of the valley.

It's an interesting little place with small balconies, and is constructed in a mixture of modern and traditional styles. The beds are comfortable and hot water is promised. Expect to pay Dr25 per person. Anywhere else it would be a well-recommended stop, but choices abound further up.

At Km25 is the village of Aït Oudinar, where you'll find the *Auberge des Gorges du Dadès* (☎ 831710) perched right over the river. You have a choice of simple rooms for Dr40/60 (shared hot showers) or classier, self-contained rooms for Dr100/140. Breakfast is included in the price. Most of the rooms, especially the more expensive ones, overlook the river.

There is also space for camping and you can sleep on couches in the salon, or in the Berber tent outside, for just Dr10 a head.

There is a little cluster of hotels further up the valley at Km27.

The *Hôtel Restaurant Camping du Peuplier*, owned by Mohammed Echaouiche, has four basic rooms (three with shower) for Dr30/40. Hot water is unlikely. You can also camp right by the stream for Dr3 per person – you can't get much cheaper than that.

Next up is the *Hôtel La Gazelle du Dadès* (☎ 831753), which has a very pleasant little rooftop terrace. It's a bit difficult to believe the manager's advertised room rates, but if they are accurate, this place automatically becomes the deal of the week. Rooms with three comfortable beds cost Dr30, for however many people. Rooms with three beds and private shower are Dr60, again for the whole room. They are clean and there is hot water. Sleeping on cushions in the salon or on the roof costs just Dr10 a head.

Next door is the *Hôtel La Kasbah de la Vallée* (☎ 831717), which is possibly the best of the bunch. There are four rooms without shower which cost Dr60 for a double, and 20 rooms with shower and toilet for Dr80/120/150 (hot water in the morning

and evening only). Demi-pension is available for Dr170. You can sleep in the salon (up to 10 or so people) for Dr25, on the large roof terrace for Dr20, in the Berber tent by the river (summer only) for Dr15, or camp for Dr10.

The hotel has a large, comfortable salon-style restaurant upstairs (with a fireplace) and an excellent cook, Mbark Bouighisse (a full meal will cost around Dr70). After dinner there's usually some informal Berber music to enjoy. You can also hire bicycles here (Dr70 per day) and in the summer it's possible to go rafting.

A little further up is the simple *Hôtel Tisadrine* which offers double rooms without/with shower for Dr40/100, including breakfast.

Nearby, the new *Hôtel Le Vieux Chateaux du Dadès* (☎ 831710) has clean, bright rooms, all with bathroom, for Dr110/ 150.

Right next door is *Chez Elizabeth*, built in earthen kasbah style, which has a few beautifully decorated rooms for about the same price. You can eat very well here, too (Elizabeth even bakes cakes).

Five kilometres higher up (beyond the most dramatic stretch of the gorge) are two rather more simple places: the *Hôtel Taghia*, which has rooms for up to three people for Dr60, and *La Kasbah des Roches*, a bright little cafe offering two rooms that sleep two or three for Dr40.

Nearly all the hotels in the gorge have their own restaurants and there's nothing to stop you trying the food in a place other than the one you're staying in.

It may be the mountain air combined with the natural beauty of the gorge, but the simple Moroccan staples you'll eat up here are generally exceedingly good.

Getting There & Away

If you happen to be around at the right time, you may be able squeeze into one of the Berber lorries that ply between Boumalne and outlying villages on market days. Market day in Boumalne is Wednesday so there are likely to be trucks heading up the gorge in the afternoon.

Central Morocco
Top: View to the desert from the rooftops of Zagora.
Middle: Kilometres of dunes north and west of Laayoune.
Bottom Left: Tamdaght Kasbah; if you're lucky, Larbi Embarak might show you around.
Bottom Right: On the way to the end of the road, Olad Driss near M'Hamid.

DAMIEN SIMONIS

GEOFF CROWTHER

GEOFF CROWTHER

Central Morocco
Top Left: Aït Benhaddou Kasbah, scene of more than 20 films.
Bottom Left: One of Morocco's most magnificent natural sights – the Todra Gorge.
Bottom Right: Dwarfed by the cliffs – travellers in the Todra Gorge.

Grands taxis are few and far between, but they do run (a place should cost about Dr10 to Aït Oudinar). Hiring a taxi for a few hours, including photo stops and the like, should cost in the region of Dr100 to Dr150.

A straightforward ride to Aït Oudinar should cost around Dr60, but you'll have to employ all your bargaining skills. Otherwise you could get up to the gorge by a combination of hitching and walking.

TINERHIR
About 53km north-east of Boumalne is the bustling town of Tinerhir which has spread quite a way beyond the boundaries of the original town.

The highway is known as Ave Mohammed V as it passes through the town on the way to Er-Rachidia. There are three banks, a couple of petrol stations and several restaurants along here.

You'll find a branch of the BMCE and the post office on Ave Hassan II, a block in to the south. Most of the town's hotels and restaurants can be found on or near Ave Hassan II.

Immediately north and south-east of the town are some lush palmeraies dotted with kasbahs and ksour which are well worth exploring. An enormous souq takes place about 2km west of the centre on Sunday and Monday.

Adjacent to the BMCE is a branch of the family-run Maison Berbère, which sells an excellent range of carpets, as well as a good selection of jewellery. The Todra Gorge lies 15km to the north of Tinerhir.

Places to Stay – bottom end
Camping About 2.5km west of the town centre is *Camping Ourti*. It's awkwardly located and pretty spartan. It costs Dr8 per person, Dr6 to pitch a tent, Dr7 for a car and Dr10 for electricity. Hot showers are free. If the pool is in use, it costs another Dr10. There are also basic rooms for Dr35 a person.

Hotels There is a handful of budget hotels virtually in a row on Ave Hassan II. The

Hôtel Salam (☎ 835020), next to the CTM office, has basic singles/doubles for Dr60/100. There is a hot shared shower.

The *Hôtel El Fath*, at No 56, has clean, acceptable rooms for Dr35/75. They promise hot water in the shared shower. The *Hôtel Al-Qods*, at the end of the block, has bright, simple rooms for Dr30/60/90.

The *Hôtel El Houda* (☎ 834613), off Ave Hassan II at No 11 Rue Moulay Ismail, has clean rooms for Dr30/60.

Another reasonable option is the *Hôtel L'Oasis* on Ave Mohammed V. It's next to the Total petrol station and has its own restaurant. Perfectly clean, comfortable rooms cost Dr35/70. There's a shared (hot) shower on the ground floor.

Places to Stay – middle
The recently upgraded *Hôtel Todra* (☎ 834 249), on Ave Hassan II, has plenty of dark wood-panelling, a pleasant balcony terrace and a new bar and restaurant. Large rooms with shower cost from Dr103/125 plus taxes.

Back behind Ave Hassan II near the central market area is the popular *Hôtel de l'Avenir* (☎/fax 834599). Very pleasant rooms cost Dr60/100/130, including breakfast. There's a hot shared shower.

The new *Hôtel Tomboctou* (☎ 834604; fax 833505), off Mohammed V on Ave Bir Anzarane, is housed in a beautiful old kasbah. Very comfortable rooms cost Dr210/250. The manager, Roger Mimó, has a good knowledge of mountain trekking possibilities and can organise mountain bike trips in the area.

The *Hôtel Kenzi Bougafer* (☎ 833280; fax 833282) is a three-star hotel on the road to Ouarzazate, opposite Camping Ourti. The location isn't great, but the rooms are fine and cost Dr360/420.

The four-star *Hôtel Sargho* (☎ 834181; fax 834352) sits on top of the hill overlooking the town. The views are superb and the hotel has an enormous swimming pool, a bar and a restaurant. Singles/doubles cost Dr320/400 plus taxes. Visa cards are accepted.

Places to Eat

The best place to look for cheap Moroccan food is in the little market area south of Ave Hassan II. There are loads of simple little stalls here. Meat-eaters are pointed to the butchers, to buy fresh meat and take it back to the 'restaurant'. If you don't want to play this game, the right gesticulations will get the message across that you'd prefer it if they took care of it for you.

There are a few simple restaurants on Ave Hassan II, including the *Café des Amis*, which serves excellent brochettes and accompaniments. You'll find more choices along Ave Mohammed V.

The *Café Centrale* and the *Restaurant Essaada* are both good for simple Moroccan standards. Slightly fancier are the *Restaurant La Kasbah* and the restaurant attached to the *Hôtel L'Oasis*, both of which offer three-course meals for around Dr70.

The restaurant at the *Hôtel de l'Avenir* serves a very good paella.

Getting There & Away

Bus Buses leave from the Place Principale, off Ave Mohammed V in the centre of town.

CTM has a couple of buses that pass through Tinerhir on their way east and west. Only 10 seats are set aside for passengers boarding at Tinerhir. At 11.30 am and 1.30 pm buses go to Er-Rachidia. The first costs Dr28 and the second Dr30. At 8 am a bus passes through on its way to Marrakesh (Dr80) via Ouarzazate (Dr35.50). Another bus leaves for Ouarzazate at 2.30 pm (Dr30). Otherwise, several private buses also leave from the same area.

Taxi Grands taxis to Ouarzazate (Dr45) and Er-Rachidia (Dr35) leave from the eastern end of the same gardens, near the Hôtel Al-Qods. This is also the place to hunt for occasional transport (taxis, lorries or pick-up trucks) up the Todra Gorge and beyond.

As a rule, if there is no standard taxi leaving for the gorge (stress that you want to pay for a place in a normal shared taxi), you may need to bargain to hire one specially to take you up.

THE TODRA GORGE

Only 15km from Tinerhir, at the end of a valley thick with palmeraies and Berber villages, is the magnificent Todra Gorge. A massive fault in the plateau dividing the High Atlas from the Jebel Sarhro, with a crystal-clear river running through it, the gorge rises to 300m at its narrowest point.

It's best in the morning, when the sun penetrates to the bottom of the gorge, turning the rock from rose pink to a deep ochre. In the afternoon it gets very dark and, in winter, bitterly cold.

Although the main gorge can be explored in half a day, those with more time might like to explore further up the gorge or walk through the palmeraies on the way to Tinerhir. There are numerous ruined kasbahs flanking the palmeraies and plenty of photographic opportunities.

As with the Dadès Gorge, the more ambitious might consider making their way further up into the Atlas mountains. A combination of souq lorries, 4WD taxis and hiking could take you north to Aït Hani, from where you could push on over the Tizi Tirherhouzine towards Imilchil, or do the long loop south through the Dadès Gorge that would bring you back to the main highway linking Ouarzazate and Er-Rachidia.

A network of difficult pistes links the sporadic villages here in the High and Middle Atlas, many of which are snowbound in winter. You could spend weeks exploring them, but you should bear in mind that you'll be far away from banks, post offices and even basic health services most of the time, so come prepared. The hotels in Tinerhir and the gorge can put you in touch with local guides.

Climbing is becoming increasingly popular on the vertical rock face of the gorge. There are some sublime routes here, some of them bolted. The two hotels inside the mouth of the gorge can provide information about routes.

Places to Stay & Eat

Camping Along the road to the gorge, about 9km from Tinerhir, are three good camp sites. They're all next to each other in the palmeraies and are all equipped with showers and toilets. There's a small shop that sells basic supplies across the road from the first of them.

The first you come upon on the way up from Tinerhir is the *Auberge de l'Atlas* (☎ 834209). It's very good, but marginally more expensive than the other two. It costs Dr9 per person, Dr13 for a car, Dr11 to pitch your tent and Dr10 for electricity. It has simple rooms for Dr45 and Berber tent accommodation for Dr20 per head.

Camping Le Lac costs Dr8 per person, Dr8 per car, Dr7 to pitch a tent and Dr10 for electricity. The site also has six basic rooms (Dr60) and a restaurant. The nearby *Camping Auberge* charges similar prices.

Hotels Just inside the mouth of the gorge are two ideal places to stay. The *Hôtel Restaurant Yasmina* (☎ 834207) is the more expensive, with good rooms costing Dr83/110 (more in summer). There are simple rooms available for Dr70 and in summer you can sleep on the roof for Dr15 a head. The hotel has bicycles for hire, a télé-boutique and in the cafe there's an open fire.

The *Hôtel Restaurant Les Roches* (☎ 834 814) offers double rooms without shower for Dr60 and rooms with shower for Dr150 (including breakfast). You can sleep in the Berber tent for Dr20 per person.

You can get reasonable food in both places, which in summer serve meals in large tents set out by the river. Neither hotel sells alcohol, so bring your own.

If these two are full, the *Hôtel Le Mansour*, a kilometre or so back downstream (15km from Tinerhir) and just outside the entrance of the gorge proper, has basic singles/doubles for Dr30/60. It does have a pleasant cafe and restaurant. Next door, the *Hôtel Etoile des Gorges* (☎ 835158) offers similarly basic rooms for slightly more. There's a decent restaurant here, too.

Getting There & Away

See the previous Tinerhir entry for transport to the gorge.

Ziz Valley & the Tafilalt

ER-RACHIDIA

At the crossroads of important north-south and east-west routes across Morocco, Er-Rachidia (named after the first Alawite leader, Moulay ar-Rashid) was originally built by the French as an administrative and military outpost. A fairly large army garrison is still maintained here.

A series of dams and an irrigation system was built in the area after massive flooding of the Oued Ziz in the late 1960s. And thanks to these measures the region is now relatively prosperous – this is the place where the locals nicknamed one of their new suburbs Dallas! Depending on where you're coming from, Er-Rachidia can be a relaxing place to hole up for a day or two.

The main highlight is to the north of town – the **Ziz Gorges** which link Er-Rachidia to the small town of Rich and on to Fès and Meknès. This magnificent route past palm-fringed towns and ksour begins with the French-built Tunnel du Légionnaire 20km south of Rich and stretches to the dam just north of Er-Rachidia. If you take this road, ensure you get a daytime bus or grand taxi.

Information

Tourist Office There's a Syndicat d'Initiative (☎ 572733), open Monday to Friday, south off Ave Moulay Ali Cherif, near the Shell petrol station.

Money There are at least four banks in town, including a BMCE on Place Moulay Hassan and a Banque Populaire near the main street heading out to Erfoud.

Post & Communications The post office is on Blvd Mohammed V. The phone office, to the left of the post office, is open daily from 8.30 am to 9 pm. There are a few card phones outside. As elsewhere, Er-Rachidia has a fair scattering of téléboutiques.

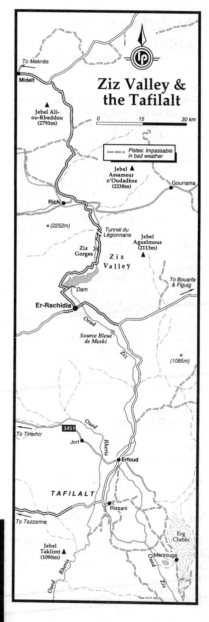

**Ziz Valley &
the Tafilalt**

0   15   30 km

=== Pistes: Impassable
in bad weather

To Meknès

Midelt

Jebel Ali-
ou-Rbeddou
(2793m)

Jebel
Assameur
n'Oudadène
(2238m)

Gourrama

Rich

x (2252m)

Tunnel du
Légionnaire

Jebel
Aguelmous
(2113m)

Ziz
Gorges

Ziz
Valley

To Bouarfa
& Figuig

Dam

Er-Rachidia

Oued

Source Bleue
de Meski

Ziz

x
(1085m)

Oued

To Tinerhir

3451

Jorf

Rheris

Erfoud

TAFILALT

Rissani

To Tazzarine

Erg
Chebbi

Jebel
Taklimt
(1090m)

Merzouga

Oued

Rheris

Oued

Ziz

CENTRAL MOROCCO

Places to Stay – bottom end

Camping The closest camp ground is *Camping Source Bleue de Meski* (see the Around Er-Rachidia section later in this chapter).

Hotels The three cheapest places are all extremely basic and located just off Place Moulay Hassan. All have cold communal showers.

At the western end of the square in a side street are the *Hôtel Royal* and the *Hôtel Marhaba*. Singles/doubles in both are Dr40/60. Slightly better is the *Hôtel Zeitoun*, on Rue Abdallah ben Yassine, with rooms for Dr30/50.

Better is the *Hôtel Restaurant Renaissance* (☎ 572633) on Rue Moulay Youssef. There are simple rooms that sleep one or two for Dr30 and rooms with shower that sleep two or three for Dr68. The staff speak French and English.

Places to Stay – middle

The best choice in town by far is the *Hôtel M'Daghra* (☎ 574047) on Rue M'Daghra, almost opposite the bus station. Comfortable, clean rooms with guaranteed hot showers cost Dr101/152/183.

The one-star *Hôtel Oasis* (☎ 572519; fax 570126), on Rue Sidi Bou Abdallah, recently lost a star and consequently feels a bit sorry for itself. Rooms without shower cost Dr121/142 and rooms with bathroom cost Dr153/179. The hotel has its own bar and restaurant.

A little cheaper is the *Hôtel Meski* (☎ 572065), on Ave Moulay Ali Cherif. It's just far enough towards the road to Fès to be inconvenient for those arriving in the centre of town, but offers reasonable value. Singles/doubles with private shower, but shared toilet, cost Dr96/122. The hotel also has a restaurant.

Places to Stay – top end

The only top-end hotel is the four-star *Hôtel Kenzi Rissani* (☎ 572186; fax 572585), on Route d'Erfoud, just across the Ziz bridge. Singles/doubles cost Dr450/550 plus taxes,

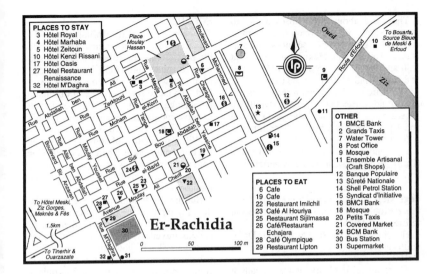

PLACES TO STAY
3 Hôtel Royal
4 Hôtel Marhaba
5 Hôtel Zeitoun
10 Hôtel Kenzi Rissani
17 Hôtel Oasis
27 Hôtel Restaurant
   Renaissance
32 Hôtel M'Daghra

PLACES TO EAT
6 Cafe
19 Cafe
22 Restaurant Imilchil
23 Café Al Houriya
25 Restaurant Sijilmassa
26 Café/Restaurant
   Echajara
28 Café Olympique
29 Restaurant Lipton

OTHER
1 BMCE Bank
2 Grands Taxis
7 Water Tower
8 Post Office
9 Mosque
11 Ensemble Artisanal
   (Craft Shops)
12 Banque Populaire
13 Sûreté Nationale
14 Shell Petrol Station
15 Syndicat d'Initiative
16 BMCI Bank
18 Mosque
20 Petits Taxis
21 Covered Market
24 BCM Bank
30 Bus Station
31 Supermarket

Er-Rachidia

and the hotel has all the amenities you would expect, including bar, restaurant and swimming pool.

Places to Eat
Restaurants One of the most popular places to eat is the *Restaurant Sijilmassa*, on the main street – look out for the sign, 'All food is here', in English, French, Spanish and Italian! It has the usual standard Moroccan dishes and a full meal will cost about Dr35. You can eat inside or at the outdoor tables.

Also good is the *Restaurant Imilchil*, opposite the covered market. It, too, has a sign in French, reading, 'Look no further, all food here'.

In much the same league is the busy *Restaurant Lipton*, across the main road from the Hôtel Restaurant Renaissance, which offers decent tajines and other staples.

For a splurge, try a meal at the licensed *Restaurant Oasis*, which is attached to the hotel of the same name. There's a very good but pricey restaurant at the Hôtel Kenzi Rissani.

For breakfast, there are a couple of good cafes on Rue M'Daghra, down by the bus station. You'll also find a hole-in-the-wall doughnut seller down here.

Self-Catering Those wishing to put their own meals together should have a look around the covered market, where a wide variety of very reasonably priced food is available.

There's a good supermarket on Rue M'Daghra where you can stock up on supplies.

Getting There & Away
Bus All buses operate out of the central bus station, which is on Rue M'Daghra. CTM has a daily departure to Marrakesh (Dr110.50) at 5.45 am via Tinerhir and Ouarzazate (Dr65.50). It also runs two buses to Meknès (Dr80) at 7.30 and 10 pm and one to Rissani (Dr18) at 5 am via Erfoud.

Quite a few other bus companies have services running through Er-Rachidia. There are several daily buses to Fès (Dr78.50). Most run via Azrou and a couple go through Sefrou.

There are about eight buses a day to Meknès (Dr77.50) via Azrou from 6 am to midnight. There are two services to Casablanca (Dr120) via Meknès and Rabat at 5.30 and 9 pm. Three others go via Azrou at 8, 10.30 and 11.15 pm (Dr113).

There are six daily departures to Rissani via Erfoud. Buses to Ouarzazate (Dr60) via Tinerhir and Boumalne leave at 11.30 am and 1 pm. There is a bus for Tinerhir only at 6.30 am.

At 3 and 5 pm buses leave for Bouarfa (Dr50; five hours), near the Algerian border.

Taxi Most of the grands taxis leave from Place Moulay Hassan. The fare per person to Erfoud is Dr16.

Heading north, the fare to Azrou is Dr75, while a seat for Fès or Meknès goes for Dr100.

There are also plenty of taxis heading south for Aoufous, which you could take to get dropped off at the Meski turn-off for the Source Bleue de Meski.

AROUND ER-RACHIDIA
Source Bleue de Meski
The Source Bleue de Meski, about 23km south of Er-Rachidia, is a wonderful natural spring and swimming pool that is understandably popular with the locals.

On spring and summer weekends heat-plagued Er-Rachidians flock here in droves, but for the rest of the time it's pretty quiet. For the hot and sweaty traveller heading between Er-Rachidia and Erfoud it is a recommended stop.

You can stay at the *Camping Source Bleue de Meski* for Dr7 a person, Dr10 for a tent place and Dr10 per car. The spring is signposted and is about 1km west of the main road. Any bus or grand taxi going south to Erfoud or Aoufous from Er-Rachidia will be able to drop you off at the turn-off.

When leaving, you should be able to flag down a grand taxi or hitch a ride to Er-Rachidia or even Erfoud from the main road.

ERFOUD
The oasis region of the Tafilalt was one of the last to succumb to French control under the protectorate, its tribes putting up sporadic resistance until 1932. Two years later, Morocco was officially considered 'pacified'. To make sure this state of affairs did not change, Erfoud was built as an administrative and garrison town to keep a watchful eye on the Tafilalt tribes.

With a population of about 7000, Erfoud is a fairly quiet place. There is a range of accommodation options here and it's a useful staging point from which to head further into the desert.

Sunrise excursions to the Erg Chebbi dunes near Merzouga to the south are becoming part of the standard menu for passing travellers. You are likely to be resolutely hassled by hotel touts on arrival, but once you're ensconced in a hotel, the welcome committees seem to vanish as quickly as they materialised.

Hotels, restaurants, the post office and so on are located on the town's main street, Ave Mohammed V, and to a lesser extent on Ave Moulay Ismail, which intersects Ave Mohammed V at the post office and links Erfoud to the Er-Rachidia, Rissani and Tinerhir highways.

Information
The post and phone offices are on the corner of Ave Mohammed V and Ave Moulay Ismail. They are open normal office hours. The small téléboutiques dotted around town keep longer hours.

There's a Banque Populaire diagonally across from the post office. You can change money at the Hôtel Salam, but watch out for inferior rates and commission charges.

Dunes
Most of the bottom-end hotels will do their best to dig up a clattering old 4WD taxi to take visitors on a sunrise excursion to the Erg Chebbi.

Nice as it is, a lightning glimpse of the dunes really isn't sufficient. If you have the time, take the opportunity to spend a couple of leisurely days among them. There's a good choice of cheap hotels right by the dunes and in the nearby village of Merzouga (see the Merzouga section later in this chapter).

If you do want to whiz out there and back from Erfoud, the taxi will pick you up at about 4 am and have you back in Erfoud by 10 am. The taxi costs around Dr300 (for up to seven people). Finding other travellers to make up numbers shouldn't be too difficult.

Places to Stay – bottom end

Camping Camping Erfoud, next to the river, is just a 10 minute walk from the bus area. It's fairly basic, however, and there is little shade. It costs around Dr10 per person and the same to pitch a tent.

Hotels The cheapest option is the Hôtel Merzouga (☎ 576532), on Ave Mohammed V, which has clean, basic singles for Dr60 and doubles for Dr80 (with showers ingeniously installed in the toilets!). The Hôtel Essaada, east along Ave Moulay Ismail, is much the same; rooms with shower cost Dr60/70.

The Hôtel La Gazelle (☎ 576028), on Ave Mohammed V, has pleasant rooms with shower for Dr60/110. There's hot water in the evening. The hotel has a decent restaurant downstairs.

Places to Stay – middle

The cheapest place in this category is the Hôtel Lahmada (☎/fax 576097), on Ave Moulay Ismail.

The rooms are spotless and have private bathrooms. Singles are Dr85, doubles Dr110 and triples Dr145. The hotel has a restaurant and a terrace.

On Ave Mohammed V, the Hôtel Sable d'Or (☎ 576348), has clean, comfortable rooms with private shower, toilet, table and chair, and there's hot water 24 hours a day.

The management is friendly and there's a rooftop terrace with great views over the town. Rooms cost Dr110/127. The hotel has a good restaurant.

The Hôtel Ziz (☎ 576154; fax 576811), on Ave Mohammed V just around the corner from the bus area, has refurbished rooms with en suite bathroom for Dr168, Dr197 and Dr250 plus taxes.

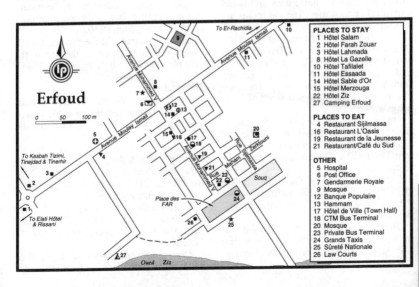

Erfoud

0   50   100 m

To Er-Rachidia

To Kasbah Tizimi,
Tinejdad & Tinerhir

To Elati Hôtel
& Rissani

Place des
FAR

Souq

Oued   Ziz

PLACES TO STAY
1 Hôtel Salam
2 Hôtel Farah Zouar
3 Hôtel Lahmada
8 Hôtel La Gazelle
10 Hôtel Tafilalet
11 Hôtel Essaada
14 Hôtel Sable d'Or
15 Hôtel Merzouga
22 Hôtel Ziz
27 Camping Erfoud

PLACES TO EAT
4 Restaurant Sijilmassa
16 Restaurant L'Oasis
19 Restaurant de la Jeunesse
21 Restaurant/Café du Sud

OTHER
5 Hospital
6 Post Office
7 Gendarmerie Royale
9 Mosque
12 Banque Populaire
13 Hammam
17 Hôtel de Ville (Town Hall)
18 CTM Bus Terminal
20 Mosque
23 Private Bus Terminal
24 Grands Taxis
25 Sûreté Nationale
26 Law Courts

CENTRAL MOROCCO

The hotel has a relaxing courtyard salon and one of the few bars in town.

For the money, the *Hôtel Farah Zouar* (☎/fax 576230) is worth considering. It's on the corner of the Rissani and Tinerhir roads. If the prices remain low, this is possibly the best deal in town. Rooms cost Dr150/200 (or Dr250 for a rather comfortable suite). Like most, the hotel comes with its own restaurant.

Places to Stay – top end

The least expensive place to stay in this category is the new three-star *Kasbah Tizimi* (☎ 576179; fax 577375), about 700m out along the road to Tinerhir.

Built in traditional kasbah style around a leafy courtyard, the hotel offers cool, comfortable rooms with bathroom for Dr215/264 plus taxes. The hotel has a restaurant.

The three-star *Hôtel Tafilalet* (☎ 576535; fax 576036), on Ave Moulay Ismail, has self-contained singles/doubles for Dr240/300.

The newer rooms on the far side of the swimming pool are superb and feature a large, sunny balcony, a comfortable bedroom and a separate dining area, all floored with local earthen tiles. The old rooms are nowhere near as attractive.

The hotel has its own bar and restaurant (breakfast is Dr30). Visits to Rissani, Taouz and Merzouga by 4WD, including a night under tents in the desert, can be organised from here, but they're not cheap. The hotel also runs a cheap place just south of Merzouga village.

Outside town, on the road to Rissani, is the four-star *Elati Hôtel* (☎ 577372; fax 577086). Spacious rooms with bathroom cost Dr400/500. The hotel has a bar and restaurant.

Top of the line is the *Hôtel Salam* (☎ 576665; fax 576426), virtually across the road from the Hôtel Farah Zouar. Rooms here are Dr438/557.

There are two wings, and the rooms in the new one are much better than the others. The hotel also has a restaurant, bar and sauna.

Swimming Pools

There's a small pool at the camp site, but it's not always in use. All four top-end hotels have swimming pools.

Hammams

There's a hammam for men and one for women just behind the Hôtel Sable d'Or.

Places to Eat

The *Restaurant/Café du Sud*, next to the Hôtel Ziz, is popular with locals. Freshly cooked brochettes served with salad, bread and fruit cost Dr35.

The extremely friendly *Restaurant de la Jeunesse*, on Ave Mohammed V, has good Moroccan dishes for reasonable prices.

Restaurant Sijilmassa on Ave Moulay Ismail is also popular with locals. The food is nothing special, but it's a pleasant place for tea or coffee at least.

The restaurant at the *Hôtel La Gazelle* has a comfortable Moroccan-style dining room where you can get a three-course evening meal for about Dr40. The *Restaurant L'Oasis* on Ave Mohammed V offers reasonable food for a similar price.

Another place worth trying is the restaurant at the *Hôtel Sable d'Or*, which offers a range of dishes from Dr30.

Of the restaurants in the top-end hotels, the most inviting choice is the one in the very pleasant *Kasbah Tizimi*.

Things to Buy

Erfoud is full of shiny black fossilised marble, which is quarried nearby in the desert. You can buy pieces in several shops around town.

Getting There & Away

Bus The CTM terminal is on Ave Mohammed V. CTM runs three services to Fès at 7 am, 11 am and 11 pm.

There's a direct bus to Meknès (Dr114) at 7.30 pm and another via Er-Rachidia (Dr15) at 8 am. A noon service runs to Midelt.

There are several private bus lines, all of which leave from Place des FAR. There are services to Meknès, Er-Rachidia, Rissani and Tinejdad (Dr19), which is along the minor 3451 heading west to Tinerhir.

A local bus runs to Tazzarine (Dr30) via Rissani at 10 am on Sunday, Tuesday and Thursday. Minibuses also shuttle between Erfoud and Rissani.

Taxi Grands taxis are, as a rule, a much more reliable bet. They also leave from Place des FAR and run regularly to Rissani (Dr6.50) and Er-Rachidia (Dr16).

MERZOUGA & THE DUNES
About 50km south of Erfoud is the tiny village of Merzouga and nearby the famous **Erg Chebbi**, Morocco's only genuine Saharan *erg* – one of those huge, drifting expanses of sand dunes that typify much of the Algerian Sahara.

It's a magical landscape which deserves much more than just a sunrise glimpse. The dunes themselves are fascinating, changing colour from pink to gold to red at different times of the day. It is a great place to appreciate the immense, clear desert sky (for details on tours to the dunes, see the Erfoud entry earlier in this section).

For bird-watchers, this is the best area in Morocco for spotting many desert species, including the desert sparrow, Egyptian nightjar, desert warbler, fulvous babbler and the blue-cheeked bee-eater.

Sometimes in spring a shallow lake appears north-west of Merzouga attracting flocks of pink flamingo and other water birds.

You can get out here by public transport, drive down yourself or arrange a sunrise tour (see the previous Erfoud section). The pistes can be rough (and getting stuck in sand is a real possibility), but a Renault 4 can make it down, winding across rough, black hammada.

The drive from Erfoud takes just over an hour and if you follow the line of telegraph poles you can't really go wrong.

Places to Stay
All up, you'll find a good dozen or so sim-

ple hotel/cafes dotted along the western side of Erg Chebbi and in the village of Merzouga itself. Most are basic and cost about Dr30/60. Many places allow you to sleep on the roof for about Dr20 per person.

The *Auberge La Caravane*, run by Zaid Boumia and his five brothers, is a welcoming place with basic rooms and a good restaurant where you can listen to excellent Berber music in the evenings.

The *Kasbah Asmaa* family-run hotels have a place nearby where you can sleep in a vast Berber tent for about Dr20 per person or set up your own tent.

Other popular places include the *Café Yasmine*, *Café du Sud*, *Café Dunes d'Or*, *Auberge Erg Chebbi*, *Café Oasis* and the *Hôtel la Grande Dune*. All offer basic meals.

An excellent place to stay in the village is the French-run *Ksar Sania* (☎/fax 577230 in Erfoud). Built in traditional kasbah style, the hotel offers comfortable singles for Dr70, doubles for Dr100 (all with collective hot shower). You can also sleep in the large nomad tent for Dr25 or camp for Dr15. The hotel restaurant offers a delicious French menu for Dr80 (cheaper individual dishes are available too).

Other places in the village include the *Auberge Merzouga*, *Café des Dunes*, *Auberge des Amis* and *Camping El Kheima*, which is set in a palmeraie.

You can arrange camel treks into the dunes from most of these hotels. Asking prices can be high, but are always open to negotiation.

Getting There & Away
Apart from the 'sunrise tours' from Erfoud, a red and white camionette leaves for Merzouga and the dunes every day at 2 pm from the taxi place in Rissani.

A place costs Dr20 and the trip takes around an hour and a half. There are also 4WD taxis between Merzouga and Rissani on market days (Sunday, Tuesday and Thursday).

There's no timetable as such and demand for them can vary enormously. The fare per person is about Dr20. If you're driving your own car from Rissani you are advised to engage a local guide since the route is not as straightforward as that from Erfoud.

RISSANI

Situated in the heart of the Tafilalt oases, the small town of Rissani is in a sense the end of the road, where the Ziz Valley peters out into the hot nothingness of stone and sand that stretches out to the south.

Just outside Rissani to the west lie the ruins of the fabled city of Sijilmassa, once the capital of a virtually independent Islamic principality adhering to the Shiite 'heresy' in the early days of the Arab conquest of North Africa.

Uncertainty reigns over exactly when it was founded, but by the end of the 8th century it was playing a key role on the trans-Saharan trade routes. Internal feuding led to its collapse some time in the 14th century.

Centuries later, it was from Rissani that the Filali (from whom the ruling Alawite dynasty is descended) swept north to supplant the Saadians as the ruling dynasty in Morocco.

It did not happen overnight, however. The founder of the dynasty, Moulay Ali ash-Sharif, began expanding his power in the early 17th century in a series of small wars with neighbouring tribes.

His sons continued a slow campaign of conquest, but only in 1668 was Moulay ar-Rashid recognised as sultan.

His brother and successor, Moulay Is-mail, later became the uncontested ruler of Morocco, and underlined his power by establishing a new capital at Meknès.

Members of the Filali still inhabit the ksour in this area, but Sijilmassa itself has fallen into ruin and there's little to indicate its past glories except for two decorated gateways and a few other structures.

The ruins are off to the right-hand side of the 'Circuit Touristique' (Tourist Circuit) as you enter Rissani from the north.

Information

The centre of town is quite small. There is a post and phone office open during normal office hours and at least two téléboutiques where you can make phone calls.

There is also a Banque Populaire and a branch of the BMCE, where you can change cash or travellers cheques.

Souq

There's a pleasant shady market place in the south-eastern corner of the town where a large souq takes place on Sunday, Tuesday and Thursday. Don't miss the 'donkey park'.

There are also a few carpet and jewellery shops in Rissani worth a look, including the Maison Berbère, Maison Toureg and the Maison du Sud, just inside the market gateway.

Circuit Touristique

This 21km loop around the palmeraies south of Rissani (on fairly rough stretches

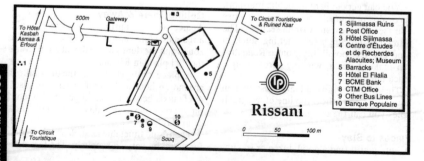

CENTRAL MOROCCO

The Tuareg

While travelling in the south of Morocco you'll hear much about the famous Tuareg (twah-reg) nomads of the central Sahara. Thought to be of Berber origin, they migrated south a thousand or more years ago and played a central role in the great caravan routes linking Morocco to the Sahara and West Africa. If not trading, they were raiding.

Robbery was considered an honourable occupation and they were renowned for their bravery and their fierce raids on camel caravans. They would also attack the villages of other tribes, stealing crops and livestock and enslaving the inhabitants.

The French put an end to much of this activity by restricting nomadic movement and abolishing slavery (although in remoter parts of Niger it persisted until the 1960s). Without their slaves, the Tuareg eventually turned to herding and had to move south to the desert's rim in search of greener pastures. Today, only a few still follow their traditional nomadic lifestyle.

Tuaregs can be recognised by their light-coloured skin and grey or blue eyes, often the only feature showing through the distinctive blue *taguelmoust* (shawl or scarf) that the men wear wrapped around the head to keep out the desert winds and sand. Tuareg are often called 'blue men' because indigo was used to dye their robes and was also rubbed onto the skin as protection from the sun.

Though Muslim, the customs of the Tuareg are distinct from those of the Arabs. Tuareg women enjoy a freedom and status unheard of in the Muslim world. The Tuareg are one of the few matrilineal ethnic groups in West Africa. Tuareg women do not wear veils, can own property, maintain it separately from their husband's during marriage, keep their social status while marrying into a lower caste, and divorce their husbands. ■

of road) takes you through villages and past several ruined ksour.

A couple of kilometres to the south-east is the zawiyya (closed to non-Muslims) of Moulay Ali ash-Sharif.

Just nearby, and worth a look, are the 19th century ruins of the Ksar d'Akbar, which once housed disgraced or unwanted members of the Alawite dynasty.

A kilometre or so further on is the Ksar Oulad Abdelhalim, built for Sultan Moulay Hassan's elder brother around 1900. There is still a substantial amount of beautiful decoration remaining.

The road continues past another group of ksour and just before you head back into town, some barely visible ruins of Sijilmassa.

Places to Stay & Eat

The cheapest place to stay is the *Hôtel El Filalia* (☎ 575096), which is basic, but adequate. This hotel is where the buses drop off and pick up passengers.

It offers rooms with two single beds for Dr50 and others with one double and one single bed for Dr65. The hotel can organise excursions if you want.

Better is the *Hôtel Sijilmassa* (☎ 575042; fax 575042), on Place al-Massira al-Khadra (Green March), which is clean, comfortable and offers spacious rooms with private shower and toilet for Dr80/120/160/190. The hotel has a rooftop terrace with great views of the town and a restaurant on the ground floor.

About 3km out along the road to Erfoud is the welcoming *Hôtel Kasbah Asmaa* (☎ 575494; fax 575494), which is part of the Kasbah chain. Comfortable rooms with bathroom cost Dr200/250/300.

There is a rather large suite for Dr500, a swimming pool, a good restaurant and a bar. The hotel can organise trips to the dunes.

If you're not staying at the Sijilmassa or Kasbah Asmaa, there are a number of simple restaurants fronting the market where you can eat cheaply and well.

A speciality of Rissani is a local version

CENTRAL MOROCCO

of pizza – a huge round of bread stuffed with meat, eggs and spices.

Getting There & Away

Buses and grands taxis leave from the area in front of the Hôtel El Filalia. CTM has a bus to Meknès (Dr120) via Erfoud and Er-Rachidia at 8 pm. Other companies put on three departures to Fès via Erfoud at 6 and 10 am and 11.30 pm (this last one via Sefrou).

A bus also leaves for Casablanca via Erfoud at 8 pm. The fare to Erfoud is generally Dr5, and minibuses make the trip regularly on market days.

Grands taxis (Dr6.50) are probably the best bet though. A red and white camionette leaves for Merzouga and the dunes from near the taxi area every day at 2 pm. A place costs Dr20.

4WD taxis run between Rissani and Merzouga on market days, and also cost about Dr20 per person. Departures are uncertain and depend on demand.

CENTRAL MOROCCO

Berber bird symbol
These broad cross-shapes are called 'birds' and are believed to have magic powers.

Glossary

This glossary is a list of Arabic (a), Berber (b), French (f) and Spanish (s) terms you may come across in Morocco.

agadir (b) – fortified communal granary
'aid (a) – feast (also *'eid*)
'ain (a) – water source, spring
aït (b) – 'family (of)', often precedes tribal and town names
akbar (a) – great
Al-Andalus – Muslim Spain and Portugal
Allah (a) – God
Almohads – puritanical Muslim group (1130-1269), originally Berber, which arose in response to the corrupt ruling Almoravid dynasty
Almoravids – fanatical Muslim group (1054-1160) which ruled Spain and the Maghreb
'ashaab – herbal remedies

bab (a) – gate
babouches – traditional leather slippers
bain (f) – see *hammam* and *douches*
baksheesh (a) – tip
bali (a) – old
baraka (a) – divine blessing or favour
Barbary – European term used to describe the North African coast from the 16th to 19th centuries
basilica – type of Roman administrative building; later used to describe churches
Bedouin (a) – nomadic Arab desert tribe
beni (a) – 'sons of', often precedes tribal name (also *banu*)
Berbers – indigenous inhabitants of North Africa
bidonville (f) – slum area, especially in Casablanca
borj (a) – fort (literally, tower)
brochette (f) – kebab
burnous (a) – traditional full-length cape with a hood, worn by men throughout the Maghreb

caid – see *qaid*

calèche (f) – horse-drawn carriage
caliph – 'successor of Mohammed'; ruler of the Islamic world
calle (s) – street
camionette (f) – Berber truck
capitol – main temple of Roman town, usually situated in the forum
caravanserai – traditional courtyard inn, used by travelling merchants and their livestock
cascades (f) – waterfall
chergui (a) – dry, easterly desert wind (also known as *sirocco*)
corniche (f) – coastal road
couscous – semolina, staple food of North Africa

dar (a) – a traditional town house
douar (a) – word generally used for village in the High Atlas
douche (f) – public showers (see *hammam*)

'eid (a) – feast (also *'aid*)
erg (a) – region of sand

Fatimids – Muslim dynasty (909-1171) which defeated the Aghlabid dynasty; descendants of the Prophet's daughter Fatima and her husband, Ali (see *Shiites*)
forum – open space at centre of Roman towns
foum (a) – usually mouth of a river or valley (from Arabic for mouth)
funduq (a) – caravanserai (often used to mean hotel)

gardiens de voitures (f) – carpark attendants
gare routière (f) – bus station
ghar (a) – cave
ghurfa (a) – room
gîte (f) – hiker's accommodation
grand taxi (f) – (long-distance) shared taxi
guerba – waterbag made from the skin of a goat or sheep, seen hanging on the side of many Saharan vehicles

guichets automatiques (f) – automatic teller machine (ATM)

hajj (a) – pilgrimage to Mecca; hence *haji*, one who has made the pilgrimage
hammada – stony desert
hammam (a) – Turkish-style bathhouse with sauna and massage; there's at least one in virtually every town in the Maghreb. Also known by the French word *bain* (bath) or *bain maure* (Moorish bath).
harem (a) – (literally) a sacred area; the family living area of a house or palace, primarily the domain of women
harira – soup or broth with lentils and other vegetables
heddaoua (b) – wandering Berber minstrels
hijab (a) – veil and women's head scarf
hijra (a) – the flight of the Prophet Mohammed from Mecca to Medina in 622; the first year of the Islamic calendar
hôtel de ville (f) – town hall

ibn (a) – son of (also *bin*, *ben*)
Idrissids – Moroccan dynasty (800-1080)
iftar (a) – (also *ftur*) the breaking of the fast at sundown during Ramadan
imam (a) – Islamic prayer leader
Interzone – the name (coined by author William Burroughs) for the period 1923-56, when Tangier was controlled by nine countries; notable for gun-running, prostitution, currency speculation and smuggling
itissalat al-Maghrib (a) – public telephone office (see also *téléboutique*)

jamal (a) – camel
jami' (a) – Friday mosque (also *djemaa*, *'jama* or *jemaa*)
jardin (f) – garden
jebel (a) – hill, mountain (sometimes *djebel* in former French possessions)
jedid (a) – new (sometimes spelled *jdid*)
jellaba (a) – flowing men's garment, usually made of cotton
jezira (a) – island

kasbah (a) – fort, citadel; often also the administrative centre (also *qasba*)

khutba – Friday sermon preached by the imam of a mosque
koubba (a) – (also *qubba*) sanctuary or shrine; (see also *marabout*)
ksar (a) – (plural: *ksour*) fortified stronghold (also *qasr*)

Maghreb (a) – west (literally, where the sun sets); used to describe the area covered by Morocco, Algeria and Tunisia
marabout – holy man or saint; also often used to describe the mausolea of these men, which are places of worship in themselves
masjid (a) – another name for a mosque, particularly in a *medersa* (see also *jami'*)
mechouar (a) – royal assembly place
medersa (a) – college for teaching theology, law, Arabic literature and grammar; wide-spread throughout the Maghreb from the 13th century (also *madrassa*)
medina (a) – old city; used these days to describe the old Arab part of modern towns and cities
mellah (a) – Jewish quarter of medina
mihrab (a) – prayer niche in the wall of a mosque indicating the direction of Mecca (the *qibla*)
minbar (a) – pulpit in mosque; the *imam* delivers the sermon from one of the lower steps because the Prophet preached from the top step
moulay – ruler
moussem – pilgrimage to *marabout* tomb; festival in honour of a *marabout*
muezzin (a) – mosque official who sings the call to prayer from the minaret
mumtaz (a) – top class in buses
musée (f) – museum

navette (f) – shuttle bus/train/boat

oued (a) – riverbed, often dry (sometimes *wad* or *wadi*)
oulad (a) – 'sons (of)' – often precedes tribal or town name

palais de justice (f) – law court
palmeraie (f) – oasis-like area around a town where date palms, vegetables and fruit are grown

pasha – high official in Ottoman Empire (also *pacha*)
patisserie (f) – cake and pastry shop
pensión (s) – guesthouse
petit taxi (f) – local taxi
pharmacie de garde (f) – late-night pharmacy
pisé (f) – building material made of sun-dried clay or mud
piste (f) – poor unsealed tracks, often requiring 4WD vehicles
place (f) – square, plaza
plage (f) – beach
plat du jour (f) – daily special (in a restaurant)
pressing – laundry

qaid (a) – local chief, loose equivalent of mayor in some parts of Morocco (also *caid*)
qasba (a) – see *kasbah*
qasr (a) – see *ksar*
qebibat (a) – cupola
qibla (a) – the direction of Mecca, indictaed by a *mihrab*
qissaria(t) (a) – covered market sometimes forming commercial centre of a medina
qubba (a) – see *koubba*
Qur'an – sacred book of Islam

Ramadan (a) – ninth month of the Muslim year, a period of fasting
ras (a) – headland
refuge (f) – mountain hut, basic hikers' shelter
reg (b) – stony desert
ribat (a) – combined monastery and fort
rôtisseries (f) – roast chicken fast food outlets

Saadians – Moroccan dynasty (1500s)
saha(t) (a) – square (or French *place*)
sebkha (a) – saltpan
shari'a (a) – Islamic law
sharia (a) – street
sherif (a) – descendant of the Prophet
Shiites – one of two main Islamic sects, formed by those who believed the true *imams* were descended from Ali (see also *Sunnis*)
sidi (a) – (also *si*) honorific (like Mr)

sirocco (a) – easterly desert wind (also known as *chergui*)
skala (a) – fortress
souq (a) – market
Sufism – mystical strand of Islam; adherents concentrate on their inner attitude in order to attain communion with god
Sunnis – one of two main Islamic sects, derived from followers of the Umayyad caliphate
Syndicat d'Initiative (f) – government-run tourist office

tabac (f) – tobacconist and newsagency
tajine – stew, usually with meat as the main ingredient
tapas (s) – various kinds of savoury snacks traditionally served in Spanish bars
tariq (a) – road, avenue
téléboutique (f) – privately operated telephone service
tizi (b) – mountain pass (French *col*)
tour (f) – tower
Tuareg – nomadic Berbers of the Sahara; they are among several Berber tribes known as the Blue Men because of their indigo-dyed robes, which gives their skin a bluish tinge

Umayyads – Damascus-based caliphate dynasty (661-750)

ville nouvelle (f) – 'new city' – town built by the French, generally alongside existing towns and cities of the Maghreb
vizier – another term for a provincial governor in the Ottoman Empire, or adviser to the sultan in Morocco

wali – Sufi holy man or saint
Wattasids – Moroccan dynasty (1400s)
wilaya (a) – province

zankat (a) – lane, alley (also *zanqat*)
zawiyya (a) – religious fraternity based around a *marabout*; also, location of the fraternity (also *zaouia*)
zeitouna (a) – olive tree or grove
zellij (a) – ceramic tiles used to decorate buildings

Index

THANKS
From Frances
With thanks to all of the following for making the trip possible: to Ali El Kasmi, Director of the Moroccan Tourist Office, London. Also in London, to Debbie at Sky International. To the many tourism *délégués* across Morocco, particularly to Abdelkrim Ouachikh at Meknès, Mohammed El Hanine in Tangier, Abderrazzak El Hajjari of Tetouan, and Rachid Ihdeme and his wife Nadia at Ifrane. Above all, thanks to Abderrahim Bentbib, délégue of Marrakesh, for his generosity and wonderful conversations.

For untiring and invaluable help with research, thanks particularly to Ali Bahaijoub, of the Maghreb Press Agency in London, and Mr Jalil Noury, of the Ministry of Environment in Rabat. Thanks to Mlle Bentaleb Zhor at the Rabat Tourism Office and Mr Ben Hammi at the Division de Cartographie for their helping obtaining official maps.

For information on Volubilis, thanks to Site Curator Hassan Limane. For help with Spanish Morocco, thanks to Caridad Batalla at the Ministry of Foreign Affairs in Madrid. Thanks also to Dave Gosney of Gostour Guides for his assistance with bird sites. In London, thanks to Bob Deitch and Paul Talako for their help with Internet research, and to Azhar at the Earl's Court photocopying shop for his good humour.

For insights into Casablanca, thanks to Oalle Flyger and Rohan Watt; at Marrakesh to Antony Dupont from Explore and Jamal Bikri the Tourist Inspector; at Fès, Stella Fleming at the American Language Center. In Melilla, thanks to Marrakesh Ahmed, Head of Customs, and to Ramón Antón Mota, Chief of Police. A big thank you also to Mohammed Abdelilah Belghazi, founder and owner of the extraordinary Berghazi Museum, to Hassan Cherradi, director of the Musée Jamai, Meknès, and to Ahmed Dinari, for his hospitality and tours around the Dadès Gorge.

Finally, thanks to the unsung team at Lonely Planet, and a huge thanks to Dorinda, my co-author, for choosing not to have babies with Berbers after all, and contributing her excellent share of the book.

With thanks to the following for making the trip memorable: to Mustapha for the midnight tour of Chefchaouen's medina and kif dens disguised in his grandfather's burnous; to Aabdennebi El Haloui for his fluent-Arabic-in-ten-hours; to the guides at Volubilis, especially Abdel Majid Aouad, for two heavenly days among the ruins. To Claire Oxford, Sara Topping and Sarah Wilson for a night of vengeance in a seedy bar in Fès. To Ahmed the Berber boy and his dog for helping me dig my car from a sand dune, and finally thanks to all those many individuals whose names I never knew, but whose warmth, candour and generosity never failed to astound me, and which I shall not forget. To all of them:

بارك الله فيك

My modest contribution to this book is dedicated to my mother, who never saw it.

From Dorinda
In London, many thanks to Ali El Kasmi, Jamal El Jaidi and Hassan Benlamlih of the Moroccan National Tourist Office; staff at the Moroccan Embassy, Hassan Alaoui of the Middle East Broadcasting Corporation and Mr Madani of the Maghreb Bookshop.

In Morocco, thanks are due to Ahmed El Khemlichi of the Agadir Tourist Office; Rick & Teresa Kramer in Rabat; Abdellatif Fouad of Safi; Abdellah El Moumni in Taroudannt; Brahim Aziam, Brahim Toudaoui and Mohammed Amgif in Imlil; Phillip Masbridge of Exodus; Mike McHugo of Discover; Belghit Tihami in Rissani; Amar Oussou of the Er-Rachidia Tourist Office; Ebrahim Jarrou, Abdeslam Belfquih, Abdelhak Ziani, and Youseff Sonissi in Tan Tan; Larbi Lahyane and Mossa Hamogh in Tiznit; and Hammou Sahbi in the Dadès Valley.

A round of applause also to Dawn Chapman, Brian Lackmacker, John Tuckey, Annie and Ruthie Holder in London, and Mark Baker and Maureen O'Donnell in Paris.

I'm particularly grateful for all the information and insights received from fellow travellers and for the open-hearted hospitality shown to me by the people of Morocco.

From the Publisher

Thanks to the many travellers who wrote in with helpful hints, useful advice, and interesting and funny stories.

Muriel & Eli Abt, Justin Anderson, David Anstee, Julian Ash, Alan Balchin, Roy Ball, Janet Berdai, Claire Bondin, Taco Brandsen, Joel Brazy, Timothy Brennan, Jeremy Brock, D Budd, Joseph Caputo, Stephen Chalkley, Michele Claus, Louise Cooke, Elly Cotsell, Catherine Couture, Bryce Crocker, Clare Crowley, Michael Cummins, Mrs Cunningham, Guy D Drury, Roy Davey, Peter Dhondt, Jake Doxat, Tim Eyre, Tom Fearnahough, Brita Flinner, Deidre Galbraith, Peter Gardiner, Adam Gaubert, Astrid Gauffin, John Gilroy, Connor Gorry, Peter Gray, JW Grayson, A & J Greenless, Mickey Gutman, Elena Hall, Fred Harshbarger, Mike & Kate Harvey, Richard Hay, Camilla Hayes, Rory Hensey, P Bustos Heppe, Colman Higgins, Yasuko Higuchi, Prof Peter Hillman, AP Hilton, Malcolm Holmes, Sydney Hope, Andy Howes, Paula Hutt, Chris Jackson, Stephen Jakobi, Bridgett James, Sabine Jefferies, Sheila Jefferson, Hans Jochen, Joshua Kaufmann, M Kent, Takahashi Kentaro, W Labi, Andrew Lee, Glen Lorentzen, Jon Marks, Lee Marshall, Christine McBride, Bryce McBride, Sarah McGuire, D & B McHugo, Clare Mercer, Don Moore, Frank Nemek, Daniela Neu, Mike & Phil Nolan, Bradley Norris, Doug Oldfield, Glen Oliff, Danic Parenteau, Robert Patterson, Benjamin Pearman, A & D Ponter, Stuart Poole, Michele Puliti, John Pyle, JD Rabbit, Kristi Robison, Jason Rothman, Patricia Rothman, Victor Sadilek, J Saunders, Frank Schaer, Frank Schmidt, Sebastian Schmitz, R & P Schroeter, Peter Shanks, Ernest Shenton, Adam Simmons, Simon Skerritt, Brooks Slaybaugh, Iain Smith, Birgitta Steen, Eszter Szira, Thomas Tallis, Michael Thogersen, Eric Timewell, Maurice van Sante, Pierre Vanderhout, Veeke Verstraete, D Visscher, Rob Voncken, Michael Ward, Elizabeth Wells, Teresa Wolf, A Wolff.

LONELY PLANET PHRASEBOOKS

Building bridges,
Breaking barriers,
Beyond babble-on

Nepali phrasebook — Listen for the gems

Ethiopian Amharic phrasebook — Speak your own words

Latin American Spanish phrasebook — Ask your own questions

Ukrainian phrasebook — Master of your own image

Greek phrasebook

Vietnamese phrasebook

- handy pocket-sized books
- easy to understand Pronunciation chapter
- clear and comprehensive Grammar chapter
- romanisation alongside script to allow ease of pronunciation
- script throughout so users can point to phrases
- extensive vocabulary sections, words and phrases for every situations
- full of cultural information and tips for the traveller

'...vital for a real DIY spirit and attitude in language learning' – Backpacker

'the phrasebooks have good cultural backgrounders and offer solid advice for challenging situations in remote locations' – San Francisco Examiner

'...they are unbeatable for their coverage of the world's more obscure languages' – The Geographical Magazine

---

Arabic (Egyptian)
Arabic (Moroccan)
Australia
 Australian English, Aboriginal and Torres Strait languages
Baltic States
 Estonian, Latvian, Lithuanian
Bengali
Burmese
Brazilian
Cantonese
Central Europe
 Czech, French, German, Hungarian, Italian and Slovak
Eastern Europe
 Bulgarian, Czech, Hungarian, Polish, Romanian and Slovak
Egyptian Arabic
Ethiopian (Amharic)
Fijian
French
German
Greek
Hindi/Urdu
Indonesian

Italian
Japanese
Korean
Lao
Malay
Mandarin
Mediterranean Europe
 Albanian, Croatian, Greek, Italian, Macedonian, Maltese, Serbian, Slovene
Mongolian
Moroccan Arabic
Nepali
Papua New Guinea
Pilipino (Tagalog)
Quechua
Russian
Scandinavian Europe
 Danish, Finnish, Icelandic, Norwegian and Swedish
South-East Asia
 Burmese, Indonesian, Khmer, Lao, Malay, Tagalog (Pilipino), Thai and Vietnamese

Spanish (Castilian)
 Also includes Catalan, Galician and Basque
Spanish (Latin American)
Sri Lanka
Swahili
Thai
Thai Hill Tribes
Tibetan
Turkish
Ukrainian
USA
 US English, Vernacular Talk, Native American languages and Hawaiian
Vietnamese
Western Europe
 Basque, Catalan, Dutch, French, German, Greek, Irish, Italian, Portuguese, Scottish Gaelic, Spanish (Castilian) and Welsh

---

LONELY PLANET JOURNEYS

JOURNEYS is a unique collection of travel writing – published by the company that understands travel better than anyone else. It is a series for anyone who has ever experienced – or dreamed of – the magical moment when they encountered a strange culture or saw a place for the first time. They are tales to read while you're planning a trip, while you're on the road or while you're in an armchair, in front of a fire.

JOURNEYS books catch the spirit of a place, illuminate a culture, recount a crazy adventure, or introduce a fascinating way of life. They always entertain, and always enrich the experience of travel.

THE RAINBIRD
A Central African Journey
Jan Brokken
translated by Sam Garrett

The Rainbird is a classic travel story. Following in the footsteps of famous Europeans such as Albert Schweitzer and H.M. Stanley, Jan Brokken journeyed to Gabon in central Africa. A kaleidoscope of adventures and anecdotes, *The Rainbird* brilliantly chronicles the encounter between Africa and Europe as it was acted out on a side-street of history. It is also the compelling, immensely readable account of the author's own travels in one of the most remote and mysterious regions of Africa.

Jan Brokken is one of Holland's best known writers. In addition to travel narratives and literary journalism, he has published several novels and short stories. Many of his works are set in Africa, where he has travelled widely.

SONGS TO AN AFRICAN SUNSET
A Zimbabwean Story
Sekai Nzenza-Shand

Songs to an African Sunset braids vividly personal stories into an intimate picture of contemporary Zimbabwe. Returning to her family's village after many years in the West, Sekai Nzenza-Shand discovers a world where ancestor worship, polygamy and witchcraft still govern the rhythms of daily life – and where drought, deforestation and AIDS have wrought devastating changes. With insight and affection, she explores a culture torn between respect for the old ways and the irresistible pull of the new.

Sekai Nzenza-Shand was born in Zimbabwe and has lived in England and Australia. Her first novel, *Zimbabwean Woman: My Own Story*, was published in London in 1988 and her fiction has been included in the short story collections *Daughters of Africa* and *Images of the West*. Sekai currently lives in Zimbabwe.

This project has been assisted by the Commonwealth Government through the Australia Council, its arts funding and advisory body.

LONELY PLANET TRAVEL ATLASES

Lonely Planet has long been famous for the number and quality of its guidebook maps. Now we've gone one step further and produced a handy companion series: Lonely Planet travel atlases – maps of a country produced in book form.

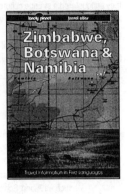

Unlike other maps, which look good but lead travellers astray, our travel atlases have been researched on the road by Lonely Planet's experienced team of writers. All details are carefully checked to ensure the atlas corresponds with the equivalent Lonely Planet guidebook.

The handy atlas format means no holes, wrinkles, torn sections or constant folding and unfolding. These atlases can survive long periods on the road, unlike cumbersome fold-out maps. The comprehensive index ensures easy reference.

- full-colour throughout
- maps researched and checked by Lonely Planet authors
- place names correspond with Lonely Planet guidebooks
  – no confusing spelling differences
- legend and travelling information in English, French, German, Japanese and Spanish
- size: 230 x 160 mm

Available now:
Chile & Easter Island • Egypt • India & Bangladesh • Israel & the Palestinian Territories •Jordan, Syria & Lebanon • Kenya • Laos • Portugal • South Africa, Lesotho & Swaziland • Thailand • Turkey • Vietnam • Zimbabwe, Botswana & Namibia

---

LONELY PLANET TV SERIES & VIDEOS

Lonely Planet travel guides have been brought to life on television screens around the world. Like our guides, the programmes are based on the joy of independent travel, and look honestly at some of the most exciting, picturesque and frustrating places in the world. Each show is presented by one of three travellers from Australia, England or the USA and combines an innovative mixture of video, Super-8 film, atmospheric soundscapes and original music.

Videos of each episode – containing additional footage not shown on television – are available from good book and video shops, but the availability of individual videos varies with regional screening schedules.

Video destinations include: Alaska • American Rockies • Australia – The South-East • Baja California & the Copper Canyon • Brazil • Central Asia • Chile & Easter Island • Corsica, Sicily & Sardinia – The Mediterranean Islands • East Africa (Tanzania & Zanzibar) • Ecuador & the Galapagos Islands • Greenland & Iceland • Indonesia • Israel & the Sinai Desert • Jamaica • Japan • La Ruta Maya • Morocco • New York • North India • Pacific Islands (Fiji, Solomon Islands & Vanuatu) • South India • South West China • Turkey • Vietnam • West Africa • Zimbabwe, Botswana & Namibia

The Lonely Planet TV series is produced by:
Pilot Productions
The Old Studio
18 Middle Row
London W10 5AT UK

For video availability and ordering information contact your nearest Lonely Planet office.

Music from the TV series is available on CD & cassette.

PLANET TALK

Lonely Planet's FREE quarterly newsletter

We love hearing from you and think you'd like to hear from us.

When...is the right time to see reindeer in Finland?
Where...can you hear the best palm-wine music in Ghana?
How...do you get from Asunción to Areguá by steam train?
What...is the best way to see India?

For the answer to these and many other questions read PLANET TALK.

Every issue is packed with up-to-date travel news and advice including:

* a letter from Lonely Planet co-founders Tony and Maureen Wheeler
* go behind the scenes on the road with a Lonely Planet author
* feature article on an important and topical travel issue
* a selection of recent letters from travellers
* details on forthcoming Lonely Planet promotions
* complete list of Lonely Planet products

To join our mailing list contact any Lonely Planet office.

Also available: Lonely Planet T-shirts. 100% heavyweight cotton.

LONELY PLANET ONLINE

Get the latest travel information before you leave or while you're on the road

Whether you've just begun planning your next trip, or you're chasing down specific info on currency regulations or visa requirements, check out Lonely Planet Online for up-to-the minute travel information.

As well as travel profiles of your favourite destinations (including maps and photos), you'll find current reports from our researchers and other travellers, updates on health and visas, travel advisories, and discussion of the ecological and political issues you need to be aware of as you travel.

There's also an online travellers' forum where you can share your experience of life on the road, meet travel companions and ask other travellers for their recommendations and advice. We also have plenty of links to other online sites useful to independent travellers.

And of course we have a complete and up-to-date list of all Lonely Planet travel products including guides, phrasebooks, atlases, Journeys and videos and a simple online ordering facility if you can't find the book you want elsewhere.

www.lonelyplanet.com
or
AOL keyword: lp

LONELY PLANET PRODUCTS

Lonely Planet is known worldwide for publishing practical, reliable and no-nonsense travel information in our guides and on our web site. The Lonely Planet list covers just about every accessible part of the world. Currently there are eight series: *travel guides, shoestring guides, walking guides, city guides, phrasebooks, audio packs, travel atlases* and *Journeys* – a unique collection of travel writing.

EUROPE

Amsterdam • Austria • Baltic States phrasebook • Britain • Central Europe on a shoestring • Central Europe phrasebook • Czech & Slovak Republics • Denmark • Dublin • Eastern Europe on a shoestring • Eastern Europe phrasebook • Estonia, Latvia & Lithuania • Finland • France • French phrasebook • Germany • German phrasebook • Greece • Greek phrasebook • Hungary • Iceland, Greenland & the Faroe Islands • Ireland • Italian phrasebook • Italy • Lisbon • Mediterranean Europe on a shoestring • Mediterranean Europe phrasebook • Paris • Poland • Portugal • Portugal travel atlas • Prague • Russia, Ukraine & Belarus • Russian phrasebook • Scandinavian & Baltic Europe on a shoestring • Scandinavian Europe phrasebook •Slovenia • Spain • Spanish phrasebook • St Petersburg • Switzerland •Trekking in Spain • Ukrainian phrasebook •Vienna •Walking in Britain • Walking in Switzerland • Western Europe on a shoestring • Western Europe phrasebook

Travel Literature: The Olive Grove: Travels in Greece

NORTH AMERICA

Alaska • Backpacking in Alaska • Baja California • California & Nevada • Canada • Florida • Hawaii • Honolulu • Los Angeles • Mexico • Miami • New England • New Orleans • New York City • New York, New Jersey & Pennsylvania • Pacific Northwest USA • Rocky Mountain States • San Francisco • Southwest USA • USA phrasebook • Washington, DC & the Capital Region

CENTRAL AMERICA & THE CARIBBEAN

Bermuda • Central America on a shoestring • Costa Rica • Cuba •Eastern Caribbean •Guatemala, Belize & Yucatán: La Ruta Maya • Jamaica

SOUTH AMERICA

Argentina, Uruguay & Paraguay • Bolivia • Brazil • Brazilian phrasebook • Buenos Aires • Chile & Easter Island • Chile & Easter Island travel atlas • Colombia • Deep South • Ecuador & the Galápagos Islands • Latin American Spanish phrasebook • Peru • Quechua phrasebook • Rio de Janeiro • South America on a shoestring • Trekking in the Patagonian Andes • Venezuela

Travel Literature: Full Circle: A South American Journey

ANTARCTICA

Antarctica

ISLANDS OF THE INDIAN OCEAN

Madagascar & Comoros • Maldives• Mauritius, Réunion & Seychelles

AFRICA

Africa - the South • Africa on a shoestring • Arabic (Moroccan) phrasebook • Cape Town • Central Africa • East Africa • Egypt • Egypt travel atlas• Ethiopian (Amharic) phrasebook • Kenya • Kenya travel atlas • Malawi, Mozambique & Zambia • Morocco • North Africa • South Africa, Lesotho & Swaziland • South Africa, Lesotho & Swaziland travel atlas • Swahili phrasebook • Trekking in East Africa • West Africa • Zimbabwe, Botswana & Namibia • Zimbabwe, Botswana & Namibia travel atlas

Travel Literature: The Rainbird: A Central African Journey • Songs to an African Sunset: A Zimbabwean Story

MAIL ORDER

Lonely Planet products are distributed worldwide. They are also available by mail order from Lonely Planet, so if you have difficulty finding a title please write to us. North American and South American residents should write to Embarcadero West, 155 Filbert St, Suite 251, Oakland CA 94607, USA; European and African residents should write to 10a Spring Place, London NW5 3BH; and residents of other countries to PO Box 617, Hawthorn, Victoria 3122, Australia.

NORTH-EAST ASIA

Beijing • Cantonese phrasebook • China • Hong Kong • Hong Kong, Macau & Guangzhou • Japan • Japanese phrasebook • Japanese audio pack • Korea • Korean phrasebook • Mandarin phrasebook • Mongolia • Mongolian phrasebook • North-East Asia on a shoestring • Seoul • Taiwan • Tibet • Tibet phrasebook • Tokyo

Travel Literature: Lost Japan

MIDDLE EAST & CENTRAL ASIA

Arab Gulf States • Arabic (Egyptian) phrasebook • Central Asia • Central Asia phrasebook • Iran • Israel & the Palestinian Territories • Israel & the Palestinian Territories travel atlas • Istanbul • Jerusalem • Jordan & Syria • Jordan, Syria & Lebanon travel atlas • Lebanon • Middle East • Turkey • Turkish phrasebook • Turkey travel atlas • Yemen

Travel Literature: The Gates of Damascus • Kingdom of the Film Stars: Journey into Jordan

ALSO AVAILABLE:

Travel with Children • Traveller's Tales

INDIAN SUBCONTINENT

Bangladesh • Bengali phrasebook • Delhi • Hindi/Urdu phrasebook • India • India & Bangladesh travel atlas • Indian Himalaya • Karakoram Highway • Nepal • Nepali phrasebook • Pakistan • Rajasthan • Sri Lanka • Sri Lanka phrasebook • Trekking in the Indian Himalaya • Trekking in the Karakoram & Hindukush • Trekking in the Nepal Himalaya

Travel Literature: In Rajasthan • Shopping for Buddhas

SOUTH-EAST ASIA

Bali & Lombok • Bangkok • Burmese phrasebook • Cambodia • Ho Chi Minh City • Indonesia • Indonesian phrasebook • Indonesian audio pack • Jakarta • Java • Laos • Lao phrasebook • Laos travel atlas • Malay phrasebook • Malaysia, Singapore & Brunei • Myanmar (Burma) • Philippines • Pilipino phrasebook • Singapore • South-East Asia on a shoestring • South-East Asia phrasebook • Thailand • Thailand's Islands & Beaches • Thailand travel atlas • Thai phrasebook • Thai audio pack • Thai Hill Tribes phrasebook • Vietnam • Vietnamese phrasebook • Vietnam travel atlas

AUSTRALIA & THE PACIFIC

Australia • Australian phrasebook • Bushwalking in Australia • Bushwalking in Papua New Guinea • Fiji • Fijian phrasebook • Islands of Australia's Great Barrier Reef • Melbourne • Micronesia • New Caledonia • New South Wales • New Zealand • Northern Territory • Outback Australia • Papua New Guinea • Papua New Guinea phrasebook • Queensland • Rarotonga & the Cook Islands • Samoa • Solomon Islands • South Australia • Sydney • Tahiti & French Polynesia • Tasmania • Tonga • Tramping in New Zealand • Vanuatu • Victoria • Western Australia

Travel Literature: Islands in the Clouds • Sean & David's Long Drive

THE LONELY PLANET STORY

Lonely Planet published its first book in 1973 in response to the numerous 'How did you do it?' questions Maureen and Tony Wheeler were asked after driving, bussing, hitching, sailing and railing their way from England to Australia.

Written at a kitchen table and hand collated, trimmed and stapled, *Across Asia on the Cheap* became an instant local bestseller, inspiring thoughts of another book.

Eighteen months in South-East Asia resulted in their second guide, *South-East Asia on a shoestring*, which they put together in a backstreet Chinese hotel in Singapore in 1975. The 'yellow bible', as it quickly became known to backpackers around the world, soon became *the* guide to the region. It has sold well over half a million copies and is now in its 9th edition, still retaining its familiar yellow cover.

Today there are over 240 titles, including travel guides, walking guides, language kits & phrasebooks, travel atlases and travel literature. The company is the largest independent travel publisher in the world. Although Lonely Planet initially specialised in guides to Asia, today there are few corners of the globe that have not been covered.

The emphasis continues to be on travel for independent travellers. Tony and Maureen still travel for several months of each year and play an active part in the writing, updating and quality control of Lonely Planet's guides.

They have been joined by over 70 authors and 170 staff at our offices in Melbourne (Australia), Oakland (USA), London (UK) and Paris (France). Travellers themselves also make a valuable contribution to the guides through the feedback we receive in thousands of letters each year and on our web site.

The people at Lonely Planet strongly believe that travellers can make a positive contribution to the countries they visit, both through their appreciation of the countries' culture, wildlife and natural features, and through the money they spend. In addition, the company makes a direct contribution to the countries and regions it covers. Since 1986 a percentage of the income from each book has been donated to ventures such as famine relief in Africa; aid projects in India; agricultural projects in Central America; Greenpeace's efforts to halt French nuclear testing in the Pacific; and Amnesty International.

'I hope we send people out with the right attitude about travel. You realise when you travel that there are so many different perspectives about the world, so we hope these books will make people more interested in what they see. Guidebooks can't really guide people. All you can do is point them in the right direction.'

– Tony Wheeler

LONELY PLANET PUBLICATIONS

Australia
PO Box 617, Hawthorn 3122, Victoria
tel: (03) 9819 1877 fax: (03) 9819 6459
e-mail: talk2us@lonelyplanet.com.au

USA
Embarcadero West, 155 Filbert St, Suite 251,
Oakland, CA 94607
tel: (510) 893 8555 TOLL FREE: 800 275-8555
fax: (510) 893 8563
e-mail: info@lonelyplanet.com

UK
10a Spring Place,
London NW5 3BH
tel: (0171) 428 4800 fax: (0171) 428 4828
e-mail: go@lonelyplanet.co.uk

France:
71 bis rue du Cardinal Lemoine, 75005 Paris
tel: 1 44 32 06 20 fax: 1 46 34 72 55
e-mail: 100560.415@compuserve.com

World Wide Web: http://www.lonelyplanet.com
or *AOL keyword: lp*